Mastering Cybersecurity

Strategies, Technologies, and Best Practices

Dr. Jason Edwards

Apress®

Mastering Cybersecurity: Strategies, Technologies, and Best Practices

Dr. Jason Edwards
Cibolo, TX, USA

ISBN-13 (pbk): 979-8-8688-0296-6   ISBN-13 (electronic): 979-8-8688-0297-3
https://doi.org/10.1007/979-8-8688-0297-3

Managing Director, Apress Media LLC: Welmoed Spahr
Acquisitions Editor: Susan McDermott
Development Editor: Laura Berendson
Project Manager: Jessica Vakili

Cover designed by eStudioCalamar

Distributed to the book trade worldwide by Apress Media, LLC, 1 New York Plaza, New York, NY 10004, U.S.A. Phone 1-800-SPRINGER, fax (201) 348-4505, e-mail orders-ny@springer-sbm.com, or visit www.springeronline.com. Apress Media, LLC is a California LLC and the sole member (owner) is Springer Science + Business Media Finance Inc (SSBM Finance Inc). SSBM Finance Inc is a **Delaware** corporation.

For information on translations, please e-mail booktranslations@springernature.com; for reprint, paperback, or audio rights, please e-mail bookpermissions@springernature.com.

Apress titles may be purchased in bulk for academic, corporate, or promotional use. eBook versions and licenses are also available for most titles. For more information, reference our Print and eBook Bulk Sales web page at http://www.apress.com/bulk-sales.

Any source code or other supplementary material referenced by the author in this book is available to readers on GitHub (https://github.com/Apress). For more detailed information, please visit https://www.apress.com/gp/services/source-code.

If disposing of this product, please recycle the paper

This book is dedicated to all the people who have supported and inspired me throughout my journey in the field of cybersecurity.

First and foremost, I want to thank my family: my wife, Selda, and my children, Michelle, Chris, Ceylin, and Mayra; my sisters, Robin, Kelly, and Lynn; and my close family members, sister-in-law Meltem and her husband Derek, and sister-in-law Nilos and her husband Ken. Thank you for your unwavering support and love.

To my good friends Wil, Wendell, Rob, Kurt, Griffin, Amil, and Brady, your friendship has been invaluable to me.

I would like to extend my gratitude to the teachers and staff at Hallmark University. Teaching in their master's course was the genesis for this book.

A special thank you to those who reviewed my book: Clarke C., Derek B., Jeff S., Kristyn L., Chinho K., Subash P., Kul S., Jim H., Gordon B., Angela D., Jerry S., Leead N., Kesha L., Michael C., Kelley D., Luis G., Christopher H., and Janice P. Your feedback was invaluable.

To all my students at various universities and programs, you have inspired me more than you know.

Finally, to everyone who follows me on LinkedIn: www. linkedin.com/in/jasonedwardsdmist/. Thank you for your continued support and engagement.

To those embarking on or considering a career in cybersecurity, let this book serve not just as a guide but as a testament to the power of collaboration, curiosity, and continuous learning. The path to mastering cybersecurity is challenging but immensely rewarding. It offers the opportunity to impact safeguarding our digital world significantly. May you find inspiration in these pages and from the people mentioned above to pursue your passions, overcome obstacles, and contribute to a safer, more secure future for all.

With heartfelt appreciation,

Jason Edwards

Table of Contents

About the Author

Dr. Jason Edwards is an accomplished cybersecurity leader with extensive experience in technology, finance, insurance, and energy sectors. Holding a Doctorate in Management, Information Systems, and Technology, he specializes in guiding companies through complex cybersecurity challenges. His career includes leadership roles at Amazon, USAA, Brace Industrial Group, and Argo Group International. A former military cyber officer and adjunct professor, Jason is recognized for his service in the U.S. Army, where he earned a Bronze Star for his contributions during the Iraq and Afghanistan wars. He is also an avid reader and popular on LinkedIn.

The original version of the book has been revised. A correction to this book can be found at https://doi.org/10.1007/979-8-8688-0297-3_19

CHAPTER 1

The Criticality and Evolution of Cybersecurity

In the digital era, the importance of cybersecurity is paramount. This critical field has evolved from a niche technical concern to a global security and economic stability cornerstone. The world's interconnectedness means that cybersecurity is not just about protecting information; it's about safeguarding our way of life. From the individual user's data to national security secrets, the spectrum of what needs protection is vast and varied. Understanding the global impact of cybersecurity involves recognizing its role in safeguarding individual and corporate data and preserving the functioning of essential services like healthcare, finance, and government.

Cyber threats have real-world consequences that extend far beyond the digital realm. These threats manifest in various forms, from the theft of sensitive personal information to large-scale attacks on critical infrastructure. The financial repercussions can be staggering for individuals who fall victim to fraud or identity theft and businesses that suffer data breaches. Beyond financial losses, the erosion of trust can be devastating for companies and institutions. For individuals, the impact of a cyber attack can range from the inconvenience of dealing with compromised accounts to serious concerns about personal safety and privacy.

Dr. J. Edwards, *Mastering Cybersecurity*, https://doi.org/10.1007/979-8-8688-0297-3_1

The Ever-Changing Landscape of Cyber Threats

Delving into the evolution of cyber threats provides a fascinating glimpse into the changing nature of technology and crime. The historical perspective on cybersecurity reveals humble beginnings, where early computer viruses and malware were often more about exploration and experimentation. However, these initial forays laid the groundwork for more serious and damaging exploits.

As technology permeated every aspect of life, cyber threats grew sophistication and impact. The Internet's exponential growth provided fertile ground for cybercriminals to operate on an unimaginable scale. Businesses, governments, and individuals became targets in a world where digital assets are as valuable as physical ones. The early 2000s saw a significant shift in the threat landscape with the emergence of organized cybercrime syndicates and state-sponsored cyber espionage. These entities brought sophistication and resources that dramatically escalated the stakes.

An alarming level of sophistication characterizes today's cyber threats. Cybercriminals employ advanced techniques such as ransomware, phishing, and social engineering to exploit vulnerabilities. Integrating artificial intelligence and machine learning in cyberattacks presents new challenges, making threats more adaptive and complex to predict. The Internet of Things (IoT) expansion has exponentially increased the number of vulnerable devices, making cybersecurity more complex and crucial than ever.

State-sponsored cyber activities have added a new dimension to this landscape. These activities range from espionage and data theft to direct attacks on critical infrastructure, blurring the lines between cybercrime and cyber warfare. This evolution indicates a shift from cyber threats being a mere nuisance to a critical component of national and international security strategy.

Preparing for the Future

This dynamic landscape requires a proactive and constantly evolving approach to cybersecurity. It's not enough to react to threats as they emerge; there must be anticipation and preparation for future challenges. Understanding the history and evolution of cyber threats is crucial for developing effective defense strategies. It informs us about the potential direction of future cyber attacks and helps craft more robust and adaptive security measures.

The increasing sophistication of cyber threats necessitates more vital collaboration between governments, private sectors, and individuals. Developing comprehensive cybersecurity policies, investing in cutting-edge security technologies, and fostering a culture of cyber awareness are critical to staying ahead of cybercriminals. Additionally, as cyber threats evolve, so must the legal and ethical frameworks governing cybersecurity, ensuring they are equipped to handle new challenges.

The Role of Cybersecurity Professionals

Cybersecurity professionals stand as the first line of defense in the landscape of ever-evolving cyber threats. They safeguard information systems, prevent data breaches, and combat cybercrime. This dynamic field requires a unique blend of skills and qualities beyond technical expertise. Professionals in this domain must possess a deep understanding of the latest cybersecurity trends and technologies and a keen analytical mind to foresee and mitigate potential threats.

A curious and proactive mindset often characterizes a successful cybersecurity professional. They must be adept at problem-solving and thinking critically to identify vulnerabilities and devise robust security solutions. Adapting to a rapidly changing environment is critical, as new threats and technologies emerge constantly. Strong ethical principles are also essential, given the sensitive nature of the data and systems they protect. Communication skills are vital, too, as cybersecurity professionals often need to explain complex technical issues to nontechnical stakeholders.

Career Opportunities in Cybersecurity

Cybersecurity offers various career opportunities, reflecting the diverse threats and technologies involved. Career paths in this field vary widely, from technical roles like network security engineers and ethical hackers to strategic positions like cybersecurity analysts and chief information security officers. The demand for cybersecurity professionals continues to grow, driven by the increasing frequency and sophistication of cyber threats. This growth translates into a robust job market with opportunities for advancement and specialization.

Cybersecurity careers are diverse and offer the potential for high job satisfaction and competitive salaries. Professionals in this field have the opportunity to work in various sectors, including government, finance, healthcare, and technology. The dynamic nature of the field ensures that the work is challenging and ever-changing, providing continuous learning and professional growth opportunities.

Educational Opportunities in Cybersecurity

The educational landscape for aspiring cybersecurity professionals is diverse, offering various pathways to enter and excel in the field.

1. **Boot Camps**: Cybersecurity boot camps are intensive, short-term training programs designed to equip students with foundational skills in a condensed time frame. These programs often focus on hands-on learning and real-world scenarios, making them a practical choice for those looking to transition into the field quickly.

2. **Online Learning**: The rise of online education has significantly expanded learning opportunities in cybersecurity. Online courses and degree programs offer flexibility and accessibility, allowing students to learn at their own pace and from any location. These platforms cater to a range of learners, from beginners seeking basic knowledge to experienced professionals looking to upskill.

3. **Colleges and Universities**: Traditional colleges and universities offer cybersecurity programs at the undergraduate and graduate levels. These programs typically provide a comprehensive education covering cybersecurity's theoretical and practical aspects. They also offer the benefits of a traditional college experience, including access to campus resources, networking opportunities, and a broader educational context.

Each educational pathway has strengths and caters to different learning styles and career goals. Boot camps are ideal for those seeking rapid skill acquisition, online learning offers flexibility and a wide range of options, and college programs provide in-depth knowledge and a traditional academic environment.

ThriveDX

ThriveDX (www.thrivedx.com) specializes in providing immersive, hands-on cybersecurity training designed to reskill individuals and assist them in transforming their careers. They cater to a broad audience, including individuals seeking to become cybersecurity professionals and universities looking to enhance their educational offerings with comprehensive, hands-on cybersecurity education. This focus on practical, experiential learning is critical to their approach, enabling learners to acquire and retain essential cybersecurity skills effectively.

The programs offered by ThriveDX are developed by world-leading cybersecurity experts and cover a range of levels from entry level to advanced. Their "learn-by-doing" methodology is particularly beneficial for rapid skill acquisition and retention, catering to individuals starting a new tech career and universities and organizations seeking to fortify their cybersecurity capabilities. This broad spectrum of training solutions is tailored to meet the specific needs of different learners, underscoring ThriveDX's commitment to providing relevant and effective cybersecurity education.

Cybrary

Cybrary (www.cybrary.it) offers an accessible and affordable training platform focused on cybersecurity. It provides various educational services, including curated career paths, threat-informed training, and certification preparation for professionals at all levels. The platform is known for its user-friendly interface and is trusted by leading organizations, offering free and paid learning options. The free access allows users to learn fundamental cybersecurity concepts, while the paid version offers a more comprehensive learning experience. Additionally, Cybrary occasionally offers discounts on its insider plan, making it even more affordable for learners.

Cybrary's training is designed to align with real-world job opportunities, aiming to develop a highly skilled cybersecurity workforce. The platform offers self-paced online courses, enabling learners to develop and showcase their skills and achievements to reach their career goals. This approach to professional development emphasizes practical skills and knowledge that are directly applicable to the cybersecurity industry. The platform's focus on real-world applicability ensures that learners acquire skills that are not only theoretical but also useful in their professional lives.

Professor Messer

Professor Messer (www.professormesser.com/) offers a range of IT certification training resources, mainly focused on CompTIA certifications such as A+, Network+, and Security+. For the CompTIA A+ certification, Professor Messer provides a variety of training materials for both the 220-1101 Core 1 and 220-1102 Core 2 exams. These resources include free video courses, course notes, practice exams, downloadable videos, pop quizzes, study group replays, and study recommendations. These comprehensive materials cater to different learning styles and provide a thorough understanding of the exam contents.

In addition to A+ certification, Professor Messer also offers resources for Network+ and Security+ certifications. For Network+, learners can access free videos, course notes, downloadable content, study group replays, and specific study recommendations. Similarly, for the Security+ SY0-601 certification, the platform includes free videos, course notes, practice exams, downloadable videos, study group replays, and unique "Take Ten Challenges" to test knowledge. These offerings demonstrate Professor Messer's commitment to providing in-depth, accessible, and varied learning tools for individuals aiming for IT certifications.

Hack The Box

Hack The Box (www.hackthebox.com/) is a prominent gamified cybersecurity platform that focuses on upskilling, certification, and talent assessment in the cybersecurity domain. It serves many users, including individuals, businesses, government institutions, and universities. The platform's primary aim is to enhance its users' offensive and defensive security skills. It's particularly beneficial for cybersecurity professionals and organizations seeking to continuously improve their readiness against cyber-attacks by developing their capabilities across red, blue, and purple teams. This comprehensive approach ensures the skills learned are applicable and valuable in real-world scenarios.

The platform offers a unique learning experience for different audiences. It allows individuals to learn hacking from scratch to become proficient security professionals. This path includes certification and is geared toward improving employability in the cybersecurity field. For businesses, Hack The Box is a resource for security managers and Chief Information Security Officers (CISOs) who want their teams to be well-trained and prepared for cyber-attacks. Additionally, for universities, the platform offers distinct cybersecurity training, focusing on developing enduring skills for professors and students. This diversity in educational offerings caters to the specific needs of each group, ensuring that the training is relevant and practical.

About the Book

This comprehensive guide to cybersecurity is designed to be a practical and informative resource for anyone interested in the field, whether they are beginners, students, or professionals seeking to expand their knowledge. Each chapter of this book delves into a specific aspect of cybersecurity, starting from the fundamentals in the introduction to cybersecurity and progressively covering advanced topics such as artificial intelligence in cybersecurity and blockchain security.

To maximize the benefit of this book, the readers should approach each chapter methodically. Every chapter is structured to give a holistic view of its topic. It begins with an overview and a detailed exploration of key concepts. What sets this book apart is its inclusion of a real-world case study in each chapter, providing practical insights into how cybersecurity principles are applied in actual scenarios. This enhances understanding and bridges the gap between theory and practice.

Moreover, each chapter features a "Career Corner" that discusses relevant certifications and career paths in cybersecurity. This section is invaluable for those looking to advance their careers or break into cybersecurity. It offers guidance on what skills and qualifications are sought in the industry. To reinforce learning and ensure a solid grasp of the material, each chapter concludes with 15 questions and answers. These are designed to test comprehension and encourage critical thinking about the chapter's content.

By engaging with all these elements – the comprehensive discussions, case studies, career insights, and Q&A sections – the readers will gain a deep and practical understanding of cybersecurity, preparing them for academic and professional success in this dynamic and crucial field.

CHAPTER 2

Threat Landscape

Maintaining a high awareness level is beneficial and essential in cybersecurity's intricate and ever-evolving realm. This critical aspect is the foremost line of defense in an environment where threats are diverse and increasingly sophisticated. The primary objective of this section is to offer a detailed and thorough understanding of the vast array of cyber threats that pervade the digital landscape. These threats, varied in nature and impact, pose significant risks to various entities ranging from individual users to large corporations and governments.

The cyber world, akin to a vast ocean, is teeming with potential dangers that lurk beneath its surface. These dangers manifest in various forms, each with its unique characteristics and methods of attack. Understanding these threats requires recognizing their existence and deep comprehension of their mechanisms and how they can infiltrate systems and networks. The spectrum of these threats includes, but is not limited to, malware, phishing, denial-of-service attacks, man-in-the-middle attacks, advanced persistent threats, cryptojacking, and zero-day exploits. Each poses a unique set of challenges and requires specific strategies to counteract them.

Moreover, the targets and victims of these cyber threats are as diverse as the threats themselves. Individual users, often the most vulnerable, face risks ranging from identity theft to financial loss. Regardless of size and industry, businesses are prime targets for cybercriminals seeking to exploit financial gains, disrupt operations, or steal sensitive data. Governmental institutions are not immune either; they are frequently

© Dr. Jason Edwards 2024, corrected publication 2024
Dr. J. Edwards, *Mastering Cybersecurity*, https://doi.org/10.1007/979-8-8688-0297-3_2

targeted for espionage, sabotage, or to undermine public trust. The healthcare sector faces threats that can have dire consequences, such as compromising patient data or disrupting critical medical services. Educational institutions, with their wealth of research and personal data, are increasingly falling prey to cyber attacks. Financial institutions stand at an exceptionally high risk due to the monetary assets and sensitive financial information they hold.

This comprehensive overview is designed to serve as a foundational understanding, setting the stage for deeper exploration into each type of threat and their respective countermeasures. By the end of this section, the readers should have a solid grasp of the cyber threat universe, equipping them with the knowledge to identify and mitigate these risks effectively. The goal is to inform and empower individuals and organizations to better protect themselves in this digital age, where cybersecurity is no longer optional but necessary.

Threats

In the digital age, the landscape of cyber threats is vast and varied, encompassing a range of tactics and methodologies cybercriminals employ to exploit, disrupt, and infiltrate. These methods, constantly evolving in complexity and ingenuity, pose a significant risk to individuals and organizations. Among the most prevalent and damaging of these methods are malware attacks, phishing schemes, denial-of-service (DoS) and distributed denial-of-service (DDoS) attacks, man-in-the-middle (MitM) operations, advanced persistent threats (APTs), cryptojacking, and zero-day exploits. Each threat carries unique challenges and requires specific knowledge and strategies to mitigate effectively.

Malware, a broad category encompassing various forms of malicious software such as viruses, worms, trojan horses, and ransomware, is designed to damage, disrupt, or gain unauthorized access to computer systems. Phishing, conversely, employs deception to steal sensitive data like login credentials and credit card numbers, often through seemingly legitimate emails or messages. DoS and DDoS attacks aim to damage networks or resources with overwhelming traffic, while MitM attacks involve intercepting and manipulating communications between unsuspecting parties. APTs represent a more stealthy and prolonged threat, where attackers gain and maintain access to a network undetected. Cryptojacking and zero-day exploits further add to the arsenal of cyber threats, with the former unauthorizedly using someone else's computer resources for cryptocurrency mining and exploiting previously unknown software vulnerabilities. Each threat underscores the need for robust cybersecurity measures and continuous vigilance in the ever-changing digital landscape.

Malware

Malware, an abbreviation for malicious software, encompasses a variety of harmful software types, including viruses, worms, trojan horses, and ransomware. Each type has unique characteristics and methods of infection and damage. Viruses, for example, attach themselves to clean files and spread uncontrollably, corrupting file systems. Worms, in contrast, self-replicate without human intervention, often exploiting network vulnerabilities. Trojan horses deceive users by masquerading as legitimate software, thereby gaining unauthorized access to systems.

Ransomware represents a particularly menacing form of malware. It encrypts a victim's data, demanding a ransom for the decryption key. This type of malware can cause significant operational disruptions and financial losses. The impact of malware is not just limited to individual users; it extends to large organizations and can lead to massive data breaches, financial loss, and damage to reputation.

The prevention and mitigation of malware attacks involve a combination of robust antivirus software, user education, and adherence to cybersecurity best practices, such as regular software updates and cautious downloading of files or applications from the Internet. Understanding the various forms of malware is critical for effective cybersecurity measures, as it enables individuals and organizations to recognize potential threats and respond accordingly.

Phishing

Phishing is a deceptive cyber tactic employed by attackers to obtain sensitive information from unsuspecting victims. This method typically involves sending fraudulent emails or messages that mimic legitimate sources, such as banks, government agencies, or well-known companies. The objective is to trick recipients into revealing personal information like login credentials, credit card numbers, and social security numbers.

These attacks can be highly sophisticated, using social engineering techniques to create a sense of urgency or fear, prompting victims to respond quickly without questioning the authenticity of the request. Phishing messages often contain links to fake websites that closely resemble legitimate ones, where victims unknowingly enter their sensitive information.

To combat phishing, individuals and organizations must be vigilant and skeptical of unsolicited communications. Key preventive measures include not clicking on links or downloading attachments from unknown sources, verifying the authenticity of requests for personal information, and using anti-phishing tools provided in most modern web browsers and email services. Education and training in identifying phishing attempts are crucial in building a first line of defense against these cyberattacks.

Denial-of-Service (DoS) and Distributed Denial-of-Service (DDoS) Attacks

Denial-of-service (DoS) and distributed denial-of-service (DDoS) attacks aim to disrupt the normal functioning of a targeted server, service, or network by overwhelming it with a flood of Internet traffic. DoS attacks typically originate from a single source, whereas DDoS attacks are launched from multiple compromised devices, often distributed globally. This multitude of sources makes DDoS attacks more difficult to stop and can have a more significant impact.

These attacks work by overloading the target with more requests than it can handle, causing the system to slow down significantly or crash altogether, denying service to legitimate users. Common methods include exploiting server vulnerabilities or using a network of bots, known as a botnet, to flood the target with traffic. The motivations behind these attacks can vary from simple vandalism and personal grudges to extortion and political activism.

To defend against DoS and DDoS attacks, organizations must employ various strategies, such as maintaining robust network architecture with redundancy, implementing proper security measures to prevent the exploitation of vulnerabilities, and utilizing DDoS mitigation services that can absorb and disperse the influx of traffic. Regular monitoring of network traffic to detect unusual patterns can also provide early warning signs of an impending attack.

Man-in-the-Middle (MitM) Attacks

Man-in-the-middle (MitM) attacks occur when an attacker secretly intercepts and possibly alters the communication between two parties who believe they are directly communicating. These attacks can occur in any form of online communication, such as email, social media, or online banking. The attacker might intercept data in transit, eavesdrop on conversations, or impersonate one of the parties to gain sensitive information.

MitM attacks often exploit security weaknesses in a network or the methods used for data transmission. For example, unsecured Wi-Fi networks are prime targets for these attacks. Attackers can set up a rogue Wi-Fi network or compromise an existing one to intercept data transmitted by users connected to the network.

To protect against MitM attacks, individuals and organizations should use secure, encrypted communication channels, such as HTTPS, and be wary of connecting to unsecured Wi-Fi networks. Regular security audits and network monitoring can also help detect and prevent these attacks. Awareness and education about the risks and signs of MitM attacks are essential for users to protect their sensitive data.

Advanced Persistent Threats (APTs)

Advanced persistent threats (APTs) represent a category of cyberattacks where an unauthorized user gains access to a network and remains undetected for an extended period. These attacks are typically targeted to steal data or monitor network activity rather than causing immediate damage. APTs are often sponsored by nation-states or large criminal organizations, making them highly sophisticated and challenging to detect and remove.

APTs involve a prolonged, stealthy, and complex infiltration process. Attackers use various methods to gain entry, including spear-phishing, exploiting vulnerabilities, or using malware. Once inside, they establish a foothold, often creating backdoors and using techniques to remain undetected. The ultimate goal of an APT is not immediate disruption but long-term espionage, data theft, or gaining strategic advantages.

Combatting APTs requires a multifaceted approach, including implementing layered security defenses, continuous monitoring of network activity, regular security audits, and employee training to recognize potential threats. Early detection and swift response are vital to mitigating the impact of APTs. Organizations need to assume a stance of constant vigilance and readiness to respond to these advanced threats.

Cryptojacking

Cryptojacking is the unauthorized use of someone else's computing resources to mine cryptocurrency. This cyber attack is stealthy and can go undetected for a long time, as it does not typically cause immediate or apparent harm to the victim. Instead, it silently consumes system resources, such as CPU and electricity, which can result in degraded system performance and increased energy costs.

Attackers deploy cryptojacking through various methods, including embedding malicious code in websites or distributing malware through phishing emails. When a user visits an infected website or downloads infected software, the cryptojacking script automatically executes, harnessing the computing power of the user's device to mine cryptocurrency for the attacker.

To protect against cryptojacking, users should employ ad blockers or anti-crypto mining extensions on their browsers, maintain updated antivirus software, and be cautious about the websites they visit and the software they download. Organizations should also monitor their networks for unusual activity, such as spikes in CPU usage, which could indicate the presence of cryptojacking malware.

Zero-Day Exploits

Zero-day exploits are cyberattacks that target software or hardware vulnerabilities unknown to the vendor or the public. The term "zero-day" refers to the developer having had zero days to fix the vulnerability, as it is only discovered once an attack has occurred. Attackers highly value these exploits, as they can be used to penetrate systems that are otherwise well-protected.

17

Zero-day exploits pose a significant challenge because they exploit unknown flaws; thus, no specific defenses exist. These vulnerabilities can be found in operating systems, browsers, applications, or firmware and are often sold on the dark web or used by nation-states or cybercriminal groups for targeted attacks.

Organizations and individuals should adopt a proactive and layered security approach to mitigate the risk of zero-day exploits. This includes keeping software and systems updated, implementing intrusion detection systems, conducting regular security audits, and educating users about safe computing practices. Since these vulnerabilities are unknown until exploited, maintaining a robust and adaptable security posture is crucial for defense against these unpredictable threats.

Social Engineering

Social engineering attacks are a form of manipulation that exploits human psychology, rather than technical hacking techniques, to gain access to buildings, systems, or data. These attacks often involve tricking individuals into breaking standard security procedures. For example, attackers might impersonate police officers, bank officials, or other persons of authority to extract sensitive information. These tactics rely heavily on human interaction, often manipulating people into breaking standard security procedures.

One common form of social engineering is pretexting, where an attacker fabricates a scenario to engage a target, increasing the chance of the target divulging information. For instance, an attacker might call an individual and pose as a customer service agent to gain personal information. Another method is baiting, where an attacker leaves a malware-infected physical device, like a USB flash drive, in a place where it is likely to be found. The finder then picks up the device and plugs it into a computer, inadvertently installing the malware.

To defend against social engineering attacks, it's crucial to be aware of the different tactics attackers use and to maintain a healthy level of skepticism, especially when dealing with unsolicited requests for information. Regular employee training and awareness programs can teach them to recognize and respond appropriately to social engineering tactics. Organizations should also have clear policies and procedures for verifying identities and handling sensitive information.

Insider Threats

Insider threats come from individuals within an organization, such as employees, contractors, or business partners, who have inside information concerning the organization's security practices, data, and computer systems. An insider threat could manifest as an employee who steals information for personal gain or a disgruntled worker who wants to harm the company. These threats are challenging to detect as they come from legitimate users with authorized access to sensitive data.

Insiders may not always act with malicious intent. Sometimes, they inadvertently become a threat through careless or negligent behavior, such as falling for a phishing scam, using weak passwords, or mishandling data. However, malicious insiders are particularly dangerous as they have knowledge of the organization's vulnerabilities and can cause significant damage.

Organizations must implement strict access controls and monitor user activities to mitigate insider threats. Regular security training and awareness programs can help reduce the risks of negligent behavior. It's also essential to have policies and procedures to detect suspicious activity and respond to insider threats. Employee behavior monitoring, regular audits, and segregation of duties are some measures that can help detect and prevent insider threats.

Supply Chain Attacks

Supply chain attacks target the less secure elements in a supply chain. Attackers infiltrate a supplier or service provider and use that as a conduit to access a more secure target. For instance, by compromising a software vendor, attackers can distribute malware to all the vendor's clients through software updates. These attacks can be particularly devastating because they exploit trusted business relationships.

One of the most challenging aspects of supply chain attacks is detecting them. Since they come through legitimate channels, they can bypass many traditional security measures. These attacks require deep trust between suppliers and their customers, and attackers can exploit this trust. The interconnected nature of supply chains means that a single compromised component can affect all the entities relying on it.

Protecting against supply chain attacks requires a multifaceted approach. Organizations should conduct due diligence on their suppliers' security practices and ensure that their security measures extend to their supply chain. Regular audits and network activity monitoring can help detect anomalies that might indicate a breach. Additionally, implementing strict access controls and network segmentation can limit the spread and impact of a potential attack that comes through a supplier.

Ransomware

Ransomware is malware that encrypts the victim's files, making them inaccessible, and demands a ransom payment to decrypt them. These attacks can affect individuals, businesses, and even governmental organizations. Attackers typically demand the ransom in a cryptocurrency like Bitcoin to avoid tracking. The impact of ransomware can be devastating, leading to significant financial losses and disruption of operations.

Ransomware is often spread through phishing emails containing malicious attachments or links, exploiting kits on compromised websites, or exploiting network vulnerabilities. Once installed on a system, it encrypts files and displays a message demanding a ransom for the decryption key. The dilemma for victims is whether to pay the ransom or lose access to their files permanently. Even if the ransom is paid, there is no guarantee that the files will be decrypted.

The best defense against ransomware is to prevent it from infecting systems in the first place. This can be achieved through regular software updates, robust antivirus programs, and educating users about the risks of opening email attachments or clicking links from unknown sources. Regularly backing up important data and storing it offline can also minimize the damage caused by a ransomware attack, as it allows the restoration of encrypted files without paying a ransom.

SQL Injection

SQL injection is a cyber attack technique that targets databases using malicious SQL code. This attack exploits vulnerabilities in the database query software, allowing attackers to interfere with an application's database queries. It can be used for unauthorized viewing of data, deleting data, or even issuing commands to the database.

This attack works by inserting or "injecting" a SQL query via the input data from the client to the application. A successful SQL injection exploit can read sensitive data from the database, modify database data (insert/update/delete), execute administration operations on the database (such as shutting down the DBMS), and sometimes issue commands to the operating system.

Protecting against SQL injection requires secure coding practices. Developers should use prepared statements and parameterized queries, which ensure that an attacker cannot change the intent of a query, even if an attacker inserts SQL commands. Web applications should also implement robust data validation and sanitation measures. Regular security audits and vulnerability assessments can help identify and fix SQL injection vulnerabilities before attackers can exploit them.

Potential Targets and Victims

In the complex and ever-evolving landscape of the digital age, the spectrum of cyber threats extends far and wide, casting a shadow over a diverse array of potential victims. From solitary individuals navigating the online world to vast government networks safeguarding national security, the range of targets vulnerable to cyberattacks is as varied as it is vast. Each category of potential victim, including individual users, businesses of all sizes, governmental bodies, healthcare institutions, educational organizations, and financial institutions, confronts its unique cybersecurity challenges and threats. These threats not only differ in their nature and execution but also the motivations driving them, whether it be financial gain, espionage, sabotage, or mere disruption.

Understanding these varied targets' nuances and specific vulnerabilities is critical to formulating effective defense mechanisms and strategies. Often less guarded, individual users face personal data breaches, identity theft, and financial losses. Regardless of scale, businesses grapple with threats to their operational integrity, data security, and corporate reputation. Governmental agencies must contend with sophisticated state-sponsored attacks aimed at destabilizing national security or stealing sensitive information. Healthcare and educational institutions, repositories of valuable and sensitive personal data, are at risk of data breaches and ransomware attacks, with far-reaching consequences. Financial institutions, guardians of monetary assets and confidential financial data, remain high-value targets for cybercriminals seeking lucrative payoffs.

This section aims to shed light on the various potential targets and victims of cyber threats. It explores in detail the nature of the risks faced by each group, the potential motivations of the attackers, and the significant implications these attacks can have. Understanding these aspects is essential for any comprehensive approach to cybersecurity, ensuring that protective measures are robust and tailored to each potential target's specific needs and vulnerabilities. In doing so, we can better equip ourselves to defend against the ever-changing threats of the digital world, safeguarding our interests and the collective security and well-being of our interconnected societies.

Individuals are often the most vulnerable targets in the cyber threat landscape, frequently falling prey to attacks like phishing, malware, and hacking of personal online accounts. Personal devices such as smartphones, tablets, and computers can be compromised, leading to the theft of sensitive personal information, including financial details, personal identification information, and private communications. The impact of such breaches can range from financial loss to identity theft and significant personal privacy violations.

Cybercriminals often exploit the lack of cybersecurity awareness among individuals. Common tactics include phishing emails or messages that trick users into revealing their credentials or installing malicious software. Social engineering techniques also manipulate individuals into divulging confidential information or performing actions that compromise their security. The interconnected nature of digital life means that a breach in one area can lead to vulnerabilities in others, such as using the same passwords for multiple accounts.

To protect themselves, individuals need to adopt a proactive approach to cybersecurity. This includes using strong, unique passwords for each online account, enabling two-factor authentication where available, and being cautious about the information shared online. Regularly updating software, using reputable antivirus solutions, and being aware of common cyber threats can significantly reduce the risk of becoming a victim of cyber attacks.

Businesses of all sizes, from small startups to large corporations, are frequent targets of cyberattacks. The motivations for targeting businesses vary but often include financial gain, data theft, corporate espionage, and, in some cases, simply disrupting business operations. The types of data at risk include customer information, proprietary business data, employee records, and financial information.

Cyberattacks on businesses can lead to severe consequences, including financial losses, damage to the company's reputation, and loss of customer trust. In some cases, the impact of a cyber attack can be so severe that it leads to the closure of the business, especially if the company cannot recover the stolen data or cope with the financial implications of the breach. Businesses also face the risk of legal consequences if they fail to protect customer data adequately.

To defend against cyber threats, businesses must implement comprehensive cybersecurity strategies. This includes regular security assessments, employee training to recognize and avoid cyber threats, robust data encryption, and backup solutions. Businesses should also develop an incident response plan to address breaches quickly and effectively. Collaboration with cybersecurity experts and staying updated with the latest security trends and technologies are crucial for maintaining a solid defense against cyber threats.

Governments are high-profile targets for cyberattacks, often facing state-sponsored or politically motivated attacks. These attacks can target critical national infrastructure, sensitive government data, and even election systems. The motives behind these attacks range from espionage and political manipulation to undermining public trust in government institutions.

The consequences of cyberattacks on government entities are far-reaching. They can disrupt public services, compromise national security, and erode citizens' trust. These attacks can sometimes escalate into international incidents, especially when attributed to foreign governments.

The data involved in such attacks is often highly sensitive, including classified information, personal records of citizens, and details of national security strategies.

Protecting government infrastructure from cyber threats requires a multilayered security approach. This includes regular security audits, investing in advanced cybersecurity technologies, and training government employees in cybersecurity best practices. International cooperation is also essential in combating cyber threats, as these often transcend national borders. Governments must also develop rapid response protocols to mitigate the impact of cyberattacks when they occur.

Cybercriminals increasingly target healthcare institutions due to the sensitive nature of the patient data they hold. This data includes personal health information, insurance details, and financial information. Cyberattacks on healthcare institutions can take various forms, such as data breaches, ransomware attacks, and phishing schemes.

The implications of cyberattacks on healthcare institutions are profound. A breach in patient data not only compromises the privacy of individuals but also erodes trust in healthcare providers. Ransomware attacks, in particular, can be life-threatening if they disrupt critical healthcare services, such as access to patient records or the functionality of medical devices. Furthermore, recovering from such attacks can be costly and time-consuming, diverting resources from patient care.

To safeguard against these threats, healthcare institutions must prioritize cybersecurity. This includes implementing strong data encryption, conducting regular security training for staff, and establishing rigorous access controls to sensitive information. Regular risk assessments and a robust incident response plan ensure preparedness against potential cyber threats.

Educational institutions, including schools and universities, are targets for cyberattacks, often aimed at accessing staff and students' research data and personal information. These institutions hold a wealth of information, from intellectual property in research departments to personal records of the educational community. Cyberattacks in educational settings can range from data breaches and identity theft to ransomware attacks that lock down essential educational resources.

The impact of such attacks on educational institutions can be significant. Apart from the immediate disruption to educational services, there is a long-term risk of loss of intellectual property and sensitive personal data. This can lead to financial losses, damage to the institution's reputation, and legal implications if the institution is found to have inadequately protected data.

Educational institutions must adopt comprehensive cybersecurity measures to protect against these threats. This involves securing their networks, regularly updating and patching systems, and implementing strict access controls. Educating staff and students about cybersecurity risks and safe online practices is also essential. Additionally, having an incident response plan is crucial for quickly addressing and mitigating the impact of any cyber incident.

Financial institutions, such as banks and other financial entities, are prime targets for cybercriminals due to the significant amounts of monetary assets and financial data they manage. These institutions face various cyber threats, including but not limited to data breaches, system hacking, and insider threats. The primary motivation for attacking these institutions is financial gain, but it can also include attempts to destabilize the financial system of a country.

The impact of cyberattacks on financial institutions can be catastrophic. Apart from direct financial loss, these attacks can undermine customer confidence and result in long-term reputational damage. In some cases, cyberattacks on financial institutions can have broader economic implications, affecting the stability of financial markets and consumer trust in the banking system.

To combat these threats, financial institutions must employ state-of-the-art cybersecurity measures. This includes continuously monitoring their systems for suspicious activity, using advanced encryption techniques for data protection, and regularly conducting cybersecurity drills. Employee training in recognizing and responding to cyber threats is also vital. Collaboration with regulatory bodies and other financial institutions to share threat intelligence and best practices can further strengthen the cybersecurity posture of the entire financial sector.

Evolution of Threats

The cybersecurity landscape is constantly changing, shaped by the evolving nature of threats that emerge and transform over time. Understanding the historical trends in these cyber threats is not just an exercise in academic analysis but a crucial element for developing effective and dynamic cybersecurity strategies. As cybercriminals adapt and refine their methods, so must our defenses evolve. This evolution of threats involves recognizing patterns from the past, identifying current vulnerabilities, and anticipating future challenges. By analyzing how cyber threats have changed over the years and projecting potential future trends, we can better prepare and protect against the next generation of digital threats. This comprehensive understanding forms the bedrock upon which robust and resilient cybersecurity frameworks are built, ensuring preparedness in an ever-changing digital landscape.

Early Viruses and Worms

In the initial stages of cyber threats, viruses and worms were primarily seen as a nuisance rather than a critical threat. These early forms of malware often involved individuals testing their programming skills or seeking to make a statement. Viruses required a host program to spread, and worms, which could replicate independently, typically cause inconvenience by slowing down systems or corrupting files. Still, they were not typically designed with malicious intent. Their creation and spread were more about demonstrating technical prowess or making a statement than causing genuine harm.

However, even in these early stages, the potential for serious damage was evident. As these viruses and worms became more widespread, they posed significant challenges to personal and organizational computer systems. Instances of widespread infections underscored the need for robust cybersecurity measures. These early experiences with malware laid the groundwork for developing antivirus software. They raised awareness about digital security, setting the stage for more complex cybersecurity strategies in response to evolving threats.

Rise of Financially Motivated Malware

With the proliferation of online banking and ecommerce, the landscape of cyber threats underwent a significant transformation. Cybercriminals quickly recognized the potential for financial gain and began to develop malware aimed at economic exploitation. This shift marked the emergence of financially motivated malware that stole credit card numbers, online banking credentials, and other financially sensitive information. This type of malware represented a significant escalation from the earlier nuisance-based viruses and worms, as it directly targeted financial assets and personal identities.

The advent of this financially motivated malware led to an increase in the sophistication and stealthiness of attacks. Cybercriminals employed advanced techniques to evade detection and ensure the success of their exploits. These attacks were far-reaching, affecting not just individual users but also businesses and financial institutions, leading to substantial financial losses and eroding trust in digital transactions. This era underscored the need for enhanced security measures in the financial sector, including more secure transaction protocols and increased public awareness about the importance of cybersecurity in financial dealings.

State-Sponsored Cyber Espionage

As the digital age progressed, nations began to recognize the strategic value of cyberspace as a domain for espionage and warfare. State-sponsored cyber espionage emerged as a significant trend, with governments either directly engaging in or sponsoring cyberattacks to spy on or disrupt other countries' operations and target critical infrastructures. These operations were often highly sophisticated, leveraging a nation's resources to develop complex cyber attack capabilities.

This form of cyber espionage represented a new threat, involving not just theft of information but also the potential to disrupt critical national infrastructures, such as power grids, communication networks, and defense systems. The implications of state-sponsored cyberattacks were profound, extending beyond mere data theft to encompass national security concerns and international relations. The rise of state-sponsored cyber espionage highlighted the need for robust national cybersecurity defenses and international cooperation to address and mitigate these threats.

Sophistication of Attacks

Over time, cyberattacks have become increasingly sophisticated, employing advanced techniques and technologies to evade detection and achieve their objectives. One notable development in this regard is the advent of polymorphic malware, which can change its code or behavior to evade detection by security software. This type of malware represents a significant challenge to traditional antivirus programs that recognize known malware signatures.

Attackers have employed advanced evasion tactics, such as using encrypted channels to communicate with compromised systems or leveraging legitimate websites and services to host or distribute malware. These sophisticated methods make detecting and preventing attacks increasingly tricky, requiring more advanced and adaptive cybersecurity measures. The evolution in the sophistication of attacks underscores the ongoing arms race in cybersecurity, where defenders must continually adapt and innovate to keep pace with increasingly advanced and elusive threats.

Future Predictions

As we look toward the future of cybersecurity, it becomes increasingly clear that the digital threat landscape is poised to evolve in complexity and scale. Advancements in technology present new opportunities for innovation and efficiency and open the door to a new generation of cyber threats that are more sophisticated and harder to detect. The future of cyber threats is likely to be characterized by cutting-edge technologies, including artificial intelligence (AI), the proliferation of Internet of Things (IoT) devices, the expanding reliance on cloud services, and the emergence of deepfakes and disinformation campaigns. Additionally, quantum computing presents a paradigm shift in cybersecurity, potentially challenging the foundations of current encryption methods.

AI-powered attacks represent a significant shift in the capabilities of cybercriminals, enabling them to automate attacks and make them more adaptive and evasive than ever before. The rapid growth in the number of IoT devices, often designed with minimal security features, is set to create a vast network of vulnerable points that can be exploited. Despite its numerous benefits, cloud computing also introduces new risks, as centralized data storage becomes a tempting target for attackers. The rise of deepfakes and sophisticated disinformation campaigns poses a threat not only to individual privacy and security but also to the fabric of society by undermining trust in digital content. Meanwhile, the potential of quantum computing to break current encryption algorithms could lead to a complete overhaul of cybersecurity strategies, requiring the development of new encryption techniques to protect sensitive data. These anticipated developments underscore the need for proactive and forward-thinking approaches in cybersecurity to safeguard against the emerging digital threats of the future.

AI-Powered Attacks

As artificial intelligence (AI) continues to advance rapidly, its implications for cybersecurity are profound. AI-powered attacks are poised to become one of the most sophisticated cyber threats. These attacks leverage AI algorithms to automate cyber attack tasks, such as identifying vulnerabilities or optimizing malware. This automation allows cybercriminals to launch more frequent and complex attacks with reduced human oversight. AI can also be used to personalize attacks, such as crafting phishing messages that are more likely to deceive specific individuals, thereby increasing the success rate of these attacks.

Moreover, AI-powered attacks can adapt in real time to defensive measures. For instance, AI can analyze the responses of security systems and modify its attack strategies dynamically to avoid detection. This ability to learn and adapt makes AI-powered attacks particularly dangerous, as they can evolve to circumvent even the most advanced security protocols. Such attacks could outpace the capabilities of traditional cybersecurity tools, requiring new strategies and technologies to counter them effectively.

The increasing use of AI in cyberattacks also raises concerns about developing autonomous cyber weapons that could operate without human control. The ethical and security implications of such advancements are significant. It underscores the need for robust AI security frameworks and ethical guidelines to prevent the misuse of AI technologies in cyber warfare and cybercrime.

IoT Vulnerabilities

The Internet of Things (IoT) represents a rapidly expanding frontier in the digital world, with an ever-increasing number of connected devices being integrated into daily life. However, this proliferation of IoT devices also brings significant security challenges. IoT devices are designed with convenience and functionality rather than security, making them vulnerable to cyberattacks. These devices, ranging from smart home appliances to industrial sensors, can serve as entry points for attackers to infiltrate networks and access sensitive data.

IoT vulnerabilities are primarily due to inadequate security measures, such as weak passwords, unencrypted communications, and a lack of regular software updates. Cybercriminals can exploit these vulnerabilities to gain unauthorized access, steal data, or even take control of the devices for malicious purposes. For instance, a compromised IoT device can be used as a botnet to launch large-scale distributed denial-of-service (DDoS) attacks.

The growing reliance on IoT devices necessitates a greater focus on securing them. This includes the development of more robust security standards for IoT devices, regular security audits, and consumer education on the importance of IoT security. Manufacturers also play a critical role in ensuring that their devices are secure by design and receive timely updates to address emerging threats.

Cloud Attacks

As businesses and individuals increasingly rely on cloud computing for storing data and running applications, the security of cloud services has become a paramount concern. Cloud attacks refer to cyberattacks that specifically target vulnerabilities in cloud computing environments. These attacks can take various forms, such as data breaches, account hijacking, and service disruptions. The centralized nature of cloud services makes them an attractive target for cybercriminals, as a successful attack can yield access to vast amounts of sensitive data.

One of the key challenges in cloud security is the shared responsibility model, where security is a joint effort between the cloud service provider and the client. Misconfigurations by users, such as improper access controls or unsecured interfaces, can leave cloud services vulnerable to attacks. Additionally, as cloud services are accessible from anywhere, they are susceptible to a wide range of attacks, including phishing, malware, and exploitation of software vulnerabilities.

To combat cloud attacks, it is essential to implement robust security measures, including encryption, strong access controls, and continuous monitoring of cloud environments. Regular security assessments and compliance with industry standards can also help mitigate cloud computing risks. As cloud technology evolves, so must the strategies to secure it against potential cyber threats.

Deepfakes and Disinformation

The rise of deepfakes and sophisticated disinformation campaigns presents a new and complex challenge in cybersecurity. Deepfakes use advanced AI and machine learning techniques to create realistic but fake audio and video content, making it possible to fabricate believable media content that can deceive individuals, manipulate public opinion, or even influence political events. The ability to convincingly replicate someone's appearance and voice has significant implications for personal and national security.

Disinformation campaigns, often amplified by deepfakes, can spread false information at an unprecedented scale, with the potential to cause social unrest, damage reputations, or interfere in electoral processes. The challenge lies not only in the technological sophistication of these methods but also in their psychological impact. Deepfakes and disinformation can erode trust in media and institutions, making it difficult for individuals to discern truth from falsehood.

Addressing the threats posed by deepfakes and disinformation requires a combination of technological solutions, such as tools to detect manipulated media and broader efforts to educate the public about these threats. Policymakers and tech companies must also collaborate to develop standards and regulations that prevent the misuse of deepfake technology while preserving freedom of expression and innovation.

Quantum Computing

The advent of quantum computing promises to revolutionize various fields, but it also poses significant challenges to cybersecurity. Quantum computers, with their ability to perform complex calculations at unprecedented speeds, can potentially render many of the current encryption methods obsolete. Traditional encryption algorithms, which rely on the difficulty of factoring large numbers – a computationally intensive task for classical computers – could be easily broken by a sufficiently powerful quantum computer.

This vulnerability presents a substantial security risk, as much of the world's digital communications and data encryption rely on these algorithms. The emergence of quantum computing could lead to sensitive information, from government secrets to personal financial data, becoming accessible to those with quantum computing capabilities. This scenario is often referred to as "quantum supremacy" in the context of cybersecurity.

To prepare for this quantum future, researchers and security experts are developing quantum-resistant encryption methods, known as post-quantum cryptography. These new algorithms are designed to be secure against conventional and quantum computing attacks, ensuring the continued protection of digital information. The transition to post-quantum cryptography will be a significant undertaking, requiring widespread updates to existing digital infrastructure. However, it is a necessary step to safeguard against the cybersecurity challenges posed by the advent of quantum computing.

Career Corner

Threat intelligence is a crucial aspect of modern cybersecurity, focusing on understanding and analyzing potential cyber threats to prevent attacks before they occur. Threat intelligence care is challenging and rewarding, requiring a blend of technical expertise, analytical skills, and a keen understanding of cyber adversaries' tactics and motivations. As cyber threats continue to evolve, professionals in this field are in high demand.

One of the primary career paths in threat intelligence is a Threat Intelligence Analyst. These professionals collect, analyze, and interpret data from various sources to identify potential security threats. Their role involves staying updated on the latest cyber threats, understanding cyber adversaries' tactics, techniques, and procedures, and providing actionable intelligence to help organizations strengthen their security posture. They work closely with security teams to inform them about the nature of threats and recommend defensive strategies.

Another critical role in this field is that of a Cyber Threat Researcher. These individuals delve deeper into the specifics of malware, hacking groups, and cyber attack strategies. They often work for cybersecurity firms, government agencies, or large corporations with a significant online presence. Their research contributes to developing more effective security solutions and strategies to counteract evolving cyber threats.

For those interested in a career in threat intelligence, several certifications can enhance one's knowledge and credibility. The Certified Threat Intelligence Analyst (CTIA) credential from the EC-Council is a popular choice, offering extensive training in threat intelligence principles, including data collection, analysis, and report generation. The Global

Information Assurance Certification (GIAC) also offers the Cyber Threat Intelligence (GCTI) certification, which focuses on skills required to analyze and combat advanced threats.

In addition to formal certifications, practical experience is highly valued in the threat intelligence field. Participating in threat intelligence sharing communities, attending relevant cybersecurity conferences, and staying abreast of the latest trends and technologies in cybersecurity are essential for career development. Professionals often start in broader cybersecurity roles, gaining experience in network security or incident response before specializing in threat intelligence.

Cybersecurity firms and consulting agencies are joint employers for threat intelligence professionals. These organizations serve a wide range of clients and offer the opportunity to work on diverse and challenging projects. Government agencies, particularly those focused on national security, are also significant employers in this field, given their need for robust threat intelligence capabilities to defend against domestic and international cyber threats.

The future of threat intelligence careers looks promising as cyber threats grow in complexity and frequency. The rise of AI and machine learning in cybersecurity offers new opportunities for threat intelligence professionals to develop more advanced analytical tools and techniques. As the landscape of cyber warfare evolves, threat intelligence becomes increasingly integral to national security, corporate cybersecurity, and critical infrastructure protection.

In summary, careers in threat intelligence are at the forefront of the fight against cybercrime, offering dynamic and impactful opportunities for professionals in the cybersecurity field. With the right combination of education, certification, and practical experience, individuals can build rewarding careers, helping organizations stay one step ahead of cyber threats. The field of threat intelligence not only demands technical acumen and a detective-like mindset, making it a perfect fit for those who enjoy unraveling complex cyber puzzles.

Case Study: MITRE ATT&CK

The MITRE ATT&CK framework, a critical tool in understanding and combating cyber threats, offers a structured approach to analyzing and responding to adversary tactics and techniques. Standing for Adversarial Tactics, Techniques, and Common Knowledge, this framework was developed by MITRE, a well-respected nonprofit organization known for its federal government–sponsored research and development centers. The ATT&CK framework is unique in its comprehensive cataloging of real-world observations of cyberattacks, making it an invaluable resource for developing specific threat models and methodologies across the private sector, government, and cybersecurity communities.

At the heart of the MITRE ATT&CK framework lies its detailed breakdown of the various stages of a cyber attack. It delineates the entire attack lifecycle, from initial reconnaissance, where attackers gather information on their target, to the final stage of data exfiltration, where compromised data is transferred from the target network. The framework categorizes adversary tactics, their overarching objectives during an attack, and the techniques, which are the specific methods used to achieve these objectives. For example, under the tactic of "Execution," one might find techniques like "Scripting" or "Command and Scripting Interpreter" detailing how attackers execute their code on a victim's system. Under "Persistence," techniques such as "Boot or Logon Autostart Execution" are listed, demonstrating how attackers maintain their foothold in a system.

One of the most prominent features of the MITRE ATT&CK framework is its emphasis on post-compromise techniques. This approach is crucial in today's cybersecurity landscape, where, despite best efforts, attackers often successfully breach perimeter defenses. The framework categorizes these techniques into several tactics, such as "Privilege Escalation," "Defense Evasion," and "Credential Access," offering insights into the actions of attackers after they have penetrated a network. This perspective is invaluable for organizations in recognizing and countering threats that have bypassed initial defenses, a scenario increasingly common in sophisticated cyberattacks.

The MITRE ATT&CK framework is dynamic and regularly updated to include new findings about emerging threats, reflecting the fast-evolving nature of cyberattacks. This constant evolution is driven by contributions from cybersecurity professionals globally, ensuring that the framework remains an up-to-date, community-driven compilation of adversary behaviors. The collaborative nature of the ATT&CK framework guarantees its relevance and accuracy, cementing its status as a critical resource for enhancing cybersecurity measures.

Furthermore, the MITRE ATT&CK framework's versatility across different industries and technological environments stands out. Its technology-agnostic nature ensures its applicability to various organizations, regardless of their specific IT infrastructure. This flexibility is particularly beneficial in diverse applications, from guiding incident response and threat hunting to influencing the development of cybersecurity tools and methodologies.

The MITRE ATT&CK framework is extensively employed in various cybersecurity exercises. Red teams, or groups of security professionals who simulate cyberattacks to test defenses, leverage the framework to craft more effective and comprehensive attack simulations. This approach thoroughly evaluates an organization's defenses against a spectrum of known tactics and techniques. Similarly, the ATT&CK framework is an essential reference point for threat hunters in identifying unusual activities and potential threats within their networks. Integrating cybersecurity practices with the ATT&CK framework enables organizations to elevate their detection, understanding, and response capabilities, thereby fortifying their defenses against the multifaceted threats in the digital world.

By categorizing and detailing each phase of a cyber attack, the MITRE ATT&CK framework provides a clear road map for understanding and mitigating cyber threats. Its comprehensive nature, focus on post-compromise scenarios, and continuous updates make it an indispensable tool in the arsenal of cybersecurity professionals worldwide. Whether used for enhancing organizational security postures, conducting cybersecurity training, or developing defensive strategies, the ATT&CK framework remains a cornerstone in the ongoing battle against cyber adversaries.

Chapter Questions

1. What is the primary purpose of ransomware in cyberattacks?

    A. To encrypt a victim's data and demand a ransom for decryption

    B. To steal personal information for identity theft

    C. To create a backdoor for future attacks

    D. To disrupt services with a flood of Internet traffic

2. What is the attacker's main action in a man-in-the-middle (MitM) attack?

    A. Encrypting sensitive data

    B. Intercepting and possibly altering communication

    C. Launching a denial-of-service attack

    D. Injecting malicious SQL queries

3. Which of the following best describes a zero-day exploit?

    A. An attack on the day software is released

    B. An attack that targets vulnerabilities unknown to the vendor

    C. A ransomware attack demanding payment within one day

    D. A phishing attack sent through an email

4. What type of cyber attack employs deceptive tactics to obtain sensitive information, often through emails mimicking legitimate sources?

    A. SQL injection

    B. Phishing

    C. Cryptojacking

    D. Advanced persistent threat (APT)

5. Advanced persistent threats (APTs) are characterized by

    A. Quick and immediate disruption of services

    B. Short-term, high-impact attacks for financial gain

    C. Prolonged and stealthy presence in a network

    D. High-frequency attacks from multiple sources

6. What common cyber threats do individual users frequently encounter?

    A. State-sponsored cyber espionage

    B. Quantum computing breaches

    C. Phishing, malware, and hacking of personal accounts

    D. Supply chain attacks

7. What is a primary cybersecurity challenge faced by businesses?

    A. Polymorphic malware

    B. Deepfake technology

    C. Threats to operational integrity and data security

    D. IoT vulnerabilities

8. Which type of cyberattacks are governmental bodies particularly vulnerable to?

    A. Cryptojacking

    B. Ransomware

    C. State-sponsored cyber espionage

    D. Phishing schemes

9. Healthcare institutions are increasingly targeted by cybercriminals for what reason?

    A. Their extensive use of cloud services

    B. The sensitive nature of patient data

    C. The high volume of financial transactions

    D. Their reliance on outdated technology

10. What are educational institutions often targeted for in cyberattacks?

    A. Their political influence

    B. Intellectual property and personal data

    C. Banking information

    D. Healthcare information

11. What motivates cyberattacks on financial
     institutions?

     A. Disrupting educational resources

     B. Financial gain from assets and data

     C. Gaining medical insights

     D. Political manipulation

12. What do early viruses and worms typically cause in
     the context of cyber threats?

     A. Financial gain for attackers

     B. System slowdowns and file corruption

     C. Breaking encryption algorithms

     D. State-sponsored espionage

13. What marked the rise of financially motivated
     malware?

     A. The advent of quantum computing

     B. Proliferation of online banking and ecommerce

     C. The introduction of deepfake technology

     D. Increased use of IoT devices

14. State-sponsored cyber espionage often targets what?

     A. Educational research data

     B. Patient health information

     C. National infrastructure and sensitive data

     D. Financial transaction records

15. What is a characteristic of the evolution of cyberattacks over time?

    A. Decreased sophistication and complexity

    B. Increased use of AI-powered attacks

    C. Reduced frequency of attacks

    D. Focus on targeting individuals only

CHAPTER 3

Social Engineering

In the realm of cybersecurity, social engineering refers to a broad spectrum of malicious activities accomplished through human interactions. It involves manipulating people into breaking standard security procedures and divulging confidential information. Social engineering is predicated on the attacker's ability to exploit their target's trust, leveraging human psychology rather than technical hacking techniques. This method of deception is particularly insidious because it targets a common vulnerability – the human tendency to trust.

At the heart of social engineering lies the art of manipulating individuals for gain. Attackers skillfully influence their targets to take actions that may not be in their best interest, such as revealing sensitive information or granting access to restricted areas. This manipulation is achieved through various means, including but not limited to impersonation, persuasion, and exploiting the natural human inclination to be helpful and cooperative. The success of these tactics hinges on the attacker's ability to establish trust or authority in the target's mind.

The effectiveness of social engineering is rooted in its exploitation of human psychology. Attackers leverage a deep understanding of human behavior, emotions, and cognitive biases to deceive their targets. They may prey on fear, urgency, or the desire to be helpful, often creating scenarios where the target feels compelled to act quickly, bypassing normal decision-making processes and security protocols. This psychological manipulation is a key differentiator that sets social engineering apart from other cyber threats.

Dr. J. Edwards, *Mastering Cybersecurity*, https://doi.org/10.1007/979-8-8688-0297-3_3

Deceptive tactics used in social engineering are numerous and varied. They range from phishing – sending emails that appear to be from reputable sources – to baiting where an attacker leaves a malware-infected device, like a USB stick, in a place where it will be found and used. Other tactics include pretexting, where an attacker fabricates a situation to steal information, and tailgating, where unauthorized persons gain physical access to restricted areas by following closely behind authorized individuals.

Understanding the historical context and evolution of social engineering is crucial in comprehending its current impact on cybersecurity. Initially, social engineering tactics were more rudimentary and executed in person or through traditional mail. Scams and cons of the past were based on the same principles of trust and manipulation but lacked the technological aspect of modern attacks.

Early examples of social engineering in the pre-digital era were often carried out through phone scams or in-person impersonations. These early methods set the groundwork for what would evolve into more sophisticated attacks with the rise of the Internet and digital communications. The digital era brought new opportunities for social engineers, with tactics like phishing and spear-phishing becoming prevalent due to the widespread use of email and the Internet.

The modern digital evolution of social engineering has profoundly impacted the landscape of cybersecurity. With the increasing sophistication of technical defenses, attackers have found more success exploiting human vulnerabilities than trying to breach advanced security systems. This shift has made social engineering one of the most significant threats in the cyber world today, necessitating a reevaluation of traditional cybersecurity strategies.

The importance of understanding social engineering cannot be overstated in today's pervasive threat landscape. Both individuals and organizations face significant risks from these types of attacks, which can lead to financial loss, data breaches, and damage to reputation.

Mitigation requires not only technical measures but also, and perhaps more importantly, awareness and education. By educating individuals and employees about the tactics used in social engineering and fostering a culture of skepticism and verification, we can significantly reduce the risks posed by these psychological manipulation strategies.

Psychology of Social Engineering

The psychology of social engineering is deeply rooted in understanding human behavior and decision-making. It revolves around the cognitive processes that drive how individuals perceive, interpret, and react to various situations. These processes blend logical thinking and emotional responses, which social engineers expertly manipulate. By studying how people make decisions, social engineers tailor their approaches to exploit specific human cognition and behavior vulnerabilities.

At the core of these cognitive processes are various mental shortcuts and biases that people unconsciously use in their daily decision-making. These cognitive biases are systematic patterns of deviation from rational judgment. They arise from the brain's attempt to simplify information processing and can significantly impact the effectiveness of social engineering tactics. Social engineers exploit these biases to steer their targets' decisions and actions.

One common cognitive bias exploited in social engineering is the confirmation bias, where individuals favor information that confirms their preexisting beliefs or hypotheses. Social engineers manipulate this bias by presenting information that aligns with their target's expectations, thereby gaining their trust and compliance. The anchoring effect, another bias, causes individuals to rely too heavily on the first piece of information they receive. In social engineering, attackers use this bias by setting an initial context or "anchor" that influences the target's subsequent decisions and judgments.

47

The availability heuristic is also a critical cognitive bias in social engineering. It refers to the tendency of individuals to overestimate the importance of information that is readily available to them. Social engineers leverage this by emphasizing certain information or scenarios that are more memorable or emotionally charged, thus influencing their target's perception and decision-making process.

Emotional manipulation is another cornerstone of social engineering tactics. Social engineers can leverage emotions such as fear and trust to influence their targets' behavior. By instilling fear, they can coerce targets into acting hastily without thorough consideration. Similarly, by gaining trust, they can lower the target's defenses and willingness to question their motives or actions.

Appealing to emotions is a powerful tool in the arsenal of a social engineer. They often create scenarios that evoke strong emotional responses, such as sympathy or empathy, to manipulate their targets into divulging confidential information or performing specific actions. Creating a sense of urgency is another emotional manipulation technique, where the target is rushed into making decisions, thereby circumventing logical thought processes and critical evaluation.

In analyzing persuasion techniques used in social engineering, several principles stand out. The principle of reciprocity, for example, exploits the human tendency to want to give something back when something is received. Social engineers use this by doing a small favor or offering help, expecting that, in return, their target will be more inclined to assist them.

Authority influence is another persuasive technique where social engineers impersonate or claim to have authority or expertise. People are generally more willing to follow instructions or give away information if they believe the request comes from a position of authority. Lastly, scarcity tactics create a perception of limited time or resources, pressuring the target to act quickly. This technique plays on the fear of missing out, prompting hasty actions without adequate scrutiny. Understanding these psychological factors is crucial in recognizing and defending against social engineering attacks.

Social Engineering Attacks

Social engineering attacks are diverse techniques that exploit human psychology for malicious purposes. One of the most common forms of these attacks is phishing, which can take various forms. Email phishing is perhaps the most familiar, involving attackers sending emails that appear to be from reputable sources to trick recipients into providing sensitive information or clicking on malicious links. These emails often mimic the look and language of legitimate correspondence from banks, service providers, or even friends and colleagues, making them difficult to distinguish from genuine communications.

Phishing also extends to text messages, known as SMS phishing or smishing. In these attacks, the perpetrator sends text messages that entice the recipient to click on a malicious link or provide personal information. These messages might appear from a trusted organization and often create a sense of urgency to prompt immediate action. Vishing, or voice phishing, is another variant where attackers use phone calls to extract sensitive information. In these scenarios, the attacker often poses as a legitimate representative of an organization to elicit information or direct action from the target.

Impersonation and pretexting are sophisticated tactics used in social engineering attacks, involving the attacker posing as an authority figure or creating a convincing scenario to exploit the target's trust. By adopting the identity of someone in authority, such as a police officer, IT technician, or corporate executive, attackers can manipulate their targets into divulging confidential information or performing actions that compromise security. Crafting convincing scenarios requires detailed knowledge of the victim or their organization, making these attacks particularly insidious and effective.

Baiting and tailgating are other prevalent methods in social engineering. Baiting involves luring targets with the promise of goods or services to steal their personal information or infect their systems with malware. This could be in the form of a free software download or access to exclusive content. Tailgating, on the other hand, is a physical security breach tactic where an unauthorized person gains access to a restricted area by following someone authorized. This attack exploits the social norm of politeness and the natural inclination to help others, allowing attackers to infiltrate secure environments.

Elicitation and manipulation are subtle yet powerful techniques in social engineering. These methods involve extracting information through seemingly innocuous conversation, where the attacker engages the target in a discussion and subtly steers it to gather the desired information. Attackers often manipulate targets emotionally, leveraging human tendencies like the desire to be liked or the fear of confrontation. Gaining trust through rapport and empathy is critical in these interactions, as it lowers the target's defenses and makes them more susceptible to divulging sensitive information.

Each social engineering attack demonstrates the complexity and variety of tactics attackers use to exploit human psychology. They underline the necessity for constant vigilance in personal and professional contexts to safeguard against these manipulative techniques. Understanding the nature of these attacks is the first step in developing effective strategies to counter them, emphasizing the importance of awareness and education in the ongoing battle against cybersecurity threats.

Tools and Techniques in Social Engineering

Social engineering attacks employ technology-based tools and psychological techniques to manipulate and deceive their targets. On the technological front, malware and trojans play a significant role. These malicious software programs are often disguised as legitimate files and, once opened, give attackers unauthorized access to the victim's system. This attack can be particularly damaging, as it allows the perpetrator to gather sensitive information or gain control over computer systems stealthily.

Another tool in the arsenal of social engineers is exploiting software vulnerabilities. Attackers often target known weaknesses in software systems to gain unauthorized access or cause disruption. These vulnerabilities can be in operating systems, applications, or even less obvious places like web browsers and plug-ins. Keeping software updated and patched is crucial in defending against these attacks.

Digital manipulation tools also play a crucial role in social engineering. These tools range from simple photo-editing software to more advanced programs that create deepfakes – highly realistic and convincing audio and video forgeries. Such tools are used to fabricate evidence, impersonate individuals, or create misleading content, which can be instrumental in manipulating targets.

On the psychological side, creating a false sense of security is a common technique. Social engineers design scenarios that make their targets feel safe and in control while subtly guiding them toward actions that compromise security. This could involve mimicking familiar interfaces or providing reassurances of security and confidentiality.

Appealing to personal interests is another psychological technique used in social engineering. By tailoring their approach to their targets' individual interests or hobbies, attackers increase the likelihood of engagement and compliance. This technique relies on gathering information about the target, often through social media or other public platforms.

Feigning empathy and understanding is a subtle yet effective psychological tool. Social engineers often pretend to understand and empathize with their target's situation, building a rapport that facilitates manipulation. This approach can lower the target's defenses, making them more susceptible to influence and persuasion.

Manipulation tactics in social engineering also involve gaslighting and creating confusion. These tactics are designed to undermine the target's confidence in their judgment, making them more dependent on the attacker for information and direction. Gaslighting can be particularly harmful, as it can lead to long-term psychological effects.

Social media exploitation is a growing field in social engineering. Attackers use platforms like Facebook, Twitter, and LinkedIn for manipulative tactics, including impersonation of authority figures. Social engineers can build trust and credibility among a broad audience by creating fake profiles or cloning existing ones.

Social engineering through social media often involves profile cloning and impersonation. Attackers replicate social media profiles of real individuals, using them to gain the trust of friends and colleagues of the person being impersonated. This tactic can particularly effectively infiltrate social or professional networks for malicious purposes.

Lastly, exploiting psychological vulnerabilities is a key aspect of social engineering. This includes creating urgency with online messages, which pressures the target into making hasty decisions, often bypassing logical thought processes. Persuasive content creation and leveraging emotional triggers, such as fear, curiosity, or excitement, are common tactics. These methods exploit the inherent human response to certain stimuli, making individuals more susceptible to manipulation and deceit.

Understanding the diverse tools and techniques used in social engineering is essential for developing effective defenses against these threats. As these methods evolve and become more sophisticated, constant vigilance and education remain key in the fight against social engineering attacks.

Defense Against Social Engineering

The battle against social engineering attacks is multifaceted, with a significant emphasis on security awareness training. Educating both individuals and employees about the nature of these threats is crucial. Awareness programs can equip people with the knowledge to recognize the signs of a social engineering attack, reducing the likelihood of successful manipulation. Training sessions should cover various types of attacks, their indicators, and appropriate responses.

One of the key components of defense is educating individuals and employees about the importance of recognizing and reporting suspicious activity. Encouraging vigilance in everyday communications and interactions plays a vital role in safeguarding personal and organizational information. Employees should be trained to report any unusual requests for information or unexpected changes in communication patterns.

Promoting a security culture within an organization is essential in defending against social engineering. This involves creating an environment where security is a shared responsibility and where there is open communication about potential threats. A strong security culture helps foster an atmosphere of awareness and preparedness, making it more difficult for social engineers to exploit vulnerabilities.

Identifying signs of phishing attacks is critical in defending against social engineering. Employees should be taught to look out for suspicious sender email addresses, which often mimic legitimate ones with slight variations. Other red flags include unexpected email content or attachments, especially those that evoke a sense of urgency or use threatening language.

It's also important to train individuals to recognize mismatched URLs and website inconsistencies, common in phishing attacks. Attackers often create websites similar to legitimate ones but with slight discrepancies. Teaching employees to verify URLs and look for signs of legitimacy can prevent them from falling victim to these schemes.

Another crucial defense strategy is recognizing indicators of vishing attacks or voice phishing. These indicators can include calls from unknown numbers, blocked caller IDs, and unsolicited requests for personal information. Employees should be wary of calls that pressure them to make quick decisions, especially if the caller uses an authoritative or persuasive tone.

Spotting signs of smishing attacks, which are phishing attempts conducted via SMS, is equally important. These attacks often manifest as unsolicited text messages containing links or attachments. Texts requesting personal or financial information or those using urgent or alarming language should be treated with skepticism. Inconsistencies between the sender and the message content are also warning signs.

Offering guidance on responding to suspected attacks is a vital defense component. Employees should be instructed to report suspicious activities to IT or security teams. They should also be taught how to verify requests through trusted channels, such as contacting the supposed sender through a known and verified method.

Encouraging individuals to avoid clicking on suspicious links or sharing personal information is key. They should also be reminded not to respond directly to suspicious messages from emails, SMS, or phone calls. Instead, they should use official channels to verify the message's authenticity.

Finally, educating others within the organization about these threats helps create a network of vigilant defenders. Sharing experiences and knowledge about social engineering attacks can raise awareness and prepare the organization to recognize better and respond to future threats. This collective vigilance is a powerful tool in the ongoing effort to protect against social engineering attacks.

Ethical Considerations in Social Engineering

Social engineering, while a significant threat in the realm of cybersecurity, presents a complex landscape of legal and ethical implications. The practice of manipulating individuals to obtain unauthorized access to information or systems falls squarely into a legal gray area. While some methods may not explicitly break the law, they often involve deception and exploitation of trust, which can lead to serious legal consequences. It's crucial to understand that engaging in social engineering without explicit authorization can result in legal action, including fraud charges or identity theft.

The legal consequences of social engineering are substantial. In many jurisdictions, acts of social engineering, especially when they result in data breaches or financial loss, can lead to criminal charges. Penalties can range from fines to imprisonment, depending on the severity of the breach and the laws in the affected region. Understanding these legal repercussions is essential for anyone involved in cybersecurity, whether as a practitioner or a researcher.

From an ethical standpoint, some clear boundaries and responsibilities must be considered. One of the most significant is the respect for privacy and consent. Social engineering, by its very nature, often involves accessing personal or sensitive information without the knowledge or consent of the individual. Ethical conduct in this field necessitates a strong respect for individual privacy rights and a commitment not to overstep these boundaries.

Ethical hacking and penetration testing represent a constructive approach to employing social engineering techniques. Ethical hacking involves testing systems' security with the owner's permission to identify and rectify vulnerabilities. When social engineering is used in this context, it must be done with clear ethical guidelines, ensuring that all activities are legal and consensual.

In the realm of ethical hacking, social engineering must be carefully managed. This includes obtaining explicit permission and consent from all targets involved in the testing process. Any social engineering tactics should be carefully planned and executed to avoid unnecessary harm or distress to the individuals involved.

When findings from ethical hacking or penetration testing are reported, this must be done responsibly. Sensitive information must be handled carefully, ensuring it does not fall into the wrong hands or cause unnecessary harm. Reports should be detailed and provide clear recommendations for addressing identified vulnerabilities.

Promoting responsible disclosure is another key aspect of ethical considerations in social engineering. When vulnerabilities or breaches are discovered, they should be reported responsibly, ideally directly to the affected parties. This allows organizations to take appropriate measures to secure their systems and protect their users' data.

Finally, encouraging ethical behavior within the cybersecurity community is crucial. This involves fostering a culture where privacy, consent, and legal compliance are prioritized and responsible practices are the norm. By promoting these values, the cybersecurity community can ensure that social engineering is used as a force for good, contributing to the overall security and resilience of digital systems and networks.

Social Engineering in the Digital Age

In the digital age, online scams and fraud have become pervasive, presenting new challenges in cybersecurity. Phishing websites and emails are at the forefront of these threats. They deceive users into providing sensitive information by mimicking legitimate websites or contacts. These phishing attempts can range from emails purporting to be from reputable companies asking for personal details to more sophisticated spear-phishing attacks targeting specific individuals or organizations.

Online financial fraud is another significant concern in the digital age. Cybercriminals use tactics like fake investment opportunities or fraudulent banking websites to trick individuals into handing over financial information or directly transferring funds. These scams can lead to substantial financial losses for victims and are often difficult to trace and prosecute due to the anonymity afforded by the Internet.

Identity theft is a particularly insidious outcome of social engineering online. Attackers use personal information gathered through deception to impersonate individuals, access their financial accounts, commit fraud, or obtain documents in the victim's name. The repercussions of identity theft can be long-lasting and devastating, affecting not just financial health but also personal reputation.

The realm of cyberspace has opened up new avenues for social engineering. Manipulating online communities and impersonating online personas are common strategies used by cybercriminals. They create fake profiles or hijack existing ones to gain trust, spread misinformation, or direct users to malicious sites. This manipulation is often subtle and can be challenging to detect.

Influence campaigns are another aspect of social engineering in the digital age. These campaigns are designed to sway public opinion or promote specific agendas through a coordinated effort to disseminate targeted content. While not always malicious, these campaigns can be used to spread false information or create social discord when driven by nefarious actors.

The role of social media in social engineering cannot be understated. Platforms like Facebook, Twitter, and Instagram have become fertile ground for social engineers. The vast amount of personal information on these platforms makes it easier for attackers to target individuals, often using the information people share about themselves.

Privacy and oversharing risks are significant concerns on social media. Users often unknowingly provide valuable information that social engineers can exploit. This includes details about personal life, work, and even location data, which can be pieced together to create compelling social engineering attacks.

Combating online manipulation requires a multifaceted approach. Suggesting strategies to protect themselves online include adhering to online privacy best practices. This involves being cautious about the information shared on social media; using strong, unique passwords for different accounts; and being skeptical of unsolicited requests for information.

Finally, raising awareness about online threats and encouraging critical thinking in the digital realm is crucial. Educating Internet users about the tactics used by social engineers, the signs of a potential scam, and the importance of verifying information can go a long way in safeguarding against these modern threats. By fostering a more informed and cautious online community, the effectiveness of social engineering tactics can be significantly diminished.

Social Engineering in the Workplace

Social engineering in the workplace represents a complex blend of external and internal security challenges, with insider threats particularly concerning. Employees, intentionally or unintentionally, can become significant threats to an organization's security. They may unwittingly divulge sensitive information or provide access to restricted areas, making insider threat detection and prevention a crucial aspect of workplace security. Establishing comprehensive measures to identify potential insider threats and implementing strategies to prevent them is essential for maintaining organizational security.

Employee awareness programs play a pivotal role in mitigating the risk of insider threats. Educating staff about the various forms of social engineering, how to recognize them, and the appropriate response measures can significantly reduce vulnerabilities. Awareness programs should be regular and up to date, ensuring that employees are informed about the latest tactics used by social engineers and the best practices for safeguarding against them.

Corporate espionage is another critical aspect of social engineering in the workplace. This involves competitors using manipulative tactics to infiltrate an organization and acquire confidential information. Espionage can severely compromise a company's competitive edge and market position. Protecting company secrets against such espionage requires a combination of tight security protocols, employee vigilance, and robust legal protections.

Identifying and responding to espionage attempts is a challenging yet vital task. This involves recognizing potential espionage activities, such as unusual requests for information from unknown entities or suspicious behavior by employees or third parties. Establishing clear protocols for reporting and investigating these incidents is crucial for effective response and mitigation.

Employee awareness and training cannot be overstated in its importance. Security training programs should be comprehensive, covering not just the theoretical aspects of social engineering but also practical simulations and exercises. This helps employees understand the real-world implications of social engineering attacks and prepares them to act effectively under threat.

Cultivating a security-aware culture within the workplace is about more than just training; it's about embedding security into the organizational ethos. Encouraging employees to take ownership of security and to report suspicious activity without fear of reprisal creates an environment where security is everyone's responsibility. This culture acts as a formidable barrier against social engineering attempts.

Certain best practices are recommended for protecting organizations against social engineering. Establishing robust security policies and controls that encompass both technological and human elements is fundamental. These policies should be regularly reviewed and updated to address evolving threats.

Third-party risk management is another critical aspect of safeguarding against social engineering in the workplace. Organizations should conduct thorough security assessments of their vendors and partners. This includes evaluating their security practices and ensuring they adhere to the same rigorous standards to prevent potential breaches that could affect the organization.

Vendor security assessments are an integral part of third-party risk management. These assessments should scrutinize the security measures vendors have in place, including their employee training programs, data protection protocols, and incident response strategies. Collaborating with vendors to enhance their security postures can significantly reduce the risk of social engineering attacks from third-party vulnerabilities.

In summary, combating social engineering in the workplace requires a multifaceted approach. It involves strengthening technical defenses and fostering a culture of security awareness among employees. Regular training, vigilant insider threat detection, and robust third-party risk management are key components in building a resilient defense against the diverse tactics used in social engineering.

Social Engineering in Everyday Life

In everyday life, the threat of social engineering is pervasive and can significantly impact personal safety and security. Protecting personal information from those who might manipulate it for malicious purposes is crucial. This includes being cautious about sharing sensitive details online, over the phone, or even in face-to-face interactions. Personal information is valuable and can be used against individuals in various ways.

Home security and physical safety measures are also essential in guarding against social engineering. Simple steps like securing personal mail, shredding sensitive documents, and being aware of who has access to your home can prevent potential social engineering attacks. Additionally, ensuring that home network security is robust can protect against digital intrusions that may start with social engineering tactics.

Privacy in public spaces is another area of concern. In our interconnected world, it's easy to overlook how much personal information can be inadvertently shared in public settings. Being mindful of conversations held in public and being cautious about the information shared on public Wi-Fi networks are vital precautions to take.

Recognizing and responding to manipulation in daily life requires keen observation and awareness. Social engineering attempts can be subtle, such as a stranger striking up a conversation and casually asking seemingly harmless questions. Being alert to the context and content of such interactions is crucial in detecting potential manipulation.

Safeguarding personal boundaries is vital in building resilience against social engineering. This means being assertive in declining requests for personal information or favors from strangers or acquaintances when they seem inappropriate or out of context. Setting and enforcing these boundaries can deter social engineers who rely on exploiting politeness or the reluctance to say no.

Building resilience against manipulation tactics involves a proactive approach. This includes educating oneself about common social engineering strategies and understanding the underlying psychological principles. Awareness of these tactics makes recognizing and resisting them easier in everyday situations.

Developing critical thinking skills is crucial for building resilience against social engineering. This means not taking information at face value, questioning the motives behind requests, and analyzing situations for potential risks. Critical thinking helps in making informed decisions rather than reacting impulsively.

Staying informed and vigilant about new social engineering tactics and trends is also essential. As methods evolve, keeping up to date with the latest information can provide valuable insights into how to protect oneself. This could involve following trusted security blogs, participating in community awareness programs, or attending relevant workshops.

Encouraging others to be security-conscious is part of creating a more resilient community. Sharing knowledge and experiences about social engineering with friends, family, and colleagues can raise collective awareness and protection. It's about fostering an environment where security is a shared responsibility.

In conclusion, social engineering in everyday life poses real risks, and being prepared is key. By emphasizing personal safety and security, recognizing manipulation attempts, and employing strategies to build resilience, individuals can significantly reduce their vulnerability to these threats. Developing a security-conscious mindset, coupled with informed and vigilant practices, is the best defense against the subtle yet pervasive threat of social engineering.

Future Trends and Emerging Threats in Social Engineering

As we look to the future, evolving social engineering tactics are expected to become even more sophisticated and challenging to detect. Advances in technology will provide social engineers with new tools and methods for exploiting vulnerabilities. These advancements will enhance existing tactics and introduce new ones, leading to an ever-evolving landscape of threats.

With technological progress comes the development of new vulnerabilities that social engineers can exploit. As systems and networks become more complex, the opportunities for manipulation and deceit grow. Attackers will likely capitalize on any weaknesses in software, hardware, or human elements. This continuous emergence of vulnerabilities will require constant vigilance and adaptation from security professionals.

Future attack vectors in social engineering are likely to include more advanced forms of deception. The range of potential attack vectors expands as the line between the virtual and physical worlds blurs. This could mean more personalized and believable scams, targeting individuals through multiple channels and employing digital and physical tactics.

Emerging technologies such as artificial intelligence (AI) and deepfakes are set to play a significant role in future social engineering attacks. AI can automate and personalize phishing attacks at an unprecedented scale, while deepfake technology can create highly realistic and convincing video or audio content. These technologies could enable attackers to impersonate trusted figures with remarkable accuracy, making it increasingly difficult to distinguish between genuine and fraudulent communications.

The Internet of Things (IoT) introduces many vulnerabilities that could be exploited in social engineering attacks. With increasing number of connected devices in homes and workplaces, attackers have more entry points to exploit. These devices often lack robust security measures, making them easy targets for attackers seeking access to broader networks.

While offering potential security benefits, blockchain technology also presents unique implications for social engineering. The decentralized nature of blockchain can make it challenging to track and prevent fraud once it occurs. Additionally, the hype and complexity surrounding blockchain and cryptocurrencies might be exploited by social engineers to deceive individuals who lack understanding in this area.

Looking forward, social engineering is expected to face numerous trends and challenges. Attackers will likely continue refining their tactics, using emerging technologies and societal changes. The evolution of social engineering will likely keep pace with technological advancements, requiring constant updates to defense strategies.

In preparing for these evolving threats, organizations and individuals must remain proactive. This includes staying informed about the latest trends in social engineering, regularly updating security protocols, and fostering a culture of awareness and skepticism. Investing in ongoing training and education will also be essential to keep up with the changing nature of threats.

AI's role in attacks and defense is set to become increasingly prominent. While attackers can use AI to enhance their tactics, it also offers powerful tools for defense. AI and machine learning can help detect and respond to social engineering attacks more efficiently, analyzing patterns and predicting potential threats.

In conclusion, the future of social engineering presents a landscape of challenges and opportunities. While emerging technologies will provide new tools for attackers, they also offer innovative ways to defend against these threats. Staying ahead of these trends will require a dynamic and informed approach to cybersecurity, blending technological solutions with a deep understanding of human psychology and behavior.

Career Corner

Social engineering encompasses a diverse range of career paths, each requiring unique skills and knowledge. Professionals in this domain typically work in areas related to cybersecurity, ethical hacking, psychological analysis, and corporate security. The core of these careers involves understanding human behavior and manipulation tactics, combined with technical knowledge of cybersecurity principles. This dual focus makes careers in social engineering both challenging and rewarding.

One popular career choice in this field is that of an ethical hacker or penetration tester. These professionals use social engineering techniques to test and strengthen organizations' security systems. They simulate social engineering attacks to identify vulnerabilities in both human and technological defenses. This role requires a deep understanding of both cybersecurity and human psychology.

Another career path is that of a cybersecurity analyst specializing in social engineering. These individuals focus on developing strategies to protect against social engineering attacks. They analyze past incidents, conduct risk assessments, and develop policies and training programs to enhance organizational resilience against these threats.

Several certifications can provide the necessary knowledge and credentials for those interested in pursuing a career in this field. The Certified Ethical Hacker (CEH) certification, offered by the EC-Council, is one of the most recognized in the industry. It covers various topics, including social engineering tactics, and equips professionals with practical skills in ethical hacking.

The Certified Information Systems Security Professional (CISSP) certification is another prestigious credential that includes components related to social engineering. Offered by International Information System Security Certification Consortium (ISC2), it is a globally recognized certification demonstrating expertise in designing and managing security programs.

Additionally, for those specifically interested in the human aspect of security, certifications like the CompTIA Advanced Security Practitioner (CASP) or Human Hacking Conference certifications focus on psychological manipulation, behavior analysis, and the art of influence. These certifications delve deeper into the psychological aspects of social engineering, providing valuable insights for professionals aiming to specialize in this area.

In conclusion, careers in social engineering are diverse and evolving, with opportunities in various sectors, including cybersecurity, corporate security, and ethical hacking. A combination of technical expertise, psychological understanding, and continuous learning is essential to excel in this field. Relevant certifications can provide a solid foundation and recognition in the industry, opening doors to various challenging and rewarding career opportunities.

Case Study: Sony Pictures Entertainment Hack

The Sony Pictures Entertainment Hack of 2014 is one of the most notorious and damaging cyberattacks in corporate history, highlighting the devastating impact of social engineering in cybersecurity. This attack began with a series of carefully crafted phishing emails targeted at

Sony employees. These emails were designed to appear legitimate and trustworthy, prompting unsuspecting employees to reveal their login credentials. The attackers, believed to be associated with a group called "Guardians of Peace," skillfully exploited the human element of security, bypassing technical safeguards by manipulating staff.

Once the attackers gained access through these phishing emails, they were able to infiltrate Sony's network, obtaining a wide range of sensitive data. This data breach was a minor leak and a massive spill of confidential information that had far-reaching consequences. The leaked data included personal information about Sony employees, such as Social Security numbers, salary details, and personal emails. This personal data breach compromised employees' privacy and exposed them to potential identity theft and financial fraud.

The scope of the attack extended beyond personal employee data. The hackers accessed and leaked a trove of internal communications within Sony. This included sensitive emails between Sony executives and other Hollywood personalities, revealing behind-the-scenes conversations and decisions. The leak of these emails was not only embarrassing on a personal level for those involved but also damaging to Sony's business relationships and reputation in the highly competitive entertainment industry.

In addition to personal and corporate information, the attackers released copies of unreleased Sony films to the public. This part of the breach had significant financial implications for Sony, undermining these films' potential box office performance. The premature release of these films dealt a blow to Sony's revenue and disrupted the carefully planned release schedules, which are crucial in the film industry.

The aftermath of the Sony hack was a period of intense scrutiny and criticism for the company. The incident raised serious questions about Sony's cybersecurity practices and preparedness for such sophisticated attacks. It highlighted the need for corporations to invest in technical defenses and train employees to recognize and resist social engineering tactics. The Sony hack became a case study in the cybersecurity world, emphasizing the importance of a holistic approach to security that includes both technical measures and human factor considerations.

Finally, the Sony Pictures Entertainment Hack served as a wake-up call for businesses and organizations worldwide about the severity and reality of cyber threats. It demonstrated that even large, technologically advanced companies are vulnerable to attacks that exploit human psychology. This event spurred many companies to reevaluate and strengthen their cybersecurity strategies, mainly focusing on employee education and awareness programs to combat social engineering tactics. The Sony hack remains a stark reminder of the ever-present danger of cyberattacks and the critical importance of comprehensive cybersecurity measures in the digital age.

Chapter Questions

1. What is the primary goal of social engineering in cybersecurity?

    A. To improve system performance

    B. To manipulate people into divulging confidential information

    C. To enhance network security

    D. To provide user training

2. Which tactic is commonly used in social engineering?

    A. Encrypting data

    B. Installing firewalls

    C. Impersonation

    D. Writing code

3. What differentiates social engineering from other cyber threats?

   A. Reliance on technical hacking techniques

   B. Focus on exploiting human psychology

   C. Use of antivirus software

   D. Implementation of firewalls

4. What is a crucial characteristic of phishing attacks?

   A. Speeding up computer processes

   B. Sending emails from unknown sources

   C. Appearing to be from reputable sources

   D. Enhancing user interface designs

5. In social engineering, what does pretexting involve?

   A. Encrypting user data

   B. Fabricating a situation to gain information

   C. Improving software algorithms

   D. Conducting regular system audits

6. Which is a common cognitive bias exploited in social engineering?

   A. Code dependency

   B. Confirmation bias

   C. Algorithm preference

   D. System familiarity

7. What is the purpose of tailgating in social engineering?

   A. Speeding up network connections

   B. Gaining physical access to restricted areas

   C. Installing security software

   D. Enhancing Wi-Fi signals

8. How does emotional manipulation function in social engineering?

   A. By improving logical thinking

   B. By leveraging feelings like fear and trust

   C. Enhancing technical skills

   D. Teaching programming languages

9. What principle do social engineers exploit by doing small favors?

   A. Network enhancement

   B. Reciprocity

   C. Code simplicity

   D. Software optimization

10. What is a significant risk in the digital age due to social engineering?

   A. Faster Internet speeds

   B. Identity theft

   C. Enhanced graphics

   D. Improved user interfaces

11. What should individuals do to safeguard against
     social engineering?

     A. Increase their Internet usage

     B. Share more personal information online

     C. Develop critical thinking skills

     D. Avoid using digital devices

12. In the workplace, what is essential to combat social
     engineering?

     A. Decreasing employee salaries

     B. Limiting Internet access

     C. Employee awareness programs

     D. Banning mobile phones

13. What emerging technology poses new risks for
     social engineering?

     A. Typewriters

     B. Artificial intelligence (AI)

     C. Fax machines

     D. Rotary phones

14. What is a future challenge in social engineering due
     to technological advancements?

     A. Reduced Internet availability

     B. More sophisticated deception methods

     C. Slower computing speeds

     D. Decreased use of digital devices

15. In preventing social engineering, what role does AI play?

    A. Decreasing technology usage

    B. Enhancing attack methods

    C. Reducing digital communication

    D. Detecting and responding to attacks

CHAPTER 4

Cryptography

Cyber cryptography is an essential field within digital security, focusing on encrypting and decrypting information. It operates at the intersection of mathematics, computer science, and electrical engineering. This discipline ensures that sensitive data remains secure from unauthorized access, manipulation, or theft.

Cryptography's role in digital security is multifaceted, chiefly regarding protecting data confidentiality, integrity, and authenticity. Confidentiality hides information from unauthorized users, integrity ensures data is not altered or tampered with, and authenticity verifies the source of information. These principles are crucial in maintaining digital communications and data storage security.

In everyday digital life, cryptography is omnipresent, though often unnoticed. It secures online transactions, protects emails, and maintains the integrity of messaging apps. From SSL/TLS protocols in web browsing to encryption in cloud storage, cryptography is the invisible guard of digital interactions.

The history of cryptography extends back to ancient civilizations. Early methods included simple substitution ciphers used by Egyptians and Spartans for military communication. Over time, these techniques evolved, growing more complex and sophisticated.

© Dr. Jason Edwards 2024, corrected publication 2024
Dr. J. Edwards, *Mastering Cybersecurity*, https://doi.org/10.1007/979-8-8688-0297-3_4

Key milestones in cryptographic history include the Renaissance-era development of the polyalphabetic cipher and the 20th century's electronic ciphers. The German Enigma machine and its Allied decryption during World War II marked a significant advancement in cryptographic technology. These developments influenced military strategy and shaped the future course of cryptography.

Cryptography's influence on historical events is significant. For instance, its use in World War II was decisive in the Allies' victory. Throughout history, cryptography has played a critical role in shaping the outcomes of wars, political events, and international relations.

In today's digital age, the role of cryptography has expanded exponentially due to the growth of digital data. As society shifts more of its functions online, the volume of sensitive data transmitted over the Internet increases, necessitating stronger cryptographic protections.

The pervasive nature of online communication underscores the importance of cryptography. From securing social media interactions to protecting digital financial transactions, cryptographic algorithms ensure the privacy and security of online communications.

The rise of sophisticated cyber threats has further highlighted the necessity for advanced cryptographic solutions. As cybercriminals employ more complex methods, cryptography must continuously evolve to defend against these evolving digital threats. Today, cryptography secures information and underpins the trust and reliability of the entire digital infrastructure.

Principles of Cryptography

Cryptography is the science of securing information by converting it from its original form to an unrecognizable format and vice versa. The process begins with encryption, where plaintext (readable data) is transformed into ciphertext (encoded data) using an algorithm and a key.

This transformation ensures the data remains incomprehensible to unauthorized entities in transit or storage. Encryption is fundamental to protecting information in the digital realm, where data vulnerability is a constant concern.

Plaintext, ciphertext, and keys are central to the encryption process. Plaintext is the original, readable data that needs protection. Ciphertext, conversely, is the encrypted version of the plaintext rendered unintelligible. Keys are crucial cryptographic tools that encode and decode the data, acting as the lock and key mechanism in digital security.

Decrypting ciphertext to obtain plaintext is the reverse process of encryption. It involves using a key, which could be the same as (symmetric encryption) or different from (asymmetric encryption) the encryption key. This process ensures that the intended recipient of the data can convert the unreadable ciphertext back into its original, comprehensible format. Decryption is vital for accessing and utilizing encrypted data in its intended form.

Confidentiality in cryptography refers to keeping data secret from unauthorized parties. It is achieved through effective encryption, ensuring that sensitive information remains inaccessible to anyone who is not the intended recipient. This principle is crucial in maintaining the privacy and security of digital data, especially in fields like banking, healthcare, and government operations.

Integrity in cryptographic terms means ensuring that data has not been altered or tampered with during transmission or storage. It involves mechanisms to detect any unauthorized changes to the data. Maintaining integrity is essential in scenarios where the accuracy and consistency of data are critical, such as financial transactions or legal documents.

Authenticity in cryptography is about verifying the source of data. It ensures that the data originates from a legitimate source and has not been sent by an imposter. This aspect of cryptography is often achieved through digital signatures and certificates, assuring the identity of the data sender.

Symmetric cryptography uses the same key for both encryption and decryption. This approach is efficient and fast, making it suitable for scenarios where large volumes of data need to be encrypted. However, it poses critical distribution and management challenges, as the same key must be securely shared between the sender and receiver.

Asymmetric cryptography, in contrast, uses a pair of keys – a public key for encryption and a private key for decryption. This method overcomes the critical distribution problem inherent in symmetric cryptography, as the public key can be shared openly. While asymmetric cryptography is more secure, it is generally slower and more computationally intensive than symmetric methods.

The use cases and advantages of each cryptographic approach vary. Due to its speed and efficiency, symmetric cryptography is often used for encrypting data at rest, like files on a hard drive. Asymmetric cryptography is typically used for securing data in transit, such as in SSL/TLS for Internet communications, because of its ability to exchange keys over an unsecured channel.

In conclusion, understanding the principles of cryptography, including the basics of encryption and decryption, is essential in the digital age. Confidentiality, integrity, and authenticity form the foundation of data security, while the choice between symmetric and asymmetric cryptography depends on specific use cases and requirements. As the digital world continues to evolve, so will the cryptography field, adapting to new challenges and technologies to secure our digital lives.

Cryptographic Algorithms

Symmetric key algorithms are a cornerstone of modern encryption techniques. A single key is used for data encryption and decryption in symmetric encryption. This method's efficiency and speed make it ideal for many applications, particularly where large volumes of data need secure handling.

Popular symmetric key algorithms include AES (Advanced Encryption Standard) and DES (Data Encryption Standard). AES is widely used due to its balance of security and efficiency, offering critical sizes of 128, 192, and 256 bits. Though an older standard, DES laid the groundwork for modern symmetric encryption. However, AES has primarily superseded it due to its shorter key length and vulnerability to brute-force attacks.

Key length is a critical factor in the security of symmetric algorithms. Longer keys offer greater security as they are harder to crack using brute-force methods. However, longer keys also require more computational power for encryption and decryption, creating a balance between security and performance in the design of symmetric algorithms.

On the other hand, asymmetric vital algorithms utilize two separate keys – a public key for encryption and a private key for decryption. This method addresses the critical distribution challenge inherent in symmetric key encryption. Asymmetric algorithms are fundamental in secure online communications and digital signatures.

RSA (Rivest-Shamir-Adleman) and ECC (Elliptic Curve Cryptography) are prominent examples of asymmetric algorithms. RSA is known for its use in securing web communications and digital signatures. At the same time, ECC provides similar security to RSA but with smaller key sizes, making it more efficient, especially in mobile applications.

Key pair generation and usage are crucial aspects of asymmetric encryption. The security of asymmetric algorithms relies on the mathematical challenge of deriving the private key from the public key, a computationally infeasible task. These keys are used in various applications, from encrypting emails to authenticating digital documents.

Hash functions, like SHA-256, play a vital role in modern cryptography. The primary purpose of hash functions is to create a unique, fixed-size hash value from input data. This feature is critical in ensuring data integrity and is widely used in various security applications.

Common hash functions, such as SHA-256, part of the SHA-2 family, are integral in maintaining data integrity and security. These functions convert input data into a unique string, deriving the original input from the hash value nearly impossible. They are crucial in digital signatures, password storage, and ensuring data integrity in transit.

The role of hash functions extends to ensuring data integrity and authenticating digital signatures. By providing a way to check the integrity of data without revealing its contents, hash functions help verify that data has not been tampered with. This makes them invaluable in building secure digital systems and protocols, where data authenticity and integrity are paramount.

In summary, cryptographic algorithms, whether symmetric, asymmetric, or hash functions, form the backbone of digital security. Each type of algorithm serves distinct purposes, from securing data transmission to verifying data integrity. As the digital landscape evolves, so do these algorithms, continually adapting to meet the ever-growing demands of cybersecurity.

Cryptographic Protocols

SSL (Secure Sockets Layer) and TLS (Transport Layer Security) are fundamental protocols for secure web communication. These protocols are designed to provide secure transmission of data between web servers and clients, typically browsers. They protect sensitive information like login credentials and financial transactions from interception and tampering.

The SSL/TLS handshake process is critical to establishing secure connections. This process involves negotiating cryptographic parameters between the client and server, including key exchange, authentication, and cipher selection. The handshake ensures that both parties have a shared secret key for encryption, and it verifies the server's identity to the client, often through digital certificates.

However, SSL/TLS protocols are not immune to vulnerabilities. Over time, various weaknesses have been identified and exploited in different versions of these protocols. Mitigating these vulnerabilities involves regular updates, turning off outdated versions, using strong cipher suites, and implementing additional security measures like Perfect Forward Secrecy.

IPsec (Internet Protocol Security) is a suite of protocols used to secure Internet Protocol (IP) communications. It encrypts and authenticates each IP packet of a communication session. IPsec is widely used to secure data flow between two points on a network, ensuring the data's confidentiality, integrity, and authenticity.

IPsec operates in two modes: tunnel and transport. Tunnel mode encrypts the entire IP packet, mainly used in VPN (Virtual Private Network) scenarios. In contrast, transport mode encrypts only the packet's payload, typically used for end-to-end communication. Additionally, IPsec supports various authentication methods, such as pre-shared keys and digital certificates.

Implementing IPsec is particularly crucial in the context of VPNs. VPNs use IPsec to create secure connections between remote users and networks, ensuring that data transmitted over potentially unsecure networks like the Internet is protected. This makes IPsec a key component in maintaining the confidentiality and integrity of data in corporate and public networks.

SSH (Secure Shell) is a protocol used primarily for secure remote command-line access and administration of servers. It provides a secure channel over an unsecured network, enabling users to execute commands and manage files on remote servers. System administrators widely use SSH for secure network management.

SSH uses key pairs and supports passwordless authentication, enhancing security. Users can generate a pair of cryptographic keys (public and private keys) and use them for authentication. The private key is kept secret, while the public key can be safely shared and used to authenticate the user, offering a more secure alternative to traditional password-based authentication.

SSH security best practices include using strong, unique passwords for initial setup, disabling root login, regularly updating SSH software, and using key-based authentication. Implementing these practices helps protect against various security threats, including brute-force attacks and unauthorized access.

In conclusion, cryptographic protocols like SSL/TLS, IPsec, and SSH are essential in providing security over networks and the Internet. Each protocol serves a specific purpose, from securing web communications to protecting network traffic and enabling secure remote access. Understanding and correctly implementing these protocols is crucial in safeguarding digital communications against cyber threats.

Cryptographic Key Management

Cryptographic key management begins with key generation, a crucial process for the security of encryption systems. Effective key generation methods ensure the creation of strong and unpredictable keys. These keys are vital for maintaining the integrity and confidentiality of encrypted data, forming the foundation of secure cryptographic systems.

Pseudorandom number generators (PRNGs) are significant in the key generation process. PRNGs produce number sequences that approximate randomness properties, which are essential for cryptographic key creation. The security of cryptographic systems heavily relies on the unpredictability of these keys, making the quality of PRNGs a pivotal factor.

Key entropy and randomness are central to the strength and security of cryptographic keys. High entropy ensures greater randomness and unpredictability, making the keys more resistant to attacks. This unpredictability is crucial in thwarting attempts to break cryptographic systems through computational or guessing attacks.

Secure storage of cryptographic keys is another essential aspect of effective key management. Protecting these keys from digital and physical threats is important to maintain their confidentiality and integrity. Implementing robust access controls and secure storage methods is key to achieving this protection.

Hardware Security Modules (HSMs) are specialized devices that securely store cryptographic keys. They provide a physically secure environment, protecting keys from unauthorized access and digital attacks. HSMs are particularly important in high-security environments like financial institutions and government agencies.

Protecting cryptographic keys from physical and digital threats requires a comprehensive approach. This includes implementing stringent access control measures, encrypting stored keys, and ensuring physical security protocols are in place where keys are stored or actively used.

The process of key distribution is a critical component of cryptographic key management. It involves securely sharing cryptographic keys between parties who need to communicate securely. The main challenge in crucial distribution is to share these keys without exposing them to potential interception or compromise.

Key exchange protocols, such as the Diffie-Hellman key exchange, are essential to distribute cryptographic keys securely. These protocols enable the establishment of a shared secret key between parties over an insecure channel. This method ensures secure communication and is crucial in maintaining the privacy and integrity of transmitted data.

Key rotation and expiration are essential practices in cryptographic key management. Regular rotation of keys helps mitigate long-term security risks, and setting expiration policies ensures that keys are updated periodically. These practices are vital to maintaining the security and effectiveness of cryptographic systems.

Effective management of crucial rotation and expiration requires balancing security needs with operational practicality. While frequent updates can enhance security, they may also impact ongoing operations. Carefully planned policies and procedures are necessary to ensure operational efficiency and sustained security in cryptographic practices.

Public Key Infrastructure (PKI)

Certificate Authorities (CAs) are pivotal components of Public Key Infrastructure (PKI), crucial in managing public-key encryption. They issue digital certificates that authenticate the identity of entities and their public keys. As trusted third parties, CAs ensure the legitimacy and trustworthiness of digital interactions, making them foundational to secure online communications.

The PKI system has a trust hierarchy with root Certificate Authorities at its apex. Root CAs issue certificates to subordinate CAs, establishing a chain of trust. This hierarchy is essential for ensuring the authenticity of each certificate, as each level of CA verifies the integrity of the level below.

The validation and revocation of certificates are critical functions of CAs. Validation checks confirm a certificate's validity and integrity, while revocation invalidates a certificate prematurely due to compromise or changes in the entity's status. These processes are vital for maintaining the security and reliability of the PKI system.

Digital certificates are the linchpins of PKI, linking public keys with their respective entities. Each certificate contains crucial information like the entity's public key, the issuing CA, and the certificate's validity period. These components collectively establish the identity of entities and secure the communication between parties.

The X.509 certificate format is a standard in PKI systems for digital certificates. This format outlines the structure of certificates, specifying how to present essential information like the public key, issuer, and subject. The ubiquity of X.509 certificates in Internet security protocols underscores their importance in digital security.

Certificate fields and extensions are integral to the functionality of digital certificates. Fields include basic information such as the serial number, issuer, and validity period. Extensions provide details like key usage policies and alternative names, enhancing the certificate's security and versatility.

Trust models in PKI, such as the hierarchical and web of trust models, are essential for establishing and maintaining security. The hierarchical model relies on a top-down approach to trust, with root CAs at the top. In contrast, the web of trust model facilitates decentralized trust, where trust relationships are formed through a network of individual users.

In the hierarchical model, building trust in a certificate chain is crucial. Each certificate in the chain is verified up to the root CA, ensuring the authenticity of the entire chain. This model is central to how PKI manages trust, providing a structured approach to certificate validation.

Trust anchors are the foundation of the trust models in PKI. They are the trusted root certificates from which the trustworthiness of other certificates is derived. In a hierarchical model, trust anchors validate the legitimacy of the certificate chain, while in a web of trust, they are key to establishing decentralized trust relationships.

Cryptographic Attacks

Brute-force attacks are a standard method used in cryptographic attacks, where attackers try every possible key combination to decrypt encrypted data. This approach relies on sheer computational power and time, testing all possible keys until the correct one is found. Although straightforward, it's a significant threat to systems with weak or short encryption keys.

Defending against brute-force attacks involves implementing strategies like rate limiting, lockouts after several failed attempts, and monitoring unusual login activities. These strategies help slow down or halt brute-force attempts, making it impractical for attackers to try every possible combination. Additionally, using CAPTCHAs can further deter automated brute-force tools.

Password complexity and length are crucial in thwarting brute-force attacks. The longer and more complex a password is, the more difficult it becomes for attackers to execute a brute-force attack successfully. Encouraging the use of long, complex passwords or passphrases among users is a crucial defense strategy against such attacks.

Man-in-the-middle (MITM) attacks occur when an attacker secretly intercepts and potentially alters the communication between two parties. In these attacks, the attacker aims to breach the confidentiality or integrity of the information being exchanged. MITM attacks can occur in various forms, such as eavesdropping on network traffic or impersonating one of the parties in the communication.

Detecting and preventing MITM attacks involves implementing robust encryption protocols like SSL/TLS, using VPNs for secure communication, and employing endpoint security measures. Regularly updating and patching network devices and software also play a crucial role in preventing MITM vulnerabilities. Educating users about secure browsing practices and recognizing suspicious activity is equally important.

Examples of real-world MITM incidents include attacks on unsecured Wi-Fi networks, DNS spoofing, and HTTPS spoofing. These incidents highlight the importance of secure communication protocols and constant vigilance in network security practices. Understanding the tactics used in these incidents helps develop more effective defense strategies against MITM attacks.

Side-channel attacks exploit information gained from the physical implementation of a cryptographic system. These attacks observe indirect information like timing, power consumption, or electromagnetic emissions from computing devices. Such attacks can reveal sensitive information about the cryptographic operations, potentially compromising the entire system.

Types of side channels include timing attacks, which analyze the time taken for operations, power analysis attacks that monitor energy consumption, and electromagnetic attacks that observe electromagnetic emissions. Each can provide clues about the cryptographic process, such as key values or algorithmic steps.

Mitigating side-channel attacks requires a comprehensive approach that includes hardware and software strategies. Implementing noise and randomization in cryptographic operations, using constant-time algorithms, and designing hardware resistant to physical leakages are effective mitigation techniques. Regular security audits and testing are essential in identifying and addressing side-channel vulnerabilities.

Quantum cryptanalysis introduces new challenges in cryptography with the advent of quantum computers. These advanced computers use quantum mechanics principles, potentially making them capable of breaking current cryptographic algorithms much faster than classical computers.

Quantum algorithms, such as Shor's algorithm, can theoretically break widely used cryptographic schemes like RSA and ECC by efficiently solving problems that are hard for classical computers. This possibility has significant implications for the security of current cryptographic systems.

In response to these challenges, post-quantum cryptography solutions are being developed. These solutions involve designing cryptographic algorithms resistant to quantum computing attacks, ensuring the security of cryptographic systems even in the era of quantum computing. The field of post-quantum cryptography is rapidly evolving, with ongoing research to create secure and practical algorithms for the quantum age.

Cryptographic Best Practices

Choosing robust cryptographic algorithms is essential for adequate digital security. When selecting an algorithm, several factors need to be considered, such as its resistance to known vulnerabilities and suitability for the intended application. The strength and reliability of an algorithm are critical to ensuring the data's confidentiality and integrity.

The National Institute of Standards and Technology (NIST) provides guidelines and recommendations widely respected in cryptography. These guidelines help select robust and tested cryptographic algorithms, ensuring compliance with security standards. It's essential to stay updated with NIST's recommendations as they evolve with emerging threats and technological advancements.

Balancing security with performance is a key consideration in selecting cryptographic algorithms. While strong encryption provides high security, it can also demand more computational resources, which may impact system performance. Therefore, choosing an algorithm that balances security strength and operational efficiency well is necessary, especially for systems with high throughput or real-time requirements.

Determining appropriate key lengths is crucial in maintaining the strength of cryptographic systems. Longer keys generally offer greater security, making them harder to crack through brute-force or other methods. However, the choice of crucial length should also consider the system's performance requirements and the sensitivity of the protected data.

Regularly updating key lengths as technology advances is vital for avoiding potential attacks. As computational power increases, previously secure key lengths may become vulnerable. Continuously assessing and updating key lengths ensures that cryptographic systems remain resistant to advances in attack methodologies.

Assessing key strengths against potential attacks involves evaluating the likelihood and capability of various attack vectors. This assessment helps choose critical lengths and algorithms that provide adequate protection against current and emerging threats, ensuring the long-term security of cryptographic implementations.

Best practices for storing cryptographic keys are fundamental to the overall security of cryptographic systems. Secure storage prevents unauthorized access and potential compromise of keys. This involves using secure environments, such as Hardware Security Modules (HSMs), and implementing strong access controls.

Handling keys in memory and storage securely is crucial to prevent leaks and unauthorized access. Keys should be encrypted when stored and carefully managed to avoid exposure. Effective key management includes secure generation, distribution, rotation, and destruction of keys.

Role-based access control and auditing are essential practices for secure key management. Access to cryptographic keys should be strictly controlled and limited to authorized personnel based on their roles. Regular auditing helps track key usage and detect any unauthorized access or anomalies, further strengthening the security of cryptographic critical management systems.

Cryptography in Real-World Applications

In the realm of secure email communication, implementing encryption is crucial. Protocols like PGP (Pretty Good Privacy) and S/MIME (Secure/Multipurpose Internet Mail Extensions) are widely used. PGP encrypts emails using symmetric and asymmetric cryptography, while S/MIME provides certificate-based email security, ensuring privacy and sender authenticity.

Email security protocols such as STARTTLS play a critical role in secure communication. STARTTLS upgrades a plain text connection to a secure encrypted connection, preventing eavesdropping and tampering by third parties. Primary email services like Gmail and Outlook use this protocol to enhance the security of everyday email communications.

However, challenges exist in the widespread adoption and implementation of email encryption. Many users and organizations find setting up and maintaining encrypted email systems complex. Additionally, the interoperability between different email encryption standards can be problematic, affecting adoption rates among general users.

Cryptography techniques in ecommerce and online banking are fundamental to protecting sensitive transactions. These techniques ensure the confidentiality and integrity of financial data as it travels over the Internet. Encryption guards against interception and manipulation of transaction data, a crucial aspect of digital financial security.

SSL/TLS (Secure Sockets Layer/Transport Layer Security) protocols are extensively used in ecommerce. They establish a secure and encrypted connection between a customer's browser and the ecommerce website. This encryption is essential for protecting credit card numbers and personal information during online transactions and building trust in digital marketplaces.

Protecting financial transactions in online banking involves multiple layers of cryptographic techniques. Banks employ encryption algorithms to safeguard user data and transactions. They also use secure hash functions to maintain data integrity, ensuring that the transaction data is not tampered with during transmission.

Cryptocurrency and blockchain technology are prime examples of cryptography in action. Blockchain technology uses cryptographic algorithms to create a secure and immutable ledger of transactions. Each block in the chain is secured with a cryptographic hash of the previous block, making it tamper-resistant.

Securing digital wallets and cryptocurrency transactions is another critical application of cryptography. Digital wallets use cryptographic keys to allow users to access and manage their cryptocurrency. These keys are essential for signing transactions and proving cryptocurrency ownership, ensuring secure and authentic transactions.

Mining and consensus algorithms in blockchain technology also rely on cryptographic principles. Mining involves solving complex cryptographic puzzles to validate transactions and add new blocks to the chain. Consensus algorithms like Proof of Work and Proof of Stake use cryptographic methods to agree on the state of the blockchain, ensuring its integrity and trustworthiness.

Cryptography is vital in various real-world applications, from securing email communications to protecting financial transactions in ecommerce and banking. The technology is also fundamental in the functioning and security of cryptocurrencies and blockchain. As the digital landscape continues to evolve, cryptography applications expand, demonstrating its critical importance in maintaining security and trust in the digital world.

Cryptography in Network Security

Virtual Private Networks (VPNs) are a cornerstone of secure communication in network security. They create an encrypted tunnel for data to travel securely over a public network, like the Internet. VPNs ensure that data remains confidential and secure from interception, making them essential for remote access and protecting sensitive information.

VPN protocols and encryption standards are key to their security effectiveness. Protocols such as OpenVPN, L2TP/IPsec, and IKEv2/IPsec offer different levels of security and compatibility. They use various encryption standards, like AES and Triple DES, to encrypt data traffic, providing a secure channel for communication over potentially unsecured networks.

Deploying and configuring VPNs requires careful consideration of security needs and network architecture. Configuration involves selecting appropriate encryption protocols and setting up authentication methods. Properly deployed VPNs ensure secure access for remote users and protect data in transit, making them a fundamental part of network security strategies.

Firewall policies and rule sets are essential in defining and controlling network traffic. They determine which traffic is allowed or blocked based on predefined security rules. Firewalls act as gatekeepers, preventing unauthorized access while allowing legitimate communication to flow freely.

The role of cryptography in firewall protection is significant, particularly in establishing secure connections and verifying data integrity. Cryptography is used in firewalls to encrypt traffic between trusted networks or to authenticate messages. This cryptographic protection is crucial in defending against network threats and maintaining secure communication channels.

Intrusion detection and prevention systems (IDPS) are crucial for maintaining network security. These systems actively monitor network traffic for suspicious activities and potential threats. They use various methods, including cryptographic techniques, to detect and prevent unauthorized access, ensuring the network's integrity and security.

Monitoring network traffic for suspicious activities involves analyzing data packets for anomalies or known attack patterns. Cryptography plays a role in this process by securing the data used in monitoring and verifying the integrity of network traffic. This helps in accurately detecting potential threats and preventing false positives.

Using cryptography in threat detection enhances the effectiveness of intrusion detection and prevention. It enables the secure analysis of traffic patterns and the authentication of network entities. In the event of a detected threat, incident response and mitigation strategies are employed, often involving cryptographic protocols to isolate and contain the threat, minimizing damage and restoring network integrity.

Cryptography and Privacy

Privacy-enhancing technologies (PETs) are crucial in the digital era for protecting user privacy. These technologies employ cryptographic techniques to safeguard personal data against unauthorized access and misuse. PETs enable users to share data while preserving confidentiality, playing a significant role in online privacy.

Privacy-preserving data analysis is an application of PETs that allows the extraction of helpful information from datasets without compromising individual privacy. This involves techniques like data masking and aggregation to protect individual data points. Cryptography is central to these techniques, ensuring data remains secure even during analysis.

Differential privacy and anonymization are critical concepts in privacy protection. Differential privacy provides a mathematical framework for quantifying and managing privacy risks in data analysis. On the other hand, anonymization involves removing or altering personally identifiable information in datasets, making it impossible to link data back to individuals.

The General Data Protection Regulation (GDPR) is the European Union's comprehensive data protection law. It sets stringent requirements for data handling and privacy, impacting organizations worldwide. GDPR emphasizes the rights of individuals regarding their data and sets out obligations for data processors and controllers.

GDPR has significantly impacted data encryption and security practices. It encourages the use of encryption and pseudonymization to protect personal data. Under GDPR, organizations are motivated to implement solid cryptographic measures to ensure compliance and secure personal data.

Compliance with GDPR and data breach notification is mandatory for organizations processing EU residents' data. In the event of a data breach, GDPR requires timely notification to the relevant authorities and, in some cases, to the individuals affected. This regulation has increased the adoption of cryptographic measures to safeguard data and prevent breaches.

Zero-knowledge proofs are a privacy-preserving cryptographic technique. They allow one party to prove to another that a statement is true without revealing any information beyond the validity of the statement itself. This technique is valuable in scenarios where privacy or confidentiality is paramount, such as identity verification processes.

Homomorphic encryption is a groundbreaking technique that enables computation on encrypted data without requiring access to the unencrypted data. This allows for secure data processing and analysis, ensuring that sensitive data remains protected during operations. Homomorphic encryption is increasingly essential in cloud computing and data analysis contexts.

Secure multiparty computation (MPC) is another cryptographic technique that facilitates collaborative computation over data while keeping the individual inputs private. In MPC, multiple parties can jointly compute a function over their inputs while keeping those inputs secret. This approach is instrumental in scenarios where sharing raw data is not desirable or feasible due to privacy concerns.

Cryptography is vital in enhancing privacy in various domains, from complying with data protection laws like GDPR to implementing advanced techniques like zero-knowledge proofs, homomorphic encryption, and secure multiparty computation. As the digital landscape evolves, the importance of cryptography in protecting privacy continues to grow, making it an essential tool for data security and confidentiality.

Emerging Trends in Cyber Cryptography

Post-quantum cryptography is becoming increasingly relevant as quantum computing evolves. This new field of cryptography focuses on developing secure cryptographic algorithms against the potential capabilities of quantum computers. The primary goal is to prepare cryptographic systems for a future where traditional encryption methods may no longer be secure.

Cryptographic algorithms resistant to quantum attacks are at the core of post-quantum cryptography. These algorithms are designed to be secure against the large-scale quantum computers of the future, which could potentially break current encryption methods. Developing these algorithms involves creating and testing new cryptographic techniques based on complex mathematical problems that even quantum computers cannot quickly solve.

Research and standardization efforts in post-quantum cryptography are ongoing. Organizations like the National Institute of Standards and Technology (NIST) are leading the way in standardizing post-quantum cryptographic algorithms. These efforts are crucial for transitioning the world's cryptographic infrastructure to a quantum-resistant footing.

Homomorphic encryption represents a significant advancement in cryptography, enabling computations on encrypted data. Data can be processed and analyzed without decrypting, maintaining privacy and security. Homomorphic encryption has revolutionary implications for secure cloud computing and data analysis.

Use cases for homomorphic encryption are particularly promising in cloud computing and data privacy. It enables organizations to securely process sensitive data in the cloud without exposing it. This is especially important for industries such as healthcare and finance handling large volumes of confidential data.

However, homomorphic encryption faces challenges regarding computational efficiency and practical applications. While it offers unprecedented data security, its current implementations are often slower than traditional methods. Researchers are actively working on making homomorphic encryption more practical for broader applications.

Zero-knowledge proofs are an emerging cryptographic trend, providing a way for one party to prove to another that a statement is true without revealing any information beyond the fact that the statement is true. This concept is revolutionary for authentication and privacy, as it allows for the verification of information without any data exchange.

Applications of zero-knowledge proofs are particularly prominent in authentication and privacy. They enable secure identity verification and transactions without exposing underlying data or credentials. This has implications for various sectors, including finance, online services, and blockchain technologies.

ZK-SNARKs (Zero-Knowledge Succinct Non-Interactive Arguments of Knowledge) and other advanced proof systems are at the forefront of zero-knowledge proof technology. These systems enable the verification of transactions or information in a highly efficient and secure manner. ZK-SNARKs, for example, are a key component in some privacy-focused cryptocurrencies, enabling secure, private transactions.

In summary, emerging trends in cyber cryptography, such as post-quantum cryptography, homomorphic encryption, and zero-knowledge proofs, are shaping the future of digital security. These advancements prepare the cryptographic landscape for quantum computing challenges and enhance the ability to perform secure computations and verifications. As these technologies develop, they will be critical in securing digital information in an increasingly complex and interconnected world.

Challenges and Future Directions

One of the primary challenges in cryptography is balancing robust security with usability. Strong cryptographic systems often come with complexity that can hinder user adoption. Designing cryptographic solutions that are both secure and user-friendly is crucial to ensure that they are widely adopted and effectively used.

User adoption challenges in cryptography stem from the need for user interface and procedure simplicity. Many users find cryptographic systems and protocols daunting, which can lead to underutilization or incorrect usage. Overcoming these challenges involves educating users and designing more intuitive cryptographic interfaces and interactions.

Human factors play a significant role in the effectiveness of cybersecurity measures. Understanding how users interact with cryptographic systems is crucial for designing solutions that cater to their needs and limitations. Human error remains one of the most significant vulnerabilities in cybersecurity, making user-centered design an essential consideration.

Ethical considerations in cryptography involve the implications of cryptographic technologies on privacy and security. As these technologies become more pervasive, they raise questions about the balance between security and individual rights. The ethical use of cryptography is essential to ensure that it benefits society while respecting individual freedoms and privacy.

Dual-use technologies in cryptography present ethical dilemmas. The same cryptographic tools that protect privacy and secure data can also be used for unlawful surveillance and infringing on personal freedoms. Navigating these ethical dilemmas involves creating policies and guidelines for the responsible use and implementation of cryptographic technologies.

The responsible use of cryptography is a growing concern, especially as cryptographic tools become more powerful and accessible. Ensuring that these tools are used ethically and in a way that benefits society requires collaboration between technologists, ethicists, and policymakers. Responsible use encompasses the design of cryptographic systems and their deployment and application.

Speculations on the future of cryptographic research suggest both challenges and breakthroughs. The field will likely evolve rapidly, with research focusing on post-quantum cryptography, advanced cryptographic protocols, and privacy-preserving technologies. These advancements will play a crucial role in addressing the growing complexities of digital security.

The potential breakthroughs in cryptography could bring significant disruptions to the current cybersecurity landscape. Emerging technologies like quantum computing could challenge existing cryptographic systems, necessitating new approaches and solutions. As the digital world becomes more interconnected, the evolution of cryptography will be key to safeguarding the future of digital security.

Career Corner

In cybersecurity, specializing in social engineering involves understanding and countering human-centric security vulnerabilities. This niche requires professionals to be adept at identifying, analyzing, and mitigating the risks posed by social engineering tactics. Various certifications cater to this aspect of cybersecurity, offering pathways to develop and validate expertise in dealing with these human-focused threats.

One prominent certification is the Certified Social Engineering Prevention Specialist (CSEPS). This program is tailored for professionals specializing in preventing social engineering attacks. CSEPS certification covers various topics, including recognizing social engineering techniques, developing effective training programs to educate employees, and implementing robust security policies to mitigate these risks. It is ideal for individuals looking to become experts in safeguarding organizations against deceptive practices that exploit human psychology.

The Certified Ethical Hacker (CEH) the EC-Council offers is another significant credential. While it encompasses a broad spectrum of cybersecurity topics, CEH focuses on social engineering methods as part of its curriculum. It equips professionals with the skills to think like hackers and identify vulnerabilities in systems and networks, including those arising from human interactions and behaviors. This certification is precious for those aspiring to penetration testing and cybersecurity analysis roles, where understanding social engineering tactics is crucial.

For a more comprehensive understanding of cybersecurity, including the human elements, the Certified Information Systems Security Professional (CISSP) is a highly respected certification. While it covers various areas of information security, CISSP also addresses the aspects of social engineering, making it suitable for professionals seeking a holistic view of cybersecurity threats, including those targeting human vulnerabilities.

The Advanced Social Engineering and Manipulation (ASEM) certification is specifically designed for cybersecurity professionals focusing on the intricacies of social engineering. It delves deep into the psychology behind these attacks, strategies used by attackers, and defense mechanisms to protect against them. This certification is ideal for those who wish to develop specialized skills in identifying and responding to sophisticated social engineering tactics.

Career paths in cybersecurity related to social engineering are diverse and evolving. Roles such as Social Engineering Analyst, Cybersecurity Trainer, or Awareness Program Coordinator are increasingly common in organizations. These professionals are crucial in educating staff about social engineering threats and developing strategies to counter them. Security Consultants specializing in social engineering offer expertise in assessing vulnerabilities and advising on best practices to mitigate such risks.

In conclusion, certifications like CSEPS, CEH, CISSP, and ASEM provide valuable pathways for those interested in specializing in social engineering within cybersecurity. These certifications not only enhance professional knowledge but also open doors to various career opportunities, where the focus is on safeguarding against the ever-evolving landscape of social engineering threats.

Chapter Questions

1. What does cyber cryptography focus on in digital security?

   A. Encrypting and decrypting information

   B. Tracking user behavior

   C. Enhancing website performance

   D. Physical security of servers

2. What does confidentiality in cryptography ensure?

   A. Data is not altered or tampered with

   B. Information is hidden from unauthorized users

   C. Encryption keys are distributed securely

   D. Data originates from a legitimate source

3. Which protocols are used in web browsing for secure online transactions?

   A. HTTP and FTP

   B. SSL/TLS

   C. TCP/IP

   D. SSH and SCP

4. Which cipher was used by Egyptians and Spartans for military communication?

   A. Polygraphic cipher

   B. Enigma machine

   C. Simple substitution cipher

D. Vigenère cipher

5. What was a significant advancement in
    cryptographic history during World War II?

    A. Development of RSA

    B. Introduction of Public Key Infrastructure

    C. Allied decryption of the Enigma machine

    D. Invention of the Internet

6. What does symmetric cryptography use for
    encryption and decryption?

    A. Different keys for each process

    B. The same key for both processes

    C. A public key only

    D. Biometric data

7. What is a critical factor in the security of symmetric
    algorithms?

    A. User authentication

    B. Key length

    C. The number of users

    D. The algorithm's popularity

8. What type of cryptography uses a public key for
    encryption and a private key for decryption?

    A. Symmetric

    B. Asymmetric

    C. Hash function

D. Multiparty computation

9. What is the primary purpose of hash functions in cryptography?

    A. To encrypt large volumes of data

    B. To create a unique, fixed-size hash value from input data

    C. To establish secure connections

    D. To distribute cryptographic keys

10. In which cryptographic system are root Certificate Authorities at the top of the trust hierarchy?

    A. Symmetric key system

    B. Public Key Infrastructure (PKI)

    C. Hash function system

    D. Multiparty computation system

11. What is the primary goal of post-quantum cryptography?

    A. To improve encryption speeds

    B. To develop algorithms secure against quantum attacks

    C. To reduce the size of cryptographic keys

    D. To replace all current cryptographic methods

12. What does homomorphic encryption enable?

    A. Computations on encrypted data

    B. Faster decryption processes

    C. Secure distribution of keys

    D. Generation of digital certificates

13. What are zero-knowledge proofs used for in cryptography?

    A. To prove a statement is true without revealing any information about the statement

    B. To encrypt emails

    C. To authenticate network devices

    D. To store cryptographic keys securely

14. What does the balance between security and usability in cryptography address?

    A. The cost of cryptographic systems

    B. The complexity of cryptographic systems for user adoption

    C. The physical security of cryptographic hardware

    D. The speed of cryptographic algorithms

15. What ethical consideration is involved in the use of cryptographic technologies?

    A. The balance between security and individual rights

    B. The color scheme of user interfaces

    C. The geographic location of servers

    D. The choice of programming language

CHAPTER 5

Network Security

Network security is a critical concern in the digital age, an era where data and digital operations are central to businesses and individuals. Ensuring the safety and integrity of networks is not just a technical challenge but a fundamental requirement for the continuity and success of modern enterprises. As technology evolves, so does the complexity of the threats, making it imperative for organizations to update and strengthen their security measures continuously. The consequences of neglecting network security can be devastating, ranging from financial losses to severe reputational damage.

The significance of network security cannot be overstated in an era where dependence on digital networks is ubiquitous. This necessity extends beyond mere protection against external threats; it also involves safeguarding systems from internal vulnerabilities. A robust network security framework ensures that sensitive data is well-protected while maintaining the network's overall functionality and reliability. It is the backbone of an organization's defense against the ever-evolving landscape of cyber threats.

At the heart of network security is protecting sensitive data, encompassing personal information, financial records, intellectual property, and other critical data types. Effective network security measures are essential in preventing data breaches that can lead to significant losses for individuals and organizations. The focus is not only on preventing unauthorized access but also on ensuring the integrity and confidentiality of the data. In a world where data breaches are increasingly common, robust network security is crucial for maintaining trust and confidence among stakeholders.

© Dr. Jason Edwards 2024, corrected publication 2024
Dr. J. Edwards, *Mastering Cybersecurity*, https://doi.org/10.1007/979-8-8688-0297-3_5

Network security is integral to ensuring business continuity. In an interconnected world, any disruption to network operations can have immediate and far-reaching impacts on business functionality. Effective network security measures help prevent such disruptions, whether from cyber-attacks, technical failures, or human errors. The goal is to create a resilient infrastructure that can withstand various threats and maintain operational integrity under diverse conditions.

The evolution of network threats has been rapid and relentless. What started as simple viruses and worms has evolved into sophisticated cyber-attacks, including advanced persistent threats (APTs) that can lurk undetected in networks for extended periods. These evolving threats require a dynamic and proactive approach to network security. Understanding the nature of these threats is crucial for developing effective strategies to combat them.

The spectrum of network threats is broad and varied, from viruses and worms to advanced persistent threats (APTs). APTs, in particular, represent a significant escalation in network attacks' sophistication and potential impact. They are characterized by their stealth, persistence, and targeted nature, often aimed at siphoning off valuable data or disrupting critical operations. The emergence of APTs underscores the need for comprehensive security strategies beyond traditional antivirus and firewall solutions.

Social engineering and phishing represent some of the most insidious network threats. These tactics exploit human psychology rather than technological vulnerabilities, tricking users into divulging sensitive information or granting access to restricted systems. The success of these methods highlights the importance of incorporating human factors into network security strategies. Training and awareness programs are essential in equipping individuals to recognize and respond appropriately to these threats.

Insider threats and espionage are particularly challenging aspects of network security. These threats come not from external attackers but from individuals within the organization with legitimate network access. Insider threats can be challenging to detect and prevent if motivated by malice, financial gain, or external coercion. Implementing strict access controls, monitoring unusual network activity, and fostering a culture of security awareness are vital in mitigating these risks.

Understanding key network security concepts is fundamental to developing effective security strategies. Among these concepts, the principles of confidentiality, integrity, and availability, collectively known as the CIA triad, are foundational. Confidentiality ensures that sensitive information is accessible only to authorized individuals, integrity guarantees that the information is accurate and unaltered, and availability ensures that authorized users have reliable access to the information and resources they need.

The concept of "defense in depth" is a foundational principle in network security, drawing inspiration from military strategies where multiple layers of defense are implemented to protect against adversaries. In network security, defense in depth involves creating multiple redundant security measures and controls throughout the network infrastructure. This approach ensures that if one defense layer fails or is breached, additional layers continue to provide protection, mitigating the risk of a total system compromise. The idea is not solely to prevent attacks but also to create a resilient environment where the impact of a successful attack can be minimized and contained.

At its core, network defense in depth integrates various security components, including firewalls, intrusion detection and prevention systems (IDS/IPS), network segmentation, access controls, and encryption. Firewalls act as the first line of defense, controlling incoming and outgoing traffic based on predefined security rules. IDS/IPS systems monitor network traffic to detect and respond to suspicious activities. Network segmentation divides the network into smaller parts, making it harder for an attacker to move laterally within the network. Access controls ensure that only authorized users can access specific resources, and encryption protects the confidentiality and integrity of data in transit and at rest. Additionally, in-depth defense encompasses technological solutions and involves policies, procedures, and awareness training to create a comprehensive security posture. This multilayered strategy is crucial in an evolving threat landscape, where the variety and sophistication of cyber attacks continue to grow, necessitating a dynamic and robust approach to network security.

Network Architecture and Topology

Network architecture and topology are fundamental aspects of modern computing environments, shaping how data is transmitted and managed across different areas. Exploring different network architectures helps us understand how they cater to specific requirements and challenges. Whether a small office network or an extensive enterprise system, the architecture lays the groundwork for efficient and secure data communication.

Local area networks (LANs) are network architecture typically used within a single building or a small group of buildings. They enable the sharing of resources and facilitate communication among devices in close proximity. LANs are known for their high speed and relatively low cost, making them ideal for more minor, localized networking needs. They are crucial in connecting personal computers, printers, and other devices within an office or home environment.

In contrast, wide area networks (WANs) span larger geographic areas, often connecting multiple LANs. They can encompass a city, a region, or even global connections. WANs are essential for businesses that operate over multiple locations, providing a cohesive network infrastructure for communication and data sharing. Due to their scale, WANs face unique management, security, and reliability challenges.

Virtualized and cloud networks represent the evolution of traditional networking concepts, moving away from physical hardware-centric models. These networks leverage cloud computing to create flexible, scalable, and efficient networking solutions. Virtualized networks allow for multiple, isolated networks on the same physical infrastructure, while cloud networks offer resources as services over the Internet, leading to cost savings and enhanced agility.

Understanding different types of network topologies is critical for designing efficient networks. Network topology arranges a computer network's different elements (links, nodes, etc.). It defines how these elements are interconnected and how data flows between them. The choice of topology impacts the network's performance, reliability, and scalability.

Star, mesh, bus, ring, and hybrid topologies are the most common types of network structures. Each has unique characteristics and suitability for different scenarios. For instance, a star topology, where each node is connected to a central hub, is known for its simplicity and easy troubleshooting. Mesh topology offers high redundancy but can be complex and expensive, while bus and ring topologies are simpler but may have limitations regarding scalability and fault tolerance.

The security implications of each network topology are significant. For example, mesh networks offer robustness due to multiple redundant paths, but they can be complex to secure. In contrast, star topologies may be more accessible to secure due to their centralized nature but can become a single point of failure. Understanding these implications is key to designing networks that are not only efficient but also secure.

The importance of redundancy in network design cannot be overstated. Redundancy ensures that alternative paths are available for data transmission if one path or node fails, thereby maintaining network availability. This is particularly crucial in mission-critical environments where downtime can have significant consequences. Redundant network design includes additional or backup components, such as routers, switches, and communication lines, to prevent single points of failure.

Various types of network architectures, such as client-server, peer-to-peer (P2P), and cloud-based architectures, each come with their own set of strengths and weaknesses in terms of security:

1. **Client-Server Architecture**: In this model, clients request resources or services from a central server. This architecture's strength lies in centralized control and management, making enforcing security policies and updates easier. However, it has a significant weakness: the central server represents a single point of failure. If compromised, it could jeopardize the entire network.

2. **Peer-to-Peer (P2P) Architecture**: P2P networks distribute resources among peers without a central server. This decentralization can be a strength, as it eliminates single points of failure and can be more resilient to attacks. However, it also poses a security challenge, as controlling and monitoring each node is more complex, making it susceptible to malware and distributed attacks.

3. **Cloud-Based Architecture**: With resources hosted in the cloud, this architecture offers scalability and flexibility. The security strength of cloud-based architectures lies in the expertise and resources cloud service providers can offer. However, reliance on third-party providers creates data security and privacy challenges, and the shared responsibility model requires a clear understanding and delineation of security roles.

Implementing network segmentation is a strategic approach to enhancing network security and performance. It involves dividing a more extensive network into smaller, isolated segments or subnetworks. This segmentation can reduce congestion, improve performance, and provide an additional layer of security. By segmenting networks, organizations can limit the spread of security breaches within their networks, as each segment can have its security protocols and controls.

VLANs (virtual local area networks) and subnetting are standard techniques used in network segmentation. VLANs allow for creating distinct broadcast domains within a single LAN, enabling better network traffic control and segmentation. Subnetting, on the other hand, divides an IP network into smaller, more manageable segments. These techniques are crucial for isolating and securing different network parts, especially in complex and large-scale environments.

Creating demilitarized zones (DMZs) is another crucial strategy in network architecture. A DMZ is a physical or logical subnetwork that contains and exposes an organization's external-facing services to an untrusted network, usually the Internet. The purpose of a DMZ is to add a layer of security, isolating the internal network from the external one. It acts as a buffer zone, preventing external users from gaining direct access to sensitive data stored on internal servers.

Network Threat Landscape

The threat landscape in network security is a dynamic and constantly evolving challenge, requiring a deep understanding of the types of threats that networks face. Recognizing these threats is the first step in developing effective security measures. The variety of threats, from malware to sophisticated social engineering attacks, highlights the need for comprehensive security strategies.

Malware, including viruses, worms, and Trojans, represents a significant portion of network threats. These malicious software programs are designed to damage, disrupt, or gain unauthorized access to computer systems. Viruses attach themselves to clean files and spread throughout a system, worms exploit network vulnerabilities to spread across networks, and Trojans disguise themselves as legitimate software to trick users into installing them.

Social engineering attacks, such as phishing and spear-phishing, target the human element of security. Phishing involves sending fraudulent communications that appear to come from a reputable source, typically via email, to steal sensitive data like login credentials and credit card numbers. Spear-phishing is a more targeted form where the attacker customizes their approach to target specific individuals or organizations.

Denial-of-service (DoS) and distributed denial-of-service (DDoS) attacks aim to disrupt normal network services. DoS attacks overwhelm a network or server with traffic, rendering it inaccessible to intended users. DDoS attacks are similar but come from a network of compromised computers, making them more challenging to mitigate. These attacks can weaken organizations, causing significant downtime and loss of service.

Recognizing insider threats is a critical aspect of network security. Insider threats can come from two main types: malicious insiders, who intentionally cause harm to the organization, and negligent insiders, who unintentionally cause harm through carelessness or lack of awareness. Both insiders pose significant risks due to their access to sensitive information and internal systems.

Insider attacks and data exfiltration involve unauthorized access, use, or transmission of an organization's confidential information. These attacks can be particularly damaging as insiders already have legitimate access to the organization's network, making their activities harder to detect. Insider threat detection methods include monitoring user behavior, implementing strict access controls, and using advanced analytics to identify unusual patterns.

Identifying vulnerabilities and exploits is a crucial step in protecting networks. Vulnerabilities are weaknesses in software or hardware that attackers can exploit to gain unauthorized access or cause harm. Common vulnerabilities include unpatched software, coding errors, and weak authentication mechanisms. Hardware vulnerabilities, though less common, can also pose significant risks.

Standard exploitation techniques attackers use include SQL injection, where malicious code is inserted into a database query, and cross-site scripting (XSS), where attackers inject malicious scripts into web pages viewed by others. Understanding these techniques helps develop defenses against them, such as input validation and regular security assessments.

In summary, the threat landscape in network security is complex and multifaceted, encompassing a wide range of potential risks. From malware and social engineering to insider threats and exploitation techniques, understanding these threats is essential for developing effective security measures. As technology evolves, so do the threats, requiring continuous vigilance and adaptation in security practices.

Network Monitoring and Management

Network monitoring and management are essential to maintaining a healthy, secure, and efficient network infrastructure. Network monitoring involves continuously observing and analyzing network performance and traffic to identify anomalies, potential threats, and performance issues. Utilizing software and hardware tools, network administrators can monitor various aspects of the network, including bandwidth usage, server performance, uptime of network services, and the health of individual network devices. This continuous monitoring is crucial for detecting issues that could escalate into serious problems, allowing for timely intervention and maintenance.

An essential aspect of network monitoring is fault management. It involves identifying, diagnosing, and resolving network issues to ensure minimal downtime and service disruption. Fault management relies on alert systems that notify network administrators of problems like server crashes, overloaded routers, or failed network connections. These alerts can be configured based on specific thresholds or anomalies in network behavior. Once alerted, network professionals can quickly address the issue, often using remote diagnostic tools and management protocols like SNMP (Simple Network Management Protocol) to investigate and resolve the problem.

Performance management is another critical facet of network monitoring. It focuses on ensuring that the network operates at an optimal level and meets the performance standards required by the organization. This includes monitoring network bandwidth, latency, and error rates to ensure efficient data transfer and communication. Performance management tools can help identify bottlenecks or hardware inefficiencies that may slow down the network, enabling administrators to make informed decisions about upgrades or optimizations. Network managers can also plan for future capacity needs by analyzing trends and historical data, ensuring the network can scale to meet growing demands.

Security management is integral to network monitoring, involving continuously scrutinizing network traffic to detect and prevent unauthorized access, data breaches, and other security threats. This includes using firewalls, intrusion detection systems (IDS), and intrusion prevention systems (IPS) to monitor and control access to the network. Regularly updating antivirus and anti-malware software, applying security patches, and monitoring for unusual activity are all part of a robust security management strategy. Additionally, implementing security policies and protocols, such as secure access controls and encryption, further strengthens the network against potential threats.

Finally, network management encompasses the administration and maintenance of network resources, ensuring that all network components function correctly and efficiently. This includes the configuration and optimization of network devices, such as routers, switches, and servers, as well as the management of software applications and services that run on the network. Effective network management ensures the high availability and reliability of network services, which are critical for the day-to-day operations of any organization. It also involves strategic planning for network expansion, upgrades, and integration of new technologies, aligning the network with the organization's evolving needs and technological advancements. Through diligent monitoring and management, network administrators can ensure a stable, secure, high-performing network infrastructure supporting the organization's objectives and growth.

Access Control and Authentication

Access control and authentication are critical pillars of network security, ensuring only authorized users can access specific resources and data. Understanding access control models is essential for implementing adequate security policies. These models define how permissions are granted and what resources users can access within a network.

Discretionary access control (DAC) is an access control model where the resource owner decides who can access it. In DAC systems, users have some flexibility in determining how they share the resources they control. This model is widely used because of its simplicity and flexibility, but it can also be less secure since it relies on user discretion to manage access rights.

Mandatory access control (MAC) is a more stringent model. In MAC, access rights are regulated based on predefined rules set by a central authority. This model is typically used in environments that require a higher level of security, such as military or government systems. Under MAC, users cannot change access permissions; they can only access resources according to the rules established by the system administrator.

113

Role-based access control (RBAC) is another model where access rights are assigned based on the role within an organization. In RBAC, roles are created for various job functions, and permissions to perform certain operations are assigned to specific roles. Users are then assigned roles, and through those roles, they acquire the permissions to perform particular system functions. This model is effective in larger organizations with many users and complex permissions.

Authentication methods are crucial for verifying the identity of users before granting access to resources. Passwords and passphrases are the most common forms of authentication. They are easy to implement but can be vulnerable if not appropriately managed, such as using weak passwords or failing to change them regularly.

Multifactor authentication (MFA) enhances security by requiring multiple verification forms before granting access. This typically involves something the user knows (like a password), something the user has (like a smartphone or a security token), and something the user is (like a fingerprint or other biometric data). MFA significantly reduces the risk of unauthorized access, as it is more difficult for attackers to compromise multiple authentication factors.

Biometrics and smart cards are advanced authentication methods. Biometrics uses unique physical identification characteristics, such as fingerprints or iris patterns. Intelligent cards containing embedded microprocessors provide a secure way to store and transmit authentication information. These methods offer higher security levels but can be more complex and costly.

Authorization and permissions are about defining and managing the access rights users have. The principle of least privilege (PoLP) is a critical concept in this area, stating that users should be granted only the permissions they need to perform their tasks. This minimizes the risk of accidental or malicious misuse of privileges.

Access control lists (ACLs) define who can access what resources in a network. They are a list of permissions attached to an object and specify which users or system processes are granted access to objects and what operations are allowed on given objects.

Identity and Access Management (IAM) systems manage user identities and their corresponding access permissions within an organization. IAM systems ensure users are who they claim to be and have appropriate access to company resources based on their roles and responsibilities. IAM is a crucial component of any organization's security strategy, encompassing the policies and technologies that ensure secure access to resources.

In summary, access control and authentication are fundamental aspects of network security, involving various models, methods, and systems to ensure that only authorized users can access network resources. Implementing effective access control and authentication mechanisms is essential for protecting sensitive data and systems from unauthorized access and potential security breaches.

Network Encryption and Data Protection

Network encryption and data protection are critical to securing digital information, whether in transit or at rest. Understanding cryptographic fundamentals is essential for implementing effective encryption strategies. Cryptography forms the basis for securing data against unauthorized access and breaches.

Symmetric and asymmetric encryption are the two primary types of cryptographic algorithms. Symmetric encryption uses the same key for encryption and decryption, making it faster but less secure if compromised. In contrast, asymmetric encryption uses a pair of keys – a public key for encryption and a private key for decryption. This method is more secure but requires more computational resources.

Public and private keys are integral to asymmetric encryption. The public key is shared openly and used for encrypting data, while the private key is kept secret and used for decryption. This system is widely used in various security protocols, including SSL/TLS, for securing Internet communications. These keys allow for secure data exchange even over unsecured channels.

Hash functions and digital signatures are essential for verifying data integrity and authenticity. A hash function converts data into a fixed-size string of characters representing the data's fingerprint. Digital signatures use asymmetric encryption to validate the authenticity of a document or message, ensuring that it hasn't been tampered with during transmission.

Securing data in transit is crucial to protect information as it moves across networks. SSL/TLS protocols are widely used for this purpose, providing a secure channel over an insecure network like the Internet. These protocols encrypt data before it's sent and decrypt it upon arrival, ensuring it remains confidential and intact during transit.

VPN technologies create secure, encrypted connections over a public network, like the Internet, ensuring safe and private data transmission. VPNs are commonly used for secure remote access to an organization's network or to protect data when using public Wi-Fi networks.

Secure email communication is another critical aspect of data protection. Encrypting emails ensures that only the intended recipient can read them, protecting sensitive information from interception or unauthorized access. Various encryption methods are available for email, ranging from encrypting the connection with SSL/TLS to encrypting the content of the emails themselves.

Data encryption at rest is essential for protecting stored data against unauthorized access and breaches. Full-disk encryption (FDE) is a method to encrypt all the data on a disk drive. FDE ensures that if a device is lost or stolen, its data remains secure and inaccessible without the correct encryption key.

File and folder encryption provides a more granular level of control, allowing specific files or folders to be encrypted. This method helps protect sensitive files on shared systems or networks. Users can access only the files for which they have the decryption key, adding a layer of security to sensitive data.

Hardware Security Modules (HSMs) are physical devices that provide an extra layer of security for managing digital keys and performing cryptographic operations. HSMs are used in high-security environments to manage the encryption keys and perform encryption and decryption operations securely outside the primary computing environment. This helps protect against both physical and logical attacks on the encryption keys.

In summary, network encryption and data protection involve various techniques and technologies to secure data in transit and at rest. From cryptographic fundamentals to specific encryption methods and protocols, understanding and effectively implementing these measures are crucial for protecting sensitive information in today's digital world.

Firewalls and Intrusion Detection/ Prevention Systems

Understanding firewalls is fundamental to network security. A firewall is a barrier between a trusted internal network and untrusted external networks, like the Internet. It filters incoming and outgoing network traffic based on an organization's established rules and policies. By scrutinizing network traffic, firewalls prevent unauthorized access to a network, effectively shielding it from many cyber threats.

There are different types of firewalls, each with unique characteristics and uses. Stateful firewalls keep track of the state of active connections and make decisions based on the context of the traffic. Stateless firewalls, on the other hand, filter traffic based solely on the source and destination without considering the traffic's history. Proxy firewalls filter network traffic at the application level, acting as an intermediary between end users and the resources they are accessing.

Firewall rules and policies are crucial for effective network management. These rules define which traffic should be allowed or blocked based on specific criteria such as IP addresses, port numbers, and protocols. Firewall policies should be regularly reviewed and updated to adapt to the evolving threat landscape and network requirements. A well-configured firewall can significantly enhance the overall security posture of a network.

Intrusion detection and prevention capabilities are essential for identifying and responding to threats. Intrusion detection systems (IDS) monitor network traffic for suspicious activity and alert network administrators of potential threats. IDS can be deployed as network based to monitor traffic to and from all devices on the network or host based to monitor activity on individual devices.

Signature-based detection in IDS involves comparing observed events in the network to a database of known threat signatures. This method detects known threats but may fail to identify new, previously unknown attacks. Anomaly-based detection, on the other hand, looks for deviations from a baseline of regular network activity, potentially identifying novel or sophisticated threats.

Real-time alerts and reporting are crucial features of IDS. They enable network administrators to detect and respond to potential threats promptly. The reporting mechanism of an IDS provides detailed information about the nature of the detected threat, helping in the analysis and mitigation of the attack. Timely alerts help in minimizing the potential impact of security breaches.

Intrusion prevention systems (IPS) are proactive security measures. While IDS alerts administrators to potential threats, IPS takes active steps to block or prevent those threats. IPS can take actions such as dropping malicious packets, blocking traffic from suspect IP addresses, or alerting administrators. This proactive approach helps to prevent intrusions before they can cause harm to the network.

Blocking suspicious traffic is a primary function of IPS. By inspecting network packets and taking actions based on defined security policies, IPS can prevent attacks from spreading within a network. Inline and out-of-band deployment are two common approaches for IPS. Inline IPS is placed directly in the path of network traffic, allowing immediate blocking of threats. At the same time, out-of-band IPS analyzes copies of network traffic, reducing potential delays but requiring additional steps to block malicious traffic.

Fine-tuning IPS policies is essential for effective intrusion prevention. Overly aggressive policies can result in false positives, unnecessarily blocking legitimate traffic, while lax policies may fail to detect and stop real threats. Regularly updating and adjusting IPS policies ensures the system remains effective against evolving threats without impeding network performance. This balance is crucial for maintaining security and functionality in dynamic network environments.

Network Security Best Practices

Patch management strategies are a cornerstone of network security. They involve identifying, acquiring, testing, and installing patches on systems and software. Effective patch management helps address vulnerabilities that attackers could exploit. It's a continuous process, requiring regular monitoring and application of patches to ensure security and functionality.

The importance of regular updates in maintaining network security cannot be overstressed. Software and system vulnerabilities are continually identified; regular updates are necessary to mitigate these risks. Organizations can protect themselves against many known security threats by keeping systems up to date. Failing to update systems regularly leaves them vulnerable to attacks that exploit outdated software or firmware.

Patch testing and deployment are critical steps in the patch management process. Before deploying patches across the network, they should be tested in a controlled environment to ensure they do not cause unintended side effects. Once tested, patches need to be systematically deployed across the affected systems. This approach minimizes the risk of introducing new issues while addressing security vulnerabilities.

Vulnerability scanning is a proactive measure for identifying potential weaknesses in a network. It involves using specialized software tools to scan systems and applications for known vulnerabilities. Regular vulnerability scanning is essential for maintaining an up-to-date understanding of the network's security posture and identifying areas requiring attention.

Network segmentation best practices involve dividing a network into smaller, distinct segments. This approach isolates critical systems and reduces the overall attack surface. An attack on one segment can be contained by segmenting the network, preventing it from spreading to other parts of the network. This is particularly important for protecting sensitive data and critical infrastructure.

Isolating critical systems is a crucial aspect of network segmentation. Systems essential for business operations or storing sensitive data should be isolated from general network areas. This isolation helps protect these critical systems from broader network threats and reduces the risk of targeted attacks.

Creating secure zones within a network is another aspect of effective segmentation. These zones can be used to group systems with similar security requirements, making it easier to apply consistent security policies. Secure zones can be defined based on factors like the sensitivity of data, user access levels, or the specific functions of the systems.

Reducing the attack surface of a network is crucial for minimizing the potential entry points for attackers. This can be achieved through network segmentation and by removing unnecessary services, closing unused ports, and enforcing strict access controls. A smaller attack surface makes a network more secure and easier to manage and monitor.

Secure remote access solutions are essential for modern networks, especially with the increasing prevalence of remote work. Virtual Private Networks (VPNs) provide a secure connection over the Internet, encrypting data and hiding the user's IP address. VPNs are widely used for secure remote access, ensuring that data remains confidential and protected from interception.

Remote Desktop Protocols (RDP) allow users to remotely connect to and control a computer. While convenient, RDP can be vulnerable if not properly secured. Strong authentication measures and limiting access to RDP are essential for mitigating security risks.

Secure Shell (SSH) is another tool for secure remote administration. SSH provides a secure channel over an unsecured network, encrypting the data between the client and the host. It's commonly used for managing servers and network devices remotely, ensuring that commands and data are protected from eavesdropping and interception.

Security assessment and penetration testing are proactive approaches to uncover vulnerabilities and weaknesses in a network. These practices involve simulating attacks on the network to identify security gaps. Ethical hacking and penetration testing provide valuable insights into how real-world attackers might exploit network vulnerabilities.

Vulnerability scanning, an integral component of security assessments, is crucial in identifying known weaknesses in systems and software. By scanning the network for vulnerabilities, organizations can gain a clear view of potential security risks, allowing them to address these issues proactively. Regular scanning helps maintain an up-to-date understanding of the network's security posture but also assists in prioritizing remediation efforts based on the severity and potential impact of the identified vulnerabilities. Furthermore, consistent vulnerability scanning enables organizations to adapt their security strategies to evolving threats, ensuring their defenses remain robust against new attacks.

Ethical hacking and penetration testing go beyond vulnerability scanning by actively trying to exploit vulnerabilities, mimicking the tactics and techniques of real attackers. These exercises provide a practical assessment of the network's defenses and can reveal complex security issues that scanning might not detect.

Reporting and remediation are crucial final steps in security assessments. After identifying vulnerabilities, detailed reports should be prepared, outlining the findings and recommending actions for remediation. Timely remediation of identified vulnerabilities is critical to maintaining a strong security posture and protecting the network against attacks.

Wireless Network Security

Securing Wi-Fi networks is a critical aspect of wireless network security. As Wi-Fi becomes increasingly prevalent in personal and professional settings, protecting these networks from unauthorized access and cyber threats is paramount. This involves implementing robust encryption protocols, securing network access points, and continuously monitoring network activity. Properly secured Wi-Fi networks protect sensitive data and ensure the network's integrity and availability for authorized users.

WPA3 and WPA2 encryption are fundamental to Wi-Fi security. WPA2, the second generation of Wi-Fi Protected Access, has been the standard for secure wireless networks, offering robust protection through solid encryption. WPA3, the latest iteration, enhances security further by offering features like individualized data encryption and protection against brute-force attacks. Upgrading to WPA3 where possible and ensuring WPA2 is properly configured are critical steps in safeguarding Wi-Fi networks.

Guest network isolation is an effective practice in wireless security. Businesses and individuals can provide Internet access without exposing their primary network and sensitive resources by setting up a separate network for guests. This separation ensures that guests cannot access the internal resources of the host network, thus mitigating potential risks associated with nonsecure devices or malicious intent. Guest networks should be secured with a different password and, if possible, isolated on a different frequency band.

MAC address filtering is another layer of security for Wi-Fi networks. This technique allows or blocks devices based on their unique Media Access Control (MAC) address. While MAC address filtering can add a layer of security by restricting network access to known devices, it is not foolproof, as MAC addresses can be spoofed. Therefore, MAC address filtering should be used with other security measures rather than as a stand-alone solution.

Bluetooth and IoT device security are increasingly important with the proliferation of connected devices. If not properly secured, Bluetooth connections can be vulnerable to eavesdropping and man-in-the-middle attacks. Similarly, Internet of Things (IoT) devices, which often lack robust built-in security, can become entry points for attackers. Ensuring that Bluetooth connections are encrypted and that IoT devices are secured is essential in a comprehensive wireless network security strategy.

IoT vulnerabilities and challenges pose significant risks to network security. Many IoT devices have limited processing power and memory, making it difficult to implement traditional security measures. Additionally, the diversity and widespread use of IoT devices in various applications create challenges in maintaining consistent security standards. The lack of regular updates and patches for many IoT devices further exacerbates their cyberattack vulnerability.

Security protocols for IoT are crucial in mitigating these risks. Developing and implementing robust security protocols for IoT devices involves ensuring secure communication channels, regular firmware updates, and robust authentication and authorization processes. IoT device authentication and authorization ensure that only legitimate devices can access the network and communicate with other devices. This can involve using certificates, secure passwords, or other forms of digital authentication to verify the identity of devices and control their access to network resources. Establishing these security measures is vital for protecting networks from the unique vulnerabilities of IoT devices.

Emerging Trends in Network Security

The Zero Trust security model represents a significant shift in network security philosophy. It operates on the principle that no user or device should be automatically trusted inside or outside the network. This model responds to the evolving complexity of modern network environments, where the traditional perimeter-based security approach is no longer sufficient. Zero Trust requires continuous verification of every access request, ensuring that only authenticated and authorized users and devices can access network resources.

Zero Trust principles revolve around "never trust, always verify." This approach entails strict identity verification, micro-segmentation of networks, and most minor privilege access controls. By assuming that threats can exist outside and inside the network, Zero Trust principles aim to minimize the attack surface and reduce the impact of potential breaches. Implementing these principles requires a comprehensive understanding of network architectures, data flows, and user behaviors.

Implementing Zero Trust Architecture involves several key steps. First, organizations must identify sensitive data and assets and then map the flow of this data across the network. Then, they enforce strict access controls and policies around this data, continuously monitoring and validating user and device trustworthiness. The implementation of Zero Trust is an ongoing process, requiring regular reviews and adjustments to adapt to new threats and changes in the network environment.

Micro-segmentation is a core component of the Zero Trust model. It involves dividing a network into smaller, more secure zones to control individual access to specific areas within the network. This approach limits an attacker's ability to move laterally across a network if they gain access. Micro-segmentation enhances security by providing granular control over traffic flows, reducing the risk of widespread network breaches.

Artificial intelligence (AI) and machine learning (ML) are increasingly integral to network security. These technologies enable the analysis of vast amounts of data to identify patterns and anomalies indicative of cyber threats. AI and ML can automate complex processes for detecting and responding to security incidents, increasing efficiency and reducing the reliance on manual intervention. Integrating these technologies is transforming how security is managed, allowing for more proactive and predictive security measures.

AI and ML are revolutionizing threat detection and analysis. These technologies can rapidly analyze data from various sources, identifying threats that might elude traditional security measures. AI-driven systems can adapt and learn from new security threats, constantly improving their detection capabilities. This results in faster, more accurate threat detection, enabling quicker response times to potential security incidents.

Security automation is becoming an essential tool in managing network security. Automation allows for the rapid execution of security tasks, such as patching vulnerabilities or responding to incidents, without human intervention. This speeds up response times and reduces the likelihood of human error. Security automation ensures consistent application of security policies, improving overall network defense.

Behavior-based analytics is another emerging trend in network security. This approach involves monitoring user and device behavior to detect anomalies that may indicate a security threat. Security systems can more accurately identify potentially malicious activities by understanding typical behavior patterns. Behavior-based analytics is particularly effective in detecting insider threats and advanced persistent threats that might go unnoticed.

Blockchain and distributed ledger technology (DLT) are beginning to find applications in network security. Their inherent characteristics, such as decentralization, transparency, and immutability, make them suitable for enhancing security in various ways. Blockchain can be used to create secure and unalterable logs of network transactions, helping detect and prevent tampering and fraud.

Use cases of blockchain in network security include secure identity management, decentralized access control, and data integrity verification. By leveraging blockchain, networks can establish more secure and transparent systems for managing access and data. This technology also offers potential solutions for secure IoT networks, where the integrity and security of devices are critical.

Challenges in adopting blockchain and DLT in network security include scalability, integration with existing systems, and regulatory compliance. While blockchain offers unique advantages, its practical implementation requires careful consideration of these challenges. Organizations must assess the suitability of these technologies for their specific security needs and the implications of their integration into existing network infrastructures.

Decentralized identity and access control are emerging as critical applications of blockchain technology in network security. This approach gives users more control over their identity and access rights, reducing reliance on centralized identity providers. Decentralized systems can enhance security and privacy by allowing users to selectively manage and share their identity information. Decentralized models offer a promising solution as organizations seek more secure and efficient ways to manage identity and access.

Emerging trends in network security, such as the Zero Trust model, AI and ML in security, and blockchain technology, are reshaping the landscape of network defense. These innovations offer new tools and approaches to protect against increasingly sophisticated cyber threats. As these technologies continue to evolve, they hold the potential to significantly enhance the security, efficiency, and resilience of network systems.

Software-Defined Networking and the Cloud

Software-Defined Networking (SDN) represents a transformative approach to network management that fundamentally changes how networks are configured and operated. SDN decouples the network control and forwarding functions at its core, enabling network management through software-based controllers. This separation allows for more agile and centralized control over network resources, unlike the traditional approach, where network devices like routers and switches manage data processing and traffic control. By centralizing control, SDN gives administrators a holistic view of the entire network, simplifying configuration and optimization processes. This architecture enhances efficiency and allows for more dynamic network management, adapting quickly to changing business needs and network conditions.

One of the key benefits of SDN is its inherent ability to support more scalable and flexible network environments. In an SDN architecture, network administrators can programmatically configure network resources through software applications using open APIs. This programmability enables rapid deployment and reconfiguration of network services without manual intervention at each network device. It paves the way for automated network configurations, streamlined service provisioning, and more efficient use of network resources. As a result, SDN is particularly advantageous in environments that require quick scalability and adaptability, such as data centers and cloud computing platforms.

SDN's role in cloud computing is particularly significant. In cloud environments, where resources must be allocated, scaled, and managed dynamically, SDN provides the necessary agility and flexibility. It enables cloud service providers to optimize network traffic flow, manage bandwidth more effectively, and ensure higher levels of performance and reliability for cloud services. By integrating SDN, cloud providers can offer enhanced services like on-demand bandwidth, improved cloud resource connectivity, and advanced virtual network services tailored to the specific needs of their customers.

Another aspect where SDN proves beneficial is in facilitating network virtualization. Network virtualization involves creating a virtual version of network resources and services and decoupling them from the underlying physical infrastructure. SDN enhances network virtualization by providing a centralized control mechanism to manage these virtual resources. This capability is crucial in cloud environments, where resources must be isolated and segmented for different tenants. SDN's centralized control simplifies the management of these complex, multitenant environments, improving operational efficiency and resource utilization.

Furthermore, SDN contributes to enhanced network security in cloud environments. The centralized control of SDN allows for more consistent and comprehensive implementation of security policies across the network. It enables real-time visibility into network traffic, allowing for the immediate detection and mitigation of security threats. In the cloud, where data security and privacy are paramount, SDN's ability to dynamically adjust network configurations and enforce security policies is invaluable. It provides a framework for implementing advanced security measures like micro-segmentation, isolating workloads, and containing security breaches within a small network segment.

Software-Defined Networking is a pivotal technology in evolving network architecture and cloud computing. It provides the flexibility, scalability, and control necessary to manage complex network environments efficiently. SDN is instrumental in the continued growth and innovation of cloud services by enabling programmable network management, enhancing network virtualization capabilities, and bolstering network security. As businesses increasingly rely on cloud-based solutions and services, SDN's role in facilitating efficient, secure, and adaptable network environments becomes ever more crucial, marking it as a critical technology in the future landscape of networking and cloud computing.

Future of Network Security

Predicting future threats and trends in network security is an ongoing challenge. As technology evolves, so do the tactics and strategies of cyber attackers. Staying ahead of these changes requires constant vigilance and adaptation. Security professionals must address current threats and anticipate emerging risks, adapting their defense mechanisms accordingly. This proactive approach is crucial in maintaining adequate security in a rapidly changing digital landscape.

Quantum computing presents both opportunities and challenges for cryptography. While quantum computers can break current encryption methods, they can also create nearly unbreakable encryption. This duality means that the rise of quantum computing will likely lead to a significant shift in cryptographic techniques. Security professionals must prepare for this future by researching and developing quantum-resistant encryption methods.

IoT and 5G security challenges are set to become more prominent. The proliferation of IoT devices and the rollout of 5G networks will increase the volume and speed of data transmission, presenting new security vulnerabilities. These technologies will require robust security frameworks to protect against potential threats, including device hijacking, data breaches, and network attacks. Addressing these challenges will be critical for ensuring the security and reliability of IoT and 5G networks.

AI-driven attacks and defenses are expected to become more sophisticated. Cyber attackers will likely use AI to develop more complex attack strategies as AI technology advances. Conversely, AI will also be a powerful tool in detecting and countering cyber threats. The arms race between AI-driven security measures and AI-powered attacks will shape the future network security landscape.

Preparing for cybersecurity challenges involves technological solutions and addressing skills and training needs. As cyber threats become more complex, the demand for skilled cybersecurity professionals will grow.

Organizations must invest in training programs to effectively develop the expertise needed to counter future threats. This will include technical skills and an understanding of the broader cybersecurity landscape.

Threat intelligence sharing is a crucial strategy for staying ahead of emerging threats. Organizations can collectively improve their defense strategies by sharing information about new threats and vulnerabilities. This collaborative approach allows for a more comprehensive understanding of the cyber threat landscape and a quicker response to new risks. Effective threat intelligence sharing requires trust and cooperation among stakeholders, including private companies, government agencies, and international entities.

Continuing education and career paths in cybersecurity will be vital for professionals looking to stay current in this rapidly evolving field. Continuous learning and professional development are necessary to keep pace with new technologies, techniques, and threats. Cybersecurity professionals must be lifelong learners, constantly updating their knowledge and skills to protect against the latest cyber threats.

Cybersecurity certification paths provide structured learning and validation of expertise. Certifications such as CISSP, CISM, and CEH are recognized across the industry and can be crucial for career advancement. Pursuing these certifications helps professionals demonstrate their expertise and commitment to the field. Additionally, certifications often expose professionals to various topics and best practices, enhancing their understanding of network security.

Research and development opportunities in cybersecurity are abundant and crucial for advancing the field. As new technologies and threats emerge, there is a continuous need for innovative solutions and defenses. R&D in cybersecurity involves developing new technologies and studying cyber attackers' tactics and psychology. This research is essential for staying ahead of attackers and developing effective countermeasures.

Ethical considerations in security research are increasingly important. As cybersecurity researchers explore new ways to defend against attacks, they must also consider the ethical implications of their work. This includes ensuring that research does not inadvertently cause harm or violate privacy and legal standards. Ethical guidelines and reviews are essential in guiding researchers to conduct their work responsibly.

In conclusion, the future of network security is poised to be shaped by a range of factors, from advancements in quantum computing and AI to the growing challenges of IoT and 5G. Preparing for these changes requires a multifaceted approach, encompassing technological innovation, skills development, collaboration, and ethical consideration. As the landscape of cyber threats evolves, so must the strategies and expertise of those tasked with defending against them.

Career Corner

Network security, a critical information technology component, protects computer networks and data from unauthorized access, misuse, or destruction. This domain has gained immense importance due to the increasing frequency and sophistication of cyberattacks and the growing complexities of digital infrastructures. As a field, network security offers a challenging and rewarding career path, pivotal in safeguarding digital assets and information.

Professionals in the field of network security can assume a variety of roles. Network Security Analysts are at the forefront, monitoring and protecting an organization's network infrastructure. They identify vulnerabilities, implement security measures, and respond to security breaches, often within security operations centers. Cybersecurity

Engineers take on the task of designing and implementing secure network solutions. Their expertise in hardware and software security aspects is crucial in developing robust defenses against cyber threats.

Penetration Testers, also known as Ethical Hackers, play a unique role by simulating cyberattacks on systems, networks, and applications to unearth vulnerabilities. Their work is instrumental in strengthening the security posture of an organization. On the strategic front, Chief Information Security Officers (CISOs) oversee the organization's overall information security strategy. This senior-level role involves technical expertise and strong leadership in developing and implementing comprehensive security policies and ensuring regulatory compliance.

In addition to practical experience, certifications are highly valued in the network security domain, as they validate a professional's expertise and commitment to the field. The Certified Information Systems Security Professional (CISSP) is a globally recognized certification ideal for seasoned professionals, covering extensive areas like risk management and security operations. The Certified Ethical Hacker (CEH) certification is tailored for those interested in the offensive aspects of network security, focusing on skills such as penetration testing.

Cisco's certifications also play a significant role in the industry. The Cisco Certified Network Professional (CCNP) Security certification is designed for professionals seeking advanced skills in securing Cisco networks, covering secure access, firewall technologies, and intrusion prevention. The Cisco Certified Internetwork Expert (CCIE) Security is a prestigious certification for experts, concentrating on advanced security topics, including complex security solutions and architectures. For those starting, the Cisco Certified Network Associate (CCNA) Security certification validates the ability to secure Cisco networks, encompassing foundational topics like intrusion prevention and network infrastructure security. Additionally, the Cisco Cybersecurity Specialist (CCST) certification emphasizes cybersecurity and threat detection skills, vital for roles in cybersecurity operations centers.

Network security is dynamic and requires professionals to continually update their knowledge and skills. Staying abreast of the latest security trends, technologies, and best practices is crucial for success. Whether one opts for a hands-on technical role or a strategic leadership position, the opportunities in network security are vast and essential, reflecting the critical need for this expertise in the modern digital landscape.

Case Study: The Target Breach

The Target data breach, which occurred in 2013, is one of the most significant cybersecurity incidents, illustrating the consequences of inadequate network design and security measures. The breach resulted in the theft of approximately 40 million credit and debit card records and 70 million records containing Target customers' personal information. This incident caused significant financial losses and severely damaged the company's reputation and trust among consumers.

The initial intrusion into Target's network was traced back to a phishing attack against a third-party vendor, an HVAC company, which had access to Target's network for maintenance purposes. The attackers gained the vendor's credentials and used them to enter Target's network. This breach highlights a critical vulnerability in Target's network design: the insufficient segmentation between the network used by third-party vendors and the network where customer data and payment systems were stored. The lack of robust segregation allowed the attackers to move laterally within the network, escalating their access privileges and reaching sensitive network areas containing customer data.

Once inside the network, the attackers installed malware on Target's point-of-sale (POS) systems. This malware was designed to capture credit card information as transactions were processed. The malware's deployment and ability to transmit stolen data back to the attackers were facilitated by weaknesses in Target's internal network security and monitoring systems. The company's failure to adequately monitor and control internal network traffic allowed the malware to remain undetected for an extended period, exacerbating the scale of the data breach.

The Target attack underscores the importance of comprehensive network security practices, particularly in access management and network segmentation. Granting broad network access to third-party vendors without stringent controls and oversight can lead to significant vulnerabilities. Effective network design should include rigorous access controls and network segmentation, ensuring that external parties do not have access to critical internal resources and that sensitive areas of the network are isolated from each other.

Another critical lesson from the Target breach is the necessity of proactive and effective network monitoring and intrusion detection systems. Target reportedly had a FireEye security system in place, which generated alerts during the early stages of the attack. However, these alerts were not adequately acted upon. This incident highlights the need to implement sophisticated security systems and ensure that the alerts they generate are appropriately managed and investigated.

In conclusion, the Target data breach is a stark reminder of the potential consequences of insufficient network security and design. It emphasizes the need for rigorous access controls, especially concerning third-party vendors, adequate network segmentation to limit the spread of an attack, and the critical importance of proactive network monitoring and response. The lessons learned from this breach have since influenced how companies approach network security, underscoring the importance of continuous vigilance and improvement in cybersecurity strategies.

Chapter Questions

1. What is the primary goal of network security in modern enterprises?

    A. To enhance user experience

    B. To ensure business continuity and success

    C. To increase network speed

    D. To reduce IT costs

2. What is a fundamental aspect at the heart of network security?

    A. Increasing network connectivity

    B. Protecting sensitive data

    C. Enhancing user interface

    D. Expanding digital operations

3. What type of threat has evolved from simple viruses to advanced persistent threats (APTs)?

    A. Physical security breaches

    B. Network hardware failures

    C. Network threats

    D. Software licensing issues

4. What is the primary purpose of implementing the Zero Trust security model?

    A. To reduce network costs

    B. To speed up data processing

    C. To avoid internal audits

    D. To continuously verify every access request

5. In network security, what does the CIA triad stand for?

    A. Connectivity, integrity, and availability

    B. Confidentiality, integrity, and availability

    C. Centralization, integrity, and accessibility

    D. Confidentiality, installation, and accessibility

6. Which technology is crucial for threat detection and analysis in network security?

    A. Virtual reality

    B. Artificial intelligence and machine learning

    C. Blockchain

    D. Quantum computing

7. What does MAC address filtering in Wi-Fi networks do?

    A. Speeds up the network

    B. Filters devices based on their unique MAC address

    C. Decreases network range

    D. Encrypts data packets

8. Which type of firewall filters traffic based on the state of active connections?

   A. Stateless firewall

   B. Stateful firewall

   C. Proxy firewall

   D. Personal firewall

9. What is the main benefit of using VPN technologies in network security?

   A. To enhance the user interface

   B. To create secure, encrypted connections over public networks

   C. To reduce network costs

   D. To increase Internet speed

10. What is the primary purpose of vulnerability scanning in network security?

    A. To increase network speed

    B. To identify potential weaknesses in a network

    C. To enhance the graphical user interface

    D. To reduce IT staff workload

11. What type of access control model is based on roles within an organization?

    A. Discretionary access control (DAC)

    B. Mandatory access control (MAC)

    C. Role-based access control (RBAC)

    D. Token-based access control

12. What is the main objective of implementing patch management strategies?

   A. To enhance network speed

   B. To address vulnerabilities that attackers could exploit

   C. To reduce network costs

   D. To improve user interface design

13. What is the critical feature of intrusion prevention systems (IPS)?

   A. Increasing network speed

   B. Blocking suspicious traffic

   C. Reducing IT costs

   D. Enhancing graphical user interfaces

14. What is the main challenge in adopting blockchain technology in network security?

   A. Enhancing the user experience

   B. Dealing with scalability and integration with existing systems

   C. Reducing the cost of network hardware

   D. Improving the speed of Internet connections

15. What does the future of network security likely involve regarding technology advancement?

   A. Decreased reliance on technology

   B. Sole focus on physical security measures

   C. Increased use of AI and quantum computing

   D. Elimination of the need for cybersecurity professionals

CHAPTER 6

Application Security

Application security is a critical aspect of the safeguarding of digital assets. It involves protecting applications from threats and vulnerabilities. With the increasing number of cyber-attacks, securing applications is more prominent than ever. This section emphasizes how application security is essential in protecting not just data but also the functionality and reputation of organizations.

Security breaches pose significant risks to organizations, leading to potentially catastrophic consequences. These breaches can result in the loss of sensitive data, financial loss, and damage to the organization's reputation. Additionally, they can disrupt operations and erode customer trust, impacting long-term business viability. Understanding these risks is crucial for any organization relying on digital platforms.

A security breach can severely damage an organization's reputation and erode customer trust. When customers lose confidence, it directly affects the business's bottom line. This loss of trust can take years to rebuild and may require significant investment. Therefore, maintaining robust application security is a technical necessity and critical to sustaining customer relationships and trust.

The financial and legal implications of a security breach are far-reaching. Organizations may face hefty fines, legal actions, and the cost of rectifying the breach. There are indirect costs, such as increased insurance premiums and investment in enhanced security measures. These financial burdens highlight the importance of proactive application security measures to avoid such costly incidents.

© Dr. Jason Edwards 2024, corrected publication 2024
Dr. J. Edwards, *Mastering Cybersecurity*, https://doi.org/10.1007/979-8-8688-0297-3_6

The threat landscape in the realm of application security is constantly evolving. New attack vectors emerge regularly, challenging existing security measures. Organizations must stay informed about the latest threats and adapt their security strategies accordingly. This chapter discusses the dynamic nature of cyber threats and the importance of continuous vigilance and adaptation in security practices.

Understanding the fundamentals of application security is essential for effective defense strategies. This involves recognizing common vulnerabilities, implementing best practices, and developing a robust security culture. This chapter outlines the basic application security principles, providing a foundation for more advanced topics discussed in later sections.

The CIA triad – confidentiality, integrity, and availability – forms the core principles of application security. Confidentiality ensures that sensitive information is accessible only to authorized individuals. Integrity involves maintaining the accuracy and reliability of data. Availability ensures that information and resources are accessible when needed. This section explains how these principles guide effective security strategies.

The security development lifecycle (SDLC) is a critical process in application development. It integrates security considerations throughout the development stages, from planning to deployment and maintenance. Incorporating security from the beginning of the development process is more effective than addressing it after a system is built. This chapter explores the steps and benefits of integrating SDLC in application development.

Threat modeling and risk assessment are vital in identifying and mitigating security threats. These practices involve analyzing an application to identify vulnerabilities and potential attack scenarios. Organizations can prioritize security efforts and allocate resources effectively by understanding these risks. This section delves into methodologies and best practices for conducting thorough threat modeling and risk assessments.

Security by Design refers to incorporating security measures from the outset of application design. This approach ensures that security is an integral part of the application rather than an afterthought. The principles of Security by Design include minimizing attack surfaces, securing defaults, and the principle of least privilege. This chapter discusses how these principles can be effectively applied to create more secure applications.

Secure Coding Practices

Secure coding practices are essential for developing robust and secure applications. One of the key practices is input validation and output encoding. This involves ensuring that all data entering an application is valid and safe. This protects the application from malicious inputs and helps maintain data integrity and reliability. Implementing these practices is a foundational step in securing applications against common attacks.

Preventing Cross-Site Scripting (XSS) is another critical aspect of secure coding. XSS attacks involve injecting malicious scripts into web applications, which unsuspecting users execute. To prevent XSS, developers must rigorously validate and sanitize all user inputs. This includes employing techniques like whitelisting allowable characters and escaping special characters that could be used in scripts.

Mitigating SQL injection vulnerabilities is crucial in protecting databases from unauthorized access. SQL injection occurs when attackers manipulate a standard SQL query through user input. This can lead to unauthorized access to or manipulation of database information. To prevent this, developers should use parameterized queries and avoid dynamic SQL generation based on user input. Regularly updating and patching database management systems is vital in reducing these vulnerabilities.

Validating and sanitizing user input is a comprehensive approach to ensure the security of an application. Input validation checks whether the provided data meets the expected criteria, such as format and type. On the other hand, sanitization involves cleaning the input to remove any potentially malicious data. These practices are essential in building applications that are resilient to various forms of input-based attacks.

Output encoding and context-aware escaping are vital in ensuring that the data an application outputs is safe. This is particularly important in web applications, where malicious scripts can be embedded in outputs rendered by a browser. By encoding outputs, especially those that include user-generated content, applications can prevent the execution of harmful scripts.

Authentication and authorization are critical components of application security. Authentication verifies the identity of a user, while authorization determines their access levels within the application. Implementing strong and effective mechanisms for both is essential in controlling access to sensitive information and functionalities.

Implementing robust authentication mechanisms involves more than just traditional username and password combinations. Multifactor authentication, biometric verification, and behavioral analytics are robust authentication methods. These techniques significantly enhance security by adding additional layers of verification, making unauthorized access much more difficult.

Role-based access control (RBAC) is an effective way to manage user permissions in an application. RBAC assigns users roles, and each role is granted specific access rights. This model simplifies managing user permissions and ensures that individuals only have access to the information and functionality necessary for their role.

Session management and protection are crucial in maintaining the security of user sessions within an application. This involves securely managing session tokens used to authenticate users during a session. Proper management includes generating secure, unique session tokens and ensuring they are transmitted and stored securely.

OAuth 2.0 and OpenID Connect are popular frameworks for authorization in modern web applications. OAuth 2.0 provides delegated authorization, allowing applications to access resources on behalf of a user. OpenID Connect, built on OAuth 2.0, adds an authentication layer. These frameworks are essential in implementing secure third-party authorization in applications.

Error handling and logging are essential for both application functionality and security. Proper error handling ensures the application responds gracefully to unexpected conditions, preventing potential security vulnerabilities. This includes avoiding disclosing sensitive information in error messages, which attackers could exploit.

Proper error message handling is crucial in not exposing the internal workings of an application to potential attackers. Error messages should be informative enough for legitimate users to understand what went wrong but not so detailed that they provide clues that could aid an attacker. Balancing this is key to maintaining both usability and security.

Logging security events and incidents is essential for monitoring and responding to potential security threats. Logs should record sufficient detail to reconstruct events but must be managed securely to prevent unauthorized access. This includes protecting log files from tampering and ensuring that sensitive data within logs is handled appropriately.

Log analysis and monitoring are vital for detecting and responding to security incidents. Analyzing logs can help identify patterns indicative of malicious activity. Security Information and Event Management (SIEM) systems can automate much of this process, aggregating and analyzing logs from various sources to detect anomalies and potential security incidents.

Security Information and Event Management (SIEM) integration is a powerful tool in a comprehensive security strategy. SIEM systems collect and analyze log data from various sources, providing real-time analysis of security alerts. This integration enables organizations to detect, understand, and respond to security incidents more effectively, enhancing overall security posture.

Secure communication is a fundamental aspect of protecting data in transit. Data transmitted over networks should be encrypted to prevent interception and unauthorized access. This is particularly important for sensitive information like login credentials, personal data, and financial transactions.

Transport Layer Security (TLS/SSL) is the standard protocol for securing data transmitted over the Internet. TLS/SSL encrypts data between the user's browser and the server, ensuring that it cannot be easily intercepted and read by unauthorized parties. Implementing TLS/SSL is a basic but essential practice for securing web applications.

API security best practices are crucial in protecting the interfaces through which applications communicate. This includes securing endpoints, validating and sanitizing inputs, and implementing rate limiting to prevent abuse. Attackers often target APIs due to their access to sensitive data and systems, prioritizing their security.

JSON Web Tokens (JWT) are popular for securing authentication and authorization processes. JWTs are compact, URL-safe tokens that can securely transmit information between parties. They are often used in modern web applications for token-based authentication and to pass the identity of authenticated users between an identity provider and a service provider.

Secure API design patterns involve more than just securing individual endpoints. They encompass a holistic approach to designing APIs with security as a fundamental consideration. This includes using HTTPS for all API traffic, implementing proper authentication and authorization checks, and ensuring that sensitive data is handled securely throughout the API.

Security Testing and Assessment

Security testing and assessment is a critical phase in the application development lifecycle, aimed at identifying and mitigating potential security vulnerabilities. One of the most recognized forms of this testing is penetration testing. This involves simulating cyber attacks on software systems to evaluate their defenses. Penetration testing provides real-world insight into how an application might respond to an attack, revealing vulnerabilities that must be addressed.

Black-box testing techniques are a key component of security assessments. In black-box testing, the tester has no prior knowledge of the system's internal workings. This approach simulates an external hacking attempt and effectively uncovers data input, output, and operational behavior issues. It provides a realistic scenario of how an attacker might interact with the application.

White-box testing methodologies take a different approach. Here, the tester has complete system knowledge, including access to source code, architecture diagrams, and other documentation. This comprehensive understanding allows for a more thorough examination of the application, including internal security mechanisms, code paths, and data processing.

Red team vs. blue team exercises are dynamic and engaging security testing methods. The red team, playing the role of attackers, tries to exploit vulnerabilities in the system. The blue team, responsible for defense, detects and responds to these attacks. This exercise is invaluable in understanding the effectiveness of current security measures and training teams for real-world scenarios.

Reporting and remediation of findings are crucial steps after any security testing. It involves documenting vulnerabilities, assessing their severity, and recommending remedial actions. Effective reporting ensures that stakeholders understand the risks and can prioritize fixes. Remediation follows, where vulnerabilities are addressed, often leading to improvements in security controls and processes.

Code review and static analysis are foundational practices in securing application code. Static analysis tools automatically examine source code for patterns that may indicate security vulnerabilities. However, tools cannot catch everything, making manual code review essential. This combination helps identify issues that automated tools might miss and provides a deeper understanding of the code's security posture.

Automated code scanning tools play a significant role in continuous security assessment. These tools scan the codebase for known vulnerabilities and coding errors that could lead to security issues. Automation is precious in large projects or continuous integration/continuous deployment (CI/CD) environments, where code changes frequently.

Manual code review best practices involve a detailed source code examination by security experts. These reviews focus on understanding the logic, identifying security flaws, and ensuring adherence to best coding practices. Manual review is often more time-consuming than automated scanning but provides depth and insight that automated tools cannot.

Code review checklists are essential for conducting thorough and consistent manual code reviews. These checklists cover various security aspects, such as input validation, authentication, authorization, and error handling. They ensure that reviewers systematically examine all relevant security aspects of the code.

Secure coding guidelines and coding standards form the backbone of developing secure applications. They provide developers with rules and best practices, reducing the likelihood of introducing security vulnerabilities into the code. Adhering to these guidelines and standards is a proactive measure in building security into the application.

Dynamic analysis and vulnerability scanning are techniques used to test applications in runtime. These methods identify security issues that become apparent only when the application runs, such as user sessions, data handling, and interaction with other systems. Dynamic analysis complements static code analysis by uncovering issues not visible in the source code alone.

OWASP ZAP (Zed Attack Proxy) and Burp Suite are popular tools for web application scanning. They are used in dynamic analysis to test web applications for vulnerabilities like XSS, SQL injection, etc. These tools simulate attacks on web applications, helping testers identify potential security issues in a controlled environment.

Dynamic Application Security Testing (DAST) tools are automated solutions that help identify web application vulnerabilities in their running state. These tools interact with the application from the outside, mimicking the actions of a user or an attacker. DAST tools are essential for detecting issues not apparent in the static code but emerge when the application is operational.

Identifying and prioritizing vulnerabilities is a critical process following security testing. Not all vulnerabilities pose the same risk level, and remediation resources are often limited. Therefore, it's important to assess the severity of each vulnerability and prioritize them based on factors like potential impact, exploitability, and the value of the affected asset.

Threat intelligence feeds and indicators of compromise (IoC) are valuable resources in identifying emerging threats and potential vulnerabilities in systems. Threat intelligence involves gathering and analyzing information about current and emerging threats and attack methods. Indicators of compromise are pieces of forensic data, such as system log entries or files, that can be used to detect unauthorized activity.

Threat modeling and risk assessment are systematic processes for identifying and mitigating potential security issues. They involve understanding how an attacker might target a system and what assets are at risk. Organizations can better understand their security needs by modeling potential threats and prioritizing efforts to address the most significant risks.

Integrating threat modeling into the software development lifecycle (SDLC) ensures that security considerations are included from the earliest stages of development. This proactive approach means that security is considered at every phase of the SDLC, from requirements gathering to design, implementation, testing, and maintenance.

Threat modeling tools and frameworks assist in systematically identifying and assessing potential threats. These tools help visualize the system's security architecture, identify potential threat agents, and evaluate the risks associated with different system components. Using such tools enhances the effectiveness and efficiency of the threat modeling process.

Attack surface reduction techniques minimize the opportunities for attackers to exploit a system. This can involve removing unnecessary features, limiting access points, and segmenting networks. Reducing the attack surface is a key strategy in making systems more secure and resilient against attacks.

Continuous threat modeling and risk reassessment are essential in today's rapidly evolving threat landscape. As new threats emerge and systems change over time, it's essential to reassess the security posture of applications regularly. Continuous threat modeling ensures security measures remain effective and relevant, adapting to new developments and insights.

Dynamic Analysis and Vulnerability Scanning

Security testing and assessment are crucial to developing and maintaining secure systems. Black-box testing, a key methodology in this domain, involves testing an application without knowing its internal workings. The principles of black-box testing focus on assessing the system from an external perspective, mimicking an attacker's approach. This testing effectively reveals vulnerabilities in the system's interfaces and external behaviors.

The advantages of black-box testing include its ability to test various applications without access to source code and its effectiveness in finding data input and output issues. However, its limitations lie in the lack of insight into the internal logic and structure of the application, which can lead to missed vulnerabilities that are not apparent from the outside.

Common black-box testing techniques include systematic input testing, testing for response behavior, and testing application workflows. Techniques like fuzz testing, where the system is bombarded with random, malformed data, effectively uncover issues that arise with unexpected inputs. Input validation testing, another common technique, checks how the application handles various types of user inputs, especially malicious ones.

Parameter manipulation is a specific black-box testing technique that involves altering query parameters, POST requests, and URL data to test how the system responds to unexpected input. This can reveal vulnerabilities in how the application processes and validates user input. Security scanning tools such as Nessus and OpenVAS are instrumental in automating some aspects of black-box testing and scanning applications for known vulnerabilities and security weaknesses.

White-box testing, in contrast, involves a thorough understanding of the application's internals. The principles of white-box testing revolve around leveraging this in-depth knowledge to test the application's internal logic, code structure, and pathways. This approach allows for a more comprehensive assessment compared to black-box testing.

The advantages of white-box testing include identifying hidden vulnerabilities in the code and covering all possible execution paths. However, its limitations include requiring specialized knowledge of the application's codebase and the potential to miss runtime vulnerabilities that only appear in a live environment.

Source code analysis and binary analysis are two facets of white-box testing. Source code analysis involves reviewing the actual lines of code, while binary analysis deals with compiled code. Both are critical in identifying potential security flaws. White-box testing tools and techniques, including static analysis tools like Fortify and Checkmarx, assist in automating the process of reviewing code for security vulnerabilities.

Dynamic analysis tools such as AppScan and WebInspect complement these static tools by testing the application's running state. Manual code review remains a best practice in white-box testing, providing an in-depth and nuanced view of potential security issues. Code review checklists and guidelines help ensure that reviews are thorough and consistent.

The role of code review in security assessment cannot be overstated. It allows for meticulously examining the source code to identify security flaws that automated tools might miss. The benefits of static code analysis, including the detection of vulnerabilities at an early stage, make it a vital component of security testing. Static code analysis tools can quickly scan large codebases, identifying potential vulnerabilities based on predefined rules and patterns.

Comparatively, Dynamic Application Security Testing (DAST) tools focus on identifying runtime vulnerabilities, offering a different perspective than static analysis. Automated tools complement them, and manual code review offers the depth needed to understand identified vulnerabilities' context and potential impact. Code review workflows and methodologies vary but typically involve peer, tool-assisted, and iterative reviews throughout the development lifecycle.

Identifying security vulnerabilities in source code is just the first step. Remediation guidance and recommendations are crucial for effectively addressing these vulnerabilities, ensuring they are identified and properly fixed. Dynamic Analysis and Vulnerability Scanning then takes over, focusing on identifying vulnerabilities during the application's runtime.

Dynamic analysis principles involve testing the application's operational state, simulating user interactions, and data processing. The advantages of dynamic analysis include its ability to identify vulnerabilities that only appear in runtime, such as those related to user sessions and live data processing. However, its limitations include potential performance impacts on the application and the inability to cover every possible execution path.

OWASP ZAP (Zed Attack Proxy) is a widely used tool for dynamic analysis. Its features and capabilities make it suitable for comprehensive testing of web applications. Spidering and scanning features allow it to crawl through web applications, identifying pages and inputs for testing. Active and passive scanning capabilities enable it to test applications for various vulnerabilities.

Reporting and integration features of tools like OWASP ZAP and Burp Suite facilitate the documentation and management of identified vulnerabilities. Burp Suite, another popular tool, offers features like proxies for intercepting requests and scanning for vulnerabilities. Its Collaborator feature allows for more extensive and collaborative testing scenarios.

Common Vulnerability and Exposure (CVE) is a reference system for publicly known cybersecurity vulnerabilities. The CVE numbering and tracking system provides a standardized method for identifying and discussing specific vulnerabilities. The impact of CVE on security assessments is significant, as it helps standardize vulnerability management and communication.

Integrating CVE data into vulnerability management processes helps organizations stay informed about emerging threats and vulnerabilities. This integration ensures that security testing and assessments are up to date and effective in identifying and mitigating known vulnerabilities.

Security in the Development Lifecycle

Security in the Development Lifecycle is a comprehensive approach to integrating security into software development. Secure software development methodologies are frameworks that incorporate security considerations throughout the software development process. These methodologies ensure that security is not an afterthought but a fundamental component of the development lifecycle.

Agile security practices adapt the principles of Agile development to include security considerations. Agile methodologies, known for their flexibility and iterative approach, can effectively integrate security by incorporating security-focused user stories, regular security reviews, and sprint-based security tasks. This approach ensures that security is addressed continuously and evolves with the application.

DevSecOps integration takes this further by embedding security practices directly into the DevOps workflow. DevSecOps involves the collaboration of development, operations, and security teams, ensuring that security is a shared responsibility and seamlessly integrated into the entire software delivery process. This approach encourages faster, more efficient, and more secure software deployment.

Comparing Waterfall, Agile, and DevOps from a security perspective involves understanding how each methodology incorporates security. In Waterfall, security is often addressed at distinct phases, potentially leading to siloed efforts. Agile, with its iterative approach, allows for more frequent security assessments. DevOps, especially with a DevSecOps approach, integrates security into all stages of the development and deployment process.

Integrating security into CI/CD pipelines is crucial for automating and enhancing security practices. Continuous integration (CI) and continuous deployment (CD) enable the automatic integration and deployment of code changes. Integrating automated security testing into these pipelines ensures that security checks are performed consistently and early in development.

Automated security testing in CI/CD pipelines can include various tools and techniques, from static and dynamic analysis to dependency checks and vulnerability scanning. This automation helps identify and address security issues quickly, reducing the time and effort required for manual security reviews.

Infrastructure as Code (IaC) security involves managing and provisioning infrastructure through code, allowing for automated, consistent, and repeatable deployment processes. By treating infrastructure as code, organizations can apply the same security and review processes used for application code, ensuring the underlying infrastructure is secure.

Security as code (SaC) extends this concept, treating security policies and configurations as code that can be version controlled, reviewed, and automated. This approach ensures that security configurations are consistent, traceable, and subject to the same rigorous review process as application code.

For developers to write secure code by design, secure coding guidelines and standards are essential. These guidelines cover various aspects of coding, such as input validation, authentication, and error handling. Adherence to these standards helps in preventing common security vulnerabilities.

The OWASP Top Ten and other security resources comprehensively overview the most critical web application security risks. These resources are invaluable for developers to understand and mitigate prevalent security threats. Similarly, the CERT Secure Coding Standards offer detailed guidelines for writing secure code in various programming languages.

Custom coding standards and policies allow organizations to tailor security practices to their needs and risk profiles. These standards can be developed based on industry best practices, regulatory requirements, and unique organizational contexts. Implementing these standards ensures that the software meets the organization's security requirements.

Compliance-driven security practices are critical in industries regulated by specific security standards and laws. Adhering to these compliance requirements is not just a legal obligation but also a way to ensure that applications meet specific security baselines. These practices often involve regular audits, adherence to specific security frameworks, and documentation of compliance efforts.

Developer training and awareness are fundamental in fostering a security-focused development culture. Security training programs and resources help developers understand security best practices, common threats, and the importance of security in their daily work. This training is essential for empowering developers to contribute proactively to the application's security. Secure coding education and workshops provide hands-on experiences and practical knowledge in secure software development. These educational initiatives can range from online courses to in-person workshops, offering developers the skills and knowledge to write secure code effectively.

Fostering a security-aware culture within the development team is about more than just training; it involves creating an environment where security is valued and prioritized. This culture encourages open discussion about security, rewards secure coding practices, and views security as integral to software quality. Developer-centric security tools and practices are designed to integrate seamlessly into the developer's workflow. These tools, such as integrated development environment (IDE) plug-ins for security scanning or pre-commit hooks for automated security checks, make it easier for developers to incorporate security into their daily work without significant disruptions.

Secure APIs and Web Services

Secure APIs and Web Services protect digital interactions and data exchanges in today's interconnected world. API security fundamentals focus on safeguarding these interfaces from unauthorized access and breaches. Effective security measures encompass robust authentication, thorough authorization, and meticulous data validation to ensure the integrity and confidentiality of data.

API authentication mechanisms play a critical role in verifying the identities of users or systems accessing the API. These mechanisms vary from simple API keys to more advanced methods like OAuth tokens or JSON Web Tokens (JWTs). The choice of an authentication method is crucial and should align with the API's specific security requirements and operational context.

In API security, authorization and scope management are essential for ensuring that authenticated entities have the right level of access. This involves setting and enforcing access policies that control what an authenticated user or system can do. Effective scope management prevents excessive permissions, adhering to the principle of least privilege, essential for minimizing the risk of unauthorized data access.

Rate limiting and throttling are key security techniques in API management. They control the number and frequency of user requests, preventing overuse and potential denial-of-service attacks. Implementing these measures helps maintain the API's availability and performance, ensuring a reliable and consistent user experience.

API versioning and deprecation are strategic components for the evolution of API services. Proper versioning allows for introducing new features or changes without disrupting existing clients. A clear and well-communicated deprecation strategy is vital for guiding users away from outdated versions that may pose security risks toward more secure and updated versions.

Web service security involves a range of practices to protect the functionalities and data exposed through web services. This includes implementing secure communication protocols like HTTPS to encrypt data in transit and robust input validation and output encoding to prevent common vulnerabilities.

Secure communication, primarily through HTTPS, is indispensable for APIs. Encrypting data in transit with HTTPS protects it from interception and tampering. This security measure is particularly crucial for APIs handling sensitive or personal information, ensuring confidentiality and integrity of data exchanges.

Input validation and sanitization are pivotal in safeguarding APIs against injection attacks and ensuring the integrity of the data processed. Proper input validation checks inputs against expected formats and types, while sanitization cleanses data of any malicious content. These practices are crucial for defending against various attack vectors targeting API vulnerabilities.

Best practices in API security encompass a holistic approach to securing API endpoints. This includes using strong, multifaceted authentication methods, enforcing robust access controls, encrypting sensitive data, and regularly auditing security measures. Staying abreast of and implementing these best practices is crucial for developing and maintaining secure APIs.

Handling sensitive data within APIs requires extra layers of security. This involves implementing encryption in transit and at rest and ensuring access to this data is strictly controlled and monitored. Additionally, precautions should be taken to avoid exposing sensitive information in API logs or error messages, as attackers can exploit these.

API testing and validation are critical processes in the API development lifecycle, ensuring that APIs function correctly and securely. This involves testing APIs for common vulnerabilities, checking their responses under various conditions, and validating that they meet specified requirements. Regular testing and validation are key to maintaining the security and reliability of APIs.

API security testing tools automate the detection of vulnerabilities in APIs. These tools can perform various tests, from static analysis of API code to dynamic testing of running APIs. Leveraging such tools helps identify potential security issues efficiently, enabling quicker and more effective remediation.

Fuzz testing and input validation are specialized techniques in API security testing. Fuzz testing involves sending random, malformed, or unexpected inputs to the API to assess its response to abnormal conditions. Input validation testing, on the other hand, verifies that the API correctly processes and sanitizes user inputs, a crucial aspect of protecting against injection attacks.

Automated API security testing streamlines the process of identifying and addressing security vulnerabilities. This automation facilitates continuous and consistent testing throughout the API development and deployment lifecycle. By integrating automated security testing into the workflow, developers can ensure that security is a continuous and integral part of the API's lifecycle.

API gateways and API firewall solutions provide an additional layer of security for APIs. These solutions act as intermediaries, inspecting and filtering API traffic. They help enforce security policies, authenticate requests, and prevent unauthorized access. Implementing such solutions is an effective way to enhance the security of APIs, especially in complex and high-traffic environments.

Secure API design principles focus on creating inherently secure APIs by design. This involves considering security at every stage of the API design process, from planning to implementation and beyond. Adhering to these principles helps prevent security vulnerabilities from being introduced into the API.

API documentation plays a crucial role in the security of APIs. Well-documented APIs help developers understand how to interact with the API securely. Documentation best practices include providing clear, comprehensive information on authentication, authorization, rate limiting, and other security-related aspects of the API.

API security reviews and validation are essential to ensure that APIs are secure and function as intended. These reviews involve scrutinizing the API design, implementation, and documentation for potential security flaws. Regular validation and review of APIs help maintain their security posture over time, adapting to new threats and changing requirements.

Mobile Application Security

Mobile Application Security is an increasingly important aspect of digital security as mobile devices become central to our daily lives. Mobile app security fundamentals involve protecting applications from various types of attacks and ensuring the safety and privacy of user data. This includes implementing strong encryption, secure communication, and robust authentication mechanisms.

The unique challenges in mobile app security arise from the diverse range of devices, operating systems, and user behaviors. Mobile apps often operate in a more fragmented and less controlled environment than desktop applications. This diversity requires a flexible and adaptable security approach catering to various platforms and ecosystems.

Mobile app attack vectors are numerous and varied, including insecure data storage, weak server-side controls, and vulnerabilities within the mobile operating system. Attackers can exploit these vulnerabilities to access sensitive data, perform unauthorized actions, or compromise the app's integrity. Understanding these attack vectors is crucial for developing effective security measures.

Mobile platforms and ecosystems, such as iOS and Android, have their security features and challenges. App store security and review processes also play a crucial role in ensuring the safety of mobile apps. These platforms provide various tools and guidelines for developers to create secure apps but also require adherence to specific security standards to be listed in their app stores.

Secure coding for mobile apps is essential to prevent vulnerabilities that attackers can exploit. This includes practices like input validation, where user input is checked for correctness and safety, and secure data storage, ensuring that sensitive data is stored safely and is protected from unauthorized access.

Secure communication and API usage are critical in protecting the data transmitted between the mobile app and backend services. This involves using protocols like HTTPS for data in transit and ensuring that the APIs the app interacts with are secure. Implementing these measures is vital to safeguard user data from interception or tampering.

User authentication and authorization are key components of mobile app security. Mobile app developers often implement various authentication methods, including traditional password-based authentication and more modern approaches like biometric authentication. These methods must be securely integrated into the app to ensure only authorized users can access sensitive features or data.

Mobile app encryption and obfuscation techniques protect the app's code and data. Encryption safeguards data stored within the app or transmitted over the network, while obfuscation helps protect the app's code from being reverse-engineered. Additionally, credential storage and key management are crucial for maintaining the integrity and confidentiality of user credentials and encryption keys. Proper management of these elements is vital for maintaining the overall security of the app and protecting user privacy.

OWASP and Web Application Security

The Open Web Application Security Project (OWASP) is an international nonprofit organization dedicated to improving software security. It provides unbiased, practical information about application security and is known for its openness, community involvement, and commitment to delivering high-quality, freely available security resources.

OWASP's history and mission are rooted in its commitment to improving software security. Founded in 2001, it has grown into a respected authority in the web application security field. OWASP's mission is to make software security visible so that individuals and organizations can make informed decisions about actual software security risks.

The importance of OWASP in application security cannot be overstated. It is a comprehensive resource for developers, security professionals, and organizations to understand, evaluate, and improve web application security. OWASP's contributions help standardize and disseminate security best practices globally, making it an indispensable resource in the field.

OWASP projects and resources offer a wide range of tools, documents, forums, and chapters to aid in securing web applications. These resources are designed to be accessible and practical, providing valuable guidance and tools for tackling real-world security challenges in web applications.

At the heart of OWASP's contributions is the OWASP Top Ten, a regularly updated list of the most critical web application security risks. This list is the go-to resource for understanding and mitigating web applications' most common and impactful security weaknesses.

Each item in the OWASP Top Ten represents a key vulnerability category, such as injection flaws, broken authentication, or sensitive data exposure. The list provides an in-depth analysis of these vulnerabilities, including how they can be exploited, their potential impact, and their prevalence in web applications.

Common attack scenarios and examples are provided for each vulnerability listed in the OWASP Top Ten. These scenarios offer insights into how attackers exploit these vulnerabilities in real-world settings, aiding developers and security professionals in understanding and recognizing potential threats.

Mitigation and prevention techniques for each vulnerability are critical to the OWASP Top Ten. These techniques offer practical guidance on securing web applications against the listed vulnerabilities, helping organizations build more secure software and protect against common web threats.

Incorporating the OWASP Top Ten into an application security program is essential for any organization developing web applications. It provides a framework for identifying and prioritizing security efforts addressing the most significant risks. Integrating the OWASP Top Ten into security practices and development processes helps create a more robust security posture.

Beyond the Top Ten, OWASP provides many other projects and resources, such as the OWASP Web Security Testing Guide, Application Security Verification Standard (ASVS), Code Review Guide, Cheat Sheets, and various tools. These resources cover a broader range of security topics and provide in-depth guidance and tools for specific aspects of application security.

Integrating OWASP into an application security program involves more than just awareness of its resources. It includes incorporating OWASP guidelines and tools into the software development lifecycle (SDLC), using them for training and education, and engaging with the OWASP community through events and contributions. This integration helps organizations stay ahead in the constantly evolving field of web application security.

The future of OWASP is shaped by its ongoing projects, initiatives, and the contributions of its global community. Staying updated with OWASP releases and participating in its projects are excellent ways for individuals and organizations to contribute to and benefit from the collective knowledge and effort in web application security.

In conclusion, OWASP's role in the evolving threat landscape is pivotal. As new security challenges emerge, OWASP continues to update and expand its resources to address these issues, maintaining its position as an invaluable resource for anyone developing, securing, or managing web applications.

Future Trends and Emerging Threats

The landscape of cybersecurity is continually evolving, with AI and machine learning emerging as significant players in security. These technologies are increasingly being used to predict and identify cyber threats by analyzing patterns and anomalies in data. AI-driven systems can process vast amounts of data at incredible speeds, enhancing security teams' capabilities in detecting and responding to threats.

Behavioral analytics and anomaly detection are pivotal in identifying potential security threats. Analyzing user behavior patterns, these systems can detect deviations that might indicate a security incident. This approach is particularly practical in identifying insider threats and compromised accounts, which traditional security measures might not detect.

The automation of threat intelligence is transforming how organizations handle security data. AI-driven systems can sift through massive datasets to identify potential threats, making threat intelligence more efficient and actionable. This automation enables security teams to focus on strategic decisions and responses rather than sifting through data manually.

AI-driven threat hunting and response represent a proactive approach to cybersecurity. Instead of waiting for security breaches to occur, these systems actively search for potential threats and vulnerabilities. AI enhances this process by predicting where threats are most likely to occur and suggesting effective response strategies.

Adversarial machine learning presents a unique challenge in cybersecurity. It involves manipulating AI models to make incorrect predictions or classifications. This emerging threat demonstrates the need for robust and secure AI systems in security applications, especially as AI becomes more prevalent in cybersecurity.

The Internet of Things (IoT) introduces new security challenges and solutions. As the number of connected devices increases, so does the attack surface for potential cyber threats. IoT devices often lack the robust security measures in traditional IT infrastructure, making them vulnerable to attacks.

Vulnerabilities in connected IoT devices can lead to unauthorized access and data breaches. Many of these devices are built with convenience rather than security, leading to potential risks. Securing these devices requires a different approach, focusing on IoT technology's unique characteristics and constraints.

Edge computing, where data processing occurs closer to the data source, brings security challenges. Edge computing environments can be diverse and distributed, making traditional centralized security measures less effective. Security in edge computing requires a decentralized approach, ensuring data is protected as it's processed at the network's edge.

Authentication and encryption are crucial for securing IoT devices. Due to the constrained nature of many IoT devices, implementing robust security measures is challenging. However, advances in lightweight cryptographic algorithms and authentication protocols are making it increasingly feasible to secure even the most resource-constrained IoT devices.

IoT security standards and frameworks are being developed to address the unique challenges of IoT security. These standards provide guidelines for secure design, development, and deployment of IoT devices and systems. Adherence to these standards is crucial for ensuring the security and privacy of IoT ecosystems.

Blockchain and cryptocurrency security are increasingly important as these technologies gain mainstream adoption. Blockchain presents unique security challenges, including securing the ledger, managing private keys, and defending against consensus attacks in decentralized networks.

Intelligent contract vulnerabilities are a particular concern in blockchain security. These self-executing contracts can contain flaws that attackers can exploit, leading to significant financial losses. Secure development practices and thorough testing are essential to mitigate these risks.

Cryptocurrency wallet security is critical for protecting digital assets. Cybercriminals often target wallets due to the high value of cryptocurrencies. Secure storage, strong authentication mechanisms, and awareness of phishing threats are key to protecting these assets.

Regulatory challenges in blockchain technology arise due to its decentralized nature and the rapid evolution of the technology. Regulators are grappling with applying existing laws to blockchain and developing new regulations that ensure security and privacy without stifling innovation.

Privacy-enhancing technologies in blockchain are being developed to address concerns around data privacy. These technologies aim to enable secure and private transactions on the blockchain, ensuring that sensitive data is protected while benefiting from blockchain technology's transparency and security.

Cloud-native security and serverless computing present new security considerations. In serverless architectures, where cloud providers dynamically manage the allocation of machine resources, traditional security perimeters are no longer applicable. Security in these environments must be dynamic, adapting to serverless functions' ephemeral and distributed nature.

Security challenges in serverless architecture include securing dependencies, managing permissions and access controls, and protecting against vulnerabilities in third-party services. Serverless security best practices involve implementing robust access controls, continuously monitoring functions for vulnerabilities, and using secure coding practices.

Cloud-native threat detection and prevention require a different approach than traditional IT environments. In cloud-native architectures, security solutions must be adaptable, scalable, and capable of monitoring a distributed and dynamic environment.

Microservices security considerations are vital in a cloud-native environment. Each microservice represents a potential attack vector, requiring individual security measures. Effective microservices security involves securing the communication channels between services, implementing service-specific authentication and authorization, and continuously monitoring for vulnerabilities.

Case Study: 7-Eleven SQL Injection Attack

The SQL injection attack on the 7-Eleven convenience store chain, resulting in the theft of credit card information, is a stark reminder of the vulnerabilities in modern digital systems. This incident illustrates the profound impact a well-executed SQL injection attack can have on businesses and consumers. SQL injection, an attack that exploits vulnerabilities in a database-driven application, allows attackers to manipulate SQL queries and potentially access and manipulate sensitive data. In the case of 7-Eleven, this vulnerability led to unauthorized access to a vast amount of sensitive customer credit card information.

The attack began when the attackers identified a vulnerability in the application's database interaction. By injecting malicious SQL commands into the system, they could bypass normal authentication processes and gain unauthorized access to the database. This access allowed them to view, copy, and potentially modify the database contents, including private customer data. The simplicity and effectiveness of the attack underscore the importance of rigorous input validation and parameterized queries in protecting against SQL injection vulnerabilities.

Once inside the system, the attackers could exfiltrate credit card information stored in the database. This data breach had significant implications, potentially exposing thousands of customers to financial fraud and identity theft. The sensitive nature of the stolen information, including credit card numbers, expiration dates, and possibly CVV codes, made the breach particularly severe. The incident not only compromised the financial security of the affected customers but also eroded their trust in the 7-Eleven brand.

The repercussions of the attack were far-reaching, impacting not only 7-Eleven's customers but also the company itself. The breach likely resulted in substantial financial losses due to fraud-related expenses, legal fees, and potential fines for failing to protect customer data. In addition, the company faced reputational damage, which can have long-term effects on customer loyalty and business performance. This incident highlights the need for businesses to invest in robust cybersecurity measures and regularly audit and update their security protocols.

In response to the attack, 7-Eleven needed to implement immediate remedial actions to secure its systems. This involved fixing the specific vulnerability that allowed the SQL injection and thoroughly reviewing their network and application security posture. Enhancing their security measures to prevent similar breaches in the future was paramount. Implementing advanced security monitoring tools, conducting regular vulnerability assessments, and training staff in cybersecurity best practices became essential components of their strategy.

Looking forward, the SQL injection attack on 7-Eleven is a cautionary tale for other businesses about the dangers of cyber threats. It emphasizes the importance of proactive and comprehensive approaches to cybersecurity, particularly in an age where digital transactions are ubiquitous. For businesses that handle sensitive customer data, especially financial information, it's crucial to employ a multilayered security approach. This includes technical measures like firewalls, encryption, and secure coding practices and organizational measures such as employee training and a robust incident response plan. The 7-Eleven incident is a stark reminder of cyber threats' continuous and evolving nature and the need for vigilance in cybersecurity practices.

Career Corner

Application security is a crucial and specialized field in the technology industry that protects software applications from various cyber threats. It offers a range of career opportunities for individuals with the necessary skills and qualifications. One might consider a career as an Application Security Analyst in this field. This role involves scrutinizing software applications for vulnerabilities, conducting security audits and risk assessments, and implementing policies to protect applications against threats. The analyst's work is vital in identifying potential security issues before they can be exploited.

Security Software Developers also play a significant role in application security. Their job goes beyond traditional software development; they integrate security into the software development process. They must be proficient in coding and possess a deep understanding of secure coding practices to prevent vulnerabilities in the software they develop.

As application security is highly technical and constantly evolving, professionals in this area are encouraged to pursue relevant certifications to enhance their skills and employability. Certifications such as the Certified Information Systems Security Professional (CISSP), which covers a broad range of security topics, including software development security, and the Certified Ethical Hacker (CEH), ideal for those aspiring to become penetration testers, are highly regarded in the industry. The Offensive Security Certified Professional (OSCP) is another prestigious certification focusing on hands-on penetration testing skills.

The Certified Secure Software Lifecycle Professional (CSSLP) is an excellent choice for those looking to integrate security into the software development lifecycle. It ensures that professionals are equipped with the skills to incorporate security practices into each phase of software development.

In conclusion, application security is a field that offers a variety of challenging and rewarding career paths. From analyzing and testing for vulnerabilities to developing secure software and ensuring compliance with security standards, professionals in this field play a critical role in protecting software applications. Continual learning and certification are key to success in this dynamic and ever-evolving field.

Chapter Questions

1. What is the primary goal of application security?

   A. To enhance user experience

   B. To protect digital assets from threats

   C. To increase application speed

   D. To reduce application development costs

2. What is a significant consequence of a security breach?

   A. Increased operational efficiency

   B. Loss of sensitive data

   C. Improved customer satisfaction

   D. Reduced maintenance costs

3. Why is maintaining robust application security crucial for businesses?

   A. To simplify IT operations

   B. To increase sales

   C. To sustain customer trust and relationships

   D. To reduce employee workload

4. What can result from a security breach besides data loss?

    A. Decreased insurance premiums

    B. Legal actions and financial penalties

    C. Streamlined business processes

    D. Increased stock prices

5. Why must organizations continuously adapt their security strategies?

    A. To comply with changing customer preferences

    B. To keep up with evolving cyber threats

    C. To reduce software development time

    D. To increase market share

6. What is the foundation of effective application security defense strategies?

    A. Frequent software updates

    B. Understanding fundamental security principles

    C. Investing in marketing strategies

    D. Outsourcing IT services

7. What does the "confidentiality" aspect of the CIA triad ensure in application security?

    A. Data is always available

    B. Data is accurate and unaltered

    C. Only authorized individuals access sensitive information

    D. Applications perform optimally

8. What is the benefit of integrating the security development lifecycle (SDLC) into application development?

   A. Reducing development costs

   B. Enhancing user interface design

   C. Incorporating security from the start

   D. Speeding up the development process

9. What is the purpose of threat modeling in application security?

   A. To predict financial trends

   B. To identify and assess potential security threats

   C. To optimize application performance

   D. To streamline project management

10. What is a principle of Security by Design?

    A. Maximizing feature sets

    B. Prioritizing usability over security

    C. Incorporating security measures from the design phase

    D. Focusing solely on aesthetics

11. Why is input validation crucial in secure coding practices?

    A. To enhance the user interface

    B. To protect against malicious inputs

    C. To increase application speed

    D. To comply with marketing strategies

12. What is the primary goal of black-box testing in security assessments?

    A. To evaluate the application's user interface

    B. To test the application without internal knowledge

    C. To assess the application's marketing impact

    D. To reduce development costs

13. Why are manual code reviews important in white-box testing?

    A. To ensure a user-friendly design

    B. To provide an in-depth security analysis

    C. To speed up the development process

    D. To reduce software licensing costs

14. What is the advantage of using Dynamic Application Security Testing (DAST) tools?

    A. They replace the need for manual testing

    B. They identify runtime vulnerabilities

    C. They reduce marketing expenses

    D. They enhance user experience

15. Why is integrating threat modeling into the software development lifecycle (SDLC) important?

    A. To focus on marketing strategies

    B. To ensure security considerations throughout the development

    C. To reduce software development time

    D. To enhance the graphical interface

CHAPTER 7

Mobile Security

Understanding the importance of mobile security is the first critical step in this journey. Due to their ubiquity and the sensitive nature of the data they often contain, mobile devices are attractive targets for cybercriminals. The risks associated with mobile devices include the potential for data theft, unauthorized access, and the introduction of malware.

The proliferation of mobile devices in recent years has only amplified these risks. With billions worldwide relying on smartphones and tablets for personal and professional use, the attack surface for potential security breaches has expanded dramatically. This proliferation has made understanding and implementing effective mobile security measures more important.

The consequences of mobile security breaches can be severe. They range from the loss of sensitive personal information, such as financial data and personal identification, to significant operational impacts for businesses, including data breaches and the loss of intellectual property. The ramifications of these breaches are not just limited to the immediate loss of data but can also have long-lasting reputational and financial impacts.

Turning to mobile operating systems, each has its unique security features. Android, for instance, offers a range of security capabilities, including application sandboxing, which isolates apps from each other and the system, and Google Play Protect, which scans apps for malicious behavior. These features are designed to protect users from a variety of threats.

© Dr. Jason Edwards 2024, corrected publication 2024
Dr. J. Edwards, *Mastering Cybersecurity*, https://doi.org/10.1007/979-8-8688-0297-3_7

iOS, Apple's mobile operating system, also boasts robust security features. These include data encryption, app sandboxing, and regular software updates that address security vulnerabilities. iOS's closed ecosystem also contributes to its security, allowing Apple to have strict control over the apps available in its App Store, reducing the risk of malware.

Other mobile operating systems have security considerations, and it's essential to understand these, especially in a corporate environment where different devices may be in use. Additionally, the security differences between various versions of these mobile operating systems can be significant, as newer versions typically include updated security features and patches for known vulnerabilities.

The mobile threat landscape constantly evolves, with new threats emerging regularly. These include malware, phishing, and network-based attacks designed to exploit mobile device and network vulnerabilities. Attack vectors on mobile devices often exploit security gaps in apps, operating systems, or user behavior.

Real-world examples of mobile security incidents underscore the severity and diversity of these threats. From large-scale data breaches resulting from compromised mobile devices to targeted attacks exploiting specific vulnerabilities, these incidents highlight the ongoing need for vigilance in mobile security. Additionally, emerging threats in mobile security, such as advanced persistent threats (APTs) and zero-day exploits, represent a constantly evolving challenge for individuals and organizations alike.

Legal and regulatory considerations play a significant role in mobile security. Data privacy laws and regulations, such as the General Data Protection Regulation (GDPR) in the European Union, impose strict requirements on how personal data is handled and protected. Organizations must ensure that their mobile security practices comply with these laws to avoid substantial penalties and reputational damage.

Industry compliance standards, such as those in the financial and healthcare sectors, also dictate mobile security measures. These standards are designed to protect sensitive information and ensure that organizations maintain a certain level of security in their mobile device usage.

Mobile security is closely tied to user privacy, with regulatory bodies crucial in defining and enforcing standards. These bodies, such as the Federal Trade Commission (FTC) in the United States, work to protect consumers and ensure that organizations are transparent about their data collection and protection practices.

Finally, mobile security best practices are essential for mitigating the risks of mobile device use. The principle of least privilege, which involves granting users only the permissions they need to perform their tasks, is a crucial tenet of adequate security. This minimizes the potential impact of a security breach by limiting access to sensitive information and system functions.

Regular software updates and patching are also critical. These updates often include fixes for security vulnerabilities discovered since the software's last version. By keeping their devices and apps up to date, users can protect themselves against known threats.

Data encryption on mobile devices is another critical best practice. Encryption protects data stored on the device and transmitted to and from it, making it unreadable to unauthorized parties.

Secure mobile app development is crucial in preventing security vulnerabilities from being introduced into the app ecosystem. Developers must follow best practices for secure coding and regularly test their apps for vulnerabilities.

Lastly, user education and awareness are perhaps the most critical elements of mobile security. Educating users about the risks associated with mobile device use and best practices for mitigating these risks can significantly reduce the likelihood of security incidents. This education should cover topics such as recognizing phishing attempts, using strong passwords, and the risks associated with connecting to unsecured Wi-Fi networks. Organizations can create a more secure mobile environment by empowering users with knowledge.

Securing Mobile Devices

Securing mobile devices is a critical aspect of contemporary digital security, encompassing a range of strategies and technologies designed to protect sensitive data and maintain the integrity of mobile communications. One fundamental component of this security is device authentication and access control. This involves using personal identification numbers (PINs), passwords, and biometric data such as fingerprints or facial recognition to verify the user's identity. These methods ensure only authorized individuals can access the device, safeguarding the information.

Further enhancing device security, two-factor authentication (2FA) adds a layer of protection. This method requires users to provide two different forms of identification before gaining access to their device. Typically, this involves something the user knows (like a password or PIN) and something the user has (like a mobile phone or security token). This dual-layer approach significantly reduces the risk of unauthorized access.

In the event of loss or theft, it is crucial to lock down a device remotely and erase its data. This functionality lets users or administrators quickly secure a device, preventing unauthorized access to sensitive information. The capability for remote wipe ensures that confidential data can be erased from the device, even if it is no longer in the owner's possession.

The use of robust authentication methods further bolsters the security of mobile devices. These methods go beyond basic passwords and PINs, incorporating advanced algorithms and security protocols to ensure only authorized users can access the device. Strong authentication plays a vital role in protecting against unauthorized access and cyber-attacks.

Mobile Device Management (MDM) systems are essential tools in the arsenal of mobile security. MDM is a technology that allows IT administrators to control and secure mobile devices within an organization. This is particularly important in corporate environments, where the security of mobile devices is paramount to protect sensitive business data.

The role of MDM in mobile security cannot be overstated. It provides a centralized platform for managing all mobile devices within an organization, ensuring that they comply with the company's security policies. MDM systems enable administrators to remotely configure devices, enforce security policies, and even remotely wipe devices if they are lost or stolen.

MDM features and capabilities include tracking and inventorying mobile devices, enforcing security policies, managing applications, and controlling data access. These features help ensure that devices are used appropriately and that sensitive data remains secure. MDM solutions are particularly effective in managing the complexities of diverse device ecosystems, offering scalability and flexibility to adapt to various business needs.

Implementing MDM policies is a critical step in securing mobile devices. These policies might include requirements for solid passwords, restrictions on which applications can be installed, and settings for data encryption. Effective policy implementation ensures that all devices comply with the organization's security standards, reducing the risk of data breaches and other security incidents.

Managing Bring Your Own Device (BYOD) programs is another important aspect of MDM. BYOD policies allow employees to use their devices for work, increasing productivity and employee satisfaction. However, this also introduces security risks, as personal devices may not have the same level of security as corporate-owned devices. MDM systems help mitigate these risks by enforcing security policies on personal devices used for work purposes, ensuring that they meet the organization's security standards.

Another critical aspect of mobile device security is the secure boot process and the Trusted Execution Environment (TEE). The secure boot process ensures that only trusted software is loaded during startup. This prevents malicious software from compromising the device at boot time. Conversely, the TEE provides a secure area within the device's central processor, where sensitive data can be stored and processed in isolation from the rest of the device's operating system. This isolation helps protect sensitive data and operations from malicious software.

TrustZone technology and TEE architecture provide a foundation for secure computing on mobile devices. TrustZone, a set of security extensions for ARM processors, creates an isolated environment that can operate alongside the primary operating system. This secure environment, or TEE, is designed to run sensitive code, process secure transactions, and handle encrypted data, providing a robust defense against cyber attacks.

Secure storage and execution are essential components of mobile device security. They ensure that sensitive data, such as passwords, financial information, and personal details, are stored and processed to minimize the risk of unauthorized access or tampering. This is particularly important in an era where mobile devices are increasingly used for sensitive transactions, from online banking to personal communications.

Hardware Security Modules (HSMs) are pivotal in enhancing mobile device security. HSMs are physical devices that provide secure cryptographic processing, key storage, and critical management. They protect cryptographic keys and perform encryption and decryption operations within a tamper-resistant hardware environment, significantly increasing the security of mobile devices against sophisticated attacks.

Mobile device hardware security is another crucial aspect of moving to the hardware realm. Secure bootloaders are integral to this, ensuring the device boots using only verified and trusted software. This helps prevent attacks that target the boot process, such as rootkits and bootkits, which can be particularly damaging as they load before the operating system and are difficult to detect.

Hardware-based encryption is another vital feature of mobile device security. It uses dedicated hardware on the device to encrypt and decrypt data, providing a more secure and efficient method of protecting sensitive information compared to software-based encryption. This form of encryption is particularly effective in safeguarding data stored on the device and transmitted to and from the device.

Protection against physical attacks is also a significant concern in mobile device security. This includes designing devices to resist tampering and unauthorized access to internal components. It's essential to protect against various physical threats, such as attempting to extract data directly from the device's hardware or modifying it to bypass security measures.

Secure enclaves and secure elements further enhance the hardware security of mobile devices. A secure enclave is a protected area within the processor that is isolated from the rest of the device, providing a secure environment for sensitive operations like fingerprint processing and encryption key management. Similarly, secure elements are specialized chips that provide tamper-resistant storage for sensitive data like cryptographic keys, further safeguarding the device against physical and logical attacks.

App store security is a vital aspect of mobile device security, considering apps' central role in mobile device functionality and user experience. The app store review process is a crucial component of this, with app stores employing various methods to vet applications before they are available for download. This process helps ensure that apps are free from malware and adhere to certain quality and security standards, protecting users from inadvertently downloading harmful software.

Sideloading risks are an essential consideration in app security. Sideloading refers to the process of installing applications from sources outside of the official app store. While this can provide users with a broader range of apps, it also bypasses the security measures of

179

the app stores, increasing the risk of installing malicious or insecure applications. Users must be aware of these risks and exercise caution when sideloading apps.

App permissions and privacy are critical aspects of app store security. When installing an app, users are often asked to grant various permissions, such as access to their camera, contacts, or location. Users need to understand these permissions and the potential privacy implications. Apps should only request permissions necessary for their functionality, and users should be wary of apps that request excessive permissions, as this could indicate a security or privacy risk.

Finally, third-party app marketplaces present a unique set of security challenges. While these marketplaces can offer a wider variety of apps, they often lack the rigorous security measures of official app stores. This can lead to a higher prevalence of malicious apps, posing significant user risks. Therefore, while these marketplaces can be a valuable resource, users must exercise increased vigilance when downloading apps to ensure the security of their mobile devices.

Mobile App Security

Mobile app security is an increasingly crucial aspect of digital security in our interconnected world. At its core, app security fundamentals involve a deep understanding of the app threat landscape. This understanding encompasses recognizing the various threats that can target mobile applications, including malware, data breaches, and unauthorized access. These threats pose significant risks to users and organizations, highlighting the need for robust app development and maintenance security measures.

Secure code development practices are a critical component of mobile app security. These practices involve writing code to minimize vulnerabilities and prevent security breaches. Developers must be trained in secure coding techniques and aware of common security pitfalls to produce apps resistant to hacking and other cyber attacks.

Code signing and app integrity play a pivotal role in maintaining the security of mobile apps. Code signing is digitally signing executables and scripts to confirm the software author and guarantee that the code has not been altered or corrupted since it was signed. This ensures the app's integrity and builds trust among users that the app they are downloading is secure and reliable.

Adhering to secure coding guidelines is essential for developers. These guidelines provide a framework for writing code that is functional and secure. They cover a range of practices, from input validation to error handling and encryption, and are crucial for minimizing the risk of vulnerabilities in mobile apps.

Mobile app permissions are another vital aspect of app security. Different types of app permissions include access to the device's camera, microphone, contacts, and location. These permissions can be necessary for the app's functionality and raise privacy considerations. Developers must be judicious in requesting permissions and ensure they are essential for the app's operation.

Privacy considerations in app permissions are increasingly under scrutiny. Apps must handle user data responsibly, ensuring that personal information is collected, used, and shared following privacy laws and user expectations. This is crucial in maintaining user trust and complying with regulatory requirements.

User consent and transparency are essential when it comes to app permissions. Users should be informed about what permissions an app requires and why. This transparency enables users to make informed decisions about granting these permissions based on their understanding of what data the app will access and how it will be used.

The principle of least privilege is a fundamental security concept that should be applied in the context of app permissions. This principle dictates that an app should have only the permissions it needs to function. Limiting the permissions granted to an app significantly reduces the potential for damage if the app is compromised.

Secure data storage and transmission are critical to protect sensitive information handled by mobile apps. Data encryption on mobile devices is a critical technique in this regard. Encryption transforms data into a coded form that can only be accessed with the correct key, thus safeguarding the data from unauthorized access or breaches.

Secure data transmission is another essential aspect, typically achieved through protocols like SSL/TLS (Secure Socket Layer/Transport Layer Security). These protocols encrypt data in transit between the mobile device and servers, preventing interception or tampering by malicious actors.

Data caching and local storage on mobile devices present unique security challenges. While caching can improve app performance, it can also pose a risk if sensitive data is stored insecurely on the device. Developers must ensure that locally stored data is adequately protected, particularly on shared or easily lost devices.

Data backup security is crucial in mobile app security. Backups should be encrypted and stored securely to prevent unauthorized access. This ensures that users' data remains protected even during data loss or a device compromise.

Vulnerability scanning and penetration testing are essential in identifying and addressing security weaknesses in mobile apps. App vulnerability assessments involve scanning the app for known vulnerabilities, which can then be addressed to prevent exploitation by attackers.

Conducting penetration tests, where ethical hackers attempt to breach app security, provides valuable insights into potential vulnerabilities. These tests simulate real-world attack scenarios, giving developers a clear understanding of where their app's security needs strengthening.

Remediation strategies are critical after identifying vulnerabilities. These strategies involve fixing the identified vulnerabilities and understanding the underlying causes to prevent similar issues in future development.

Bug bounty programs can be a practical part of a mobile app's security strategy. These programs incentivize independent security researchers to find and report vulnerabilities in the app, often in exchange for rewards. This approach can uncover vulnerabilities internal testing might miss, further strengthening the app's security.

A wide array of options are available to developers regarding app security testing tools and frameworks. These tools help identify vulnerabilities, enforce security policies, and ensure compliance with security standards. They range from static and dynamic analysis tools to network security and encryption testing tools.

Automating security testing can significantly improve the efficiency and effectiveness of the testing process. Automated tools can scan code for vulnerabilities more quickly and thoroughly than manual methods, allowing for more frequent and comprehensive testing.

Testing in both the development and post-release phases is crucial. Security testing should be integrated into the development lifecycle, with regular tests conducted as the app is being developed. Post-release, continuous monitoring, and testing ensure the app remains secure against new threats.

Security code review techniques are an essential part of the testing process. These techniques involve manually reviewing code to identify security flaws and ensure adherence to best practices. This human element complements automated tools, providing a deeper understanding of the code and its potential vulnerabilities.

Mobile app security is a multifaceted challenge requiring technical measures, best practices, and ongoing vigilance. From secure code development to user consent, data protection, and vulnerability management, each aspect plays a crucial role in safeguarding mobile apps against the myriad of threats in the digital landscape.

Network Security for Mobile

Network security for mobile devices is an intricate and vital aspect of modern digital security, given our increasing reliance on mobile technology. It encompasses various strategies and technologies to protect information and maintain privacy in a mobile-connected world. This section explores the critical elements of network security specifically designed for mobile environments, addressing their unique challenges. Each aspect is crucial for safeguarding mobile devices against the myriad of threats in the digital landscape.

Understanding mobile network architecture is essential for understanding how network security functions in a mobile context. Cellular networks, the backbone of mobile communications, have evolved significantly, offering enhanced speed and capacity with each new generation. These networks provide the primary connectivity for mobile devices, facilitating a wide range of services from voice calls to Internet access. The security and integrity of these networks are paramount for the safe operation of mobile devices.

Wi-Fi networks and hotspots complement cellular networks in providing mobile connectivity. They offer an alternative, often at higher speeds and lower costs, but vary widely in security, with public hotspots generally being less secure than private, password-protected networks. The security of Wi-Fi networks is particularly crucial in public spaces, where the risk of unauthorized access and data interception is higher. Understanding and securing these networks are essential components of comprehensive mobile network security.

Virtual Private Networks (VPNs) have bolstered mobile network security. They encrypt data transmitted from mobile devices, ensuring privacy and security, especially when using less secure or public networks. VPNs create a secure tunnel for data transmission, shielding sensitive information from potential interception or eavesdropping. VPNs are essential for users who frequently connect to public Wi-Fi networks or require secure communication over potentially insecure networks.

The introduction of 5G technology represents a significant evolution in mobile network architecture, with implications for network security. 5G networks offer faster speeds and more reliable connections but bring new security challenges and considerations. The architecture of 5G networks is more complex, and securing these networks requires advanced strategies to protect against potential vulnerabilities. As 5G becomes more widespread, the focus on its security aspects becomes increasingly critical for the overall safety of mobile communications.

Man-in-the-Middle Attacks (MITM)

Man-in-the-middle (MITM) attacks are a prevalent threat to mobile network security. In such attacks, an attacker intercepts communication between two parties to either eavesdrop or alter the communication. This interception can happen in various ways, such as compromised Wi-Fi networks or using sophisticated software tools. Understanding how MITM attacks work is vital to developing effective prevention strategies.

Preventing MITM attacks involves a combination of technical measures and user awareness. Secure network practices are fundamental, such as using encrypted connections and avoiding unsecured Wi-Fi networks. Additionally, organizations can implement network security solutions like intrusion detection systems that monitor for signs of MITM attempts. Educating users about the risks of MITM attacks and how to recognize suspicious network activity is also a critical component of prevention.

Detecting MITM activity is challenging, as these attacks are designed to be stealthy and unobtrusive. However, some signs can indicate a potential MITM attack, such as unexpected certificate warnings, unusual network slowdowns, or changes in the appearance of websites. Network monitoring tools and security software can also help in detecting anomalies that may suggest a MITM attack is occurring. Prompt detection is key to mitigating the impact of these attacks.

SSL (Secure Socket Layer) pinning and certificate validation are technical strategies to combat MITM attacks. SSL pinning involves hardcoding the certificate known to be used by the server within the app, which helps ensure that the app communicates only with the intended server. Certificate validation involves verifying the authenticity of the SSL certificates presented by the server, ensuring a legitimate Certificate Authority issues them. These practices are essential in ensuring secure data transmission and preventing interception by attackers.

Public Wi-Fi Security

Public Wi-Fi networks, while convenient, pose significant security risks. These networks are often unsecured, making them vulnerable to cyberattacks, including eavesdropping and data interception. The openness of public Wi-Fi networks makes it easy for attackers to access unencrypted data or even inject malicious content. Users must be cautious when connecting to these networks and aware of the risks involved.

Safe practices for using public Wi-Fi are crucial in mitigating these risks. Users should avoid conducting sensitive transactions, like online banking or shopping, over public networks. Additionally, ensuring that websites use HTTPS and being cautious about the personal information shared while connected to public Wi-Fi can significantly reduce security risks. These practices are simple yet effective in enhancing security on public networks.

VPNs and secure hotspots offer robust solutions for secure connectivity on public Wi-Fi networks. A VPN encrypts the data transmitted over the network, protecting it from potential interception. Secure hotspots, which are password-protected and use encryption, provide a safer alternative to open public Wi-Fi networks. These tools are indispensable for users who need to connect to the Internet securely while on the go.

Wireless network encryption is another critical aspect of public Wi-Fi security. Networks that use WPA2 (Wi-Fi Protected Access 2) encryption offer higher security than unencrypted networks. Users should always choose networks with solid encryption standards to secure their data. This encryption is a fundamental barrier, preventing unauthorized access and safeguarding data transmitted over the network.

Mobile Data Encryption

Encryption standards for mobile data are essential in protecting sensitive information. Modern encryption algorithms, such as AES (Advanced Encryption Standard), protect data transmitted from and stored on mobile devices. These standards ensure that even if data is intercepted, it remains unreadable and secure from unauthorized access. Implementing these standards is a cornerstone of robust mobile data security.

Encrypted messaging and calls have become increasingly important in maintaining privacy in communications. Many mobile apps now offer end-to-end encryption, ensuring that only the sender and the recipient can access the content of the messages or calls. This encryption protects against eavesdropping and interception, providing a secure medium for private communication. Users are increasingly seeking out apps that offer this level of security for their personal and professional communications.

Secure mobile browsing is another critical component of mobile data encryption. This involves using browsers and apps that encrypt web traffic, protecting users' online activities from surveillance and data theft. Features like HTTPS, SSL/TLS encryption, and secure browsing modes are essential for maintaining privacy and security while browsing the Internet on mobile devices. These features help shield users from various online threats, including MITM attacks and data breaches.

Data-at-rest encryption refers to encrypting data stored on a mobile device. This type of encryption is crucial in protecting information if the device is lost or stolen. Encrypting stored data ensures that sensitive information, such as personal photos, emails, and documents, remains secure and inaccessible without the correct authentication. This encryption is a vital layer of defense in safeguarding personal and corporate data stored on mobile devices.

Mobile Network Security Best Practices

Adopting network layer security protocols is a fundamental best practice in mobile network security. IPsec (Internet Protocol Security) and SSL/TLS provide a secure environment for data transmission over mobile networks. These protocols encrypt data at the network layer, offering an additional layer of security against unauthorized access and data breaches. Implementing these protocols ensures secure communication and data transfer over mobile networks.

Regular security updates are crucial for maintaining the security of mobile networks. Manufacturers and software developers frequently release updates that address vulnerabilities and enhance security features. Users should ensure their devices and apps are updated to the latest versions to protect against known threats. These updates are a key defense mechanism in the ever-evolving landscape of mobile security threats.

User education on safe network usage plays a significant role in mobile network security. Educating users about the risks associated with mobile networks and the best practices for safe usage is vital. This education should cover topics such as recognizing phishing attempts, the importance of using strong passwords, and the dangers of connecting to unsecured networks. An informed user base is a crucial defense against network security threats.

Mobile device firewall settings are essential in protecting against unauthorized network access. Firewalls monitor and control incoming and outgoing network traffic based on predetermined security rules. Configuring these settings appropriately on mobile devices can prevent malicious traffic from compromising the device. This measure and other security practices form a comprehensive approach to securing mobile devices against network-based threats.

Mobile App Development Security

Mobile app development security is a critical aspect of the broader field of cybersecurity, focusing on creating secure software applications for mobile devices. This area encompasses various practices, techniques, and methodologies that aim to incorporate security into every stage of the app development process. Organizations can significantly reduce vulnerabilities, protect sensitive data, and enhance user trust by prioritizing security in mobile app development.

Secure Software Development Lifecycle (SDLC)

The secure software development lifecycle (SDLC) is a framework that integrates security practices into the software development process. The SDLC comprises several phases: planning, design, development, testing, deployment, and maintenance. Each phase has specific security considerations that must be addressed to ensure the overall security of the final product. Incorporating security at every stage of the SDLC is vital for developing robust and secure software.

Security considerations in each phase of the SDLC include threat modeling in the planning stage, secure design principles in the design stage, secure coding practices during development, thorough security testing, and ongoing security monitoring and patching post deployment. Addressing security at each phase helps in the early identification and mitigation of potential security risks, thereby enhancing the overall security posture of the application.

Integrating security into the SDLC is not a one-time activity but a continuous process. It involves regularly updating security practices, tools, and methodologies to keep pace with evolving threats. This integration can be achieved through training, adopting secure coding standards, and using security tools throughout development. By embedding security into the SDLC, organizations can ensure that security considerations are an integral part of the development process rather than an afterthought.

Agile and DevSecOps approaches have transformed how security is integrated into the SDLC. Agile methodologies focus on iterative development and collaboration, while DevSecOps introduces security practices into the DevOps approach, emphasizing continuous integration, delivery, and security. These approaches promote a culture where security is a shared responsibility among all team members, ensuring faster and more efficient delivery of secure applications.

Code Review and Static Analysis

Code review is a critical best practice in mobile app development security. It involves manually examining the source code to identify security vulnerabilities, coding errors, and adherence to coding standards. Effective code review practices include peer review, where developers review each other's code, and expert review, where security experts examine the code for complex vulnerabilities. Regular code reviews help in the early detection and remediation of potential security issues.

Automated static analysis tools are essential in complementing manual code review processes. These tools scan the source code without executing it, identifying patterns that indicate security vulnerabilities, coding standards violations, and other issues. Automated static analysis helps scale the code review process, enabling the examination of large codebases more efficiently and consistently.

Identifying and remedying vulnerabilities is a primary objective of code reviews and static analysis. Developers must find vulnerabilities, understand their implications, and implement effective remediation strategies. This involves fixing coding errors, addressing design flaws, and updating security practices. Regular training and updates in security knowledge are essential for developers to stay ahead of evolving threats.

Secure code review checklists are valuable tools that guide developers and reviewers through the code review process. These checklists outline key security considerations, common vulnerabilities to look for, and best practices to follow. They serve as a reference point to ensure that no critical security aspects are overlooked during the review process, contributing to the overall robustness of the application.

Secure APIs and Web Services

APIs (Application Programming Interfaces) are integral to mobile app functionality but can also introduce security threats if not properly secured. API security threats include unauthorized access, data breaches, and denial-of-service attacks. Mitigating these threats requires a comprehensive approach to API security, encompassing robust authentication, authorization, and data protection measures.

API authentication and authorization are critical components of API security. Authentication verifies the identity of users or systems attempting to access the API, while authorization determines what actions they are allowed to perform. Implementing strong authentication and authorization mechanisms, such as OAuth or API keys, is essential for controlling access to APIs and protecting them from unauthorized use.

API security best practices involve a range of strategies to protect APIs from potential threats. These include validating and sanitizing input, implementing rate limiting to prevent abuse, encrypting data in transit, and regularly auditing and testing APIs for vulnerabilities. Adhering to these best practices helps maintain the integrity, confidentiality, and availability of the API and the data it handles.

Web services security standards, such as WS-Security and OAuth, provide guidelines and protocols for securing web services. These standards define mechanisms for message integrity, confidentiality, and authentication. By adhering to these standards, developers can ensure that their web services are secure and resilient against cyber attacks, thus protecting the data and functionality they expose.

Secure Authentication and Authorization

OAuth and OpenID Connect are widely used standards for secure authentication and authorization in mobile apps. OAuth provides a framework for granting access tokens, allowing apps to access resources on behalf of the user without exposing their credentials. OpenID Connect, built on OAuth 2.0, adds an identity layer, enabling apps to verify the end user's identity. These standards are crucial for implementing robust, flexible authentication and authorization mechanisms in mobile apps.

Role-based access control (RBAC) restricts access to resources based on the roles of individual users within an organization. In mobile apps, RBAC helps manage user permissions effectively, ensuring users can access only the resources necessary for their role. This approach minimizes the risk of unauthorized access and simplifies user permissions management.

Token-based authentication is a secure method of handling user authentication in mobile apps. It involves issuing a token upon successful authentication, which the user then presents to access protected resources. This method is more secure than traditional methods, like session-based authentication, as the token can be easily invalidated, and sensitive information is not stored on the device.

Single Sign-On (SSO) solutions provide a user-friendly way to manage authentication across multiple applications. With SSO, users can log in once and access all associated applications without needing to authenticate separately. SSO improves user experience while maintaining security, reducing the number of credentials users need to remember and manage.

Secure Data Handling

Data classification and protection are fundamental to secure data handling in mobile app development. Data classification involves categorizing data based on sensitivity and the required protection level. Once classified, appropriate protection measures, such as encryption and access controls, can be applied to ensure that sensitive data is adequately safeguarded against unauthorized access and breaches.

Input validation and sanitization are critical practices in preventing common vulnerabilities like SQL injection and cross-site scripting (XSS). These practices involve checking incoming data for validity and cleaning it of any potentially harmful elements before processing. Proper input validation and sanitization help ensure that only expected and safe data is processed by the app, thus preventing exploitation by attackers.

Data encryption in transit and at rest is essential for protecting sensitive information handled by mobile apps. Encryption in transit protects data as it moves between the app and servers, while encryption at rest secures data stored on the device. Implementing strong encryption standards is crucial for maintaining the confidentiality and integrity of data, making it unreadable and unusable in case of unauthorized access.

Secure session management is a crucial aspect of secure data handling. This involves securely managing user sessions, ensuring that session tokens are protected, and implementing measures like session timeouts and token invalidation. Effective session management prevents session hijacking and other attacks that exploit weaknesses in session handling, thereby safeguarding user data and interactions within the app.

Mobile Threat Detection and Prevention

In mobile security, intrusion detection systems (IDS) are vital tools for identifying and responding to potential security breaches. IDS are designed to detect anomalies and suspicious activities that could indicate a threat, such as unusual behavior patterns, unauthorized access attempts, or other signs of compromise. By identifying these threats early, IDS enables quick responses to mitigate potential risks and protect mobile devices.

Intrusion Detection Systems (IDS) for Mobile

Intrusion detection systems (IDS) for mobile devices are crucial components in the landscape of mobile security. These systems specialize in identifying unusual activities and potential threats, which is vital in safeguarding mobile devices from cyber risks. IDS for mobile devices focuses on detecting anomalies and suspicious activities that might indicate a security breach. This includes monitoring for irregular behavior patterns, unusual data traffic, and signs of unauthorized access attempts. By identifying these irregularities, IDS can alert users or administrators to potential security incidents, allowing prompt action to mitigate any threats.

IDS are categorized mainly into two types: network-based and host-based. Network-based IDS monitors network traffic to and from mobile devices, looking for malicious activity or unauthorized access indicators. They are particularly effective in identifying attacks originating from or targeting network communications. On the other hand, host-based IDS are installed directly on the mobile device and monitor the device's internal operations. They track changes to system files, logs, and other operations to detect signs of compromise or malware within the device. Each type offers distinct advantages and, when used together, provides a comprehensive approach to intrusion detection.

Real-time threat monitoring is a crucial feature of modern IDS, especially in the mobile context, where threats can emerge rapidly. Real-time monitoring enables these systems to provide immediate alerts about potential security issues, facilitating quick response to mitigate risks. This is crucial in a mobile environment where delayed detection can lead to significant data breaches or other security incidents. By continuously scanning and analyzing data, real-time IDS help maintain the ongoing security of mobile devices against an ever-evolving landscape of cyber threats.

Mobile Security Information and Event Management (SIEM)

Mobile Security Information and Event Management (SIEM) systems play a critical role in enhancing the security of mobile devices and networks. These systems focus on collecting and analyzing various security data from various sources. This data can include network traffic, user activities, system logs, and application events. By aggregating and examining this information, SIEM systems provide a comprehensive view of the security status of mobile environments, helping to identify potential threats and vulnerabilities.

An essential function of SIEM systems is the correlation of security events. This process involves analyzing disparate data points to identify patterns or anomalies that might indicate a security incident. By correlating events across different sources and times, SIEM systems can uncover complex, multistage attacks that might otherwise go unnoticed. This capability is significant in mobile environments, where the diversity of devices and applications can create a complex security landscape.

SIEM solutions for mobile environments are equipped to handle the unique challenges mobile devices pose. These solutions consider the mobility, varied data sources, and specific types of threats encountered in mobile ecosystems. By tailoring their functionalities to the mobile context, these SIEM systems provide more effective monitoring, detection, and response capabilities, ensuring that mobile devices and their data are adequately protected.

Incident response is a critical component of Mobile SIEM systems. When a threat or anomaly is detected, the SIEM system can initiate a response protocol to mitigate the risk. This could include automated actions, such as isolating a compromised device from the network or alerting security personnel for further investigation. The ability of SIEM systems to quickly and effectively respond to incidents is essential in minimizing the impact of security breaches and maintaining the overall integrity of mobile security.

Secure Communication and Data Privacy

Secure communication and data privacy are paramount in the mobile domain, where sensitive information is often transmitted over potentially insecure networks. Mobile Virtual Private Networks (VPNs) and secure tunneling techniques ensure this communication remains confidential and protected from unauthorized access.

Virtual Private Networks (VPNs) are fundamental for achieving secure communication on mobile devices. VPNs create a private network from a public Internet connection, providing a secure and encrypted tunnel for data transmission. This encryption ensures that data sent and received over the VPN is protected from eavesdropping and interception, even when using public Wi-Fi networks. By routing mobile data traffic through this secure tunnel, VPNs help maintain the privacy and integrity of the data.

There are various VPNs, each utilizing different protocols to establish secure connections. Standard VPN protocols include OpenVPN, L2TP/IPsec, and IKEv2. Each protocol has its strengths and is suited to different use cases, with considerations around speed, security, and compatibility. Choosing the right VPN type and protocol depends on the user's specific requirements, such as the level of security needed and the type of network they are connecting to.

Secure tunneling is a crucial aspect of VPNs, ensuring data privacy during transmission. This process involves encapsulating data packets within encrypted tunnels, making the data unreadable to anyone who might intercept it. Secure tunneling is significant for mobile users who frequently connect to public or unsecured Wi-Fi networks, with higher data interception risk.

Mobile VPN apps and settings allow users to configure and use VPNs on their devices easily. These apps provide a user-friendly interface for selecting VPN servers, adjusting security settings, and connecting to the VPN. Many mobile VPN apps also offer additional features, such as automatic connection to the VPN when accessing unsecured networks, ensuring continuous protection for mobile communications. Proper configuration and regular app updates are essential for adequate security and privacy protection.

End-to-End Encryption

End-to-end encryption (E2EE) is critical in safeguarding communication privacy, particularly in the mobile landscape, where data transmission frequently occurs over public or unsecured networks. E2EE ensures that only the communicating users can access the messages or calls, significantly enhancing the security and confidentiality of the exchanged information.

The principles of end-to-end encryption involve encrypting data at the source (the sender's device) and decrypting it only at the destination (the recipient's device). This means the data remains encrypted and inaccessible to anyone, including service providers and potential interceptors, as it travels across the network. By employing E2EE, sensitive information such as personal messages, financial details, and private documents can be securely transmitted, with assurance that only the intended recipient can decrypt and read the content.

Secure messaging apps have become increasingly popular due to their implementation of end-to-end encryption. These apps, such as Signal, WhatsApp, and Telegram, encrypt messages so that only the sender and the receiver can view them. This level of security is crucial for maintaining privacy in digital communications and protecting users from eavesdropping and data breaches. The widespread adoption of these secure messaging apps reflects a growing public awareness of and demand for privacy in digital communications.

Securing voice and video calls is another application of end-to-end encryption. Like messaging, E2EE in voice and video calls ensures unauthorized parties cannot intercept or access the conversation. This is particularly important in a mobile context where calls often traverse various networks and infrastructures. Secure voice and video call encryption is increasingly integrated into standard communication apps, providing users with easy-to-use options for private and secure conversations.

Email encryption solutions are essential for securing email communications, which often contain sensitive information. E2EE can be implemented in email through PGP (Pretty Good Privacy) or S/MIME (Secure/Multipurpose Internet Mail Extensions). These solutions encrypt the email content, ensuring only the intended recipient with the corresponding decryption key can access the message. While historically more complex to set up, modern email encryption tools have become more user-friendly, making secure email communication accessible to a broader audience. Employing these encryption solutions in email is vital for protecting sensitive information against unauthorized access and ensuring data privacy in digital correspondence.

Location Privacy and Tracking

Location privacy and tracking are increasingly pertinent concerns in the era of mobile connectivity, where devices constantly communicate their whereabouts. The convenience and functionality offered by location services also bring potential privacy risks and challenges that need careful management.

Location services on mobile devices use GPS, cellular network data, Wi-Fi, and sometimes Bluetooth to determine and share the device's geographical position. These services enable many applications, from navigation and location-based recommendations to tracking fitness activities and finding nearby services. While incredibly useful, these services also raise privacy concerns, as they involve collecting and sometimes sharing precise location data.

The risks of location tracking are multifaceted. Persistent tracking can reveal sensitive information about a person's habits, routines, and preferences. If accessed by unauthorized parties, this data can lead to privacy invasions or even physical security risks. Additionally, location data can be used for targeted advertising or sold to third parties, sometimes without the user's explicit consent, leading to potential misuse or overcommercialization of personal information.

Protecting location privacy involves several strategies. Users can control their location settings, choosing when and how their location data is shared and with whom. This includes disabling location services when not needed or granting permissions only to trusted applications. Awareness and careful management of these settings are crucial for controlling personal data. Furthermore, technologies like VPNs can mask a device's location, providing an additional layer of privacy.

Geofencing and location-based services represent both an application of and a challenge to location privacy. Geofencing uses GPS or RFID technology to create a virtual geographic boundary, triggering a response when a mobile device enters or leaves a particular area. While useful for parental control, employee monitoring, or personalized marketing, geofencing also raises privacy concerns. Users should be aware of how their location data is being used in these contexts and have the option to opt in or out of such services. The balance between the benefits of location-based services and the protection of individual privacy is a critical consideration in the evolving landscape of mobile technology.

Mobile Payment Security

Mobile payment security is an increasingly important aspect of financial transactions in the digital age, where convenience and speed are paramount. With the rise of mobile payment technologies, ensuring the security of these transactions is essential to protect against fraud and unauthorized access.

Mobile wallets have become a popular way to store payment information on mobile devices. These digital wallets can store credit and debit card information, loyalty cards, and coupons, allowing quick and easy payments. Security measures for mobile wallets typically include strong encryption, biometric authentication (such as fingerprint or facial recognition), and tokenization, which replaces sensitive card details with a unique identifier during transactions. These features help to secure payment information both in storage and during transactions.

Contactless payments, facilitated by Near Field Communication (NFC) technology, allow users to make payments by simply tapping their mobile device against a payment terminal. This method is convenient and secure, as it usually involves multiple layers of security, including encryption and dynamic authentication tokens. These tokens change with each transaction, making it difficult for fraudsters to replicate or use the information for unauthorized transactions.

Mobile payment apps have revolutionized the way individuals transfer money and make payments. These apps often have robust security features like two-factor authentication, end-to-end encryption, and real-time transaction monitoring to detect and prevent fraudulent activities. Many of these apps also allow users to instantly lock their accounts if suspicious activity is detected, adding an extra layer of security.

NFC and QR code payments are other popular forms of mobile payments. NFC payments, as mentioned, use contactless technology, while QR code payments involve scanning a code to initiate a transaction. Both methods offer a secure and convenient way to pay, with the benefit of minimizing physical contact. This feature has become particularly valuable in the context of public health. QR code payments typically involve scanning a code displayed by the merchant or generating a code in the customer's payment app, which the merchant then scans. NFC and QR code payments leverage encryption and tokenization to secure transaction data, ensuring that sensitive payment information is protected throughout the process.

Risks and Vulnerabilities in Mobile Payments

The convenience of mobile payments is accompanied by various risks and vulnerabilities that users and service providers must be aware of and address. As mobile payment technologies become more widespread, the potential for security breaches, fraud, and other malicious activities also increases.

Payment card data theft is one of the primary risks associated with mobile payments. This type of theft can occur if a mobile device is lost or stolen or through cyber attacks like hacking or phishing. When payment card details stored on a mobile device are accessed without authorization, it can lead to unauthorized transactions and financial losses. To mitigate this risk, it's crucial for mobile payment solutions to have strong security measures such as encryption and the ability to wipe sensitive data in case the device is compromised remotely.

Payment fraud and scams are another significant concern. These can take various forms, from fraudulent transactions using stolen card details to social engineering scams that trick users into authorizing payments or divulging sensitive information. Cybercriminals continually develop sophisticated methods to carry out such scams, making vigilance and awareness essential for users of mobile payment systems. Financial institutions and payment service providers also play a crucial role in detecting and preventing fraud through monitoring and security systems.

Mobile payment apps can be risky if not adequately secured or downloaded from unreliable sources. Risks include vulnerabilities within the app that hackers could exploit to steal data or money. Users must download payment apps from trusted sources, such as official app stores, and keep them updated to ensure they have the latest security features. App developers and providers must also prioritize security in their design and regularly update apps to address new threats.

Point-of-sale (POS) security is an essential consideration in mobile payments. As more retailers and businesses adopt mobile POS systems to accept payments, the security of these systems becomes paramount. These systems can be vulnerable to various forms of attack, including skimming devices and malware. Ensuring the security of POS systems involves implementing solid data encryption, regular security updates, and training staff to recognize and respond to security threats. Both businesses and customers must be aware of these risks to protect sensitive payment information during transactions.

Secure Mobile Payment Solutions

Secure mobile payment solutions are essential in the digital era, where mobile transactions are commonplace. Implementing robust security measures in mobile payments is crucial for protecting against fraud and unauthorized access. These solutions include tokenization, biometric authentication, secure elements (SE), and secure payment APIs, each playing a vital role in safeguarding mobile transactions.

Tokenization in mobile payments is a process where sensitive data, like credit card numbers, is replaced with a unique, algorithmically generated token. This token represents the original data but does not carry the same risk if intercepted, as it is useless outside the context of the specific transaction for which it was created. Tokenization significantly enhances payment security by ensuring that actual card details are not transmitted or stored on the device during the transaction, thereby reducing the risk of data breaches and card fraud.

Biometric payment authentication has gained popularity for its enhanced security and user convenience. This technology uses unique biological characteristics, such as fingerprints, facial recognition, or iris scans, to verify a user's identity before authorizing a payment. Biometric authentication provides a higher level of security than traditional methods like PINs or passwords, as biometric traits are difficult to replicate or steal.

The Secure Element (SE) is a tamper-proof chip embedded in mobile devices that provides an additional layer of security for payment transactions. The SE stores sensitive data, like payment credentials, and performs cryptographic operations. It acts as a vault, isolating this information from the device's central operating system and applications. This isolation protects the data from software-based attacks and unauthorized access, making SE a critical component in contactless and mobile payment security.

Secure payment APIs are crucial for developing safe and reliable mobile payment applications. These APIs provide a standardized way for apps to access payment services while ensuring data is transmitted securely. They handle tasks like encryption, tokenization, and communication with payment gateways, ensuring developers can build payment functionalities into apps without compromising security. A well-designed payment API is critical in the ecosystem of mobile payments, as it allows for seamless and secure transactions, maintaining the integrity of the payment process and protecting user data.

Mobile Banking Security

Mobile banking security is a critical concern in the financial sector as more consumers turn to their smartphones for banking needs. The security of mobile banking apps, awareness of potential threats, and adherence to best practices are all essential to safeguard personal financial information and transactions.

Secure mobile banking apps are the foundation of mobile banking security. Financial institutions invest heavily in securing their apps, incorporating features such as strong encryption, secure login processes, and automatic logout after periods of inactivity. Many banks also use biometric authentication, like fingerprint or facial recognition, to add an extra layer of security. These apps must undergo regular security audits and updates to address emerging threats and vulnerabilities continually.

Mobile banking threats are diverse and constantly evolving. They include risks such as phishing attacks, where users are tricked into revealing sensitive information; malware that can steal data or log keystrokes; and man-in-the-middle attacks, which intercept communication between the user and the bank. Users need to be aware of these threats and cautious about downloading apps, clicking on links in emails or messages, and connecting to public Wi-Fi networks while conducting banking transactions.

Transaction verification and alerts are essential features of mobile banking security. Many banks offer the option to set up alerts for various types of account activities, such as large transactions, foreign transactions, or changes to personal information. These alerts can be sent via email, text message, or through the banking app, providing immediate notification of any unusual activity. Some banks also use transaction verification methods, like one-time passwords or push notifications, to confirm that the user authorizes a transaction.

Mobile banking best practices are essential for individual users to protect their financial information. These practices include regularly updating the banking app and the device's operating system; using strong, unique passwords for banking apps; and never sharing login credentials. Users should also be cautious of unsolicited communications claiming to be from their bank and should always verify the authenticity of such communications. Additionally, regularly monitoring account statements and transactions can help in the early detection of any unauthorized activities. By following these best practices, users can significantly reduce the risk of falling victim to mobile banking fraud and other security threats.

Mobile Payment Compliance

Mobile payment compliance is crucial to ensuring the security and integrity of mobile financial transactions. This involves adhering to established standards and regulations, conducting thorough security audits, and having robust procedures for reporting security incidents.

The Payment Card Industry Data Security Standard (PCI DSS) is a set of security standards designed to ensure that all companies that accept, process, store, or transmit credit card information maintain a secure environment. This standard is particularly relevant to mobile payment solutions, which often involve processing and storing sensitive payment card information. Compliance with PCI DSS involves implementing a range of security measures, such as encryption of cardholder data, maintaining a secure network, and conducting regular security testing.

Regulatory compliance in mobile payments extends beyond PCI DSS. Different countries and regions have regulations governing electronic and mobile payments, such as the General Data Protection Regulation (GDPR) in the European Union, which includes provisions for protecting personal data in payment transactions. Compliance with these regulations is essential not only for legal reasons but also for maintaining customer trust and protecting against financial and reputational damage.

Mobile payment security audits are essential for ensuring industry standards and regulations compliance. To identify and rectify potential security vulnerabilities, these audits thoroughly examine the mobile payment system's infrastructure, applications, and processes. Regular audits help maintain high-security standards, ensuring that the mobile payment solutions are resilient against evolving cyber threats and compliant with relevant regulations.

Reporting payment security incidents is a critical component of mobile payment compliance. In the event of a security breach or incident, prompt and transparent reporting is necessary, both to regulatory authorities and affected customers. This reporting is a regulatory requirement and essential to maintaining customer trust. Having a well-defined incident response plan, including procedures for reporting and managing security incidents, is essential for any organization involved in mobile payments. This plan ensures that incidents are handled efficiently and effectively, minimizing potential damage and ensuring compliance with legal and regulatory requirements.

Mobile Security for Enterprises

Enterprise mobile security presents challenges and risks as organizations increasingly integrate mobile devices into their business operations.

Enterprise Mobile Security Challenges

The prevalence of Bring Your Own Device (BYOD) policies in modern enterprises introduces inherent risks. Employees using their devices for work can inadvertently introduce vulnerabilities due to varying security measures compared to corporate-owned devices. This disparity can lead to increased risks of data breaches and malware infections. Consequently, organizations must implement stringent security measures to mitigate the risks associated with BYOD.

Mobile Device Management (MDM) systems are essential in managing these challenges. MDM solutions allow organizations to enforce consistent security policies, manage applications, and protect sensitive corporate data across all employee devices. They provide crucial tools for maintaining control and security in diverse mobile device usage environments. Implementing MDM is a crucial strategy for enterprises to ensure that corporate and personal mobile devices adhere to required security standards.

Enterprises also face threats to their data from various mobile-related vulnerabilities. These threats range from sophisticated cyberattacks targeting mobile devices to human errors leading to data exposure. Protecting enterprise data from such mobile threats necessitates a comprehensive security approach that includes technology solutions and employee awareness. Enterprises must adopt proactive security measures to safeguard sensitive information.

The issue of shadow IT and unauthorized apps presents a significant challenge in mobile security for enterprises. Employees may use unapproved software or applications, potentially exposing the organization to security vulnerabilities. Managing the risks associated with shadow IT requires vigilance and a clear policy from the IT department. Enterprises must establish clear guidelines and monitoring systems to control unsanctioned software and maintain security.

Mobile Device and App Management

Mobile Application Management (MAM) is a crucial aspect of enterprise mobile security. MAM solutions enable organizations to manage and secure the applications on employee devices effectively. They facilitate the deployment and updating of applications while enforcing security policies at the application level. MAM provides an essential layer of control and security, particularly in environments where employees use a mix of personal and corporate devices.

Mobile Threat Defense (MTD) solutions are integral to an enterprise's mobile security strategy. These solutions offer protection against a broad spectrum of mobile threats through threat detection, vulnerability assessments, and incident response mechanisms. MTD solutions are critical for safeguarding mobile devices and data against evolving security threats, ensuring the ongoing protection of enterprise resources.

The concept of Enterprise App Stores is gaining traction as a method to distribute secure and approved applications to employees. By offering a controlled selection of apps, enterprises can reduce the risks of downloading apps from public app stores. Enterprise App Stores are a secure way to ensure employees can access necessary tools while maintaining compliance with organizational security policies.

Remote wipe and lockdown capabilities are essential features in enterprise mobile security. In cases where a device is lost or stolen, these features enable IT administrators to erase sensitive data remotely or lock the device to prevent unauthorized access. Remote wipes and lockdowns protect corporate data from potential security breaches, making them vital tools in the enterprise mobile security arsenal.

Securing Mobile Email and Documents

Mobile email security best practices are vital for protecting sensitive business communications. These practices include using secure email gateways, implementing robust encryption for email data, and enforcing strong authentication methods. Ensuring mobile email security is crucial as email is often a primary communication channel in enterprises, frequently containing confidential information.

Secure document sharing and collaboration tools are increasingly important in the enterprise context. These tools utilize encryption and access control mechanisms to ensure that sensitive documents are shared securely and accessed only by authorized personnel. They facilitate safe collaboration and information sharing, essential in today's mobile-driven business environment.

Containerization is a technology that isolates enterprise data from personal data on employees' mobile devices. This separation creates a secure environment for corporate data, safeguarding it from unauthorized access and potential threats. Containerization is particularly beneficial in BYOD environments, as it allows employees to use their devices for work without compromising enterprise data security.

Establishing and enforcing mobile security policies is fundamental to enterprise mobile security. These policies provide guidelines on acceptable use, security protocols, and procedures for reporting security incidents. Implementing and enforcing these policies are vital to maintaining an enterprise's secure and compliant mobile environment. They serve as a framework for safe mobile device and application usage, ensuring employees understand their security responsibilities.

Mobile Security Awareness and Training

Employee training on mobile security is a critical component of an enterprise's security strategy. Educating staff about security best practices, recognizing potential threats, and safe mobile usage can reduce the likelihood of security incidents. Regular and practical training ensures that employees are aware of the risks associated with mobile device usage and understand how to mitigate these risks.

Security awareness programs in enterprises are designed to inform employees about the latest security threats and the organization's security policies. Frequent updates and communication of these programs help cultivate a security awareness culture. This ongoing education is essential in equipping employees with the knowledge to recognize and respond appropriately to security threats.

Reporting security incidents promptly and accurately is crucial to an enterprise's security posture. Clear procedures and channels for reporting security incidents enable swift action and mitigation of potential risks. Encouraging a culture where employees feel comfortable reporting security concerns without fear of reprisal is vital for early detection and response to security incidents.

Conducting mobile security drills and exercises is an effective way to test and reinforce an enterprise's security preparedness. These exercises simulate real-world scenarios, allowing employees to practice their response to security incidents. Regular drills help identify improvement areas in the organization's security protocols and ensure employees are prepared to handle potential security challenges effectively.

Mobile Security Compliance and Auditing

Regulatory compliance is a significant aspect of enterprise mobility. Enterprises must adhere to various laws and regulations that govern the protection and privacy of data, especially in sectors handling sensitive information. Compliance with these regulations prevents legal repercussions, helps maintain customer trust, and safeguards the enterprise's reputation.

Mobile security auditing and reporting are essential for ensuring that an enterprise's mobile security measures are effective and comply with regulatory standards. Regular audits help to identify vulnerabilities and areas for improvement in the organization's mobile security practices. Effective reporting mechanisms ensure that security incidents or compliance issues are documented and addressed promptly.

Data protection in enterprise mobility involves safeguarding sensitive information accessed and stored on mobile devices. This includes implementing encryption, access controls, and Data Loss Prevention strategies. Protecting data in a mobile environment is challenging but essential, as mobile devices are often more susceptible to loss, theft, and unauthorized access than traditional computing devices.

Developing an enterprise mobile security road map is crucial for strategic planning and improving mobile security measures. This road map should outline the organization's objectives, strategies, and tactics for securing mobile devices and data. It guides the implementation and updating of security measures, ensuring the enterprise's mobile security posture evolves to meet changing threats and business needs.

Future Developments in Mobile Security

The future of mobile security is set to be shaped by a range of innovative technologies and approaches. As mobile devices and applications become increasingly sophisticated, so must the measures to protect them.

Integrating AI and machine learning in mobile security is transforming threat detection capabilities. AI can be leveraged to identify new and evolving threats quickly, while machine learning algorithms can analyze patterns to detect anomalies that may indicate a security breach. Behavioral biometrics is becoming an essential tool for authentication, using machine learning to analyze patterns in user behavior for more secure access. Predictive analysis is also used for risk assessment, helping organizations anticipate potential vulnerabilities and respond proactively.

The advent of 5G networks and edge computing presents new security challenges and opportunities. 5G networks, with their increased speed and connectivity, necessitate enhanced security protocols to protect against sophisticated attacks. Edge computing, which processes data closer to where it is generated, also requires robust security to protect the data outside traditional centralized networks. Zero Trust Networking, which assumes no user or device is trustworthy, is becoming more relevant in the 5G era. Ensuring privacy in edge processing is also critical, as more sensitive data is processed outside traditional data centers.

Blockchain technology is increasingly being explored for mobile security applications. Thanks to its decentralized and tamper-proof nature, it offers a secure way to manage mobile identities and transact payments. Decentralized apps (DApps) on the blockchain can enhance security, reducing risks associated with centralized data storage. Blockchain can also create tamper-proof records for mobile devices, enhancing security and trust.

Quantum computing poses both challenges and opportunities for mobile encryption. The immense processing power of quantum computers could threaten current encryption methods, necessitating the development of post-quantum cryptography for mobile security. Preparing for quantum-resistant mobile security is crucial to protect against future threats. Quantum Key Distribution (QKD) offers a promising approach to secure communications in the face of quantum computing advancements.

Advancements in biometric technologies are enhancing mobile security. Facial recognition technology is becoming more sophisticated, offering more secure and convenient user authentication. Behavioral biometrics and continuous authentication provide ongoing security checks without disrupting the user experience. Biometric liveness detection helps prevent spoofing attacks. However, these advancements also bring ethical and privacy considerations that must be addressed.

Integrating the Internet of Things (IoT) with mobile devices opens new security challenges. IoT-enabled mobile devices increase the complexity of the security ecosystem. Securing the IoT ecosystem with mobile technologies is crucial to protect device-to-device communication. Developing and adhering to IoT security standards and protocols is essential to maintain the integrity of these interconnected systems.

Privacy-centric features in mobile operating systems are becoming more critical. Users are gaining more control over their data sharing, with privacy labels and transparency in app functionalities becoming standard. Emerging privacy regulations are shaping how mobile apps and devices handle user data, emphasizing the need for robust privacy controls.

Automated threat detection and response systems are becoming essential in mobile security. These systems can quickly identify and mitigate threats, reducing the reliance on manual intervention. Threat intelligence sharing platforms facilitate the exchange of security information, enhancing collective defense. Predictive threat intelligence uses machine learning to forecast potential threats, enabling proactive security measures.

As AR and VR technologies become more prevalent in mobile devices, new security challenges emerge. AR/VR apps introduce unique privacy concerns, creating new authentication and security challenges in virtual environments. Integrating AR/VR in mobile devices also presents a new attack surface that must be secured.

The mobile security landscape is continually shaped by evolving data protection regulations. Industry-specific mobile security standards are being developed to address unique challenges in sectors like finance and healthcare. Regulatory bodies are responding to new technologies, creating compliance challenges for organizations. Navigating these regulations and developing compliance solutions are critical for mobile security strategy.

Cross-industry collaboration is vital for effective cybersecurity. Public-private partnerships enhance collective defense strategies. Sharing threat intelligence globally helps in combating widespread cyber threats. Collective defense approaches, where information and resources are pooled, are becoming more critical in addressing complex security challenges.

User-centric security design focuses on creating solutions that are both secure and user-friendly. The balance between usability and security is crucial to ensure that security measures are effective and adopted by users. Education and training in mobile security are essential for empowering users to protect themselves. Incorporating behavioral psychology can help design security solutions that align with user behavior and expectations.

Sustainable mobile security practices are increasingly important, aligning with broader environmental concerns. Ethical hacking and responsible disclosure are crucial in identifying and addressing security vulnerabilities. Green computing principles are being integrated into mobile security solutions. Ethical considerations around AI and data usage are also shaping the future of mobile security, ensuring that technologies are used responsibly and ethically.

Case Study: The Phone Hack of CIA Director John Brennan

In 2015, a significant security breach occurred involving John Brennan, the then Director of the Central Intelligence Agency (CIA). This case study delves into the details of the phone hack, examining the methods used by the hackers, the nature of the information compromised, and the subsequent implications.

The breach was not a sophisticated cyber-attack by a foreign state but rather the work of a teenager operating from within the United States. The hacker, who claimed to be motivated by political reasons, managed to gain unauthorized access to Brennan's email account. This incident raised serious concerns about the security practices of high-ranking government officials, especially regarding the use of personal email accounts for potentially sensitive communications.

The attack began with a social engineering tactic known as "pretexting," where the hacker posed as a Verizon technician to trick customer service representatives into revealing Brennan's personal account details. Armed with this information, the hacker employed a password reset mechanism to access Brennan's AOL email account. This method of attack highlighted the vulnerabilities inherent in relying on personal, less secure email services for official communications.

The breach exposed several sensitive documents, including personal information about more than 20 CIA employees, confidential communications regarding intelligence operations, and even sensitive information related to national security. The hacker also accessed Brennan's contact list, which included numerous high-profile government officials. The extent of the breach underscored the potential risks posed by the mishandling of secure information.

The primary perpetrator was a teenager, part of a group known as "Crackas With Attitude." This group was known for targeting US government officials, allegedly in protest against US foreign policy. The relative ease with which a teenager could penetrate the personal communications of the CIA Director stunned the cybersecurity community and government officials alike.

The John Brennan phone hack serves as a stark reminder of the importance of cybersecurity, even for high-ranking government officials. It demonstrates the need for stringent security measures, especially regarding personal email accounts and sensitive information. The incident prompted a reevaluation of security protocols for government officials, emphasizing the importance of secure communication channels and the dangers of overreliance on personal, less protected digital platforms.

Career Corner

Mobile device and application security is a rapidly growing field within cybersecurity, focused on protecting mobile devices, their applications, and the data they process and store. This specialization offers diverse career opportunities for those with the requisite skills and passion for mobile technology and security.

A career path in this field is that of a Mobile Security Analyst. Individuals in this role evaluate mobile devices and applications for vulnerabilities. They conduct security assessments, analyze risks, and implement strategies to protect mobile devices and apps from cyber threats, including malware, unauthorized data access, and network-based attacks.

Another vital role is that of a Mobile Application Penetration Tester. These professionals use their expertise to identify and exploit vulnerabilities in mobile applications. By simulating cyberattacks, they play a crucial role in discovering and mitigating potential security weaknesses before they can be exploited maliciously, thus contributing significantly to the application's overall security.

Mobile Security Developers also have a crucial role in this sector. Their responsibilities extend beyond typical app development; they are skilled in coding secure mobile applications and are familiar with various mobile operating systems and platforms. Their expertise in secure coding practices is essential in preventing vulnerabilities and ensuring the safety of mobile apps from development through to deployment.

For those interested in a broader perspective, the role of a Mobile Device Management (MDM) Specialist is critical. These professionals are responsible for implementing and managing mobile device security policies within an organization. They oversee the deployment, security, monitoring, integration, and management of mobile devices in the workplace, ensuring they comply with organizational security standards.

Given mobile devices' technical and ever-evolving nature and application security, professionals are often encouraged to pursue specialized certifications. The Certified Information Systems Security Professional (CISSP) and the Certified Ethical Hacker (CEH) are valuable for a broad understanding of cybersecurity, which includes mobile security aspects. Additionally, certifications like the CompTIA Security+ and the Offensive Security Certified Professional (OSCP) can provide foundational and advanced knowledge in cybersecurity relevant to mobile security.

The Global Information Assurance Certification (GIAC) offers the Mobile Device Security Analyst (GMOB) certification, specifically tailored to mobile device and application security professionals. This certification demonstrates the skills to effectively manage and secure mobile devices and apps.

In summary, a mobile device and application security career is both challenging and rewarding, offering numerous opportunities for growth and specialization. Professionals in this field play a vital role in the security landscape, from analyzing and testing mobile apps and devices for vulnerabilities to developing secure mobile applications and managing device security in organizational settings. Continuous learning through experience and certifications is crucial to keeping pace with the rapidly evolving threats and technologies in mobile security.

Chapter Questions

1. What primary risk is associated with enterprises' Bring Your Own Device (BYOD) policies?

   A. Increased productivity

   B. Enhanced user satisfaction

   C. Introduction of vulnerabilities

   D. Improved device management

2. What is the main purpose of Mobile Device Management (MDM) systems in enterprises?

   A. To reduce operational costs

   B. To enforce consistent security policies

   C. To enhance employee collaboration

   D. To monitor employee productivity

3. Which technology is vital for securing voice and video calls on mobile devices?

   A. GPS tracking

   B. End-to-end encryption (E2EE)

   C. Biometric authentication

   D. Public Wi-Fi networks

4. What is a significant challenge in public Wi-Fi network security?

   A. High costs

   B. Limited availability

   C. Vulnerability to cyberattacks

   D. Slow connection speeds

5. Why is data encryption necessary for mobile device security?

   A. To increase data storage

   B. To speed up device performance

   C. To protect data from unauthorized access

   D. To reduce data usage

6. What is the primary function of Virtual Private Networks (VPNs) in mobile security?

   A. Enhancing device processing power

   B. Providing a secure and encrypted data tunnel

   C. Increasing Internet browsing speed

   D. Offering free Internet access

7. What is the purpose of threat intelligence automation in mobile security?

    A. To improve user interface design

    B. To reduce the cost of security software

    C. To predict and respond to threats quickly

    D. To increase battery life

8. Which aspect of mobile app security is addressed by code signing?

    A. Enhancing app functionality

    B. Guaranteeing app integrity

    C. Increasing app download speed

    D. Reducing app size

9. In mobile security, what is the principle of least privilege aimed at?

    A. Maximizing user access

    B. Minimizing the potential impact of a breach

    C. Increasing operational efficiency

    D. Reducing software development time

10. What is the primary concern with using public Wi-Fi networks for mobile devices?

    A. High data charges

    B. Limited connectivity range

    C. Risk of data interception

    D. Battery drainage

11. What role does behavioral biometrics play in mobile security?

A. Providing entertainment value

B. Enhancing device aesthetics

C. Authenticating user identity

D. Increasing screen resolution

12. Why is regular software updating critical in mobile security?

A. To introduce new features

B. To fix known security vulnerabilities

C. To increase advertisement revenue

D. To change the user interface

13. What is the significance of SSL/TLS in mobile data transmission?

A. To reduce data transmission time

B. To encrypt data during transmission

C. To increase the data limit

D. To improve GPS accuracy

14. How does Mobile Threat Defense (MTD) contribute to enterprise mobile security?

A. Enhancing email functionality

B. By providing threat detection and response

C. Reducing mobile data costs

D. By improving application design

15. What is the primary purpose of implementing secure mobile payment solutions like tokenization?

    A. To increase transaction speed

    B. To enhance user experience

    C. To reduce payment processing fees

    D. To protect against data breaches and fraud

CHAPTER 8

Cloud Security

Cloud computing has revolutionized our interactions with technology, offering a paradigm shift from traditional computing. At its core, cloud computing delivers services over the Internet, including servers, storage, databases, networking, software, analytics, and intelligence. This innovative approach allows for flexible resources, rapid innovation, and economies of scale. Users typically pay only for their cloud services, helping lower operating costs, run infrastructure more efficiently, and scale as business needs change.

At its most basic, cloud computing is defined as providing various services over the Internet. These services range from software and databases to networking and data storage. Unlike traditional computing, where data is stored on personal computers or servers physically present on-site, cloud computing stores data on servers in remote data centers. The core concepts of cloud computing revolve around on-demand availability, broad network access, resource pooling, rapid elasticity, and measured service. This model ensures that resources are available whenever needed, without the up-front cost and complexity of owning and maintaining physical IT infrastructure.

The key characteristics of cloud computing include resource pooling, where multiple customers use shared computing resources; on-demand self-service, allowing users to access services without long delays; scalability and rapid elasticity, which enable swift adjustment of resources based on demand; measured service, ensuring users pay only for what they use; and broad network access, making services available over any standard Internet connection. These characteristics offer unparalleled flexibility and efficiency, distinguishing cloud computing from traditional methodologies.

Cloud Service Models

Infrastructure as a Service (IaaS) forms the foundation of the cloud service pyramid. It provides the fundamental computing resources required for any digital operation. This includes virtual machines (VMs) with varying capacities, scalable storage solutions, and extensive networking capabilities. IaaS operates on a pay-as-you-go model, offering significant flexibility and cost-effectiveness. Users can rent the infrastructure according to their needs, avoiding the high capital expenditure of setting up physical servers. IaaS is particularly beneficial for businesses with fluctuating workloads, as it allows them to scale their infrastructure up or down based on demand. Significant examples of IaaS include Amazon Web Services (AWS), Microsoft Azure, and Google Compute Engine (GCE), each offering robust, scalable, and reliable infrastructure services.

Platform as a Service (PaaS) takes a step further by including the operating systems, middleware, and development tools necessary for software development. This model is designed to provide developers with a platform to build, test, deploy, and manage applications without the complexity of maintaining the underlying infrastructure. PaaS offers a seamless environment for development, often integrating database management systems, support for several programming languages, and tools for application design and testing. PaaS is ideal for developers and companies focusing on software creation and deployment. It streamlines the development process and allows developers to concentrate on the creative side of application development. Leading examples of PaaS are Microsoft Azure's App Service, Google App Engine, and Heroku.

Software as a Service (SaaS), the most user-friendly layer of cloud services, delivers software applications over the Internet on a subscription basis. SaaS applications are accessible through web browsers, eliminating the need for users to install and maintain software on their devices. This model is characterized by its ease of use, scalability, and maintenance handled by the service provider. SaaS solutions are widely used in business environments for email, customer relationship management (CRM), and enterprise resource planning (ERP) applications. They are also prevalent in personal use scenarios, such as document and photo editing software. Popular SaaS offerings include Microsoft Office 365, Salesforce, and Google Workspace. The SaaS model is particularly advantageous for small- to medium-sized businesses, as it provides access to sophisticated applications at a fraction of the cost of licensing traditional software.

A Brief History of the Cloud

While seemingly modern, the concept of cloud computing has its roots in the 1960s. During this time, the idea of an "intergalactic computer network," a term coined by J.C.R. Licklider, who was instrumental in developing the Advanced Research Projects Agency Network (ARPANET), emerged. Licklider envisioned a world where everyone could be interconnected and access programs and data from anywhere. This vision laid the groundwork for what would eventually become cloud computing. In the 1970s and 1980s, this concept started to take a more tangible form with the advent of virtual machines, allowing multiple distinct computing environments to reside in one physical hardware environment.

Precursors to modern cloud computing also included grid and utility computing. Grid computing, a form of distributed and parallel computing, involves a network of loosely connected computers working together to perform large tasks. On the other hand, utility computing is the packaging of computing resources, such as computation and storage, as a metered service similar to a traditional public utility, like electricity. These concepts were pivotal in shaping the basic structure of cloud computing, emphasizing on-demand resource usage and network-based access to a shared pool of configurable computing resources.

The emergence of modern cloud computing can be traced back to the late 1990s and early 2000s. The launch of Salesforce in 1999 marked a significant milestone, introducing the concept of using the Internet to deliver software applications to end users. This was soon followed by Amazon's development of Amazon Web Services (AWS) in 2002, which provided a suite of cloud-based services, including storage, computation, and even human intelligence through the Amazon Mechanical Turk. In 2006, Amazon launched Elastic Compute Cloud (EC2). This commercial web service allowed small companies and individuals to rent computers to run their computer applications, which was a significant step forward in cloud computing.

As cloud computing evolved, several key milestones marked its advancement. In 2009, Google and others started to offer browser-based enterprise applications through services such as Google Apps. The same year, Microsoft Azure was launched, offering a cloud computing service for building, testing, deploying, and managing applications and services through Microsoft-managed data centers. Furthermore, the introduction of OpenStack 2010, an open source cloud computing platform, significantly contributed to the democratization and standardization of cloud technology.

The Three Leading Cloud Providers

The cloud computing market is dominated by three leading providers: Amazon Web Services (AWS), Microsoft Azure, and Google Cloud Platform (GCP). Each of these giants offers a broad range of cloud services and has carved out a significant presence in the market. AWS, launched in

2006, is often credited with pioneering the cloud computing wave and maintaining the largest market share. Microsoft Azure, introduced in 2010, follows closely, targeting enterprises and individual developers. Google Cloud Platform, entering the market in 2011, has rapidly gained traction, particularly among data-centric and AI-focused projects.

Amazon Web Services (AWS) is the frontrunner in the cloud industry, providing a vast array of services. AWS offers everything from essential infrastructural services like compute power, storage, and networking to more advanced services like machine learning, artificial intelligence, and data analytics. AWS's market dominance is due to its wide range of services and its extensive global infrastructure. The company has established a network of data centers worldwide, ensuring high availability, low latency, and robust disaster recovery capabilities for its clients.

Microsoft Azure is another significant player in the cloud space. Azure offers a diverse array of services, including solutions for computing, analytics, storage, and networking. Its strong emphasis on hybrid cloud capabilities sets Azure apart, allowing businesses to integrate their on-premises data centers with the Azure cloud seamlessly. This strategy has made Azure particularly appealing to enterprises not ready to migrate to the cloud entirely. Additionally, Microsoft's established presence in enterprise software gives Azure a unique edge, especially among organizations that already rely on Microsoft's software and services.

Google Cloud Platform (GCP) provides services that leverage Google's core strengths in data management and artificial intelligence. GCP offers services like Google Compute Engine, Google App Engine, and Google Kubernetes Engine, which are particularly popular among developers looking for highly scalable and reliable cloud services. GCP's emphasis on data and AI is evident in its offerings, which include advanced machine learning tools and analytics solutions that integrate seamlessly with Google's AI and data platforms. While AWS and Azure hold larger market shares, GCP has carved out a niche, particularly among tech-savvy startups and data-driven enterprises.

Outside these three giants, the cloud computing landscape includes notable players like IBM, Oracle, and Alibaba, each offering niche services and specialized solutions. These providers cater to specific market needs and are integral to the diverse cloud computing ecosystem. The competitive landscape in cloud computing is dynamic, with each provider constantly innovating and expanding its offerings to capture a larger market share and meet the evolving needs of businesses and developers.

Importance of Security in the Cloud

The importance of security in cloud computing cannot be overstated, particularly as the reliance on cloud services grows across various sectors. With the increasing adoption of cloud technologies, businesses and individuals are shifting significant portions of their data and operations to cloud environments. While offering flexibility and scalability, this transition brings new challenges and risks regarding data security and privacy. The shared responsibility model in cloud computing underscores the necessity for cloud service providers and users to manage and protect data diligently.

As cloud services become increasingly integral to business operations and personal activities, the security challenges inherent in cloud computing become more pronounced. These challenges range from safeguarding data against unauthorized access and cyber attacks to ensuring compliance with various regulatory requirements. The multitenancy nature of cloud computing, where multiple users share the same infrastructure resources, also introduces complexities in maintaining data isolation and preventing breaches. Additionally, the distributed nature of cloud services can complicate the tracking and management of data across various global jurisdictions, each with its own set of privacy laws and regulations.

One of the critical implications of adopting cloud services is the need for robust data and privacy protection measures. With stringent regulations like the General Data Protection Regulation (GDPR) in the

European Union and similar laws worldwide, businesses must ensure that their cloud infrastructure complies with these legal requirements. This includes implementing proper encryption, access controls, and data governance policies. Moreover, the increasing awareness and concern over personal data privacy have made consumers more conscious of how their data is handled and stored, prompting businesses to adopt stricter privacy measures in their cloud operations.

Another essential aspect of cloud computing is ensuring business continuity and disaster recovery. Cloud environments offer sophisticated tools and infrastructures for backing up data and maintaining operations, even during system failures, natural disasters, or cyber-attacks. The ability of cloud services to replicate data across multiple geographical locations ensures that businesses can quickly recover and restore their operations with minimal downtime. This resilience is crucial for maintaining customer trust and avoiding significant financial losses due to interruptions in service.

In summary, while cloud computing presents enormous benefits regarding efficiency, scalability, and innovation, it also necessitates a heightened focus on security and privacy. Addressing these challenges is crucial for maintaining the integrity and reliability of cloud services. As the cloud continues to evolve, ongoing efforts to enhance security measures, comply with legal requirements, and ensure robust disaster recovery mechanisms will be imperative for businesses and cloud providers.

Cloud Deployment Models

Cloud computing offers several deployment models to cater to diverse public, private, and hybrid needs. Each model presents its unique set of features, advantages, and challenges. The public cloud is managed by third-party providers and shared among multiple organizations, offering scalability and cost-effectiveness. Private clouds are dedicated to a single organization, providing enhanced control and security, while hybrid clouds blend both attributes, offering flexibility and tailored privacy control.

The public cloud is characterized by its open nature, where computing resources are hosted and managed by third-party providers and shared across multiple organizations. This model's key characteristics include high scalability, flexibility, and cost-effectiveness, as resources are typically available on a pay-as-you-go basis. Public clouds are ideal for businesses needing rapid scalability, those with variable workloads, or companies that prefer not to invest in heavy infrastructure. However, they also bring data security and compliance risks, as the shared environment can pose potential vulnerabilities. Leading public cloud providers include Amazon Web Services (AWS), Microsoft Azure, and Google Cloud Platform (GCP), each offering various services and global reach.

In contrast, private clouds are dedicated to a single organization and offer greater control and security. These clouds can be hosted on-premises or by a third-party provider but are exclusively used by one enterprise. The main features of private clouds include enhanced security and customization options, as they can be tailored to meet specific business needs and compliance requirements. Private clouds are particularly suitable for organizations with strict data security and privacy concerns, such as government agencies or financial institutions. While offering greater security, private clouds require significant investment in terms of infrastructure and management.

Hybrid clouds combine public and private cloud elements, allowing businesses to leverage the advantages of both. In a hybrid cloud, sensitive operations can be run on the private cloud, while less critical functions can use the cost-effective public cloud. This model offers flexibility and scalability, enabling businesses to manage varying workloads and data privacy requirements efficiently. Hybrid cloud deployment requires careful planning and robust integration of both environments to ensure seamless operation and security. Security strategies in hybrid clouds involve implementing consistent security policies, encryption, and identity management across public and private components.

Each cloud deployment model serves distinct purposes and offers different benefits and challenges. Public clouds provide scalability and cost savings, private clouds offer enhanced security and control, and hybrid clouds bring the best of both worlds, allowing businesses to balance flexibility and security. Understanding these models is crucial for organizations to make informed decisions about their cloud computing strategies, ensuring they align with their operational needs and security requirements.

Fundamentals of Cloud Security

Cloud security is critical to managing cloud environments, ensuring that data and applications hosted in the cloud are protected from various threats and vulnerabilities. The core principles of cloud security are rooted in the confidentiality, integrity, and availability (CIA) triad. This foundational concept is crucial in developing robust security strategies for cloud-based systems. Confidentiality ensures that sensitive information is accessed only by authorized individuals, integrity maintains the accuracy and completeness of data, and availability ensures that information and resources are accessible when needed.

The CIA triad applies to cloud environments with some unique considerations due to the nature of cloud computing. In cloud environments, confidentiality involves securing data in transit and at rest, employing encryption methods, and implementing strict access controls. Integrity in the cloud is maintained through regular audits, consistent data backup practices, and checksums or hash functions to detect alterations. Availability in the cloud is ensured through redundant resources, robust disaster recovery plans, and reliable uptime commitments from cloud service providers.

A fundamental concept in cloud security is the shared responsibility model. This model outlines the division of security responsibilities between the cloud service provider (CSP) and the customer. While the CSP is responsible for securing the infrastructure that runs cloud services, the customer is responsible for securing their data within the cloud. This includes managing user access, protecting client-side data, and ensuring application security. Understanding this model is vital for cloud customers to know their roles and responsibilities in maintaining cloud security.

The roles of the cloud provider and the customer in the shared responsibility model can vary based on the service model – Infrastructure as a Service (IaaS), Platform as a Service (PaaS), or Software as a Service (SaaS). In an IaaS model, the CSP manages the physical infrastructure, while the customer is responsible for the operating system, applications, and data. In PaaS, the provider also manages the operating system and runtime, and in SaaS, the provider is responsible for securing the entire stack. Customers must clearly understand these distinctions to manage their part of the security effectively.

The implications of the shared responsibility model for security responsibilities are significant. Customers cannot assume that the provider handles all aspects of security. They must actively secure their data and applications, including implementing robust encryption, access control policies, and monitoring systems. This active role in security is crucial to protect against data breaches, unauthorized access, and other cyber threats.

Threats and vulnerabilities in the cloud are diverse and constantly evolving. Common threat vectors include data breaches, compromised credentials, hijacked accounts, and insider threats. Vulnerabilities specific to cloud environments can arise from misconfigured cloud storage, inadequate access controls, or vulnerabilities in shared technology. Organizations must stay vigilant and informed about the latest threat landscape in cloud computing.

Risk assessment and management are key components of a comprehensive cloud security strategy. Risk assessments involve identifying, analyzing, and evaluating risks specific to cloud deployments. This process helps organizations understand their exposure to potential threats and make informed decisions about security controls. Developing risk mitigation strategies involves implementing measures to reduce the impact of identified risks, such as enhancing security protocols, training employees, and establishing incident response plans.

Compliance and legal considerations are also integral to cloud security. Organizations must ensure that cloud deployments, such as GDPR, HIPAA, and PCI-DSS, meet regulatory requirements. This includes understanding data sovereignty issues, adhering to data protection regulations, and ensuring that contracts with cloud providers align with compliance needs. Navigating cloud security's legal and contractual aspects requires a thorough understanding of the regulatory landscape and cloud service agreements' specific terms and conditions. By addressing these aspects, organizations can ensure their cloud deployments are secure and compliant with legal and regulatory standards.

Security Controls in the Cloud

Identity and Access Management (IAM) is pivotal in cloud security, ensuring only authorized users can access specific resources. Proper user authentication is a cornerstone of IAM, involving verifying users' identities before granting access to systems or data. This process typically includes username and password verification, but increasingly, organizations are moving toward more secure methods.

One such method is role-based access control (RBAC), which assigns users to specific roles and grants access based on those roles. RBAC minimizes the risk of unauthorized access by ensuring users have access only to the resources necessary for their roles. Implementing multifactor authentication (MFA) adds a layer of security. MFA requires users to provide two or more verification factors to gain access, significantly reducing the risk of compromised credentials.

Encryption is another critical element of cloud security, safeguarding data by converting it into an unreadable coded form without the decryption key. Encrypting data at rest protects it from unauthorized access when stored in cloud servers. Securing data in transit, as it moves between client devices and cloud servers, is equally important. This is typically achieved through encryption protocols like TLS (Transport Layer Security). Key management, involving the creation, distribution, and management of encryption keys, is vital. Best practices in key management include using robust algorithms, regularly rotating keys, and ensuring that keys are stored securely.

Network security is crucial in protecting data and resources in the cloud. Configuring a Virtual Private Cloud (VPC) allows organizations to create a segregated cloud section, providing control over the virtual network environment. Network segmentation further enhances security by dividing networks into smaller parts, limiting attacks spread within the network. Implementing intrusion detection and prevention systems (IDS/IPS) is also key, as these systems monitor network traffic for suspicious activities and take action to prevent or mitigate attacks.

Application security in the cloud requires a multifaceted approach. Secure development practices involve incorporating security considerations throughout the software development lifecycle. This includes code reviews, vulnerability testing, and compliance checks. Web Application Firewalls (WAF) protect web applications by filtering and monitoring HTTP traffic between a web application and the Internet. WAFs can prevent attacks from application vulnerabilities, such as SQL injection, cross-site scripting (XSS), and file inclusion. API security measures are also crucial, as APIs are often used to interact with cloud services. This includes securing endpoints, authenticating and authorizing API calls, and encrypting data transmitted through APIs.

Monitoring and incident response are essential for maintaining ongoing security in the cloud. Real-time security monitoring involves continuously observing cloud resources and networks for signs of security breaches or anomalies. This proactive approach allows for immediate detection and response to potential threats. Incident detection and response plans are critical for addressing security incidents effectively. These plans outline the procedures for responding to security breaches, including containment, eradication, and recovery. Post-incident forensics and analysis are also important, as they help understand how the breach occurred and improve security measures to prevent future incidents. This comprehensive approach to cloud security – from Identity and Access Management to incident response – ensures a robust defense against the evolving landscape of cyber threats.

Cloud Security Best Practices

Cloud security best practices are essential in protecting cloud environments from evolving threats and vulnerabilities. Secure cloud architecture design is one of the most critical aspects involving the creation of inherently secure cloud environments. This approach requires designing for security from the ground up, integrating security into every layer of the cloud architecture. Security by Design principles emphasize including security features and considerations early in the design process rather than as an afterthought.

Defense in depth is a strategy that layers multiple security measures to protect data and resources in the cloud. This approach mitigates the risk that if one security control fails, others will still be in place to provide protection. It involves a combination of preventive, detective, and responsive security controls, ranging from firewalls and encryption to intrusion detection systems and security monitoring.

Security automation and orchestration are becoming increasingly important in managing the complexity and scale of cloud security. Automating security tasks helps reduce the likelihood of human error and frees up resources to focus on more strategic security initiatives. Security orchestration involves integrating various security tools and processes for a coordinated response to security incidents. This orchestration enables a rapid response to threats and helps manage complex security environments more effectively.

Continuous security improvement is vital in the cloud, where the threat landscape constantly evolves. This includes regular reviews and updates of security policies, procedures, and controls. Patch management is a critical component involving the timely and secure application of software patches to address vulnerabilities. Patching challenges in cloud environments include ensuring compatibility across various cloud services and managing patches in a distributed environment.

User training and awareness play a crucial role in cloud security. It is essential to educate users on cloud security best practices, potential threats such as phishing, and their role in maintaining security. Phishing awareness and prevention training can significantly reduce the risk of security breaches that originate from user actions. This training should be ongoing to keep pace with the evolving nature of cyber threats.

Disaster recovery and business continuity are crucial for maintaining operations during security breaches or other disruptions. Cloud-based disaster recovery strategies offer flexibility and scalability, allowing organizations to recover from an incident quickly. Ensuring business continuity in the cloud involves planning how critical operations will continue during and after a disaster. This includes backup and redundancy planning, ensuring that data and applications can be restored quickly and efficiently during a disaster.

In summary, cloud security best practices encompass a comprehensive approach, from secure architecture design and defense in depth to user education and disaster recovery planning. These practices ensure that cloud environments are secure and resilient in the face of threats and capable of rapid recovery when incidents occur. Implementing these best practices is essential for organizations to protect their cloud-based resources and maintain trust with their customers and stakeholders.

Cloud Identity and Access Management (IAM)

Cloud Identity and Access Management (IAM) is a framework used in cloud computing for managing digital identities and controlling how users can access cloud resources. This system is essential for verifying and validating user identities and assigning and enforcing access privileges to cloud services and data. Cloud IAM ensures that only authorized individuals access specific resources, safeguarding sensitive data and applications. Its importance is amplified in cloud environments where resources are remotely accessible and susceptible to various security threats.

The significance of IAM in cloud computing lies in its ability to offer robust security and operational efficiency. IAM systems prevent unauthorized access and potential data breaches by managing user access to critical information and cloud resources. This is particularly crucial in the cloud, where the scalability and accessibility of resources make security management more challenging. IAM also ensures compliance with various regulatory standards, making it an indispensable tool for organizations operating in the cloud.

IAM's role in cloud security and access control is multifaceted. It is the first defense against unauthorized access, providing mechanisms for securely managing user identities and access rights. Through practices like role-based access control and multifactor authentication, IAM enhances security by ensuring that users have access only to the resources necessary for their job functions. This protects against external threats and mitigates internal risks, such as insider threats.

Cloud service providers (CSPs) typically integrate IAM into their offerings, recognizing its critical role in security and management. These providers design IAM services to be flexible and scalable, catering to the diverse needs of their customers. By offering IAM as part of their services, CSPs enable organizations to manage user access and security policies effectively, ensuring a secure and efficient cloud environment.

IAM systems vary across cloud deployment models – public, private, and hybrid – each presenting unique challenges and requirements. IAM must address a broader range of external users and services in public clouds, requiring robust and scalable solutions. Private clouds, often used by a single organization, focus on detailed internal access control and integration with existing systems. Hybrid clouds combine these aspects, requiring IAM solutions that seamlessly operate across public and private components, thus ensuring consistent security and access management across the entire cloud infrastructure.

Data Security in the Cloud

In cloud computing, data encryption strategies are vital for safeguarding sensitive information. Encryption is a primary defense mechanism against unauthorized access, ensuring that data remains secure and confidential. It involves converting data into a coded format accessible only to those with the decryption key. Employing robust data encryption strategies in the cloud is essential for protecting against external threats, complying with data protection regulations, and maintaining customer trust.

Data at rest refers to data stored instead of transmitted over a network. Encrypting data at rest is crucial in the cloud, as it adds a significant layer of security, protecting data from being accessed if storage devices or systems are compromised. Encryption is essential for safeguarding sensitive data stored in the cloud, such as personal information, financial records, and intellectual property. Encryption at rest ensures that even if data is accessed illegally, it remains unintelligible and useless without the corresponding decryption keys.

Encrypting data at rest in cloud environments cannot be understated. As cloud storage facilities are often shared among multiple users and potentially accessible from anywhere, the risk of unauthorized access and data breaches increases significantly. Encryption at rest is a critical barrier, rendering data unreadable to anyone who does not possess the correct decryption keys. This protects sensitive data from cyber threats and helps organizations meet compliance requirements and maintain the confidentiality and integrity of their data.

Effective key management is a cornerstone of robust data encryption. Managing encryption keys involves securely storing, maintaining, and controlling access to the keys used to encrypt and decrypt data. In cloud environments, key management must be handled with utmost care to prevent unauthorized access to keys, as the security of encrypted data is directly linked to the security of the keys. This involves setting up secure key storage, implementing access controls, and monitoring key usage.

Most cloud providers offer built-in encryption services to secure data at rest and in transit. These services typically include automated encryption solutions, making it easier for customers to implement encryption without extensive cryptographic expertise. Cloud provider encryption services often come with integrated critical management solutions, simplifying data encryption and managing the associated keys. Users can leverage these services to ensure their data is encrypted according to best practices while benefiting from the provider's expertise and infrastructure.

Data in transit encryption focuses on securing data while it's being transmitted over a network. This is crucial in cloud computing, where data travels across various networks and devices. Encrypting data in transit protects it from being intercepted and read by unauthorized entities.

This type of encryption is significant when transmitting sensitive data over public networks, where the risk of eavesdropping and data interception is higher.

Securing data during transmission involves implementing encryption protocols safeguarding data as it moves from one location to another. Protocols like Transport Layer Security (TLS) and Secure Sockets Layer (SSL) are commonly used. They encrypt the data before it is sent over a network and decrypt it upon arrival at its destination. This ensures that even if data is intercepted during transmission, it cannot be deciphered by unauthorized parties.

Encryption protocols and algorithms are fundamental to ensuring secure data transmission and storage. Protocols like TLS and SSL provide secure channels for data transmission, while various encryption algorithms determine how data is encrypted and decrypted. The choice of encryption algorithm depends on the level of security required and the nature of the data. Advanced algorithms such as AES (Advanced Encryption Standard) are widely used for their strength and reliability.

Best practices in crucial management are essential for maintaining the security of encrypted data. This involves centralized or decentralized critical management systems, depending on the organization's needs and infrastructure. Centralized key management offers easier control and auditing, while decentralized systems can provide higher security by spreading the risk. Key rotation and lifecycle management are also critical, ensuring that keys are regularly updated and retired securely when no longer used.

Choosing between centralized and decentralized key management depends on the organization's specific security requirements and operational complexity. Centralized critical management systems consolidate vital activities in a single location, simplifying administration and auditing. Decentralized systems, on the other hand, distribute the management of keys across multiple locations or systems, enhancing security by reducing the potential impact of a single point of failure.

Key rotation and lifecycle management are critical components of effective key management. Regularly rotating keys minimizes the risk of crucial compromise over time. Lifecycle management involves creating, using, storing, and retiring or deleting keys. Proper lifecycle management ensures that keys are always secure and effective and that outdated or compromised keys are removed.

Hardware Security Modules (HSMs) in the cloud provide a highly secure way of managing and storing encryption keys. HSMs are physical devices designed to safeguard cryptographic keys and perform encryption and decryption processes within a tamper-resistant hardware environment. Cloud providers often offer HSM services, allowing users to benefit from high-level security for their keys without the need to manage their physical hardware.

Data Masking and Redaction

Data masking and redaction are crucial data security and privacy techniques, especially in cloud environments where data is often accessible to many users and systems. The primary purpose of these methods is to protect sensitive information from unauthorized access while allowing for the functional use of data. This is particularly important for organizations that handle personal, financial, or otherwise confidential information. Organizations can leverage their data for operational purposes without compromising security or privacy by obscuring specific data elements.

Compliance with privacy regulations is another key driver for the adoption of data masking and redaction techniques. Laws such as the General Data Protection Regulation (GDPR) and the California Consumer Privacy Act (CCPA) mandate strict controls over how personal data is handled and accessed. Data masking and redaction help organizations meet these regulatory requirements by ensuring that sensitive information

241

is not exposed to unauthorized personnel within and outside the organization. This is essential for legal compliance, customer trust, and the organization's reputation.

There are various techniques for data masking, each suited to different requirements and data types. Static data masking involves creating a sanitized copy of the data where sensitive information is replaced or obfuscated. This masked data can be used in nonproduction environments for testing or development purposes, ensuring that the personnel in these environments do not have access to real sensitive data. On the other hand, dynamic data masking involves masking data in real time as users request it. This method is particularly useful in production environments where data needs to be protected from certain users without affecting the database's overall functionality.

Data redaction approaches take these concepts further by removing or obscuring specific information within a dataset. Redaction is often used in documents and databases to permanently conceal parts of the data, such as names, social security numbers, or credit card details. Redaction policies and rules ensure that only the necessary data is visible to authorized users, minimizing the data exposure risk. Dynamic redaction offers real-time protection by automatically redacting sensitive information based on predefined rules and user privileges. This approach is invaluable in environments where data access needs constantly change and where maintaining the balance between data utility and privacy is crucial.

Data Loss Prevention (DLP) in the Cloud

Data Loss Prevention (DLP) in the cloud is critical to modern cybersecurity strategies, particularly as organizations increasingly move sensitive data to cloud-based environments. Understanding Data Loss Prevention involves recognizing its role in identifying, monitoring, and protecting data from unauthorized access or leaks. DLP solutions are designed to safeguard sensitive information, ensuring it doesn't leave the network without proper authorization. This is crucial in preventing data breaches and maintaining compliance with data protection regulations.

The first step in implementing an effective DLP strategy is identifying sensitive data that requires protection. This involves classifying data and information types based on their sensitivity and the potential risk associated with their exposure. Classifying data correctly is essential for applying the appropriate level of security and ensuring that DLP tools effectively protect the most critical information.

Implementing cloud-based DLP solutions requires a comprehensive approach encompassing policy enforcement, integration with cloud services, and continuous monitoring. DLP policy enforcement in cloud services ensures data handling practices adhere to established security protocols and compliance requirements. This includes setting rules for data access, transfer, and storage and defining the actions to be taken when these rules are violated.

Integration of DLP solutions with cloud applications is another critical component. This integration allows for seamless data monitoring and protection as it moves through and is stored in various cloud applications. It ensures that security measures are consistently applied across all cloud-based platforms and services, providing a holistic approach to data protection.

Monitoring and incident response are vital for a proactive DLP strategy. Real-time DLP alerts and notifications play a crucial role in this regard, as they enable quick identification of potential data leaks or policy violations. This immediate awareness allows rapid response to prevent data loss or mitigate its impact. Effective incident handling and reporting mechanisms are also essential, as they provide insights into the nature and frequency of data security incidents, helping in refining DLP strategies and improving overall data protection measures.

Data Loss Prevention in the cloud is a multifaceted process that involves identifying and classifying sensitive data, enforcing robust DLP policies, integrating DLP solutions with cloud applications, and maintaining vigilant monitoring and responsive incident handling. As cloud environments continue to grow in complexity and importance, the role of DLP in safeguarding sensitive information becomes increasingly critical for organizations seeking to protect their data assets while complying with regulatory standards.

Data Backup and Recovery

Data backup and recovery are essential to a robust cloud computing strategy, ensuring data integrity and business continuity. The importance of data backup in the cloud is amplified due to the nature of cloud storage and the various risks associated with digital data management. Backups provide a safety net against data loss, whether due to human error, technical malfunctions, or malicious attacks; in an era where data is increasingly valuable, reliable backup solutions are crucial for any organization's resilience and operational stability.

Protection against data loss is a primary objective of data backup strategies in the cloud. This includes safeguarding against accidental deletions, corruption of data, and system failures. Additionally, with the rise in ransomware attacks, where data is held hostage by malicious actors, having an up-to-date backup can be the difference between a minor setback and a catastrophic loss. A robust backup strategy is critical in disaster recovery, enabling organizations to restore data and resume operations with minimal downtime quickly.

Cloud backup strategies have evolved to offer automated, efficient, and secure solutions. Automated backup solutions are particularly effective in cloud environments, as they can be set to capture and store data regularly without manual intervention. This ensures that backups are consistently up to date and reduces the risk of human error. Deciding on backup frequency and establishing retention policies are also crucial steps. These decisions should align with the organization's data management needs and regulatory requirements, ensuring that important data is retained for as long as necessary but not excessively.

Offsite and cloud-to-cloud backups are additional strategies to enhance data protection. Offsite backups involve storing data in a location separate from the primary data center, which can be crucial in a physical disaster like a fire or flood. Cloud-to-cloud backup involves storing copies of data in multiple cloud environments, which provides an extra layer of security and redundancy. This approach is beneficial for mitigating risks associated with reliance on a single cloud provider.

Data recovery in the cloud is a critical counterpart to data backup. It involves procedures for restoring data from backups in the event of data loss or corruption. Effective data recovery strategies are characterized by clear data restoration procedures, ensuring that data can be quickly and accurately reinstated. These strategies ensure business continuity, minimizing the operational impact of data loss incidents. This involves restoring data and ensuring that systems are returned online and functioning as expected.

Data backup and recovery in the cloud are vital for protecting against data loss, mitigating the impact of ransomware and disasters, and ensuring ongoing business operations. Through automated backups, regular testing of recovery procedures, and the implementation of offsite and cloud-to-cloud backups, organizations can safeguard their critical data and maintain business continuity in the face of various challenges. As cloud computing continues to evolve, so will the strategies and technologies for effective data backup and recovery, remaining a cornerstone of digital resilience.

Data Privacy and Compliance

Data privacy and compliance are increasingly critical in the digital landscape, especially with the widespread adoption of cloud computing. Privacy considerations in cloud data storage involve ensuring that personal and sensitive data is handled in a manner that respects individual privacy rights and complies with legal standards. Given the distributed nature of cloud services, this is a challenging task, which often involves storing and processing data across multiple jurisdictions.

Compliance with privacy regulations like the General Data Protection Regulation (GDPR) in the European Union and the California Consumer Privacy Act (CCPA) in the United States is essential for organizations using cloud services. These regulations set stringent guidelines for data protection and grant individuals significant control over their personal information. In addition, international data transfers in cloud environments must be managed carefully to ensure compliance with the varied data protection laws applicable in different countries. The complexities of these laws require cloud users and providers to be vigilant in their data handling practices to avoid legal pitfalls.

Apart from general privacy laws, there are also industry-specific compliance frameworks that organizations must adhere to. For instance, the Health Insurance Portability and Accountability Act (HIPAA) sets standards for protecting sensitive patient health information. At the same time, the Payment Card Industry Data Security Standard (PCI DSS) provides guidelines for handling credit card information. Compliance with these standards is critical for organizations using cloud services in the respective sectors. Cloud providers often facilitate this by obtaining relevant compliance certifications, demonstrating that their infrastructure and services meet regulatory requirements.

Auditing and reporting are critical to maintaining data privacy and compliance in the cloud. Regular auditing of cloud data access and usage helps organizations track how data is being handled and by whom.

This is essential for identifying potential privacy breaches and ensuring data handling practices align with compliance requirements. Generating compliance reports is another crucial aspect, providing transparency and accountability in cloud data management.

Third-party audits and assessments play a significant role in verifying compliance with privacy and regulatory standards. These independent evaluations objectively assess an organization's data privacy practices and compliance status. They are particularly useful for identifying gaps in compliance and providing guidance on addressing these issues. Maintaining data privacy and compliance in cloud environments requires a comprehensive approach involving careful consideration of legal requirements, rigorous auditing, and continuous improvement in data handling practices.

Network Security in the Cloud

Virtual Private Cloud (VPC) is a fundamental concept in cloud computing, offering enhanced security and control within cloud environments. Understanding VPC involves recognizing it as an isolated network within the public cloud, essentially a private cloud residing within a public cloud infrastructure. This isolation allows organizations to run their cloud resources in a virtual network they define and control. VPCs provide the flexibility to configure network settings, select IP address ranges, and create subnets, offering a customized networking solution in the cloud.

One of the key benefits of a VPC in cloud security is its ability to define isolated network environments. This isolation is crucial for organizations looking to maintain high security and control over their cloud-based resources. Organizations can use a VPC to create a secure environment logically separated from other users on the same cloud platform. This segregation is particularly important for handling sensitive data or running mission-critical applications that require enhanced security measures.

Network segmentation in the cloud is another critical aspect of VPCs. The importance of segregating resources in a cloud environment cannot be overstated, as it allows for better control and management of network traffic. By implementing VPC subnets and zones, organizations can divide their cloud network into smaller, more manageable segments. This segmentation enables them to apply specific security and compliance policies to different parts of their network, depending on their unique requirements and risk profiles.

Within a VPC, security groups and network access control lists (ACLs) are essential tools for managing access and enhancing security. Security group rules allow granular control over inbound and outbound traffic at the instance level. These rules can be configured to allow or deny traffic based on various criteria, such as IP addresses, ports, and protocols, providing a flexible way to manage access to cloud resources. On the other hand, network ACLs offer an additional layer of security at the subnet level. They act as a firewall for controlling traffic in and out of one or more subnets, offering another level of defense.

Layered defense with security groups and ACLs in a VPC is a best practice in cloud security. This approach combines the strengths of both security groups and network ACLs to create a comprehensive security strategy. While security groups provide instance-level traffic control, network ACLs add a layer of protection at the subnet level. This layered approach ensures that cloud resources are safeguarded from various angles, significantly reducing the risk of unauthorized access and potential security breaches. By effectively utilizing these tools within a VPC, organizations can create a robust and secure cloud environment that aligns with their specific security needs.

Protection Against Distributed Denial-of-Service (DDoS) Attacks

Protection against distributed denial-of-service (DDoS) attacks is crucial in maintaining the availability and functionality of cloud-based services. In the cloud, the DDoS threat landscape presents unique challenges due to the scalable and accessible nature of cloud resources. DDoS attacks in cloud environments can be more complex and potent, leveraging the vast resources of the cloud itself. These attacks aim to overwhelm a network, service, or application, rendering it unavailable to legitimate users, which can have significant consequences for businesses relying on cloud services.

DDoS attacks come in various forms, each with its method of disrupting services. Common types include volumetric attacks, which flood a network with excessive traffic; protocol attacks, which exploit weaknesses in the network layer; and application-layer attacks, which target specific aspects of an application or service. Amplification attacks and botnets are particularly prevalent in DDoS scenarios. Amplification attacks involve exploiting vulnerable network protocols to multiply traffic, while botnets use networks of infected computers to generate massive amounts of traffic directed at the target.

DDoS mitigation strategies are essential for defending against these attacks. Content Delivery Networks (CDNs) significantly mitigate DDoS attacks by distributing the load across multiple servers and locations, thereby diluting the impact of an attack aimed at a single point. Additionally, Web Application Firewalls (WAFs) provide protection at the application layer, filtering and monitoring HTTP traffic to and from a web service, and can effectively mitigate application-layer DDoS attacks.

Cloud-based DDoS protection services offer another layer of defense, providing specialized resources and expertise to detect and mitigate large-scale DDoS attacks. These services typically include advanced traffic monitoring and threat detection capabilities, enabling them to respond quickly and efficiently to DDoS threats. They can absorb and disperse the huge volumes of traffic associated with DDoS attacks, ensuring that cloud services remain operational.

Proactive DDoS preparedness is key in effectively managing these risks. This involves implementing the right tools and technologies and developing comprehensive DDoS response plans. These plans should outline precise procedures for detecting, responding to, and recovering from DDoS attacks. They must include coordination mechanisms among stakeholders, such as cloud service providers, security teams, and network operators.

Traffic monitoring and anomaly detection are critical components of DDoS defense. Continuous monitoring of network traffic allows for the early detection of unusual traffic patterns or spikes that may indicate a DDoS attack. By leveraging anomaly detection technologies, organizations can quickly identify potential attacks and take immediate action to mitigate them.

Defending against DDoS attacks in the cloud requires a multifaceted approach that combines advanced technology solutions like CDNs and WAFs, cloud-based DDoS protection services, and proactive planning and response strategies. Through vigilant monitoring and rapid response, organizations can protect their cloud services from the disruptive and damaging effects of DDoS attacks.

Intrusion Detection and Prevention Systems (IDS/IPS)

Intrusion detection and prevention systems (IDS/IPS) play a pivotal role in the security architecture of cloud environments. These systems are designed to detect and prevent unauthorized access and malicious activities in cloud networks. The role of IDS is to monitor network traffic for suspicious activities and alert administrators, while IPS actively takes steps to block these threats. Together, they form a critical line of defense, helping to maintain the integrity and security of cloud-based resources.

IDS and IPS solutions come in two main types: network-based and host-based. Network-based IDS/IPS monitor traffic across the entire network, identifying potential network threats. On the other hand, host-based systems are installed on individual servers or devices, providing more granular monitoring and protection at the machine level. Both types have unique advantages, and their choice often depends on specific security needs and the cloud environment's architecture.

The deployment strategies for IDS/IPS in the cloud are crucial for their effectiveness. One common approach is inline deployment, where the IDS/IPS is placed directly in the path of network traffic. This allows for real-time detection and prevention of threats but can introduce latency. Alternatively, out-of-band deployment involves placing the system outside the traffic flow and analyzing copies of data packets. While this reduces latency, it might not be as effective in real-time threat mitigation as inline deployment.

Cloud-native IDS/IPS solutions are specifically designed for cloud environments. These solutions are built to be scalable and flexible, aligning with the dynamic nature of cloud services. They can handle the vast amounts of data and rapidly changing network configurations typical in cloud systems. Cloud-native IDS/IPS also integrates seamlessly with other cloud services, providing more comprehensive and cohesive security coverage.

Regarding threat detection, IDS/IPS systems employ signature-based and behavioral detection methods. Signature-based detection uses known patterns or "signatures" of malicious activities to identify and block threats. This method is effective against recognized threats but can be limited in detecting new, unknown attacks. On the other hand, behavioral anomaly detection focuses on identifying unusual behavior or deviations from regular network activity, which could indicate a potential threat. This approach is instrumental in cloud networks, where the flexible and scalable nature of the cloud can result in rapidly changing network behaviors.

Recognizing known threats with signatures is a fundamental aspect of intrusion detection. IDS/IPS systems can quickly identify and respond to familiar attacks by maintaining and updating a database of known threat signatures. However, as new threats constantly emerge, relying solely on signature-based detection is not sufficient in the evolving threat landscape of cloud computing.

Behavioral anomaly detection in cloud networks adds a layer of security. This method involves establishing a baseline of normal network activities and continuously monitoring for deviations from this baseline. Anomalies could indicate potential security threats like data breaches or unauthorized access attempts. Behavioral detection is particularly effective in cloud environments, where traditional security perimeters are less defined and network traffic patterns are more fluid.

Intrusion detection and prevention in the cloud are vital components of a comprehensive cloud security strategy. IDS/IPS systems, whether network-based or host-based, provide essential protection against various threats. Effective deployment strategies and signature-based and behavioral detection methods ensure robust security in dynamic cloud environments. As cloud computing continues to evolve, so will the technologies and strategies for effective intrusion detection and prevention.

Secure Network Communication

Securing data in transit is a critical aspect of cloud security to protect data as it moves across the Internet or other networks. When data is in transit, it is potentially more vulnerable to interceptions and attacks, making its security a top priority for organizations leveraging cloud services.

The foundational security measures for protecting data in transit include Transport Layer Security (TLS) and Secure Sockets Layer (SSL) protocols. These protocols encrypt data as it is transmitted, ensuring it remains confidential and intact between the sender and the recipient.

VPNs (Virtual Private Networks) and encrypted tunnels are also key tools in securing data in transit. They create a secure and encrypted connection over a less secure network, typically the Internet. By routing data through these encrypted tunnels, VPNs ensure that data remains private and secure from potential eavesdropping or interception. This is especially important for remote workers or when accessing cloud services over unsecured networks.

Mutual authentication adds an extra layer of security in data transmission. The sending and receiving parties must verify each other's identities before initiating a data transfer. This process helps prevent man-in-the-middle attacks and ensures that data is only exchanged between authorized entities. Mutual authentication is often implemented with TLS/SSL protocols to provide a more comprehensive security approach.

Implementing secure API gateways is crucial in managing and securing data flow between software applications and services, particularly in cloud environments. API gateways act as intermediaries, receiving API requests, applying policies like rate limiting and access controls, and then routing these requests to the appropriate services. This control point helps in safeguarding APIs from malicious attacks and unauthorized access.

API security considerations extend beyond just the gateways. OAuth protocols and API key management are essential in authenticating and authorizing API transactions. OAuth provides a secure and efficient way for users to grant websites or applications access to their information on other websites without giving them passwords. API key management involves issuing and revoking keys to authenticate API clients, ensuring only authorized clients can access API services.

Rate limiting and access control are further measures to protect APIs and data in transit. Rate limiting controls the number of requests a user can make in a certain period, which helps mitigate denial-of-service attacks and ensures fair usage of APIs. Access control defines who can access what resources and operations in an API, limiting access to sensitive data.

Network monitoring and logging are essential for ensuring data security in transit. Real-time network traffic analysis allows organizations to monitor data flows for unusual or suspicious activity, enabling quick detection and response to potential threats. Log retention and analysis are equally important, as they provide historical data that can be used for forensic analysis in a security incident.

Incident detection through network logs involves analyzing log data to identify patterns or signs of malicious activities. Logs can provide invaluable insights into how a security incident occurred and the extent of its impact. This information is crucial for remediation and recovery efforts, improving security measures, and preventing future incidents.

Securing data in transit in cloud environments requires a multifaceted approach, combining encryption, secure protocols, VPNs, API security measures, and vigilant network monitoring. By implementing these strategies, organizations can ensure their data's confidentiality, integrity, and availability as it moves across different networks and platforms.

Zero Trust Network Architecture

The principles of Zero Trust represent a fundamental shift in the approach to cybersecurity, especially in cloud computing. The core philosophy of Zero Trust is encapsulated in the mantra "never trust, always verify." Unlike traditional security models that assume everything inside an organization's network can be trusted, Zero Trust operates under the assumption that trust is never given implicitly and must be continually earned, regardless of a user's location or network.

Micro-segmentation is critical to implementing Zero Trust and the principle of least privilege access. Micro-segmentation involves dividing the network into smaller, distinct zones, allowing organizations to tailor security settings to the specific needs of each segment and minimize lateral movement within the network. Least privilege access means giving users and devices the minimum access required to perform their functions, reducing the risk and impact of a potential breach.

Implementing Zero Trust in cloud environments requires a focus on identity-centric security. This approach emphasizes verifying the identity of users and devices seeking access to resources rather than merely focusing on securing the network's perimeter. This means incorporating robust identity verification methods and ensuring that security policies are consistently enforced, regardless of where the resources are hosted or accessed.

Continuous authentication and authorization are critical components of the Zero Trust model. Trust is not a one-time validation but a continuous process in this framework. This means regularly revalidating the credentials and permissions of users and devices to ensure they still meet the stringent security requirements set by the organization. This approach helps in quickly identifying and responding to potential security breaches.

The benefits of adopting a Zero Trust model are significant, particularly in reducing the attack surface available to potential intruders. Organizations can significantly mitigate the risk of unauthorized access and data breaches by enforcing strict access controls and verifying trust. However, the challenges of Zero Trust should not be underestimated. Implementing a Zero Trust Architecture can add complexity to the network and systems, potentially impacting user experience. Managing this complexity while maintaining a compelling user experience is crucial for successfully adopting Zero Trust principles.

In conclusion, Zero Trust represents a proactive and dynamic approach to security, particularly suited to the complexities of cloud computing. Its emphasis on never implicitly trusting and consistently verifying, combined with strategies like micro-segmentation and least privilege access, offers a robust framework for securing modern IT environments. While enhanced security benefits are clear, the complexity and user experience challenges need careful management to ensure a successful implementation.

Cloud Application Security

Cloud application security is an increasingly vital field in cybersecurity, primarily due to the unique challenges presented by cloud-based applications. These challenges stem from the cloud's inherent characteristics: its distributed nature, scalability, and the shared environment cloud services operate. Understanding and addressing these challenges is crucial, as cloud applications often handle sensitive data and are integral to the operations of many businesses.

The importance of cloud application security cannot be overstated. With the growing adoption of cloud services, vulnerabilities in cloud applications can have far-reaching consequences, including data breaches, compliance issues, and compromised business operations. Security in cloud applications varies depending on the cloud service model being used – Infrastructure as a Service (IaaS), Platform as a Service (PaaS), or Software as a Service (SaaS). Each model has different implications for application security, and understanding these nuances is key to implementing effective security measures.

A fundamental aspect of cloud application security is the shared responsibility model. This model delineates the security responsibilities of the cloud service provider and the customer. While providers are responsible for securing the infrastructure, customers must ensure the security of their applications and data. This model underscores the importance of a proactive approach to security in cloud-based applications.

Secure cloud software development is central to creating safe cloud applications. This involves adopting principles of secure coding specific to the cloud environment, where scalability, multitenancy, and integration with various cloud services are expected. The secure software development lifecycle (SDLC) for cloud applications ensures that security is a priority at every stage of development, from planning and design to deployment and maintenance. Threat modeling, which involves identifying potential security threats and vulnerabilities, is a key part of this process.

Secure code reviews and testing are critical in identifying and rectifying security issues before deploying applications. Additionally, integrating DevSecOps practices – where security is embedded within the development and operations processes – helps build more secure cloud applications. This approach encourages continuous security assessment and improvement, making it an essential strategy in cloud application development.

Web application security is another crucial area, particularly given the prevalence of web-based cloud applications. Common web application vulnerabilities, such as those listed in the OWASP Top Ten, must be addressed rigorously. Using Web Application Firewalls (WAFs) in the cloud provides an additional layer of protection, filtering, and monitoring of HTTP traffic to and from web applications to prevent attacks.

API security and authentication are also vital in cloud environments, as APIs are often used to interact with cloud services. Ensuring that APIs are secure and that only authenticated users can access them is essential for protecting the integrity of cloud applications. Similarly, serverless web application security is an emerging area of focus, with unique security considerations due to the serverless computing model's stateless and ephemeral nature.

Container and serverless security are integral to cloud application security. Securing containers involves ensuring that container images are free from vulnerabilities, which can be achieved through best practices like regular container image scanning. Serverless computing presents security challenges, requiring a different approach to traditional application security. Implementing security in serverless architectures involves careful planning and using specific tools and practices designed for these environments, such as monitoring and logging for serverless applications.

Cloud-native application security is about building applications in the cloud with security as a foundational element. This includes considerations for microservices security, where each microservice has its security requirements. Service mesh and sidecar proxies can enhance security in microservices architectures. Additionally, the concept of immutable infrastructure, where resources are not modified after deployment, offers security benefits by reducing the attack surface.

Finally, implementing a Zero Trust Architecture in cloud-native applications ensures that trust is never assumed and must always be verified, regardless of where the request originates or what resource it accesses. This approach is particularly well-suited to cloud environments' dynamic and distributed nature.

Securing cloud applications requires a comprehensive and multifaceted approach. It involves understanding the unique challenges of the cloud, adhering to the shared responsibility model, and implementing best practices throughout the software development lifecycle. Organizations can effectively safeguard their cloud applications against security threats with the right strategies and tools.

Cloud Security Monitoring and Incident Response

Cloud security monitoring and incident response are critical components of a comprehensive cloud security strategy. They involve the continuous surveillance of cloud environments and the prompt handling of security incidents. Real-time monitoring in the cloud is essential due to cloud services' dynamic and scalable nature, which can complicate the detection of security threats. Prompt and effective monitoring allows for the early detection of potential security incidents, minimizing their impact.

The challenges in monitoring and incident response in cloud environments stem from the complexity and heterogeneity of cloud architectures. Additionally, the shared responsibility model in cloud computing implies that cloud service providers and customers play a role in incident handling. While providers are typically responsible for the security of the cloud infrastructure, customers must secure their data and applications on the cloud.

The incident response lifecycle in the cloud follows a structured process, including preparation, detection, analysis, containment, eradication, recovery, and post-incident activities. Security Information and Event Management (SIEM) systems are vital in this lifecycle, providing a holistic view of security events across cloud environments. SIEM solutions in the cloud aggregate and analyze log data, helping in the early detection of security incidents and providing actionable insights.

Log collection and analysis are fundamental to SIEM operations in the cloud. This involves gathering logs from various cloud resources and services and then analyzing them for signs of suspicious activities. Correlation and alerting capabilities in cloud SIEM systems enable the identification of patterns that might indicate a security breach, triggering alerts for further investigation.

Best practices for cloud SIEM include integrating cloud services with the SIEM system ensuring comprehensive coverage of all cloud assets. This integration is crucial for maintaining visibility and control over security events across diverse cloud services and platforms.

Cloud security analytics take the capabilities of SIEM a step further by incorporating advanced techniques like behavioral analytics and anomaly detection. Behavioral analytics focuses on understanding standard patterns of user and entity behavior in cloud environments, allowing for the identification of deviations that might indicate a security threat. Anomaly detection in cloud traffic helps identify unusual patterns that could signify an attack.

Machine learning and AI for threat detection represent a significant advancement in cloud security. These technologies enable the automated identification of complex and evolving threats, enhancing the efficiency and effectiveness of security monitoring. User and Entity Behavior Analytics (UEBA) leverage these technologies to detect insider threats, compromised accounts, and other sophisticated attacks.

Predictive analytics in cloud security aim for proactive security measures, using data analysis to predict and mitigate potential security incidents. Regarding incident and response, cloud-specific threat detection techniques are essential, as cloud environments often present unique security challenges. Incident triage and prioritization help manage the response process effectively, ensuring that the most critical incidents are addressed first.

Containment and eradication strategies in the cloud focus on isolating affected systems and removing threats. Legal and compliance considerations are also crucial in cloud incident response, particularly in relation to data breaches and regulatory requirements. Learning from cloud incidents is vital for improving future response strategies and security postures.

Forensics and investigations in the cloud address the unique challenges of conducting digital investigations in cloud environments. Cloud forensics tools and techniques are tailored to navigate the complexities of cloud architectures, ensuring effective data recovery and preservation. Maintaining the chain of custody in digital evidence gathered from the cloud is crucial, particularly when preparing for legal proceedings.

Security incident playbooks for cloud environments provide structured response plans for different incidents. Creating cloud-specific incident response plans and developing playbooks for common scenarios ensure that organizations are prepared to respond quickly and effectively to security incidents. Automating incident response processes can significantly enhance the speed and efficiency of the response.

Cross-functional collaboration in incident response is essential, involving coordination between security teams, IT personnel, legal departments, and other relevant stakeholders. Continuous improvement of incident response processes through regular reviews and updates ensures organizations remain prepared to handle emerging threats and challenges in cloud environments.

Cloud security monitoring and incident response are dynamic and multifaceted processes, requiring advanced technology solutions, careful planning, and cross-functional collaboration. Organizations can effectively safeguard their cloud environments against various security threats by adopting a proactive and comprehensive approach to these processes.

Cloud Security Best Practices

Secure cloud architecture design is a critical aspect of cloud computing, ensuring that security is embedded into the fabric of the cloud environment. Employing Security by Design principles involves incorporating security elements from the initial stages of cloud architecture development. This approach ensures that security is not an afterthought but a fundamental architecture component. It involves thoroughly understanding the cloud environment's unique characteristics, including its distributed nature, scalability, and shared resources. By incorporating security from the ground up, organizations can build cloud architectures that are inherently more secure and resilient to threats.

Designing resilient architectures in the cloud involves creating systems that can withstand various failures and attacks without compromising data integrity or availability. This requires an in-depth defense strategy, where multiple layers of security controls are implemented at different levels of the architecture. These layers might include network security measures like firewalls and intrusion detection systems, application-level security controls like Identity and Access Management, and data encryption. Layered security controls ensure that if one layer is compromised, others continue to provide protection, significantly enhancing the overall security of the cloud environment.

Redundancy and failover planning are also integral to secure cloud architecture design. Redundancy refers to the duplication of critical components or functions of a system to increase the system's reliability, usually in the form of a backup or fail-safe. This might involve multiple applications running in different geographic locations or cloud zones in cloud environments, ensuring that if one instance fails, others can take over with minimal disruption. Failover planning involves defining how the system will transfer control to the redundant or backup systems in case of a failure, ensuring continuity of service.

Cloud-native security considerations focus on leveraging the inherent security advantages of cloud-native services, such as elasticity, scalability, and managed services. These services, offered by cloud providers, often come with built-in security features that can be effectively utilized to enhance the overall security posture. Security in microservices architectures, a typical pattern in cloud-native applications, involves securing each service and its communications. Container security is another crucial aspect involving securing the container runtime environments, the application code running within containers, and the orchestration tools that manage the containers.

Secure cloud architecture design requires a comprehensive approach incorporating security at every level from the ground up. By employing defense-in-depth strategies, ensuring redundancy and robust failover planning, and leveraging cloud-native security features, organizations can build cloud architectures that are resilient, secure, and capable of withstanding a variety of security challenges. This holistic approach to security is essential in today's increasingly complex and threat-prone digital landscape.

Security Automation and Orchestration

Security automation and orchestration have become integral components of modern cybersecurity strategies, especially in complex cloud environments. Automating security tasks is essential for efficiency and effectiveness, allowing organizations to identify and address vulnerabilities and threats swiftly. This includes continuous security scanning and remediation processes, where systems are regularly scanned for vulnerabilities, with automated tools implemented to patch or remediate these issues. This automation speeds up the response to potential threats and ensures a consistent and thorough approach to security.

Infrastructure as Code (IaC) is a key practice in automating cloud security. IaC allows the management and provisioning of infrastructure through machine-readable definition files rather than physical hardware configuration or interactive configuration tools. This approach enables the automation of security configurations and compliance settings, ensuring that security standards are consistently applied across all cloud resources. This systematic approach helps maintain a strong security posture and enables rapid scaling and adaptation of infrastructure while maintaining security controls.

Orchestration for rapid response is another crucial aspect of cloud security. It involves coordinating various automated tasks and security systems to respond to incidents efficiently. Automated incident response workflows play a significant role here, streamlining the process of detecting, analyzing, and responding to security incidents. Organizations can ensure a quick and coordinated response to threats by automating these workflows, minimizing potential damage.

Integrating Security Information and Event Management (SIEM) and Security Orchestration, Automation, and Response (SOAR) tools enhances security automation and orchestration. SIEM systems provide real-time analysis of security alerts generated by applications and network hardware, while SOAR tools bring together security orchestration, automated incident response, and interactive investigations. The integration of these tools enables a more streamlined and practical approach to security monitoring, threat detection, and incident response.

Continuous security improvement is an ongoing process in the realm of cloud security. Feedback loops are vital for enhancing security measures, where insights from security incidents and operations are used to refine and improve security strategies and tools. This approach ensures that security measures evolve in response to new threats and changing cloud environments.

Security metrics and performance monitoring are essential for evaluating the effectiveness of security automation and orchestration. By continuously monitoring these metrics, organizations can gauge the effectiveness of their security measures, identify areas for improvement, and ensure that their security posture aligns with their evolving needs and the changing threat landscape.

Security automation and orchestration streamline and enhance the effectiveness of cloud security. By automating key security tasks, implementing orchestration for rapid incident response, integrating advanced SIEM and SOAR tools, and continuously improving security practices through feedback and performance monitoring, organizations can maintain robust security in their cloud environments. This proactive and dynamic approach is key to addressing cloud security's complex and evolving challenges.

Disaster Recovery and Business Continuity

Disaster recovery and business continuity are pivotal components of an organization's overall risk management strategy, particularly in cloud environments. Cloud-based disaster recovery strategies offer a scalable and flexible approach to backing up critical data and ensuring business operations can continue during a disaster. These strategies often involve replicating and backing critical data to cloud environments, which can be geographically diverse, offering protection against localized physical disasters.

Failover and redundancy planning are integral to these strategies. Failover involves automatically switching to a standby database, server, or network if the primary system fails or is temporarily shut down for servicing. This ensures that services remain available even in the event of system failure. Redundancy planning goes hand in hand with failover, involving creating duplicate systems or components that can be activated if the primary ones fail. These measures are crucial in minimizing downtime and maintaining business operations.

Ensuring business continuity in the cloud requires a comprehensive approach focusing on technical solutions and organizational preparedness. Cloud service resilience and availability are critical factors to consider. This involves selecting cloud service providers with robust infrastructure and proven track records of high uptime and quick recovery capabilities. Additionally, it's important to have communication and collaboration tools that employees can use to continue working and stay connected during disruptions, regardless of their physical location.

Backup and redundancy planning in the cloud should be thorough and regularly tested. This involves backing up data and ensuring that applications, servers, and systems can be quickly restored and returned online during a disaster. These plans are regularly tested and updated to ensure they remain effective and aligned with the organization's evolving needs and technologies.

Data restoration procedures are a crucial part of disaster recovery plans. These procedures should be clear, well-documented, and tested to ensure rapid recovery during a disaster. The goal is to minimize data loss and restore critical functions quickly to reduce the impact on business operations.

Disaster recovery and business continuity in the cloud require a multifaceted approach that includes cloud-based data replication and backup, failover and redundancy planning, careful selection of cloud services for resilience and availability, and practical communication tools. Additionally, regular testing and updating of backup, redundancy, and data restoration procedures are essential to ensure rapid recovery and minimal disruption during a disaster. By implementing these strategies, organizations can protect their critical data and ensure continuous operation, even in unforeseen events.

Future Trends in Cloud Security

Emerging technologies in cloud security are shaping the future of how we protect cloud environments, introducing new concepts and strategies that are more adaptive and intelligent. Among these, Zero Trust Architecture (ZTA) stands out. ZTA is based on the principle of "never trust, always verify," a significant shift from traditional security models that operate on implicit trust within a network. Implementing ZTA in cloud environments involves rigorous identity verification, micro-segmentation, and continuous monitoring, ensuring that each access request is authenticated and authorized.

Artificial intelligence (AI) and machine learning (ML) are increasingly pivotal in cloud security. These technologies enable advanced threat detection and anomaly analysis by learning normal network behaviors and identifying deviations that may indicate a security threat. Predictive security analytics powered by AI and ML can anticipate potential security incidents before they occur, allowing for proactive threat mitigation.

Quantum computing presents both opportunities and threats in the field of cloud security. While it promises groundbreaking computational power, it poses significant risks to current encryption methods. The impact of quantum computing on encryption is profound, as it could render current cryptographic algorithms obsolete, exposing data to new vulnerabilities. In response, quantum-safe cryptography solutions are being developed, offering encryption that can withstand the computing power of quantum technology.

Cloud-native security focuses on protecting cloud-native technologies such as microservices and containers. Security for microservices and containers involves isolating and securing each application component independently. Service mesh and sidecar security offer additional layers of control and security, enabling secure communication between microservices and providing individualized security policies for each service.

Security automation and orchestration are becoming essential in managing the complexity of cloud security. This involves automating repetitive security tasks and orchestrating responses to security incidents. Continuous security improvement is key to this, where security systems are constantly updated and refined based on new threats and vulnerabilities. Automated incident response workflows allow for rapid and coordinated responses to security incidents, reducing the time and resources required to handle threats.

The landscape of cloud security is rapidly evolving with the adoption of emerging technologies like Zero Trust Architecture, AI and ML for threat detection, quantum-safe cryptography, and cloud-native security strategies. These technologies are reshaping how security is implemented in the cloud, offering more dynamic, intelligent, and practical solutions to protect against an ever-changing array of threats.

Edge and IoT Security in the Cloud

Edge and IoT (Internet of Things) security in the cloud is increasingly crucial as these technologies become more prevalent in our digital world. Edge computing brings computation and data storage closer to the location where it is needed, improving response times and saving bandwidth. IoT devices, ranging from simple sensors to complex machines, are often deployed at the edge, generating vast amounts of data. However, security challenges in edge and IoT deployments are significant, primarily due to these devices' distributed nature and vast scale. These devices operate in diverse and often untrusted environments, making them susceptible to various security threats, including physical tampering and remote cyber-attacks.

One of the primary challenges is the resource constraints in edge devices. Many IoT devices have limited processing power, memory, and storage, which can restrict the types of security measures that can be implemented directly on the devices. This limitation makes traditional security solutions, like comprehensive antivirus software or complex encryption algorithms, impractical for many edge devices. As a result, alternative approaches to security that are lightweight yet effective and can be deployed at scale must be developed.

Cloud-based edge security solutions address these challenges by providing centralized security management for distributed edge devices. By leveraging the cloud, security management can be scaled efficiently to handle thousands or even millions of edge devices, ensuring consistent security policies and practices across the entire network. Secure communication protocols are also vital in this context, as data often needs to be transmitted over potentially insecure networks. Protocols that ensure data integrity and confidentiality are crucial for protecting the data as it moves from edge devices to the cloud and back.

In the realm of IoT, device security is paramount. This includes ensuring that each IoT device can be securely authenticated and authorized to communicate with other devices and systems. Over-the-air (OTA) updates and patch management are critical for maintaining the security of IoT devices, allowing for timely updates and patches to fix vulnerabilities as they are discovered. Additionally, adherence to IoT security standards and frameworks is essential for establishing a baseline of security practices and protocols. These standards provide guidelines for IoT device manufacturers and users, helping to ensure that devices are not only secure but also interoperable with other systems and devices in the IoT ecosystem.

Securing edge and IoT deployments in the cloud is complex but crucial. Edge devices' distributed nature and resource constraints require innovative and scalable security solutions. Cloud-based security management, secure communication protocols, effective IoT device security measures, and adherence to established standards and frameworks are essential components of a robust edge and IoT security strategy. As the use of edge and IoT technologies grows, so will the importance of implementing effective security measures to protect these critical systems.

Ethical Hacking and Red Teaming in the Cloud

Ethical hacking and red teaming have become vital components in strengthening cloud security. These proactive security testing practices involve simulating real-world attacks to identify vulnerabilities and weaknesses in cloud environments before malicious actors can exploit them. Ethical hackers and red teams use the same tools and techniques as attackers to improve security rather than cause harm. This approach is particularly important in cloud environments where the shared infrastructure, dynamic nature, and vast scale present unique security challenges.

Vulnerability assessments and penetration testing are key elements of ethical hacking in the cloud. These activities involve systematically evaluating the cloud environment to identify security weaknesses, such as unpatched software, misconfigured services, or weak encryption protocols. Cloud configuration audits are also crucial, as they review and assess cloud services and infrastructure setup to ensure they adhere to best security practices and compliance standards. The goal is to identify and address vulnerabilities before attackers discover and exploit them.

Continuous security testing is essential in the rapidly evolving cloud landscape. Unlike traditional environments, where periodic assessments may suffice, cloud environments require ongoing evaluation due to their fluid and dynamic nature. This includes monitoring for new cloud-specific attack vectors, which can arise from the complex interplay of cloud services, APIs, and third-party integrations. Continuous testing helps ensure that security measures are effective against the latest threats and that any new vulnerabilities introduced through updates or changes are quickly identified and remediated.

The benefits of ethical hacking and red teaming in the cloud are manifold. Firstly, they significantly strengthen an organization's security posture by uncovering and helping to remediate vulnerabilities. This proactive approach to security helps build resilience against potential cyberattacks. Furthermore, these practices are invaluable in measuring the effectiveness of incident response mechanisms. By simulating real-life attack scenarios, organizations can evaluate how well their security teams respond to breaches, identify gaps in their response strategies, and improve their readiness to handle actual security incidents.

Ethical hacking and red teaming are crucial strategies in cloud security. By proactively identifying and addressing vulnerabilities, continuously testing security measures, and evaluating incident response effectiveness, organizations can significantly enhance their defense against the increasing threats in the cloud computing environment. These practices fortify the security infrastructure and foster a culture of continuous improvement and vigilance in cybersecurity.

Predictions for the Future of Cloud Security

The future of cloud security is poised to evolve in response to an ever-changing threat landscape and technological advancements. As attackers adapt their techniques, cloud security must also advance to counter these threats effectively. One significant concern is the rise of advanced persistent threats (APTs) in the cloud. APTs, characterized by their stealthy and continuous nature, pose a significant risk as they can infiltrate cloud systems and remain undetected for extended periods. The focus will likely shift toward more sophisticated detection and response mechanisms to combat these threats.

Integrating cloud security with DevOps practices and forming DevSecOps are vital trends. This approach embeds security into every stage of the software development lifecycle, promoting a culture where security is everyone's responsibility. Secure software supply chain practices will become increasingly important, ensuring that all software components, from development to deployment, are secure and free from vulnerabilities. This holistic approach to security will be crucial in preventing supply chain attacks and ensuring the integrity of cloud-based applications.

Regulatory and compliance changes are also expected to impact cloud security significantly. Evolving data privacy laws and the impact of geopolitical factors will necessitate more agile and adaptive security and compliance strategies. As regulations become more stringent and geographically varied, cloud service providers and users must ensure their practices align with the latest legal requirements. This could lead to development of more sophisticated compliance tools and services to help organizations navigate this complex landscape.

Security as a Service (SECaaS) is anticipated to grow, with more organizations outsourcing security functions to specialized cloud-native security services. This model offers the benefits of expert security management without requiring extensive in-house capabilities. It enables organizations to access various security services tailored to their needs, from threat intelligence to identity management.

The role of AI in cybersecurity will become more prominent, offering augmented threat detection and response capabilities. AI and machine learning can analyze vast amounts of data to identify patterns and anomalies that may indicate a security threat, enhancing the speed and accuracy of threat detection. The collaboration between human expertise and machine intelligence will be vital in developing more effective security strategies. This human-machine collaboration in security will leverage the strengths of both – the intuitive and creative problem-solving abilities of humans and the data-processing power of AI.

Advanced threats, the integration of security into DevOps practices, evolving regulatory landscapes, and the increasing adoption of SECaaS will characterize the future of cloud security. AI will play a significant role in augmenting threat detection and response capabilities, and the collaboration between human and machine intelligence will be crucial in developing effective security strategies. These changes will require organizations to be adaptable, vigilant, and proactive in their approach to cloud security.

Case Study: The Capital One Data Breach

The Capital One data breach, which occurred in March 2019, is a significant case study in cloud security. This incident exposed the personal information of over 100 million Capital One customers and applicants, making it one of the most significant breaches in the financial sector. The breach offers critical insights into cloud security vulnerabilities and the importance of robust security practices.

Capital One utilized Amazon Web Services (AWS) as its cloud service provider. The breach was orchestrated by a former AWS employee, who exploited a non-AWS misconfigured Web Application Firewall to gain unauthorized access to Capital One's data stored on AWS servers. The attacker was able to exploit a specific vulnerability known as a "Server-Side Request Forgery" (SSRF) attack, which allowed her to access information that should have been securely stored.

The data accessed included customers' personal information such as names, addresses, phone numbers, email addresses, dates of birth, and self-reported income. The breach also compromised sensitive financial information, including credit scores, limits, balances, payment history, and transaction data. About 140,000 Social Security numbers and 80,000 linked bank account numbers of secured credit card customers were also exposed.

This incident highlights several critical lessons in cloud security. Firstly, it underscores the criticality of proper configuration and security practices. A robust cloud platform like AWS requires meticulous configuration and regular security assessments to prevent such vulnerabilities. The breach also emphasizes the importance of monitoring and promptly responding to security alerts. Capital One was alerted to the breach by an external party rather than through its internal systems, indicating a potential gap in monitoring and response mechanisms.

Another significant aspect of this breach is the insider threat. The fact that the attacker was a former employee of the cloud service provider raised questions about employee access to sensitive data and the need for robust access controls and monitoring, even after an employee's tenure ends. This aspect of the breach demonstrates the importance of comprehensive security protocols encompassing technical measures and human elements, such as employee access rights and ongoing monitoring of those rights.

Capital One quickly fixed the vulnerability in response to the breach and began working with federal law enforcement. The company also committed to enhancing its cybersecurity measures and increasing investments in cloud security. This response highlights the need for swift action and transparency in the wake of security incidents and a commitment to continuous improvement in security practices.

The Capital One data breach is a stark reminder of the potential vulnerabilities in cloud environments and the need for comprehensive security strategies. This case study exemplifies the importance of regular security assessments, proper configuration, monitoring and response systems, and managing insider threats to prevent such breaches in the future.

Career Corner

Cloud security, an increasingly vital field within cybersecurity, focuses on protecting data and applications hosted in cloud environments from various threats. This specialization is essential in the era of widespread cloud adoption, offering a variety of career paths for those with the appropriate skills and a keen interest in cloud computing and security.

A prominent career in cloud security is that of a Cloud Security Engineer. Individuals in this role design and implement secure cloud-based environments. Their responsibilities include assessing the security needs of cloud infrastructures, designing and applying security measures to safeguard cloud services and data, and managing cloud security technologies. They play a crucial role in ensuring the integrity, confidentiality, and availability of data stored in the cloud.

Another critical position is that of a Cloud Security Analyst. These professionals monitor and evaluate cloud systems for potential vulnerabilities and threats. They conduct security assessments, risk analyses, and compliance audits to ensure cloud services meet security standards and best practices. Their expertise is vital in identifying and mitigating risks in cloud environments.

The role of a Cloud Security Architect is also significant. These individuals are responsible for designing an organization's cloud infrastructure framework with a strong focus on security. They work to create secure cloud architectures and strategies, integrating security at every level of cloud deployment and operations.

For those with a consulting perspective, a Cloud Security Consultant offers expert advice and solutions for cloud security issues. They work with organizations to assess cloud security needs, design security strategies, and assist in implementing effective cloud security measures.

Given cloud security's technical and dynamic nature, professionals in this field are encouraged to pursue relevant certifications. Certifications such as the Certified Information Systems Security Professional (CISSP), which includes cloud security in its curriculum, and the Certified Cloud Security Professional (CCSP), tailored explicitly for cloud security expertise, are highly regarded in the industry.

Other relevant certifications include the AWS Certified Security – Specialty, which focuses on security in Amazon Web Services, one of the leading cloud platforms. Similarly, the Microsoft Certified: Azure Security Engineer Associate and the Google Cloud Professional Cloud Security Engineer certifications are valuable for those specializing in Azure and Google Cloud Platform security.

In conclusion, a career in cloud security is both challenging and promising, offering a range of opportunities for specialization. From engineering and analyzing cloud security to architecting secure infrastructures and consulting on cloud security strategies, professionals in this field are essential for the secure operation and management of cloud environments. Continuous learning through certifications and staying abreast of the latest cloud security trends and technologies is crucial in this rapidly evolving field.

Chapter Questions

1. What is the primary benefit of cloud computing over traditional computing?

    A. Higher initial setup costs

    B. Physical data storage

    C. Flexible resources and rapid innovation

    D. Limited scalability

2. Which of the following is a core concept of cloud computing?

    A. Limited network access

    B. On-demand availability

    C. On-premises data storage

    D. Fixed resource pooling

3. What characterizes the public cloud deployment model?

   A. Restricted to a single organization

   B. Requires heavy infrastructure investment

   C. Hosted by third-party providers and shared among organizations

   D. Limited scalability and flexibility

4. Which cloud service model includes operating systems, middleware, and development tools?

   A. Infrastructure as a Service (IaaS)

   B. Platform as a Service (PaaS)

   C. Software as a Service (SaaS)

   D. Hardware as a Service (HaaS)

5. What is the main feature of the Software as a Service (SaaS) model?

   A. Providing virtual machines

   B. Delivering software over the Internet on a subscription basis

   C. Offering physical IT infrastructure

   D. Providing development tools for software creation

6. What was the primary vision of J.C.R. Licklider that laid the groundwork for cloud computing?

   A. Localized computing

   B. An intergalactic computer network

   C. Stand-alone servers

   D. Physical data storage solutions

7. What is a crucial characteristic of grid computing?

    A. Centralized data processing

    B. A form of distributed and parallel computing

    C. Exclusive use by single organizations

    D. Limited to on-premises infrastructure

8. Which cloud provider is known for its strong emphasis on hybrid cloud capabilities?

    A. Amazon Web Services (AWS)

    B. Microsoft Azure

    C. Google Cloud Platform (GCP)

    D. IBM Cloud

9. What is a primary concern when implementing cloud services, especially with growing reliance on them?

    A. Decreasing flexibility

    B. Data security and privacy

    C. Reduced scalability

    D. Increased operational costs

10. What is the customer responsible for in the cloud computing shared responsibility model?

    A. Securing the cloud infrastructure

    B. Managing the physical servers

    C. Securing their data within the cloud

    D. Maintaining the underlying hardware

11. What is the role of role-based access control (RBAC) in cloud security?

    A. Assigns users to specific roles and grants access based on those roles

    B. Manages the physical security of cloud data centers

    C. Encrypts data at rest

    D. Monitors network traffic

12. What is a critical component of data encryption in the cloud?

    A. Frequent data deletion

    B. Effective key management

    C. Using a single encryption algorithm

    D. Centralized data storage

13. What is the purpose of using Transport Layer Security (TLS) in cloud computing?

    A. To manage user identities

    B. To secure data during transmission

    C. To provide physical security for servers

    D. To store data in encrypted form

14. Which approach represents a fundamental shift in cybersecurity, particularly in cloud computing?

    A. Open Trust Architecture

    B. Zero Trust Architecture

    C. Complete Trust Architecture

    D. Limited Trust Architecture

15. What is the primary goal of ethical hacking and red teaming in cloud security?

    A. To simulate real-world attacks and identify vulnerabilities

    B. To decrease the efficiency of cloud services

    C. To focus on physical security breaches

    D. To reduce cloud service offerings

CHAPTER 9

Internet of Things (IoT) Security

The Internet of Things (IoT) represents a transformative concept in the digital era, fundamentally altering how we interact with the technological and physical worlds. At its core, IoT refers to the interconnected network of physical devices, vehicles, home appliances, and other items embedded with electronics, software, sensors, actuators, and connectivity, enabling these objects to connect, collect, and exchange data. This groundbreaking idea extends Internet connectivity beyond traditional devices like desktop and laptop computers, smartphones, and tablets to a diverse range of devices and everyday things that utilize embedded technology to communicate and interact with the external environment via the Internet.

IoT encompasses a wide variety of "smart" devices, from industrial machines that transmit data about the production process to sensors that track information about the natural environment. These devices use Internet protocols and modern analytic techniques to collect, send, and process data acquired from their environments. IoT applications connect devices across different sectors, including energy, health, transportation, and more, enabling sectors to work smarter. IoT is about creating a seamless integration between the physical and digital worlds. The data these devices collect and exchange are used to enhance efficiency, safety, and decision-making.

Dr. J. Edwards, *Mastering Cybersecurity*, https://doi.org/10.1007/979-8-8688-0297-3_9

The evolution of IoT is a chronicle of how technology has progressed from rudimentary sensors and actuators to sophisticated networks of interconnected devices capable of independent decision-making. The origins of IoT can be traced back to the early days of the Internet and the first connected device, a modified Coke machine, at Carnegie Mellon University in the early 1980s. Since then, technological advances, such as the reduction in size and cost of sensors and processors and the expansion of Internet connectivity, have enabled a wide range of devices to communicate and interact. Over the years, IoT has evolved from a novel concept to an integral part of our daily lives, transforming various sectors such as healthcare, agriculture, and manufacturing.

The applications of IoT are diverse and growing rapidly as technology advances. In smart homes, IoT technology can automate lighting, heating, and air conditioning, increasing comfort and reducing energy use. In healthcare, wearable devices monitor patients' vital signs in real time, providing critical data to healthcare providers. IoT-based smart farming systems can monitor crop and soil conditions in agriculture, optimizing water use and fertilizers. Industrial IoT (IIoT) revolutionizes manufacturing with sensors and automation, improving efficiency and safety. Additionally, IoT facilitates smart city initiatives, from improving traffic management to reducing energy consumption in buildings, thereby enhancing urban life.

Significance of IoT Security

The significance of IoT security cannot be overstated in today's interconnected digital landscape. As IoT devices increasingly permeate every aspect of our lives – from smart home devices to industrial control systems – the need for robust security measures becomes paramount. The fundamental challenge in IoT security lies in protecting a diverse array of devices, often with limited processing power and memory, from a growing range of cyber threats. Effective IoT security ensures the confidentiality, integrity, and availability of the data these devices collect and transmit while safeguarding the devices' functionality. This is crucial for protecting personal and corporate data and ensuring the safety and reliability of critical infrastructure and services.

The adoption of IoT technologies has been growing unprecedentedly, driven by advancements in sensor technology, wireless communications, and data analytics. This growth is evident across various sectors, including healthcare, where IoT devices monitor patient health; in smart cities, where sensors manage traffic flows and energy use; in agriculture, where IoT aids in precision farming; and in manufacturing, where IoT optimizes production processes. The proliferation of IoT devices transforms organizations' operations, offering new opportunities for innovation, efficiency, and customer engagement. However, this rapid expansion also brings challenges, particularly in managing and securing the vast amounts of data generated by these devices.

With the growing adoption of IoT, security risks and concerns have become increasingly prominent. IoT devices, often designed with convenience and functionality in mind rather than security, can present vulnerabilities that hackers may exploit. These vulnerabilities range from weak passwords and unsecured network services to outdated firmware and encryption. The risks are compounded by the scale and diversity of IoT devices, making it challenging to implement uniform security protocols. Moreover, the interconnected nature of IoT devices means that compromising one device can potentially lead to broader network breaches, making the entire ecosystem vulnerable. Therefore, understanding and mitigating these risks is crucial for the secure deployment of IoT technologies.

The impact of IoT security breaches can be far-reaching and devastating. A breach in an IoT system can lead to unauthorized access to sensitive personal and corporate data, disruption of critical services, and even physical harm in the case of connected medical devices or industrial control systems. For businesses, a security breach can result in significant financial losses, damage to reputation, and legal repercussions. On a larger scale, breaches in IoT infrastructure can affect public safety and national security. For instance, a compromised smart grid could lead to widespread power outages, while a breach in connected transportation systems could endanger lives. Therefore, understanding the potential impacts of IoT security breaches is essential for developing effective strategies to mitigate these risks.

IoT Fundamentals

The Internet of Things (IoT) ecosystem is a complex and dynamic network encompassing various technologies, devices, and systems. The IoT ecosystem is designed to capture, transmit, and process data from the physical world to enable smarter decision-making and automated actions. This ecosystem consists of interconnected devices equipped with sensors, actuators, and software, which communicate with each other and centralized systems over various networks. Integrating these elements allows for the seamless collection, exchange, and analysis of data, transforming it into meaningful and actionable insights. The IoT ecosystem is not just about the technology; it also involves the regulatory, social, and economic contexts within which these technologies operate and the security and privacy concerns that arise from such interconnected systems.

Devices, Sensors, and Actuators

Devices, sensors, and actuators are the fundamental building blocks of the IoT ecosystem. Devices in IoT can range from simple temperature sensors to complex industrial machines. Sensors collect data from the environment – such as temperature, humidity, pressure, or motion – providing a digital representation of physical phenomena. On the other hand, actuators are mechanisms that can change the state or position of a device or system based on the data received or commands given. They are essential for enabling IoT devices to interact with and affect the physical world. These devices, sensors, and actuators are usually equipped with microcontrollers and are designed to operate with low power consumption and minimal human intervention.

Communication Networks

Communication networks are crucial for the functioning of the IoT ecosystem, providing the backbone for data transfer among devices and between devices and central systems. These networks can vary greatly regarding range, bandwidth, and protocol. They include short-range wireless technologies like Bluetooth and Wi-Fi and long-range systems like LoRaWAN and cellular networks. The choice of communication technology depends on various factors, including the amount of data to be transmitted, the required transmission speed, energy consumption, and the environmental context. The evolution of communication networks, especially with the advent of 5G, is set to dramatically enhance the capabilities of IoT, enabling faster, more reliable, and more secure connections.

Cloud and Data Analytics

Cloud computing and data analytics are integral to the IoT ecosystem, providing the computational power and intelligence needed to process and make sense of the vast amounts of data generated by IoT devices. Cloud platforms offer scalable and flexible resources for storing, managing, and analyzing this data. They also provide the necessary infrastructure for deploying machine learning and artificial intelligence algorithms to extract valuable insights from IoT data. These insights range from simple notifications and alerts to complex predictive maintenance and decision-making processes. Integrating cloud computing and advanced analytics with IoT devices enhances operational efficiency and enables new services and business models.

Key Components of IoT

The Internet of Things (IoT) is an intricate system composed of several key components that work together to collect, transmit, and process data, enabling intelligent decision-making and automated actions. The primary components of IoT include sensors and actuators, edge devices, connectivity technologies, data processing platforms, and user interfaces. Sensors gather data from the environment, which is then processed by edge devices or sent to central systems for analysis. Connectivity technologies facilitate communication between devices and central systems, while data processing platforms, often in the cloud, analyze this data to extract actionable insights. Finally, user interfaces allow humans to interact with the IoT system, enabling monitoring and control. Each component plays a vital role, and their integration is essential for the effective functioning of an IoT system.

Edge devices in IoT are critical components that operate at the boundary between the physical world and the digital network. These devices, which include gateways, routers, and embedded PCs, are responsible for initial data processing, filtering, and analysis. By processing data locally, edge devices can reduce latency, decrease bandwidth usage, and enhance the responsiveness of IoT applications. They are especially important when real-time decision-making is crucial, such as autonomous vehicles or industrial automation. Edge computing also addresses privacy and security concerns by processing sensitive data locally rather than sending it across the network to a centralized cloud.

Connectivity technologies in IoT are diverse, each suited to different requirements in terms of range, bandwidth, power consumption, and security. Short-range wireless technologies like Bluetooth, Zigbee, and Wi-Fi are commonly used for home automation and consumer devices. For broader coverage, cellular networks, including 4G LTE and 5G, offer higher bandwidth and are ideal for mobile or geographically dispersed devices. Low-power wide area networks (LPWAN), such as LoRaWAN and NB-IoT, are designed for long-range communication with minimal power consumption, suitable for sensors and devices in remote locations. The choice of connectivity technology is crucial and depends on the specific needs of the IoT application, including range, data requirements, power constraints, and cost.

Data processing is a central element of the IoT ecosystem, involving collecting, storing, and analyzing data generated by IoT devices. This process begins with data aggregation and filtering at the device or edge level, followed by more complex processing and analysis, often in cloud-based systems. Advanced data processing techniques, including machine learning and artificial intelligence, are employed to identify patterns, make predictions, and provide insights. This processing can lead to actionable information, such as predictive maintenance alerts in industrial settings or personalized recommendations in consumer applications. Efficient and effective data processing is essential for deriving value from IoT systems, enabling smarter decisions, and automating responses to changing conditions.

IoT Applications and Use Cases

The applications and use cases of the Internet of Things (IoT) are incredibly diverse, touching virtually every aspect of our personal and professional lives. By enabling the connection and communication between devices and systems, IoT can make our environments smarter, more efficient, and more responsive to our needs. Key application areas include smart homes, industrial settings (IoT or IIoT), healthcare, wearables, smart cities, agriculture, and transportation. Each area leverages IoT to capture data from the environment, process it, and use it to automate tasks, improve efficiency, enhance safety, and provide previously inaccessible insights. The adaptability of IoT technologies allows them to be tailored to the specific needs of different sectors, offering customized solutions that can address a wide range of challenges and opportunities.

In smart homes, IoT technologies are revolutionizing how we interact with our living spaces. Smart home IoT devices include thermostats, lighting systems, security cameras, and voice assistants, all interconnected and often controllable via smartphones or other interfaces. These devices can learn from user behaviors to optimize heating, lighting, and energy consumption, increasing comfort and reducing utility costs. Security is another major application, with smart locks, cameras, and alarms providing enhanced safety measures. Integrating these devices into a cohesive system allows for a level of automation and personalization that was unimaginable just a few years ago.

Industrial IoT (IIoT) refers to the application of IoT technologies in manufacturing and industrial processes. In this sector, IoT devices monitor and optimize industrial operations, improve safety, and reduce operational costs. Key IoT technologies include sensors for tracking machine performance, production line monitoring systems, and automated quality control mechanisms. These technologies enable predictive maintenance, where potential issues are identified and addressed before they can cause downtime. IIoT also facilitates enhanced resource management, real-time data analysis for decision-making, and the integration of different parts of the supply chain into a cohesive and responsive whole.

IoT applications in healthcare profoundly impact patient care, hospital management, and health monitoring. Wearable devices like fitness trackers, heart rate monitors, and smartwatches collect real-time health data, providing valuable insights into an individual's health and wellness. This data can be used for personal health monitoring or shared with healthcare providers for more personalized care. IoT devices track patients' vital signs, manage medication delivery, and monitor hospital assets. These applications not only improve patient outcomes but also increase the efficiency of healthcare delivery. IoT in healthcare is a critical step toward more proactive and preventive health management, personalized medicine, and enhanced patient engagement.

The Growing Threat Landscape

The Internet of Things (IoT) expansion has been paralleled by a growing threat landscape, posing significant challenges to cybersecurity. With millions of devices connected to the Internet, each becomes a potential entry point for malicious actors. The diversity and ubiquity of IoT devices and their often limited security capabilities make them attractive targets for cybercriminals. These vulnerabilities can lead to many threats, from individual privacy breaches to large-scale attacks on critical infrastructure. The threat landscape is not static; it evolves continuously as new technologies emerge and attackers develop more sophisticated methods. This dynamic nature of threats necessitates ongoing vigilance and adaptation in IoT security strategies.

Cyberattacks on IoT devices have become increasingly common and sophisticated. These attacks exploit vulnerabilities in IoT devices to gain unauthorized access, disrupt functionality, or use compromised devices as part of larger botnets for coordinated attacks. Common types of cyberattacks on IoT devices include denial-of-service attacks, which overwhelm devices with data and render them inoperative, and man-in-the-middle attacks, where attackers intercept and manipulate transmitted data. These attacks can have serious consequences, mainly when they target critical infrastructure or systems essential for safety and security.

IoT devices often collect and transmit sensitive data, making them a prime target for data breaches. These breaches can result in the unauthorized access and misuse of personal information, leading to privacy violations and identity theft. Additionally, the interconnected nature of IoT devices means that a breach in one device can potentially expose data across the entire network. The accumulation of vast amounts of data, often without adequate security measures, exacerbates privacy concerns, highlighting the need for robust data protection and privacy policies in the IoT ecosystem.

The economic and safety implications of IoT security breaches can be profound. Economically, breaches can lead to significant financial losses due to intellectual property theft, costs associated with responding to the breach, and reputational damage. This can also translate to lost customer trust and potential legal liabilities for the business. From a safety perspective, attacks on IoT devices can have dire consequences, especially when they target critical systems like healthcare devices, industrial control systems, or transportation infrastructure. Such attacks can endanger human lives and cause substantial physical damage.

Common IoT Security Vulnerabilities

Common security vulnerabilities in IoT devices include inadequate authentication mechanisms, weak encryption, unpatched software, and lack of proper device management. Many IoT devices are released with default passwords or simple authentication methods, making them easy targets for unauthorized access. Weak or nonexistent data encryption in transit and at rest further exposes these devices to eavesdropping and data tampering. Additionally, many devices lack the capability or support to receive regular software updates, leaving known vulnerabilities unaddressed.

Inadequate authentication is a critical vulnerability in many IoT devices. Devices often come with default usernames and passwords that are easily guessable and widely known, presenting an easy target for attackers. Some devices do not implement robust authentication, allowing unrestricted access to sensitive functions. The lack of robust authentication mechanisms exposes devices to unauthorized control and access, which can be particularly dangerous when the devices have significant control over physical systems.

Weak encryption is another common issue in IoT security. Many IoT devices either do not encrypt data or use outdated or weak encryption standards. This vulnerability allows attackers to intercept, read, and manipulate sensitive data transmitted between devices and servers. Without strong encryption, the confidentiality and integrity of data are severely compromised, posing significant risks to user privacy and data security.

The absence of effective device management and maintenance is a significant security challenge in the IoT landscape. Many IoT devices cannot be remotely updated or patched, meaning known security vulnerabilities remain unaddressed. Without proper management, devices can continue to operate with outdated software, default configurations, and unpatched security flaws. This lack of ongoing management and maintenance makes IoT devices and networks susceptible to exploitation and attacks.

Principles of IoT Security

The confidentiality, integrity, and availability (CIA) triad forms the bedrock of cybersecurity principles, especially vital in IoT. Confidentiality ensures that sensitive data is kept secret and only accessible to those with authorized access. This is crucial in IoT, where devices often collect personal or commercially sensitive information. Integrity pertains to the accuracy and consistency of data across its lifecycle. In IoT systems, ensuring data integrity means that the data remains unaltered during transit and storage, providing reliable information for decision-making processes. Availability, the third pillar, guarantees that data and services are available to authorized users when needed. This is particularly important in IoT applications like healthcare monitoring or industrial automation, where system availability can be a matter of safety and operational continuity. The challenge in IoT security is to balance these three principles, often in devices with limited computational resources, to ensure a robust and resilient system.

Ensuring data privacy in IoT is a multifaceted challenge that involves protecting personal and sensitive data from unauthorized access and exploitation. As IoT devices permeate our personal and professional spaces, they often collect vast amounts of data, some of which can be highly personal, such as health metrics or household habits. Protecting this data involves complying with various privacy regulations like GDPR in Europe or CCPA in California, which dictate how data should be collected, stored, and used. Beyond legal compliance, ensuring data privacy also means implementing technical measures like strong encryption and access controls and fostering a culture of privacy awareness among users and developers. Privacy by design, where privacy considerations are integrated into the development process of IoT devices and systems, is increasingly becoming a standard approach in this field.

Data integrity assurance in the context of IoT goes beyond merely preventing unauthorized data alteration. It encompasses a range of practices and technologies designed to ensure that data remains accurate, reliable, and trustworthy throughout its lifecycle. In IoT systems, where decisions and actions are often automated based on sensor data, compromised data integrity can lead to erroneous decisions with potentially severe consequences. Techniques to ensure data integrity include cryptographic checksums and hashes to detect alterations, digital signatures for authentication, and robust error detection and correction algorithms. Regular audits and monitoring of data flows also play a crucial role in maintaining data integrity, especially in complex IoT ecosystems involving numerous devices and data streams.

Service continuity in IoT systems is critical, particularly in applications that support critical infrastructure, healthcare, or essential services. Ensuring service continuity involves designing resilient systems for failures, attacks, and natural disasters. This involves redundant hardware and network paths and resilient software architectures that can adapt and recover from disruptions. Disaster recovery planning and regular testing of backup systems and procedures are essential to ensure that services can be quickly restored after an outage. Furthermore, considering the potential impact of IoT service interruptions on safety, productivity, and user trust, service continuity planning must be an integral part of the IoT system design and operation.

Authentication and Authorization

In IoT, authentication and authorization ensure that only legitimate users and devices can access the network and perform actions within their rights. Authentication in IoT can be challenging due to the diverse range of devices and the potential limitations in their computational capabilities. Solutions range from traditional username-password setups to more sophisticated methods like biometric authentication or digital certificates. Once authenticated, authorization mechanisms determine what resources and actions the user or device can access and perform. This is where role-based access control (RBAC) and attribute-based access control (ABAC) models play a crucial role, defining permissions based on roles or attributes ensuring a principle of least privilege is maintained.

In the IoT ecosystem, ensuring the authenticity of user and device identities is paramount to maintaining system security. This involves robust identity verification mechanisms to prevent unauthorized access and potential malicious activities. For users, this might include multifactor authentication (MFA) that combines something they know (like a password), something they have (like a mobile device), and something they are (like a fingerprint). For devices, identity verification often involves unique identifiers and cryptographic methods. Securely managing these identities, particularly in large-scale IoT deployments with potentially millions of devices, requires comprehensive identity management systems that can handle registration, authentication, and authorization efficiently and securely.

Role-based access control (RBAC) is a widely adopted approach in IoT security that restricts system access to authorized users. It is an approach that assigns users and devices to certain roles, and each role is granted specific access rights and permissions. This model simplifies management and enhances security by ensuring that individuals or devices have access only to the information and functionality necessary for their roles. In IoT, where systems can be complex and multifaceted, RBAC helps streamline access control by grouping permissions into roles rather than assigning permissions to each user or device individually. This enhances security and improves scalability and ease of administration in large and diverse IoT environments.

Fine-grained permissions in IoT security refer to the detailed control over access rights and operational capabilities of users and devices within the network. Unlike broader permission sets, fine-grained permissions allow for a more nuanced and specific allocation of access, minimizing the risk of excessive privileges that attackers could exploit. This approach is critical in complex IoT systems where different devices and users may need particular access rights based on their functions. Implementing fine-grained permissions involves sophisticated access control mechanisms that can handle the intricacies of varying access needs, ensuring that each entity in the IoT ecosystem has precisely the access required for its role, no more, no less.

Encryption and Data Protection

Encryption plays a critical role in data protection within the IoT ecosystem. It involves encoding data so only authorized parties can decode and read it. In IoT, where devices often transmit sensitive data over potentially insecure networks, encryption helps protect against eavesdropping and unauthorized access. Data protection in IoT also involves securing data at rest (stored data) and in transit (data being transmitted). This requires using robust and current encryption standards and algorithms and ensuring that cryptographic keys are securely managed and protected. Effective encryption and data protection strategies are essential to maintaining the confidentiality and integrity of data in the IoT ecosystem.

End-to-end encryption is a security measure where data is encrypted on the sender's device and only decrypted on the receiver's device. In the context of IoT, this means that data remains encrypted as it travels through various networks and intermediaries, protecting it from interception and tampering. This is particularly important in IoT applications that handle sensitive data, such as healthcare monitoring or smart home systems. End-to-end encryption ensures that even if data is intercepted during transmission, it remains unreadable and secure. Implementing end-to-end encryption in IoT systems requires careful consideration of the computational capabilities of devices and the need for efficient encryption protocols that do not overly burden these devices.

Secure data storage in IoT protects data at rest from unauthorized access and breaches. This involves implementing robust access controls, encryption, and regular security audits. Data storage security is a critical aspect of IoT, as these devices often collect and store vast amounts of sensitive data, ranging from personal information to industrial operational data. Measures for securing data storage include encrypting the data before it is stored, ensuring that storage systems are regularly updated and patched, and implementing access control mechanisms to restrict data access to authorized personnel only. Regular security audits and vulnerability assessments can also help identify and mitigate potential security gaps in storage systems.

Secure data transmission in IoT is crucial for maintaining the confidentiality and integrity of data as it moves between devices and between devices and central systems. This includes using secure communication protocols like TLS/SSL, data encryption during transmission, and network security measures to protect against interception and attacks. Ensuring the security of data transmission in IoT is challenging due to the diversity of devices, their varying capabilities, and the types of networks involved. Nevertheless, it is essential for preventing data breaches and maintaining the trustworthiness of IoT systems.

IoT Device Security

IoT device security is critical, encompassing several layers of protection to safeguard devices from physical tampering, unauthorized access, and cyberattacks. It begins with secure hardware design, incorporating tamper-resistant chips and secure boot processes. Hardware Security Modules (HSMs) and secure element integration ensure cryptographic operations are performed securely. Device security also involves robust firmware and software security, including secure boot processes, regular firmware updates, and version control. Effective device identity management is another cornerstone, involving unique identification and using public and private keys and device certificates to ensure secure communication and authentication within the IoT ecosystem.

Secure boot and firmware updates are foundational to maintaining the integrity and security of IoT devices. A secure boot process ensures a device starts with verified and untampered software, preventing malicious code execution at startup. This process typically involves verifying the digital signature of the firmware to ensure it's from a trusted source. Over-the-air (OTA) updates allow devices to receive and install firmware updates remotely, ensuring they benefit from the latest security patches and feature enhancements. Implementing secure OTA updates is critical to protect against firmware tampering and to ensure that devices are not compromised during the update process.

The secure boot process is a critical security measure for IoT devices, ensuring they boot with verified and trusted software. It involves a series of checks during device startup to validate the integrity and authenticity of the firmware and software. This process typically relies on cryptographic techniques, such as digital signatures and hashing, to verify that the software has not been altered or tampered with since its original release. A secure boot process prevents rootkits, bootkits, and other low-level malware from compromising the device.

Over-the-air (OTA) updates are crucial to maintaining and enhancing IoT device security post deployment. These updates allow devices to receive new firmware and software remotely, eliminating the need for physical access to each device for upgrades. Secure OTA update mechanisms must include encryption to protect the update data in transit, authentication to ensure that updates come from a trusted source, and mechanisms to prevent or recover from failed updates. OTA updates address security vulnerabilities as they are discovered and enable enhancements in device functionality and performance.

Version control in IoT device management is crucial for tracking and managing the different versions of firmware and software that a device might run over its lifetime. Effective version control helps ensure that devices operate with the most up-to-date and secure software. It allows for the orderly deployment of updates, rollback of changes in case of issues, and auditing software versions for security compliance. In the context of IoT, where devices are often deployed in large numbers and remote locations, robust version control is essential for streamlined and secure device management.

Secure Hardware Design

Secure hardware design is fundamental to IoT device security, addressing vulnerabilities at the physical level. This includes the design of tamper-resistant and tamper-evident components, using Hardware Security

Modules (HSMs), and integrating secure elements for key storage and cryptographic operations. Secure hardware design aims to protect against physical attacks, such as side-channel attacks, and to provide a secure foundation for the device's overall security. This involves considering security at every stage of the hardware design process, from selecting components to the printed circuit board (PCB) layout.

Hardware Security Modules (HSMs) are dedicated hardware devices designed to securely manage, process, and store cryptographic keys and perform sensitive operations like encryption and digital signing. In the context of IoT, HSMs provide a secure enclave for cryptographic operations, protecting against physical and logical attacks. Their use is critical in scenarios where high-security assurance is required, such as in financial services or critical infrastructure. HSMs are designed to be tamper-resistant, ensuring that cryptographic keys and other sensitive data are protected even in a physical breach.

Secure element integration in IoT devices involves incorporating specialized chips to store sensitive information such as cryptographic keys and personal data securely. These secure elements provide a tamper-resistant environment, protecting stored data even if the device is compromised. They are commonly used in applications requiring high levels of security, such as payment systems or identity verification. Integrating secure elements into IoT devices helps safeguard against various attacks, including hardware tampering and unauthorized access to sensitive data.

Hardware-based cryptography in IoT devices involves performing cryptographic operations using dedicated hardware, offering enhanced security compared to software-based solutions. This approach uses specialized processors or chips designed for efficient and secure execution of cryptographic algorithms. Hardware-based cryptography provides better protection against certain types of attacks, such as side-channel attacks, and can offer improved performance for encryption, decryption, and key generation. The use of hardware-based cryptographic methods is essential in high-security applications and contributes significantly to the overall security posture of IoT devices.

Device Identity Management

Device identity management in IoT is a critical aspect of security, involving the management of identities assigned to each device within the network. This process includes creating, storing, distributing, and revoking identities. Unique device identification is critical, ensuring each device can be individually authenticated and authorized. Public and private keys, often managed through Public Key Infrastructure (PKI), are crucial in securing communications and verifying device identities. Additionally, using device certificates provides a means to establish trust among devices in the network, facilitating secure interactions and data exchange.

Unique device identification is a security measure in IoT that assigns a distinct identifier to each device in the network. This unique ID is crucial for accurately identifying, authenticating, and managing IoT devices. It enables administrators to track device configurations, monitor device behavior, enforce security policies, and manage access controls. Unique device identification is also essential for the secure onboarding of devices into the network. It plays a key role in the lifecycle management of IoT devices, from deployment to decommissioning.

Public and private keys are foundational to securing communications in the IoT ecosystem. These keys are part of asymmetric cryptography, where the public key is openly shared for encrypting messages or verifying digital signatures. In contrast, the private key is kept secret and used for decryption or signing. In IoT, this cryptographic approach is used for secure device authentication, ensuring that communications are encrypted and can only be decrypted by the intended recipient. Managing these keys securely, including protecting the private keys from unauthorized access and ensuring the authenticity of public keys, is critical for maintaining the security of IoT communications.

Device certificates in IoT are digital documents that use public key cryptography to verify the identity of a device. These certificates, issued by a trusted Certificate Authority (CA), bind a device's public key to its identity, providing a reliable way to authenticate devices within the network. Device certificates are crucial in establishing secure connections between IoT devices and between devices and servers. They are used in various security protocols, such as TLS/SSL, to ensure that the devices in communication are legitimate and trustworthy. Effective management of device certificates, including their issuance, renewal, and revocation, is vital for maintaining the security and integrity of IoT systems.

Network Architecture and Protocols

The network architecture and protocols in IoT are fundamental to IoT devices' efficient and secure communication. These architectures are designed to handle the unique challenges posed by IoT, such as large numbers of devices, varying data transmission rates, and diverse communication requirements. IoT network topologies, including star, mesh, and hybrid topologies, are selected based on specific application needs and can significantly impact the performance and scalability of IoT systems. Advanced computing architectures like edge computing and fog computing are employed to manage data processing closer to the data source, reducing latency and bandwidth usage. In terms of communication protocols, IoT utilizes a variety of protocols, including MQTT, Constrained Application Protocol (CoAP), and HTTP/HTTPS, each offering different features suited to various IoT applications. Network segmentation and isolation techniques, such as VLANs, subnetting, firewall rules, and micro-segmentation, are crucial for enhancing network security and managing traffic efficiently.

IoT Network Topologies

IoT network topologies are crucial in designing and implementing IoT systems, influencing their scalability, reliability, and efficiency. Different topologies offer varying advantages and are suited to different types of IoT applications. Star topology, where each device connects directly to a central hub, is simple and easy to manage but can become a bottleneck and a single point of failure. Mesh topology, in which devices connect directly, offers better reliability and range but can be more complex to manage. Hybrid topologies combine elements of both star and mesh topologies, aiming to leverage the advantages of each. The choice of topology depends on factors like network size, device capabilities, and application-specific requirements.

Star, mesh, and hybrid topologies are the primary network structures used in IoT deployments. In a star topology, all peripheral nodes (devices) are connected to a central node. This setup simplifies the network design and makes it easier to control and troubleshoot, but it can create a single point of failure. Mesh topology, conversely, allows devices to interconnect with multiple other devices, enhancing network resilience and extending coverage. However, mesh networks can become complex to manage as they scale. Hybrid topologies combine features of both star and mesh architectures, offering a balance between simplicity and robustness, and can be tailored to specific IoT use cases.

Edge computing architectures in IoT refer to computing done at or near the data source rather than relying solely on a central data processing warehouse. This approach reduces latency, saves bandwidth, and improves response times by processing data locally. Edge computing is particularly beneficial when real-time data processing is critical or connectivity to a central cloud is limited or unreliable. By leveraging edge computing, IoT systems can perform more efficiently, providing faster insights and actions based on the data collected by IoT devices.

Fog computing is a paradigm that extends cloud computing to the edge of the network, facilitating the operation of compute, storage, and networking services between end devices and cloud computing data centers. It is beneficial in IoT for managing data at the network level, offering a decentralized computing infrastructure that reduces the amount of data sent to the cloud for processing. Fog computing enables more efficient data processing, storage, and analysis, improving system performance and reducing latency in IoT applications.

IoT Communication Protocols

IoT communication protocols are rules and standards that define how IoT devices communicate and exchange data. These protocols must cater to the unique requirements of IoT, such as low power consumption, minimal bandwidth usage, and the ability to handle large numbers of connections. Protocols like MQTT, CoAP, and HTTP/HTTPS each have distinct characteristics that make them suitable for different IoT applications. MQTT is known for its lightweight and efficient pub/sub model, CoAP is designed for resource-constrained devices, and HTTP/HTTPS provides a familiar and widely used framework for data exchange, albeit with higher overhead.

MQTT (Message Queuing Telemetry Transport) is a lightweight messaging protocol for low-bandwidth, high-latency, or unreliable networks, common in IoT environments. It follows a publish-subscribe pattern, making it highly scalable and efficient for IoT applications that require minimal data packets and conserve battery life. MQTT is widely used in scenarios where a small code footprint is required or network bandwidth is at a premium, such as in home automation, industrial automation, and sensor networks.

CoAP (Constrained Application Protocol) is a web transfer protocol explicitly designed for use with constrained nodes and networks in IoT. It is similar to HTTP but optimized for IoT devices with limited processing capabilities and operating in low-power environments. CoAP supports RESTful API design and is particularly useful in M2M (machine-to-machine) environments, where minimal overhead and low power usage are crucial.

HTTP/HTTPS are well-established protocols in the Internet world and are also used in IoT for device-to-server communication. HTTP is a request-response protocol commonly used for transferring data over the Web. At the same time, HTTPS is the secure version of HTTP, using SSL/TLS to encrypt data for secure communication. In IoT, HTTP/HTTPS is often used for applications where existing web infrastructure and compatibility are essential, though they typically require more power and bandwidth than MQTT or CoAP.

Network Segmentation and Isolation

Network segmentation and isolation are essential to network security practices in IoT. They divide the network into smaller, distinct segments or subnetworks, each with access controls and policies. This helps limit the spread of attacks within the network, as each segment is isolated. Techniques like VLANs, subnetting, firewall rules, and micro-segmentation are used to implement network segmentation and isolation. These practices are crucial in IoT environments to manage traffic efficiently, reduce network congestion, and improve overall security.

VLANs (virtual local area networks) and subnetting are techniques to divide a more extensive network into smaller, segmented parts. VLANs allow for the creation of separate, isolated networks within the same physical infrastructure, enabling better control and security. Subnetting, on the other hand, divides an IP network into subnetworks, improving performance and organization. VLANs and subnetting are essential in managing and securing IoT networks, as they help separate IoT device traffic from other network traffic, reduce risks, and improve performance.

Firewall rules are fundamental to network security, a barrier between trusted and untrusted networks. In IoT, firewalls are used to control the traffic allowed into and out of the network based on a set of predefined security rules. These rules can be configured to permit or block specific types of traffic based on factors like IP addresses, port numbers, and protocols. Proper configuration of firewall rules is crucial in protecting IoT devices and networks from unauthorized access and cyberattacks.

Micro-segmentation is a security technique that involves dividing a network into smaller, more granular segments or zones, each with its security controls. In an IoT context, micro-segmentation allows for individual or groups of devices to be isolated, reducing the attack surface and limiting the potential impact of a breach. This approach is particularly practical in complex IoT environments, where devices with different security levels coexist. Micro-segmentation enables more precise security policy enforcement and better containment of threats within the network.

Secure Communication

Secure communication in IoT is crucial for protecting data integrity and confidentiality as it moves between devices, gateways, and servers. This involves implementing robust encryption standards, secure transport protocols, and authentication mechanisms. Techniques like TLS/SSL encryption, VPNs, and secure tunneling protocols ensure that data transmitted over networks is protected from interception and tampering. For application-level security, protocols like MQTT and CoAP incorporate security features to safeguard message exchanges. Access control, certificate-based authentication, and API security measures, including OAuth 2.0 authorization and rate limiting, ensure that only authorized entities can access and interact with IoT systems.

Data Encryption and Transport Security

Data encryption and transport security are fundamental to protecting data as it traverses networks in an IoT ecosystem. This involves encrypting data at rest and in transit to prevent unauthorized access and ensure confidentiality. Encryption transforms the data into a format that can only be read by someone with the key to decrypt it. Regarding transport security, protocols like TLS/SSL provide secure data transmission channels. This is particularly important in IoT, where sensitive data is often communicated over public or shared networks.

TLS (Transport Layer Security) and SSL (Secure Sockets Layer) are cryptographic protocols that provide secure communication over a computer network. In the context of IoT, TLS/SSL encryption is used to establish a secure channel between IoT devices and servers, protecting the data exchanged from eavesdropping, tampering, and message forgery. This is accomplished through asymmetric and symmetric encryption, ensuring that only the intended recipient can decrypt and read the transmitted data. TLS/SSL is a best practice for securing communications in IoT applications.

Virtual Private Networks (VPNs) are increasingly used in IoT to create secure connections over the Internet. VPNs for IoT ensure that data transmitted from devices to servers is encrypted and routed through a private network, shielding it from potential threats on public networks. This is particularly useful for remote IoT devices that transmit sensitive data over long distances. IoT deployments can benefit from enhanced security and greater control over network traffic and device access by using VPNs.

Secure tunneling protocols in IoT create a safe passage for data to travel across untrusted networks. These protocols encapsulate data packets, encrypting them to ensure their confidentiality and integrity during transit. This is essential for protecting data from potential interception and tampering, especially when it traverses shared or public networks. Protocols like IPSec and L2TP are commonly used to provide a secure tunnel for data transmission in IoT applications.

MQTT and CoAP Security

MQTT (Message Queuing Telemetry Transport) and CoAP (Constrained Application Protocol) are popular IoT protocols that have been enhanced with security features to protect data transmission. MQTT security can be enhanced using TLS for transport security, client authentication, and authorization controls. CoAP, designed for resource-constrained devices, supports DTLS (Datagram Transport Layer Security) for secure communication. Both protocols also include message authentication and integrity-checking provisions, ensuring that the data sent and received is from a legitimate source and has not been tampered with.

Message authentication in IoT is crucial for verifying that an authentic source has sent a message and has not been altered during transit. This is typically achieved using cryptographic techniques such as digital signatures or MAC (Message Authentication Codes). In the context of IoT, where devices often communicate sensitive data, message authentication ensures that the information exchanged between devices and servers is reliable and trustworthy.

Access control lists (ACLs) are used in IoT to specify which users or devices have permission to access or manipulate resources within a network. ACLs are fundamental to network security, providing a simple yet effective way to control traffic and prevent unauthorized access. By defining rules that allow or deny traffic based on various criteria, such as IP addresses or port numbers, ACLs help secure IoT ecosystems by ensuring that only authorized entities can access critical resources.

Certificate-based authentication is a robust security mechanism in IoT, utilizing digital certificates to authenticate devices and users. These certificates, issued by a trusted Certificate Authority (CA), serve as proof of identity and facilitate secure communication. In IoT systems, certificate-based authentication is particularly effective in ensuring the legitimacy of devices in the network, as it is more secure than traditional password-based methods and can be efficiently managed even in large-scale deployments.

API Security

API (Application Programming Interface) security is vital in IoT to protect the interfaces through which applications communicate. This involves securing the APIs from unauthorized access, attacks, and data breaches. Techniques to secure APIs include using HTTPS for encryption, implementing strong authentication and authorization controls, and validating input to prevent injections and other attacks. API security is crucial in maintaining the integrity and confidentiality of data exchanged between different components of an IoT system.

RESTful API security is essential in IoT, as many IoT devices and services communicate using REST-based APIs. Securing these APIs involves implementing measures such as HTTPS for encrypted communication, user authentication, and data validation. It also includes more specific protections like OAuth for authorization and JWT (JSON Web Tokens) for secure transmission of information between parties. Ensuring the security of RESTful APIs is critical to preventing unauthorized access and data breaches in IoT applications.

OAuth 2.0 is an authorization framework widely used in IoT for securing access to APIs. It allows users to grant third-party applications limited access to resources stored on another service without exposing their credentials. In IoT, OAuth 2.0 can be used to authorize devices and services to access specific resources or perform actions on behalf of a user. This framework is handy when IoT devices must securely interact with cloud services or other APIs.

Rate limiting and throttling are essential security measures in IoT to control the traffic a server accepts or a client sends. Rate limiting restricts the number of requests a user or device can make to an API in a given period, while throttling dynamically adjusts the traffic rate based on the server load. These practices prevent abuse of APIs, mitigate denial-of-service attacks, and ensure the availability of services even under high demand. Implementing rate limiting and throttling is crucial for maintaining the stability and reliability of IoT systems.

Cloud Services in IoT

Cloud services play a pivotal role in the Internet of Things (IoT) ecosystem, offering scalable, flexible, and powerful platforms for managing, processing, and analyzing vast amounts of data generated by IoT devices. These services encompass cloud-based IoT platforms, device management, data analytics, and robust security measures. Popular platforms like AWS IoT, Azure IoT, and Google Cloud IoT provide comprehensive suites of tools and services tailored for IoT applications. Critical aspects of utilizing cloud services in IoT include ensuring secure device management, implementing rigorous security protocols, managing identity and access, ensuring compliance with privacy regulations, and securing data storage and transmission.

Cloud-Based IoT Platforms

Cloud-based IoT platforms are integral to the IoT ecosystem, offering a centralized framework for connecting, monitoring, and managing IoT devices and data. These platforms provide essential services such as device registration, data collection, and real-time analytics. Major cloud providers like AWS IoT, Azure IoT, and Google Cloud IoT offer specialized IoT services that enable seamless integration of devices with cloud resources.

These platforms are designed to handle IoT deployments' scalability, heterogeneity, and communication requirements, facilitating efficient data processing, device management, and application development.

AWS IoT, Azure IoT, and Google Cloud IoT are leading cloud-based platforms that offer comprehensive services for IoT applications. AWS IoT provides a suite of services that support the secure, bidirectional communication of IoT devices with cloud applications. Azure IoT offers a range of tools for building and managing IoT solutions, including device provisioning, data processing, and analytics capabilities. Google Cloud IoT leverages Google's data analytics expertise, offering powerful data processing and machine learning tools for IoT data. Each platform has unique features and services, catering to different requirements and use cases in the IoT domain.

Device management in the cloud is a critical aspect of IoT, involving the configuration, monitoring, and maintenance of IoT devices at scale. Cloud-based IoT platforms provide tools for registering devices, tracking their status, performing remote updates, and managing device security. Effective device management in the cloud ensures IoT devices operate efficiently, securely, and reliably, even in large and complex deployments. This includes capabilities for over-the-air (OTA) updates, remote troubleshooting, and device lifecycle management.

Data analytics and insights in IoT are facilitated by cloud services, enabling the transformation of vast amounts of IoT data into actionable intelligence. Cloud platforms offer advanced analytics tools, including machine learning and artificial intelligence, to process and analyze data from IoT devices. These insights can drive decision-making, optimize operations, and enable new services and business models. Cloud-based analytics allows for real-time processing and predictive analytics, providing deep insights into device performance, user behavior, and environmental conditions.

Security Considerations in the Cloud

Security in cloud-based IoT solutions involves safeguarding data, protecting cloud resources, and ensuring the privacy and integrity of IoT operations. This includes strong encryption, robust access controls, and secure communication protocols. Cloud platforms must also manage the security challenges inherent in multitenant environments and ensure compliance with industry standards and regulations. Continuous monitoring and threat detection are essential to prevent, detect, and respond to potential security incidents in the cloud.

Identity and Access Management (IAM) in cloud-based IoT systems is crucial for controlling who can access what resources and actions they can perform. IAM involves managing user identities, assigning permissions, and enforcing policies that govern the authentication and authorization of users and devices. This ensures that only authorized personnel and devices can access specific cloud resources, enhancing security and compliance. IAM solutions often include features like multifactor authentication, role-based access control, and activity logging for audit purposes.

Cloud security groups are virtual firewalls that provide a layer of protection for cloud resources by controlling inbound and outbound traffic to IoT devices and services. These groups define rules that specify which traffic is allowed to and from devices and services based on criteria such as IP addresses, port numbers, and protocols. By using security groups, cloud environments can enforce network segmentation and isolation, reducing the risk of unauthorized access and lateral movement within the network.

Compliance and audit trails are essential in cloud-based IoT systems, ensuring adherence to legal, regulatory, and policy requirements. Cloud providers typically offer tools and services to help organizations meet compliance standards related to data protection, privacy, and industry-specific regulations. Audit trails record and monitor activities within the cloud environment, providing visibility into operations and changes and aiding in forensic investigations and compliance reporting.

Data Storage and Privacy

Data storage and privacy in cloud-based IoT systems involve securely storing and managing sensitive data while respecting user privacy. This includes implementing secure storage solutions, encrypting data at rest, and adhering to privacy regulations like GDPR or CCPA. Cloud providers offer various storage options, including databases and object storage, with security features to protect data integrity and confidentiality. Managing privacy involves carefully handling personal data, providing transparency to users, and ensuring control over their data.

Secure cloud storage solutions in IoT are designed to safely store and manage the vast amounts of data generated by IoT devices. These solutions offer data encryption, access control, and redundancy to ensure data integrity and availability. Secure cloud storage enables IoT applications to scale efficiently, accommodating growing data volumes while maintaining high levels of security and compliance.

Data encryption at rest is a security measure that involves encrypting data while it is stored, preventing unauthorized access, and ensuring confidentiality. In cloud-based IoT systems, encryption at rest is a fundamental practice to protect sensitive data from potential breaches and leaks. This includes encrypting data in databases, file systems, and other storage mediums, using robust encryption algorithms, and securely managing encryption keys.

Privacy regulations and compliance in cloud-based IoT systems involve adhering to laws and standards that govern data privacy and protection. This includes compliance with regulations like the General Data Protection Regulation (GDPR) in the European Union, the California Consumer Privacy Act (CCPA) in the United States, and other regional and industry-specific standards. Ensuring compliance requires implementing privacy-by-design principles, providing data subjects with control over their data, and maintaining transparency in data processing activities.

Backend Security

Backend security in the Internet of Things (IoT) is crucial for safeguarding the systems that manage, process, and store data from IoT devices. This encompasses secure API design, robust access control, secure data processing, and effective data management policies. Implementing API security best practices, such as input validation and rate limiting, is critical to protecting backend systems from attack vectors. Authentication mechanisms, including multifactor and token-based authentication, are fundamental in verifying user identities and controlling access. Secure data processing, which includes data validation, sanitization, and secure data pipelines, ensures that data is handled securely throughout its lifecycle. Data retention policies are critical in managing data storage and maintaining compliance with privacy regulations.

Secure API Design

Secure API design is vital in backend security, as APIs are often the primary interface for data exchange between IoT devices and backend systems. A secure API design involves implementing robust authentication, authorization, encryption, and data validation mechanisms. It also requires careful consideration of the API's architecture to minimize vulnerabilities, such as those outlined in the OWASP Top Ten for APIs. Secure API design protects against common threats, including unauthorized access, data breaches, and denial-of-service attacks.

API security best practices are essential for securing communication between IoT devices and backend servers. These include using HTTPS for encrypted data transmission, implementing strong authentication and authorization mechanisms, and regularly auditing and testing APIs for vulnerabilities. Input validation and sanitization are crucial to prevent injection attacks, while rate limiting and throttling help mitigate denial-of-service attacks. Following these best practices ensures that APIs remain secure and resilient against cyber threats.

Input validation and sanitization are critical security measures in backend systems, especially in APIs. These processes ensure that only properly formatted data is accepted and potentially harmful data is either rejected or cleaned. Input validation checks data against rules, like data type, length, and format, to ensure it meets the expected criteria. Sanitization modifies the input to remove or neutralize any malicious content. Together, these practices protect against input-based attacks, such as SQL injection and cross-site scripting (XSS).

API rate limiting is a critical security control that limits the number of requests a user or device can make to an API within a specific time frame. This is crucial for preventing abuse and overuse of APIs, which can lead to service outages or vulnerabilities to brute-force attacks. Rate limiting also helps manage resources effectively and ensure the API's availability for all legitimate users. Implementing rate limiting can involve setting global limits, per-user limits, or more sophisticated dynamic limits based on user behavior.

Access Control and Authentication

Access control and authentication are fundamental aspects of backend security, ensuring that only authorized users and devices can access backend systems and data. This involves verifying the identity of users or devices (authentication) and determining their access rights (authorization). Effective access control mechanisms prevent unauthorized access and limit the potential damage in case of compromised credentials.

User authentication in IoT backend systems verifies a user's identity to grant access to secured resources. Traditional username and password authentication can be supplemented with more secure methods like token-based or certificate-based authentication. Strong user authentication is crucial for protecting backend systems from unauthorized access and safeguarding sensitive data.

Multifactor authentication (MFA) adds a layer of security to user authentication processes. MFA requires users to provide two or more verification factors, significantly reducing the likelihood of unauthorized access. These factors can include something the user knows (like a password), something the user has (like a smartphone or a security token), and something the user is (like a fingerprint or facial recognition). MFA is essential in protecting access to backend systems in IoT, where sensitive data and critical functionalities are involved.

Token-based authentication is a secure method commonly used in IoT backend systems. It involves issuing a token upon successful authentication, which the user or device then presents to access the backend system. These tokens, often JSON Web Tokens (JWT), provide a secure and efficient authentication method and can include additional information, such as user roles and permissions. Token-based authentication is favored for its scalability and statelessness, making it suitable for distributed IoT environments.

Secure Data Processing

Secure data processing in IoT backend systems ensures that data is securely handled, processed, and stored. This includes implementing data validation and sanitization to protect against data corruption and injection attacks. Secure data pipelines ensure that data moves securely between different backend system components, maintaining data integrity and confidentiality. This is critical in IoT, where large volumes of data from various sources must be processed and analyzed securely.

Data validation and sanitization in backend systems are key to ensuring the integrity and security of the data handled by IoT applications. Validation involves checking incoming data for correctness, relevance, and security, ensuring it conforms to the expected format and content. Sanitization involves cleaning the data to remove any potentially malicious elements that could be used to exploit vulnerabilities in the system. Together, these processes help in protecting backend systems from various forms of data-centric attacks.

Secure data pipelines are essential for safely transporting and processing data in IoT backend systems. They involve implementing security measures at each stage of the data pipeline, from collection and transmission to processing and storage. This includes encrypting data in transit and at rest, performing regular security audits, and ensuring proper access controls are in place. Secure data pipelines help maintain data confidentiality, integrity, and availability throughout its lifecycle.

Data retention policies in IoT backend systems define how long data should be kept and when it should be disposed of. These policies are crucial for managing the vast amounts of data generated by IoT devices, ensuring compliance with legal and regulatory requirements, and protecting user privacy. Effective data retention policies balance the need for data for business or analytical purposes with privacy and security considerations, ensuring data is not kept longer than necessary and is securely deleted or anonymized when its retention period expires.

IoT Security Lifecycle

The IoT Security Lifecycle is a comprehensive approach to ensuring the security of IoT systems from inception through deployment and operation. It encompasses secure development practices, regular security testing and validation, and effective incident response and patch management. This lifecycle approach ensures that security is not an afterthought but an integral part of the IoT ecosystem, encompassing secure coding standards, rigorous code review and testing processes, secure development tools, and regular security assessments. Effective incident response and timely patch management are crucial for maintaining security throughout the device's operational life.

Secure Development Practices

Secure development practices are fundamental to the IoT Security Lifecycle, incorporating security considerations into the software development process. This approach emphasizes security from the early stages of design and development, reducing the likelihood of vulnerabilities in the final product. Secure development practices include threat modeling, risk assessment, and adherence to security best practices and standards throughout the development process.

Secure coding standards are guidelines and best practices for writing secure code. They are crucial in preventing common coding errors leading to security vulnerabilities. Adhering to secure coding standards helps developers avoid pitfalls such as buffer overflows, injection flaws, and insecure cryptographic practices. OWASP Top Ten and CERT Coding Standards provide comprehensive guidance for writing more secure code in various programming languages.

Code review and testing are critical components of secure software development, involving examining and testing source code to identify and fix security flaws. Code reviews can be conducted manually by peers or automatically using static analysis tools. Testing includes a range of techniques, from unit testing to integration and system testing, to ensure that security controls are adequate and that the application behaves as expected under various conditions, including attack scenarios.

Secure development tools are software applications that help developers identify and fix security vulnerabilities in their code. These tools include Static Application Security Testing (SAST) tools, which analyze source code for vulnerabilities; Dynamic Application Security Testing (DAST) tools, which test running applications; and dependency checkers, which identify security flaws in third-party libraries and components. Using these tools is integral to the secure development process, helping automate identifying security issues.

Security Testing and Validation

Security testing and validation involve systematically assessing an IoT system to ensure it meets security requirements and identifies vulnerabilities. This process includes various types of testing, such as penetration testing, vulnerability scanning, and security audits. The goal is to proactively uncover security weaknesses and address them before the system is deployed or before attackers can exploit them.

Penetration testing, or pen testing, is a simulated cyber attack against a system to check for exploitable vulnerabilities. In the context of IoT, pen testing involves attempting to breach various components of the IoT ecosystem, including devices, networks, and backend systems. This type of testing helps identify weaknesses in security defenses and provides insights into how an attacker could gain unauthorized access or cause harm.

Vulnerability scanning involves using automated tools to scan IoT systems for known vulnerabilities. These tools check devices, networks, and applications against databases of known vulnerabilities and provide reports on potential security issues. Regular vulnerability scanning is crucial for maintaining an up-to-date understanding of IoT systems' security posture and ensuring known vulnerabilities are identified and addressed promptly.

Security assessment tools are used to evaluate the security of IoT systems. These tools range from vulnerability scanners, which automate the process of finding known vulnerabilities, to more sophisticated tools that assess compliance with security standards, perform risk assessments, and help in threat modeling. These tools are essential to security testing and validation, providing a systematic approach to uncovering and mitigating potential security risks.

Incident Response and Patch Management

Incident response and patch management are crucial for dealing with security incidents and vulnerabilities in IoT systems. An effective incident response plan involves procedures for detecting, reporting, and responding to security incidents. This includes identifying the scope of the incident, containing the impact, eradicating the threat, and recovering from the incident. Patch management always updates systems and software to address known vulnerabilities, ensuring that IoT devices and software are protected against known threats.

Incident identification and reporting are the initial steps in the incident response process. This involves the detection of potential security incidents and their timely reporting to the appropriate personnel or incident response team. Effective incident identification relies on monitoring systems and tools to detect and alert suspicious activities. Reporting mechanisms should be straightforward and accessible, ensuring incidents are promptly and effectively communicated.

An incident response plan is a predefined set of procedures and guidelines for an organization to follow during a security incident. This plan should include roles, responsibilities, response procedures, communication protocols, and recovery strategies. A well-developed incident response plan enables an organization to respond quickly and effectively to security incidents, minimizing their impact and reducing the recovery time.

Timely patching and updates are essential for maintaining the security of IoT systems. This involves regularly updating software and firmware to patch known vulnerabilities, thereby protecting systems from exploitation by attackers. Effective patch management requires a process for tracking available updates, assessing their relevance and impact, and deploying them in a timely manner. This helps address specific vulnerabilities and maintains IoT systems' overall security and integrity.

AI and Machine Learning in IoT Security

Integrating artificial intelligence (AI) and machine learning (ML) in IoT security transforms how threats are detected, analyzed, and mitigated. These technologies enable more sophisticated and dynamic approaches to security, moving beyond traditional rule-based systems. AI and ML can analyze vast amounts of data generated by IoT devices, identify patterns, and detect anomalies that may indicate security threats. This includes real-time threat detection and prevention analysis, anomaly detection, behavior analysis, and predictive security measures. AI and ML's adaptive algorithms continually improve their effectiveness, learning from new data and evolving threat landscapes.

Threat Detection and Prevention

AI and ML are highly effective in threat detection and prevention within IoT ecosystems. By analyzing network traffic, user behavior, and device activity, these systems can identify potential security threats more quickly and accurately than traditional methods. AI algorithms can recognize patterns indicative of cyberattacks, such as distributed denial-of-service (DDoS) attacks or unauthorized access attempts, enabling proactive measures to prevent breaches before they occur.

Anomaly detection in IoT security involves using AI and ML to identify unusual patterns or activities that deviate from the norm and could indicate a security threat. This includes detecting abnormal device behavior, unusual network traffic, and other indicators of potential security incidents. By continuously monitoring for anomalies, AI and ML systems can quickly flag potential issues for further investigation, helping to catch novel or sophisticated attacks that might elude traditional detection methods.

319

Behavior analysis using AI and ML involves studying user and device behavior patterns to identify potential security risks. This can include analyzing how devices interact within the network and how users access resources. Deviations from these established patterns can be flagged for further investigation. This approach is beneficial in identifying insider threats or compromised devices behaving in unexpected ways.

Predictive security leverages AI and ML to forecast potential security incidents before they occur. By analyzing trends and patterns in data, AI models can predict where vulnerabilities are likely to be exploited and which types of attacks are probable. This forward-looking approach allows organizations to preemptively strengthen their defenses in areas most likely to be targeted, enhancing overall security posture.

Quantum Computing and Post-Quantum Cryptography

The advent of quantum computing presents both opportunities and challenges for IoT security. Quantum computers have the potential to break many of the cryptographic algorithms currently in use, posing a significant threat to IoT security. This has led to the development of post-quantum cryptography, which involves designing cryptographic algorithms that are secure against the capabilities of quantum computers.

Quantum computing poses a significant threat to traditional cryptographic systems used in IoT security. Like Shor's algorithm, quantum algorithms could decrypt many forms of encryption currently relied upon to secure data and communications. This poses a risk to IoT devices and networks, which often depend on encryption for secure data transmission and authentication.

Post-quantum cryptographic algorithms are being developed to secure communications against the threat posed by quantum computing. These algorithms are designed to be secure against the computational capabilities of quantum computers, ensuring the long-term security of data and communications. Research in this field is ongoing, with several algorithms being considered for standardization by organizations like the National Institute of Standards and Technology (NIST).

Preparing for quantum-safe IoT security involves anticipating the impact of quantum computing and transitioning to cryptographic methods that will remain secure in a post-quantum world. This includes keeping abreast of developments in post-quantum cryptography, assessing the quantum readiness of current security systems, and planning for the gradual implementation of quantum-resistant algorithms. Preparing for this transition is crucial for maintaining IoT ecosystems' long-term security and integrity.

Case Study: The Mirai Botnet Attack

In late 2016, the digital world witnessed one of the most significant distributed denial-of-service (DDoS) attacks, orchestrated using the Mirai botnet. This attack targeted systems operated by Dyn, a company providing Domain Name System (DNS) services to major websites. The attack's scale was unprecedented, and its impact was felt globally, as it disrupted access to popular websites, including Twitter, Netflix, and The New York Times. The attack was notable for its scale and method: it utilized a network of compromised Internet of Things (IoT) devices.

The Mirai botnet operated by infecting IoT devices with malware. These devices included unsecured Internet-connected cameras, DVRs, and routers. The malware exploited weak security using default usernames and passwords that the device owners never changed. Once infected, the attackers controlled these devices remotely, forming a large botnet – a network of infected machines that can be coordinated to execute attacks.

The attack was executed in waves, sending millions of requests to Dyn's servers, overwhelming them, and effectively disrupting their ability to direct users to various websites. This type of DDoS attack, known as a TCP connection flood, exploits the normal three-way handshake process of TCP/IP communications, creating massive incomplete connection requests that eventually overload the server.

The consequences of the Mirai botnet attack were far-reaching. Major websites experienced substantial downtime, leading to significant disruptions and financial losses. The attack highlighted the vulnerabilities inherent in many IoT devices and underscored the importance of securing these devices against potential threats. Moreover, it raised awareness about the potential for large-scale disruptions that could be caused by exploiting the increasing number of connected devices in homes and businesses.

In response to the attack, security teams at Dyn and affected companies worked diligently to mitigate the impact. The source code of the Mirai malware was eventually released publicly, ironically aiding security experts in understanding and combating the threat. The incident prompted many IoT device manufacturers to reevaluate and strengthen their security measures. It also increased consumer awareness about securing home and office networks.

The Mirai botnet attack was a wake-up call about the risks of unsecured IoT devices in the burgeoning age of Internet connectivity. It demonstrated that even seemingly innocuous devices could be harnessed for malicious purposes. The attack underscored the need for more vital security protocols in IoT devices, robust network infrastructure, and awareness of cybersecurity practices among users. It also highlighted the need for collective cybersecurity efforts involving manufacturers, consumers, service providers, and regulatory bodies to safeguard against such large-scale attacks in the future.

Career Corner

A career in the security of Internet of Things (IoT) devices is an exciting and rapidly growing field within cybersecurity, centered around protecting connected devices and networks in the IoT ecosystem from various cyber threats. This specialization is increasingly vital as the number of connected devices rises, expanding the potential attack surface for cyber threats.

One pivotal career in this area is that of an IoT Security Engineer. These professionals are responsible for designing and implementing security measures to protect IoT devices and networks. Their tasks include developing secure IoT frameworks, applying encryption techniques, and ensuring secure communication between devices and networks. Their role is crucial in preventing unauthorized access and protecting against potential security breaches in IoT systems.

Another essential position is the IoT Security Analyst. Individuals in this role focus on monitoring and assessing IoT systems for vulnerabilities and threats. They perform security audits, conduct risk assessments, and implement security policies and procedures to mitigate risks associated with IoT devices. Their work is critical to identifying potential weaknesses in IoT systems and preventing cyber attacks.

The role of an IoT Security Architect is also of great importance. These professionals are tasked with designing the overall security architecture for IoT systems. They develop strategies to integrate security into the IoT infrastructure from the ground up, ensuring that security considerations are embedded in the design and operation of IoT devices and networks.

For those interested in a broader perspective, an IoT Security Consultant provides expert advice on IoT security matters. They help organizations understand the unique security challenges of IoT systems and develop tailored strategies to address them. Consultants often assist in implementing and managing these security solutions, ensuring the organization's IoT ecosystem is robust and resilient against cyber threats.

In IoT security, pursuing relevant certifications can enhance one's expertise and career prospects. The Certified Information Systems Security Professional (CISSP) is a valuable certification for a broad understanding of cybersecurity, including aspects relevant to IoT. Additionally, specialized certifications like the Certified Internet of Things Practitioner (CIoTP) or the Certified IoT Security Practitioner (CIoTSP) can provide more focused knowledge and skills in IoT security.

In summary, a career in IoT device security offers a range of challenging and rewarding opportunities. From engineering and analyzing security for IoT systems to architecting and consulting on IoT security strategies, professionals in this field are crucial for safeguarding the increasingly connected world. Continual learning and staying current with emerging trends and technologies in IoT security are essential in this dynamic and fast-evolving field.

Chapter Questions

1. What is the primary goal of IoT?

   A. To improve device battery life

   B. To connect physical devices to the Internet

   C. To increase data storage capacity

   D. To replace traditional computing devices

2. What is a crucial feature of IoT devices?

   A. High processing power

   B. Large storage capacity

   C. Ability to connect and exchange data

   D. Use of only wired connections

3. Which of the following is a primary application of IoT technology?

    A. Gaming consoles

    B. Industrial automation

    C. Graphic design

    D. Video streaming

4. What does IoT security primarily aim to protect?

    A. Device color and design

    B. Confidentiality, integrity, and availability of data

    C. Battery life of devices

    D. The physical size of the devices

5. What is a common challenge in IoT security?

    A. High energy consumption

    B. Diverse range of devices with limited security

    C. Color variation in devices

    D. Limited range of device functionality

6. Which technology is vital in IoT for data processing and analysis?

    A. Mechanical gears

    B. Cloud computing

    C. Paper-based records

    D. Wired telegraph systems

7. What is the purpose of edge computing in IoT?

    A. To increase data storage on the device

    B. To reduce data processing time by processing data near
       the source

    C. To improve the physical appearance of devices

    D. To eliminate the need for sensors

8. What is a key feature of MQTT protocol in IoT?

    A. High graphics rendering

    B. Lightweight messaging

    C. Complex user interfaces

    D. High power consumption

9. What is the role of AI and ML in IoT security?

    A. To improve device aesthetics

    B. To predict fashion trends

    C. To detect and prevent threats

    D. To reduce device weight

10. What kind of threat does quantum computing pose
    to IoT security?

    A. Decreased device durability

    B. Breaking traditional cryptographic algorithms

    C. Reducing battery life

    D. Compromising device color schemes

11. Why is role-based access control important in IoT?

    A. To enhance device aesthetics

    B. To reduce manufacturing costs

    C. To control resource access based on user roles

    D. To increase battery life

12. What is the main benefit of secure boot in IoT devices?

    A. Enhancing device color quality

    B. Starting devices with verified and trusted software

    C. Increasing device size

    D. Improving entertainment features

13. What is the purpose of data encryption in IoT?

    A. To improve device flexibility

    B. To protect data confidentiality during transmission

    C. To enhance device aesthetics

    D. To increase data storage capacity

14. What is the significance of secure API design in IoT backend systems?

    A. To make the API visually appealing

    B. To protect against unauthorized data access

    C. To increase API weight

    D. To improve API entertainment value

15. Why is incident response planning crucial in IoT?

    A. To enhance device design

    B. To effectively address security incidents

    C. To reduce device manufacturing cost

    D. To improve device marketing strategies

CHAPTER 10

Digital Forensics

Digital forensics is a multidisciplinary field combining elements of law and computer science to collect and analyze data from computer systems, networks, wireless communications, and storage devices in a way that is admissible as evidence in a court of law. The scope of digital forensics has grown to include a broad range of devices and data types, from computers to smartphones and from emails to digital documents. This area of expertise is critical in criminal and civil contexts, where digital evidence can be crucial. It involves not only the extraction of data from digital devices but also the interpretation of this data, understanding its relevance to an investigation, and presenting it in a way understandable to nontechnical decision-makers.

What Are Digital Forensics?

Digital forensics, at its core, is the practice of uncovering and interpreting electronic data to preserve any evidence in its most authentic form. This practice involves using specialized techniques to retrieve information that may have been deleted, encrypted, or damaged. Digital forensics professionals work in various settings, from law enforcement to corporate environments, to analyze data breaches and cybercrime and conduct fraud investigations. The field encompasses a range of activities, including the identification, preservation, extraction, and documentation of computer evidence, as well as the analysis of network traffic and digital communications.

Dr. J. Edwards, *Mastering Cybersecurity*, https://doi.org/10.1007/979-8-8688-0297-3_10

The field of digital forensics has evolved significantly over the past decades, expanding its scope to keep pace with the rapid growth of digital technology. Initially focused primarily on computer crime, it now covers various digital devices and data sources. The evolution of this field has been driven by the increasing sophistication of both technology and cybercriminals. This growth has necessitated the development of more advanced forensic techniques and tools, expanding the skill set required of practitioners. Digital forensics now plays a crucial role in various scenarios, from criminal investigations to corporate litigation and national security.

In the modern digital age, the significance of digital forensics cannot be overstated. With the proliferation of digital devices and the immense volume of digital data generated daily, the need for digital forensic expertise is more prominent than ever. Digital evidence is now a cornerstone in criminal investigations, civil litigation, and corporate investigations. The ability to recover and analyze digital data can be decisive in solving crimes, understanding cyberattacks, and resolving disputes in court. The field's importance extends beyond law enforcement; it is vital in protecting organizations against data breaches and ensuring compliance with data protection regulations.

Historical Overview

Tracing the historical development of digital forensics reveals its roots in the increasing use of computers in the late 20th century. The field emerged as a response to the growing need to analyze data in computer systems and storage devices for legal purposes. Early efforts were often ad hoc, with investigators adapting existing technology tools for forensic purposes. As computers became more prevalent in society and criminal activities, the demand for structured digital forensic methodologies and dedicated forensic tools grew, leading to the establishment of digital forensics as a recognized discipline.

Several vital milestones mark the evolution of digital forensics. These include the development of the first standardized methodologies for digital evidence collection and analysis, creation of specialized software tools for data recovery and analysis, and the establishment of professional organizations dedicated to the field. Significant legal cases have also shaped the practice of digital forensics, setting precedents for how digital evidence is handled and interpreted in legal contexts. The expansion of the field to include mobile and network forensics represents another critical milestone, reflecting the changing nature of technology and crime.

The evolution of forensic tools and techniques has been a continuous process driven by the ever-changing landscape of technology and cybercrime. Early tools were often simple software programs designed to recover deleted files or to clone hard drives. Today, digital forensic tools are sophisticated systems capable of extracting data from various devices, including smartphones, cloud storage, and IoT devices. These tools have also become more user-friendly, allowing forensic practitioners to conduct more complex analyses more efficiently. Developing techniques for dealing with encrypted data, large datasets, and complex digital environments is ongoing, illustrating the field's constant adaptation to new challenges.

Influential cases in digital forensic history have often served as catalysts for change in the field. High-profile criminal cases where digital evidence played a key role have highlighted the need for standardized practices and robust forensic tools. Legal challenges to digital evidence have led to stricter evidence handling and analysis guidelines. These cases have shaped the technical aspects of the field and its legal and ethical framework, emphasizing the importance of maintaining the integrity of digital evidence throughout the investigative process.

Importance in Modern Technology

The importance of digital forensics in modern technology extends beyond criminal investigations. It is increasingly relevant in safeguarding corporate and national security. Businesses rely on digital forensic experts to investigate data breaches, insider threats, and fraud. Digital forensics helps uncover and mitigate cyber espionage and terrorism-related activities in national security. The field also plays a critical role in developing secure technologies, as understanding the methods used to compromise systems can inform better security practices.

Digital forensics has become integral to law enforcement and legal systems worldwide. Forensic experts work closely with law enforcement agencies to collect and analyze digital evidence for use in criminal investigations. In the courtroom, digital forensic evidence can be critical in proving or disproving allegations, making the role of the digital forensic expert vital in the judicial process. The field's principles and practices have been incorporated into legal frameworks, guiding how digital evidence is collected, preserved, and presented in court.

Digital forensics is increasingly relevant in the corporate sector as businesses face growing cyber threats. Companies employ digital forensic experts to investigate security incidents, such as data breaches and cyberattacks, to understand their cause and impact. These investigations help mitigate damage, identify security weaknesses, and improve overall cybersecurity posture. Digital forensics also ensures compliance with data protection and privacy regulations, making it an essential aspect of corporate governance.

Digital forensics has a significant impact on privacy and data security. As forensic techniques become more sophisticated, they raise important questions about balancing investigative needs and individual privacy rights. Digital forensic experts must navigate these issues, ensuring their methods are practical and respectful of legal and ethical boundaries. The field's advancements also enhance data security by exposing vulnerabilities and informing the development of more secure technologies.

Legal and Ethical Considerations

The legal framework and standards for digital forensics provide the foundation for how digital evidence is handled, analyzed, and presented in legal proceedings. These frameworks are crucial for ensuring that digital evidence is admissible in court and that the rights of individuals are protected. Standards cover a range of practices, including the collection, preservation, analysis, and documentation of digital evidence. They ensure that forensic procedures are consistent, reliable, and can withstand legal scrutiny. Developing these standards often involves collaboration between legal experts, law enforcement, and forensic professionals, reflecting the field's interdisciplinary nature.

The laws governing digital evidence vary by jurisdiction but generally include provisions for how digital data can be legally obtained, stored, and used in legal cases. These laws address the unique nature of digital data, such as its ease of duplication, alteration, and transmission. Key legal concepts include the chain of custody, data privacy, and the rights of individuals and organizations. Laws must continually adapt to keep pace with technological advancements, ensuring that they remain relevant and effective in regulating the use of digital evidence.

International standards and protocols are critical in digital forensics, especially when digital data often crosses international borders. These standards facilitate cooperation and consistency in handling digital evidence across countries and legal systems. They include guidelines for data collection, evidence preservation, and information sharing, considering different nations' diverse legal environments and privacy laws. International protocols also help combat transnational cybercrimes by providing a common framework for investigation and prosecution.

Compliance with legal requirements is fundamental in digital forensics. Forensic practitioners must ensure that their methods and practices adhere to relevant laws and regulations to maintain the admissibility and credibility of digital evidence. This compliance involves understanding and following procedures related to search and seizure, data privacy, and evidence handling. Failure to comply with these legal requirements can result in the exclusion of digital evidence in court proceedings or even legal repercussions for the forensic experts involved.

Ethical Challenges

Digital forensics practitioners face various ethical challenges in their work. These challenges include respecting the privacy and rights of individuals while conducting investigations, avoiding conflicts of interest, and maintaining professional integrity. Ethical guidelines in digital forensics help practitioners navigate these challenges, ensuring that they conduct their work in a manner that is not only legally compliant but also morally sound.

Balancing privacy and investigation is a key ethical challenge in digital forensics. Investigators must often access sensitive and personal data during work, raising concerns about individual privacy rights. The challenge lies in conducting thorough investigations while minimizing unnecessary invasions of privacy. This balance requires a clear understanding of legal boundaries and ethical principles and the application of minimally intrusive investigation techniques.

Digital forensic investigators frequently encounter ethical dilemmas, such as deciding how much data to collect, determining what constitutes relevant evidence, and dealing with privileged or personal information. These dilemmas require careful consideration and often involve weighing the investigative needs against ethical and legal constraints. Forensic professionals must make these decisions based on a solid understanding of ethical principles, legal requirements, and the potential impact of their actions.

Maintaining integrity and impartiality is essential in digital forensics. Investigators must conduct their work objectively, without bias or influence from external parties. This includes presenting findings honestly and accurately, regardless of whether they support the case of the prosecution or defense. Upholding these principles is crucial for maintaining the trust and credibility of the forensic process and its outcomes.

Privacy Issues

Privacy issues are at the forefront of digital forensics, particularly as the volume of personal data in digital form continues to grow. Forensic investigators must navigate various privacy laws and expectations, ensuring their practices do not infringe on individual rights. This includes obtaining proper authorization for data access and handling personal information with care and discretion.

Data protection laws, such as the General Data Protection Regulation (GDPR) in the European Union, significantly impact digital forensics. These laws regulate how personal data can be collected, used, and shared, with strict penalties for non-compliance. Digital forensic practitioners must be well-versed in these laws to ensure their investigative practices do not violate data protection regulations.

Encryption and anonymity present significant challenges in digital forensics. Criminals often use these techniques to hide illicit activities, making it difficult for investigators to access and analyze relevant data. Forensic experts must develop and employ advanced methods to deal with encrypted or anonymized data while ensuring these methods are legally and ethically sound.

Consent and authorization are critical in digital forensic investigations. In many cases, investigators must obtain consent from individuals or authorization from legal authorities before accessing and analyzing digital data. This requirement helps protect individual rights and ensures the investigation is conducted lawfully. Obtaining proper consent or authorization is a complex process that involves understanding the legal nuances of each case and the jurisdictions involved.

Digital Evidence

Digital evidence encompasses diverse data collected from electronic devices, which is crucial in modern investigations. This evidence includes but is not limited to emails, text and instant messages, digital documents, images, audio and video files, and social media interactions. Additionally, digital evidence can be derived from less conventional sources such as GPS data, Internet of Things (IoT) devices, cloud storage, and even metadata embedded in digital files. Each type of digital evidence has unique characteristics and requires specific methods for retrieval and analysis. The variety and complexity of these data types highlight the need for forensic experts to be versatile and knowledgeable across different technology platforms.

The realm of digital forensics deals with a vast array of data formats and sources, reflecting the complexity and diversity of the digital landscape. Data formats range from essential text files and images to complex database structures, encrypted files, and proprietary formats specific to particular software or devices. Sources of digital evidence are equally varied and include personal computers, smartphones, tablets, network servers, cloud services, and, increasingly, smart devices and wearables. Each format and source presents unique challenges in data extraction, preservation, and analysis, requiring forensic practitioners to have a deep understanding of various technologies and the ability to adapt to new and evolving digital environments.

In digital forensics, evidence is categorized into volatile and nonvolatile types, each with its own set of challenges for collection and analysis. Volatile evidence includes temporary data that can be lost when a device is powered down or reset, such as information in a computer's RAM or cache memory. Capturing this type of evidence requires timely and specialized techniques to ensure it is preserved before it disappears. On the other hand, nonvolatile evidence refers to data stored on permanent storage mediums, like hard drives, solid-state drives, and flash memory. This type of evidence is generally more stable but requires careful handling to avoid alteration or damage during the forensic process. Understanding the nature of volatile and nonvolatile evidence is crucial for forensic professionals to ensure comprehensive and effective evidence recovery.

Metadata and logs are foundational elements of digital evidence, often providing critical information in forensic investigations. Metadata, essentially data about other data, can include details like the creation date and time of a file, the author, modifications made, and, in the case of digital photographs, information about the camera used and the photograph's location. Logs, such as system logs, application logs, or security logs, record actions and events within a system or network, offering invaluable insights into user behaviors and system activities. Understanding and effectively analyzing metadata and logs can reveal much information, often providing key evidence in reconstructing events or understanding user actions.

Evidence Collection and Preservation

The collection and preservation of digital evidence are critical processes in digital forensics, requiring meticulous attention to detail and adherence to established protocols. The process involves methodically extracting data from various devices and ensuring it is preserved as close to its original form as possible. This includes protecting evidence from alteration, damage, or loss during the collection, transportation, and storage stages. Effective collection and preservation strategies are crucial for maintaining the integrity and reliability of digital evidence, which is essential for its admissibility and effectiveness in legal proceedings.

Adhering to standard procedures for evidence collection is essential in digital forensics to ensure the reliability and legality of the evidence. These procedures typically involve a systematic approach that includes careful planning and preparation, securing the necessary legal authorizations, using appropriate tools and techniques for data extraction, and ensuring that all potentially relevant data is captured. This process must be thorough and methodical, with each step carefully documented to maintain the integrity of the evidence. Following these standardized procedures is vital not only for the validity of the forensic investigation but also for the admissibility of the evidence in legal proceedings.

Ensuring the integrity of data in digital forensics is paramount. It involves confirming that digital evidence has remained unaltered from the point of collection to its analysis and eventual presentation in court. Forensic experts employ various techniques to safeguard data integrity, such as using cryptographic hash functions to create unique digital fingerprints of data. These fingerprints can be used to verify that the data has not been changed or tampered with at any stage of the forensic process. Maintaining data integrity is essential for the credibility of the forensic investigation and for the evidence to be considered valid in legal contexts.

Thorough documentation and reporting are fundamental aspects of the digital forensics process. This involves creating detailed and accurate records of all activities and observations made during the forensic investigation. Documentation should cover the entire process, from the initial receipt of the digital evidence to the final analysis and reporting. This recordkeeping is crucial for transparency, allowing for the verification of the forensic process and the findings. On the other hand, effective reporting is about communicating the investigation results clearly and concisely, often to audiences who may not have a technical background. This requires forensic professionals to be skilled in technical analysis and effectively understandably convey complex information.

Chain of Custody

The chain of custody in digital forensics is a critical concept that refers to the documentation of the evidence from the moment of collection to its presentation in court. This process involves meticulously recording every instance of the evidence's handling, transfer, examination, and storage. A proper chain of custody is crucial in establishing the authenticity and integrity of the evidence. It provides a documented trail that confirms that the evidence has been controlled, handled, and preserved to prevent tampering, substitution, or contamination.

The importance and purpose of maintaining a rigorous chain of custody in digital forensics cannot be overstated. It guarantees that the evidence presented in legal proceedings is the same as that collected initially and has been protected from tampering or contamination throughout the investigation process. A well-documented chain of custody is essential for establishing the credibility of the evidence in the eyes of the court and the involved parties. It assures the legal system and stakeholders that the evidence has been managed securely and consistently, upholding the principles of justice and due process.

Maintaining and documenting the chain of custody involves a comprehensive and secure process of logging all interactions with the evidence. This process includes recording details of each person who handled the evidence, the dates and times of transfers or examinations, and the purpose of each interaction. Secure storage and controlled access are vital to maintaining the chain of custody, ensuring that unauthorized personnel cannot access the evidence. This meticulous approach is critical for preserving the evidence's integrity and providing an unambiguous account of its handling throughout the investigative process.

Breaches in the chain of custody can have profound legal implications in digital forensics. If the chain's integrity is compromised, it can lead to challenges regarding the authenticity and reliability of the evidence. Such breaches can result in the evidence being deemed inadmissible in court or, at the very least, cast doubt on its validity, potentially undermining the outcome of the investigation or trial. Therefore, strict adherence to the chain of custody protocols is paramount to upholding the forensic process's credibility and the evidence's legal integrity.

Forensic Analysis Tools and Techniques

In digital forensics, a wide range of software and hardware tools are employed to assist in the investigation and analysis of digital evidence. Software tools are designed for various tasks such as data recovery, analysis of file systems, decryption, and network analysis. On the other hand, hardware tools include write blockers that prevent data alteration during analysis, forensic duplicators for creating exact copies of storage devices, and specialized devices for mobile and network forensics. The selection of appropriate tools depends on the specific requirements of the investigation, including the type of device being examined and the nature of the data involved. The effectiveness of these tools is critical in uncovering hidden or deleted data, decrypting encrypted files, and reconstructing fragmented data.

Forensic software encompasses a range of applications designed to investigate digital evidence. This software allows forensic experts to perform various tasks, from simple data retrieval to complex analysis and reporting. Standard features include creating disk images, recovering deleted files, analyzing file structures, and examining file metadata. More advanced forensic software can handle tasks like carving out data from unallocated disk space, decrypting files, and analyzing Internet and email histories. The versatility and power of forensic software make it an indispensable tool in the digital investigator's arsenal.

Essential hardware in digital forensics includes devices and tools that facilitate the examination and analysis of digital evidence. This hardware ranges from basic computer systems with forensic software to specialized equipment like forensic workstations, write blockers and hardware imagers. Forensic workstations are high-powered computers optimized for data processing and analysis. Write blockers are critical for preventing accidental data modification during forensic examination. Hardware imagers are used to create exact, sector-by-sector copies of storage devices. Mobile device forensic tools also extract data from smartphones and tablets, often requiring specialized connectors and software.

The debate between open source and commercial forensic tools centers on cost, support, functionality, and reliability. Open source tools are freely available and can be modified to suit specific needs, but they may lack the comprehensive support and regular updates provided by commercial products. While often more expensive, commercial tools typically offer a broader range of features, regular updates, and professional support. The choice between open source and commercial tools depends on the specific requirements of the forensic task, budget constraints, and the preference or policy of the forensic analysis organization.

Data Recovery and Analysis

Data recovery and analysis are fundamental aspects of digital forensics. This process involves retrieving data from digital storage devices, including data that may have been deleted, hidden, or damaged. The analysis then examines this data to extract meaningful information relevant to the investigation. Techniques employed in data recovery and analysis must be meticulous and robust to ensure the integrity of the evidence and the accuracy of its conclusions.

Techniques for data recovery in digital forensics are diverse and complex, tailored to the specific challenges presented by different types of data and storage devices. These techniques include file carving, which involves extracting files from raw data; slack space analysis, which retrieves data stored in the space between file clusters; and partition recovery, which accesses data from deleted or damaged disk partitions. Advanced recovery techniques may also repair corrupted files and reconstruct fragmented data, allowing forensic experts to recover initially inaccessible information.

Analyzing deleted, encrypted, or damaged files is challenging in digital forensics. Deleted file analysis involves retrieving files removed from the file system whose data remains on the storage medium. Encrypted file analysis requires decryption, which can be complex depending on the encryption method. Damaged file analysis involves repairing or reconstructing files that have been corrupted or partially overwritten. These tasks require a deep understanding of file systems, encryption algorithms, and data recovery techniques.

Data carving and reconstruction methods are crucial in digital forensics for recovering data from unallocated or damaged areas of storage devices. Data carving involves searching for data patterns or file signatures in raw disk space to extract or fragment files. Reconstruction methods are employed to piece together fragmented or partially overwritten files, often a painstaking process requiring specialized software. These methods are particularly useful in cases where file system metadata is absent or corrupted, allowing investigators to uncover hidden or seemingly lost evidence.

Network Forensics

Network forensics involves monitoring and analyzing computer network traffic for information gathering, legal evidence, or intrusion detection. This subfield of digital forensics focuses on identifying and responding to network-based threats, including hacking, denial-of-service attacks, and unauthorized data exfiltration. Techniques used in network forensics include capturing and analyzing network packets, examining network logs, and monitoring traffic in real time. Network forensic investigations often require specialized tools and expertise to interpret complex data.

Investigating network logs is a key component of network forensics. Network logs record various events and transactions, such as authentication attempts, connections to and from the network, and system errors or warnings. Analyzing these logs can provide valuable insights into network activities, identify anomalies or signs of malicious activity, and help reconstruct events for investigative purposes. Effective log analysis requires understanding network protocols, system architecture, and typical network usage patterns within an organization.

Tools for network analysis in digital forensics range from essential utilities for capturing and inspecting network traffic to more sophisticated systems for comprehensive network monitoring and intrusion detection. These tools allow forensic experts to capture real-time data traveling over a network, analyze packet contents, and trace the source and destination of network communications. Advanced tools can automate the detection of suspicious patterns, perform deep packet inspection, and provide visualizations of network interactions. These tools are essential for identifying breaches, unauthorized access, and other malicious activities within a network.

Identifying and tracing network attacks is a critical aspect of network forensics. This process involves analyzing network data to detect signs of intrusion, such as unusual traffic patterns, unauthorized access attempts, or the presence of malware. Tracing the source of an attack can be challenging, as attackers often use techniques to conceal their identity and location. Network forensic investigators use a combination of data analysis, knowledge of network protocols, and understanding of attack methodologies to trace the origin of attacks and their mechanisms. This information is crucial for resolving security incidents, improving network defenses, and preventing future attacks.

File Systems and Data Storage

Understanding file systems is crucial in digital forensics, as they dictate how data is stored, organized, and retrieved on a storage medium. A file system manages files and directories, maintaining the data structure stored on hard drives, SSDs, and other media. Different file systems have different structures and methods for managing data, affecting how forensic analysis is conducted. Knowledge of file system architecture, including metadata, file allocation tables, and directory structures, is essential for forensic experts to navigate, recover, and analyze data effectively. This understanding helps in piecing together deleted files, uncovering hidden data, and reconstructing file systems from corrupted or damaged storage media.

There are several types of file systems, each with its own set of features, structures, and use cases. Common file systems include NTFS (New Technology File System), used primarily in Windows environments; FAT (File Allocation Table) and exFAT, commonly found in removable storage devices; and EXT (Extended File System), used in Linux and Unix systems. Each file system has a unique way of organizing and managing files, which impacts how data is stored and retrieved. Understanding these differences is critical for forensic practitioners when conducting examinations, as the specific type of file system can significantly influence the approach and tools used for data recovery and analysis.

File system analysis techniques in digital forensics involve examining the structures and contents of a file system to extract and analyze data. This includes interpreting file metadata, analyzing file allocation tables, and examining directory structures. Forensic analysts use these techniques to locate hidden or deleted files, understand file access and modification patterns, and recover fragments. Advanced analysis may involve reconstructing damaged file systems or piecing together file fragments from unallocated space. Mastery of these techniques allows forensic experts to extract maximum information from a file system, which is often crucial in investigations.

File system artifacts are remnants of file activity crucial in digital forensic investigations. These artifacts include file slack (unused space at the end of a file), timestamps, log files, and file fragments left in unallocated space. Analyzing these artifacts can provide valuable insights into user actions, file usage, and system processes. For instance, timestamps can reveal when a file was created, modified, or accessed, while file slack can contain remnants of previously deleted data. Understanding and interpreting these artifacts is essential for forensic practitioners, who often hold key evidence in an investigation.

Storage Media Types

Various storage media types are encountered in digital forensics, each with its characteristics and challenges. Common media types include hard disk drives (HDDs), solid-state drives (SSDs), and flash memory devices like USB drives and memory cards. Each type of storage media has a different data storage and retrieval method, which affects how data is recovered and analyzed. HDDs store data magnetically on rotating platters, SSDs use integrated circuits, and flash memory relies on electronically programmable memory cells. Understanding these differences is essential for forensic analysts to effectively retrieve data from these devices.

Hard drives, SSDs, and flash memory are the most common types of storage media used in digital devices. Each has distinct characteristics that impact how data is stored and recovered. Hard drives store data on magnetic disks and have mechanical parts, making them susceptible to physical damage but more accessible to recover data from in some scenarios. SSDs, with no moving parts, are more durable but use complex algorithms for data storage, which can complicate data recovery. Flash memory, used in USB drives and SD cards, is similar to SSDs but has different wear-leveling and data management techniques. Forensic experts must adapt their approach depending on the type of storage media to recover and analyze data effectively.

Optical and magnetic media, such as CDs, DVDs, and magnetic tapes, are less common but still relevant in digital forensics. Optical media stores data by altering the physical properties of the disk, which a laser can read. Magnetic media, like tapes, store data magnetically and are often used for backup and archival purposes. These media types require specialized equipment and techniques for data extraction, and their physical nature makes them susceptible to damage and degradation over time.

Cloud storage and remote servers represent a modern and complex aspect of data storage relevant to digital forensics. Data stored on cloud services or remote servers is not physically accessible like data on a local device, presenting unique challenges for forensic analysis. This type of storage often involves encryption, multitenant environments, and jurisdictional issues, complicating the process of data acquisition and analysis. Understanding the architecture of cloud services and the legal considerations for accessing data stored remotely is essential for forensic practitioners working in today's interconnected digital environment.

Data Carving and File Recovery

Data carving and file recovery are key techniques in digital forensics used to retrieve data that is not readily accessible through standard file system analysis. Data carving involves searching for and reconstructing files based on known file signatures or patterns, often used to recover files from unallocated space or after file system corruption. File recovery techniques vary depending on the storage medium and the nature of the data loss, ranging from simple undeletion to complex reconstruction of fragmented or partially overwritten files. Mastery of these techniques enables forensic experts to recover vital data that might otherwise be considered lost.

The principles of data carving in digital forensics revolve around identifying and extracting data segments based on specific patterns or signatures without relying on file system metadata. This technique is particularly useful in recovering deleted files or extracting data from damaged or formatted storage media. Data carving requires a deep understanding of file formats and identifying file signatures amidst raw binary data. It is a time-consuming and often complex process, requiring sophisticated software tools and high expertise.

Various tools and techniques are employed in digital forensics for file recovery. These tools range from essential software for undeleting files to more advanced applications capable of reconstructing files from fragments scattered across a storage medium. Techniques include scanning for known file headers and footers, analyzing file fragments, and using algorithms to piece together partially overwritten files. The choice of tools and techniques depends on factors such as the file system type, the nature of the data loss, and the condition of the storage medium.

Recovering fragmented and overwritten data presents significant challenges in digital forensics. Fragmentation occurs when files are not stored in contiguous blocks, making recovery complex as pieces of the file are scattered across the storage medium. Overwritten data involves new data partially or fully replacing the original file data, complicating the recovery process. Dealing with these challenges requires advanced techniques and tools capable of piecing together file fragments and extracting usable information from partially overwritten files. These tasks demand high skill and expertise and a deep understanding of storage media behavior and file system mechanics.

Operating System Forensics

Windows forensics is a significant branch of digital forensics, focusing on the Microsoft Windows operating system, widely used in personal and corporate environments. Forensic analysis of Windows systems involves understanding the intricacies of its file systems (like NTFS and FAT), registry, system files, and artifacts. The Windows operating system produces rich data and artifacts crucial in investigations, including user activity, system logs, installed software, and network information. Effective Windows forensics requires a deep understanding of where and how Windows stores its data and the ability to interpret it to reconstruct user actions and system events.

Analyzing Windows file systems is a critical aspect of Windows forensics. The New Technology File System (NTFS) is commonly used in modern Windows installations. It contains complex features like file compression, encryption, and alternate data streams that can hide significant forensic data. Forensic investigators need to understand the allocation and structure of files and directories in NTFS and older file systems like FAT and exFAT. This analysis includes recovering deleted files, understanding ownership and permissions, and analyzing file metadata for forensic clues.

The Windows Registry is a crucial source of forensic information in Windows environments. It contains a wealth of data about the system configuration, installed software, user profiles, and system and network activity. Forensic analysis of the Windows Registry can reveal user account information, application settings, connected devices, and much more. Investigators must be adept at navigating and interpreting the complex and often voluminous data in the registry to extract relevant forensic information.

Recovering Windows artifacts and logs is an important part of Windows forensics. Windows operating systems produce artifacts, including temporary files, prefetch files, and system logs that record many system and user activities. Analyzing these artifacts can provide insights into user behavior, system usage, and potential security incidents. Logs, such as Event Logs, can be precious in reconstructing events and identifying irregular activities on a Windows system.

Linux and Unix Forensics

Linux and Unix forensics involves examining systems running on Linux or Unix-like operating systems, which are widely used in server environments and by tech-savvy users. These operating systems have different file systems (like ext3/4, XFS, and Btrfs), command histories, and log file structures compared to Windows. Forensic investigations in these environments require specialized knowledge of these systems' structures and behaviors and understanding of the tools and commands commonly used by Linux and Unix users.

Understanding Unix file systems and structure is vital in Linux and Unix forensics. File systems such as ext3/4, XFS, and Btrfs have unique features and store data in different formats than Windows files. Investigators must understand the allocation, management, and structure of these file systems. This includes knowledge of inode structures, journaling features, and methods of file storage, which are crucial for effective data recovery and analysis in Unix-like environments.

Analyzing Linux logs and artifacts is a key component of Linux and Unix forensics. Linux systems generate logs that record system events, user activities, and network connections. These logs, typically found in the /var/log directory, are valuable sources of forensic evidence. Additionally, artifacts such as bash history, cron jobs, and user-created scripts can provide insights into user behavior and system usage. Effectively analyzing these logs and artifacts can uncover crucial information about system configurations, user activities, and potential security incidents.

There are tools specifically designed for forensic analysis of Linux and Unix systems. These tools cater to the unique aspects of Linux and Unix environments, such as different file system structures, log formats, and command-line tools. Some forensic tools are open source and can be modified to suit specific investigative needs, while others are commercial products that provide a more integrated and user-friendly forensic solution. These tools help in data carving, log analysis, and recovery of deleted files specific to Linux and Unix file systems.

MacOS Forensics

MacOS forensics focuses on Apple's MacOS operating system, which is used widely in personal computing and creative industries. MacOS has unique aspects, and security features differentiate it from Windows and Linux systems. Forensic analysis of MacOS requires an understanding of its file system (like APFS and HFS+), system artifacts, and the nuances of MacOS security features. MacOS generates specific types of artifacts, such as plist files and Time Machine backups, which are valuable in forensic investigations.

MacOS has unique aspects that forensic investigators need to consider. This includes its proprietary file systems like HFS+ and the newer APFS, with features like space sharing, snapshots, and encryption. MacOS also integrates closely with other Apple products and services, such as iCloud, which can contain significant user data. Understanding these unique aspects is crucial for effectively analyzing MacOS systems in forensic investigations.

MacOS file systems, particularly the newer Apple File System (APFS), have unique characteristics important in forensic analysis. APFS is designed for SSDs and includes features like encryption, space efficiency, and snapshots, which can complicate forensic analysis. MacOS also incorporates various security features like FileVault for disk encryption and Gatekeeper for software security, which can affect how data is accessed and analyzed. Forensic experts must navigate these features to recover and analyze data on MacOS devices.

Recovering data from MacOS devices involves dealing with specific file system structures and backup mechanisms. Tools and techniques must be tailored to handle the intricacies of APFS and HFS+ and extract data from

MacOS-specific features like Time Machine backups. Additionally, dealing with encrypted volumes using FileVault requires specialized approaches to access and analyze the data. Effective data recovery from MacOS devices is essential for thorough forensic investigations in MacOS environments.

Mobile Device Forensics

Mobile device forensics presents unique challenges that distinguish it from traditional computer forensics. The primary challenges include the vast diversity of devices and operating systems, the frequent updates and changes in technology, and the compact and integrated nature of mobile hardware. Additionally, mobile devices often contain a mix of personal and professional data, raising complex privacy and ethical issues. The data on these devices is typically encrypted and protected by security features like passcodes, biometrics, and secure boot mechanisms, making forensic extraction difficult. Moreover, the constant connectivity of mobile devices means that data can be remotely wiped or altered, adding another layer of complexity to mobile forensic investigations.

The diversity of mobile devices and operating systems adds significant complexity to mobile forensics. There are numerous manufacturers, each with multiple device models running different versions of operating systems such as Android, iOS, and others. These variants may have unique hardware configurations, file systems, and security mechanisms. This diversity requires forensic professionals to have a broad and continually updated knowledge base and access to various tools capable of handling different devices and operating systems.

Modern mobile devices have robust encryption and security features to protect user data. This includes full-disk encryption, which renders data inaccessible without the correct passcode or biometric authentication, and sandboxing environments, particularly in iOS, which isolate applications and their data. These security features present significant hurdles in

351

forensic analysis, as accessing encrypted data can be challenging, if not impossible, without the proper tools or user credentials. Forensic experts must stay abreast of the latest advancements in decryption and data extraction techniques to overcome these challenges.

Legal and ethical considerations are paramount in mobile device forensics. The invasive nature of mobile forensic analysis, which can uncover a wealth of personal and sensitive information, requires strict adherence to legal protocols and ethical standards. This includes obtaining proper authorization, warrants, or consent before conducting forensic activity. Respecting user privacy, maintaining data integrity, and ensuring that the rights of individuals are not violated are crucial aspects of the forensic process. Forensic professionals must navigate these legal and ethical landscapes carefully to ensure that their investigations are effective and lawful.

Tools and Techniques for Mobile Analysis

Many tools and techniques are employed in mobile device forensics to overcome the challenges presented by diverse devices and robust security features. These include hardware and software tools designed to bypass security mechanisms and extract and analyze data from mobile devices. Tools vary in capabilities, with some specialized for specific device types or operating systems. Techniques for mobile forensics also evolve rapidly to keep pace with advancements in mobile technology and security.

Mobile forensic tools range from commercial products to open source solutions, offering different functionalities. Commercial tools often provide a more comprehensive and user-friendly interface with support for various devices and regular updates. Open source tools can be more flexible and customizable but may require more technical expertise. These tools bypass security locks, extract data from physical memory, analyze file systems, and recover deleted data.

Techniques for data extraction in mobile forensics include logical, physical, and cloud extraction methods. Logical extraction involves accessing and copying data through the device's standard communication protocols and interfaces. In contrast, physical extraction entails accessing the device's raw memory to recover all data, including deleted files. Cloud extraction is becoming increasingly important, as many mobile devices back up data to cloud services. Each method has its strengths and limitations, and the choice of technique depends on the case's specific requirements and the device's security features.

Analyzing app data and cloud storage is crucial to mobile device forensics. Mobile applications often store a wealth of user data, including messages, photos, and location history. Extracting and interpreting this data can provide valuable insights into user behavior and activities. Additionally, with the increasing integration of mobile devices with cloud services, forensic investigators frequently need to access and analyze data stored remotely. This requires technical capabilities and an understanding of the legal and jurisdictional issues of accessing cloud data.

Network and Cloud Forensics

Investigating network intrusions is critical to network forensics, focusing on identifying and analyzing unauthorized or malicious activities within a network. This process involves examining network traffic, logs, and system alerts to detect anomalies that indicate a security breach. Network forensic investigators use specialized tools and techniques to track the activities of intruders, understand their methods, and assess the impact of the intrusion. This investigation is crucial for mitigating ongoing threats, preventing future attacks, and providing evidence for legal proceedings.

Identifying signs of intrusion in network forensics involves detecting activities indicative of unauthorized access or malicious behavior. These signs can include unusual outbound traffic, spikes in data transmission, unrecognized user accounts, and alerts from intrusion detection systems. Investigators must be skilled in interpreting these signs, often found in detailed logs and network data, to promptly identify and respond to potential security breaches. This process requires a thorough understanding of normal network behaviors to distinguish between benign anomalies and genuine threats.

Analyzing network traffic and logs is fundamental in network forensics. Traffic analysis involves examining the data packets moving through the network to identify suspicious patterns or anomalies. Log analysis reviews the records generated by network devices, servers, and applications, providing insights into system operations and user activities. Effective analysis helps reconstruct the events leading up to and following a security incident, making it an invaluable tool in network intrusion investigations.

Cloud Storage and Services

Cloud storage and services have become integral to modern computing, offering scalable and flexible data storage and processing solutions. However, using cloud services introduces specific challenges and complexities in forensic investigations. Data in cloud environments is stored on remote servers, often distributed across multiple jurisdictions, and managed by third-party service providers. This arrangement can complicate identifying, acquiring, and analyzing digital evidence.

Cloud forensics faces several challenges, including the dynamic nature of cloud environments, the lack of physical control over storage infrastructure, and the dependence on cloud service providers for data access. Cloud services' scalable and elastic properties mean data can be rapidly moved, modified, or deleted, complicating the forensic process. Additionally, multitenancy in cloud environments raises concerns about data privacy and the potential for cross-contamination of evidence.

Forensic approaches to cloud environments require adapting traditional digital forensic methods to the cloud's virtualized and distributed nature. This includes developing strategies for remote data acquisition, ensuring the integrity of collected data, and navigating the legal and technical complexities of working with cloud providers. Forensic practitioners must also use cloud-specific tools and techniques to extract and analyze data from cloud services while maintaining the chain of custody.

Analyzing data from cloud services involves technical expertise and understanding the cloud service models (IaaS, PaaS, SaaS) and their respective data management practices. Investigators need to know how to access and interpret logs provided by cloud services, including user access logs, transaction logs, and system operation logs. Practical analysis requires collaboration with cloud service providers and understanding the legal frameworks governing data access and privacy.

Legal and Technical Challenges in Cloud Forensics

Cloud forensics is fraught with legal and technical challenges. Legally, jurisdictional boundaries, data sovereignty, and compliance with various data protection laws complicate acquiring and analyzing cloud data. Technically, cloud services' distributed and multitenant nature poses challenges in isolating and extracting relevant data without compromising other users' data. Navigating these challenges requires a blend of legal knowledge, technical expertise, and diplomatic skills to liaise with cloud providers and legal authorities.

Jurisdictional issues in cloud forensics arise because cloud data can be stored in multiple locations across the globe, often crossing international borders. Different countries have different laws and regulations regarding data access, privacy, and cybercrime, which can conflict or complicate forensic investigations. Determining which jurisdiction's laws apply, obtaining the necessary legal authorizations, and working with international entities are key challenges in cloud forensic investigations.

Data acquisition from cloud providers is a critical step in cloud forensics. This process often involves legal procedures, such as serving warrants or subpoenas, to compel cloud providers to release data. Forensic investigators must work closely with cloud providers to understand their data storage architectures and obtain the required data forensically soundly. This collaboration is essential to ensure the data acquired is relevant, complete, and admissible in legal proceedings.

Privacy and legal implications are at the forefront of cloud forensics. Investigators must balance the need to acquire potentially sensitive data with individuals' and organizations' legal requirements and privacy rights. Adhering to laws such as the General Data Protection Regulation (GDPR) in the European Union or the Electronic Communications Privacy Act (ECPA) in the United States is crucial. These laws govern the access and handling of data and impose strict penalties for violations, making compliance a critical concern in cloud forensic investigations.

Cryptocurrency and Blockchain Forensics

Understanding blockchain technology is essential in the realm of cryptocurrency and blockchain forensics. A blockchain is a decentralized, distributed ledger that records transactions across multiple computers in a way that makes it difficult to alter retroactively. This technology underpins most cryptocurrencies and has unique characteristics like immutability, transparency, and decentralization. Forensic experts focusing on blockchain and cryptocurrency must thoroughly understand how blockchains work, including mining, consensus algorithms, and smart contracts, to analyze transactions and trace digital assets effectively.

Basics of Blockchain and Cryptocurrencies

The basics of blockchain and cryptocurrencies involve understanding how digital transactions are conducted and recorded on a blockchain. Cryptocurrencies like Bitcoin, Ethereum, and others use blockchain technology to facilitate secure and transparent digital transactions. These transactions are verified and recorded in blocks linked together in a chain, creating a permanent and tamper-evident record. Each cryptocurrency operates on its underlying blockchain technology, with varying complexity and features. Understanding these fundamentals is crucial for forensic investigators to navigate the world of digital currencies and their associated transactions.

Blockchain technology plays a pivotal role in digital transactions, particularly in cryptocurrencies. It provides a secure and decentralized framework for conducting transactions without the need for traditional financial intermediaries. This decentralization is achieved through a network of nodes that validate and record transactions, ensuring the integrity and transparency of the transaction data. The role of blockchain in digital transactions has significant implications for forensic analysis, as it creates a public ledger that can be scrutinized for investigative purposes.

Forensic analysis of blockchain transactions involves examining the public ledger to trace the movement of digital assets and identify patterns that may indicate illicit activities. Each transaction on a blockchain is recorded with details such as the amount transferred, the public addresses of the sender and receiver, and the timestamp. Forensic experts use these details to track the flow of cryptocurrencies, identify links between different transactions and addresses, and uncover the identities of the parties involved in suspicious activities.

Investigating Cryptocurrency Transactions

Investigating cryptocurrency transactions requires a blend of technical expertise and investigative skills. Investigators analyze the transaction history on the blockchain to follow the trail of digital currencies, identify the parties involved, and uncover the purpose of the transactions. This process can be challenging due to the pseudonymous nature of cryptocurrencies, which can obscure the identity of the individuals behind the transactions.

Tracing Bitcoin and other altcoin transactions is a key aspect of cryptocurrency forensics. While transactions are publicly recorded on the blockchain, they are associated with digital addresses rather than personal identities. Tracing involves mapping these transactions to real-world identities, often correlating blockchain data with external information sources. This tracing can reveal patterns of money laundering, fraud, and other illicit activities conducted using cryptocurrencies.

There are specialized tools available for cryptocurrency analysis that aid forensic investigators in tracing transactions, analyzing patterns, and identifying links between different blockchain addresses. These tools can aggregate and visualize transaction data from various blockchains, making it easier to analyze complex networks of transactions. They often include features for tagging known addresses, clustering related addresses, and integrating off-chain intelligence.

One of the significant challenges in cryptocurrency forensics is the anonymity and encryption inherent in blockchain technology. Many cryptocurrencies offer varying degrees of anonymity, with some designed to obscure transaction details and user identities. Encryption further complicates forensic efforts, as it protects transaction details and wallet information. These challenges require advanced forensic techniques and collaboration with regulatory bodies and financial institutions.

Legal Considerations

Legal considerations in cryptocurrency and blockchain forensics are complex and evolving. As cryptocurrencies operate in a relatively new and rapidly changing legal landscape, forensic investigators must navigate various laws and regulations that can vary significantly by jurisdiction. These considerations include compliance with anti-money laundering (AML) and counter-terrorism financing (CTF) laws and understanding the legal implications of cross-border transactions.

The regulatory framework for cryptocurrencies varies globally, with different countries adopting diverse approaches to regulation. Some countries have established clear guidelines and regulations for using cryptocurrencies, while others have imposed restrictions or outright bans. Forensic investigators must be aware of these regulatory environments, as they can impact the methods and scope of cryptocurrency investigations.

Legal challenges in crypto investigations often arise from the borderless nature of cryptocurrencies and the varying legal statuses they hold in different jurisdictions. Issues such as jurisdictional authority, the legality of asset seizures, and the admissibility of blockchain evidence in court are common. These challenges require forensic experts to have a firm understanding of both international law and the specific legal context of the countries involved in their investigations.

International cooperation and jurisdiction issues are critical in cryptocurrency and blockchain forensics due to the global nature of digital currencies. Investigating and prosecuting cryptocurrency crimes often requires collaboration across countries and legal systems. Navigating jurisdictional issues, such as which country has the authority to investigate and prosecute, and coordinating with international law enforcement agencies are essential for successful outcomes in these complex investigations.

Advanced Topics in Digital Forensics

Artificial intelligence (AI) in forensics represents a significant evolution, bringing sophisticated analytical capabilities to various aspects of digital investigations. AI and machine learning algorithms can process and analyze large volumes of data more quickly and accurately than traditional methods. This capability is invaluable in identifying patterns, anomalies, and correlations in digital evidence, which might be challenging or time-consuming for human investigators to detect. The use of AI in forensics is growing, with applications in areas such as image and video analysis, network traffic analysis, and malware detection.

AI and Machine Learning Applications

AI and machine learning applications in digital forensics are diverse and expanding. Machine learning algorithms can be trained to recognize specific types of digital artifacts, such as images or emails, relevant to criminal investigations. AI can also be used for predictive modeling, helping to anticipate potential security breaches or cyber-attacks by analyzing patterns in data. In addition, natural language processing, a branch of AI, is used to analyze and interpret large sets of unstructured textual data, which is common in digital forensics.

Automation in Evidence Analysis

Automation in evidence analysis, facilitated by AI and machine learning, is revolutionizing digital forensics. Automated tools can sift through vast amounts of data to identify relevant pieces of evidence, reducing the time and labor required for data analysis. This automation accelerates the investigative process and reduces the likelihood of human error. However, forensic experts need to understand the underlying algorithms and ensure that the automated processes are reliable and transparent.

The prospects of AI in digital forensics are vast but come with challenges. As AI technology advances, forensic tools are anticipated to become more sophisticated, enabling more thorough and efficient investigations. However, this advancement also raises concerns about the accuracy of AI algorithms, the potential for bias in automated systems, and the interpretability of AI-driven conclusions in forensic investigations.

Forensics in Emerging Technologies

Forensics in emerging technologies, such as the Internet of Things (IoT), virtual reality (VR), and augmented reality (AR), presents new frontiers for digital forensic investigations. These technologies generate new types of data and evidence that forensic experts must learn to acquire, analyze, and interpret. For instance, IoT devices can provide critical investigation information, from smart home devices recording user activities to wearable technology tracking movements.

IoT forensics involves investigating a multitude of devices that are interconnected and constantly exchanging data. These devices, from smart appliances to wearable health monitors, create a complex web of evidence sources. The challenge in IoT forensics lies in the diversity of devices, each with its own operating system, data formats, and communication protocols, as well as in the volume and nature of the data they generate.

Forensics in virtual and augmented reality are emerging as these technologies become more widespread. Investigating crimes in virtual environments or analyzing data from AR devices requires new forensic tools and techniques. This includes understanding the data structures, user interactions within these environments, and the legal implications of collecting and analyzing such data.

The challenges with new technology forensics include staying abreast of rapid technological advancements, developing tools and methods to handle novel data types, and ensuring legal compliance in obtaining and analyzing evidence. As technology evolves, so do the tactics of those exploiting it for illicit purposes, requiring forensic experts to adapt and update their skills continually.

Future Trends and Challenges

Future trends in digital forensics will likely involve adapting to increasingly sophisticated cybercrimes and navigating the complexities of emerging technologies. Challenges include managing the sheer volume of data, dealing with encryption and privacy issues, and maintaining the integrity of evidence in a rapidly evolving digital landscape. Forensic professionals must anticipate technological advancements and develop new methodologies to stay ahead of criminals.

Anticipating technological advancements is crucial for the evolution of digital forensics. Forensic experts must keep pace with current technologies and anticipate and prepare for future trends. This includes understanding potential new cyber threats, staying informed about computing and data storage advancements, and predicting how emerging technologies might be exploited for criminal activities.

Developing skills for future forensics involves continuous learning and adaptation. Forensic professionals need ongoing education and training to keep their skills relevant and up to date. This includes familiarizing themselves with the latest forensic software and tools, understanding new and emerging technologies, and staying informed about legal and ethical developments in the field.

The ethical and legal challenges ahead in digital forensics are significant. As technology advances, forensic experts face new ethical dilemmas, including issues related to privacy, data protection, and the use of AI and automated tools in investigations. Legally, they must navigate a landscape of evolving laws and regulations that govern digital evidence and cybercrime. Balancing technological capabilities with ethical and legal responsibilities will be a continuing challenge for forensic professionals.

Case Study: The DNC Hack of 2016 – A Digital Forensics Case Study

In 2016, the Democratic National Committee (DNC), the governing body of the US Democratic Party, experienced a significant cyber-attack. This incident, unfolding during a critical phase of the US Presidential election, had far-reaching political and cybersecurity implications. Digital forensic analysis played a pivotal role in uncovering the details of the hack, providing insights into the methodologies used by the attackers, and shaping the response to this significant cybersecurity breach.

The breach was first identified when anomalous network activity was detected. The DNC swiftly engaged CrowdStrike, a cybersecurity firm, to conduct an in-depth forensic analysis. This response highlighted the growing recognition of digital forensics as essential in understanding and mitigating cyber threats. The initial phase of the forensic investigation focused on identifying the breach's scope and the methods employed by the attackers.

CrowdStrike's forensic team employed various techniques to analyze the DNC's network. This included examining server logs, conducting malware analysis, and assessing network traffic patterns. The team looked for digital fingerprints left by the attackers, which involved identifying malicious software and unusual access patterns. One of the key challenges was differentiating between legitimate network activities and those related to the hack.

The forensic investigation led to significant findings. Two groups, identified as Fancy Bear and Cozy Bear, were found to be involved in the breach. These groups were believed to be associated with Russian intelligence services. The forensic evidence pointed to sophisticated malware and phishing techniques to access the DNC's network and exfiltrate data. This data included emails and other documents later publicly leaked, adding a complex political dimension to the cyberattack.

The forensic findings had substantial implications. They clarified the attack's nature and indicated a state-sponsored cyber-espionage effort, which heightened tensions between the United States and Russia. The incident underscored the vulnerabilities in political organizations' cybersecurity practices and sparked a global conversation about the security of political systems in the digital age. It also highlighted the critical role of digital forensics in attributing cyberattacks and shaping strategic responses.

The DNC hack of 2016 serves as a seminal case in digital forensics, illustrating its vital role in addressing complex cyberattacks. The incident emphasized the need for robust cybersecurity measures, especially for politically sensitive entities. It also showcased how digital forensic investigations could unravel the complexities of sophisticated cyber-espionage activities, providing crucial insights for future cybersecurity strategies and policies. The case remains a significant reference point in understanding the intersection of cybersecurity, politics, and international relations in the digital era.

Career Corner

A career in digital forensics is a specialized and intriguing field within cybersecurity, dedicated to uncovering and analyzing digital evidence from various electronic devices and cyber environments. This field is crucial in investigating cybercrimes and recovering digital data in legal and corporate settings.

One of the key roles in digital forensics is that of a Digital Forensic Investigator. These professionals are skilled in examining digital devices like computers, smartphones, and networks to uncover evidence of crimes or malicious activities. They use various tools and techniques to recover data, analyze system logs, and trace unauthorized activities. Their work is often pivotal in legal investigations, where they may also present their findings in court.

Another significant career path is that of a Forensic Computer Analyst. Individuals in this role specialize in analyzing data on computers and digital storage devices. They look for hidden, encrypted, or deleted information relevant to investigations. Their expertise is essential in solving crimes that involve digital components, from fraud to cyber attacks.

The role of a Cybersecurity Forensic Analyst is also crucial in the digital forensics landscape. These professionals focus specifically on analyzing breaches and attacks in cybersecurity environments. They are responsible for identifying how a cyber breach occurred, what data was compromised, and who might be responsible. Their analysis helps strengthen cybersecurity measures against future attacks.

Becoming a Law Enforcement Digital Forensic Examiner can be a fulfilling career choice for those interested in law enforcement. These examiners work directly with law enforcement agencies, helping to solve crimes by analyzing digital evidence. Their work often involves close collaboration with other law enforcement professionals and requires a strong understanding of legal procedures.

In terms of certifications, several are recognized in digital forensics. The Certified Computer Examiner (CCE) and the Certified Forensic Computer Examiner (CFCE) certifications are among the most respected, focusing specifically on computer forensics. The Global Information Assurance Certification (GIAC) offers several relevant certifications, including the GIAC Certified Forensic Analyst (GCFA) and the GIAC Certified Forensic Examiner (GCFE), which cover advanced skills and techniques in digital forensics.

A career in digital forensics requires a combination of technical skills, attention to detail, and a methodical approach to investigation. Professionals must stay updated with the latest technological advancements and forensic techniques. Whether working in law enforcement, corporate settings, or private consulting, digital forensic experts play a crucial role in uncovering digital evidence and resolving complex cyber-related cases. Continuous learning and certification are crucial to success in this evolving and highly specialized field.

Chapter Questions

1. What is the primary focus of digital forensics?

    A. Enhancing network security

    B. Collecting and analyzing data for legal evidence

    C. Developing new data storage technologies

    D. Creating digital documents and emails

2. Which area has digital forensics expanded to include?

    A. Only computer-based investigations

    B. Primarily, network security breaches

    C. A broad range of devices and data types

    D. Exclusive focus on encrypted data

3. What drove the evolution of digital forensics in recent decades?

    A. Decreased use of digital devices

    B. Simplification of cybercriminal tactics

    C. The increasing sophistication of technology and cybercriminals

    D. The decline in digital data volume

4. Why is digital forensic expertise more prominent now than ever?

   A. Because of the decrease in digital crime

   B. Due to the limited use of digital devices

   C. Owing to the proliferation of digital devices and data

   D. The reduced need for legal evidence

5. What was a key factor in the historical development of digital forensics?

   A. The decreasing cost of digital storage

   B. Reduced usage of computers

   C. The increasing use of computers in society

   D. The decline in cybercrime

6. Which is a crucial component of digital evidence?

   A. Network security protocols

   B. Metadata and logs

   C. Physical documents only

   D. Solely encrypted data

7. What is essential in ensuring the admissibility of digital evidence in court?

   A. The speed of data recovery

   B. The use of open source tools

   C. Maintaining the integrity of data

   D. The brand of forensic software used

8. What is a significant challenge in mobile device forensics?

   A. Uniformity of devices and operating systems

   B. Infrequent updates and changes in technology

   C. The diversity of devices and operating systems

   D. The decreasing use of mobile devices

9. In network forensics, what is critical to identifying security breaches?

   A. Analyzing financial transactions

   B. Examining network traffic and logs

   C. Monitoring employee behavior

   D. Checking hardware configurations

10. What is a key challenge in cloud forensics?

   A. Stable nature of cloud environments

   B. Physical control over storage infrastructure

   C. Dynamic nature of cloud environments

   D. Limited data volume in cloud services

11. What has significantly influenced modern digital forensics?

   A. Declining use of AI in investigations

   B. Increasing use of paper records

   C. Introduction of AI and machine learning

   D. Decreased data privacy concerns

12. What type of forensics involves investigating interconnected devices?

    A. Paper document forensics

    B. Network forensics

    C. IoT forensics

    D. Cryptocurrency forensics

13. What is a future trend anticipated in digital forensics?

    A. Reduced complexity in cybercrimes

    B. Decrease in data volume

    C. Adapting to sophisticated cybercrimes

    D. Shift away from digital evidence

14. In digital forensics, what is crucial when dealing with emerging technologies?

    A. Ignoring technological advancements

    B. Developing tools for novel types of data

    C. Focusing only on current technologies

    D. Reducing legal compliance

15. What ethical and legal challenge is significant in digital forensics?

    A. Ignoring privacy and data protection

    B. Navigating evolving laws and ethical dilemmas

    C. Focusing solely on technical capabilities

    D. Avoiding new forensic tools and techniques

CHAPTER 11

Vulnerability Assessment and Penetration Testing

Vulnerability assessment is a comprehensive process aimed at identifying, quantifying, and prioritizing vulnerabilities within a system. This system can range from a computer network to a building, a supply chain, a health system, or any other entity that faces potential risks. The concept revolves around understanding and uncovering weaknesses that threats could exploit, whether cyber-attacks, natural disasters, or operational failures. The importance of vulnerability assessment is manifold. It serves as a crucial element in risk management, providing insights that guide the development of strategies to protect assets and ensure continuity. By conducting regular assessments, organizations can stay ahead of emerging threats, adapt to changing environments, and maintain operational integrity. Furthermore, vulnerability assessments are pivotal in compliance with regulatory standards, ensuring that organizations meet required security benchmarks and avoid penalties.

The field of vulnerability assessment has seen significant evolution and development over the years, adapting to the changing landscape of threats and the increasing complexity of systems. Initially focused on physical security measures, the field expanded to encompass IT systems, reflecting

© Dr. Jason Edwards 2024, corrected publication 2024
Dr. J. Edwards, *Mastering Cybersecurity*, https://doi.org/10.1007/979-8-8688-0297-3_11

the growing reliance on technology and the Internet. As threats became more sophisticated, vulnerability assessments adapted, incorporating advanced techniques and technologies like artificial intelligence and machine learning to predict and identify potential vulnerabilities. Expanding this field into cybersecurity, public health, and climate change underscores its adaptability and relevance in various sectors. This evolution is not only a response to the diverse range of threats faced today but also a reflection of the increasing recognition of the interconnected nature of risks. Modern vulnerability assessments must consider various factors, including cyber threats, physical security, human error, supply chain disruptions, and environmental impacts, making it a complex but indispensable field.

Vulnerability assessments have a broad scope, encompassing various components such as hardware, software, environmental factors, human elements, and organizational processes. The scope also varies depending on the assessment scale, which can range from localized evaluations of specific systems to comprehensive analyses at a global level. Despite their broad applicability, vulnerability assessments come with certain limitations. They are typically specific to the time and context in which they are conducted, meaning their findings may become outdated as conditions change. These assessments' effectiveness and accuracy heavily depend on the quality and completeness of the data available and the methodologies employed. Additionally, there is always an element of uncertainty, as not all potential threats can be anticipated or identified. The dynamic nature of risks, particularly in fields like cybersecurity, means that assessments must be regularly updated to remain relevant.

In the context of vulnerability assessment, several key terminologies are essential for a comprehensive understanding. A vulnerability is a weakness or flaw in a system that can be exploited by threats, leading to potential harm or disruption. Risk is the potential for loss or damage when a threat takes advantage of a vulnerability. This concept is central to understanding the purpose of vulnerability assessments: to identify and address these vulnerabilities to mitigate risk. Threat assessment is closely related, involving identifying and evaluating potential threats to a system. Risk management involves identifying, assessing, and controlling threats to an organization's resources and earnings, including implementing measures to mitigate identified risks. Mitigation refers to the actions taken to reduce a vulnerability's impact or lessen the damage caused by a threat. Resilience, another critical term, describes the ability of a system or organization to withstand and recover from adverse events. These terminologies form the foundation of vulnerability assessment, each contributing to a deeper understanding of the complexities and challenges in protecting systems from a wide range of threats.

Setting Up a Vulnerability Assessment Program

The initial step in setting up a vulnerability assessment program involves defining its objectives and goals. These objectives should align with the organization's broader security and risk management strategies. The primary goal is to identify and assess vulnerabilities within the system – be it in software, hardware, processes, or human elements – and determine their potential impact. Objectives might include ensuring compliance with legal and regulatory requirements, protecting sensitive data, or maintaining operational continuity. Clear objectives guide the assessments' scope and depth and help set priorities. Goals should be specific, measurable, achievable, relevant, and time-bound (SMART), providing a clear direction for the program. Additionally, these goals should be regularly reviewed and updated to adapt to the evolving security landscape and organizational changes, ensuring that the program remains effective and relevant.

Resource allocation is a critical component in establishing a vulnerability assessment program. It involves distributing necessary resources – such as personnel, time, tools, and budget – to carry out the assessments effectively. Deciding on the allocation requires a thorough understanding of the program's goals and the scope of assessments. Financial resources are needed for tools and technologies that aid in vulnerability scanning and analysis and for training and potentially hiring specialized staff. Time allocation is also crucial, as regular assessments and follow-up actions must be scheduled without disrupting normal business operations. The allocation of human resources involves selecting or hiring personnel with the necessary expertise and skills. Proper resource allocation ensures the program has the necessary support to function efficiently and effectively, leading to more accurate and actionable assessment outcomes.

The team structure responsible for the vulnerability assessment program is fundamental to its success. A well-structured team should include individuals with diverse skills and expertise, such as IT professionals, security analysts, network administrators, and compliance officers. The roles and responsibilities within the team need to be clearly defined to ensure efficient operation. This might include individuals responsible for conducting the assessments, analyzing the findings, implementing mitigation strategies, and overseeing the overall process. In larger organizations, the team may also require roles for coordinating with different departments and handling communication and reporting. The team should operate with a transparent chain of command and have established protocols for decision-making and escalation. A well-defined team structure facilitates effective collaboration and ensures that each aspect of the vulnerability assessment process is adequately managed.

Planning and scheduling are crucial for the smooth operation of a vulnerability assessment program. This phase involves developing a detailed plan that outlines the methodologies to be used, the systems and assets to be assessed, the frequency of assessments, and the process for reporting and addressing findings. The plan should be tailored to the organization's specific needs and risk profile, considering the complexity and criticality of different systems. Scheduling is essential to ensure that assessments are conducted at appropriate intervals – whether regular routine checks or more extensive annual audits. The schedule should account for the availability of resources and aim to minimize disruption to business operations. It should also include time for reviewing and updating the assessment process, allowing the program to evolve and improve over time. Effective planning and scheduling provide a road map for the program, ensuring that assessments are thorough, timely, and aligned with organizational goals.

Types of Vulnerabilities

Network architecture weaknesses refer to the inherent flaws or deficiencies in the design and structure of a network that attackers can exploit. These weaknesses often stem from outdated or improperly configured hardware, lack of redundancy, or insufficient segmentation. For example, a network may have a single point of failure, such as a central router or server, which, if compromised, could disrupt the entire network. Inadequate security controls and lack of regular updates can also lead to vulnerabilities in the network infrastructure. It's essential to conduct regular reviews and updates of the network architecture to identify and address these weaknesses. This includes implementing robust security measures, such as firewalls, intrusion detection systems, and regular patch management to safeguard against potential attacks. A well-designed network architecture should facilitate efficient and secure data flow and include measures for rapid detection and response to security incidents.

Protocol and service vulnerabilities involve weaknesses in the software rules and algorithms that govern data transmission across the network. Many network protocols were not designed with robust security features, making them susceptible to eavesdropping, spoofing, and denial-of-service (DoS) attacks. For instance, older protocols like HTTP and FTP transmit data in unencrypted form, exposing sensitive information to potential interception. Similarly, services running on network devices, like DNS and DHCP, can be targeted to disrupt network operations or redirect traffic to malicious sites. To mitigate these vulnerabilities, using secure protocols (such as HTTPS and SFTP) and regularly updating and patching network services are crucial. Additionally, monitoring network traffic for unusual patterns can help detect exploits targeting these protocols and services early.

Wireless networks introduce specific security challenges due to their nature of transmitting data over the air, making them vulnerable to eavesdropping and unauthorized access. Weaknesses in wireless security protocols, such as WEP (Wired Equivalent Privacy), have been well-documented, leading to more secure standards like WPA3 (Wi-Fi Protected Access 3). However, issues like weak encryption, poor configuration, and the use of default passwords can still leave wireless networks exposed. Ensuring the security of a wireless network involves implementing strong encryption, using robust authentication mechanisms, and regularly updating firmware and software on wireless devices. Additionally, measures like network cloaking, where the network name (SSID) is not broadcasted, and limiting the range of the wireless signal can also help reduce the risk of unauthorized access.

Network segmentation and isolation are critical strategies for enhancing network security. Segmentation involves dividing the network into smaller, manageable segments based on function, department, or security level. This approach limits the spread of attacks within the network, as attackers can only access a network segment at a time. Effective segmentation requires firewalls, access control lists, and virtual LANs (VLANs) to regulate traffic between segments. Isolation, conversely, refers to completely separating certain parts of the network from the rest, often used for highly sensitive data or critical systems. This can be achieved through physical means, like separate cabling and switches, or virtually, using technologies like Virtual Private Networks (VPNs) and private clouds. Properly implemented, network segmentation and isolation reduce the attack surface and simplify monitoring and management of network security.

Software Vulnerabilities

Common software flaws are weaknesses or errors in software design, implementation, or configuration that attackers can exploit. These flaws include many issues, such as buffer overflows, injection flaws (like SQL injection), improper error handling, and insecure data storage. Buffer overflows occur when a program writes more data to a buffer than it can hold, potentially allowing attackers to execute arbitrary code. Injection flaws happen when an attacker can insert or manipulate queries in a software application, leading to data theft or loss. Insecure data storage and improper error handling can expose sensitive information or create vulnerabilities that attackers can exploit. Understanding these common flaws is essential for developers and security professionals to identify and remediate vulnerabilities in software. Regular code reviews, security testing, and adherence to best practices in software development can significantly reduce the occurrence and impact of these common software flaws.

Secure coding practices are essential in developing software that is resistant to attacks. These practices involve writing code with security in mind from the outset, adhering to principles that minimize the occurrence of vulnerabilities. This includes validating input to prevent injection attacks, using secure functions to avoid buffer overflows, and handling errors in a way that doesn't expose sensitive information. Secure coding also involves following best practices for authentication and authorization, ensuring data is encrypted when necessary, and maintaining session security. Educating developers about secure coding practices and integrating security into the software development lifecycle are crucial steps in producing more secure software. Tools like static and dynamic code analyzers can also help identify potential security issues in the codebase.

Patch management is a critical aspect of maintaining software security. It involves regularly updating software to address security vulnerabilities discovered since the software was released. Effective patch management includes identifying the software components that need updates, understanding the security issues addressed by each patch, and prioritizing and applying these patches in a timely manner. This process is crucial in preventing attackers from exploiting known vulnerabilities, a common attack vector. Challenges in patch management include ensuring compatibility with existing systems and minimizing disruption during the update process. Automation of patch management processes can help maintain the currency and security of software across an organization's digital infrastructure.

Dependency and third-party risks arise from using external code, libraries, or services in software development. These external components can introduce vulnerabilities into an application, especially if they are not adequately vetted or regularly updated. Dependency risks are prevalent in modern software development practices like using open source libraries, where the security of the dependent code can vary widely. Third-party risks include vulnerabilities in software or services provided by vendors, which might not be under the direct control of the organization using them. Managing these risks involves conducting thorough security assessments of third-party vendors, regularly reviewing and updating dependencies, and monitoring for security advisories related to used components. It's also essential to have a contingency plan in place in case a third-party service becomes compromised or unavailable. Addressing dependency and third-party risks is vital to a comprehensive software security strategy, ensuring that vulnerabilities are not introduced through external sources.

Hardware Vulnerabilities

Physical device security addresses the risks associated with the physical components of technology, such as servers, workstations, networking equipment, and mobile devices. These risks include theft, tampering, unauthorized access, and damage to physical infrastructure. Ensuring physical security involves implementing access control systems, surveillance cameras, and secure locks to protect hardware assets. Additionally, it's essential to consider environmental factors like fire, water damage, and electrical surges that can affect hardware. Strategies for enhancing physical device security also include maintaining a secure facility, training staff on security protocols, and employing intrusion detection systems. By securing the physical aspects of hardware, organizations can prevent direct access to critical systems and data, thus mitigating the risk of physical breaches that could lead to data loss, system downtime, or compromised network security.

Embedded systems, such as IoT devices, automotive controls, and industrial control systems, present unique security challenges. These systems often operate continuously and are sometimes deployed in unsecured or remote environments. Vulnerabilities in embedded systems can arise from inadequate security measures, outdated software, and the limited processing power available for security functions. Ensuring the security of these systems involves implementing robust authentication and encryption protocols, regular firmware updates, and secure coding practices during development. It's also important to consider the physical security of these devices, as they can be susceptible to tampering or theft. Manufacturers and users of embedded systems need to be vigilant about security, given that these devices can be targeted in large-scale attacks or used as entry points into broader networks.

Supply chain risks in hardware arise from the complex network of suppliers, manufacturers, and distributors involved in the production and distribution of hardware components and devices. These risks include introducing malicious hardware or firmware during manufacturing, counterfeit components, or compromised integrity due to poor manufacturing practices. Organizations must implement rigorous supplier vetting processes to mitigate these risks, conduct regular supplier audits, and establish strong quality control measures. Ensuring the traceability of components and maintaining transparency in the supply chain are also key strategies. Organizations should also be prepared to respond quickly to vulnerabilities discovered in the hardware supply chain, including the ability to patch or replace compromised components promptly.

Hardware lifecycle management involves the processes and policies for managing hardware from acquisition to disposal. This includes selecting secure and reliable hardware, maintaining it throughout its operational life, and securely disposing it at the end of its lifecycle. Effective hardware lifecycle management helps minimize vulnerabilities due to outdated or unsupported hardware. Regular maintenance and updates are essential to address emerging security threats and to ensure that hardware continues to operate effectively. When hardware reaches the end of its lifecycle, it's crucial to dispose of it securely to prevent data breaches. This includes practices like data wiping, degaussing, or physically destroying storage media. Managing the hardware lifecycle effectively is a key part of an organization's overall security strategy, ensuring that hardware-related vulnerabilities are addressed throughout the device's entire lifespan.

Human Factor Vulnerabilities

Social engineering tactics exploit human psychology rather than technical hacking techniques to gain access to systems, data, or physical locations. These tactics include phishing, pretexting, baiting, and tailgating. Phishing involves sending fraudulent communications that appear to come from a reputable source to steal sensitive data like login credentials. Pretexting is creating a fabricated scenario to obtain information. Baiting involves offering something enticing to gain access, and tailgating is unauthorized following into a restricted area. These tactics exploit the natural tendency of people to trust and be helpful. The success of social engineering underscores the importance of addressing human factors in security. Regular training and awareness programs can help individuals recognize and respond appropriately to these tactics, reducing their effectiveness.

User education and awareness are crucial in mitigating human factor vulnerabilities. Most security breaches involve some degree of human error, which can be reduced through effective education and awareness programs. These programs should cover various topics, including password security, identifying phishing attempts, safe Internet practices, and understanding company security policies. Regular training sessions, security briefings, and testing (such as simulated phishing exercises) can enhance employees' ability to recognize and avoid security threats. Additionally, creating a culture where security is a shared responsibility encourages proactive behavior from employees in reporting potential security incidents. Continuous education and fostering a security-conscious culture are essential in reducing risks associated with human factors.

Insider threats come from individuals within the organization, such as employees, contractors, or business partners, who have inside information concerning the organization's security practices, data, and computer systems. These threats can be intentional (such as stealing data for personal gain) or unintentional (such as inadvertently downloading malware). Mitigating insider threats requires a combination of technical controls, such as access controls and monitoring systems, and nontechnical strategies, like conducting background checks, enforcing least privilege principles, and maintaining a positive work environment to reduce the likelihood of malicious insider behavior. Organizations should also have policies and procedures in place to detect and manage insider threats, including clear guidelines on data access and the ethical conduct of employees.

Policy and procedure gaps can create vulnerabilities within an organization's security framework. These gaps might arise from outdated policies, lack of clear guidelines, insufficient enforcement, or policies that do not cover all aspects of the organization's operations. For instance, a lack of clear policies on remote work can leave systems exposed to increased risk. Addressing these gaps requires thoroughly reviewing existing policies and procedures, ensuring they are up to date, comprehensive, and aligned with current security best practices and compliance requirements. Policies should be communicated to all organization members, and their understanding and compliance should be regularly assessed. Additionally, procedures for reporting and responding to security incidents should be clear and well-documented. Regular audits and reviews are crucial in identifying and addressing policy and procedure gaps, ensuring the organization's security posture remains strong and effective against evolving threats.

Assessment Techniques

Vulnerability scanning involves using specialized tools and technologies to identify, assess, and report on security weaknesses in networks, systems, and applications. These tools range from basic port scanners to advanced software that can simulate attacks and analyze vulnerabilities in depth. They work by comparing information about the target system against databases of known vulnerabilities, identifying misconfigurations, and detecting security gaps. Some tools focus on specific areas, such as network vulnerability or web application scanners, while others offer comprehensive scanning across various domains. Advanced scanning technologies incorporate artificial intelligence and machine learning to improve the accuracy and efficiency of vulnerability detection. The choice of tools and technologies should align with the organization's specific needs, taking into account factors like the complexity of the environment, the type of assets to be scanned, and compliance requirements.

Vulnerability databases are critical components in the vulnerability scanning process. They are repositories that contain information about identified security weaknesses in software and hardware. These databases provide details such as the nature of the vulnerability, its severity, potential impact, and available patches or workarounds. Well-known databases include the National Vulnerability Database (NVD), Common Vulnerabilities and Exposures (CVE), and vendor-specific databases. Keeping these databases up to date is crucial for effective vulnerability scanning, as they form the basis on which scanning tools assess and identify vulnerabilities. Regular updates ensure the scanning process can detect the latest known vulnerabilities, providing organizations with timely information to protect against emerging threats.

Vulnerability scanning methodologies encompass the strategies and approaches used in conducting scans. These methodologies vary based on the objectives of the scan, the type of systems being assessed, and the depth of analysis required. Common approaches include network-based scanning, which assesses the network for potential vulnerabilities from an outsider's perspective, and host-based scanning, which evaluates individual systems for weaknesses. Another method is application scanning, focusing specifically on software applications. Scans can be configured to be nonintrusive, causing minimal impact on system performance, or intrusive, simulating actual attacks to understand the real-world impact of vulnerabilities. The choice of methodology often depends on the balance between the thoroughness of the scan and the potential risk of disrupting system operations.

Automated and manual scanning are two distinct approaches to vulnerability scanning, each with strengths and limitations. Automated scanning uses software tools to scan systems and networks for vulnerabilities, providing a quick and efficient way to identify known security issues. It is particularly effective for regular assessments of a large number of assets and for maintaining ongoing security monitoring. However, automated scans may not detect complex or context-specific vulnerabilities and can result in false positives. Manual scanning, on the other hand, involves security experts actively analyzing and probing systems to uncover vulnerabilities. This approach allows for a more nuanced understanding of the security environment and can identify issues that automated tools may miss. Manual scanning is often used for in-depth assessments, such as penetration testing. A balanced approach, combining automated and manual scanning, can provide a comprehensive view of an organization's security posture, leveraging the efficiency of automation and the depth of manual expertise.

Penetration Testing

Penetration testing methodologies involve systematic approaches to simulate cyberattacks on a system, network, or application to identify and exploit security vulnerabilities. Common methodologies include black-box testing, where the tester has no prior knowledge of the target system; white-box testing, where the tester has complete knowledge of the system, including access to source code and architecture; and gray-box testing, which is a blend of both, with limited knowledge of the system. These methodologies determine the approach and techniques used in the penetration test, such as social engineering, network service attacks, or application-level exploits. The choice of methodology often depends on the specific goals of the test, the nature of the system being tested, and the threat model that the test aims to simulate. Each methodology provides different insights into the target's security posture, helping organizations understand potential weaknesses from various attacker perspectives.

Ethical hacking principles guide the conduct of penetration testers to ensure that their activities are legal, professional, and aimed at improving security. These principles include obtaining explicit permission before attempting to penetrate systems, respecting the privacy and confidentiality of the organization, and avoiding any actions that could harm the target system or its data. Ethical hackers must also report all findings to the organization comprehensively and understandably, enabling them to address the identified vulnerabilities. Adherence to ethical hacking principles is crucial to maintain the trust between the penetration tester and the client and to ensure that the testing activities contribute positively to the organization's security posture.

Test planning and scope are critical in successfully executing a penetration test. Planning involves defining the objectives of the test, such as identifying vulnerabilities, testing the effectiveness of security controls, or evaluating incident response procedures. The scope of the test needs to be clearly outlined, determining which systems, networks, or applications will be included in the test and the extent of the testing activities. Setting boundaries for the test is crucial to ensure that it remains focused and within legal and ethical limits. Proper planning and scoping also involve coordinating with relevant stakeholders, establishing communication protocols, and preparing contingency plans for unexpected issues during the test. A well-planned and scoped penetration test ensures that the testing activities are targeted, efficient, and effective in achieving the desired security outcomes.

Reporting and analysis are the final steps in the penetration testing process, where the findings are documented and interpreted to provide actionable insights. A comprehensive report should include a detailed description of the testing methodology, the vulnerabilities identified, the potential impact of these vulnerabilities, and recommendations for remediation. The report should be both technical, for the IT team to address the vulnerabilities, and executive-friendly, providing a high-level overview for decision-makers. Analysis of the findings involves understanding the root causes of vulnerabilities, assessing their risk, and prioritizing them for remediation based on their severity and potential impact. Effective reporting and analysis not only help address the current vulnerabilities but also improve the overall security strategy, informing future security investments, policies, and practices.

Configuration and Compliance Review

Configuration management in the context of IT security is maintaining a consistent and secure state of systems and software through controlled change and documentation. This process involves identifying and defining the configurations of various IT assets, ensuring they are optimized for security, and maintaining them in a known and trusted state. Configuration management helps prevent security breaches arising from misconfigured systems, unpatched software, or unauthorized changes. It includes tasks like standardizing configurations across similar systems, regularly updating software and hardware settings, and tracking and documenting all changes made to the system configurations. Effective configuration management requires automated tools and manual oversight to ensure that all systems adhere to the desired state and that any deviations are quickly identified and addressed.

Compliance standards are guidelines and requirements that organizations must follow to ensure that their IT systems and processes are secure and responsible. These standards can be industry specific, like HIPAA for healthcare or PCI DSS for payment card processing, or more general, like GDPR for data protection and ISO 27001 for information security management. Adhering to these standards helps organizations protect sensitive data, avoid legal and financial penalties, and maintain customer trust. Compliance involves understanding the relevant standards, implementing the required controls and procedures, and regularly updating these measures to align with any changes in the standards. Compliance is not just a one-time effort but an ongoing process that requires constant vigilance and adaptation to evolving regulatory landscapes.

Auditing and review processes are critical in ensuring that an organization's IT systems and processes meet the established security standards and comply with relevant regulatory requirements. These processes involve conducting regular examinations and assessments of the systems to verify that they are configured correctly, are operating as intended, and comply with the necessary standards. Audits can be conducted internally by the organization's staff or externally by independent auditors. The review process includes evaluating the effectiveness of current security controls, identifying gaps or weaknesses, and assessing the organization's adherence to its policies and procedures. Regular auditing and reviews are essential for maintaining a robust security posture, as they provide insights into potential improvement areas and help proactively address vulnerabilities.

Remediation and action plans are developed in response to the findings from configuration reviews and compliance audits. These plans outline the steps to address identified security vulnerabilities, non-compliance issues, and other risks. A remediation plan typically includes prioritizing the issues based on their severity and impact, determining the appropriate actions to fix them, and allocating the necessary resources. The plan should also define timelines for the implementation of these actions. In addition to resolving specific issues, action plans may involve updating policies, enhancing security controls, and improving training and awareness programs. These plans must be dynamic, allowing for adjustments as new vulnerabilities are discovered, or changes occur in the compliance landscape. Effective remediation and action planning are critical components of a proactive security strategy, ensuring that issues are identified promptly and effectively resolved.

Advanced Assessment Techniques

Red teaming and war gaming are advanced assessment techniques that simulate realistic cyber-attacks and defense scenarios to evaluate an organization's security posture. Red teaming involves a group of skilled security professionals, known as the red team, attempting to breach the organization's defenses using techniques employed by real-world attackers. This approach tests the technological defenses and the human and process elements of security. On the other hand, war gaming is a broader exercise involving attacking (red team) and defending (blue team) groups. It simulates a full-scale cyber conflict to test the organization's response and resilience under stress. These exercises provide valuable insights into vulnerabilities, the effectiveness of current security measures, and the preparedness of staff in responding to sophisticated attacks. Red teaming and war gaming are proactive strategies that help organizations stay ahead of emerging threats by identifying and addressing weaknesses before actual attackers can exploit them.

Threat hunting and anomaly detection are proactive security approaches focused on actively searching for and identifying advanced threats that evade traditional security solutions. Threat hunting involves security analysts using their knowledge, tools, and available data to search for indicators of compromise within an organization's network. This approach is hypothesis driven, often beginning with an assumption or a piece of intelligence that is then investigated. Anomaly detection, on the other hand, relies on automated systems to identify patterns or behaviors that deviate from the established norm, which could indicate a security threat. These techniques are crucial for detecting sophisticated, persistent threats that can quietly infiltrate and remain within a network for extended periods. By actively seeking out these threats, organizations can identify and mitigate them before they result in significant damage or data loss.

Code review and static analysis are techniques used to identify vulnerabilities and ensure the quality and security of software code. Code review is a manual process where developers examine source code to find errors, bugs, and security vulnerabilities. It involves systematically reading code to identify potential issues such as code injection vulnerabilities, buffer overflows, or authentication flaws. Static analysis, on the other hand, is an automated process that scans the code for similar issues without executing the program. This technique uses tools to analyze the code for patterns indicative of common security vulnerabilities. Both code review and static analysis are essential parts of the secure software development lifecycle, helping to ensure that software is secure by design and free from vulnerabilities that attackers could exploit.

Continuous monitoring strategies involve continuously observing and analyzing an organization's network and systems to detect and respond to security threats in real time. This approach goes beyond periodic assessments and audits, providing a dynamic view of the organization's security posture. Continuous monitoring utilizes various tools and technologies, such as intrusion detection systems, Security Information and Event Management (SIEM) systems, and network traffic analysis tools. These technologies collect and analyze data from various sources within the IT environment, looking for signs of unauthorized access, malware activity, or other security incidents. By continuously monitoring the network, organizations can quickly detect and respond to threats, minimize the impact of security breaches, and maintain a strong security posture in the face of constantly evolving cyber threats.

Risk Management and Mitigation

Asset identification and classification are the foundational steps in the risk identification process. This involves cataloging all assets within an organization, such as hardware, software, data, personnel, and physical resources. Once identified, these assets are classified based on their criticality and value to the organization. Classification helps understand the potential impact of a security incident on each asset. Maintaining an up-to-date inventory of assets is crucial, as the risk landscape can change with the introduction of new assets or the decommissioning of old ones. This comprehensive understanding of assets allows for a more focused and practical approach to managing risks, ensuring that security measures are aligned with the importance and sensitivity of each asset.

Threat identification involves recognizing potential sources of harm that could exploit vulnerabilities in the organization's assets. This process includes identifying a wide range of threats, from cyber-attacks, such as malware and phishing, to physical threats, like theft and natural disasters. The identification of threats is informed by various sources, including industry reports, threat intelligence feeds, historical data, and internal analysis. Understanding the nature of potential threats helps assess the likelihood of their occurrence and potential impact. This knowledge is crucial for developing effective strategies to mitigate these threats and protect the organization's assets.

Vulnerability discovery identifies weaknesses in the organization's systems and processes that threats could exploit. This involves analyzing software and hardware configurations, network architectures, and operational procedures. Techniques for discovering vulnerabilities include automated scanning tools, penetration testing, and code reviews. It is also essential to stay informed about new vulnerabilities discovered in the industry, as they may affect the organization's assets. Timely identification of vulnerabilities is critical to preventing security incidents, as it allows for implementing appropriate countermeasures before these weaknesses can be exploited.

Risk scoring and prioritization involve evaluating and ranking risks based on their potential impact and likelihood of occurrence. This process typically uses a risk matrix to assign scores to identified risks, considering factors such as the severity of impact, the value of the affected assets, the vulnerability of the assets, and the capability of the threat actors. Prioritizing risks enables organizations to allocate resources and efforts effectively, focusing on the most critical risks first. It is an essential part of risk management, ensuring that the organization can mitigate risks systematically and efficiently, balancing the need for security with operational and financial constraints. Risk scoring and prioritization are dynamic processes that should be regularly revisited as the organization's assets, threats, and vulnerabilities evolve.

Risk Evaluation

Impact analysis is a critical component of risk evaluation, focusing on understanding the consequences of a potential security incident. This analysis involves determining how much a threat could harm the organization, considering financial loss, reputational damage, operational disruption, and legal liabilities. The process requires a deep understanding of the organization's operations, the value of its assets, and the potential repercussions of their compromise. The impact analysis helps quantify the potential damage in tangible terms, providing a basis for prioritizing risks and deciding on the necessary mitigation strategies. It also aids in creating business continuity and disaster recovery plans, ensuring the organization can maintain or quickly resume critical functions in the event of a security incident.

Probability assessment in risk evaluation involves estimating the likelihood of a particular threat exploiting a vulnerability. This assessment is based on various factors, including the nature of the threat, the organization's exposure to the threat, historical incident data, and current security measures. Probability assessment helps understand how often a risk might materialize, providing essential input for prioritization and decision-making. The assessment is not always straightforward, as it often involves uncertainty and incomplete information. However, threat intelligence, industry reports, and risk assessment frameworks can provide valuable insights for making informed estimates.

Evaluating control effectiveness is an integral part of risk evaluation. This involves assessing how well security measures and controls protect against identified risks. The evaluation looks at various types of controls, including technical safeguards like firewalls and encryption, administrative controls like policies and training, and physical security measures. The effectiveness of these controls is measured based on their ability to prevent, detect, or respond to potential threats. This evaluation is crucial for identifying gaps in the current security posture and determining where additional or improved controls are needed. Regularly reviewing control effectiveness is essential, as the security landscape is constantly evolving, and controls that were effective in the past may not suffice against new or emerging threats.

Risk acceptance criteria are an organization's standards to decide which risks it can tolerate without additional mitigation measures. These criteria are based on the organization's risk appetite – the level of risk it is willing to accept in pursuit of its objectives. The criteria consider factors like the strategic importance of the activities involved, the cost of implementing additional controls vs. the potential impact of the risk, and the likelihood of the risk occurring. Establishing clear risk acceptance criteria helps make informed decisions about where to allocate resources and efforts in risk management. It also ensures that the organization's risk approach aligns with its overall strategy and business objectives. Not all risks can or should be mitigated, and effective risk management involves making strategic decisions about which risks to accept, avoid, mitigate, or transfer.

Mitigation Strategies

Implementing controls is a fundamental mitigation strategy in managing identified risks. Controls are measures taken to reduce the likelihood or impact of a risk. They can be technical, such as firewalls, encryption, and intrusion detection systems, or administrative, like policies, procedures, and compliance requirements. Physical controls, like access control systems and surveillance, are also critical. Implementing controls involves identifying the most appropriate controls based on the nature of the risk, the vulnerability involved, and the protected asset. The effectiveness of these controls needs to be continuously monitored and evaluated, with adjustments made as necessary in response to changes in the risk landscape. Effective implementation of controls is a balancing act – ensuring adequate security while maintaining operational efficiency and user experience.

Incident response planning is a proactive strategy to prepare for, manage, and recover from security incidents. A well-developed incident response plan outlines the procedures to follow when a security breach or attack occurs, detailing roles and responsibilities, communication protocols, and steps for containment, eradication, and recovery. The plan should be regularly tested and updated to ensure its effectiveness. Drills and tabletop exercises can be useful in training the response team and identifying areas for improvement. A robust incident response plan minimizes the impact of security incidents by ensuring a quick and organized response, thereby reducing downtime, mitigating damage, and maintaining trust with customers and stakeholders.

Recovery and business continuity strategies are essential to ensure an organization can quickly resume normal operations after a security incident. These strategies involve having plans for data backup, system restoration, and alternative operating procedures in case of system unavailability. Business continuity planning focuses on maintaining essential functions during and after a disaster, whereas recovery planning deals with restoring normal operations after the incident has been resolved. These plans should encompass not only IT systems but all critical business functions. Regular testing and updating of these plans are essential to ensure they remain effective in the face of evolving threats and changing business needs.

Security training and awareness programs are critical strategies in mitigating risks associated with human factors. These programs aim to educate employees about security best practices, the latest threats, and the organization's security policies and procedures. Regular training ensures that staff members know their role in maintaining security and equips them with the knowledge to recognize and respond appropriately to potential security threats. Awareness campaigns can reinforce key messages and keep security in employees' minds. Such programs help build a culture of security within the organization, where every member understands the importance of their actions in protecting its assets.

Monitoring and Review

Continuous monitoring is an essential process in cybersecurity, involving the ongoing observation and analysis of the security state of information systems. This process provides real-time insights into network and system activities, helping detect and quickly respond to threats. Continuous monitoring involves various tools and technologies, such as intrusion detection systems, network traffic analysis, and Security Information and Event Management (SIEM) systems. These tools collect and analyze data continuously, allowing for the identification of unusual or suspicious activities that might indicate a security breach. Continuous monitoring aims to maintain an up-to-date view of an organization's security posture, enabling rapid response to incidents and ongoing improvements to security controls.

Regular assessments and audits are critical for ensuring an organization's security measures are effective and comply with relevant standards and policies. These evaluations systematically review security controls, policies, procedures, and operations. Assessments can be conducted internally or by external auditors and may include vulnerability assessments, penetration testing, and reviews of policy adherence. Regular audits help identify any gaps or weaknesses in the security framework, ensuring that controls function as intended and that the organization complies with legal and regulatory requirements. They provide an opportunity for a comprehensive examination of the security posture and help maintain high-security standards over time.

Reporting and documentation are integral aspects of the monitoring and review process. Effective reporting involves communicating the findings from assessments, audits, and monitoring activities to relevant stakeholders. This includes detailed reports on security incidents, analysis of the effectiveness of controls, and recommendations for improvements. Documentation is also crucial for maintaining records of security policies, procedures, incidents, and remediation actions. Good documentation ensures that valuable information is captured and retained, facilitating decision-making, compliance, and historical analysis. Reporting and documentation also play a crucial role in accountability, providing a trail of evidence for internal and external review and ensuring transparency in security operations.

Improvement and evolution are ongoing processes in the field of cybersecurity. Security measures must be regularly reviewed and updated as threats evolve and the organization's environment changes. This involves taking the insights from continuous monitoring, assessments, audits, and reporting to make informed decisions about enhancing security strategies and practices. Improvement may involve updating technologies, refining policies, retraining staff, or reengineering processes. The goal is to adapt and evolve the security posture to stay ahead of emerging threats and to enhance the organization's ability to protect its assets continually. This improvement cycle should be ingrained in the organization's culture, ensuring that cybersecurity is not static but a dynamic and integral part of the business's growth and adaptation.

Policy and Compliance

Policy frameworks provide the structured foundation for developing and managing an organization's security policies. These frameworks ensure policies are comprehensive, consistent, and aligned with the organization's goals and regulatory requirements. A robust policy framework typically includes guidelines for policy development, standards for various security domains (like access control, data protection, and incident response), and procedures for policy management. Frameworks such as ISO/IEC 27001, NIST, and COBIT can serve as models or starting points, providing best practices and globally recognized standards. The choice of a framework often depends on the organization's specific industry, size, and regulatory environment. Implementing a policy framework helps create a cohesive and organized approach to security policy development, ensuring that all relevant risks and compliance issues are addressed.

Policy writing and documentation involve articulating the rules, guidelines, and practices defining an organization's cybersecurity approach. Effective security policies are clear, concise, and easily understandable, ensuring they are accessible to all employees, regardless of their technical background. The policy writing process includes identifying each policy's scope, specifying roles and responsibilities, and detailing procedures for compliance. Policies should be documented formally and standardized, making them easy to reference and update. Good documentation practices also involve maintaining historical versions of policies, providing context for changes and developments over time. Well-written and documented policies are crucial for setting clear expectations and guidelines for employees, helping to establish a strong security culture within the organization.

Implementation and enforcement are critical phases in the security policy lifecycle. Implementation involves implementing policies, which may require changes in technology, processes, or behavior. This stage often includes configuring systems, training employees, and integrating policies into day-to-day operations. Enforcement ensures that the policies are followed and involves monitoring compliance, addressing violations, and taking corrective actions when necessary. Mechanisms for enforcement might include regular audits, security assessments, and disciplinary measures for non-compliance. Successful implementation and enforcement require ongoing communication, support from management, and a clear understanding of the importance of adhering to security policies.

Policy review and updates are essential for ensuring security policies remain effective and relevant. The cybersecurity landscape is dynamic, with new threats emerging and technologies evolving. Regularly reviewing and updating policies ensures they protect against threats and align with best practices and compliance requirements. The review process should consider employee feedback, changes in the organization's structure or operations, and threats in the threat environment. Updates might involve refining existing policies or developing new ones to address emerging risks. Engaging stakeholders from different parts of the organization during the review process can provide valuable insights and foster a sense of ownership and commitment to the security policy framework. Regular updates and reviews are crucial to maintaining robust and effective security policies that support the organization's long-term security strategy.

Legal and Regulatory Compliance

Understanding legal requirements is critical to managing legal and regulatory compliance in cybersecurity. This involves being aware of and interpreting various laws and regulations that apply to the organization, which can vary depending on geographical location, industry sector, and the data type handled. Legal requirements may include data protection and privacy laws (such as GDPR in the European Union), sector-specific regulations (like HIPAA for healthcare in the United States), and laws governing financial transactions and reporting. Staying informed about these legal requirements is essential, as non-compliance can result in significant penalties, including fines and legal action. Organizations should have a process for regularly reviewing and understanding applicable laws and regulations, which may involve consulting with legal experts specializing in cybersecurity and data protection laws.

Compliance with industry standards is about adhering to best practices and benchmarks that are recognized within the organization's industry. These standards, including ISO/IEC 27001 for information security management, NIST frameworks, or PCI DSS for payment card security, provide guidelines for managing and securing data and IT systems. Compliance with these standards helps organizations protect against cybersecurity threats and vulnerabilities and often enhances their reputation and trustworthiness in the eyes of customers and partners. While compliance with some industry standards may be voluntary, in many cases, it is driven by market expectations or contractual obligations. Regularly assessing and aligning with these standards can also prepare organizations for compliance with legal regulations, as there is often an overlap in the principles and safeguards they prescribe.

Auditing and reporting are integral components of legal and regulatory compliance. This involves conducting regular internal and external audits to ensure the organization's cybersecurity practices meet the required legal and industry standards. Audits can identify gaps in compliance and areas where improvements are needed. The reporting aspect involves documenting compliance efforts and outcomes and, in many cases, formally reporting this information to regulatory bodies or external auditors. Effective reporting demonstrates the organization's commitment to compliance and can be essential in the event of legal scrutiny or regulatory reviews. Additionally, regular auditing and reporting can provide insights into the effectiveness of the organization's cybersecurity strategy and contribute to continuous improvement.

Dealing with non-compliance involves identifying areas where the organization fails to meet legal or regulatory standards and taking corrective action. This may include revising policies and procedures, implementing new security controls, or conducting additional employee training. It's essential to address non-compliance issues promptly to minimize legal risks and potential penalties. Dealing with non-compliance also involves understanding the root causes of compliance failures, which could be inadequate resources, lack of awareness, or rapidly changing legal requirements. Organizations should have a plan for responding to non-compliance, which includes steps for investigating issues, reporting non-compliance to relevant authorities if necessary, and implementing remediation measures. Effective management of non-compliance not only addresses immediate risks but also strengthens the organization's overall compliance posture.

Organizational Aspects

Organizational structure and culture play a pivotal role in the effectiveness of cybersecurity strategies. The structure should clearly define roles and responsibilities related to cybersecurity, ensuring that there are dedicated resources and clear lines of authority and accountability. This includes establishing specialized teams or roles such as a Chief Information Security Officer (CISO), and ensuring they have the necessary authority and visibility within the organization. Equally important is fostering a culture of security awareness where cybersecurity is viewed as a shared responsibility. A strong security culture is characterized by regular training, open communication about threats and vulnerabilities, and an environment where employees are encouraged to report potential security issues without fear of reprisal. Such a culture helps in embedding security practices into everyday activities and decisions, enhancing the overall resilience of the organization against cyber threats.

Stakeholder engagement in cybersecurity involves identifying and involving all parties with a stake in the organization's security posture. This includes internal stakeholders like employees, management, and IT staff and external parties such as customers, partners, suppliers, and regulators. Effective stakeholder engagement ensures a broad understanding of the importance of cybersecurity and its impact on the organization. Engaging stakeholders can also provide valuable insights into potential security concerns and help develop more effective strategies. Regular communication with stakeholders about cybersecurity policies, practices, and incidents can build trust and foster a collaborative approach to managing security risks.

Resource allocation for cybersecurity involves ensuring that adequate budget, personnel, and technology are dedicated to developing and maintaining an effective cybersecurity posture. This includes investing in technology solutions, hiring and training skilled cybersecurity personnel, and providing ongoing funding for cybersecurity initiatives. Effective resource allocation requires understanding the organization's specific security needs and balancing these needs with other business priorities. It also involves planning for future requirements and adapting to threat landscape changes. Organizations must regularly assess their resource allocation to ensure it aligns with their risk profile and cybersecurity strategy.

Communication and collaboration are crucial for effective cybersecurity management within an organization. Clear and continuous communication ensures that all employees know cybersecurity policies, potential threats, and best practices. This includes regular updates, training sessions, and open channels for reporting security concerns. Collaboration involves different departments and teams working together to address cybersecurity challenges. This can include joint initiatives between IT and other business units, cross-functional cybersecurity committees, or collaborative efforts with external partners and industry groups. Effective communication and collaboration help in breaking down silos, ensuring a coordinated approach to security, and enabling a quicker response to emerging threats.

Continuous Improvement

Feedback mechanisms are essential for continuous improvement in cybersecurity. They involve establishing channels through which employees, customers, and other stakeholders can provide input on the organization's security policies and practices. This feedback can be gathered through surveys, suggestion boxes, incident reporting systems, or regular meetings and discussions. Feedback mechanisms help organizations identify weaknesses or gaps in their security posture and gain insights into the effectiveness of current strategies. They also foster a culture where everyone feels involved and responsible for cybersecurity, encouraging proactive identification and reporting of security issues. Regularly collecting and analyzing feedback ensures that the organization's cybersecurity approach remains responsive to the needs and concerns of all stakeholders.

Performance metrics are quantitative measures used to assess the effectiveness of cybersecurity strategies and initiatives. These metrics can include indicators such as the number of detected incidents, response times to security breaches, system downtime due to security incidents, and the effectiveness of employee security training. By tracking these metrics over time, organizations can evaluate their cybersecurity performance and identify improvement areas. Performance metrics also provide valuable data for reporting to management and other stakeholders, demonstrating the value and impact of cybersecurity investments. Regularly reviewing and adjusting these metrics ensures they remain relevant and aligned with the organization's evolving security objectives and challenges.

Training and development are crucial for maintaining and enhancing an organization's workforce's cybersecurity skills and awareness. This involves providing regular training sessions on the latest cybersecurity threats, best practices, and company-specific security policies. It is essential to develop a comprehensive training program that includes new employees, ongoing training for existing staff, and specialized training for IT and security personnel. Training should be engaging and relevant, possibly utilizing real-world examples and interactive content. Additionally, development opportunities such as attending cybersecurity conferences and workshops or pursuing certifications can keep the IT and security teams up to date with the latest trends and technologies in the field. Continuous training and development are vital to building and maintaining a knowledgeable and security-conscious workforce.

Adaptation to changing environments is a critical aspect of continuous improvement in cybersecurity. As technology evolves, new threats emerge, and business models change, an organization's cybersecurity strategies and practices must evolve. This involves staying informed about the latest cybersecurity trends and threats, regularly reviewing and updating security policies and controls, and being flexible in adopting new technologies or strategies. Organizations should also consider external factors such as regulatory changes, industry developments, and shifts in customer expectations. Proactively adapting to these changes helps ensure the organization's cybersecurity posture remains robust and effective, protecting against current and future threats.

Future of Vulnerability Assessment

Emerging technologies in the field of cybersecurity are constantly evolving, offering new tools and methods to enhance security measures. These technologies include advanced encryption methods, blockchain for secure transactions, Internet of Things (IoT) security solutions, and quantum computing, which promises to revolutionize encryption and data protection. Integrating these technologies can strengthen an organization's defense mechanisms by providing robust security solutions and protecting a more comprehensive range of assets. However, the adoption of emerging technologies also requires careful consideration of potential new vulnerabilities they may introduce and the need for specialized skills to implement and manage them effectively.

The advancement of technology significantly impacts vulnerability assessment practices. As new technologies are adopted, they often bring new types of vulnerabilities that must be identified and assessed. This evolution requires vulnerability assessment methods and tools to adapt and evolve continually. For example, the widespread adoption of cloud computing and mobile technologies has expanded the scope of vulnerability assessments beyond traditional network boundaries. Additionally, new technologies can provide more sophisticated tools for conducting vulnerability assessments, such as improved scanning software that can detect vulnerabilities in complex systems more effectively.

Automation and artificial intelligence (AI) are becoming increasingly important in cybersecurity. These technologies automate repetitive and time-consuming tasks like monitoring network traffic, analyzing logs, and detecting anomalies. AI, particularly machine learning algorithms, can predict and identify potential threats based on patterns and behaviors, enhancing the speed and accuracy of threat detection. However, as these technologies advance, there is also a growing concern about their potential misuse, such as developing AI-driven cyber-attacks that are more sophisticated and harder to detect.

The future threat landscape in cybersecurity is expected to become more complex and challenging due to technological advancements. As technology advances, cybercriminals also leverage these technologies to create more sophisticated attack methods. This includes using AI to develop adaptive malware, exploiting IoT devices for large-scale attacks, and leveraging quantum computing to break traditional encryption methods. Organizations must stay informed about these advancements and potential threats to prepare and adapt their security strategies accordingly. This may involve investing in advanced security technologies, continuously updating security policies, and ensuring ongoing education and training for cybersecurity professionals.

Predictive Analysis

Predictive models and algorithms in cybersecurity are designed to forecast potential security incidents by analyzing trends and patterns in data. These models use historical data, current security logs, and a variety of other sources to predict where vulnerabilities might arise and where attacks are likely to occur. Machine learning algorithms are particularly adept at processing large datasets to identify subtle patterns that might indicate emerging threats. Developing and refining these models requires cybersecurity expertise and advanced analytical skills. By employing predictive models, organizations can move from a reactive security posture to a more proactive stance, addressing vulnerabilities before they are exploited.

Threat intelligence and data analytics involve collecting and analyzing data about existing and emerging threats to inform security strategies. This can include data from various sources, such as industry reports, security forums, incident logs, and intelligence feeds. Advanced data analytics tools are used to process this vast amount of information, helping security teams identify trends, correlate disparate pieces of information, and prioritize threats based on their relevance and potential impact. Effective use of threat intelligence and data analytics enables organizations to understand the evolving threat landscape and to tailor their security measures to address the most pressing threats.

Behavior analysis and anomaly detection are critical components of predictive analysis in cybersecurity. These techniques involve monitoring and analyzing user and system behaviors to identify actions that deviate from established patterns, which could indicate a security threat. Behavioral analysis can help detect insider threats, compromised accounts, or malicious actors within the network. Anomaly detection algorithms can automatically flag unusual activities for further investigation, such as unexpected access to sensitive data, unusual login times, or data transfer patterns. These techniques can detect novel or evolving threats by focusing on behavior rather than relying solely on known signatures of malware or attack methods.

Proactive security measures, guided by predictive analysis, involve anticipating and mitigating potential security incidents before they occur. This proactive approach can include strengthening defenses in areas predicted to be targeted, conducting simulations or drills based on forecasted attack scenarios, and implementing advanced threat-hunting practices. The idea is to stay ahead of threats by being prepared for various scenarios and continuously adapting security strategies based on predictive insights. Proactive security measures are increasingly necessary in a rapidly evolving digital landscape, where the speed and sophistication of attacks can outpace traditional reactive security methods.

Case Study: The Equifax Data Breach of 2017

In September 2017, Equifax, one of the largest credit reporting agencies in the United States, announced a massive data breach. This incident exposed the personal information of approximately 147 million consumers, including names, Social Security numbers, birth dates, addresses, and, in some instances, driver's license numbers. This breach is a stark reminder of the consequences of failing to address known vulnerabilities.

The breach was traced back to a vulnerability in Apache Struts, an open source web application framework used by Equifax. The vulnerability, CVE-2017-5638, allowed attackers to execute remote commands on the server. While Apache released a patch for this vulnerability in March 2017, Equifax failed to update its systems promptly. This oversight provided a window of opportunity for hackers, who began exploiting the vulnerability in May 2017, gaining unauthorized access to Equifax's systems.

The attackers maintained this access for several months, exfiltrating sensitive data undetected. During this period, Equifax had multiple opportunities to identify and mitigate the vulnerability. Regular vulnerability scanning and patch management processes could have identified this security gap and prompted timely remediation. Additionally, more rigorous network monitoring might have detected unusual activity from exploiting the vulnerability, such as the large volumes of data being accessed and exfiltrated.

The Equifax breach highlights the importance of a proactive approach to cybersecurity. Regular vulnerability assessments are crucial in identifying and addressing security weaknesses, especially when using third-party software like Apache Struts. These assessments need to be part of an ongoing cybersecurity strategy rather than one-off occurrences to ensure that new vulnerabilities are detected as they arise.

In the aftermath of the breach, Equifax faced significant repercussions, including lawsuits, a loss of consumer trust, and a decline in market value. The incident led to a congressional investigation and the eventual resignation of the CEO. Equifax also incurred substantial legal fees, improvements to its cybersecurity infrastructure, and compensation to affected consumers. This breach serves as a case study of the far-reaching impact that a single unaddressed vulnerability can have on an organization.

This Equifax data breach case study underscores the criticality of timely vulnerability detection and mitigation. It demonstrates that even large, resource-rich organizations are not immune to cyber threats if they do not maintain robust and adaptive cybersecurity practices. Regular vulnerability scanning, prompt patch management, and continuous monitoring are essential to an effective cybersecurity strategy. Organizations can significantly reduce their risk of a devastating cyberattack by prioritizing these practices.

Career Corner

Vulnerability assessment and penetration testing (pentesting) are dynamic and critical fields within cybersecurity, offering numerous career opportunities for those interested in protecting organizations from cyber threats.

A Vulnerability Assessor or Analyst career involves identifying, evaluating, and reporting on vulnerabilities in systems and networks. These professionals use various tools to conduct vulnerability scans, assess risks, and recommend mitigation strategies. Staying updated with the latest security trends and vulnerability disclosures is vital to the job. This role is crucial in helping organizations understand their security posture and take proactive steps to strengthen their defenses.

Penetration testers, or ethical hackers, simulate cyberattacks to identify and exploit vulnerabilities in an organization's systems. Their role is to think and act like a hacker (but ethically) to uncover weaknesses before malicious attackers do. This career requires a deep understanding of various hacking techniques and tools and creativity and problem-solving skills to breach complex systems. Pentesters often specialize in areas like network, application, or wireless penetration testing.

Security Consultants in vulnerability assessment and pentesting offer expert advice to organizations on protecting their systems. They assess security policies, conduct tests, and provide recommendations tailored to the client's specific needs. This role often involves technical expertise and communication skills, as consultants must translate complex security concepts into actionable advice for nontechnical stakeholders.

Certifications in Vulnerability Assessment and Penetration Testing

Certifications play a significant role in vulnerability assessment and pentesting, validating professionals' skills and knowledge. Several certifications are highly regarded in the industry.

The Certified Ethical Hacker (CEH) certification, offered by the EC-Council, is one of the most recognized credentials for penetration testing. It covers a broad range of topics in ethical hacking, including the latest hacking techniques, tools, and security threats. CEH is often considered a stepping stone for those looking to enter the field of ethical hacking.

The Offensive Security Certified Professional (OSCP) is another prestigious certification known for its rigor and hands-on approach. The OSCP certification process involves a challenging 24-hour practical exam where candidates must successfully attack and penetrate various live machines in a controlled environment. It is highly respected among cybersecurity professionals, especially those aiming to demonstrate practical pentesting proficiency.

The GIAC Enterprise Vulnerability Assessor Certification (GEVA) can be a valuable asset for those focusing on vulnerability assessment. This certification emphasizes the methodology to conduct vulnerability assessments and the techniques to identify system vulnerabilities.

In addition to these, the CompTIA PenTest+ certification is designed for intermediate-level cybersecurity professionals. It covers penetration testing and vulnerability management and includes aspects like compliance and operational requirements.

Pursuing certifications in vulnerability assessment and pentesting requires a blend of theoretical knowledge and practical experience. They enhance a professional's skill set and significantly boost their career prospects and credibility in the cybersecurity community. Regularly updating these certifications and staying abreast of the latest developments in the field are essential for anyone looking to build a career in these dynamic and ever-evolving areas of cybersecurity.

Chapter Questions

1. What is the primary goal of identifying and categorizing system vulnerabilities in cybersecurity?

    A. To enhance system performance

    B. To streamline cybersecurity efforts

    C. To comply with legal requirements

    D. To increase user convenience

2. Which of the following is a common form of system vulnerability?

    A. Frequent software updates

    B. Strong password policies

    C. Software bugs

    D. Regular data backups

3. What role do automated vulnerability scanners play in cybersecurity?

    A. They replace the need for manual testing

    B. They provide a complete solution to cybersecurity

    C. They detect known vulnerabilities efficiently

    D. They eliminate all system vulnerabilities

4. Why is manual testing necessary in vulnerability assessment?

    A. It is faster than automated testing

    B. It uncovers more nuanced and complex vulnerabilities

    C. It is less costly than automated testing

    D. It requires less expertise

5. What is the limitation of relying solely on automated vulnerability scanners?

    A. They are too complex to operate

    B. They may not detect zero-day exploits

    C. They always cause system disruptions

    D. They require constant manual intervention

6. Why is continuous monitoring essential in cybersecurity?

   A. To ensure constant system performance

   B. To comply with international standards

   C. To keep up with evolving threats and vulnerabilities

   D. To reduce the need for manual testing

7. What is the primary purpose of penetration testing in cybersecurity?

   A. To train IT staff

   B. To identify vulnerabilities in a system

   C. To comply with cybersecurity insurance requirements

   D. To impress stakeholders

8. What is the significance of the reconnaissance phase in ethical hacking?

   A. It involves the exploitation of vulnerabilities

   B. It gathers detailed information about the target system

   C. It is the final phase of ethical hacking

   D. It includes the documentation of findings

9. In penetration testing, what is the role of exploitation tools?

   A. To document the testing process

   B. To simulate real-world attacks

   C. To train cybersecurity personnel

   D. To back up system data

10. What is a critical component of reporting in cybersecurity?

    A. Predicting future stock market trends

    B. Documenting findings from assessments

    C. Advertising cybersecurity tools

    D. Recruiting IT professionals

11. How does risk assessment contribute to cybersecurity?

    A. By ensuring legal compliance

    B. By evaluating the potential impact of vulnerabilities

    C. Providing entertainment to staff

    D. By marketing the organization's security posture

12. What is the importance of a multilayered security approach?

    A. It simplifies cybersecurity management

    B. It reduces the need for IT staff

    C. It creates a more resilient defense system

    D. It focuses only on technical controls

13. Why is mitigation strategy development a collaborative effort?

    A. To increase the IT budget

    B. To ensure alignment with business goals

    C. To create a competitive advantage

    D. To comply with industry standards

14. In mitigation strategies, why is continuous adaptation necessary?

    A. To maintain a consistent approach

    B. To keep up with changing cyber threats

    C. To simplify cybersecurity protocols

    D. To reduce the need for employee training

15. Why is comprehensive communication and training necessary in cybersecurity?

    A. To boost sales and marketing

    B. To create a security-conscious culture

    C. To increase social media presence

    D. To reduce the number of IT staff

CHAPTER 12

Security Policies and Procedures

In today's digital landscape, creating effective security policies is not just a precaution but a fundamental necessity. These policies are more than mere guidelines; they are the backbone of an organization's cybersecurity strategy, playing a pivotal role in safeguarding digital assets. Their importance is profound, extending beyond basic instructions to symbolize an organization's commitment to combat many cyber threats. These policies reflect the organization's dedication to adhering to legal and regulatory standards and fostering a culture of security awareness and vigilance. As we delve into the development of these policies, it becomes clear that they are integral to the organization's ethos, embodying its core values and ethical principles and signifying a deep-seated commitment to maintaining a strong cybersecurity posture.

Security policies within the digital domain serve as a constitution for an organization, establishing the essential laws and principles that govern its cyber landscape. They clearly distinguish between permissible and prohibited actions in the digital world, a crucial feature in an environment where cyber threats continually evolve and present new challenges. These policies act as a compass, offering direction and stability, and provide a structured framework to navigate cybersecurity's complex and often intricate pathways. They are the architectural blueprint for building

© Dr. Jason Edwards 2024, corrected publication 2024
Dr. J. Edwards, *Mastering Cybersecurity*, https://doi.org/10.1007/979-8-8688-0297-3_12

and maintaining a secure, resilient digital infrastructure, capable of withstanding the test of time and adapting to the ever-changing cyber threat landscape.

The development of these policies is a testament to an organization's proactive approach to managing and mitigating cyber risks. It demonstrates an understanding that cyber threats are dynamic, requiring constant vigilance and adaptability. These policies serve as a strategic response to this dynamic environment, equipping the organization to avoid potential cyber threats. They lay the foundation for safe digital practices and ensure that every stakeholder, from the highest levels of management to the most junior employees, understands their role in maintaining cybersecurity.

These policies also act as a beacon of assurance for all stakeholders, including customers, partners, and regulatory bodies. They illustrate the organization's commitment to protecting sensitive information and maintaining trust in its digital operations. In a world where cyber threats can severely impact an organization's reputation and operational integrity, these policies offer reassurance that the organization is not only aware of these risks but is actively counteracting them. They send a clear message of the organization's commitment to defending its digital domain against any threat, ensuring the integrity, confidentiality, and availability of its digital assets.

Developing and implementing comprehensive security policies is imperative in today's digital environment. These policies encapsulate an organization's commitment to cybersecurity, providing a clear road map for navigating the complex world of digital threats and laying the groundwork for a secure and resilient digital environment. Far from being merely defensive mechanisms, these policies represent a proactive strategy and a declaration of the organization's readiness to face and overcome the challenges posed by the digital age.

Developing Effective Security Policies

In today's digital era, formulating robust security policies transcends a mere precautionary measure; it epitomizes a fundamental necessity. These policies stand at the core of an organization's cybersecurity strategy as pivotal guiding principles that underscore safeguarding digital assets. Their role is multifaceted and profound, extending well beyond basic guidelines. They embody an organization's unwavering commitment to safeguard itself against the myriad of cyber threats, ensuring adherence to legal and regulatory standards and nurturing a pervasive culture of security awareness and vigilance. As we navigate the intricate process of developing these policies, it becomes evident that their significance is manifold. They are not merely a collection of rules and protocols but mirror the organization's core values, ethical principles, and steadfast dedication to maintaining a robust cybersecurity posture.

Security policies in the digital domain are comparable to a constitution within an organization. They establish the fundamental laws and principles governing the cyber landscape, clearly distinguishing between permissible and prohibited actions in the digital sphere. This distinction is crucial in an environment where cyber threats constantly evolve, posing new and unforeseen challenges. The policies act as a compass, offering direction and stability amidst these challenges and providing a structured framework to navigate cybersecurity's intricate and often convoluted pathways effectively. They are akin to an architectural blueprint, essential for constructing and maintaining a secure, resilient digital infrastructure that can withstand the test of time and adapt to the ever-changing cyber threat landscape.

These security policies testify to an organization's proactive stance in managing and mitigating cyber risks. They reflect a deep-seated understanding that threats are not static but dynamic in the digital world, requiring continuous vigilance and adaptation. The policies are a strategic response to this dynamic environment, enabling the organization to avoid potential cyber threats. They form the bedrock upon which safe digital practices are built and maintained, ensuring that every stakeholder understands their role in upholding cybersecurity, from the highest levels of management to the most junior employees.

Moreover, these policies are a beacon of assurance for all stakeholders, including customers, partners, and regulatory bodies. They demonstrate the organization's dedication to protecting sensitive information and maintaining trust in its digital operations. In a landscape where cyber-threats can undermine an organization's reputation and operations, these policies provide a reassurance that the organization is not only aware of the risks but is also actively engaged in countering them. They send a clear message: the organization is committed to safeguarding its digital realm against any threat, ensuring the integrity, confidentiality, and availability of its digital assets.

Developing and implementing comprehensive security policies are imperative in today's digital landscape. They encapsulate an organization's ethos and commitment to cybersecurity, provide a clear road map for navigating the complex world of digital threats, and lay the foundation for a secure and resilient digital environment. These policies are not just a defensive mechanism; they are a proactive strategy, a declaration of the organization's readiness to confront and conquer the challenges posed by the digital age.

Critical Components of Security Policies

The structure of a robust security policy is intricate and multidimensional, reflecting the complexity of the digital landscape it aims to protect. The bedrock of this structure is the policy's scope, which demands precise definitions to encapsulate every relevant facet of the organization's digital operations. This meticulous delineation ensures comprehensive protection that leaves no aspect of the digital ecosystem vulnerable. The scope should be all-encompassing, ranging from the nuances of network infrastructure to the subtleties of end-user behavior, ensuring that each element falls within its protective ambit, whether tangible or intangible.

The objectives of a security policy serve as its guiding beacons, directing its course and ensuring its effectiveness. These objectives must adhere to the SMART criteria – specific, measurable, achievable, relevant, and time-bound – providing the policy with well-defined, actionable targets. Beyond mere compliance and protection, these objectives should progressively elevate the organization's cybersecurity stature. An example of such an objective might be the enhancement of system resilience against ransomware attacks by 70% over the next 18 months, combining both a specific target and a clear timeline.

Roles and responsibilities form the operational backbone of a security policy, ensuring its successful execution. This segment should function like a finely tuned instrument, where each participant, from the boardroom to the break room, is acutely aware of their role and its significance in cybersecurity. This level of clarity is pivotal, aligning every individual with the policy's goals and ensuring a collective effort toward achieving them. It's about creating a shared sense of purpose and responsibility, where everyone understands their contribution to the organization's digital safety.

Compliance requirements act as the navigational compass for the policy, guiding the organization through the intricate maze of legal and regulatory obligations. This alignment transcends mere adherence to avoid penalties; it embodies a commitment to ethical and responsible digital conduct. The policy should serve as a compliance checklist and a comprehensive guide, illuminating the path to ethical digital practices and ensuring that the organization remains on the right side of the law.

The consequences of violating the policy are its enforcement mechanism, providing it with the necessary authority and gravitas. These consequences should be communicated, acting as a robust deterrent against breaches of the policy. However, the focus should not solely be on punitive measures but also on corrective and educational aspects.

This balanced approach fosters a culture of responsibility and learning rather than fear, ensuring that the policy is not only adhered to but also respected.

In addition, the policy must integrate proactive strategies for threat anticipation and mitigation. This includes continuously monitoring and analyzing the cyber landscape to identify emerging threats and vulnerabilities. By staying ahead of potential risks, the policy ensures that the organization is not merely reactive but is actively engaged in preemptive defense.

The policy should also be adaptable and capable of evolving with the ever-changing digital environment. This flexibility is key to maintaining relevance and efficacy over time. Regular reviews and updates should be embedded in the policy's lifecycle, allowing it to adapt to new technologies, threat vectors, and regulatory changes.

Lastly, the policy should emphasize the importance of collaboration and information sharing within the organization and with external partners. This collaborative approach enriches the policy with diverse perspectives and expertise, enhancing its robustness and effectiveness.

The anatomy of a robust security policy is a complex blend of scope definition, objective setting, role clarification, compliance adherence, consequence management, proactive threat management, adaptability, and collaborative engagement. Together, these elements form a comprehensive shield, safeguarding the organization against cyber threats while fostering a culture of informed vigilance and ethical digital practice.

Tailoring Policies to Organizational Needs

Creating a security policy is not a one-off exercise but a tailored process requiring deep understanding and customization. Every organization has its unique DNA – structure, culture, operations, and risk profile. The security policy must be a bespoke suit tailored to fit these unique attributes perfectly.

The structure of an organization heavily influences its security needs. A complex, multilayered organization with diverse operations and global reach requires a policy that addresses this complexity. The policy must be versatile and able to cater to the varied facets of the organization while maintaining coherence and consistency.

Cultural alignment is essential for policy adoption. A policy that resonates with the organization's culture will likely be embraced and followed. This alignment requires understanding the organization's values, norms, and communication styles. For instance, a policy in a hierarchical organization might need to emphasize top-down communication and enforcement, whereas a flat organization might benefit from a more collaborative approach.

Risk profile assessment is the compass that guides the tailoring process. It involves thoroughly analyzing the threats and vulnerabilities specific to the organization. This assessment is not static; it needs to be dynamic, adapting to the evolving nature of cyber threats. The policy must be flexible enough to accommodate these changes, ensuring the organization remains protected against emerging risks.

Stakeholder engagement is the thread that weaves through the entire policy development process. It's about bringing together different perspectives, from the IT team to the front-line employees, ensuring the policy is comprehensive and practical. This engagement fosters a sense of ownership and accountability, making the policy a collective effort rather than a top-down mandate.

Engaging Stakeholders in Policy Development

Developing security policies is a task that thrives on wide-ranging collaboration and input from varied sources. Actively involving stakeholders from different departments and levels within the organization is not merely beneficial – it's fundamental to creating policies aligned with the organization's diverse and specific needs. The policy development process comprehensively understands the distinct challenges and risks encountered across various departments by engaging with stakeholders ranging from senior executives to operational staff. Such a multilayered engagement strategy ensures that the resulting policies are practical and relevant and enjoy broad acceptance and commitment throughout the organization.

This stakeholder engagement is multifaceted, encompassing various participatory and consultative approaches. Workshops, for example, offer a dynamic forum for open dialogue, collaborative problem-solving, and consensus building, allowing stakeholders to contribute their insights and concerns actively. Targeted interviews with specific departments or teams allow one to delve into unique operational challenges and requirements, offering a deeper, more nuanced understanding that can shape more effective policies. Regular feedback sessions are essential for maintaining a loop of continuous engagement, enabling the iterative adaptation of policies in line with evolving organizational needs and external circumstances.

In addition to these methods, roundtable discussions and surveys can be crucial. Roundtable discussions encourage a free flow of ideas and debate, fostering an environment where stakeholders feel valued and heard. Surveys can gather broad-based input across the organization, ensuring that even the voices of those who are less vocal in meetings are captured and considered in the policymaking process.

Balancing Flexibility and Rigidity

The art of crafting effective security policies lies in striking a delicate balance between flexibility and rigidity. Policies must be sufficiently rigid to establish clear, definitive guidelines and standards that provide direction and certainty. However, they also require a degree of flexibility to accommodate evolving technological landscapes, business processes, and emerging threats. This balance is crucial in preventing policies from becoming overly restrictive and impractical or, conversely, too vague and ineffective.

Achieving this equilibrium demands a dynamic and responsive policy formulation and maintenance approach. This involves regular reviews and updates and incorporating mechanisms for exceptions and adaptations under special circumstances. Such a flexible yet structured approach ensures that the policies remain relevant, effective, and responsive to internal organizational changes and external environmental shifts.

Regular Review and Update of Policies

In the fast-paced and ever-evolving cybersecurity domain, static policies quickly become obsolete. Consequently, regular and systematic reviews and updates of security policies are imperative to ensure their continued relevance and effectiveness. This process should be methodical and scheduled, such as through semiannual or annual reviews, to ensure a disciplined approach to policy maintenance.

These reviews should be comprehensive, encompassing a full reassessment of existing risks, a thorough analysis of recent security incidents and breaches, and the integration of feedback from throughout the organization. By adopting a continuous improvement mindset, these regular reviews help ensure that security policies remain ahead of the curve, effectively addressing emerging threats and aligning with the organization's evolving cybersecurity needs.

Documentation and Accessibility of Policies

Effective security policies must be well-conceived, clearly documented, and readily accessible to all organization members. The documentation of these policies should be straightforward, structured, and free of technical jargon to ensure comprehensibility across the entire workforce, regardless of their level of cybersecurity expertise. Ensuring the accessibility of these policies is crucial; they should be readily available for reference at any time, fostering a culture of continuous awareness and adherence.

To enhance accessibility, various methods can be employed. Hosting the policies on a widely accessible internal platform, such as an intranet or a dedicated portal, ensures they are always just a few clicks away for every employee. Incorporating key policy elements into employee handbooks and making them a focal point of onboarding processes for new hires can also be effective. Regular communication strategies, such as email bulletins or intranet posts highlighting and reminding employees of key policy elements, can reinforce ongoing awareness and comprehension.

Training and Awareness Programs

The culmination of effective security policy development is ensuring that these policies are understood and actively adhered to across the organization. This is achieved through comprehensive and engaging training and awareness programs tailored to the varied roles and responsibilities within the organization. Regardless of their position, each employee should clearly understand how the security policies apply to their specific role and what is expected of them in terms of compliance.

Training programs should be dynamic, engaging, and reflective of the latest developments in the organization's policies and the broader cybersecurity landscape. They should encompass a mix of theoretical learning and practical exercises, including simulations and drills, to ensure that the learning is absorbed and applied in real-world scenarios. This hands-on approach helps in firmly embedding security policies into the organizational culture, transforming them from static documents into active, living frameworks that guide daily behavior and decision-making within the organization.

In addition to traditional training methods, innovative and interactive tools, such as elearning modules, gamification, and scenario-based learning, can significantly enhance engagement and retention of policy knowledge. Regular refresher courses and updates are also crucial in keeping the training content relevant and top of mind for employees.

By adopting these comprehensive strategies for policy development, documentation, accessibility, and training, organizations can ensure that their security policies are robust, up to date, and deeply ingrained in their operational ethos and culture. This holistic approach is key to building a resilient and secure digital environment where every organization member safeguards against cyber threats.

Implementing Security Procedures

Implementing security procedures is a pivotal step in strengthening an organization's defense mechanisms against the myriad of cyber threats present in today's digital world. This task extends far beyond the mere application of outlined policies and strategies. It requires a deep understanding of these policies and a strategic approach to transform theoretical plans into actionable, practical steps. A systematic and methodical approach is vital in ensuring these security procedures are efficient and effective, ultimately enhancing the organization's overall cybersecurity posture.

In the initial stages of the implementation process, gaining a comprehensive understanding of the scope and objectives of the security procedures is fundamental. This understanding ensures that the procedures align seamlessly with the organization's broader cybersecurity goals and strategies. Following this, it becomes imperative to allocate the necessary resources judiciously. This includes not only financial resources but also the appropriate personnel and technological tools required for the successful execution of these procedures. The human element plays a crucial role in this phase, mainly through the training and education of all relevant staff members. This training ensures that every individual within the organization comprehensively understands their role and responsibilities in the newly implemented security framework.

Implementing security procedures in a phased manner is a strategy that offers considerable benefits. This gradual approach aids significantly in risk management, allowing for the systematic identification and resolution of potential issues in a smaller, more controlled environment before a broader implementation is undertaken. This step-by-step rollout helps minimize operational disruptions and facilitates smoother transitions.

Testing and validation form another critical phase in the implementation process. This stage involves conducting simulated cyber-attacks, rigorous system tests, and trial runs to ensure the efficacy and reliability of the security procedures. Such proactive measures are crucial in identifying and addressing vulnerabilities or shortcomings before full-scale deployment.

Equally important is the establishment of an effective feedback mechanism. This mechanism is designed to gather insights, observations, and recommendations from users during and after the implementation of the security procedures. This feedback is invaluable, as it provides real-world perspectives that can be leveraged to make necessary adjustments, enhancing the procedures' effectiveness and user-friendliness.

Comprehensive documentation and meticulous recordkeeping of the implementation process, including any challenges encountered and the strategies used to overcome them, are also essential. This detailed documentation is a crucial reference point for future initiatives and contributes to improving security practices.

An essential final consideration in implementing security procedures is their dynamic nature. In a world where cyber threats constantly evolve and become more sophisticated, security procedures mustn't be static. Continuous monitoring, regular assessments, and timely adjustments are necessary to ensure these procedures remain robust and effective against the ever-changing landscape of cyber threats and vulnerabilities. This ongoing vigilance and adaptability are central to maintaining a strong and resilient cybersecurity posture within the organization.

Training and Compliance Challenges

Training and ensuring compliance in the realm of security procedures pose a myriad of challenges, often beginning with resistance to change. This resistance is typically rooted in a lack of understanding or fear regarding new procedures and changes in routine. Tackling this issue effectively necessitates clear, concise, and persuasive communication highlighting the benefits and critical importance of the new security measures. It's about informing the workforce of the necessity and value of these changes for their safety and the organization's security.

Customizing training programs to cater to the specific needs and roles of different departments is crucial for enhancing the effectiveness of these programs. Tailored training ensures that the content is relevant and resonates more deeply with each group, increasing engagement and retention of information. However, the training process is not limited to imparting theoretical knowledge; it extends to ensuring that it is translated into practice. This can be achieved by incorporating practical exercises, simulations, and real-world scenarios into the training sessions, effectively bridging the gap between theory and application.

Monitoring compliance is a significant task that involves regular checks and measures. This can be done through systematic audits, periodic reviews, and the implementation of automated systems designed to track and ensure adherence to security procedures. Given the dynamic nature of the cybersecurity landscape, the training material and content must be regularly updated to reflect the latest threats, trends, and best practices. This ensures that the workforce remains well-informed and prepared to face new challenges.

Cultivating a security culture within the organization is another crucial aspect of ensuring compliance. Beyond the adherence to rules and procedures, it's about embedding security into the very fabric of the organization's culture. This involves encouraging open and transparent communication about security matters, recognizing and rewarding good security practices, and fostering an environment where security is viewed as a collective responsibility.

Furthermore, it is imperative to have a well-defined process in place for addressing instances of non-compliance. This process should include clear guidelines for remediation and, if necessary, disciplinary actions. However, the focus should be on corrective measures rather than punitive ones, aiming to educate and realign rather than merely penalize.

Encouraging feedback from employees is an essential part of this process. Active solicitation of feedback on training and compliance issues can provide valuable insights into the effectiveness of the current strategies and areas that require improvement. This feedback loop is integral to continuously evolving and enhancing security procedures, ensuring they remain effective, relevant, and aligned with the organization's ongoing needs and objectives.

Addressing the challenges in training and compliance requires a multifaceted approach. It involves clear communication, customized training programs, practical application of knowledge, regular monitoring and updates, fostering a security-centric culture, a straightforward process for handling non-compliance, and continuous feedback and improvement. These elements together form the backbone of a successful strategy for implementing and maintaining adequate security procedures within an organization.

Case Study: Yahoo Data Breaches (2013–2014)

Between 2013 and 2014, Yahoo, one of the world's largest Internet services companies, experienced a series of devastating data breaches. These incidents led to the compromise of approximately three billion user accounts, marking them as some of the most significant breaches in history. The breaches exposed usernames, email addresses, telephone numbers, dates of birth, and, in some cases, encrypted or unencrypted security questions and answers. An analysis of the breaches revealed that they were partly due to weak security measures and inadequate response strategies.

These first breaches occurred in 2013 but were not discovered until 2016. This delay in detection was a critical factor that exacerbated the breach's impact. The attackers could exploit Yahoo's weak security infrastructure, which lacked sufficient safeguards like solid encryption and intrusion detection systems. Yahoo's security team was under-resourced and lacked the authority to enforce more robust security measures.

The breach had a substantial impact on Yahoo's business and reputation. It eroded user trust, impacted the company's valuation, and led to legal and regulatory scrutiny. Yahoo's delayed disclosure of the breach also attracted widespread criticism, suggesting a lack of a transparent and effective incident response strategy. The scale of the breach underscored the importance of robust cybersecurity measures in protecting user data.

Had Yahoo implemented more robust security policies, the breach could have been either prevented or its impact significantly mitigated. Key areas for policy enhancement include data protection, access controls, and incident response. Implementing advanced encryption for data at rest and in transit could have made it more difficult for attackers to access and decipher user information. Regular security audits and penetration testing could have identified vulnerabilities before exploiting them.

Improving access control measures is another crucial area. Yahoo could have benefited from stricter access controls and more rigorous network activity monitoring. Regular updates and patches to their systems would have reduced vulnerabilities. Employee training on cybersecurity best practices could have helped recognize and mitigate phishing attempts and other common attack vectors.

Finally, a robust incident response strategy is vital in managing and mitigating breaches effectively. This includes having a dedicated cybersecurity team with the authority to implement security measures and a clear plan for action in the event of a breach. The plan should detail how to quickly identify and contain a breach, assess the damage, communicate transparently with stakeholders, and prevent future incidents.

The Yahoo data breaches highlight the critical need for comprehensive security policies to protect against cyber threats. By implementing rigorous data protection measures, access controls, and incident response strategies, organizations can significantly reduce the risk of breaches and mitigate their impact should they occur.

Career Corner

A career focused on developing security policies and procedures is a vital and strategic field within cybersecurity, centered around creating frameworks and guidelines to protect organizations from cyber threats. This specialization is essential for maintaining information integrity, confidentiality, and availability in various settings, from corporations to government agencies.

One of the central roles in this field is that of a Security Policy Analyst. These professionals are responsible for developing, analyzing, and updating security policies and procedures. Their work involves assessing organizational needs, understanding legal and regulatory requirements, and ensuring security policies are comprehensive and aligned with business objectives. They are crucial in bridging the gap between complex cybersecurity concepts and practical, enforceable policies.

Another significant career path is that of a Security Compliance Analyst. Individuals in this role focus on ensuring that an organization's security practices comply with external regulations and internal policies. They conduct audits and assessments to evaluate compliance with standards such as ISO 27001, HIPAA, or GDPR. Their expertise is essential in helping organizations navigate the complex landscape of regulatory requirements and avoid potential legal and financial penalties.

The role of a Security Procedures Developer is also critical. These professionals specialize in creating detailed procedures and guidelines that operationalize security policies. They ensure that procedures are clear, practical, and effective in mitigating risks. Their work often involves collaboration with various departments to ensure procedures are understood and implemented correctly.

A Security Policy Director or Manager could be an ideal role for those interested in overarching security strategy. These individuals oversee the development and implementation of security policies and procedures at an organizational level. They ensure that security strategies are aligned with business goals and respond to changing threat landscapes. Their leadership is key in fostering a security awareness and compliance culture throughout the organization.

In terms of certifications, several can enhance expertise in this area. The Certified Information Systems Security Professional (CISSP) is widely recognized and covers aspects of security policy development. The Certified Information Security Manager (CISM) is another respected certification, focusing on the management aspect of security policies and strategies.

Professionals in this field must possess strong analytical skills, excellent communication abilities, and a deep understanding of cybersecurity principles and business operations. They should be adept at translating complex security requirements into understandable and actionable policies and procedures.

A career in developing security policies and procedures is strategic and impactful, offering opportunities to shape how organizations protect their critical assets. From analyzing and creating security policies to ensuring compliance and implementing procedures, professionals in this field are crucial for effectively managing cybersecurity risks. Keeping up to date with evolving cybersecurity trends, regulatory changes, and best practices is essential in this dynamic and crucial field.

Chapter Questions

1. What is the primary role of security policies in an organization's cybersecurity strategy?

   A. To enhance user interface design

   B. To serve as a legal document

   C. To guide the safeguarding of digital assets

   D. To monitor employee behavior

2. What do security policies in the digital domain resemble within an organization?

   A. Marketing strategies

   B. Financial plans

   C. A constitution

   D. Operational procedures

3. What aspect of security policies demonstrates an organization's proactive stance in managing cyber risks?

   A. Marketing alignment

   B. Budget allocation

   C. Adaptation to dynamic threats

   D. Employee satisfaction

4. How do effective security policies impact stakeholders outside the organization, like customers and partners?

    A. Increasing product prices

    B. Through marketing communication

    C. By assuring the protection of sensitive information

    D. Changing operational strategies

5. Why is it essential for security policies to be adaptable?

    A. To accommodate changes in management

    B. To adapt to the evolving digital environment

    C. To adjust to financial constraints

    D. To comply with marketing trends

6. What characterizes the scope of a robust security policy?

    A. Narrow focus on a single aspect

    B. Emphasis on financial data only

    C. Comprehensive coverage of the digital ecosystem

    D. Limited to external threats

7. What is a key feature of the objectives set in a security policy?

    A. Being vague and flexible

    B. Adherence to the SMART criteria

    C. Focused only on short-term goals

    D. Oriented toward financial gain

8. What is crucial in developing security policies to ensure their effectiveness and alignment with the organization's needs?

    A. Random audits

    B. Stakeholder engagement

    C. Following industry trends

    D. Outsourcing policy development

9. What approach is vital for maintaining the relevance and effectiveness of security policies?

    A. Infrequent reviews

    B. Regular reviews and updates

    C. Maintaining static policies

    D. Annual financial audits

10. What is a critical element of the enforcement mechanism of a security policy?

    A. Focusing only on punitive measures

    B. Sole reliance on technological solutions

    C. Clear communication of policy violations' consequences

    D. Ignoring minor infractions

11. Why is continuous monitoring important in the context of security policies?

    A. To ensure employee productivity

    B. To keep up with changing cyber threats

    C. For constant budget evaluation

    D. To monitor market trends

12. What is the importance of training and awareness programs in security policy implementation?

    A. To reduce operational costs

    B. To ensure understanding and adherence across the organization

    C. For entertainment purposes

    D. To comply with international standards

13. How does tailoring security policies benefit an organization?

    A. It simplifies legal compliance

    B. It ensures that policies fit the organization's unique attributes

    C. It makes policies easier to change

    D. It reduces the need for employee training

14. Why is stakeholder engagement a multilayered strategy in the context of security policies?

    A. It is required by law

    B. To ensure policies are practical and widely accepted

    C. For financial auditing

    D. To follow industrial protocols

15. What aspect of security policies helps manage the dynamic nature of cyber threats?

A. Focusing on past incidents

B. Emphasizing static rules

C. Integrating proactive strategies for threat anticipation and mitigation

D. Limiting policies to high-level management decisions

CHAPTER 13

Data Privacy and Protection

Understanding data privacy has become a paramount concern for individuals and organizations in our increasingly digital world. Data privacy refers to correctly handling, processing, storing, and disposing of personal information. This concept hinges on respecting individuals' rights to control their data and ensuring it is not misused or improperly accessed.

The importance of data privacy cannot be overstated. In an era where personal information is a valuable commodity, safeguarding this data is a matter of personal security and maintaining public trust. Data privacy impacts everything from individual identity protection to the integrity of democratic processes. When personal information is adequately protected, it fosters an environment where individuals feel secure in sharing their data, knowing it will be used responsibly and ethically.

Historically, the concept of data privacy has evolved alongside technological advancements. In the early days of computing, data privacy concerns were limited due to the isolated nature of data systems. However, as the Internet facilitated the widespread sharing and storage of information, the need for robust data privacy measures became apparent. This evolution has led to the establishment of various laws and regulations worldwide to protect personal data.

© Dr. Jason Edwards 2024, corrected publication 2024
Dr. J. Edwards, *Mastering Cybersecurity*, https://doi.org/10.1007/979-8-8688-0297-3_13

The fundamental principles of data privacy revolve around transparency, accountability, and individual rights. Transparency requires that individuals are informed about how their data is collected, used, and shared. Accountability mandates that organizations implementing data collection and processing are responsible for managing this data securely and ethically. Furthermore, individual rights ensure that people have control over their data, including the right to access, correct, and even request the deletion of their data.

Data Protection Landscape

Navigating the data protection landscape requires a comprehensive understanding of various elements that form the intricate tapestry of data privacy. Many factors shape this landscape, including the evolving nature of technology, the increasing value of data in the digital economy, and the heightened awareness of privacy issues among consumers and regulatory bodies.

Global perspectives on data protection vary widely and are at the heart of this landscape. Different regions and countries have adopted unique approaches to data privacy, influenced by cultural values, historical experiences, and legal traditions. For instance, the European Union, with its General Data Protection Regulation (GDPR), adopts a stringent approach to data privacy, emphasizing individual rights and control over personal data. In contrast, other regions may have less comprehensive or evolving data protection laws. These diverse global perspectives create a complex environment for international businesses and organizations, which must navigate varying requirements across different jurisdictions.

Regulatory frameworks form the cornerstone of the data protection landscape. These frameworks comprise laws, directives, and guidelines that dictate how personal data should be collected, processed, and protected. The GDPR in Europe, the California Consumer Privacy Act

(CCPA) in the United States, and other similar regulations worldwide aim to empower individuals with greater control over their data while placing obligations on data handlers to protect privacy. These frameworks continually evolve to address new challenges posed by technological advancements and changing societal norms.

Compliance challenges represent a significant aspect of data protection. Organizations are required to continually adapt to new regulations, implement adequate data protection strategies, and ensure ongoing compliance. This includes understanding the intricacies of various data protection laws, securing personal and sensitive data against breaches, and keeping up with the rapid pace of technological change. The complexities are further heightened by the potential consequences of non-compliance, including hefty fines, legal repercussions, and damage to reputation.

The data protection landscape is a dynamic and complex field influenced by global perspectives and shaped by various regulatory frameworks. Organizations face significant compliance challenges in this landscape, requiring a proactive approach to understanding and implementing effective data protection measures. As data plays a crucial role in the digital age, the importance of navigating this landscape with diligence and foresight cannot be overstated.

Types of Data

The types of data managed and protected in data privacy are diverse, each with its unique characteristics and requirements for handling. Broadly, these can be categorized into personal and sensitive data, each necessitating different levels of protection due to their nature and the potential impact on individuals if mishandled.

Personal data refers to any information that can be used to identify an individual, directly or indirectly. This includes apparent identifiers like names and social security numbers and more indirect identifiers like IP addresses or user IDs. Personal data forms the foundation of many digital processes, from customer transactions to personalized services.

In contrast, sensitive data is a subset of personal data that carries a higher risk due to its nature. It includes information such as racial or ethnic origin, political opinions, religious beliefs, biometric data, health information, and sexual orientation. The unauthorized access or mishandling of sensitive data can have particularly severe consequences for individuals, leading to discrimination, harm, or distress.

Data classification is a critical process in data protection, involving the categorization of data based on its sensitivity and the impact that its compromise could have. This process helps organizations determine the protection and security controls that should be applied to each data category. For example, due to its nature, sensitive data would typically require higher security controls than less sensitive personal data.

Anonymization and pseudonymization are techniques used to protect personal and sensitive data. Anonymization involves altering data so that individuals cannot be identified directly or indirectly, even if the data is combined with other information. Once data is anonymized, it is no longer considered personal data under many protection laws. Pseudonymization, however, involves replacing private identifiers with fake identifiers or pseudonyms. This process allows data to be matched with its source without revealing the actual source, reducing the risks associated with data processing while still allowing for valuable data analytics.

Understanding the different types of data, particularly personal vs. sensitive data, and applying appropriate data classification methods are crucial steps in data protection. Anonymization and pseudonymization further enhance privacy measures, allowing organizations to utilize data for analysis and decision-making while mitigating privacy risks.

Stakeholder Perspectives

The landscape of data protection is a multifaceted domain, deeply influenced by the perspectives and roles of various stakeholders, each contributing to the overarching framework of data privacy and security. These stakeholders include consumers, businesses, and governments with distinct perspectives and responsibilities.

Stakeholder perspectives are crucial in shaping data protection policies and practices. Consumers, who are the primary subjects of personal data, increasingly demand transparency and control over how their information is used. Their growing awareness and concern about privacy have spurred changes in how businesses and governments approach data protection. Consumers seek assurance that their data is handled responsibly, securely, and with respect for their privacy.

Consumer rights form a cornerstone of data protection. These rights are enshrined in various data protection laws and regulations worldwide. They typically include the right to be informed about how personal data is collected and used, the right to access one's data, the right to request the correction or deletion of data, and the right to object to or restrict the processing of their data. Empowering consumers with these rights protects their personal information and fosters trust in the digital ecosystem.

Business obligations in the realm of data protection are extensive and multifaceted. Companies must comply with applicable data protection laws, which often involve implementing robust data security measures, ensuring transparency in data processing activities, and respecting the privacy rights of individuals. Businesses must also be prepared to promptly respond to consumer requests regarding their data rights. Failure to comply with these obligations can result in significant legal, financial, and reputational consequences.

Governmental roles in data protection are predominantly centered around legislating and enforcing data privacy laws and regulations. Governments are responsible for establishing legal frameworks that balance the need to protect individual privacy with the economic and societal benefits of data processing. They also play a critical role in overseeing compliance, investigating data breaches, and enforcing penalties for violations. Governments often engage in public awareness campaigns and guide businesses and consumers about data protection practices.

The interplay of stakeholder perspectives, consumer rights, business obligations, and governmental roles creates the comprehensive tapestry of data protection. Each stakeholder contributes uniquely to developing, implementing, and evolving data protection standards, highlighting the collective effort required to safeguard personal information in the digital age.

Legal Frameworks and Compliance

A patchwork of laws governs the global landscape of data protection, each designed to address the unique challenges posed by the digital age. These laws aim to protect personal data, provide rights to individuals regarding their information, and place obligations on entities that process data. Among the most prominent are the General Data Protection Regulation (GDPR) in the European Union and the California Consumer Privacy Act (CCPA) in the United States. Additionally, various other regional laws contribute to the global data protection framework.

The GDPR, implemented in May 2018, represents a landmark in data protection laws. It applies to all companies processing and holding the personal data of individuals residing in the European Union, regardless of the company's location. The GDPR emphasizes transparency, security, and accountability in data processing. It grants individuals robust rights, including the right to access, correct, and delete their data and the right to data portability. Non-compliance with GDPR can result in significant fines, making it one of the world's most stringent data protection laws.

The CCPA, which took effect in January 2020, is a significant state-level privacy law in the United States. It provides California residents with rights similar to those in the GDPR, such as the right to know what personal information is being collected about them, the right to delete personal information held by businesses, and the right to opt out of the sale of their personal information. While the CCPA applies explicitly to businesses operating in California, its impact is felt nationally and globally due to the size and influence of the California economy.

Other regional laws across the globe also play critical roles in the data protection landscape. For instance, the Personal Information Protection and Electronic Documents Act (PIPEDA) in Canada, the Lei Geral de Proteção de Dados (LGPD) in Brazil, and the Data Protection Act in the United Kingdom post-Brexit each provide frameworks for data protection in their respective regions. These laws, while varying in specifics, commonly include provisions for the rights of individuals to access and control their data, requirements for data breach notifications, and guidelines for lawful data processing.

Global data protection laws like the GDPR, CCPA, and other regional laws form an intricate and evolving tapestry of regulations governing personal data handling. These laws reflect a growing global consensus on protecting personal information, providing rights to individuals, and setting standards for businesses and organizations that process data. As the digital landscape evolves, so will the laws designed to safeguard privacy and data security.

Compliance Requirements

Navigating the complex world of data protection compliance requires a thorough understanding of various requirements and principles for safeguarding personal data. Compliance requirements, data processing principles, data subject rights, and reporting obligations form the core components of this landscape, each playing a vital role in ensuring robust data protection practices.

Compliance requirements vary depending on the regulatory framework, but generally, they adhere to specific rules and guidelines about how personal data should be collected, processed, stored, and shared. For organizations, compliance means implementing appropriate technical and organizational measures to protect data and ensuring that all data processing activities are lawful and transparent. This often includes obtaining valid consent from data subjects, respecting their privacy rights, and maintaining comprehensive records of data processing activities.

Data processing principles are foundational to most data protection laws and regulations, including the GDPR and CCPA. These principles include lawfulness, fairness, and transparency, meaning that data must be processed legally, fairly, and in a way that is transparent to the data subject. Other fundamental principles include purpose limitation, data minimization, accuracy, storage limitation, and integrity and confidentiality. These principles ensure that data is processed responsibly, ethically, and securely.

Data subject rights are central to data protection laws, empowering individuals with control over their data. These rights typically include the right to be informed about data collection and use, the right to access their data, the right to rectification of incorrect data, the right to erasure ("right to be forgotten"), the right to restrict processing, the right to data portability, and the right to object to processing, including automated decision-making and profiling. Organizations must have mechanisms to respond to and honor these rights requests from individuals.

Reporting obligations in the context of data protection mainly relate to data breaches. Organizations are generally required to report certain types of data breaches to the relevant regulatory authority and, in some cases, to the affected data subjects. The GDPR, for instance, mandates that data breaches likely to result in a risk to the rights and freedoms of individuals must be reported to the supervisory authority within 72 hours of the organization becoming aware of it. Quick and transparent reporting of breaches is crucial for mitigating potential harms and maintaining trust.

Understanding and adhering to compliance requirements, data processing principles, data subject rights, and reporting obligations are critical for any organization handling personal data. These components ensure that data is handled ethically, legally, and securely, thus safeguarding the privacy and rights of individuals in the digital age.

Cross-Border Data Transfer

Cross-border data transfer is a crucial aspect of the global digital economy, involving the movement of personal data across national borders. Complex regulations and agreements govern this process to ensure that data remains protected when transferred internationally. Understanding these regulations is essential for businesses and organizations operating globally.

International agreements play a pivotal role in governing cross-border data transfers. These agreements are established between countries or regions to provide a legal framework for transferring personal data. One of the most significant examples is the European Union's adequacy decisions, which determine whether a non-EU country offers adequate data protection. If a country is deemed to have adequate protection, personal data can flow from the EU (and European Economic Area) to that country without any further safeguards being necessary.

Safe Harbor Principles were a set of privacy principles that formed the basis of an agreement between the United States and the European Union. The Safe Harbor Agreement allowed US companies to receive personal data from EU countries legally, provided they adhered to these principles, ensuring data protection compatible with EU standards. However, the European Court of Justice invalidated the Safe Harbor framework in 2015 due to concerns about US government surveillance practices. The EU-US Privacy Shield Framework subsequently replaced it, invalidated in 2020, leading to ongoing negotiations for a new framework.

Transfer mechanisms are various tools and legal arrangements used to facilitate the lawful transfer of personal data across borders without international agreements like the EU-US Privacy Shield. Standard contractual clauses (SCCs) are one of the most common mechanisms involving a set of legal terms and conditions that both the sender and the receiver of the personal data agree to, ensuring adequate data protection. Binding corporate rules (BCRs) are another mechanism used by multinational corporations, providing a company-wide policy for transferring personal data within the same corporate group but across different countries. Other mechanisms include the consent of the data subject, the performance of a contract, and specific derogations under local data protection laws.

Cross-border data transfer is a complex process governed by international agreements, principles like the now-defunct Safe Harbor, and transfer mechanisms like standard contractual clauses and binding corporate rules. These elements work together to ensure that personal data remains protected when transferred across national borders, reflecting the global nature of data privacy and the need for international cooperation in its protection.

Enforcement and Penalties

The enforcement of data protection laws and the imposition of penalties for non-compliance are critical elements in ensuring that organizations take these regulations seriously and effectively protect personal data. Regulatory bodies typically enforce, and the penalties can range from fines and sanctions to other forms of regulatory action.

Enforcement and penalties are essential because they underscore the seriousness with which data protection is regarded. Without the threat of significant consequences, organizations might not prioritize the security and proper handling of personal data. The enforcement mechanisms and the potential penalties vary depending on the jurisdiction and the specific data protection regulation.

Regulatory actions can take various forms. These actions are usually initiated by data protection authorities (DPAs), which are tasked with overseeing compliance with data protection laws. Regulatory actions can include audits, orders to comply with specific requirements (such as improving data security measures or ceasing certain data processing activities), and orders to provide information or access to data processing facilities for inspection. DPAs also play a crucial role in investigating complaints from individuals about potential breaches of data protection laws.

Fines and sanctions are the most visible and often impactful penalties for non-compliance with data protection laws. The GDPR, for example, allows for fines of up to €20 million or 4% of the company's annual global turnover, whichever is higher, of severe breaches. The CCPA also provides for financial penalties, though generally lower than those under the GDPR. The size of the fines under these regulations highlights the importance placed on data protection and is a significant deterrent against non-compliance.

In addition to fines, sanctions can also include orders to stop processing data, which can substantially impact a business's operations. In severe cases, non-compliance can lead to legal action, including civil lawsuits from individuals whose data rights have been violated.

Enforcement and penalties are crucial aspects of data protection regimes worldwide. Regulatory actions, including audits and investigations, fines and sanctions, ensure that organizations take their data protection responsibilities seriously. These measures not only help enforce compliance but also build public trust in the digital economy by demonstrating a commitment to protecting personal data.

Future of Data Protection Laws

The future of data protection laws is poised to be shaped by emerging trends and anticipated changes, which are likely to have a profound impact on businesses and their data handling practices. As technology evolves rapidly, data protection laws must adapt to address new challenges and risks associated with the processing and storing of personal data.

Emerging trends in data protection are driven mainly by technological advancements, such as the increasing use of artificial intelligence (AI), machine learning, and the Internet of Things (IoT). These technologies pose unique challenges for data privacy, including issues related to automated decision-making, profiling, and the vast amounts of data generated by IoT devices. Additionally, the growing awareness and concern over privacy among consumers are pushing for more stringent data protection measures.

Anticipated changes in data protection laws are expected to reflect these emerging trends. We may see more regulations focusing on specific technologies, such as AI and IoT, with guidelines on ethical usage, transparency, and accountability in data processing. The concept of "privacy by design," which involves integrating data protection into the development of business practices and technologies from the outset, is likely to become a more prominent and possibly a mandated aspect of data protection strategies.

The impact on businesses due to these evolving data protection laws is expected to be significant. Organizations must invest in more robust data protection measures, update their policies and practices to comply with new regulations, and possibly redesign their systems and services to incorporate privacy-by-design principles. This could entail additional costs and require specialized expertise, especially for smaller businesses and startups.

Furthermore, businesses must stay agile and informed about changes in data protection laws across different jurisdictions, mainly if they operate internationally. This may require a more proactive approach to data protection, including regular employee training, ongoing risk assessments, and implementing more sophisticated data security and privacy technologies.

The future of data protection laws will likely be characterized by a greater focus on emerging technologies, increased regulation, and a shift toward more proactive and integrated approaches to data privacy. These changes will substantially impact businesses, requiring them to adapt and invest in more robust data protection measures to ensure compliance and maintain consumer trust in this ever-evolving digital landscape.

Privacy vs. Public Interest

The tension between privacy and public interest represents a critical and often challenging aspect of data protection and policymaking. This balancing act involves weighing individual rights to privacy against the broader interests of society, which can include public safety, national security, and public health. Navigating this balance often leads to complex ethical dilemmas and case-specific judgments.

Privacy vs. public interest debates are not new but have become more pronounced in the digital age. Privacy advocates argue for the fundamental right of individuals to control their personal information and protect it from unwarranted intrusion. On the other side, there are circumstances where accessing personal data can serve the public interest, such as public health research, national security purposes, or the investigation of crimes.

The balancing act between these two considerations requires careful assessment and often involves legal and ethical complexities. For instance, during public health emergencies like the COVID-19 pandemic, many governments implemented contact tracing apps and other surveillance technologies to track the spread of the virus. While these measures were crucial for public health, they also raised concerns about the potential for long-term impacts on privacy and the normalization of increased surveillance.

Case examples highlight the complexities of this balance. A notable instance is the legal battle between the FBI and Apple Inc. in 2016, where the FBI requested Apple to unlock an iPhone used by a suspect in a terrorism case. Apple resisted, citing concerns over the implications for privacy and security for all its users. The case exemplified the delicate line between aiding law enforcement for public safety and protecting user privacy.

Ethical dilemmas arise in various forms when dealing with privacy vs. public interest. For example, the use of big data and AI in predictive policing or risk assessment in criminal justice can be seen as serving the public interest by potentially reducing crime. However, these practices also raise ethical concerns about surveillance, profiling, and potential biases against certain groups. Similarly, in healthcare, using patient data for research is vital for medical advancements but must be balanced against individual privacy rights and informed consent.

The interplay between privacy and public interest is a complex and ongoing debate. It requires a nuanced understanding of both the value of individual privacy and the broader community's needs. As technology continues to evolve, so will the nature of this balancing act, necessitating ongoing dialogue, legal considerations, and ethical reflections to navigate these challenges effectively.

Consent and Transparency

The concepts of consent and transparency are foundational to modern data protection practices. They revolve around the idea that individuals should have control over their personal information and be fully informed about how their data is collected, used, and shared. These principles are central to building trust between data subjects and controllers and are critical requirements in most data protection regulations.

Informed consent is a critical aspect of data privacy. It means that individuals must be clearly and comprehensively informed about the data being collected from them, the purpose of this data collection, how it will be used, and who it will be shared with before they consent. This consent must be freely given, specific, informed, and unambiguous – it cannot be inferred from inaction or silence. The GDPR, for instance, strongly emphasizes obtaining explicit consent for processing personal data, especially for more sensitive information.

Privacy notices play an essential role in facilitating transparency. Organizations provide these documents or statements to inform individuals about their data collection and processing practices. Privacy notices should be written in clear, straightforward language and be easily accessible. They typically include information about the types of data collected, the purposes of data processing, details on data sharing and transfer, the rights of data subjects, and how they can exercise these rights. Ensuring that these notices are comprehensible and not hidden in fine print is crucial to ensuring informed consent.

User control over personal data is another cornerstone of data protection. This concept extends beyond the initial granting of consent, allowing individuals ongoing control over their data. This includes the ability to access their data, correct inaccuracies, request the deletion of their data (the right to be forgotten), and withdraw consent for data processing at any time. Providing users with easy-to-use tools and options to manage their data empowers them and fosters a sense of trust and transparency.

Consent and transparency are vital to ensuring ethical and legal data processing practices. Informed consent ensures that individuals understand and agree to how their data is used, privacy notices are the vehicle for transparent communication between organizations and individuals, and user control allows individuals ongoing authority over their data. These elements work together to create a data protection environment that respects individual privacy and builds trust in the digital ecosystem.

Data Minimization

Data minimization is a fundamental principle in data protection, emphasizing the need to limit personal data collection, storage, and usage to what is strictly necessary. This concept aligns with the broader goals of privacy and security, ensuring that only relevant and needed data is handled, thereby reducing the risk of data breaches and misuse.

The principle of a need-to-know basis underpins data minimization. It dictates that personal data should only be accessed by individuals who require it to perform their job duties. This approach limits data exposure within an organization and aligns with best practices in data security. By restricting access to data, organizations can better protect sensitive information from unauthorized access or disclosure.

Data retention policies are critical for effective data minimization. These policies define how long different data types should be kept and outline the procedures for their eventual disposal. Retention policies are based on legal requirements, business needs, and the principle of minimizing data held. By regularly reviewing and purging unnecessary or outdated data, organizations can reduce the risk associated with data storage and maintain a leaner and more secure data environment.

Safe disposal of data is the final step in the data lifecycle and is just as important as the initial collection and processing stages. Once data is no longer needed or has reached the end of its retention period, it should be securely and permanently destroyed. This can include shredding paper records, securely erasing digital files, or wiping electronic storage devices. Proper disposal prevents the data from falling into the wrong hands and being used inappropriately or maliciously.

Data minimization and its related practices, such as operating on a need-to-know basis, adhering to data retention policies, and ensuring safe data disposal, are crucial for maintaining privacy and security in managing personal data. These practices help comply with data protection regulations and reinforce an organization's commitment to respecting and safeguarding individual privacy.

Bias and Discrimination

The issue of bias and discrimination in the context of data protection and technology is increasingly receiving attention, particularly in relation to algorithmic bias. As more decisions are automated or assisted by algorithms, the potential for these systems to perpetuate or even exacerbate existing biases and discriminatory practices becomes a significant concern.

Algorithmic bias occurs when automated decision-making systems produce results that are systematically prejudiced due to erroneous assumptions in the machine learning process or biases in the data used to train these systems. This can manifest in various sectors, from finance and healthcare to employment and law enforcement, leading to unfair or discriminatory outcomes for certain groups of people, particularly marginalized or minority communities.

Fair data practices are essential in combating algorithmic bias. These practices ensure that the data used to train algorithms represents diverse populations and does not contain inherent biases. It also includes implementing robust testing and monitoring systems to identify and address algorithm bias. Transparency in how these algorithms operate and their decision-making criteria is also crucial, as it allows for external scrutiny and accountability.

Remedial measures are necessary to address and mitigate the impacts of algorithmic bias. This can include the development of guidelines and standards for equitable and nondiscriminatory algorithmic decision-making. Regular audits and assessments of algorithms can help identify potential biases. Adjusting or retraining the algorithms with more balanced data is essential when biases are detected or redesigning the system entirely if necessary. Additionally, there should be avenues for affected individuals to challenge decisions made by automated systems and seek redress.

Addressing bias and discrimination in data and technology, particularly concerning algorithmic bias, is vital for ensuring fairness and equity in the digital age. Implementing fair data practices and taking remedial measures are essential to mitigating these biases. As technology advances and plays an increasingly significant role in decision-making processes, the need for vigilance and proactive measures in this area becomes more critical.

Responsible Data Sharing

Responsible data sharing is an essential aspect of modern data management, playing a crucial role in various fields such as research, marketing, and technology development. It involves sharing data in a way that respects privacy, ensures security, and adheres to ethical and legal standards.

Data partnerships refer to the collaboration between different organizations to share data for mutual benefit. These partnerships can enable more comprehensive data analysis, foster innovation, and drive business growth. However, they also raise concerns about privacy and security. To address these, responsible data partnerships should be governed by clear agreements that specify the terms of data sharing, including the purpose of data sharing, the types of data to be shared, and measures to protect data privacy and security.

Anonymized data plays a significant role in responsible data sharing. Anonymization involves stripping data of personal identifiers so that individuals cannot be readily identified. This process enables organizations to utilize data for analysis and decision-making while mitigating privacy risks. However, it's important to ensure that anonymization is done effectively, as poorly anonymized data can sometimes be reidentified, leading to privacy breaches.

Ethical guidelines are essential for guiding organizations in responsible data sharing. These guidelines often emphasize the need for transparency in data handling practices, respect for individual privacy, and the maintenance of data integrity. They also encourage organizations to consider the societal impacts of data sharing and to avoid actions that could lead to harm or discrimination. Adhering to ethical guidelines helps build trust with stakeholders and ensures compliance with legal and regulatory standards.

Responsible data sharing through data partnerships, anonymized data, and adherence to ethical guidelines is vital in today's data-driven world. It enables organizations to leverage the benefits of data while ensuring that privacy and ethical standards are upheld, thus maintaining public trust and complying with legal requirements.

The Role of Technology in Data Privacy

Data encryption is a fundamental security technique to protect information from unauthorized access and breaches. It involves converting data into a code to prevent unauthorized access, ensuring that only those with the key to decrypt the information can access it in its original form.

There are several types of encryption, each with specific applications and strengths. Symmetric encryption uses the same key for both encrypting and decrypting data. It's fast and efficient, making it suitable for encrypting large volumes of data. However, the need to share the key between sender and receiver can pose a security risk. Asymmetric encryption, also known as public-key encryption, uses two keys – a public key for encryption and a private one for decryption. While it's more secure than symmetric encryption, it's also slower and more complex, often used for secure communications such as email.

In the context of privacy, encryption plays a critical role. It's used to secure data at rest (such as on a hard drive) and in transit (like during an Internet transaction or data transfer). This protection is crucial for sensitive information, including personal and financial data, ensuring that it remains unreadable and secure even if data is intercepted or accessed without authorization.

Despite its advantages, encryption has some limitations. One significant challenge is the management of encryption keys. The encrypted data may become inaccessible or vulnerable if keys are lost or compromised. Additionally, encryption cannot protect against all types of cyber threats. For instance, it does not prevent data from being intercepted or accessed; instead, it renders it unreadable. There's also the issue of encryption backdoors, which are methods of bypassing encryption that hackers can exploit or use by governments for surveillance, raising ethical and privacy concerns.

Data encryption is vital in protecting privacy and offering robust security for data at rest and in transit. However, its effectiveness depends on proper key management and understanding its limitations. Encryption is a crucial part of a broader data security strategy, including other measures like access controls, network security, and ongoing monitoring.

Anonymization Techniques

Anonymization techniques protect privacy by removing or modifying personal information in datasets, ensuring that individuals cannot be readily identified directly or indirectly. These techniques are essential for enabling the use of data in research, analytics, and various other applications while safeguarding individual privacy.

There are various methods and tools used for anonymization, each with its strengths and specific applications:

1. **Data Masking**: This involves obscuring specific data within a database to protect it. For example, characters in a text string might be replaced with asterisks or other characters.

2. **Pseudonymization**: This replaces private identifiers with fake identifiers or pseudonyms. While it can reduce the risk associated with data processing, pseudonymized data can still be reidentified with additional information.

3. **Generalization**: This method reduces the precision of data, such as altering an exact birth date to just a year or a precise location to a broader area.

4. **Noise Addition**: Adding "noise" or random data to actual data can help mask the original data points, making identifying individuals from the dataset difficult.

5. **Aggregation**: This involves combining data into larger groups, making identifying individuals within these groups harder.

The effectiveness of anonymization techniques depends on various factors, including the nature of the data, the method used, and the context in which the data will be used. While these techniques can significantly reduce the risk of reidentification, they are not foolproof. Data analytics and machine learning advances can sometimes de-anonymize data, revealing personal information intended to be hidden.

Legal considerations are also crucial in the context of anonymization. Different jurisdictions may have varying definitions and standards for adequately anonymized data. For example, under the GDPR, data must be anonymized so that the individual is not identifiable by any means reasonably likely to be used. If data is successfully anonymized, it may no longer be subject to data protection laws; however, legal obligations may still apply if there is a risk of reidentification.

Anonymization techniques are valuable tools for protecting privacy in data processing and analysis. However, their effectiveness can vary and must be carefully implemented to ensure compliance with legal standards. As technology advances, the methods and effectiveness of anonymization will continue to evolve, requiring ongoing attention to technical and legal developments in the field.

Blockchain for Privacy

Blockchain technology, often associated with cryptocurrencies like Bitcoin, has broader applications, including privacy protection. Its unique features offer an innovative approach to managing and securing data in a way that can enhance privacy.

The concept and mechanism of blockchain for privacy hinge on its decentralized and immutable nature. A blockchain is a distributed ledger storing data in blocks linked together in a chain. Each block contains a cryptographic hash of the previous block, a timestamp, and transaction data. This structure makes the blockchain inherently resistant to data modification. Once recorded, the data in any given block cannot be altered retroactively without altering all subsequent blocks, which requires network consensus.

Use cases of blockchain in privacy protection are diverse:

1. **Data Security and Integrity**: Blockchain can be used to create secure and tamper-proof records of data transactions, ensuring data integrity.

2. **Identity Management**: Blockchain can provide a secure and unforgeable way of managing digital identities, reducing the risk of identity theft and fraud.

3. **Consent Management in Healthcare**: Patients' consent for data use can be managed more transparently and immutably, giving them greater control over their personal information.

4. **Supply Chain Transparency**: Blockchain can be used to track the movement of goods securely and transparently, ensuring data integrity throughout the supply chain.

Advantages of using blockchain for privacy include enhanced security, increased transparency, and improved data integrity. The decentralized nature of blockchain means there is no central point of failure, making it more resilient to attacks. The transparency of blockchain, where all transactions are verifiable by all participants, also brings a new level of accountability to data transactions.

However, there are challenges in implementing blockchain for privacy. One major challenge is scalability: as the blockchain grows, the resources required to process and store the data increase. There's also the issue of varying data privacy regulations, such as the GDPR, which mandates the right to erasure ("right to be forgotten"). This right can be at odds with the immutable nature of blockchain. Additionally, the technology is still relatively new and untested in many real-world scenarios, leading to uncertainties about its applicability and effectiveness.

While blockchain presents a promising approach to enhancing privacy and security, it has challenges. The technology offers significant advantages in terms of security and transparency, but scalability and regulatory compliance remain key issues that must be addressed. As the technology matures, we can expect more refined blockchain applications for privacy.

AI and Privacy

The intersection of artificial intelligence (AI) and privacy is an area of growing importance and concern in the digital age. AI technologies, while offering significant benefits, also pose unique challenges to privacy, particularly through automated decision-making processes.

Automated AI decision-making refers to systems' ability to make decisions without human intervention based on data analysis and machine learning algorithms. This can range from personalized content recommendations on streaming services to more consequential decisions like credit scoring, hiring, and law enforcement. While automated decision-making can increase efficiency and objectivity, it raises concerns about transparency, fairness, and accountability.

Privacy risks associated with AI and automated decision-making are multifaceted. One key concern is the extent and nature of personal data collection. AI systems often require vast amounts of data to function effectively, which can lead to excessive data collection and potential invasions of privacy. There's also the risk of unintended bias in AI systems, where algorithms might make unfair or discriminatory decisions based on flawed data or biased programming. Additionally, the opaque nature of some AI systems, often called "black boxes," can make it difficult for individuals to understand how decisions about them are being made, challenging the principles of transparency and consent in data protection.

Regulatory responses to the challenges posed by AI and privacy are evolving. Several jurisdictions are implementing or proposing regulations specifically targeting AI and automated decision-making. For example, the European Union's proposed Artificial Intelligence Act aims to regulate AI applications and mitigate risks, including those to personal privacy. The GDPR also addresses automated decision-making and profiling, granting individuals the right not to be subject to decisions based solely on automated processing, including profiling, which significantly affects them.

Moreover, regulatory responses often emphasize the need for ethical AI development and deployment. This includes ensuring transparency in AI algorithms, implementing fairness audits to detect and mitigate bias, and upholding data protection principles throughout the AI lifecycle. Ensuring human oversight in AI decision-making processes is also a key aspect, allowing for human intervention and review to ensure fair and accountable decisions.

AI and privacy are complex and rapidly evolving areas, with significant challenges related to automated decision-making and data privacy. Regulatory responses are developing to address these challenges, focusing on transparency, fairness, and accountability in AI systems. As AI technology advances, ongoing dialogue and adaptation in regulatory frameworks will be essential to safeguard individual privacy rights.

IoT and Privacy Concerns

The proliferation of the Internet of Things (IoT) has brought significant technological advancements, making everyday objects smarter and more connected. However, this increasing connectivity raises substantial privacy concerns, especially regarding the vast amounts of data collected by IoT devices and the security measures necessary to protect this data.

IoT devices, such as smart thermostats, watches, and home assistants, are designed to collect and transmit data for various purposes, including optimizing device functionality, personalizing user experiences, and gathering data for analysis. These smart devices can collect a wide range of data, from basic information like device operation times to more personal data such as location, health metrics, and even voice recordings. This extensive data collection can provide valuable insights and convenience but poses significant privacy risks.

The primary privacy concern with IoT devices is the extent and sensitivity of the data they collect. Many IoT devices collect personal data continuously, and users may not always be aware of the scope and nature of this data collection. Furthermore, the data collected by these devices can be highly personal and sensitive, potentially leading to privacy invasions if accessed by unauthorized parties.

Security measures are crucial in addressing privacy concerns in the IoT landscape. IoT devices, by their nature, are often connected to the Internet, making them vulnerable to hacking and cyberattacks. Ensuring these devices are secure is challenging due to their diversity, the limited processing power of some devices, and the complexity of the IoT ecosystem. Standard security measures include robust encryption, regular software updates and patches, secure authentication methods, and the implementation of privacy-by-design principles during device development. Privacy by design involves integrating privacy and security considerations into the product design process rather than as an afterthought.

In addition to technological measures, regulatory responses are critical in addressing IoT privacy concerns. Regulations like the GDPR in Europe have implications for IoT devices, particularly regarding data minimization, user consent, and data subject rights. Manufacturers and service providers are increasingly required to consider these regulations when designing and deploying IoT devices.

While IoT devices offer significant benefits in terms of convenience and efficiency, they also bring substantial privacy concerns related to the extensive data collection and the need for robust security measures. Addressing these concerns requires a combination of technological solutions, user awareness, and regulatory compliance to ensure that the benefits of IoT do not come at the cost of compromising individual privacy.

Privacy by Design and Default

Privacy design principles are critical in the current era, where technology and data play central roles. These principles guide organizations in integrating privacy into the design and architecture of IT systems and business practices, ensuring that privacy is not an afterthought but a foundational component.

The conceptual framework of privacy design revolves around proactively embedding privacy into developing and operating IT systems, networked infrastructure, and business practices. This approach, often called "privacy by design" (PbD), was developed by Dr. Ann Cavoukian and has been widely adopted worldwide. It includes key principles such as privacy as the default setting, end-to-end security, and visibility and transparency. By adhering to these principles, organizations can ensure that personal data is protected and that privacy rights are respected throughout the lifecycle of a project or product.

Implementation strategies for privacy design are diverse and depend on the organization's and its projects' specific context and requirements. Common strategies include conducting privacy impact assessments to identify and mitigate privacy risks early in the development process, implementing data minimization practices to collect only necessary data, and ensuring that privacy settings are set at their highest level by default. Another important strategy is fostering a culture of privacy within the organization, where employees are trained and encouraged to consider privacy implications in their daily work.

Privacy design principles provide a framework for proactively integrating privacy considerations into technology and business practices. Implementing these principles requires careful planning and a commitment to privacy at all levels of an organization. By adopting privacy design strategies, organizations can comply with regulatory requirements and build trust with customers and users by demonstrating a commitment to protecting their personal data.

Data Minimization Strategies

Data minimization is a crucial principle in data protection, emphasizing the importance of limiting data collection, storage, and usage to what is strictly necessary for the intended purpose. Adopting data minimization strategies can significantly enhance privacy and security but also presents particular challenges.

Techniques and tools for data minimization are varied and can be implemented at different stages of data handling:

1. **Limiting Data Collection**: Only collect data essential for the specified purpose. Tools like data collection forms or APIs can be designed to restrict the input to necessary fields only.

2. **Data Pseudonymization**: Replace identifying information in datasets with artificial identifiers. This reduces the risk of linking data back to individuals, minimizing the amount of "personal data" handled.

3. **Automated Data Erasure**: Implement tools and processes that automatically delete data once it is no longer necessary for the purpose for which it was collected.

4. **Regular Data Audits**: Conduct frequent audits to identify and eliminate unnecessary data. This can involve automated tools that scan databases for redundant, obsolete, or trivial information.

The benefits of data minimization are significant. Firstly, it enhances privacy and security by reducing the data volume that could be compromised. It also helps organizations comply with data protection laws, such as the GDPR, which explicitly require data minimization. Furthermore, by storing less data, organizations can reduce costs and simplify data management, improving efficiency.

However, implementing data minimization strategies comes with challenges. One primary challenge is balancing data minimization with the desire to harness big data for analytics and business intelligence. In some cases, organizations might find it difficult to predict which data will be valuable in the future, leading to reluctance to delete or not collect specific data. Another challenge lies in the technical and organizational adjustments required to implement these strategies, which can involve significant changes to existing systems and processes.

While data minimization strategies offer numerous benefits regarding privacy, security, and compliance, their implementation requires careful planning and a balance between minimizing data and retaining what is necessary for legitimate business purposes. The choice of techniques and tools will depend on the specific needs and capabilities of the organization.

User-Centric Approaches

User-centric approaches in data protection focus on placing the user at the forefront of privacy and data management strategies. These approaches emphasize empowering users with control over their data and ensuring transparency in how it is collected, used, and shared. Implementing user-centric approaches involves user control and consent considerations, user interface design, and feedback mechanisms.

User control and consent are fundamental aspects of user-centric data protection. This means providing users with clear and straightforward options to control their data. Consent mechanisms should be designed to be easily understandable, allowing users to make informed choices about their data. This includes the ability to opt in or opt out of data collection, access their data, request corrections, or delete their data. Effective user control also involves informing users about data breaches or changes in data use policies in a timely and clear manner.

User interface design plays a crucial role in implementing user-centric approaches. The interface through which users interact with their data should be intuitive and transparent. This includes precise privacy settings, easily accessible privacy policies, and straightforward tools for users to manage their data. Good design can help demystify the complexities of data protection, making it easier for users to understand and control their privacy settings.

Feedback mechanisms are essential for maintaining a user-centric approach. They involve creating channels through which users can provide feedback on their privacy experiences or report concerns and issues. This feedback can improve privacy practices and address users' needs more effectively. Additionally, regular user surveys, usability testing, and other forms of user engagement can provide valuable insights into user preferences and concerns regarding data protection.

User-centric approaches in data protection are about empowering users with control over their data and designing systems that are transparent, intuitive, and responsive to user needs. By focusing on user control and consent, user-friendly interface design, and effective feedback mechanisms, organizations can foster trust and compliance with data protection regulations while enhancing the overall user experience.

Compliance from the Start

"Compliance from the Start" is a proactive approach in data protection and privacy, emphasizing the integration of regulatory compliance into the initial stages of product development and business planning. This approach ensures that compliance with data protection laws is not an afterthought but embedded in the fabric of organizational processes and products.

Understanding and adhering to regulatory requirements is the foundation of this approach. Organizations must be well-versed in the laws and regulations relevant to their operations, such as the GDPR in Europe, CCPA in California, or other regional and sector-specific data protection laws. From the outset, this understanding should inform all aspects of product design, business processes, and data handling practices.

Early-stage integration of compliance is crucial. It involves incorporating data protection principles in project and business strategy planning and development phases. This can be achieved through practices like Privacy Impact Assessments (PIAs) to identify and mitigate potential privacy risks before they materialize. Additionally, adopting the principle of "privacy by design" ensures that privacy and data protection are considered throughout the system development lifecycle.

Continuous evaluation is an integral part of ensuring ongoing compliance. The regulatory landscape, technology, and market conditions are constantly evolving, requiring regular reassessment of compliance measures. Organizations should establish processes for regular reviews and updates of their data protection policies and practices. This includes monitoring changes in laws, emerging technologies, and evolving best practices in data protection. Continuous evaluation also involves training and awareness programs for employees to ensure they remain informed about their responsibilities and the latest developments in data protection.

Adopting a "Compliance from the Start" approach is essential in today's data-driven environment. By understanding regulatory requirements, integrating compliance measures early in project and product development, and engaging in continuous evaluation, organizations can ensure compliance with data protection laws and build trust with customers and users by demonstrating a commitment to protecting their data.

Innovations in Privacy Design

Innovations in privacy design are increasingly important in an era where data is a critical asset, and privacy concerns are paramount. Emerging technologies and future trends in this field shape how industries approach data privacy, leading to new methods and strategies for protecting personal information.

Emerging technologies play a pivotal role in advancing privacy design. For instance, blockchain technology offers new ways to secure data with its decentralized and tamper-evident ledger system, enhancing data integrity and transparency. Artificial intelligence (AI) and machine learning are being used to identify and protect sensitive data and automate privacy impact assessments. Additionally, advancements in encryption technologies, like homomorphic encryption, allow data to be processed in encrypted form, enhancing security and privacy.

Future trends in privacy design are likely to focus on enhancing user control and automating privacy protection. We expect to see more intuitive and user-friendly privacy interfaces that empower users to control their data and understand its use easily. The concept of "privacy by default" will become more prevalent, where systems are designed with the most privacy-protective settings as the default. Additionally, there is a growing trend toward federated learning, a form of machine learning where the algorithm is trained across multiple decentralized devices or servers holding local data samples without exchanging them, thus enhancing privacy.

The impact of these innovations on the industry is significant. Companies increasingly recognize that robust privacy practices are not just a regulatory requirement but a competitive differentiator that can build customer trust. Industries that handle large volumes of personal data, such as healthcare, finance, and technology, are particularly impacted. These sectors invest in innovative privacy technologies to safeguard sensitive data, comply with evolving regulations, and meet consumer expectations for privacy.

Innovations in privacy design, driven by emerging technologies and future trends, are transforming how industries approach data protection. These advancements are not only enhancing the ability to safeguard personal data but are also reshaping consumer expectations and corporate strategies around privacy. As technology evolves, so will the tools and methodologies for protecting privacy, necessitating ongoing adaptation and investment by industries.

Consumer Data Rights and Responsibilities

Understanding data rights is fundamental to data protection, empowering individuals with control over their personal information. Key rights include the right to access, the right to rectification, and the right to erasure. These rights are enshrined in various data protection laws, such as the General Data Protection Regulation (GDPR) in the European Union, providing individuals with the means to manage their data effectively.

The right to access allows individuals to obtain a copy of an organization's personal data. It is a critical right that enables individuals to understand exactly what information about them is being processed and how it is being processed. This transparency is the cornerstone of data protection, as it allows individuals to verify the lawfulness of the data processing and the accuracy of the data.

The right to rectification is the individual's right to have inaccurate personal data corrected or completed if it is incomplete. This right ensures that personal data remains accurate, up to date, and relevant. Inaccurate data can have significant consequences, particularly in contexts like credit scoring or employment, so this right is crucial for safeguarding against potential harms that might arise from incorrect information.

The right to erasure, often referred to as the "right to be forgotten," entitles individuals to have their data deleted by the data controller in certain circumstances. This right is fundamental in cases where the data is no longer necessary for the initially collected purpose or if the individual withdraws their consent for data processing. There is no other legal ground for processing it. The right to erasure is a crucial aspect of data control, allowing individuals to have a say in the lifecycle of their data.

Understanding data rights is essential in today's data-driven world. The right to access, rectification, and erasure empowers individuals to take control of their data, ensuring that their information is handled transparently, accurately, and respectfully. These rights form the backbone of adequate data protection and are critical for maintaining trust in how personal data is used and managed.

Data Portability

Data portability is crucial in data protection, granting individuals more control over their data. It refers to the right of data subjects to receive their data from one data controller in a structured, commonly used, and machine-readable format and to transmit that data to another controller without hindrance. This right is increasingly recognized in various data protection regulations, including the GDPR.

The importance of data portability lies in its empowerment of individuals. It enables them to take their data from one service provider and move it to another, fostering competition and innovation in the market. For example, it allows users to transfer their social media data or email contacts from one platform to another. This capability is especially significant in the digital age, where personal data is valuable for individuals and businesses.

However, implementing data portability presents technical challenges. One of the primary challenges is ensuring interoperability between different systems and formats. Different service providers may use various data formats and structures, making it difficult to transfer data seamlessly from one to another. Additionally, transferring data securely and efficiently without compromising data integrity or exposing it to unauthorized access during the transfer process is challenging.

Best practices in facilitating data portability include

1. **Adopting Standard Data Formats**: Using standardized data formats (JSON and XML) can simplify transferring data between different systems.

2. **Ensuring Security**: Implementing robust encryption and secure transmission protocols is crucial to protect data during transfer.

3. **Clear User Interface**: Providing a straightforward and user-friendly interface for users to request and manage the transfer of their data.

4. **Comprehensive Data Inclusion**: Ensuring that all relevant data is included in the transfer, not just a subset, so the user receives a comprehensive view of their data.

5. **Privacy Protection**: Safeguarding the privacy of other individuals implicated in the data being transferred (e.g., in social media data).

6. **Testing and Validation**: Regularly testing the data portability process to ensure it works smoothly and accurately.

In summary, data portability is a significant aspect of modern data protection, offering user empowerment and market competition benefits. While there are technical challenges in implementing data portability, following best practices can help organizations provide this right effectively while maintaining data security and integrity.

Consumer Awareness and Education

Consumer awareness and education are vital components of data protection and privacy. Educating consumers about their rights and how their data is used can significantly impact their ability to protect their personal information in an increasingly digital world.

Public campaigns play a crucial role in raising consumer awareness. These campaigns, often conducted by governmental bodies, privacy advocacy groups, or even businesses, aim to inform the public about data protection rights, risks associated with personal data sharing, and ways to safeguard their information. Effective campaigns use various media, including social media, television, print, and online platforms, to reach a broad audience. They often focus on key messages like the importance of strong passwords, the risks of sharing personal information online, and individuals' rights under data protection laws like the GDPR or CCPA.

Resources and tools are essential for empowering consumers with the knowledge and means to protect their privacy. This includes websites offering advice and best practices, downloadable guides on privacy rights, and tools that enable individuals to manage their privacy settings or check whether their data has been compromised in a breach. Many data protection authorities also provide helplines and online portals where consumers can seek advice or report privacy concerns.

Impact assessment of consumer awareness and education initiatives is important to gauge their effectiveness. This involves evaluating how well these initiatives improve public understanding of privacy issues and whether they lead to changes in consumer behavior. Surveys, feedback forms, and analytics (such as website traffic to privacy information pages) can be valuable tools in assessing the impact. A successful consumer awareness campaign increases the general knowledge about data protection and leads to more proactive consumer behavior in safeguarding personal information.

Consumer awareness and education are key to empowering individuals in the digital age. Through public campaigns, resources, and tools, consumers can be better informed about their privacy rights and how to protect their data. Assessing the impact of these initiatives is crucial to ensure they are effective and to identify areas for improvement. As digital technologies continue to evolve, ongoing efforts in consumer education will be essential in promoting a safer and more privacy-conscious digital environment.

Responsibilities of Consumers

In the data protection landscape, consumers' responsibilities are increasingly important. While organizations must protect user data, consumers also play a crucial role in safeguarding their personal information. Understanding and actively engaging in safe data practices, reporting breaches, and advocacy are key aspects of consumer responsibility.

Safe data practices are fundamental for consumers to protect their personal information. This includes using strong, unique passwords for different accounts and changing them regularly; being cautious about sharing personal information online, especially on social media; and being aware of phishing scams and other types of online fraud. Consumers should also regularly update their software and use security tools like antivirus programs and firewalls. Understanding and managing privacy settings on apps and online services is another crucial aspect, as it allows consumers to control what data they share and with whom.

Reporting breaches is another vital responsibility. If consumers suspect that their data has been compromised, it's essential for them to report this to the relevant organization and, if necessary, to data protection authorities. Prompt reporting can help mitigate the impact of a breach on the individual and alert organizations to potential security issues that might affect other users.

Advocacy is about consumers using their voices to influence better data protection practices and policies. This can involve supporting organizations prioritizing data privacy, participating in public consultations on privacy-related issues, and voicing concerns to policymakers about data protection laws and regulations. Consumers can also advocate for their rights by demanding transparency from companies about how their data is used and measures taken to protect it.

Consumers have an active role to play in protecting their data. By engaging in safe data practices, reporting breaches, and advocating for more robust data protection measures, consumers can contribute to a more secure digital environment. While the primary responsibility for data protection lies with organizations, informed and proactive consumers are an essential defense against privacy risks.

Future of Consumer Rights

The future of consumer rights in the context of data protection is set against an evolving landscape shaped by technological advancements, changing regulatory frameworks, and growing public awareness of privacy issues. Anticipated changes in this area will likely have significant global implications, reflecting the interconnected nature of the digital world.

Several factors drive the evolving landscape of consumer rights. Technological innovations, such as the rise of artificial intelligence, the Internet of Things (IoT), and increasing digital interconnectivity, are creating new challenges and opportunities in data protection. These advancements necessitate legal frameworks and consumer rights adaptations to address emerging privacy concerns and potential risks associated with these technologies.

Anticipated changes in consumer rights are likely to focus on enhancing individual control and transparency over personal data. This could include more substantial rights to access, rectify, and erase personal data, robust consent mechanisms, and greater control over how personal data is used and shared, particularly in automated decision-making and profiling. Additionally, there may be a shift toward more global standards in data protection as companies operate across borders and data flows internationally.

The global implications of these changes are significant. As countries and regions update their data protection laws, international businesses will need to navigate a complex web of regulations, potentially leading to more standardized global practices in data protection. This harmonization, however, may be challenging due to differing cultural attitudes toward privacy and varying legal traditions.

Moreover, there is likely to be an increased emphasis on cross-border cooperation in enforcing data protection laws, as privacy violations increasingly have international dimensions. Consumers worldwide may also become more empowered to demand higher data protection standards from companies, influenced by global awareness campaigns and the spread of information through digital channels.

The future of consumer rights in data protection is poised for significant evolution, driven by technological advancements and a changing regulatory landscape. These changes will have far-reaching global implications, necessitating coordinated international responses and a rethinking of traditional privacy and data protection approaches. As these trends unfold, the role of consumers in advocating for and exercising their rights will become increasingly important.

Corporate Data Governance

Governance frameworks in the context of data protection are comprehensive systems designed to ensure that organizations manage and protect data responsibly and in compliance with applicable laws and regulations. These frameworks are integral to the overall strategy for data governance and involve several key components: organizational structures, policy development, and compliance monitoring.

Organizational structures are the foundation of effective governance frameworks. They define roles and responsibilities related to data management within an organization. This typically includes appointing specific roles such as a Data Protection Officer (DPO), who oversees data protection strategy and compliance. Additionally, clear lines of accountability and reporting are established to ensure effective management and communication regarding data protection matters.

Policy development is a crucial element in governance frameworks. This involves creating comprehensive policies that address how data is collected, stored, used, and shared in line with legal and regulatory requirements. Effective data protection policies are not static; they must be regularly reviewed and updated to adapt to changes in the law, technology, and business operations. These policies must also be practical and enforceable, providing clear guidelines for employees on handling data appropriately.

Compliance monitoring is another critical component of governance frameworks. It ensures that the organization adheres to its privacy policies and legal obligations. This involves regular audits and assessments of data processing activities, identifying potential areas of risk or non-compliance, and implementing corrective actions where necessary. Compliance monitoring also includes staying abreast of changes in data protection laws and adjusting policies and practices accordingly.

Governance frameworks in data protection are essential for ensuring that organizations handle data responsibly and comply with legal requirements. These frameworks are built on robust organizational structures, well-crafted policies, and effective compliance monitoring, each playing a vital role in safeguarding data and maintaining the trust of customers, clients, and regulators.

Data Lifecycle Management

Data Lifecycle Management (DLM) is a comprehensive approach to managing an organization's data flow throughout its lifecycle, from initial creation and collection to its eventual disposal. This process is critical for ensuring data is managed securely and efficiently and complies with applicable data protection laws and regulations. DLM encompasses several vital stages: collection and storage, usage and sharing, and disposal.

Collection and Storage: The first stage of the data lifecycle involves the collection and storage of data. During this phase, it's crucial to ensure that the data collected complies with legal standards, such as obtaining proper consent where required. Once collected, data must be stored securely to protect it from unauthorized access, breaches, or other forms of compromise. This includes implementing robust security measures like encryption, access controls, and secure data storage solutions. Data minimization principles should also be applied, meaning only data necessary for a specific purpose is collected and retained.

Usage and Sharing: Once data is collected and stored, it may be used for various purposes, including business operations, analysis, and decision-making. In this phase, it's important to ensure that data is used consistently with the reasons for which it was collected and in compliance with applicable regulations. Similar considerations apply when sharing data internally within an organization or externally with third parties. Data-sharing agreements and protocols should be in place to ensure that all parties handle the data appropriately and that the privacy of the individuals concerned is maintained.

Disposal: The final stage of the data lifecycle is data disposal. When data is no longer needed or must be retained by law, it should be disposed of securely and effectively. This is crucial for protecting sensitive information from being accessed after it is useless. Data disposal can involve physical destruction (in the case of paper records) or digital methods such as wiping or degaussing for electronic data. Proper disposal ensures that data is irrecoverable, thus preventing potential data breaches and maintaining compliance with data protection regulations.

Effective Data Lifecycle Management involves carefully considering and managing how data is collected, stored, used, shared, and disposed of. By adhering to best practices in each stage of the data lifecycle, organizations can protect sensitive information, comply with data protection laws, and maintain the trust of their stakeholders.

International Data Transfers and Challenges

International data transfers are integral to the global digital economy, but they come with significant challenges, particularly in regulatory compliance. These challenges stem from different countries having different laws and standards regarding data protection, creating a complex landscape for organizations operating across borders.

Regulatory Challenges

Regulatory Challenges: One of the significant hurdles in international data transfers is navigating the myriad of data protection regulations that vary from country to country. For instance, the European Union's GDPR sets stringent requirements for transferring personal data outside the EU. These requirements are designed to ensure that the data protection accorded to personal data remains intact when transferred internationally. Non-compliance with such regulations can result in hefty fines and legal actions, making it imperative that organizations understand and comply with these laws thoroughly.

Differing Laws and Standards: Each country has its unique approach to data protection, resulting in a patchwork of laws and standards that organizations must navigate. Some countries have very stringent data protection laws (like the EU), while others may have more lenient or no specific data protection laws. This disparity poses challenges for organizations in ensuring that their data transfer practices meet the legal requirements of each jurisdiction. It also complicates creating standardized global policies for data management and protection.

Compliance Complexities: Ensuring compliance with various international data protection laws can be complex and resource-intensive. Organizations must keep abreast of the changing legal landscape, which can be particularly challenging as new laws are enacted and existing ones are updated. They also need to implement robust mechanisms and strategies for data transfer, such as Standard Contractual Clauses (SCCs), Binding Corporate Rules (BCRs), or relying on adequacy decisions. Additionally, there's the challenge of ensuring that third-party partners and service providers that handle data on behalf of the organization also comply with these diverse international data protection standards.

International data transfers present considerable regulatory challenges, stemming from differing laws and standards across jurisdictions and the complexities of ensuring compliance. Organizations transferring data across borders must deeply understand these challenges and implement comprehensive strategies to address them effectively. This includes staying informed about legal changes, implementing appropriate data transfer mechanisms, and ensuring compliance with various international data protection regulations.

Transfer Mechanisms

When transferring personal data across international borders, organizations must use specific mechanisms to ensure compliance with data protection laws. These transfer mechanisms are designed to safeguard personal data from one jurisdiction to another, particularly from regions with strong data protection laws (like the European Union) to those with less stringent or differing regulations. Key mechanisms include

Standard Contractual Clauses (SCCs), Binding Corporate Rules (BCRs), and certification schemes.

Standard Contractual Clauses (SCCs) are legal agreements to ensure that personal data transferred outside the European Economic Area (EEA) is still protected according to European Union standards. The European Commission sets these clauses and provides a contractual solution for transferring personal data to third countries. Organizations can incorporate SCCs into their contracts to meet the GDPR requirements for data transfer, ensuring that the data recipient in the non-EEA country commits to data protection standards equivalent to those in the EU.

Binding Corporate Rules (BCRs) are another suitable mechanism for multinational companies. BCRs are internal rules adopted by multinational companies that define their global policy regarding the international transfer of personal data within the same corporate group to entities in countries that do not provide adequate protection. To be effective, BCRs must be approved by data protection authorities in the EU. Once approved, BCRs allow for the free transfer of data within the corporate group, including to locations outside the EEA.

Certification Schemes, such as the EU-US Privacy Shield Framework (invalidated and is currently being renegotiated), provide a mechanism for companies to comply with data transfer requirements. These schemes involve a set of data protection standards that companies must adhere to, and upon certification, they are deemed to provide an adequate level of data protection. Certification schemes often include regular audits and require companies to adhere publicly to the framework's principles.

Each of these transfer mechanisms bridges the gap between different data protection regimes, allowing for the international flow of data while striving to maintain a high level of protection for personal data. Choosing the right mechanism depends on various factors, including the nature of the data being transferred, the countries involved, and the organizational structure of the entities participating in the transfer.

Data Sovereignty

Data sovereignty is a concept that pertains to the idea that digital data is subject to the laws of the country in which it is located or stored. This concept has become increasingly significant in the global digital economy, where data often crosses international borders and can thus be subject to various jurisdictions. Understanding data sovereignty involves recognizing the impact of local laws on data, the implications of data localization requirements, and the challenges associated with cross-border data transfers.

Local Laws Impact: Data sovereignty means that when data is stored in a particular country, it must comply with its laws and regulations regarding data protection, privacy, and usage. This can have significant implications for organizations that store or process data, as they must be aware of and comply with the legal requirements in each jurisdiction where their data resides. For example, data stored in the European Union is subject to the stringent requirements of the GDPR, which can differ significantly from the laws in other regions.

Data Localization: Some countries have implemented data localization laws that require specific types of data to be stored within the country's borders. These laws are often motivated by privacy, data security, and national sovereignty concerns. Data localization can pose challenges for global businesses, as it may require them to establish data storage and processing capabilities in each country, leading to increased operational complexities and costs.

Cross-Border Issues: Data movement across international borders can be complicated due to varying data protection laws and the principle of data sovereignty. Organizations must navigate these complexities to ensure compliance with different national regulations, which can be a significant legal and logistical challenge. This is particularly relevant for cloud services, where data might be stored and processed in multiple locations worldwide. Ensuring compliance in such scenarios requires a thorough understanding of the laws applicable in each jurisdiction and may involve data transfer mechanisms like SCCs, BCRs, or adherence to international frameworks.

Data sovereignty is a critical consideration in today's interconnected digital world. The impact of local laws, data localization requirements, and cross-border data transfer challenges all play a significant role in how organizations manage and protect data. Navigating these complexities often requires a comprehensive strategy that includes legal expertise, robust data management practices, and an understanding of the global data protection landscape.

Best Practices for Cross-Border Data Flows

Best practices for managing cross-border data flows are essential for organizations operating in the global digital economy. Ensuring international data transfers comply with national laws and regulations requires a strategic and informed approach. Critical components of this approach include conducting risk assessments, engaging in strategic planning, and seeking legal advice.

Risk Assessment: The first step in managing cross-border data flows is to conduct a thorough risk assessment. This involves identifying the types of data being transferred, understanding the data flow (where the data is coming from and going to), and recognizing the potential risks associated with these transfers. Risks can include legal and regulatory compliance risks, the risk of data breaches or unauthorized access, and the risks arising from the political and economic stability of the countries involved. Assessing these risks helps understand the potential impacts on the organization and develop strategies to mitigate them.

Strategic Planning: Once the risks are identified, strategic planning is crucial. This includes determining the most appropriate data transfer mechanisms, such as Standard Contractual Clauses (SCCs), Binding

Corporate Rules (BCRs), or reliance on adequacy decisions for transfers within certain jurisdictions. Strategic planning also involves developing data protection policies that are flexible enough to adapt to different legal requirements while maintaining a high standard of data protection across all jurisdictions. Additionally, it's essential to establish clear protocols for responding to foreign jurisdictions' legal requests and handling data breaches involving cross-border data.

Legal Advice: Given the complexity and variability of laws governing cross-border data flows, obtaining expert legal advice is essential. Legal advisors with expertise in international data protection laws can provide guidance on the requirements of different jurisdictions, help draft and review legal documents like data transfer agreements, and advise on compliance strategies. They can also provide valuable insights into the evolving legal landscape, such as updates to data protection regulations or changes in the interpretation of existing laws.

Managing cross-border data flows effectively requires a comprehensive approach that includes conducting thorough risk assessments, engaging in strategic planning, and seeking specialized legal advice. By following these best practices, organizations can ensure that their international data transfers are compliant, secure, and aligned with their broader data protection and business strategies.

Emerging Trends and Future Outlook

Rapid advancements and innovations primarily shape emerging trends and future outlooks in the realm of technology. Key particularly influential areas include artificial intelligence (AI), quantum computing, and biometric technologies. Each field evolves rapidly, offering new capabilities and presenting unique challenges and considerations.

Technological Innovations

Technological innovations are driving significant changes across various sectors. Advancements in cloud computing, the Internet of Things (IoT), and 5G technology are transforming how data is collected, processed, and utilized, leading to more interconnected and efficient systems. These innovations offer tremendous opportunities for growth and improvement in services but also raise important questions about data privacy, security, and governance.

AI developments are at the forefront of technological evolution. AI and machine learning technologies are becoming increasingly sophisticated, enabling more effective data analysis, automation, and decision-making processes. These technologies have applications in numerous fields, from healthcare and finance to transportation and customer service. However, they also bring challenges such as algorithmic bias, ethical concerns regarding autonomous systems, and the need for robust datasets that respect privacy and consent.

Quantum computing represents a significant leap in computational capabilities. Quantum computers, which use quantum bits (qubits) instead of classical bits, promise to solve complex problems much faster than traditional computers. This could revolutionize areas like cryptography, drug discovery, and climate modeling. However, quantum computing also poses a potential threat to current encryption methods, prompting a need for quantum-resistant cryptographic techniques.

Biometric technologies are increasingly being used for authentication and security purposes. Innovations in facial recognition, fingerprint scanning, and voice recognition are enhancing security and personalization in technology. While these technologies offer more secure and convenient authentication methods, they also raise significant privacy concerns, as biometric data is particularly sensitive and potentially vulnerable to misuse.

Rapid advancements in AI, quantum computing, and biometric technologies mark the future outlook in technology. These developments promise to bring about transformative changes but also necessitate careful consideration of ethical, privacy, and security implications. As these technologies continue to evolve, it will be crucial to balance innovation with responsible management and protection of data and privacy.

Evolving Legal Landscape

New regulations, international harmonization efforts, and trends in enforcement are shaping the evolving legal landscape in data protection and privacy. As technology advances and the global data economy grows, legal frameworks continually adapt to address emerging challenges and protect individual privacy rights.

New regulations are frequently introduced, and existing ones are updated to respond to the changing digital environment. For example, the European Union's General Data Protection Regulation (GDPR) set a new standard for data protection. It inspired similar laws in other jurisdictions, like the California Consumer Privacy Act (CCPA) in the United States and Brazil's Lei Geral de Proteção de Dados (LGPD). These regulations typically include requirements for data consent, rights for individuals to access and control their data, and strict guidelines for data breach notifications.

International harmonization of data protection laws is an ongoing trend, driven by the need for consistent and effective data management practices in a globally interconnected world. Efforts are being made to align different national and regional data protection standards to facilitate cross-border data flows while ensuring high levels of data protection. This includes discussions for mutual recognition of data protection regimes, such as adequacy decisions by the EU for countries outside the bloc and initiatives like the Asia-Pacific Economic Cooperation (APEC) Cross-Border Privacy Rules (CBPR) system.

Enforcement trends show a marked increase in the number and severity of penalties for data protection violations. Regulators are becoming more proactive and stringent in their enforcement actions. High-profile cases have resulted in significant fines, emphasizing the importance of compliance. Moreover, there is a growing focus on holding companies accountable for not just data breaches but also for lack of transparency, inadequate data governance practices, and failure to uphold users' privacy rights.

The evolving legal landscape in data protection and privacy is characterized by the introduction of new regulations, efforts toward international harmonization, and increasingly rigorous enforcement. These changes reflect a global shift toward greater accountability and protection of personal data in the digital age. For organizations, staying abreast of these developments and proactively adapting to them is crucial for compliance and maintaining public trust.

Privacy Challenges in New Domains

In the realm of social media, privacy challenges have evolved significantly. With an unprecedented volume of personal data shared online, users often unknowingly expose sensitive information. Key concerns include data harvesting, where companies collect extensive personal data for targeted advertising, and the lack of control over sharing or using this information. Additionally, social media platforms have become arenas for deepfake technology and identity theft, leading to further invasions of privacy. The line between public and private personas is increasingly blurred, raising questions about consent and the right to digital anonymity.

Virtual reality (VR) introduces a new dimension of privacy challenges. In VR environments, user data and biometric data such as eye movements, facial expressions, and even heart rate are collected. This highly personal and sensitive data can be used to create detailed user profiles. There is also the concern of VR spaces being monitored or recorded without explicit consent, leading to potential misuse of personal interactions and experiences. The need for robust privacy protections and ethical guidelines becomes more critical as VR technology becomes more integrated into daily life.

Autonomous vehicles (AVs) present unique privacy challenges due to the extensive data they collect. These vehicles use sensors and cameras to navigate, inadvertently capturing detailed information about the environment, including other people and private properties. Data security becomes a significant concern as the information transmitted between AVs and their control systems can be vulnerable to hacking, leading to potential privacy breaches. Additionally, tracking location and travel patterns raises concerns about surveillance and the misuse of personal data. As AVs become more prevalent, establishing clear regulations and privacy standards is essential to protect individual rights in this rapidly evolving domain.

Ethical and Societal Considerations

In the digital age, ethical considerations have become increasingly complex and multifaceted. Digital ethics covers various issues, from data privacy and cybersecurity to ethical AI and digital equity. Key concerns include the responsible use of technology, ensuring fairness in algorithmic decision-making, and protecting users from digital harms like misinformation and cyberbullying. As technology becomes more integrated into everyday life, there is a growing need for ethical frameworks that address these challenges, promoting transparency, accountability, and respect for user rights.

Social responsibility in the context of technology revolves around the idea that companies and developers should act in the best interests of society. This includes creating inclusive and accessible technologies, minimizing environmental impacts, and ensuring that technological advancements do not exacerbate social inequalities. It also involves addressing the digital divide, ensuring everyone has equal access to technology and its benefits. As technology evolves, the emphasis on social responsibility highlights the need for sustainable and equitable development practices.

Public discourse in the digital era has transformed significantly, with technology playing a pivotal role in sharing and discussing information. While technology has democratized access to information and enabled global conversations, it has also led to challenges like echo chambers, polarization, and spreading fake news. Ethical considerations in public discourse involve promoting factual, respectful, and inclusive conversations online and ensuring that platforms for public discourse do not become tools for misinformation or hate speech. Balancing freedom of expression with the need to maintain a healthy, informed public sphere is a critical challenge in this domain.

Future Directions in Data Privacy

As we look to the future, several predictions can be made regarding the evolution of data privacy. First, the increasing use of AI and machine learning will likely lead to more sophisticated data processing techniques, making privacy protection more complex. There will be a greater emphasis on privacy by design, where systems and services are built from the ground up with privacy in mind. We can also expect stronger regulations like the GDPR to emerge globally, along with advancements in encryption and anonymization technology. Furthermore, consumer awareness and demand for privacy might drive more transparent data practices and the rise of privacy-focused products and services.

Preparing for these changes involves multiple stakeholders, including businesses, governments, and individuals. Organizations must invest in robust privacy frameworks and stay abreast of evolving regulations. There will be a growing need for privacy and data protection professionals. For governments, the challenge lies in creating balanced regulations that protect individual privacy without stifling innovation. Conversely, individuals must become more informed about their digital rights and how to manage their digital footprints. Education and awareness programs will be critical in preparing society for these changes.

The long-term impacts of these developments in data privacy are profound. We might see a reshaping of the digital landscape where privacy is a fundamental right, deeply integrated into all aspects of digital interaction. This could lead to a more trust-based digital economy, with greater user control over personal data. However, there is also the potential for a digital divide, where individuals who are less informed or have fewer resources are more vulnerable to privacy breaches. In the broader sense, how we approach data privacy today will shape not just technology but also the societal norms and ethical standards of the digital future.

Case Study: Facebook-Cambridge Analytica Data Privacy Scandal

The Facebook-Cambridge Analytica scandal, which surfaced in early 2018, is a pivotal event in data privacy. This controversy revolved around the unauthorized collection and use of personal data from millions of Facebook users by Cambridge Analytica, a political consulting firm. Notably, this data was allegedly utilized to sway voter opinions in several key political events, including the 2016 US presidential election.

The manipulation of Facebook's data-sharing system was at the heart of this scandal. The breach occurred through "This Is Your Digital Life," a third-party application developed by researcher Aleksandr Kogan. Disguised as a personality quiz, the app not only harvested the data of its users but also gathered information from their Facebook friends. This process led to accumulating data from millions of users without explicit consent.

The incident highlighted several critical oversights in Facebook's approach to data privacy. The company's platform policies at the time allowed third-party applications to access extensive user data without rigorous monitoring or auditing. Furthermore, the policies were insufficient in preventing the misuse or unauthorized distribution of the collected data. Another significant issue was the lack of transparency with users about third-party applications' potential reach and use of their data.

The ramifications of the scandal were widespread and profound. Facebook faced intense criticism from users and stakeholders, sparking a global conversation about privacy rights and leading to the #DeleteFacebook movement. The breach attracted significant legal and regulatory attention, resulting in hearings in both the US Congress and the UK Parliament. Financially, Facebook saw a substantial decline in its stock value following the revelations.

In response to the crisis, Facebook undertook several measures to rectify its privacy protocols. The company revised its third-party app policies to restrict access to user data, striving to prevent similar incidents in the future. Efforts were also made to enhance the transparency of data sharing and usage policies. Additionally, Facebook improved tools and settings to give users more control over their data privacy.

The Facebook-Cambridge Analytica scandal serves as a crucial case study on the importance of data privacy in the digital age. It highlights the necessity for companies to implement stringent data access controls, uphold transparency in data usage, and conduct regular audits of data-sharing practices. This case is a powerful reminder for tech companies of their responsibility to protect user data against misuse, emphasizing that privacy should remain a primary concern in our increasingly digital world.

Career Corner

A career in privacy is an increasingly important and dynamic field within cybersecurity and data protection, focusing on safeguarding personal and sensitive information from unauthorized access and misuse. This specialization is crucial as digital technologies continue to evolve and data privacy becomes a paramount concern for individuals, corporations, and governments.

One of the critical roles in this area is that of a Privacy Analyst. These professionals are responsible for assessing and ensuring personal data privacy within an organization. They analyze data processing activities; evaluate compliance with privacy laws and regulations like GDPR, HIPAA, or CCPA; and recommend improvements to data handling processes. Their work is vital in identifying potential privacy risks and ensuring that personal data is managed responsibly and ethically.

Another significant career path is a Data Protection Officer (DPO). Especially critical in organizations that process large amounts of personal data, DPOs oversee the data protection strategy and its implementation to ensure compliance with data protection laws. They serve as the point of contact between the organization and regulatory authorities, guiding data protection impact assessments, audits, and compliance issues.

The role of a Privacy Consultant is also increasingly popular. These professionals advise organizations on privacy matters, helping them develop and implement privacy policies, manage privacy risks, and ensure compliance with privacy laws. They often work with various clients, offering tailored solutions for diverse privacy needs and challenges.

Becoming a Chief Privacy Officer (CPO) is an option for those interested in a more strategic role. CPOs are senior executives responsible for overseeing an organization's overall privacy strategy. They ensure that the organization's data handling practices are ethical, transparent, and compliant with legal standards. They also play a crucial role in fostering a culture of privacy within the organization and often liaise with other executives to align privacy practices with business objectives.

In terms of certifications, several are recognized in the field of privacy. The Certified Information Privacy Professional (CIPP) offered by the International Association of Privacy Professionals (IAPP) is a widely respected certification providing a comprehensive understanding of privacy laws and regulations. Additionally, the Certified Information Privacy Manager (CIPM) and the Certified Information Systems Security Professional (CISSP) are valuable certifications for those seeking to deepen their privacy management and cybersecurity expertise.

Professionals in the field of privacy need to have a strong understanding of legal frameworks, excellent analytical and communication skills, and a keen sense of ethical considerations. They play a crucial role in shaping how personal and sensitive information is handled, balancing the need for data-driven innovation with the right to privacy.

A career in privacy offers diverse opportunities and is integral to the responsible management of data in today's digital world. From analyzing privacy risks and ensuring legal compliance to shaping organizational privacy strategies, professionals in this field are essential in protecting personal data and upholding privacy rights. Staying abreast of evolving privacy laws, technological advancements, and ethical considerations is crucial in this rapidly evolving field.

Chapter Questions

1. What is the primary purpose of data privacy laws?

    A. To increase data storage capacity

    B. To safeguard personal information in the digital realm

    C. To enhance the speed of data processing

    D. To promote data sharing among organizations

2. What influences the design of data privacy
    regulations globally?

    A. Technological advancements only

    B. Cultural, political, and social factors

    C. The global economic climate

    D. Trends in digital marketing

3. Which legislation is recognized as a trailblazing
    model for data protection and privacy?

    A. Singapore's PDPA

    B. India's IT Rules

    C. The European Union's GDPR

    D. The United States' HIPAA

4. What fundamental principle is emphasized in GDPR
    and influences other data protection laws?

    A. Data minimization

    B. Mandatory data storage

    C. Unlimited data access

    D. Unrestricted data processing

5. What does GDPR require of organizations in terms
    of data handling?

    A. Limited data encryption

    B. Strict penalties for non-compliance

    C. Minimal user consent

    D. Data sharing with third parties

6. How does GDPR impact multinational corporations?

   A. It limits their operational scope to Europe

   B. It leads to a decrease in data collection

   C. It compels them to reassess global data handling practices

   D. It encourages data sharing without consent

7. What challenges do international data privacy laws pose for global organizations?

   A. Simplification of data processing

   B. Uniformity of rules and enforcement mechanisms

   C. Complexity in navigating diverse compliance requirements

   D. Decrease in data security measures

8. What is the focus of the CCPA in the United States?

   A. Enhancing cybersecurity

   B. Consumer rights regarding personal information

   C. Restricting digital marketing

   D. Increasing data storage

9. How do sector-specific regulations like HIPAA impact data privacy management?

   A. They simplify compliance processes

   B. They add complexity due to specific data requirements

   C. They reduce the need for encryption

   D. They encourage unrestricted data access

10. What is a primary challenge in data privacy due to technological advancements?

    A. Reduced need for data protection

    B. Increased ease of compliance

    C. The evolving nature of data privacy regulations

    D. Decreased reliance on digital data

11. How do international data privacy agreements affect multinational companies?

    A. They eliminate the need for data protection

    B. They regulate cross-border data flow

    C. They discourage data encryption

    D. They mandate data sharing with governments

12. Why are regular data audits essential for organizations?

    A. To reduce operational costs

    B. To ensure compliance with data privacy laws

    C. To increase data storage capacity

    D. To promote unrestricted data access

13. What does the principle of data minimization entail?

    A. Collecting as much data as possible

    B. Retaining only necessary data for intended purposes

    C. Sharing data with multiple third parties

    D. Storing data indefinitely

14. What is the significance of "privacy by design" in data protection?

    A. It allows unrestricted data sharing

    B. Privacy considerations are integrated from the outset

    C. It focuses solely on encryption

    D. It prioritizes data monetization

15. Why is employee training crucial in data protection?

    A. To improve sales and marketing strategies

    B. To reduce operational costs

    C. To mitigate the risk of data breaches

    D. To increase data collection

CHAPTER 14

Insider Threats

The concept of insider threats is not a new phenomenon. Organizations and nations have historically grappled with protecting sensitive information and assets from those within their ranks. The roots of such threats can often be traced back to various factors, including personal grievances, financial pressures, or ideological differences. Understanding these origins is crucial for developing effective strategies to counteract insider threats.

Insider threats come in various forms, each presenting unique challenges. They can range from intentional theft, sabotage, espionage, or data breaches to unintentional incidents caused by negligence or lack of awareness. Some insiders act alone, while others might be part of a more significant, coordinated effort. The diversity of these threats necessitates a multifaceted approach to detection and prevention.

The most daunting aspect of insider threats is their unpredictability and the difficulty in detection. Insiders inherently possess knowledge and access that external actors do not, allowing them to bypass security measures more efficiently. They often know where vulnerabilities lie and can exploit them without raising immediate suspicion. This makes identifying potential insider threats a complex task beyond standard security protocols.

Throughout history, there have been numerous high-profile insider threat incidents that have had significant repercussions. From corporate espionage cases leading to massive financial losses to national security

Dr. J. Edwards, *Mastering Cybersecurity*, https://doi.org/10.1007/979-8-8688-0297-3_14

breaches posing threats to entire countries, these incidents have served as wake-up calls, highlighting the critical need for robust insider threat programs.

Each major incident provides valuable lessons on the nature of insider threats and effective countermeasures. They underscore the importance of thorough background checks, continuous monitoring, employee engagement, and establishing a strong security culture within organizations. Learning from past incidents is essential in shaping future security strategies.

As technology and organizational structures evolve, so do the tactics of insiders. The advent of sophisticated cyber tools, the rise of remote working, and the increasing complexity of organizational data systems have all contributed to the changing landscape of insider threats. Today, the challenge lies in addressing current threats and anticipating how they might evolve, necessitating constant vigilance and adaptation in insider threat management strategies.

Psychological Profile of Insiders

The concept of insider threats transcends the mere technicalities of security breaches and infiltrates the more complex realm of human psychology. At its core, an insider threat is deeply rooted in human behavior and motives, making the psychological profiling of individuals within an organization a critical component of insider threat management. Understanding the human element in this context involves delving into the myriad psychological factors that drive individuals to become threats to their organizations. These factors range from personal grievances and ethical dissonance to external pressures and mental health issues. The complexity of human psychology means that potential insider threats are often nuanced and not immediately apparent, making their identification a challenging but essential task.

The importance of psychological profiling in managing insider threats cannot be overstated. In the realm of security, where focus is often predominantly placed on technological safeguards and physical security measures, human psychology is sometimes underemphasized. However, the reality is that individuals with legitimate access and deep knowledge of the most robust security systems can be compromised. Therefore, understanding the psychological makeup of potential insiders becomes crucial in preempting and preventing malicious actions. Psychological profiling helps identify the overt signs of a potential threat, like a sudden change in behavior or overt expressions of dissatisfaction, and more subtle indicators, such as changes in work patterns, social withdrawal, or minor policy violations. These insights enable organizations to implement more targeted and practical strategies to mitigate the risk of insider threats.

Moreover, psychological profiling is not only about identifying potential threats; it's also about understanding the overall mental well-being and morale of employees within an organization. A healthy and transparent organizational culture can significantly reduce the likelihood of insider threats. By recognizing and addressing employees' psychological needs and grievances, organizations can foster a more loyal and committed workforce, thereby naturally reducing insider sabotage or espionage propensity. This approach requires a shift in perspective, where employees are seen not just as potential threats but also as assets whose welfare and satisfaction play a critical role in the organization's overall security posture.

In essence, the psychological profile of insiders is a pivotal aspect of insider threat management. It involves a delicate balance of vigilance and empathy, combining proactive monitoring and compassionate engagement. As organizations grapple with the ever-present and evolving threat posed by insiders, the role of psychological understanding in shaping effective defense strategies becomes increasingly important. The challenge lies in integrating this understanding with other security measures to create a comprehensive and resilient approach to insider threat management.

Motivations and Triggers

Understanding the motivations and triggers behind insider threats is crucial for preventing and mitigating these risks. Individuals within an organization may turn into insider threats for various reasons, from personal to ideological. Financial gain is one of the most straightforward and common motivators. In such cases, an individual might be driven by the desire to improve their financial situation, which could stem from personal financial difficulties, greed, or the allure of a lucrative offer from a competitor or external entity. This motivation can be particularly potent in cases where the individual feels undervalued or undercompensated in their current role.

Ideological beliefs present a more complex motivation. In these scenarios, the individual's actions are driven by a belief system that may conflict with the organization's values or activities. This could involve leaking sensitive information to groups or countries with opposing ideologies or sabotaging operations to support a cause they believe in. The challenge in these cases is that such motivations can be deeply ingrained and more challenging to detect, as they are often cloaked in normal behavior.

Personal grudges or dissatisfaction also play a significant role in driving insider threats. Employees who feel mistreated, overlooked for promotions, or unfairly criticized may resent their employer. This dissatisfaction can fester into a desire to harm the organization as revenge or regain control and empowerment.

Coercion or blackmail is another significant motivator. In these instances, an individual may not initially intend to harm the organization but can be compelled to do so due to external pressures. These could stem from threats to their safety, their family's safety, or threats to expose compromising information about them.

Identifying the triggers for malicious behavior is equally important. Personal crises, such as divorce, financial problems, or significant health issues, can create immense stress and lead to desperate actions. In the workplace, promotions, demotions, or grievances can be the tipping point for an employee who feels aggrieved or undervalued. Even positive events like promotions can lead to insider threats if the individual gains access to sensitive information they cannot handle responsibly.

External influences like peer pressure or social engineering are often overlooked but can be powerful. Others might influence an employee to partake in activities against the organization, or external entities could manipulate them through sophisticated social engineering techniques.

The motivations and triggers behind insider threats are diverse and complex. They require a nuanced approach to detection and prevention, vigilance and monitoring, and understanding human behavior and psychology. By recognizing these motivations and triggers, organizations can develop more effective strategies to combat insider threats, combining technological tools with psychological insights and a supportive organizational culture.

Behavioral Warning Signs

The identification of behavioral warning signs is a critical component in mitigating insider threats. These signs often manifest as observable changes in an individual's behavior, work habits, and interactions, which can be early indicators of potential malicious activities or intentions. Recognizing these signs requires a keen understanding of standard behavior patterns and the ability to detect deviations from these patterns.

Observable changes in behavior are often the most noticeable indicators. These can include shifts in mood, unexplained increases in stress levels, or a sudden disinterest in work or social activities. Such changes might indicate underlying issues that could escalate into security risks if not addressed promptly.

Shifts in work habits and performance are also telling signs. An employee who suddenly starts working odd hours without an apparent reason or shows a decline in work quality or displays an unusual interest in areas outside their scope of work might be exhibiting warning signs. Similarly, a noticeable increase in performance without a clear justification can be equally concerning, as it might indicate unauthorized access to information or systems to gain favor or achieve specific goals.

Unusual network or data access patterns are critical technical indicators of insider threats. This includes accessing sensitive information without a need, downloading or transferring large amounts of data, or attempting to bypass security measures. Such activities often require immediate investigation as they can be precursors to data breaches or malicious insider actions.

Changes in social interactions and attitudes can provide insights into an individual's state of mind and intentions. An employee who becomes increasingly isolated, shows hostility toward colleagues or management, or expresses dissatisfaction with the organization more frequently could be at risk of becoming an insider threat.

Psychological indicators are also vital in assessing potential threats. Signs of stress or distress, such as anxiety, irritability, or depression, can impact an individual's decision-making and increase the risk of harmful actions. It is essential to approach these indicators sensitively, as they can also be signs of personal issues unrelated to malicious intent.

Signs of disgruntlement or antagonism toward the organization are particularly concerning. Employees who vocalize their dissatisfaction, criticize the organization openly, or express feelings of being treated unfairly might harbor resentment that could manifest in harmful ways.

Risk-taking or violation of policies is another significant warning sign. This includes bypassing protocols, ignoring security procedures, or engaging in unethical behavior. Such actions indicate a potential insider threat and create vulnerabilities that external actors can exploit.

In conclusion, identifying behavioral warning signs is a nuanced process that requires a balance of vigilance, empathy, and discretion. It involves understanding the individual, the work environment, and the interplay between personal and professional factors. Effective management of insider threats depends on detecting these signs early and responding appropriately, ensuring potential risks are mitigated before they materialize into serious security incidents.

Profiling and Monitoring

The process of profiling and monitoring in the context of insider threats is a meticulous and ongoing activity that plays a crucial role in preempting and mitigating risks. This approach combines the analysis of behavioral patterns with security measures to create a comprehensive risk assessment and response strategy.

Profiling for risk assessment begins with building detailed profiles of employees, especially those with access to sensitive information or critical infrastructure. These profiles are not just limited to the professional aspects such as job role, level of access, and work history but also encompass behavioral tendencies and patterns. By establishing a baseline of normal behavior for each employee, deviations that may indicate potential threats can be more easily identified. The profiling process involves a careful balance, ensuring thoroughness without infringing on personal privacy or creating an environment of mistrust.

The analysis of past incidents plays a significant role in refining these profiles. By examining previous insider threat cases within the organization or in similar entities, patterns, and common characteristics can be identified. These patterns might include specific behavioral changes before an incident, methods of data exfiltration, or types of targeted data. Learning from past incidents helps anticipate potential threats and tailor the profiling criteria accordingly.

Integrating behavioral data with security protocols is the next critical step. This integration involves using the insights gained from profiling to enhance security measures. For instance, additional network activity monitoring or more frequent access privileges audits might be warranted if an employee's profile indicates a potential risk. This integration also means updating security protocols based on behavioral trends. For example, if a trend of increased risk is identified in a particular department or job role, the security measures for that group can be adjusted to mitigate the risk.

However, it's important to note that profiling and monitoring should be conducted with respect for individual privacy and within legal boundaries. The goal is to protect the organization and its assets, including its employees, from potential harm, not to create an atmosphere of surveillance or mistrust. Transparency about the purpose and methods of profiling and monitoring and clear communication about the policies and procedures can help maintain a balance between security and privacy.

Profiling and monitoring as part of insider threat management is dynamic and sensitive. It requires continuous refinement and adaptation to changing circumstances and threats. By combining detailed profiling with integrated security protocols, organizations can create an effective line of defense against insider threats while maintaining a respectful and trustworthy work environment.

Continuous Monitoring and Evaluation

Continuous monitoring and evaluation form a cornerstone in proactively managing insider threats. This ongoing process is essential for the early detection of potential risks and ensuring that the measures remain practical and relevant over time. Continuous monitoring involves regularly observing and assessing employee behavior, network activity, and access to sensitive information. This constant vigilance helps identify anomalies or changes that could signal a potential threat. The key to effective monitoring is its integration into the organization's daily operations, ensuring that it becomes a seamless part of the security culture rather than an intrusive or disruptive element.

Implementing noninvasive monitoring techniques is critical in this process. The objective is to ensure security without creating a sense of being watched or monitored excessively. Techniques such as anomaly detection algorithms flag unusual network or data access patterns and are effective yet unobtrusive. These systems can monitor vast amounts of data and transactions to identify potential threats without impacting employee privacy. Another approach is aggregated data analysis, which focuses on patterns and trends rather than individual behavior, thereby reducing the perception of personal surveillance.

Regular reviews and updates to behavioral baselines are also essential. As individuals and organizations evolve, so do their behaviors and practices. What was considered normal a year ago might not be the norm today. Therefore, it is necessary to periodically review and update the behavioral baselines against which employee activities are measured. This ensures the monitoring remains accurate and relevant, reducing the risk of false positives or negatives. Regular reviews also allow for refining and improving monitoring techniques and tools based on the latest technological advancements and emerging threat landscapes.

Balancing privacy concerns with security needs is perhaps the most challenging aspect of continuous monitoring. It is imperative to maintain a delicate balance between protecting the organization and respecting the privacy and rights of employees. This balance can be achieved through transparent communication about the monitoring policies, ensuring that employees understand the necessity and scope of monitoring. Additionally, adhering to legal and ethical standards is paramount. The monitoring should be designed to collect only the information necessary for security purposes and should comply with data protection laws and regulations.

Continuous monitoring and evaluation are powerful tools against insider threats when implemented thoughtfully and ethically. By incorporating noninvasive techniques, regularly updating behavioral baselines, and balancing privacy concerns, organizations can create a dynamic and practical framework for identifying and mitigating insider threats, ensuring the security and integrity of their operations.

Intervention Strategies

In managing insider threats, intervention strategies are pivotal in mitigating risks before they escalate into serious security incidents. These strategies are not solely about imposing punitive measures but also about engaging in proactive and supportive actions that address the underlying issues leading to potential insider threats.

Proactive interventions are essential in this context. They involve identifying and addressing potential issues before they manifest into harmful actions. This could mean closely monitoring individuals who show signs of becoming a threat, but more importantly, it involves creating an environment where potential problems can be resolved proactively. Proactive interventions require a thorough understanding of the individual and situational dynamics that could lead to insider threats. It's about being ahead of the curve, anticipating problems, and addressing them in their nascent stages.

Employee Assistance Programs (EAPs) are critical to these intervention strategies. EAPs offer a range of services to employees, including counseling, mental health support, and advice on financial or legal issues. These programs play a dual role – they support employees in dealing with personal issues that might affect their work and also serve as a preventative measure against insider threats. By providing employees with the necessary support, EAPs help mitigate the stressors that could lead to harmful actions against the organization. They also signal to employees that the organization cares about their well-being, which can foster a more loyal and positive workforce.

Conflict resolution and mediation are other important aspects of intervention strategies. Conflicts, whether personal or professional, can be significant stressors and might contribute to someone becoming an insider threat. Effective conflict resolution mechanisms ensure that disputes are settled fairly and in a timely manner, reducing the likelihood of disgruntlement or resentment. As a part of this process, mediation involves a neutral third party facilitating a resolution acceptable to all involved parties. It helps de-escalate situations and find mutually agreeable solutions, thereby reducing the risk of conflicts evolving into serious insider threats.

Intervention strategies in the context of insider threats are about more than just monitoring and enforcement. They encompass a range of proactive measures to support employees and resolve issues before they escalate. By implementing comprehensive intervention strategies, including EAPs and effective conflict resolution mechanisms, organizations can create a safer, more secure, and more supportive work environment. This not only helps mitigate insider threats but also contributes to the overall health and productivity of the organization.

Identifying and Assessing Risks

In insider threat management, identifying and assessing risks is a critical step involving a nuanced understanding of risk factors and their implications within an organization. This process is foundational in developing effective strategies to mitigate potential threats.

Risk Assessment Models

Developing and implementing robust risk assessment models is crucial in identifying potential insider threats. These models are designed to evaluate various factors and indicators that may signify a risk within the organization. A key aspect of these models is the identification of common risk indicators. These indicators can range from employee behavior and performance changes to network and data access pattern anomalies. Recognizing these indicators requires a deep understanding of normal operational patterns so that deviations can be accurately identified.

Identifying key indicators of potential insider threats involves a detailed analysis of past incidents, employee behavior, and organizational vulnerabilities. This process is not static; it evolves as new threats emerge and the organization changes. It's about understanding the organization's specific context – its culture, structure, and the nature of its business – and how these factors can influence the likelihood and impact of insider threats.

Contextualizing these indicators within different organizational environments is another critical step. What might be considered a risk indicator in one type of organization might be normal in another. For example, a sudden increase in data access might be a significant red flag in a high-security environment. At the same time, it might be part of regular activities in a research-intensive organization. Therefore, risk indicators must be contextualized to the organization's specific environment to be meaningful.

Evaluating threat levels involves establishing criteria for assessing the severity of insider threats. This multidimensional process considers the potential impact of a threat and its likelihood. Factors such as the level of access the individual has, the sensitivity of the data or systems they can access, and their potential motives and capabilities are all considered in this evaluation.

Adapting evaluation metrics to reflect changing risks is essential in keeping the risk assessment model relevant and effective. As the organizational environment and external threat landscape evolve, so must the metrics and criteria used to evaluate risks. This means regularly reviewing and updating the risk assessment model to incorporate new threats, technological advancements, and organizational changes.

Identifying and assessing risks in the context of insider threats is a dynamic and ongoing process. It requires a thorough understanding of risk indicators, the ability to contextualize them in the organization's specific environment, and the agility to adapt evaluation metrics as circumstances change. Organizations can proactively manage insider threats and safeguard their critical assets and operations by identifying and assessing risks.

Digital Footprints and Anomalies

One of the primary ways technology aids in insider threat management is by analyzing digital footprints and anomalies. In an increasingly digital world, employees interact with numerous systems and networks, leaving behind digital footprints that can be tracked and analyzed. These footprints include email communications, network access logs, file transfer records, and even patterns of physical access through badge swipes. Anomalies in these footprints often serve as critical indicators of potential insider threats. For instance, an employee accessing sensitive data at unusual hours, downloading large amounts of data, or attempting to access restricted areas can all be signs of malicious intent.

Detecting these unusual activities requires sophisticated techniques to differentiate between normal and potentially harmful behavior. Advanced analytical tools, such as machine learning algorithms, are increasingly being used to identify patterns and anomalies that would be difficult, if not impossible, to detect manually. These algorithms can process and learn from vast amounts of data, becoming more effective at identifying potential threats over time. Behavioral analytics is another important technique that involves creating profiles of normal user behavior and monitoring deviations from these profiles. This approach is particularly practical in identifying subtle changes in behavior that might indicate a threat.

Tools for Tracking and Analyzing Digital Footprints

The tools for tracking and analyzing digital footprints are diverse and continually evolving. They range from basic Security Information and Event Management (SIEM) systems, which aggregate and analyze log data from various sources, to more advanced User and Entity Behavior Analytics (UEBA) systems. UEBA systems use machine learning, statistical analysis, and other advanced techniques to identify patterns of behavior associated with insider threats. Additionally, Data Loss Prevention (DLP) tools are used to monitor and control the transfer of sensitive information, helping to prevent data exfiltration by insiders.

Incorporating these technologies into an insider threat management program requires a strategic approach. It involves selecting the right tools based on the organization's specific needs and risks, integrating them into existing security infrastructures, and continually updating them to respond to new challenges and technological advances.

Technology is a critical ally in the fight against insider threats. Organizations can gain a significant advantage in identifying and mitigating these threats by leveraging tools and techniques for tracking digital footprints and detecting anomalies. However, it's important to remember that technology is just one part of a comprehensive insider threat management strategy, including policies, procedures, and a culture of security awareness.

Implementing Cybersecurity Strategies to Mitigate Insider Threats

A comprehensive and multilayered strategy is the cornerstone of effective cybersecurity against insider threats. This approach includes technical measures such as robust access controls, encryption, and network segmentation, as well as administrative strategies like regular security audits and policy enforcement. Access controls ensure that employees have only the necessary privileges to perform their duties, minimizing the risk of unauthorized access to sensitive information. Encryption protects the integrity and confidentiality of data, making it less susceptible to unauthorized access or exfiltration. Network segmentation divides the organization's network into separate zones, limiting the spread of potential breaches and making it easier to isolate threats.

Regular security training and awareness programs are also crucial. Employees should be educated about insider threats, recognizing potential risks, and following security protocols. Simulated attack drills, such as phishing exercises, can be particularly effective in reinforcing training and identifying areas where additional education is needed.

Continuous monitoring of user activities and data flows is another key aspect. This involves using advanced tools to detect unusual patterns of behavior that might indicate an insider threat, such as abnormal access to sensitive data or anomalous data transfers. These tools must be sophisticated enough to distinguish between normal and potentially harmful activities to minimize false positives, which can be disruptive and erode trust among staff.

Balancing Cybersecurity Measures with Employee Privacy

While implementing stringent cybersecurity measures is essential, balancing them with respect for employee privacy is equally important. Overly intrusive monitoring or control can create a climate of distrust and dissatisfaction, potentially exacerbating insider threat risks, and it is essential to find a balance that maintains security without infringing on employee privacy and rights.

This balance can be achieved by clearly communicating the rationale behind security policies and measures and ensuring transparency in monitoring tools and data handling. Privacy concerns should be addressed in the policy design phase, incorporating principles such as data minimization and limiting monitoring to professional activities and environments.

Legal compliance is another critical aspect. Cybersecurity measures should align with relevant privacy laws and regulations. This protects the organization from legal repercussions and reinforces a culture of ethical conduct and respect for individual rights.

In conclusion, cybersecurity measures against insider threats require a well-rounded approach that includes technological solutions and human-centric strategies. The key lies in implementing robust and adaptive security practices while maintaining a respectful and transparent environment that values employee privacy. This approach protects the organization from insider threats and fosters a positive and secure working environment.

Identifying and Addressing Organizational Structures That Facilitate Insider Threats

The first step in this process is to identify the aspects of organizational structure that may contribute to insider threats. These can include unclear lines of authority, inadequate segregation of duties, limited oversight of critical areas, or inefficient access control systems. For instance, if employees have access to systems or information not essential for their job functions, this over-privileging can lead to unnecessary risks. Similarly, a lack of clear reporting procedures for suspicious activities can hinder the timely detection and response to insider threats.

Once these structural weaknesses are identified, the next step is to address them through strategic organizational changes. This may involve restructuring roles and responsibilities to ensure a clear segregation of duties and reduce the risk of any individual having unchecked power or access. Enhancing oversight mechanisms is another crucial area. This can be achieved by implementing robust audit trails, regular access, and activity log reviews, particularly for sensitive systems and data.

Improving policies and procedures related to access control is also essential. Access rights should be granted based on the principle of least privilege, ensuring employees have only the access necessary to perform their duties. Regular reviews of these access rights, especially after role changes or terminations, are crucial in maintaining a secure environment.

Another aspect is fostering a culture of accountability and transparency within the organization. Employees should be encouraged and empowered to report suspicious activities or potential security lapses. This requires clear and accessible reporting channels and a supportive environment where employees do not fear retaliation for reporting concerns.

In some cases, addressing structural weaknesses may require a significant cultural shift within the organization. This involves changing policies and procedures and influencing attitudes and behaviors. Leadership plays a critical role in this process by setting the tone for the importance of security and demonstrating a commitment to addressing insider threats.

Mitigating insider threats requires a keen focus on identifying and rectifying structural weaknesses within an organization. Organizations can significantly reduce the risk of insider threats by restructuring roles and responsibilities, enhancing oversight, improving access controls, and fostering a culture of accountability and transparency. This proactive approach not only enhances security but also contributes to the overall efficiency and effectiveness of the organization.

Understanding How Organizational Culture Can Contribute to or Mitigate Insider Threats

Organizational culture can inadvertently contribute to insider threats when it fails to prioritize security, lacks clear communication, or does not foster a sense of responsibility and accountability among employees. For instance, a culture that values speed over security might encourage employees to bypass security protocols for efficiency. Similarly, a culture that does not encourage open communication can lead to situations where employees are either unaware of security policies or hesitant to report suspicious activities.

Conversely, a strong security-conscious culture can significantly mitigate the risk of insider threats. In such cultures, security is seen as a collective responsibility, and employees are vigilant, aware, and committed to protecting the organization's assets. This culture encourages transparency, open communication, and a proactive approach to identifying and addressing security concerns.

Strategies for Cultivating a Security-Conscious Culture

Developing a security-conscious culture requires deliberate and sustained efforts. One effective strategy is to integrate security into the organization's core values. This involves leadership consistently communicating the importance of security and setting an example for employees to follow. Regular training and awareness programs are also crucial in keeping security at the forefront of employees' minds. These programs should not only cover the technical aspects of security but also emphasize the role of each individual in safeguarding the organization.

Recognition and reinforcement of positive security behaviors can further strengthen the culture. Acknowledging and rewarding employees who adhere to security protocols or contribute to improving security measures can reinforce the importance of these actions. This positive reinforcement helps create an environment where security is valued and practiced consistently.

Another important aspect is to create an environment of trust and support. Employees should feel confident in reporting security concerns without fear of retaliation. Establishing clear, confidential, and accessible channels for reporting suspicious activities is key to this. Additionally, management should respond to these reports seriously and respectfully, ensuring employees feel their concerns are being addressed.

Encouraging collaboration and cross-departmental communication also play a vital role in cultivating a security-conscious culture. When departments work together and share information about potential risks and best practices, the organization's overall security posture strengthens.

The cultural factors within an organization play a pivotal role in either exacerbating or reducing insider threats. By understanding the impact of culture on security and implementing strategies to foster a security-conscious environment, organizations can create a solid first line of defense against insider threats. This requires a holistic approach that combines leadership, communication, training, reinforcement, and collaboration to build a culture where security is ingrained in every aspect of the organization's operations.

Identifying and Rectifying Policy Shortcomings That Could Lead to Insider Threats

The first step in addressing policy gaps is a comprehensive review of existing policies to identify lacking or outdated areas. This review should cover various aspects of the organization's operations, including data access and control, employee conduct, IT security, and incident response.

Particular attention should be paid to how these policies address the potential for insider threats. For instance, if policies on data access do not include provisions for monitoring and controlling the activities of privileged users, this could create an opportunity for insider abuse.

The process of rectifying these shortcomings involves not only updating and refining existing policies but also developing new ones where necessary. This might include establishing clearer guidelines on data handling, more stringent access controls, or detailed procedures for reporting and managing security incidents. These policies must be comprehensive but also clear and understandable to all employees.

Best Practices for Policy Development and Implementation

Developing effective policies requires a careful balance between thoroughness and practicality. Best practices include involving stakeholders from across the organization in policy development. This ensures that the policies are applicable and consider the unique aspects of different departments and roles. It also aids in gaining buy-in from various parts of the organization, which is crucial for effective implementation.

Another best practice is ensuring policies are communicated effectively to all employees. This involves distributing the policies and providing training and education to ensure employees understand the policies and their importance. Regular training sessions, reminders, and updates can help keep employees' minds secure.

Policies should also be dynamic and adaptable. Policies should be reviewed and updated regularly as threats evolve and the organization changes. This ensures they remain relevant and effective in addressing the current threat landscape.

Finally, the implementation of these policies should be monitored and enforced consistently. This includes regular audits to ensure compliance and mechanisms for addressing violations. These enforcement measures must be applied fairly and uniformly to maintain trust and respect for the policies.

Addressing policy gaps is a critical component of insider threat management. By identifying and rectifying shortcomings in existing policies and following best practices in policy development and implementation, organizations can significantly strengthen their defenses against insider threats. This process requires ongoing effort and commitment but is essential for maintaining the security and integrity of the organization.

Insider Threat Profiles

Creating and maintaining insider threat profiles is essential in identifying and mitigating potential security risks within an organization. These profiles, centered around behavioral baselines, are crucial tools for understanding standard behavior patterns and identifying deviations that could indicate a threat.

Creating Behavioral Baselines

The foundation of insider threat profiles is the establishment of behavioral baselines. These baselines are developed by understanding and documenting employees' normal activities, behaviors, and patterns of work conduct in various organizational roles. This understanding might include typical work hours, standard data access patterns, communication styles, and performance levels. By establishing what is considered normal in these areas, it becomes possible to detect anomalies that may signal a deviation from usual behavior, potentially indicating an insider threat.

For example, an employee who typically accesses specific data during regular business hours but suddenly starts accessing it at odd hours may trigger an alert based on this deviation from their baseline. Similarly, a noticeable change in an employee's interaction with colleagues or a sudden drop in work performance could indicate underlying issues relevant to security concerns.

Establishing Normal Behavioral Patterns for Detecting Anomalies

Establishing these normal behavioral patterns involves continuous data collection and analysis. It requires a comprehensive understanding of the various roles within the organization and the specific behaviors associated with each role. Effective establishment of these patterns also demands regular updates to the baseline to account for changes in job roles, organizational processes, or technology use.

This process is particularly challenging because it requires distinguishing between harmless deviations, a normal part of human behavior, and those that might indicate malicious intent. Therefore, establishing behavioral patterns should be nuanced, considering the context and the potential for various interpretations of behavior.

Techniques for Effective Behavioral Monitoring

Effective behavioral monitoring involves a combination of technological tools and human analysis. On the technological side, advanced software systems can monitor network activity, access logs, and other digital footprints in real time, flagging any activities that deviate from established baselines. These systems can be enhanced with machine learning algorithms that adapt and improve their detection capabilities.

However, technology alone is not sufficient. Human analysis is also critical in interpreting the data accurately. Security professionals should review the flagged activities to determine whether they represent genuine threats or benign anomalies. This analysis often requires understanding the context in which the behavior occurred, including personal, organizational, and environmental factors.

Moreover, effective behavioral monitoring should be conducted with a consideration for privacy and ethical guidelines. Employees should be made aware of the monitoring processes, which should be conducted transparently and respectfully, focusing on professional conduct and activities.

Insider threat profiles based on behavioral baselines are crucial in identifying organizational threats. Creating these profiles involves establishing standard behavioral patterns and utilizing technological tools and human expertise for effective monitoring. This process, while complex, is essential in proactively identifying and mitigating insider threats in a way that respects employee privacy and maintains organizational trust.

Identifying Roles and Departments More Susceptible to Insider Threats

Identifying high-risk roles and departments typically involves an analysis of access privileges, the sensitivity of information handled, and the potential impact of unauthorized access or data breaches. Roles with elevated access to sensitive data, critical infrastructure, or key financial systems are often considered high-risk due to the potential damage that could be caused if these privileges are misused. Departments like finance, IT, or research and development, where employees can access proprietary information, trade secrets, or significant financial assets, are also commonly identified as higher risk.

In addition to access and information sensitivity, other factors such as employee turnover rates, the stress level of roles, and the history of security incidents within departments can also be indicators of potential risk. An area with high employee dissatisfaction or frequent disciplinary issues might be more susceptible to insider threats due to disgruntled employees.

Tailoring Security Measures to Specific Internal Risk Profiles

Once high-risk roles and departments are identified, tailored security measures can be implemented to mitigate these risks. These measures should be proportionate to the level of risk and designed to address the specific vulnerabilities of each role or department.

For high-risk roles, measures might include more stringent access controls, enhanced monitoring of activities, and regular security audits. Additional layers of authentication and access logging may be necessary for these employees, along with regular reviews of access privileges to ensure they remain necessary and appropriate.

In high-risk departments, security measures could include more frequent security training focused on the specific data types or systems they handle. There may also be a need for more robust incident response plans and regular drills to ensure preparedness for potential security breaches.

It's also essential to foster a security culture within these high-risk areas. This can involve encouraging employees to be vigilant, report suspicious activities, and ensure they know the potential risks and their role in mitigating them. Regular communication about the importance of security and the potential consequences of breaches can help reinforce this culture.

Furthermore, security measures should be reviewed and updated regularly to ensure they remain effective against evolving threats and changes within the organization. Continuous risk assessment and adjustment of security protocols are key to maintaining a strong defense against insider threats in high-risk areas.

Identifying and appropriately securing high-risk roles and departments is critical to insider threat management. By understanding which areas of the organization are most vulnerable and tailoring security measures to these specific risks, organizations can effectively reduce the likelihood and potential impact of insider threats. This targeted approach, combined with a strong overall security culture, forms a comprehensive defense against the unique challenges posed by insider threats.

Implementing Systems for Continuous Monitoring of Potential Insider Threats

Continuous monitoring is a proactive security measure that plays a crucial role in the early detection of insider threats. This involves using sophisticated technology systems to track employee behavior, network activity, access to sensitive information, and other key indicators of potential threats. Such systems often employ advanced analytics, including machine learning algorithms, to identify patterns and anomalies that might suggest malicious activity or a deviation from normal behavior.

The implementation of these systems must be strategic and considerate of privacy concerns. Monitoring should be transparent and communicated clearly to all employees, ensuring they understand the rationale behind these measures. The focus should be professional activities and behavior, respecting personal boundaries while ensuring organizational security.

Effective monitoring systems are not just about technology; they also involve human oversight. Trained security professionals should analyze the data and alerts generated by these systems to determine the context and seriousness of any potential threats. This human element is crucial for accurately interpreting data and avoiding false positives, which can erode trust and morale within the organization.

Protocols for Reporting and Responding to Identified Risks

Establishing clear protocols for reporting and responding to identified risks is equally crucial to monitoring. These protocols should outline the steps employees must take if they detect suspicious behavior or security breaches, ensuring that such reports are handled promptly and effectively.

Reporting protocols should include multiple accessible channels for employees to report concerns, including anonymous options if necessary. This encourages a culture of openness and vigilance, where employees feel empowered and responsible for the organization's security.

A well-defined response protocol is essential once a potential insider threat is reported. This should include initial assessment procedures to verify the threat's credibility and a detailed investigation if necessary. The protocol should also define roles and responsibilities, ensuring a coordinated and efficient response. This includes determining who within the organization needs to be informed, how to contain and mitigate the threat, and steps for follow-up and resolution.

When a threat is confirmed, the response protocol should guide the organization in disciplinary actions, legal proceedings, or other necessary steps. It should also include provisions for post-incident analysis to learn from the event and improve future threat detection and response.

Monitoring and reporting are critical elements in managing insider threats. Implementing effective systems for continuous monitoring and clear protocols for reporting and responding to risks enables organizations to detect and address insider threats promptly. This proactive approach enhances security and fosters a culture of responsibility and vigilance.

Prevention Strategies

In insider threat management, developing a robust prevention plan is critical to safeguard an organization's assets and information. A well-crafted plan helps in averting potential threats and lays the groundwork for a swift and effective response in case of an incident. The effectiveness of a prevention plan hinges on several vital components and strategic integrations.

Critical Components of an Effective Plan

An effective prevention plan for insider threats encompasses various components, each addressing specific aspects of threat mitigation. Firstly, it should include a comprehensive risk assessment to identify potential vulnerabilities within the organization. This assessment considers factors such as the accessibility of sensitive information, the level of control over critical systems, and the potential impact of insider breaches.

Another crucial component is the establishment of strict access controls and monitoring systems. This involves implementing the least privilege principle, ensuring employees have access only to the information and resources necessary for their roles. Monitoring network and data access patterns help detect anomalies that might signal a threat.

Employee training and awareness programs are also integral to the plan. These programs aim to educate staff about insider threats, the importance of adhering to security protocols, and the procedures for reporting suspicious activities. Creating a culture of security awareness can significantly reduce the likelihood of insider incidents.

Additionally, the plan should include clear policies and procedures for handling sensitive information and guidelines on using organizational resources. Regular updates and audits of these policies ensure they remain relevant and effective against evolving threats.

Identifying Critical Elements Specific to Mitigating Insider Threats

Identifying critical elements specific to mitigating insider threats involves understanding the unique characteristics and motivations behind these threats. This includes profiling potential insider threat actors, understanding their access levels, and recognizing behavioral patterns that might indicate malicious intent. It also involves evaluating the organization's specific vulnerabilities – such as areas with insufficient oversight or departments handling critical information.

Incorporating psychological aspects, such as employee satisfaction and workplace culture, into the prevention plan is also important. Often, insider threats stem from disgruntlement or ethical disagreements; thus, maintaining a positive and transparent workplace environment can act as a deterrent.

Integrating Incident Response and Recovery Strategies

A comprehensive prevention plan should seamlessly integrate with incident response and recovery strategies. This integration ensures the organization is prepared to respond effectively, minimize damage, and recover quickly if an insider threat materializes.

The incident response strategy should include protocols for immediate containment of the threat, investigation procedures, and communication plans, both internally and externally. It should also outline the roles and responsibilities of various team members during a response.

The recovery strategy focuses on restoring systems and operations post incident while addressing exploited security gaps. It involves analyzing the incident to glean lessons and implementing measures to prevent similar occurrences in the future.

Developing a prevention plan for insider threats is a multifaceted process that requires a thorough understanding of potential risks, robust policy implementation, and integration with response and recovery strategies. By focusing on these critical elements, organizations can create a strong defense against the complex and evolving nature of insider threats.

Defining Clear Roles in Preventing Insider Threats Across Different Organizational Levels

Preventing insider threats requires a coordinated effort across all levels of an organization. At the executive level, leaders are responsible for setting the tone and culture around security. They should prioritize insider threat prevention in their strategies and ensure adequate resources are allocated for security initiatives. This includes approving policies, overseeing the implementation of security measures, and supporting a culture of security awareness.

Management and supervisory roles involve overseeing the implementation of security policies within their respective departments. They are tasked with ensuring their teams are trained and compliant with security protocols. Managers also play a key role in monitoring potential threats, as they are often best positioned to notice changes in employee behavior or deviations from standard work patterns.

IT and security teams have a more hands-on role in the technical aspects of preventing insider threats. This includes managing access controls, monitoring network and data usage, and implementing security tools and technologies. They are also responsible for staying abreast of the latest security trends and threats, ensuring the organization's defenses remain effective against evolving tactics.

Employees, regardless of their position, also play a crucial role. They are often the first line of defense responsible for adhering to security policies and procedures. Employees should be trained to recognize potential security threats and know how to report suspicious activities.

Establishing Accountability and Communication Protocols

Accountability is key to maintaining an effective insider threat prevention strategy. This means establishing clear expectations for security practices and consequences for non-compliance. Regular security audits and assessments can help ensure policy adherence and identify improvement areas.

Effective communication protocols are also essential. These protocols should outline how and when to report potential security threats, whom to report to, and the steps to follow in the event of a suspected breach. Ensuring these protocols are well-understood and easily accessible encourages prompt and appropriate reporting of security concerns.

Communication should also include regular updates and feedback from leadership about the state of security within the organization. This could involve sharing insights from recent security audits, policy changes, or updates about emerging threats. Such communication helps in keeping security a constant presence in the organizational conversation.

Defining clear roles and responsibilities across all levels of the organization is crucial in creating a comprehensive defense against insider threats. Coupled with strong accountability and clear communication protocols, these efforts help foster an environment where security is everyone's responsibility, and potential threats are more likely to be identified and addressed promptly.

Training and Awareness

Training and awareness are key components of an effective insider threat prevention strategy. They involve educating employees about the nature and risks of insider threats and encouraging proactive participation in threat prevention. Well-informed employees are an invaluable asset in identifying and mitigating potential security risks.

Employee Education Programs

Developing comprehensive employee education programs is critical in raising awareness about insider threats. These programs should cover the spectrum of potential threats, including how they might manifest within the organization. The content should be tailored to different roles and departments, addressing the specific risks and responsibilities associated with each.

Key topics to cover in these programs include identifying sensitive information, understanding access controls, recognizing suspicious behaviors or activities, and knowledge of the organization's policies and procedures related to security. Additionally, training should educate employees on the consequences of insider threats, not just for the organization but also for individual employees, including legal and disciplinary repercussions.

Interactive and engaging training methods, such as workshops, simulations, and real-life scenario analyses, can be particularly effective. These methods help employees better understand the practical aspects of insider threat prevention and how to apply policies and procedures in their daily work.

Creating Tailored Programs to Educate Employees About the Nature and Risks of Insider Threats

Tailoring education programs to the specific needs and risks of the organization ensures that the training is relevant and practical. This involves conducting a thorough risk assessment to understand where the organization is most vulnerable and customizing the training content accordingly.

For example, training might focus more on financial fraud and data protection in departments that handle sensitive financial data. In contrast, in R&D departments, the emphasis might be on intellectual property theft and confidentiality agreements.

Furthermore, training programs should be regularly updated to reflect the evolving nature of insider threats and the changing landscape of the organization. This includes incorporating lessons learned from recent incidents, both internal and external, and adjusting the training content to address new types of threats or vulnerabilities.

Encouraging Proactive Employee Participation in Threat Prevention

Encouraging proactive participation involves creating an environment where employees feel responsible for and capable of contributing to the organization's security. This can be achieved by involving them in security discussions, soliciting their policy feedback, and recognizing and rewarding proactive security behaviors.

Creating channels for employees to report suspicious activities anonymously can also encourage participation. These channels should be easily accessible and well-publicized throughout the organization.

Additionally, fostering a culture of openness and trust where employees feel comfortable discussing security concerns without fear of retaliation is crucial. This culture encourages vigilance and a sense of collective responsibility toward the organization's security.

Training and awareness programs are vital in equipping employees with the knowledge and tools to identify and prevent insider threats. By creating tailored, engaging, and regularly updated programs and fostering an environment of proactive participation, organizations can significantly enhance their ability to mitigate these complex risks.

Simulations and Drills

Simulations and drills are critical components of an insider threat prevention strategy, providing a practical and immersive way to test and improve an organization's readiness against such threats. By simulating realistic scenarios, organizations can assess their vulnerabilities, response capabilities, and the effectiveness of their security protocols.

Conducting Realistic Scenarios to Test the Organization's Readiness Against Insider Threats

Simulations and drills should be designed to mimic potential insider threat scenarios as closely as possible. This could include scenarios such as unauthorized data access, data leakage, sabotage of organizational systems, or other forms of malicious insider activity. These exercises allow employees and security teams to practice responding in a controlled environment, helping them understand their roles during an incident.

The scenarios should be varied and cover a range of potential threats to ensure a comprehensive evaluation of the organization's preparedness. Participation should be organization-wide, involving various departments and levels, to ensure a holistic test of the organization's response capabilities.

Analyzing Outcomes and Improving Preparedness

After conducting simulations and drills, analyzing the outcomes thoroughly is essential. This analysis should identify both strengths and weaknesses in the organization's response. Key aspects to evaluate include the speed and effectiveness of the response, the communication flow during the incident, the decision-making process, and the coordination among different teams.

Feedback from participants is also valuable in understanding the practical challenges faced during the simulation. This feedback can adjust policies, procedures, and training programs.

The ultimate goal of these exercises is continuous improvement. Lessons learned should be integrated into the organization's insider threat strategy to enhance preparedness and response capabilities.

Continuous Awareness Campaigns

In addition to simulations and drills, continuous awareness campaigns are essential in keeping the topic of insider threats at the forefront of employees' minds. Ongoing initiatives help maintain a high level of vigilance and reinforce the importance of security practices.

Continuous awareness campaigns should be dynamic and engaging to capture and retain employee attention. This can involve regular updates on security protocols, insights into recent security incidents (both internal and external), and reminders of best practices. These initiatives can be integrated into regular communication channels such as newsletters, intranet sites, or staff meetings.

Utilizing Varied Mediums and Messages to Reinforce the Importance of Vigilance

To ensure the effectiveness of these campaigns, it's important to utilize a variety of mediums and messages. This can include digital communications, posters, interactive webinars, and workshops. Varied mediums cater to different learning preferences and help disseminate the message more effectively across the organization.

The messaging should also be varied, addressing different aspects of insider threats. This could range from understanding the motives behind insider threats to recognizing the signs and knowing how to respond. The key is keeping the content fresh and relevant, ensuring employees remain engaged and informed.

Simulation drills and continuous awareness campaigns are integral to an insider threat prevention strategy. These activities test and improve the organization's readiness and foster a culture of security awareness and vigilance, significantly enhancing the organization's resilience against insider threats.

Access Control and Management

Access control and management are pivotal in preventing insider threats. By effectively managing who has access to what information and systems, organizations can significantly reduce their vulnerability to malicious activities from within. This involves implementing principles like least privilege and segregation of duties and conducting regular audits and reviews.

Least Privilege Principle

Applying the least privilege principle is foundational in minimizing insider threat risks. This principle dictates that employees should be granted only the access rights necessary to perform their job functions and no more. This approach limits the potential damage an individual could inflict, as it restricts their ability to access sensitive information or critical systems beyond their immediate job requirements.

Implementing the least privilege principle requires a thorough understanding of the roles and responsibilities within the organization. Access rights should be carefully assigned based on these roles, and any exceptions should be monitored and justified.

Regularly Reviewing and Adjusting Access Permissions

Reviewing and adjusting access permissions regularly is crucial to ensure the effectiveness of the least privilege principle. This involves routinely auditing user rights to ensure they are still appropriate, particularly after changes in job roles, promotions, or terminations. Regular reviews help promptly identify and rectify any instances of excessive privileges, thereby reducing the risk of insider threats.

Segregation of Duties

Implementing segregation of duties is another critical strategy in reducing insider threat risks. This approach involves dividing responsibilities and access among multiple employees to prevent any single individual from having the ability to perpetrate harmful actions independently. The organization can mitigate the risk of fraud, data theft, and sabotage by ensuring that critical processes require collaboration or approval from multiple parties.

This practice is especially important in financial transactions, system administration, and access to sensitive data. Segregation of duties ensures that critical processes are not vulnerable to single points of failure or exploitation by one individual.

Regular Audits and Reviews

Scheduling and conducting periodic audits is crucial in assessing the effectiveness of access controls. These audits should examine how access rights are granted, enforced, and revoked. They should also assess compliance with the least privilege principle and segregation of duties.

Audit findings are invaluable in identifying weaknesses in the access control system and guiding improvements. They provide insights into potential areas of risk and help in refining policies and procedures. Regular audits also demonstrate a commitment to maintaining robust security practices, which can deter potential insider threats.

Using Audit Findings to Improve Insider Threat Prevention Measures Continuously

Utilizing the insights gained from audits allows for continuously improving insider threat prevention measures. Organizations can use these findings to make informed decisions about enhancing access control systems, refining policies, and improving employee training and awareness.

In summary, effective access control and management, characterized by the application of the least privilege principle, regular reviews of access permissions, segregation of duties, and ongoing audits, are essential in mitigating the risk of insider threats. These practices protect sensitive information and critical systems and create a culture of security and vigilance within the organization.

Data Loss Prevention (DLP)

Data Loss Prevention (DLP) tools are essential in safeguarding an organization's sensitive information from insider threats. These sophisticated tools monitor, detect, and act against unauthorized access or transmission of critical data.

DLP encompasses a set of technologies and processes designed to prevent unauthorized use, access, or transfer of sensitive information. The primary aim is to protect the organization's intellectual property, regulatory compliance data, and other key information assets from external and internal threats, including accidental or intentional leaks by insiders. DLP tools are thus an integral part of an organization's overall data security framework.

Originally, DLP tools were relatively straightforward systems focused mainly on detecting and blocking data based on preset rules. However, these tools have become more sophisticated as the digital landscape has evolved. Modern DLP solutions incorporate advanced technologies like deep content inspection, natural language processing, and machine learning. These enhancements enable the tools to understand the context of data usage, adapt to changing threat patterns, and effectively protect sensitive data in various states: at rest (stored data), in motion (data being transmitted), and in use (data being processed).

The critical role of DLP in mitigating insider threats cannot be overstated. By virtue of their access to sensitive data and understanding of the organization's systems, insiders pose a unique challenge. DLP tools help address this challenge by providing a safety net that prevents sensitive data from leaving the organization's network without proper authorization. They are particularly effective in identifying and blocking attempts by insiders to exfiltrate data, whether through email, cloud services, or other means.

Key Features of DLP Systems

A cornerstone of DLP functionality is its ability to identify and classify data. These systems scan files and communications to categorize data based on sensitivity, using criteria such as content, context, and user activity. Accurate classification is vital for applying appropriate security controls. For instance, a trade secret document would require stricter controls than a publicly available company brochure.

DLP systems enable organizations to create and manage policies that define how different types of data should be handled. These policies can dictate who can access specific data, under what circumstances data can be transmitted, and what actions should be taken when a policy violation is detected. Creating nuanced policies allows organizations to enforce security without impeding legitimate business activities.

One of the most powerful features of DLP systems is real-time monitoring and alerting. These tools continuously monitor data movement within the organization's network and alert administrators to suspicious activities. This real-time capability ensures that potential threats can be identified and responded to promptly, minimizing the risk of data leakage.

Implementing DLP Solutions

Implementing a DLP solution begins with thoroughly assessing the organization's data protection needs. This assessment involves identifying the types of data that need protection, understanding how and where this data is used and stored, and determining the potential risks associated with this data.

For DLP tools to be effective, they must be seamlessly integrated with the organization's IT infrastructure. This includes alignment with existing security tools, such as firewalls and intrusion detection systems, and compatibility with the organization's data storage and communication platforms. Proper integration ensures that the DLP tools can effectively monitor and protect data across all systems and platforms.

User training and acceptance are crucial for the successful deployment of DLP tools. Employees need to understand the importance of data security, how DLP tools operate, and how they might impact their work. Effective training programs can help minimize resistance and ensure employees adhere to the new security protocols.

Challenges and Best Practices

One of the challenges in implementing DLP tools is managing false positives – legitimate activities that are incorrectly flagged as security risks. High rates of false positives can lead to operational inefficiencies and user frustration. To mitigate this accurately, DLP systems should be finely tuned to distinguish between normal and suspicious activities.

Striking a balance between security and usability is another critical aspect. While robust data protection is essential, it should not come at the cost of hindering employee productivity. DLP policies and controls should be designed to protect sensitive data while allowing employees to perform their job functions effectively.

The threat landscape and organizational environments constantly evolve, necessitating regular updates and improvements to DLP systems. This includes updating data classification criteria, refining policies, and staying abreast of new technological developments in DLP.

DLP tools are vital in the fight against insider threats, providing a robust framework for protecting sensitive data. Organizations can significantly enhance their data security posture while maintaining operational efficiency by understanding and implementing their features effectively.

User Behavior Analytics (UBA)

User Behavior Analytics (UBA) has emerged as a critical component in modern security strategies, particularly in addressing insider threats. UBA systems analyze user behavior and apply advanced analytics to identify potential security threats.

Understanding UBA

UBA plays a significant role in enhancing security by focusing on what is often the weakest link in security: human behavior. By analyzing user behavior patterns, UBA tools can identify deviations that may indicate a security threat, such as an insider attempting to steal or compromise data. Unlike traditional security measures focusing primarily on external threats, UBA provides a nuanced approach that looks at potential threats within the organization.

Traditional security tools are typically rule-based and perimeter-focused, guarding against known threats and external attacks. On the other hand, UBA uses machine learning and statistical analysis to understand normal user behavior and detect anomalies that may signify a threat. This approach allows UBA to uncover subtle and unusual behavior patterns that traditional tools might miss.

UBA is particularly effective in detecting insider threats because it can identify subtle activities that other security systems may not flag. For example, a user accessing files at unusual hours or downloading large amounts of data might go unnoticed by traditional security systems but would be detected by UBA as an anomaly.

Components of UBA Systems

UBA systems create behavioral profiles for users, establishing what normal behavior looks like for each individual. These baselines are crucial in identifying deviations that may indicate a threat. By continuously analyzing user behavior, UBA systems can update these baselines over time, adapting to changes in user activity.

At the core of UBA systems are sophisticated anomaly detection algorithms. These algorithms analyze behavioral data to identify patterns and activities that deviate from the norm. The effectiveness of these algorithms is crucial in accurately identifying potential threats without overwhelming administrators with false positives.

UBA tools often incorporate risk scoring mechanisms, which assign a risk level to user activities based on their deviation from baseline behaviors. This scoring helps prioritize alerts, allowing security teams to focus on the most critical issues first.

Deployment and Integration

Implementing UBA successfully involves several key steps. Initially, it requires a clear understanding of the organization's security goals and the types of insider threats it faces. This understanding guides the configuration of the UBA system to ensure it aligns with specific organizational needs.

UBA systems should be integrated with other security tools within the organization, such as SIEM (Security Information and Event Management) and DLP (Data Loss Prevention) systems, for maximum effectiveness. This integration allows for a more comprehensive security approach, combining the strengths of each system.

When deploying UBA, it's essential to address privacy and ethical concerns. This involves ensuring that monitoring is done in compliance with legal standards and ethical guidelines and that employees are aware of the monitoring and its purpose.

UBA in Action

There are numerous case studies where UBA has effectively identified and mitigated insider threats. These cases often involve scenarios where traditional security measures failed to detect subtle, malicious activities. Through UBA, organizations were able to identify and respond to these threats quickly, minimizing potential damage.

Deployments of UBA systems have provided valuable lessons in their capabilities and limitations. Key takeaways include the importance of continuously updating and tuning the system, the need for skilled personnel to analyze and interpret UBA data, and balancing security measures with privacy concerns.

As UBA technology evolves, future developments will likely include more advanced machine learning algorithms, better integration with other security tools, and enhanced capabilities for predicting potential threats. The ongoing refinement of UBA systems will make them even more effective in combating insider threats and protecting organizational data.

Artificial Intelligence (AI) in Insider Threats

Artificial intelligence (AI) is revolutionizing the field of insider threat detection and management, offering advanced tools and capabilities for organizations to safeguard their sensitive information. However, integrating AI into security systems brings new challenges and complexities, particularly regarding potential misuse and ethical considerations.

AI-Driven Security Systems

AI-driven security systems are increasingly integral to modern cybersecurity strategies, particularly in mitigating insider threats. These systems leverage AI algorithms to analyze vast data, identify patterns, and detect unusual activities that could signify a security breach. By processing and interpreting data at a scale and speed unattainable by human analysts, AI systems can uncover subtle anomalies in user behavior, such as irregular access patterns to sensitive data or unexpected changes in data transfer volumes. This capability to quickly and accurately identify potential threats transforms how organizations approach insider threat detection, allowing them to be more proactive rather than reactive.

The capabilities of AI in detecting and predicting insider threats are rooted in its ability to analyze complex datasets and identify correlations that may indicate malicious activity. Machine learning models, a subset of AI, are adept at evolving and improving their detection capabilities over time, learning from new data, and adapting to changing behavior patterns. This adaptability is crucial in the ever-evolving landscape of cybersecurity, where threat actors continuously modify their tactics. Additionally, AI's predictive analytics can forecast potential insider threats based on observed behaviors, allowing organizations to intervene before a threat materializes into an actual breach.

Potential Risks of AI

The deployment of AI in security contexts is not without its risks. One significant concern is the possibility of AI tools being manipulated or exploited by insider threats. Malicious insiders with technical expertise could potentially find ways to alter AI algorithms or feed them misleading data, undermining their effectiveness. Furthermore, there is the risk of overreliance on AI systems, which might lead to complacency in other critical security practices. As AI systems become more sophisticated, there is growing concern about their potential use in creating advanced cyber-attack strategies, making it challenging for organizations to keep pace with increasingly intelligent threats.

The potential of AI to be used as a tool for perpetrating insider threats is a growing concern in the cybersecurity community. Insiders with malicious intent and access to AI technologies could develop sophisticated methods to bypass traditional security measures. They could, for instance, use AI algorithms to analyze security protocols and find loopholes or automate extracting and compiling sensitive data without triggering security alerts. The stealth and efficiency afforded by AI could thus make insider attacks more difficult to detect and counter, posing a significant challenge to existing cybersecurity defenses.

Organizations must adopt a layered security approach encompassing technological and human elements to mitigate the risks associated with AI misuse effectively. Establishing robust monitoring systems that detect unusual changes or manipulations in AI operations is crucial, indicating potential tampering. Organizations should also foster a culture of security awareness, where employees are trained to recognize and report suspicious activities, including those related to AI systems. Additionally, implementing strict access controls to AI tools and maintaining up-to-date security protocols are essential in preventing unauthorized use or manipulation of AI technologies.

Ethical Considerations and AI Governance

Integrating AI into insider threat management raises important ethical considerations, particularly regarding privacy and surveillance. As AI systems often require access to vast amounts of personal and behavioral data, there is a risk of infringing on individual privacy rights. Ensuring that AI deployment in security respects privacy norms and complies with relevant data protection laws is imperative. Ethical AI governance involves transparency in AI operations, clear communication about AI's role in monitoring and threat detection, and adherence to ethical standards that protect individual rights while ensuring organizational security.

Creating and adhering to ethical guidelines for using AI in security is essential to maintaining trust and integrity within an organization. These guidelines should emphasize the responsible and fair use of AI, ensuring that AI-driven security measures do not lead to discrimination or unjust surveillance. Involving diverse stakeholders, including legal, ethical, and data privacy experts, in developing these guidelines can help address a broad spectrum of concerns. Furthermore, establishing clear policies on the extent and manner of AI utilization in security processes can help balance the need for robust security with the imperative of protecting individual rights.

AI's role in insider threat detection and prevention is becoming increasingly significant, offering powerful tools for organizations to safeguard their data and systems. However, this technological advancement also necessitates careful consideration of potential risks, ethical implications, and robust governance frameworks to ensure AI's responsible and effective use in cybersecurity.

Quantum Computing and Security Implications

Quantum computing represents a paradigm shift in computational capabilities and poses opportunities and challenges for cybersecurity, including insider threats.

Quantum computing technology is based on the principles of quantum theory, which explains the nature of energy and matter at the atomic and subatomic levels. Unlike classical computing, which uses bits as the smallest unit of data, quantum computing uses quantum bits, or qubits, which can exist in multiple states simultaneously. This allows quantum computers to process calculations simultaneously, dramatically increasing their power and efficiency.

The potential impact of quantum computing on cybersecurity is profound. On the one hand, it promises to enhance cryptographic protocols, making them more secure against conventional hacking attempts. On the other hand, its immense computing power could potentially break many of the encryption standards currently in use, posing a significant threat to data security.

Quantum Computing and Insider Threats

The advent of quantum computing could significantly enhance insider threat detection capabilities. With their ability to rapidly analyze large datasets, quantum algorithms could identify subtle patterns and anomalies indicative of insider threats more efficiently than current systems. These advanced analytical capabilities would enable organizations to detect potential threats faster and more accurately, reducing the risk of data breaches and other security incidents.

However, quantum computing could also serve as a potent tool in the hands of insiders with malicious intent. The advanced capabilities of quantum computers might enable these individuals to decrypt sensitive information, create sophisticated attack strategies, or manipulate data in ways that are currently impossible with classical computing. This potential makes quantum computing a double-edged sword in the context of insider threats.

Preparing for a Quantum Future

Given the potential impact of quantum computing on cybersecurity, organizations must start preparing for a quantum future. This preparation involves upgrading existing security protocols to ensure they are quantum resilient. Developing and implementing quantum-safe encryption methods will be crucial in protecting sensitive information against the threat of quantum computing capabilities.

Anticipating and mitigating quantum-enabled threats is another critical aspect. Organizations must stay informed about advancements in quantum computing and assess how these developments could be used against them. Proactive measures might include investing in quantum computing research, developing quantum-resistant security technologies, and incorporating quantum risk assessments into overall security strategies.

While quantum computing offers exciting possibilities in various fields, including cybersecurity, it also brings new challenges, particularly insider threats. As this technology continues to develop, organizations must remain vigilant and proactive in upgrading their security protocols, anticipating potential threats, and preparing for the impact of quantum computing on data security and privacy. This forward-thinking approach will ensure that organizations are ready to harness the benefits of quantum computing while safeguarding against its potential risks.

Case Study: The Insider Threat Incident at Lianjia

In June 2018, a significant cybersecurity incident unfolded at Lianjia, a major Chinese real estate brokerage firm previously known as Homelink. Han Bing, a database administrator at the company, used his administrative privileges to launch a devastating attack on the company's financial databases. This case study explores the events leading up to the incident, the attack itself, and its aftermath, offering insights into the complex nature of insider threats and the importance of effective cybersecurity measures and employee management.

Han Bing, who had access to the company's financial system due to his role as an IT administrator, was one of the few individuals at Lianjia with the necessary clearance to access the sensitive data that he eventually targeted. Before the incident, he had repeatedly raised concerns about security vulnerabilities within the system to his employer and supervisor. Unfortunately, these warnings were reportedly dismissed or ignored, a factor that may have contributed to his subsequent actions.

The attack was carried out using Bing's administrative credentials, granting him unfettered access to Lianjia's financial system. He employed the "shred" and "rm" commands, powerful Unix/Linux commands for deleting files. The "shred" command is particularly destructive as it overwrites the data multiple times with different patterns, rendering it irrecoverable. The "rm" command, on the other hand, removes the symbolic links to the files, effectively erasing them from the system. Bing successfully wiped crucial data using these commands from two databases and two application servers.

The consequences of Bing's actions were severe. Deleting these databases had a significant operational impact on Lianjia, which at the time had an estimated market value of around $6 billion. The restoration of the deleted data cost the company approximately $30,000. More critically, tens of thousands of Lianjia's employees could not receive their salaries for an extended period while the company struggled to resolve the issue and recover the lost data.

The investigation into the incident involved meticulous analysis of server access logs, IP and MAC addresses, Wi-Fi connectivity logs, and timestamps. This digital evidence was cross-referenced with CCTV footage, confirming Bing's involvement in a cyberattack. Despite Bing's initial refusal to grant investigators access to his laptop, citing the presence of private data, the digital forensics evidence was compelling enough to lead to his conviction.

Han Bing was found guilty of damaging computer information systems and sentenced to seven years. This incident at Lianjia is a stark reminder of the potential damage that insider threats can inflict on an organization. It highlights the importance of implementing robust cybersecurity measures and seriously addressing employee grievances and concerns. The case underscores the need for a balanced approach to cybersecurity, combining technical safeguards with attentive and responsive management practice.

Career Corner

The growing awareness and concern around insider threats have increased the demand for professionals in this area. Organizations across various industries seek experts who can identify, assess, and mitigate risks posed by insider threats. This demand spans a range of roles, each requiring a unique set of skills and expertise.

Insider Threat Analysts are crucial in detecting and analyzing potential insider threats. They monitor data and user behavior, looking for anomalies that could indicate malicious activity. Their role often involves working with large datasets and utilizing advanced analytical tools.

Insider Threat Investigators take the lead in responding to incidents. They conduct in-depth investigations into suspicious activities, gather evidence, and work closely with legal teams and law enforcement when necessary. Their work is pivotal in understanding a breach's extent and preventing future incidents.

Insider Threat Program Managers oversee the development and implementation of insider threat programs. They are responsible for designing strategies, policies, and procedures to prevent, detect, and respond to insider threats. Their role also involves training employees and fostering a culture of security awareness within the organization.

IT Security Specialists focusing on insider threats are tasked with implementing technical solutions to monitor and prevent insider activities. They handle cybersecurity tools like Data Loss Prevention (DLP) systems, User Behavior Analytics (UBA), and other monitoring software.

Certifications for Insider Threat Professionals

For those looking to specialize in insider threat management, several certifications can enhance their qualifications and career prospects.

The Certified Insider Threat Professional (CITP) certification is designed for individuals seeking to understand the nuances of insider threat detection and mitigation. This certification covers various aspects of insider threat management, including risk assessment, psychological factors, and legal considerations.

While broader in scope, the Certified Information Systems Security Professional (CISSP) includes elements related to insider threats. It covers security risk management, legal issues, and compliance, all pertinent to an insider threat specialist.

The Certified Protection Professional (CPP) certification by ASIS International is another respected credential. It focuses more on security management and addresses various aspects of internal threats, including prevention and investigation strategies.

For IT professionals, certifications like CompTIA Security+ and Certified Information Systems Auditor (CISA) offer valuable knowledge and skills in implementing and managing security technologies and policies, which are crucial in safeguarding against insider threats.

As organizations increasingly recognize the importance of protecting against insider threats, the demand for skilled professionals is growing. A career in insider threat management offers opportunities to work in diverse roles, each playing a crucial part in safeguarding an organization's assets. Coupled with the right certifications, individuals interested in this field can significantly enhance their expertise and career prospects, positioning themselves as valuable assets in this evolving and critically important area of cybersecurity.

Chapter Questions

1. What is the primary characteristic of insider threats
    in cybersecurity?

    A. They always involve external actors

    B. They originate from individuals within the organization

    C. They are less harmful than external threats

    D. They are easily detectable

2. Why are "malicious insiders" considered a
    significant insider threat?

    A. They lack access to sensitive information

    B. They intentionally cause harm to the organization

    C. They are usually external hackers

    D. They are not aware of their actions

3. What role does User Behavior Analytics (UBA) play
    in managing insider threats?

    A. It decreases network traffic

    B. It enhances server performance

    C. It analyzes patterns in user behavior to detect threats

    D. It focuses solely on external threats

4. Which method is used to identify unusual patterns that may indicate insider threats?

   A. Data encryption

   B. Password management

   C. Anomaly detection

   D. Firewall implementation

5. Why is Data Loss Prevention (DLP) important in combating insider threats?

   A. It increases data storage capacity

   B. It detects and prevents unauthorized data access and transmission

   C. It improves user interface design

   D. It focuses on external cyber-attacks

6. What is the purpose of Access Controls in the context of insider threats?

   A. To enhance website design

   B. To increase data processing speed

   C. To limit access to information based on job requirements

   D. To promote social media marketing

7. How do incident response plans assist in dealing with insider threats?

   A. They outline steps for marketing strategies

   B. They define procedures to handle detected threats

   C. They focus on recruitment processes

   D. They are used for financial auditing

8. What is a critical component of employee training and awareness in cybersecurity?

   A. Social media training

   B. Phishing awareness training

   C. Sales techniques

   D. Graphic design skills

9. Why are regular security audits and assessments crucial in a security-minded workplace?

   A. They focus on public relations

   B. They identify and address security vulnerabilities

   C. They deal with customer service training

   D. They are used for employee performance reviews

10. How does "careless insiders" impact on an organization's cybersecurity?

    A. They intentionally sabotage systems

    B. They cause breaches through negligence or lack of awareness

    C. They improve cybersecurity measures

    D. They are involved in marketing strategies

11. How does promoting a trusting but vigilant atmosphere contribute to cybersecurity?

    A. It focuses on financial investment

    B. It encourages proactive identification and reporting of threats

    C. It deals with employee entertainment

    D. It is used for product development

12. What is the significance of secure communication practices in a security-minded workplace?

    A. They help in team building

    B. They reduce operational costs

    C. They prevent sensitive information from being compromised

    D. They are used for advertising purposes

13. What motivates a "collaborative insider" to pose a threat?

    A. Lack of access to sensitive information

    B. Collaboration with external entities to compromise security

    C. A desire to improve cybersecurity

    D. Involvement in financial planning

14. Why is employee dissatisfaction a critical factor to consider in managing insider threats?

    A. It enhances team performance

    B. It can lead to intentional or unintentional security breaches

    C. It is irrelevant to cybersecurity

    D. It focuses on employee welfare programs

15. Why is encouraging the reporting of security concerns vital in a workplace?

   A. It is essential for public relations

   B. It aids in the early detection and mitigation of potential threats

   C. It is only used for employee appraisals

   D. It focuses on customer feedback

CHAPTER 15

Artificial Intelligence and Machine Learning in Cybersecurity

Artificial intelligence (AI) and machine learning (ML) are the most transformative technologies in the modern digital landscape. At its core, AI is the simulation of human intelligence in machines programmed to think and act like humans. This encompasses a broad range of capabilities, from basic problem-solving and decision-making to advanced functions like speech recognition and natural language understanding.

Machine learning, a subset of AI, involves the development of algorithms that enable computers to learn and make decisions based on data. Unlike traditional programming, where humans explicitly code the behavior, ML automatically allows the system to learn and improve from experience. This is achieved by feeding large amounts of data into algorithms, enabling the system to identify patterns, make predictions, and improve its performance over time.

Evolution in Cybersecurity

Integrating AI and ML into cybersecurity marks a significant evolution in the field. Initially, cybersecurity relied heavily on rule-based systems for threat detection and prevention. While effective against known threats, these systems struggled with the constantly changing landscape of cyber attacks.

The introduction of AI and ML brought a paradigm shift. With their ability to learn and adapt, ML algorithms became instrumental in identifying novel threats, including zero-day exploits and sophisticated malware. AI's predictive capabilities enabled proactive threat intelligence, moving cybersecurity from a reactive posture to a more anticipatory approach.

Moreover, AI-driven behavioral analysis revolutionized understanding and responding to insider threats and anomalous network activities. By analyzing patterns and detecting deviations, AI systems provide a dynamic and nuanced approach to securing digital assets.

The advent of AI and ML in cybersecurity is not just an upgrade; it's a fundamental change in how we protect digital infrastructures. As these technologies evolve, they promise to be the cornerstone of robust, adaptive, and intelligent cybersecurity solutions.

Historical Perspective

The historical journey of artificial intelligence (AI) and machine learning (ML) can be traced back to the mid-20th century. This era began a fascinating quest to create artificial beings endowed with human-like intelligence. The initial concept of AI was inspired by the desire to replicate the cognitive abilities of the human mind in machines.

In these early stages, AI research was predominantly focused on symbolic methods. The goal was to emulate human reasoning through rules and logic. Researchers and scientists attempted to encode knowledge and reasoning capabilities directly into computers. This approach led to the development of the first AI programs designed to perform specific tasks, such as solving algebraic problems and proving mathematical theorems.

A pivotal figure in the early development of AI was Alan Turing, a British mathematician and computer scientist. His work laid the theoretical foundations for computer science and AI. Turing's famous question, "Can machines think?" posed in his 1950 paper, propelled the pursuit of creating intelligent machines and set the stage for future advancements in the field.

The term "artificial intelligence" was formally coined in 1956 at the Dartmouth Conference, organized by John McCarthy and others. This landmark event brought together eminent researchers and marked the official birth of AI as an independent field of study. At this conference, AI's potential began to be fully recognized and explored.

By the 1980s, it became evident that the scope of explicit programming in AI was limited. This realization led to the emergence of machine learning as a distinct field. ML shifted the focus from hardcoding intelligence into systems to enabling them to learn and adapt from data. This period witnessed significant research in developing algorithms that could improve performance by learning from data inputs.

A breakthrough in ML was the development of neural networks inspired by the structure and function of the human brain. This technique involved creating interconnected nodes or "neurons" in a network, which could process and transmit information like biological neural networks. Neural networks became a fundamental aspect of ML, setting the stage for various modern AI applications.

Despite early enthusiasm, AI faced reduced funding and interest periods, known as the "AI winters." The first occurred in the 1970s, followed by another in the late 1980s. These periods were characterized by skepticism and disappointment over AI technologies' unmet expectations and limitations at the time.

The late 1990s and early 2000s marked the revival of AI, fueled by increased computational power, availability of large datasets, and algorithm advancements. The resurgence saw AI and ML being applied in more practical and impactful ways, from natural language processing to computer vision.

Integrating AI and ML with big data analytics and cloud computing further accelerated their capabilities. This convergence allowed for the processing and analysis of vast amounts of data, leading to more accurate and sophisticated AI models. Cloud platforms provide the necessary infrastructure and scalability for deploying AI solutions on a large scale.

Generative AI

Generative AI refers to a subset of artificial intelligence technology that focuses on creating new content based on learning from a vast array of existing data, whether text, images, music, or code. Unlike traditional AI models designed for tasks like classification or prediction, generative AI models can generate entirely new, plausible data points. This transformative ability enables AI to move from an interpretive role to a creative one.

The defining characteristic of generative AI is its ability to use learned patterns to generate new outputs similar to, but not identical to, the data it was trained on. This involves understanding and replicating complex patterns, structures, and elements inherent in the training data. The results can be novel creations that do not just mimic but also have the potential to innovate beyond the original dataset.

Generative AI differentiates itself from other AI models through its creative capability. While conventional AI models might predict or classify data based on learned patterns, generative AI creates new, original content that adheres to the learned patterns and structures of its training data.

Technical Background

Generative AI uses advanced algorithms and neural network architectures, such as Generative Adversarial Networks (GANs) and Variational Autoencoders (VAEs).

GANs consist of two parts: a generator and a discriminator. The generator creates data, while the discriminator evaluates it against the real data. The generator continuously learns to produce more accurate data, while the discriminator becomes better at distinguishing between generated and real data. This adversarial process leads to the generation of highly realistic and sophisticated outputs.

VAEs are another type of generative model that compresses data into a smaller representation and then reconstructs it to generate new data points. They are particularly effective in managing data variability and are often used for tasks requiring high precision in the generation process.

Uses in Today's World

Generative AI has many applications today, impacting various industries, from art and design to technology and science. In creative fields like art, music, and literature, generative AI is used to produce new works inspired by human creativity yet entirely machine-generated. This has opened up new possibilities in personalized content creation and has even led to AI being credited as a co-creator in some works.

Generative AI plays a significant role in design and simulation. In architecture and engineering, for instance, it can generate multiple design options based on specified criteria. In scientific research, it simulates complex systems and scenarios, providing valuable insights that would be difficult to obtain otherwise. In data science, generative AI is used for data augmentation, generating additional training data for machine learning models. This is particularly useful when real data is scarce or expensive to obtain, as the artificially generated data can enhance the performance of predictive models.

555

Generative AI represents a significant leap in the capabilities of artificial intelligence, moving from analysis and interpretation to creating new and original outputs. Its applications span various fields, offering innovative solutions and augmenting human creativity with its unique capacity to generate new content and ideas.

Fears and Facts of AI

Its portrayal profoundly influences the fears surrounding artificial intelligence (AI) in science fiction. Sci-fi narratives often depict AI as an overpowering force capable of surpassing human intelligence, potentially leading to dystopian outcomes. This portrayal has played a significant role in shaping public perceptions, instilling a sense of apprehension and skepticism about AI's real-world implications and capabilities. Science fiction has been instrumental in forming public expectations and misconceptions about AI. It often dramatizes AI capabilities, presenting futuristic scenarios that blur the line between reality and fiction.

These imaginative and engaging depictions can lead to misunderstandings about the actual state and potential of AI technologies. It's crucial to differentiate between the fictional representations of AI and its real-world applications. Unlike its sci-fi depictions, real AI is a tool designed, controlled, and governed by humans, with ethical guidelines and practical limitations. Understanding this distinction helps form a more realistic view of AI and its impact on society.

Educational Repercussions of Generative AI

Generative AI's impact on education is multifaceted, offering challenges and opportunities for learning environments. Generative AI has the potential to revolutionize education by providing personalized learning materials and creating adaptive educational pathways. It can tailor educational content to suit individual learning styles, making education more effective and accessible for diverse learners.

However, there are growing concerns about academic integrity, as students might leverage generative AI to complete assignments or essays. This raises ethical questions about authorship and effort, necessitating new academic guidelines and monitoring systems to ensure integrity in educational settings. Educators and institutions are faced with adapting their strategies to incorporate and regulate the use of AI in education. This includes developing new pedagogical approaches that leverage AI's capabilities while maintaining academic standards and fostering genuine learning.

Elimination of Jobs and Careers Because of AI

AI's integration into various industries has sparked concerns about job displacement and eliminating specific career paths. Automation and AI technologies can replace human roles in specific sectors, particularly those involving repetitive or routine tasks. This has raised concerns about job security in the manufacturing, customer service, and data entry industries. As AI takes over more routine tasks, the requirement for human roles is shifting toward more complex, creative, or interpersonal skills.

This transition necessitates retraining and upskilling for many workers to stay relevant in an AI-integrated job market. While AI introduces efficiencies and cost savings for businesses, it also presents the possibility of job displacement. Addressing this challenge requires proactive strategies, including education, training, and policymaking, to manage the transition and mitigate the impact on the workforce.

New Careers and Jobs Created Because of AI

Conversely, the advent of AI is also creating new career opportunities and job sectors. AI has led to new fields and specialties, such as machine learning engineering, AI ethics, and data science. These areas offer new career paths and opportunities for innovation and development.

There's an increasing demand for professionals working effectively alongside AI, leveraging its capabilities while providing human insight and oversight. This includes roles in AI management, supervision, and integration across various sectors. The growth of AI is not limited to technical roles; it's also expanding opportunities in nontechnical areas like policymaking, legal consulting on AI ethics, and AI-influenced design and marketing strategies.

The Future of Work with AI As a Partner

The future of work in an AI-integrated world is likely to emphasize collaboration between humans and AI systems. AI is increasingly seen as a collaborative tool that enhances human capabilities rather than replacing them. AI assists in analysis, decision-making, and creative processes in many sectors, working alongside human expertise. AI integration reshapes work environments, encouraging a hybrid model where human creativity and AI efficiency coexist. This paradigm shift requires rethinking job roles, work processes, and organizational structures.

Preparing for an AI-integrated future involves redefining education, job training, and organizational policies to embrace AI as a collaborative partner. It demands a holistic approach that considers AI's ethical, social, and economic implications in the workforce.

AI-Driven Threat Detection and Analysis

In cybersecurity, understanding the various types of cyber threats is crucial. These threats come in many forms, ranging from malware, such as viruses and ransomware, to more sophisticated forms, like advanced persistent threats (APTs) and zero-day exploits. Each type poses unique challenges and requires specific strategies for detection and mitigation. Malware can disrupt or damage systems, while APTs involve prolonged, targeted attacks against specific entities. Phishing attacks deceive users into divulging sensitive information, and DDoS attacks overwhelm systems with traffic, causing them to crash.

The threat landscape in cybersecurity is dynamic and constantly evolving. With the advancement of technology, cybercriminals have become more sophisticated, leveraging AI and ML to devise more complex attacks. Geopolitical developments, economic incentives, and the ever-expanding array of vulnerable devices and networks influence this landscape. For example, the rise of IoT devices has opened new avenues for cyber attacks. Similarly, the increasing reliance on cloud services has shifted the focus of attackers to these platforms. Understanding this evolving landscape is pivotal for developing effective AI-driven security measures.

Attack vectors are the methods or pathways through which cybercriminals launch attacks on information systems. Typical vectors include email attachments, compromised websites, and unsecured network connections. More sophisticated attacks may exploit zero-day vulnerabilities – flaws in software unknown to the vendor – or use social engineering to trick users into granting access. In the context of AI-driven threat detection, understanding these vectors is vital. It allows for developing models that can recognize patterns associated with different types of attacks and identify potential vulnerabilities in a network.

AI technologies play a crucial role in identifying and responding to emerging threats. By analyzing vast amounts of data, AI systems can detect anomalies that might indicate a cyber attack. This includes unusual network traffic, unexpected access patterns, or unfamiliar files in the system. AI's ability to learn from new data means it can adapt to recognize new threats, making it an essential tool in responding to the dynamic nature of cyber risks.

Predictive analysis, enabled by AI and ML, is transforming cybersecurity strategies. AI systems can predict potential future attacks by analyzing trends and patterns from past data. This approach allows organizations to proactively strengthen their defenses against anticipated threats rather than simply reacting to attacks as they occur. Predictive analysis can also help identify an organization's most likely attack vectors and potential targets, enabling a more focused and effective defense strategy.

AI-driven threat detection and analysis enhance traditional cybersecurity measures. Where traditional methods might rely on predefined rules and signatures, AI adds a layer of intelligence that can adapt and evolve. This includes updating threat databases in real time, identifying new forms of malware, and automating responses to security incidents. Integrating AI into traditional security frameworks results in a more robust and responsive defense system.

Behavioral analysis is another area where AI significantly contributes. By monitoring normal user and system behaviors, AI algorithms can detect deviations that may indicate a security breach. This method is particularly effective against insider threats and sophisticated attacks that might bypass conventional detection methods. Behavioral analysis helps in early detection, often before significant damage is done.

AI enables real-time threat intelligence, crucial for timely and effective responses to cyber attacks. AI systems provide up-to-date information on current threats by continuously analyzing data from various sources. This real-time intelligence allows organizations to quickly adapt their defense mechanisms to current threat scenarios, reducing the window of opportunity for attackers.

AI-driven threat detection is not just about identifying threats; it also plays a crucial role in incident response. Once a threat is detected, AI systems can automate specific responses, like isolating affected systems or blocking malicious traffic. This rapid response can limit the impact of attacks and prevent further damage. Additionally, AI can assist in post-incident analysis, helping to understand how the attack happened and improving defenses against future attacks.

AI will continue to be a pivotal force in shaping cybersecurity strategies. As cyber threats grow in complexity and volume, AI's ability to analyze large datasets, adapt to new threats, and automate responses will be invaluable. The future of cybersecurity lies in leveraging AI not just as a tool but as an integral component of a comprehensive, adaptive, and proactive security approach.

Machine Learning in Threat Detection

Anomaly detection is a critical aspect of machine learning in cybersecurity. It involves identifying unusual patterns or behaviors in data that deviate from the norm, which could indicate a potential security threat. Machine learning algorithms, especially unsupervised learning models, are particularly adept at this task. They can process vast amounts of data and identify outliers without knowing what constitutes a threat. This capability detects novel or sophisticated attacks that might not trigger traditional rule-based systems. Anomalies could range from unusual network traffic patterns to unexpected changes in system files or user behavior.

Machine learning enhances anomaly detection by continuously learning and adapting to new data. As the system is exposed to more information, it becomes better at distinguishing between benign anomalies and those indicative of a security threat. This dynamic approach is essential in an ever-changing threat landscape, where attackers continually evolve their methods to evade detection. Furthermore, ML algorithms can be trained to reduce false positives, improving the accuracy and reliability of threat detection systems.

Pattern recognition is another crucial application of machine learning in threat detection. ML algorithms are designed to recognize patterns in data, which is a fundamental aspect of identifying cyber threats. For instance, specific network traffic patterns might indicate a DDoS attack, while specific file behaviors could suggest the presence of ransomware. Machine learning models can learn to identify these patterns and flag potential threats by analyzing historical data.

Deep learning, a subset of machine learning, is particularly effective in pattern recognition tasks. Utilizing neural networks with multiple layers, deep learning models can process complex, high-dimensional data. This ability is invaluable in cybersecurity, where threats might be hidden in large and complex datasets. Deep learning models can extract features and recognize patterns not immediately apparent to human analysts or traditional algorithms.

Predictive Modeling

Predictive modeling in cybersecurity involves using machine learning to predict future threats and vulnerabilities. By analyzing historical data, ML models can identify trends and patterns likely to lead to future security incidents. This proactive approach is a significant shift from traditional reactive cybersecurity methods. Predictive modeling enables organizations to anticipate and prepare for potential threats rather than responding to them after they have occurred.

Machine learning's predictive modeling is particularly effective in adapting to the dynamic threat landscape. As new types of attacks emerge, predictive models can be updated with new data, allowing them to evolve and remain effective. This continuous learning process ensures that threat detection systems stay ahead of attackers, who are constantly developing new techniques. Predictive modeling can also significantly reduce response times to security incidents. By anticipating potential threats, organizations can implement preventative measures in advance, minimizing the impact of attacks. This proactive stance is critical in maintaining security in environments where even a tiny delay can result in significant damage.

Integrating machine learning with existing security systems enhances their capabilities. ML algorithms can complement traditional security measures, providing a more comprehensive defense strategy. This integration allows for more accurate threat detection, faster response times, and a more robust overall security posture. A key advantage of machine learning in threat detection is its continuous improvement over time. As ML models are exposed to more data, their accuracy and effectiveness increase. This continuous improvement is vital in keeping pace with the rapidly evolving nature of cyber threats.

The development of machine learning in cybersecurity is poised for significant growth. Advances in AI and ML technologies and increasing data availability will lead to more sophisticated and effective threat detection systems. Machine learning will enhance our ability to detect known threats and anticipate and prepare for future challenges in the cybersecurity landscape.

AI in Threat Intelligence

In the realm of threat intelligence, AI plays a crucial role in the collection and analysis of data. The process involves gathering vast amounts of information from various sources, including network logs, threat databases, and online forums. With its advanced data processing capabilities, AI can sift through this sea of data to extract meaningful insights. It identifies patterns, correlations, and anomalies that might indicate potential threats or vulnerabilities. This level of analysis is beyond the scope of manual processing, making AI an invaluable asset in comprehending complex cybersecurity data landscapes.

AI technologies enhance data analysis by enabling structured and unstructured data processing. Machine learning algorithms can learn from this data, improving their detection capabilities. Natural Language Processing (NLP), a subset of AI, is particularly useful in analyzing unstructured data like text in threat reports or online discussions. NLP can extract relevant information, identify trends, and even understand the sentiments in these texts, providing a deeper layer of intelligence for cybersecurity.

Real-Time Threat Intelligence

Real-time threat intelligence is another critical aspect of AI in cybersecurity. AI systems can monitor various data streams continuously, providing instant analysis and alerts. This real-time capability is essential for timely detection and response to cyber threats. For instance, if an emerging threat is detected elsewhere, AI can quickly analyze it and inform relevant stakeholders, allowing them to take preemptive measures.

The ability of AI to provide real-time intelligence is essential in the face of rapidly evolving cyber threats. AI models can adapt to new patterns and anomalies as they emerge, ensuring that the threat intelligence remains current and relevant. This adaptability is key in a landscape where attackers continually change their tactics to bypass security measures.

Integration with Existing Systems

Integrating AI into existing cybersecurity systems is a significant step in enhancing an organization's defense mechanisms. AI can complement and augment existing security tools, providing a more sophisticated layer of analysis and response. For instance, AI can be integrated with Security Information and Event Management (SIEM) systems to enhance their capability to analyze and interpret security data. This integration involves not just data sharing but also a seamless operational collaboration. AI can automate certain functions, like initial data analysis or alert prioritization, allowing human analysts to focus on more complex tasks. This synergy between AI and existing systems creates a more efficient and effective security infrastructure.

AI's role in threat intelligence is not limited to stand-alone functions. It facilitates a collaborative defense mechanism, sharing AI-driven insights across different tools and teams. This collaboration ensures a unified response to threats, enhancing the organization's overall security posture.

Integrating AI in threat intelligence also involves tailoring AI models to the specific needs and contexts of the organization. AI algorithms can be trained on data relevant to an organization's particular threats and vulnerabilities, ensuring more accurate and relevant intelligence.

A key advantage of AI in threat intelligence is its ability to learn and improve continuously. As AI systems are exposed to new data and scenarios, they become more adept at identifying and responding to threats. This continuous learning ensures that threat intelligence remains effective, adapting to the evolving cybersecurity landscape.

Looking forward, the role of AI in threat intelligence is set to become increasingly integral. As cyber threats grow more sophisticated and data sources become more diverse, the capabilities of AI to analyze, predict, and respond to threats will be essential. AI-driven threat intelligence will be a cornerstone in developing proactive and adaptive cybersecurity strategies to counter the ever-evolving challenges in the digital world.

Automated Response and Mitigation

Automated incident response is a critical component of modern cybersecurity strategies, where AI plays a pivotal role. When a security breach or threat is detected, time is of the essence. Automated response systems powered by AI can react in real time, often much faster than human teams. These systems can execute predefined actions, such as isolating affected systems, blocking malicious IP addresses, or shutting down compromised processes. This immediate response can significantly limit the damage caused by cyber-attacks and prevent further penetration into the network.

Enhancing Efficiency with Automation

AI-driven automation enhances the efficiency of incident response. Handling routine and straightforward tasks frees human security professionals to focus on more complex aspects of the response and recovery process. Moreover, AI can analyze the incident to identify the attack's nature and origin, aiding in a more informed and strategic response.

System hardening, securing a system by reducing its vulnerability surface, is another area where AI contributes significantly. AI algorithms can continuously monitor systems for vulnerabilities, such as unpatched software or insecure configurations, and recommend or implement fixes. This proactive approach to system hardening helps in preventing attacks before they occur.

AI systems can perform continuous vulnerability assessments, scanning for weaknesses across the network and prioritizing them based on potential impact. This ongoing assessment ensures that vulnerabilities are identified and addressed promptly, keeping the systems resilient against evolving threats.

Proactive vs. Reactive Approaches

The traditional approach to cybersecurity has often been reactive, dealing with threats as they occur. However, AI enables a more proactive stance. By analyzing patterns and predicting potential attack vectors, AI-driven systems can prepare defenses against likely threats before they materialize. This shift from reactive to proactive is crucial in staying ahead of sophisticated cybercriminals.

Predictive security measures, enabled by AI, involve anticipating and mitigating potential security incidents before they happen. This could include adjusting security protocols, strengthening firewalls, or educating users about imminent threats based on AI's predictive analysis. These proactive measures significantly reduce the risk of successful attacks.

Integrating AI-driven automated response and proactive strategies into broader cybersecurity policies is essential for creating a comprehensive defense mechanism. This integration ensures that all aspects of cybersecurity – from detection to response – are streamlined and effective.

AI's Role in Developing Cyber Resilience

Cyber resilience builds the capacity to anticipate, withstand, recover from, and adapt to adverse conditions, stresses, attacks, or compromises on systems. AI is central to this, providing the tools and intelligence necessary to build resilient systems and networks capable of coping with the challenges of the digital age.

AI allows for dynamic adjustment of security postures in response to changing threat landscapes. As new threats are identified and trends change, AI systems can recalibrate security measures accordingly. This dynamic adjustment is vital in maintaining an effective defense against a constantly evolving array of cyber threats.

Looking to the future, the role of AI in automated response and mitigation in cybersecurity is poised to grow. As AI technologies advance, they will provide even more sophisticated and nuanced solutions for cyber threats. The future of cybersecurity lies in leveraging AI not only as a tool for defense but also as a proactive agent in shaping more resilient and adaptive cybersecurity strategies.

AI in Network Security

In the network security landscape, AI-enabled real-time monitoring is critical. This advanced approach involves continuously surveilling network traffic, using AI algorithms to process and analyze data as it flows through the network. The capability of AI to handle vast volumes of data in real time is a game changer, allowing for the immediate detection of unusual or potentially harmful activities. This type of monitoring is vital for identifying threats when they occur, such as suspicious data transfers, unauthorized access attempts, or irregular traffic patterns that could indicate a breach or an attack in progress.

The importance of real-time monitoring extends to its ability to provide a comprehensive and instantaneous snapshot of network health. This immediate insight is crucial for maintaining the integrity and security of the network infrastructure. The AI systems employed in this task are designed to analyze traffic patterns, user behaviors, and network performance indicators, flagging anomalies that deviate from established norms. By doing so, they offer unparalleled vigilance, detecting potential security issues that could otherwise remain hidden.

Behavioral Analytics

Behavioral analytics represents a significant stride forward in network security, propelled by AI technologies. This method involves an in-depth analysis of the behavior patterns of users, devices, and the network itself. By understanding what constitutes normal operations within a network, AI systems can identify deviations that might signal a security threat. This could include unusual login times, strange data access patterns, or unexpected network traffic volume changes.

The strength of behavioral analytics lies in its ability to learn and adapt. AI systems are trained to recognize the typical behaviors within a specific network environment, making them adept at detecting anomalies that could indicate a security breach, such as a compromised account or insider threat. The sophistication of these systems allows them to differentiate between benign irregularities and genuine threats, reducing the rate of false positives and ensuring that security teams can focus on actual risks.

Threat Prediction

AI's capability in threat prediction is a transformative aspect of network security. AI algorithms can predict potential future threats and vulnerabilities by analyzing historical data, current network activities, and external threat intelligence. This forward-looking approach equips organizations with the foresight to address security risks before they materialize into serious incidents proactively.

The predictive power of AI in network security is rooted in its ability to discern patterns and trends from complex datasets. For instance, if an AI system identifies a rising trend in a specific network attack occurring globally, it can alert network administrators to bolster defenses against that threat vector. This predictive modeling goes beyond mere reaction to known threats; it involves anticipating and preparing for future challenges based on emerging trends and evolving attack methodologies.

The dynamic nature of AI-enabled network monitoring systems is a cornerstone of their effectiveness. These systems are not static; they continually learn and adapt based on new data, emerging threats, and evolving network behaviors. This continuous adaptation is crucial in the ever-changing landscape of cyber threats, where new vulnerabilities and attack strategies are constantly being developed. AI's ability to keep pace with these changes, learn from them, and anticipate future trends makes it an invaluable tool in the network security arsenal.

AI in network security, mainly through AI-enabled network monitoring, behavioral analytics, and threat prediction, represents a significant advancement in protecting digital infrastructures. By providing real-time insights, understanding complex behavior patterns, and predicting future threats, AI transforms how organizations approach and manage network security, offering a more dynamic, proactive, and effective defense against the myriad of cyber threats in the digital age.

Securing IoT and Edge Devices

Securing various connected devices presents unique challenges in the rapidly expanding Internet of Things (IoT). Artificial intelligence (AI) offers robust strategies to bolster IoT security, addressing vulnerabilities inherent in these interconnected systems. AI's role in IoT security revolves around its capability to analyze and process large volumes of data generated by IoT devices, identifying potential security threats in real time.

AI algorithms are particularly adept at detecting threats in the IoT environment, where traditional security measures often fall short. Given the diversity and volume of devices, each with its vulnerabilities, AI's ability to monitor and analyze data from multiple sources simultaneously is invaluable. AI systems can recognize patterns indicative of cyber attacks, such as network intrusions or unusual data transmissions, and can react quickly to mitigate potential risks.

Another significant aspect of AI in IoT security is its adaptability. IoT ecosystems are diverse and constantly evolving, frequently adding new devices. AI systems can learn from ongoing network activities and adapt security measures to the changing landscape. This includes updating threat detection models and adjusting security protocols to cater to new device types and configurations.

Edge Computing Considerations

Edge computing, where data processing occurs closer to the data source rather than in a centralized cloud-based system, introduces new dimensions to cybersecurity. In edge computing, AI is crucial in ensuring data is processed securely and efficiently at the network's edge.

In edge computing environments, AI enhances data processing capabilities. By leveraging AI at the edge, data can be analyzed and acted upon almost instantaneously, reducing latency and reliance on cloud-based systems. This is particularly important for IoT devices that require real-time data processing, such as those used in autonomous vehicles or industrial automation.

The decentralized nature of edge computing poses unique security challenges. AI algorithms deployed at the edge must be capable of operating independently, making real-time security decisions without always relying on central servers. This includes detecting and responding to local threats and anomalies and ensuring data integrity and confidentiality in a less controlled environment.

AI in edge computing also involves balancing efficiency and security. While edge computing aims to process data quickly and reduce latency, these benefits should not compromise security. AI algorithms must be optimized to function efficiently in edge environments, using limited resources without sacrificing their ability to effectively detect and respond to security threats.

Continuous Learning and Adaptation

AI systems in edge computing environments must continuously learn and adapt to new threats and changing network conditions. This is especially important in IoT contexts, where devices may operate in dynamic environments. AI models deployed at the edge must be regularly updated and trained to maintain their effectiveness in securing the network.

Scalability and flexibility are critical considerations in AI-driven edge security. As IoT networks expand, AI systems must scale accordingly, ensuring consistent security across many devices and data points. This requires AI models that are flexible enough to adapt to various types of devices and network configurations, providing robust security in diverse IoT and edge computing environments.

Securing IoT and edge devices requires a multifaceted approach, where AI's advanced capabilities play a central role. AI strategies for IoT security focus on advanced threat detection, adaptability to diverse ecosystems, and continuous learning. In edge computing, AI enhances data processing while addressing the unique security challenges of decentralized environments. The balance between efficiency, security, scalability, and flexibility is crucial in developing robust AI solutions for IoT and edge computing security.

Adaptive Security Architectures

Adaptive security architectures are increasingly crucial in the rapidly evolving landscape of cybersecurity. These architectures are designed to be flexible and responsive to changing threats, offering dynamic network defenses that can adjust in real time to emerging challenges. Unlike traditional, static security measures, adaptive architectures leverage AI and other advanced technologies to create a more fluid and responsive defense system.

A key feature of dynamic network defenses is their ability to adapt in real time. These systems can analyze network traffic and user behavior using AI-driven analytics, immediately identifying and responding to unusual or malicious activities. This real-time adaptation is crucial in countering sophisticated cyber attacks that evolve quickly and can bypass conventional security measures.

Dynamic defenses often include automated adjustments to security protocols and responses. For instance, if an AI system detects an anomaly that suggests a potential breach, it can automatically reconfigure network firewalls or isolate affected network segments to contain the threat. This level of automation enhances the speed and efficiency of the response to cyber incidents.

Self-Learning Systems

A cornerstone of adaptive security architectures is the inclusion of self-learning systems. These systems use machine learning algorithms to continuously learn from new data, improving their ability to detect and respond to threats over time. This continuous learning process is vital for keeping up with the ever-changing tactics used by cyber attackers.

Self-learning systems evolve by analyzing the latest cyber threats and attack patterns. As they are exposed to new types of attacks and security incidents, they adjust their detection algorithms accordingly, becoming more adept at identifying similar threats in the future. This ability to evolve with emerging threats ensures that the security architecture remains effective.

Another advantage of self-learning systems is their ability to reduce false positives. By constantly refining their understanding of what constitutes normal and abnormal behavior within a network, these systems become more accurate in identifying true threats, thereby reducing the number of false alarms that can drain security resources.

Continuous Improvement

The concept of continuous improvement is integral to adaptive security architectures. This approach ensures that security systems are not static but are continually enhanced based on new information, technological advancements, and evolving cybersecurity landscapes.

Adaptive security architectures embrace an iterative approach to security enhancements. Regular assessments and updates ensure that security measures are effective and relevant. This includes updating threat intelligence databases, refining AI algorithms, and integrating new security technologies as they become available.

Continuous improvement also involves learning from past security incidents. By analyzing breaches and attempted attacks, adaptive systems can identify potential weaknesses in the network and implement measures to strengthen these areas. This learning process is crucial for building a more resilient security posture. Ultimately, the goal of continuous improvement in adaptive security architectures is to stay ahead of cyber threats. By continuously evolving and refining their capabilities, these systems can anticipate and counteract sophisticated cyber attacks, offering a proactive rather than reactive approach to cybersecurity.

Adaptive security architectures represent a significant advancement in cybersecurity, offering dynamic network defenses, self-learning systems, and a commitment to continuous improvement. By leveraging AI and machine learning, these architectures provide a responsive and evolving defense mechanism capable of adapting to cyber threats' complex and ever-changing landscape.

Machine Learning in Identity and Access Management

Identity and Access Management (IAM) is a critical aspect of cybersecurity, involving the administration of user identities and controlling access to resources within a system. Integrating machine learning (ML) into IAM revolutionizes how organizations manage and secure user access, addressing traditional challenges and emerging threats.

Key Concepts

The fundamental concepts of IAM revolve around ensuring that the right individuals have access to the appropriate resources in an organization. This includes processes and technologies for user authentication, authorization, and the auditing of user activities. IAM systems are designed to manage digital identities, streamline access rights, and monitor user activities to ensure compliance with security policies.

Authentication and authorization are core components of IAM. Authentication verifies a user's identity, often through credentials like passwords, biometric data, or tokens. Authorization, conversely, determines what resources a user can access and what actions they can perform within the system. A robust IAM system effectively manages both these aspects to maintain a secure and efficient access environment.

Traditional IAM methods primarily rely on predefined rules and policies for granting access. These methods include password-based authentication, role-based access control (RBAC), and access reviews. While effective to an extent, they often lack the flexibility and scalability required to address the complex security demands of modern digital environments.

One of the mainstays of traditional IAM is RBAC, where resource access is based on a user's role within the organization. Users are granted permissions according to their role, simplifying access rights management. However, managing access based on roles alone can become challenging as organizations grow and roles become more dynamic.

Challenges in IAM

The evolving digital landscape presents several challenges to traditional IAM approaches. One of the primary challenges is managing a growing number of user identities, especially with the rise of remote work and the increasing use of cloud services. This expansion creates a larger attack surface and more potential vulnerabilities.

Another significant challenge is the dynamic nature of access requirements. In today's fast-paced business environment, users' access needs can change rapidly, making it difficult for traditional IAM systems to keep up. There's also the challenge of balancing security with user convenience. Strict security measures often lead to cumbersome access processes, reducing efficiency and user satisfaction. Furthermore, the threat of sophisticated cyber attacks, such as phishing and credential stuffing, has exposed weaknesses in traditional IAM methods. These methods often struggle to effectively detect and respond to such advanced threats, leading to potential security breaches.

While traditional IAM methods provide a foundational framework for managing access, they face limitations in addressing modern cybersecurity challenges' complex and dynamic nature. Integrating machine learning into IAM is emerging as a solution to these challenges, offering more adaptive, efficient, and secure management of identities and access rights.

Behavioral Biometrics and AI

Behavioral biometrics is an advanced user verification method beyond traditional physical biometrics like fingerprints or facial recognition. This technique involves analyzing patterns in human activities – such as keystroke dynamics, mouse movements, and gait analysis – to authenticate individuals. Unlike static biometrics, which can be replicated or stolen, behavioral biometrics are dynamic and unique to each individual, offering a more secure and unobtrusive authentication method.

One of the critical advantages of behavioral biometrics is its ability to provide dynamic and continuous authentication. This means that verification occurs at the login point and continuously throughout a user's interaction with a system. For instance, how users type, use a mouse, or interact with a touchscreen can continuously verify their identity, ensuring that the system remains secure even if the initial login credentials are compromised.

Behavioral biometrics rely on individual behavior patterns being unique and challenging to mimic. This uniqueness provides a highly secure form of authentication, as the behavioral traits used are not easily replicated or stolen like traditional passwords or physical biometrics.

AI in User Authentication

Integrating AI into user authentication, particularly in analyzing behavioral biometrics, marks a significant enhancement in security technologies. AI algorithms are adept at processing complex and nuanced behavioral patterns, making them ideal for interpreting the subtle characteristics used in behavioral biometrics.

AI excels in recognizing complex patterns in large datasets, a crucial capability for interpreting behavioral biometrics. By analyzing detailed user interaction data, AI algorithms can accurately identify individuals based on their behavior patterns. This level of analysis goes beyond what is possible with traditional methods, offering a more sophisticated and secure form of user authentication.

AI systems in behavioral biometrics are not static; they learn and adapt over time. As a user's behavior might change slightly – due to mood, physical conditions, or even the device being used – AI algorithms can adjust to these changes, ensuring that the authentication remains accurate and reliable.

Privacy, Security, and Ethical Considerations

While behavioral biometrics and AI offer significant advantages in terms of security, they also raise important considerations regarding privacy and data security.

The use of behavioral biometrics involves the collection and analysis of personal behavior data, which can be highly sensitive. It is crucial to ensure this data is protected and securely stored, with strict controls on who can access it. Privacy regulations, such as the GDPR in the European Union, impose strict guidelines on how personal data can be used and safeguarded.

A delicate balance must be maintained between enhancing security and protecting individual privacy. Organizations must ensure that using behavioral biometrics and AI in authentication respects user privacy and complies with legal and ethical standards. This includes being transparent about data collection methods and giving users control over their data.

The use of AI in analyzing personal data also brings ethical considerations. There must be clear guidelines and principles governing how AI is used to prevent bias in AI algorithms and ensure that AI systems' decisions are fair and transparent.

In conclusion, integrating behavioral biometrics and AI into user authentication presents a promising frontier in cybersecurity. It offers enhanced security by leveraging human behavior's unique and dynamic nature. However, addressing privacy and security concerns adequately is imperative, ensuring that these advanced technologies are used responsibly and ethically.

Anomaly Detection in User Behavior

In cybersecurity, monitoring user activities is crucial to identifying and mitigating potential threats. Anomaly detection in user behavior involves continuously observing and analyzing user actions within a network or system to identify patterns or activities that deviate from the norm. This monitoring form is integral to identifying security breaches or malicious organizational activities.

The process involves a comprehensive analysis of user activities, including login times, file access patterns, network usage, and application activities. By establishing a baseline of normal behavior for each user, the system can more effectively detect anomalies that may indicate a security concern. This kind of surveillance is often automated and powered by AI and machine learning algorithms, capable of processing vast amounts of data in real time.

Real-time monitoring and alerting are critical components of practical user behavior analysis. The system continuously scans for activities that diverge from established patterns, quickly alerting security teams to potential threats. This prompt notification enables immediate investigation and response, which is crucial in mitigating risks and preventing potential breaches.

Detecting Unusual Behaviors

Detecting unusual behaviors in user activities is a nuanced process that requires sophisticated analysis. Machine learning algorithms play a vital role in this, as they can discern between benign anomalies and actions indicative of malicious intent or compromised accounts.

AI and machine learning are adept at pattern recognition, which is essential for detecting unusual behaviors. These systems can identify deviations from standard behavior patterns by analyzing historical data and current user activities. Such deviations might include accessing files at odd hours, unusual login locations, or an atypical data transfer volume.

The strength of machine learning in anomaly detection lies in its adaptability. In dynamic work environments where user behavior can naturally vary, AI algorithms can adjust their baseline understanding of what constitutes normal behavior. This adaptability reduces false positives and ensures the system effectively identifies genuine threats.

Preventing Insider Threats

Anomaly detection is particularly effective in preventing insider threats, one of the more challenging aspects of cybersecurity. Insider threats can be difficult to detect because they often involve legitimate users misusing their access rights rather than external actors breaching the system.

By monitoring for unusual user behaviors, AI-driven systems can identify potential insider threats, intentional (malicious insiders) or unintentional (compromised accounts). For example, an employee accessing sensitive data irrelevant to their role or downloading large volumes of data can trigger alerts.

Continuous risk assessment is a proactive approach to preventing insider threats. Machine learning algorithms can continuously evaluate user behaviors and risk factors, assessing potential insider threats continuously. This allows organizations to address risks before they escalate into serious security incidents.

Anomaly detection in user behavior is a crucial component of modern cybersecurity strategies, particularly in mitigating the risk of insider threats. By leveraging advanced AI and machine learning algorithms for continuous monitoring and analysis of user activities, organizations can effectively detect unusual behaviors and take timely actions to protect their digital assets and data. This proactive approach is key to maintaining robust security in an increasingly complex and dynamic digital landscape.

Automated Access Controls

In the realm of Identity and Access Management (IAM), the implementation of automated access controls represents a significant technological leap. These systems, empowered by artificial intelligence (AI) and machine learning (ML), automate the decision-making process for granting or denying access to resources within an organization. By utilizing AI, these systems analyze user roles, behaviors, and access patterns to make informed and efficient access decisions, enhancing security and operational efficiency.

AI significantly streamlines access decision processes in automated systems. It rapidly assesses the user's role, previous access patterns, and current context to determine appropriate access rights. This not only bolsters security by ensuring that only authorized individuals gain access but also improves the overall efficiency of access management by minimizing the need for manual intervention.

Automated access controls are inherently dynamic, adapting to changes in user roles, behaviors, and perceived risks. For example, if a user's role within the organization changes, AI algorithms can automatically update their access privileges to align with their new role. Likewise, the system can restrict or modify access rights in real time if it detects any unusual or potentially risky user activity.

AI in System Hardening

AI's role in system hardening involves continuously identifying and addressing vulnerabilities within an organization's digital infrastructure. AI systems proactively scan for weaknesses by applying advanced algorithms, enabling organizations to fortify their defenses against potential cyber threats preemptively. This proactive stance is essential in a landscape where threats continually evolve and become more sophisticated.

AI-driven proactive vulnerability management entails the continuous monitoring and patching of system vulnerabilities. This process significantly reduces the risk of exploitation by cyber attackers, as AI systems can promptly detect and rectify security gaps before they are exploited. Automating this process ensures that vulnerabilities are consistently managed, maintaining a high level of system security.

Integrating AI in system hardening substantially enhances the resilience of IT systems. AI algorithms adapt to and learn from network activities and emerging threats, thereby continuously evolving the system's defenses. This learning and adaptation capability is crucial for maintaining robust security measures effective against an ever-changing array of cyber threats.

Proactive vs. Reactive Approaches

The advent of AI and ML in IAM signifies a shift from traditional reactive security measures to a more proactive approach. Rather than merely responding to security incidents as they occur, AI-driven systems are designed to anticipate potential threats and take preventative action. This paradigm shift is crucial for staying ahead of increasingly sophisticated cyber threats.

Predictive security measures enabled by AI involve using historical data and current trends to foresee and counteract potential security incidents. This approach allows organizations to implement preventative measures, such as updating security protocols or reconfiguring access rights, based on the predictive insights generated by AI algorithms. Organizations can significantly reduce the likelihood of successful cyber attacks by anticipating potential threats.

One of the critical strengths of AI and ML in automated access control is their capability for continuous improvement and adaptation. As these systems are exposed to new data and evolving security challenges, they refine their algorithms and strategies, enhancing their effectiveness over time. This constant evolution is vital for maintaining an effective defense against the dynamic nature of cyber threats, ensuring that security measures remain relevant and robust.

Future of AI and ML in Cybersecurity

The future of artificial intelligence (AI) and machine learning (ML) in cybersecurity is marked by rapid advancements and the emergence of new technologies. This evolution is driven by the need to counter increasingly sophisticated cyber threats and to adapt to the changing digital landscape.

Next-Gen AI Tools

Innovative AI tools are at the forefront of the future cybersecurity landscape. These next-generation tools are expected to be more autonomous and capable of making decisions and taking actions with minimal human intervention. With advancements in AI algorithms, these tools can predict and counteract cyber threats more efficiently, offering real-time defense mechanisms against various cyber attacks.

Enhanced Predictive Capabilities: Future AI tools in cybersecurity are anticipated to have enhanced predictive capabilities, utilizing vast amounts of data to forecast potential threats and vulnerabilities. This foresight will allow for preemptive action, strengthening defenses before attacks occur.

Autonomous Response Systems: AI tools are evolving to include autonomous response systems that instantly react to detected threats. These systems will be capable of isolating affected areas, deploying countermeasures, and even repairing damage without human intervention, significantly reducing response times and the impact of cyber attacks.

Advancements in ML

Machine learning is set to see significant advancements, particularly in its ability to learn and adapt to new threats more efficiently. Enhanced ML models will be able to analyze patterns in cyber threats and adapt their defense mechanisms accordingly.

Sophisticated Anomaly Detection: Advancements in ML will lead to more sophisticated anomaly detection systems capable of identifying subtle and complex threats that traditional security measures might miss. This includes detecting network traffic, user behavior, and system performance irregularities.

Continuous Learning and Adaptation: Future ML models in cybersecurity will continually learn from new data, improving their accuracy and efficiency over time. This continuous learning will ensure that cybersecurity systems stay updated with the latest threat intelligence, adapting to new attack methods and tactics.

Integration with Other Technologies

Integrating AI and ML with other emerging technologies is a key trend in the future of cybersecurity. This integration is expected to enhance the effectiveness and scope of cybersecurity measures.

Collaboration with IoT and Edge Computing: AI and ML will increasingly collaborate with IoT and edge computing technologies to provide comprehensive security solutions. This includes securing many IoT devices and managing data processing and security at the edge of networks.

Synergy with Blockchain and Quantum Computing: There will be a growing synergy between AI/ML and technologies like blockchain and quantum computing. Blockchain can offer decentralized and tamper-proof data management, enhancing cybersecurity, while quantum computing has the potential to significantly improve the speed and capability of AI and ML algorithms.

In conclusion, the future of AI and ML in cybersecurity is poised for transformative growth, marked by the development of next-gen tools, significant advancements in machine learning, and integration with other cutting-edge technologies. These developments are expected to revolutionize addressing cybersecurity challenges, offering more sophisticated, efficient, and adaptive solutions to safeguard digital assets and infrastructures.

Challenges and Opportunities Ahead in AI and ML for Cybersecurity

As AI and ML evolve in cybersecurity, one of the most significant challenges is balancing enhancing security and protecting privacy. This delicate equilibrium is pivotal in gaining public trust and ensuring compliance with various data protection regulations. The ethical use of data in AI and ML systems is crucial. These technologies often require access to vast amounts of personal or sensitive data to function effectively. Ensuring this data is used responsibly and ethically is critical to maintaining user trust and adhering to legal standards.

When implementing AI in cybersecurity, organizations must navigate complex privacy regulations, such as GDPR in Europe and various state-level laws in the United States. These regulations mandate strict guidelines on data handling, necessitating robust privacy protections in AI and ML systems. The development and implementation of privacy-preserving techniques in AI, such as federated learning and differential privacy, are gaining importance. These technologies allow AI to learn from data without compromising individual privacy, addressing the tension between the need for data-driven security and privacy concerns.

Handling Sophisticated Threats

AI and ML are potent tools in countering sophisticated cyber threats, but they also present new challenges as threat actors become more adept at using advanced technology. The cyber threat landscape continually evolves, with attackers employing more sophisticated methods, including AI-powered attacks. This raises the stakes for cybersecurity systems, which must constantly evolve to keep pace with these advanced threats.

Cybercriminals' potential use of AI for offensive purposes is a growing concern. As AI becomes more accessible, there is a risk of it being used to develop more effective malware, conduct social engineering attacks, or exploit vulnerabilities at an unprecedented scale. In response, cybersecurity systems must adopt more proactive defense strategies, leveraging AI and ML to detect, predict, and prevent attacks before they occur.

Skill Gaps and Training

The integration of AI and ML in cybersecurity also highlights the issue of skill gaps and the need for specialized training. The practical implementation of AI and ML in cybersecurity requires a workforce with specialized skills. There is a growing demand for professionals who are not only skilled in cybersecurity but also proficient in AI and ML technologies.

Addressing this skill gap requires a focus on education and training. Educational institutions and organizations must offer courses and training programs covering the intersection of AI, ML, and cybersecurity. The rapidly changing nature of both AI technology and the cybersecurity landscape necessitates a culture of continuous learning and adaptation among professionals. Staying abreast of the latest developments and acquiring new skills are essential for effectively harnessing AI and ML in the fight against cyber threats.

Ethical Considerations and Compliance in AI and ML for Cybersecurity

Integrating artificial intelligence (AI) and machine learning (ML) in cybersecurity raises significant ethical considerations. While beneficial in enhancing security measures, these technologies must be deployed in a manner that respects ethical principles and protects individual rights. As AI systems process and analyze vast amounts of data, it's imperative to establish stringent guidelines that prevent the unethical use of personal information, ensure the responsible handling of sensitive data, and avoid intrusive surveillance practices that could infringe on privacy.

Another critical aspect of AI ethics in cybersecurity is the challenge of eliminating biases in AI algorithms and ensuring fairness in their operations. Biases in AI can lead to unfair or discriminatory outcomes, such as targeting certain groups unfairly or failing to detect specific threats. To address this, it's crucial to implement continuous monitoring, rigorous testing, and regular adjustments of AI algorithms to ensure they operate fairly and without prejudice. This requires a diverse dataset for training AI systems and an inclusive approach in their design and development to reflect a broad range of perspectives and reduce inherent biases.

Maintaining transparency in AI systems' operations and ensuring accountability are fundamental ethical concerns. Especially in scenarios where AI systems autonomously respond to cybersecurity threats, there must be mechanisms to track and audit these decisions. Organizations should be able to explain and justify actions taken by AI systems, ensuring clear accountability, especially in cases where these decisions have significant consequences. This transparency is critical for ethical compliance and building trust among users and stakeholders regarding the use of AI in cybersecurity.

Regulatory Landscape

Organizations using AI in cybersecurity must carefully navigate the complex web of data protection and privacy laws. Regulations like the General Data Protection Regulation (GDPR) in the European Union and the California Consumer Privacy Act (CCPA) set stringent requirements for data handling, mainly concerning personal data. These laws impact the design, deployment, and operation of AI systems in cybersecurity, mandating that they protect against cyber threats and safeguard personal data rights and privacy.

As AI technology becomes more sophisticated, there is a growing necessity for regulatory frameworks specifically tailored to AI's unique capabilities and challenges in cybersecurity. Such regulations must address various issues, from ethical AI use and data handling to the deployment and control of autonomous AI systems. Developing these AI-specific regulations requires a nuanced understanding of AI technology, its potential impact, and the cybersecurity landscape.

Given the global nature of cyber threats and technology, international cooperation and standards are vital for effective AI governance in cybersecurity. Consistent international standards can help ensure that AI is used responsibly and ethically across borders, fostering a unified approach to AI governance. This global cooperation is essential for maintaining security standards and ensuring that AI-driven cybersecurity measures are ethically aligned and universally acceptable.

Balancing Innovation and Compliance

Striking a balance between encouraging innovation in AI for cybersecurity and ensuring compliance with ethical and regulatory standards is a crucial industry challenge. Regulations are essential for AI's ethical and responsible use in cybersecurity, but they must be designed to support and not hinder technological advancement. Overly restrictive regulations could impede the development of innovative AI-driven cybersecurity solutions crucial for countering modern cyber threats. It's essential to create an environment where innovation in AI can thrive while adhering to ethical principles and regulatory requirements.

Creating flexible and adaptive regulatory frameworks that can evolve with AI technology is crucial. As AI and ML continue to advance, the regulatory frameworks governing their use in cybersecurity must also adapt to remain relevant and practical. This requires a forward-thinking approach to regulation that anticipates future developments and provides the flexibility needed to accommodate technological evolution without compromising ethical standards or data protection.

A collaborative approach involving diverse stakeholders, including policymakers, technologists, cybersecurity experts, and ethicists, is necessary to achieve this balance. This collaborative effort can lead to developing regulations that effectively protect individual rights and societal values while fostering innovation in AI. It's about building a consensus on how AI should be used in cybersecurity, ensuring that it serves the greater good while promoting technological progress and maintaining public trust in these advanced systems.

Case Study: The Impact of Generative AI on Cybersecurity

A report by Deep Instinct, titled "Generative AI and Cybersecurity: Bright Future or Business Battleground?" conducted by Sapio Research, provided a critical analysis of the cybersecurity landscape influenced by generative AI. The report focused on the dual-edged impact of generative AI on cybersecurity by surveying over 650 senior security operations professionals in the United States, including CISOs and CIOs.

The study revealed a startling increase in cyber attacks, with 75% of security professionals reporting a rise in incidents over the past year. Significantly, 85% attributed this surge to malicious actors' misuse of generative AI. This highlights the emerging trend where sophisticated AI technologies, initially designed for beneficial purposes, are being leveraged to perpetrate cybercrimes, indicating a pressing need for updated defense strategies.

Despite the challenges, the report also noted the positive impacts of generative AI. About 70% of professionals observed enhanced employee productivity and collaboration due to generative AI, with 63% acknowledging improved employee morale. This paradoxical situation reflects the nuanced role of AI in cybersecurity, offering both advanced tools for defense and novel means for attackers.

The study underscored the evolving threat landscape, with ransomware identified as the primary concern for 62% of respondents, marking a significant increase from the previous year. This has led to a strategic shift in data security approaches, with nearly half of the organizations now considering paying ransoms as part of their response strategy.

The rising complexity and frequency of attacks, coupled with the integration of AI in cybersecurity, have increased stress levels among professionals, with 55% reporting heightened stress. Staffing and resource limitations were cited as the major contributors to this trend. This situation calls for a reassessment of industry practices and policies, focusing on equipping cybersecurity professionals with the tools and support necessary to counter AI-fueled cyber threats.

Career Corner

A career in artificial intelligence (AI) or machine learning (ML) is a rapidly evolving and highly dynamic field within the technology sector, focusing on developing systems that can learn, adapt, and perform tasks that typically require human intelligence. This field is at the forefront of innovation, offering many opportunities for those passionate about technology and problem-solving.

One of the fundamental roles in this domain is that of a Machine Learning Engineer. These professionals are responsible for designing and implementing ML models. They work with large datasets, apply algorithms, and use statistical methods to train models on patterns and predictions. Their work is pivotal in transforming theoretical data science models into applicable AI solutions.

Another critical position is that of a Data Scientist. While closely related to ML, data scientists have a broader focus. They analyze and interpret complex digital data to help organizations make informed decisions. Their role often encompasses aspects of computer science, statistics, and mathematics, and they are skilled in using various tools and algorithms to uncover insights from data.

AI Researchers represent a more exploratory and academic aspect of the field. They advance the underlying algorithms and technologies in AI and ML. Their work often contributes to new approaches to machine learning, a deeper understanding of neural networks, and breakthroughs in AI functionalities.

Roles like AI Application Developer or Industry-specific ML Specialist are highly relevant for those interested in applying AI and ML to specific industries. These professionals focus on applying AI and ML algorithms to solve real-world problems in healthcare, finance, automotive, or retail sectors. They tailor AI solutions to industry-specific needs, driving innovation and efficiency in various fields.

As AI and ML are highly technical and specialized, pursuing relevant advanced degrees and certifications can enhance expertise and career prospects. Degrees in computer science, mathematics, or statistics are often foundational. Certifications and courses in specific AI and ML technologies, offered by platforms like Coursera, Udacity, or edX, can provide focused knowledge and skills.

Professionals in AI and ML must possess strong technical skills, including programming proficiency in languages like Python or R, a deep understanding of algorithms and data structures, and the ability to work with large and complex datasets. Soft skills such as problem-solving, critical thinking, and effective communication are also crucial.

A career in AI or ML offers diverse and exciting opportunities. From building complex machine learning models and analyzing large datasets to researching new AI technologies and applying AI solutions in various industries, professionals in this field are critical drivers of technological innovation. Continuous learning and staying abreast of the latest advancements are essential in this rapidly advancing and highly competitive field.

Chapter Questions

1. What is the primary advantage of integrating AI in cybersecurity?

   A. Cost reduction

   B. Faster data processing and threat identification

   C. Simplifying user interfaces

   D. Eliminating the need for human analysts

2. What unique capability do ML algorithms offer in cybersecurity?

   A. Data encryption

   B. Rule-based decision-making

   C. Learning from new data to identify emerging threats

   D. Reducing the need for data storage

3. What characterizes the cyber threat landscape today?

   A. Static and predictable

   B. Decreasing in complexity

   C. Continuously evolving

   D. Focused on physical infrastructure

4. What is a significant challenge in using AI and ML for cybersecurity?

   A. The high cost of software

   B. Dependence on high-quality data

    C. Lack of available algorithms

    D. User interface design

5. How does AI aid in phishing detection?

    A. By providing antivirus solutions

    B. Analyzing email patterns and content

    C. Encrypting email data

    D. Manual screening of emails

6. Who proposed the Turing Test, and what is its purpose?

    A. John McCarthy, to define AI

    B. Alan Turing, to test if a machine can mimic human intelligence

    C. Claude Shannon, for encrypting data

    D. Marvin Minsky, to solve general problems

7. What was the first AI winter a result of?

    A. Technological advancements

    B. Reduced interest and investment in AI research

    C. Overabundance of data

    D. Ethical concerns

8. What is the role of "deep learning" in the current AI boom?

    A. Simplifying algorithms

    B. Data storage

    C. Advanced pattern recognition and prediction

    D. Rule-based decision-making

9. Which of these is a critical ethical concern in AI?

    A. Increased energy consumption

    B. Inherent biases in AI algorithms

    C. Slower processing speeds

    D. Oversaturation of AI applications

10. What does the term "explainable AI" refer to?

    A. AI that can explain its programming

    B. AI that is only used in experiments

    C. AI, whose decision-making process is understandable

    D. AI that can self-improve

11. What is one significant way AI impacts employment and society?

    A. Creating more job opportunities

    B. Leading to workforce disruptions due to automation

    C. Decreasing reliance on technology

    D. Simplifying job training

12. In cybersecurity, what do AI-driven systems automate?

    A. Data entry

    B. Response to identified threats

    C. Software development

    D. Human resource management

13. What does the use of ML in cybersecurity enhance?

   A. Website design

   B. Threat detection and response

   C. Employee productivity

   D. Marketing strategies

14. What types of models are central to generative AI?

   A. Linear regression models

   B. Generative Adversarial Networks (GANs) and Variational Autoencoders (VAEs)

   C. Statistical models

   D. Basic arithmetic models

15. Why is there a need for ethical guidelines in AI?

   A. To increase profitability

   B. To govern AI's influence on privacy, autonomy, and fairness

   C. To simplify AI technologies

   D. To reduce AI development

CHAPTER 16

Blockchain

Fundamentally, blockchain technology is a digital ledger system that records transactions across a network of computers, ensuring both security and transparency. It is revolutionary in its decentralized approach, differing significantly from traditional, centralized recordkeeping methods. The technology emerged initially as the backbone for cryptocurrencies but has since shown potential in various other sectors.

At its core, a blockchain is akin to a digital ledger but has distinct features that set it apart. It's a continuously growing list of records, referred to as blocks, linked and secured using cryptography. Each block in the chain contains a cryptographic hash of the previous block, a timestamp, and transaction data. This structure ensures that it is challenging to alter once a block is added to the chain, providing high security and trustworthiness.

One of the defining characteristics of blockchain technology is its emphasis on decentralization. Unlike centralized systems, where a single entity controls the data, blockchain distributes its data across a network of nodes (computers), eliminating any single point of failure. This decentralization ensures no central authority is required to approve transactions, leading to more democratic processes and resistance against attacks.

Transparency is another key feature of blockchains. In most blockchain networks, transactions are transparent to all participants, fostering unprecedented accountability. Every action on the ledger is visible, making it easy to review and audit, thus enhancing trust among users.

© Dr. Jason Edwards 2024, corrected publication 2024

Dr. J. Edwards, *Mastering Cybersecurity*, https://doi.org/10.1007/979-8-8688-0297-3_16

Immutability is also a cornerstone of blockchain technology. Once a transaction is recorded, it cannot be altered or deleted. This permanence is secured through cryptographic hashes, a type of digital fingerprint unique to each block. Any attempt to alter transaction data would change the hash, signaling a breach in the chain's integrity.

Blockchain technology is broadly categorized into public, private, and consortium blockchains. Public blockchains, like Bitcoin and Ethereum, are open networks where anyone can participate in the verification process. They offer high levels of transparency and security but often face challenges with scalability. On the other hand, private blockchains are controlled by single or multiple entities. Organizations typically use them for faster and more scalable operations, albeit at the cost of some decentralization. Consortium blockchains strike a balance between the two, are managed by multiple organizations, and are often used in business collaborations for shared control.

Evolution and History of Blockchain Technology

The history of blockchain technology is a fascinating journey that begins with its origins in cryptocurrency. Initially conceptualized and implemented as the technology underpinning Bitcoin, blockchain was introduced to the world in a 2008 whitepaper by an individual or group under the pseudonym Satoshi Nakamoto. The creation of Bitcoin marked the first practical solution to the double-spending problem for digital currencies using a peer-to-peer network. This innovation was not just the birth of Bitcoin but also the genesis of blockchain technology.

Since its inception with Bitcoin, blockchain technology has significantly expanded into various sectors beyond digital currencies. Industries such as finance, supply chain, healthcare, and even government operations have started to explore and adopt blockchain solutions for their unique advantages. For instance, in the financial sector, blockchain has been instrumental in developing decentralized finance (DeFi) platforms that operate without traditional financial intermediaries, offering more accessible and inclusive financial services. In supply chain management, blockchain's ability to provide transparent and immutable records has enhanced traceability and accountability, from the origin of raw materials to the final consumer products.

The expansion of blockchain into these sectors demonstrates its versatility and adaptability to a wide range of applications. It's not just a technology for creating cryptocurrencies but a foundational technology that can be used to create more efficient, transparent, and secure systems in almost any domain.

Looking to the future, the potential of blockchain technology continues to be immense, but it also faces several challenges. One of the main challenges is scalability, particularly for public blockchains like Bitcoin and Ethereum. These networks currently face limitations in transaction processing speed and capacity, which can lead to increased costs and slower transaction times. Another significant challenge is the regulatory environment. As blockchain technology intersects with more sectors, it attracts more regulatory scrutiny, which can vary significantly between countries and regions, creating a complex legal landscape for blockchain applications.

Moreover, the growing concerns around the environmental impact of blockchain technologies, especially those that rely on energy-intensive consensus mechanisms like Proof of Work (PoW), are driving the search for more sustainable alternatives. The industry is exploring new consensus mechanisms, such as Proof of Stake (PoS), that promise to reduce the environmental footprint of blockchain networks.

Fundamental Concepts of Blockchain Technology

Understanding the fundamental concepts of blockchain technology is essential to grasp its potential and how it operates. These concepts include the structure and function of blocks, nodes, and miners, the various consensus mechanisms such as Proof of Work (PoW) and Proof of Stake (PoS), and the innovative applications enabled through smart contracts and decentralized applications (DApps).

At the heart of blockchain technology are blocks, the basic units storing batches of transactions. These transactions are securely hashed and encoded into a Merkle tree. Each block is linked to the previous one through a cryptographic hash, creating an unbreakable and tamper-evident chain. The blockchain's integrity and up-to-date state are maintained by nodes, which are individual computers connected to the blockchain network. Each node has its copy of the entire blockchain and works to validate and relay transactions and blocks. Miners, often nodes with significant computational resources, play a vital role in many blockchain networks. In systems using a Proof of Work (PoW) consensus, miners solve complex mathematical problems to validate transactions and secure the network. The first miner to solve each problem adds a new block to the blockchain and is rewarded with cryptocurrency, incentivizing their participation and maintaining the network's integrity.

Consensus mechanisms are critical to the function of blockchain networks, ensuring all participants agree on the validity of transactions. Proof of Work (PoW), the original mechanism used by Bitcoin, requires miners to solve complex cryptographic puzzles to create new blocks and validate transactions. This process, while secure, is energy-intensive and can lead to scalability issues. Alternatively, Proof of Stake (PoS) presents a less energy-intensive option. In PoS systems, the creator of the next block is selected based on various factors, including random selection and the participant's stake in the network, such as the amount of cryptocurrency they hold. PoS encourages energy efficiency and faster transaction validation, addressing some of the limitations of PoW.

Smart contracts and decentralized applications (DApps) represent innovative applications of blockchain technology. Smart contracts are self-executing contracts with the terms of the agreement embedded directly into code. They operate autonomously on the blockchain, executing and enforcing contract terms without the need for intermediaries. This automation reduces the potential for error and fraud and increases efficiency. DApps extend this concept further, representing a new class of applications that run on a decentralized network, often leveraging intelligent contracts. DApps have a wide range of applications, from decentralized finance (DeFi) to gaming and social media, demonstrating the versatility and potential of blockchain technology beyond mere currency transactions.

Cryptocurrencies and Blockchain

The relationship between cryptocurrencies and blockchain is integral, with cryptocurrencies serving as one of the most prominent applications of blockchain technology. This chapter delves into an overview of cryptocurrencies, the pivotal role of Bitcoin in popularizing blockchain, the emergence of altcoins like Ethereum and Ripple, and the concepts of tokenomics and crypto-economics.

Cryptocurrencies represent digital or virtual currencies that use cryptography for security, making them nearly immune to counterfeiting. The defining feature of cryptocurrencies is their decentralized nature, typically using a blockchain for their underlying technology. This decentralization contrasts starkly with traditional fiat currencies, which governments regulate. The cryptocurrency landscape has grown exponentially, with thousands of cryptocurrencies in existence today, each with unique features and uses.

Bitcoin, the first and most well-known cryptocurrency, was created in 2009 by an individual or group known as Satoshi Nakamoto. More than just a new form of currency, Bitcoin introduced the world to blockchain technology. Its success demonstrated the viability of decentralized digital currencies and the potential of blockchain technology beyond financial applications. Bitcoin's decentralized ledger, trustless transactions, and the security of its protocol laid the foundation for the development of further blockchain applications.

Following Bitcoin's success, numerous other cryptocurrencies, commonly called altcoins, emerged. These altcoins, such as Ethereum, Ripple, Litecoin, and others, offer different features and technological improvements over Bitcoin. Ethereum, for instance, introduced the concept of smart contracts and decentralized applications, extending blockchain's utility beyond mere currency transactions. Ripple, on the other hand, focuses on fast and efficient cross-border payment solutions for financial institutions. The diversity and specialization of these altcoins have contributed significantly to the expansion and maturation of the cryptocurrency market.

Tokenomics and crypto-economics are fundamental concepts in understanding how cryptocurrencies function economically and socially. Tokenomics refers to the economic principles and incentives that govern a cryptocurrency's creation, distribution, and consumption. It includes factors like token supply, distribution methods, and how tokens are used within the ecosystem. Crypto-economics, a broader term, encompasses the study of economic interactions and incentives in decentralized environments. It combines cryptography, game theory, and economic theory elements to design and analyze protocols that govern the production, distribution, and consumption of goods and services in a decentralized digital economy. Understanding these concepts is crucial to grasp how cryptocurrencies operate and their potential impact on the global financial system.

Blockchain in Financial Transactions

Blockchain technology has significantly transformed the landscape of financial transactions. Its impact extends to various domains, including decentralized finance (DeFi), cross-border payments and remittances, and innovative fundraising methods like initial coin offerings (ICOs), security token offerings (STOs), and crowdfunding. Integrating blockchain in these areas has introduced new levels of efficiency, security, and accessibility.

Decentralized finance, or DeFi, is perhaps one of the most groundbreaking blockchain applications in finance. DeFi refers to a system where financial products are available on a public decentralized blockchain network, making them open to anyone rather than through intermediaries like banks or brokerages. This ecosystem encompasses various financial services, including lending, borrowing, trading, investment, and risk management, all operating without a central authority. DeFi platforms leverage intelligent contracts on blockchains like Ethereum, automating and securing financial transactions in a trustless environment. This innovation has opened financial services to a broader audience, offering inclusivity and opportunities for financial growth and stability.

Blockchain technology has also revolutionized cross-border payments and remittances, traditionally plagued by high costs, slow transaction speeds, and a lack of transparency. Utilizing blockchain allows these transactions to be conducted faster, more securely, and with reduced costs. Blockchain's decentralized nature eliminates the need for intermediaries typically involved in cross-border transactions, like correspondent banks, significantly reducing transaction fees and processing times. This has particularly benefited migrant workers sending remittances back to their home countries, where every saved penny on transaction fees can make a significant difference.

Initial coin offerings (ICOs), security token offerings (STOs), and crowdfunding are innovative ways blockchain is being used for fundraising. ICOs allow startups to raise capital by issuing digital tokens in exchange for cryptocurrencies like Bitcoin or Ethereum. Although ICOs have been criticized for lacking regulation and being high risk, they have been instrumental in funding many blockchain projects. STOs are a more regulated alternative, where tokenized digital securities are offered, typically representing an underlying investment asset. STOs combine elements of ICOs with traditional securities, providing more security to investors. Crowdfunding through blockchain platforms has also gained popularity, offering a decentralized way for projects to raise funds directly from a global audience. These blockchain-enabled fundraising methods have opened new avenues for startups and projects to access capital, democratizing investment.

Risks and Challenges in Cryptocurrencies and Blockchain

While cryptocurrencies and blockchain technology present numerous opportunities and innovations, they have risks and challenges. These include market volatility, the evolving regulatory landscape, and cryptocurrency security vulnerabilities. Understanding these risks is crucial for anyone engaging with this technology, whether as an investor, developer, or user.

One of the most prominent risks of cryptocurrencies is their extreme market volatility. Prices of digital currencies can experience rapid and significant fluctuations within very short periods. This volatility is attributed to several factors, including speculative trading, regulatory news, technological advancements, and changes in market sentiment. While this volatility can present opportunities for high returns, it also carries a high risk of loss. The unpredictable nature of the market can be challenging for individual investors and businesses looking to adopt cryptocurrencies as a mode of payment or investment.

Despite the inherent security features of blockchain technology, cryptocurrencies are not immune to security risks. These risks include hacking attacks on cryptocurrency exchanges, wallet vulnerabilities, and the potential for loss or theft of private keys. Smart contracts, while automated and efficient, are also prone to bugs and vulnerabilities, which can be exploited if not adequately audited and tested. Additionally, the decentralized and often anonymous nature of blockchain transactions can make it difficult to recover funds in the event of theft. These security concerns require continuous vigilance and advancements in cybersecurity measures within the blockchain ecosystem.

While cryptocurrencies and blockchain technology offer transformative potential for the financial world and beyond, they also come with significant risks and challenges. Market volatility, regulatory uncertainty, and security vulnerabilities are vital concerns that must be addressed. Developing robust solutions to these challenges and fostering a stable and secure environment are essential for the continued growth and adoption of these technologies.

Blockchain Security Fundamentals

Blockchain security is a critical aspect of the technology's design and implementation. Understanding blockchain security involves comprehending the role of cryptography, acknowledging network security considerations, and being aware of common vulnerabilities and attacks such as the 51% attack and Sybil attack. These elements are fundamental to ensuring the integrity and reliability of blockchain networks.

Blockchain security is integral to the trust and functionality of blockchain networks. It's about protecting transactions and data from unauthorized access and ensuring the network's continuous, uninterrupted operation. Blockchain's security model is based on cryptographic techniques, decentralized architecture, and consensus algorithms. This model ensures that once data is recorded on the blockchain, it becomes nearly impossible to alter without detection, thereby maintaining the integrity and history of the ledger.

Cryptography is at the heart of blockchain's security. It involves using mathematical algorithms to secure data and verify transactions. Each transaction on the blockchain is encrypted and linked to the previous transaction, creating a secure and tamper-proof chain of blocks. Cryptographic hashes, such as SHA-256 used in Bitcoin, ensure that each block is unique and any alteration to its data changes its hash value, signaling a potential compromise in the network. Additionally, public-key cryptography is used to create a secure digital identity for each user, enhancing transaction security and user privacy.

The decentralized nature of blockchain presents unique network security considerations. Since there is no central point of control, the network's security depends on the cooperation and participation of all its nodes. This decentralized consensus mechanism makes blockchains resilient to traditional cyber-attacks but introduces new challenges. Ensuring network security involves maintaining a large and diverse node population to prevent centralization, robustly encrypting data transmission, and implementing protocols to identify and isolate malicious actors quickly.

Despite its inherent security features, blockchain is not immune to attacks. Common vulnerabilities and attacks on blockchain networks include

- **51% Attack**: This occurs when a single entity or group gains control of more than 50% of a blockchain network's hashing power, allowing them to manipulate the network by double-spending coins and preventing the confirmation of new transactions.

- **Sybil Attack**: In a Sybil attack, an attacker subverts the network by creating many pseudonymous identities, using them to gain a disproportionately large influence over the network.

- **Other Vulnerabilities**: These include intelligent contract vulnerabilities, routing attacks, and phishing attacks, among others. These attacks can exploit blockchain design or implementation weaknesses, underscoring the need for continuous security enhancements and vigilant network monitoring.

The security of blockchain technology is multifaceted, relying on cryptographic principles, network architecture, and consensus algorithms to maintain the integrity and functionality of the network. While blockchain offers a robust security model, awareness and mitigation of potential vulnerabilities and attacks are essential for maintaining a secure and trustworthy blockchain ecosystem.

Security Measures and Best Practices in Blockchain

In the realm of blockchain, implementing robust security measures and adhering to best practices is paramount for maintaining the integrity and trustworthiness of the network. This involves securing nodes and network defenses, ensuring the safety of smart contracts through thorough auditing and secure development, and emphasizing user security, particularly in managing wallets and private keys.

The security of nodes, integral components of a blockchain network, is critical. These nodes store, process, and validate transactions, making their security a top priority. Node security encompasses several practices, including regular updates of blockchain software and the underlying operating system to protect against known vulnerabilities. Additionally, implementing firewalls and continuous monitoring of network traffic is essential for detecting and preventing unauthorized access and other malicious activities. Ensuring data integrity and quick recovery in case of failures or attacks also involves maintaining regular backups and redundant systems. Moreover, setting strict access controls and permissions for node operators helps prevent unauthorized access to the node's data and resources.

Smart contracts, self-executing contracts with terms directly written into code, require rigorous security measures. Before deployment, security experts should thoroughly audit intelligent contracts to identify and rectify vulnerabilities, logical errors, and potential exploits. Developers should follow secure coding practices, using established patterns and avoiding common pitfalls while keeping the code simple and transparent. Rigorous testing, including unit testing and deployments on test networks, is crucial for identifying issues before the intelligent contract goes live on the leading network.

User security is another vital aspect, especially in managing digital wallets and private keys. Users must ensure the secure storage of their private keys, ideally using hardware wallets or paper wallets, to avoid exposure to Internet-connected devices. Backup and recovery plans are also essential, enabling users to recover their assets in case of device failure or other unforeseen events. Educating users about phishing attacks and other common scams is crucial to safeguard them from threats. Ensuring the safety of private keys and wallets not only protects individual assets but also reinforces the overall security of the blockchain network.

Blockchain Applications Beyond Cryptocurrency: Supply Chain and Logistics

Blockchain technology, known primarily for its association with cryptocurrencies, has far-reaching applications beyond digital currencies. Its potential in transforming supply chain and logistics is particularly noteworthy. In this domain, blockchain offers solutions for provenance tracking and transparency and enables the innovative use of smart contracts in logistics.

In the supply chain and logistics sector, blockchain technology introduces efficiency and transparency previously unattainable with traditional systems. By leveraging a decentralized and immutable ledger, blockchain allows for real-time tracking of goods as they move through the supply chain. This enhances operational efficiency and significantly reduces the likelihood of errors and fraud. The ability to securely and transparently track the journey of a product from its origin to the consumer is revolutionizing the supply chain industry. It enables businesses to verify the authenticity of their products, manage inventory more effectively, and improve overall customer trust and satisfaction.

Provenance tracking is one of the most compelling uses of blockchain in supply chain management. It refers to the ability to trace the origin and journey of products with high accuracy and reliability. Blockchain's inherent characteristics, such as immutability and transparency, ensure that once data regarding a product's production, transportation, and storage is recorded, it cannot be altered retroactively. This provides unprecedented transparency in the supply chain, enabling consumers to verify the authenticity and ethical sourcing of products. For industries like food and pharmaceuticals, where safety and quality are paramount, blockchain's provenance tracking can significantly enhance consumer trust and compliance with safety standards.

Integrating intelligent contracts in logistics further demonstrates the versatility of blockchain technology. Smart contracts are self-executing contracts with the terms of the agreement directly written into code. In logistics, they can automate various processes, such as payments, compliance, and quality control. For example, a smart contract could automatically release payment to a supplier once a shipment reaches its destination and passes a quality check. This automation speeds up the process and reduces the likelihood of disputes, as the terms are predefined and executed automatically. Using smart contracts in logistics leads to more efficient, transparent, and reliable supply chains, benefiting all stakeholders involved.

Applying blockchain technology in supply chain and logistics exemplifies its potential beyond cryptocurrencies. By providing solutions for provenance tracking, enhancing transparency, and enabling smart contracts, blockchain is set to revolutionize this sector, offering benefits such as increased efficiency, reduced costs, and enhanced consumer trust.

Blockchain Applications Beyond Cryptocurrency

Blockchain technology is revolutionizing the supply chain and logistics sector by offering solutions beyond simple provenance tracking and transparency. Its impact on this sector represents a significant shift in how supply chains are managed and operated, bringing unprecedented efficiency and security.

In real-time data access and sharing, blockchain enables all parties in the supply chain to access up-to-date information. From the initial manufacturer to the distributors, retailers, and eventually the end consumers, every participant in the supply chain can trace the product journey in real time. This shared ledger approach ensures consistency in information across all parties, reducing the likelihood of disputes and enhancing collaborative efforts.

Implementing blockchain also leads to reduced costs and increased efficiency in supply chains. The technology automates many of the traditionally manual and time-consuming processes, such as verification of product origins and compliance checks. This automation speeds up the entire supply chain process, minimizes errors, and reduces operational costs. For instance, blockchain can simplify the documentation process in international trade, cutting through red tape and expediting customs clearances.

Moreover, blockchain introduces a new level of trust and integrity in supply chains. The immutable nature of blockchain records means that every transaction and movement of goods is recorded permanently, making it nearly impossible to tamper with the data. This aspect is particularly beneficial in sectors where authenticity and ethical sourcing are crucial, such as luxury goods or organic produce. Companies can demonstrate their commitment to ethical practices by providing transparent and verifiable records of their supply chains.

The use of smart contracts in logistics also embodies a significant innovation brought about by blockchain. These contracts can be programmed to automatically execute when certain conditions are met, such as the delivery of goods to a specific location, further streamlining processes like payments and quality assurance. This level of automation facilitates smoother operations and ensures compliance with predefined standards and agreements, leading to a more efficient and reliable supply chain.

The blockchain application in supply chain and logistics showcases its versatility and potential to transform industries beyond finance. By providing real-time data access, reducing costs, enhancing efficiency, and ensuring a higher degree of trust and integrity, blockchain is set to reshape the supply chain and logistics sector, offering tangible benefits to businesses and consumers alike.

Identity Management and Governance

Blockchain technology's influence extends into identity management and governance, introducing innovative concepts like self-sovereign identity models, transforming voting systems and public registries, and addressing critical issues such as data privacy and GDPR compliance. These applications showcase blockchain's capacity to enhance security, transparency, and efficiency in areas fundamentally important to societal function and individual rights.

In identity management, blockchain introduces the concept of self-sovereign identity. This model allows individuals to own and control their digital identities without relying on central authority. In a self-sovereign system, users can store their identity data on their devices and provide it efficiently and securely to those who need to validate it. This contrasts sharply with traditional identity systems, which often involve centralized databases and control by third-party entities. Blockchain's decentralized and secure nature makes it an ideal foundation for these self-sovereign identity systems, offering enhanced security against identity theft and fraud.

In governance, particularly voting systems, blockchain can play a transformative role. By leveraging blockchain technology, voting systems can become more secure, transparent, and tamper-proof. This application could potentially eliminate many of the traditional challenges associated with voting, such as fraud, coercion, and vote tampering. Blockchain-based voting systems allow for secure and anonymous votes, ensuring the integrity of the electoral process while maintaining voter privacy. Additionally, results can be tallied transparently, with each vote verifiably recorded on the blockchain, making the process more transparent and trustable.

Blockchain also finds significant application in public registries, such as land registries or business incorporation records. By recording these registries on a blockchain, governments and public organizations can ensure that the records are permanent, transparent, and tamper-proof. This application not only streamlines the management of public records but also significantly reduces the potential for fraud and errors, enhancing the efficiency and reliability of public services.

Regarding data privacy and compliance with regulations like the General Data Protection Regulation (GDPR), blockchain presents unique advantages and challenges. The immutable nature of blockchain can conflict with GDPR's deletable data requirement. However, innovative approaches in blockchain design, such as using off-chain data storage or privacy-focused cryptographic techniques, are being explored to reconcile blockchain with GDPR requirements. This compliance is crucial for blockchain applications involving personal data, ensuring that they adhere to the stringent data privacy and protection set forth by regulations.

Blockchain's applications in identity management and governance are vast and varied. From enabling self-sovereign identity models and securing voting systems to managing public registries and ensuring data privacy compliance, blockchain technology offers solutions that could significantly enhance how personal data is managed and how public services are delivered, paving the way for more secure, transparent, and efficient systems.

Healthcare and Legal Applications

Blockchain technology's applications in healthcare and legal sectors demonstrate its potential to revolutionize these critical areas of society. In healthcare, blockchain is being leveraged for patient data management, interoperability, and drug traceability. In the legal field, technology is finding innovative uses by integrating intelligent contracts into legal processes.

In healthcare, managing patient data poses significant challenges, particularly regarding security, privacy, and interoperability between different systems. Blockchain offers a solution by enabling secure, immutable storage of patient records. This ensures the confidentiality and integrity of the data and allows for seamless sharing among authorized healthcare providers, enhancing the quality of care. The decentralized nature of blockchain means that patient data can be accessed across different institutions and platforms, solving the long-standing issue of interoperability in healthcare IT systems. Patients can also have more control over their data, deciding who gets access to their medical information, thereby enhancing patient privacy and consent.

Drug traceability is another crucial application of blockchain in healthcare. Counterfeit drugs are a significant problem in the pharmaceutical industry, posing risks to patient safety and costing the industry billions annually. Blockchain can track pharmaceuticals' production, shipment, and delivery, ensuring the authenticity and quality of drugs from the manufacturer to the end consumer. This traceability can significantly reduce the incidence of counterfeit drugs entering the supply chain, ensuring patient safety and regulatory compliance.

In the legal sector, blockchain is transforming traditional processes through smart contracts. Smart contracts are self-executing contracts with the terms of the agreement written into code. In legal processes, they offer the potential for automating various aspects of contract execution and enforcement. For instance, smart contracts can automatically execute and enforce the terms of a contract when certain conditions are met without the need for intermediaries. This can significantly streamline legal transactions and reduce the potential for disputes. Furthermore, blockchain can provide a tamper-proof record of legal documents and transactions, enhancing the integrity of legal records.

Blockchain technology is set to impact both the healthcare and legal sectors profoundly. Its applications in patient data management, drug traceability, and smart contracts in legal processes showcase its potential to enhance security, efficiency, and transparency in these critical areas. As blockchain technology continues to evolve, it promises to bring more innovative solutions to these and other fields, further demonstrating its versatility and transformative power.

Technical Deep Dive: Blockchain Architecture

Delving into the technical aspects of blockchain architecture provides a deeper understanding of how this innovative technology functions at its core. This includes exploring the blockchain data structures, examining the anatomy of a block, understanding the chain structure and fork management, and comprehending the role of Merkle trees in ensuring data integrity.

At its foundation, a blockchain is a specific type of data structure. It consists of a series of linked and secured blocks using cryptography. Each block in a blockchain contains a collection of transactions that are recorded in a digital ledger. The blockchain data structure is designed to be tamper-evident and immutable, so once a transaction is recorded, it cannot be altered retroactively. This characteristic is crucial for maintaining trust and security in the network.

A block in a blockchain serves as a container for transactions. Each block has several key components: a block header, which includes metadata, and a list of transactions. The block header contains the block's cryptographic hash, the previous block's hash (linking it to the previous block in the chain), a timestamp, and other relevant information, such as the nonce used in the mining process. This structure ensures that every block is unique and securely linked to the chain, contributing to the overall security and integrity of the blockchain.

The chain structure in a blockchain creates the history of all transactions ever made. Each new block is added to the end of the chain, creating a chronological order of transactions. Forks can occur in the chain when two blocks are added to the chain nearly simultaneously, leading to a temporary divergence. In most cases, one of the branches becomes longer and is accepted as the truth, while the shorter branch is abandoned, a process known as fork resolution. Managing forks is essential for maintaining the consistency and integrity of the blockchain.

Merkle trees are vital in blockchain architecture, particularly in ensuring data integrity. A Merkle tree is a data structure used to summarize and verify large datasets' integrity efficiently. Each leaf node in a Merkle tree is a hash of transaction data, and each non-leaf node is a hash of its children's hashes. This structure allows for quick and secure content verification in a block, as changing a single transaction would require changes up the tree. Merkle trees are crucial in blockchain, providing a secure and efficient way to handle and verify large amounts of transaction data.

The technical aspects of blockchain architecture, from its unique data structures to the intricate design of individual blocks, the management of chain forks, and the use of Merkle trees for data integrity, all contribute to this technology's robust and secure nature. Understanding these technical details is essential for appreciating blockchain's full potential and functionality.

Consensus Mechanisms in Blockchain

The consensus mechanism is fundamental to blockchain technology, determining how transactions are verified and added to the blockchain. This critical component varies widely across blockchains and has significant implications for security, energy consumption, and scalability.

Proof of Work (PoW) and Proof of Stake (PoS) are the most well-known consensus mechanisms. PoW, the original mechanism Bitcoin uses, involves miners solving complex cryptographic puzzles to validate transactions and create new blocks. While highly secure, PoW is often criticized for its substantial energy consumption due to the intense computational work required for mining. On the other hand, PoS, which is used by cryptocurrencies like Ethereum 2.0, selects validators in proportion to their holdings in the cryptocurrency. It reduces energy consumption and improves scalability but introduces different security considerations, such as the potential for wealth concentration in the network.

Beyond PoW and PoS, there are several other consensus mechanisms, like Delegated Proof of Stake (DPoS), Proof of Authority (PoA), and Proof of Space (PoSpace). Each of these is designed to address specific limitations of PoW and PoS, offering variations in energy efficiency, transaction speed, and network scalability. These mechanisms cater to different network requirements and philosophies, indicating the diverse approaches to achieving consensus in blockchain networks.

The choice of consensus mechanism also differs significantly between private and public blockchains. Public blockchains like Bitcoin generally use PoW or PoS mechanisms, emphasizing decentralization and security. In contrast, private blockchains, used mainly by enterprises and organizations, often prefer mechanisms like PoA or DPoS. These mechanisms prioritize speed, efficiency, and control, fitting the requirements of a controlled-access environment. In private blockchains, since the participants are known and trusted to a degree, the network can afford to use less energy-intensive and faster consensus models.

Energy consumption and scalability are two of the most pressing issues in blockchain technology. PoW, in particular, has been criticized for its high energy usage, leading to a growing interest in more energy-efficient consensus mechanisms like PoS. Scalability, or the ability of the network to handle a large number of transactions, is another challenge, especially for public blockchains. The consensus mechanism is crucial in determining the network's scalability, with different mechanisms offering varying trade-offs between speed, security, and decentralization.

In conclusion, choosing a consensus mechanism is a critical decision in blockchain architecture, profoundly influencing the network's functionality, security, and efficiency. From the energy-intensive PoW to the more efficient PoS and other innovative models, each mechanism offers unique benefits and challenges, highlighting blockchain technology's diverse and evolving nature.

Advanced Topics in Blockchain Architecture

Exploring advanced topics in blockchain architecture provides insights into this technology's evolving nature and potential future directions. This includes understanding concepts like sidechains and Layer 2 solutions, interoperability between different blockchains, and the emerging trends shaping the future of blockchain architecture.

Sidechains and Layer 2 solutions represent significant advancements in addressing scalability and functionality issues in blockchain networks. Sidechains are separate blockchains connected to the main chain, allowing for asset transfer. They operate independently, with their consensus mechanisms and protocols, providing a way to offload transactions from the main chain, thereby reducing congestion and improving scalability.

Layer 2 solutions are another approach to enhancing blockchain scalability and efficiency. These solutions operate on top of the base blockchain layer (Layer 1) and include technologies like state channels, plasma chains, and rollups. They allow multiple transactions to be processed off the main chain, with only the final state recorded on Layer 1. This approach significantly increases transaction throughput and reduces transaction costs, making blockchain networks more practical for high-volume applications.

Interoperability is a critical challenge in the blockchain space, referring to the ability of different blockchain networks to communicate and interact seamlessly. As the blockchain ecosystem grows and diversifies, the need for interoperability becomes increasingly important. Solutions being explored include cross-chain protocols and bridges, which allow for transferring assets and information across different blockchain platforms. Achieving interoperability is crucial for creating a more integrated and efficient blockchain ecosystem where diverse networks can harmonize harmoniously.

Legal and Regulatory Aspects of Blockchain

Blockchain technology's legal and regulatory aspects are complex and evolving, encompassing a wide range of issues from the global regulatory landscape and compliance requirements to intellectual property considerations and the legal challenges in implementation. Additionally, the prospects of regulation in this field are crucial for its continued development and integration into mainstream applications.

The global regulatory landscape for blockchain and cryptocurrencies is diverse and continually evolving. Countries have varying approaches, some embracing the technology and others imposing strict regulations or outright bans. This varied landscape poses challenges for businesses operating in multiple jurisdictions, requiring them to navigate a patchwork of regulations. Compliance with existing laws, particularly in areas like Know Your Customer (KYC) and Anti-Money Laundering (AML), is critical for blockchain platforms, especially those dealing with cryptocurrencies. These regulations are designed to prevent illegal activities such as money laundering and terrorist financing, and complying with them is essential for the legitimacy and acceptance of blockchain technologies.

Intellectual property (IP) considerations in blockchain are emerging as essential, especially with the increasing development of unique blockchain solutions and applications. Issues revolve around patenting blockchain technologies, protecting developers' IP rights, and managing open source software in blockchain development. Navigating these IP issues is vital for fostering innovation while ensuring developers and companies can protect their inventions and investments.

The implementation of blockchain technology presents several legal challenges. The legality and enforceability of smart contracts, which are agreements in the form of computer code executed on the blockchain, raise questions about their recognition under existing contract law. Jurisdictional issues in decentralized systems are also a significant challenge, as blockchain networks often span multiple countries with different legal systems. Determining which jurisdiction's laws apply and how legal disputes can be resolved is complex in a decentralized environment. Additionally, consumer protection and liability in blockchain transactions need clarification, especially regarding errors or fraudulent activities on the blockchain.

Future Regulatory Prospects

Looking forward, blockchain's regulatory landscape will likely undergo significant changes. Potential changes in financial regulations could further integrate blockchain into the financial system or impose new requirements for blockchain-based financial products and services. Standardization efforts and industry guidelines are also emerging to create common standards and best practices for blockchain implementation. Such efforts could enhance interoperability, security, and compliance across blockchain systems. Governmental blockchain initiatives, where governments explore the use of blockchain in public services and administration, could also drive regulatory changes, promoting the adoption of blockchain technology while ensuring it aligns with public policy objectives.

The legal and regulatory aspects of blockchain are critical for its sustainable and responsible growth. Navigating the complex regulatory environment, addressing intellectual property issues, overcoming legal challenges in implementation, and adapting to future regulatory changes are all integral to successfully integrating blockchain technology into various sectors. As the technology continues to evolve, so will the legal and regulatory frameworks that govern it, shaping the future of blockchain applications and their societal impact.

Future of Blockchain and Emerging Trends

The future of blockchain technology is poised for exciting advancements, marked by innovations in consensus algorithms, integration with other cutting-edge technologies, and significant improvements in scalability and processing speed. These developments are not just technical enhancements; they represent a transformative shift in how blockchain will be utilized across various industries and sectors.

Blockchain technology is continually evolving, driven by a need to overcome current limitations and expand its applicability in various domains. This evolution is characterized by a focus on developing next-generation consensus algorithms, integrating blockchain with other technologies like AI and IoT, and enhancing the scalability and speed of blockchain networks.

The development of new consensus algorithms is a crucial area of advancement in blockchain technology. Current mechanisms like Proof of Work (PoW) and Proof of Stake (PoS) have limitations, such as high energy consumption in the case of PoW and potential security concerns in PoS. Next-generation consensus algorithms aim to address these issues by being more energy efficient, faster, and more scalable. These new algorithms are exploring ways to reduce blockchain operations' environmental impact and make blockchain networks more accessible and efficient for a broader range of applications.

Another significant trend is the integration of blockchain with artificial intelligence (AI) and the Internet of Things (IoT). By combining blockchain with AI, there is potential for enhanced data analysis, automated decision-making, and improved security and privacy in AI applications. In the realm of IoT, blockchain can provide a secure and unalterable ledger for the vast amounts of data generated by interconnected devices. This integration can lead to more secure, efficient, and transparent IoT networks where devices can communicate and transact in a trustless environment.

Scalability and speed are critical areas where blockchain technology is expected to improve substantially. As blockchain applications expand, the need for networks that can handle a large volume of transactions quickly and efficiently becomes increasingly important. Scalability enhancement will enable blockchain networks to support higher transaction volumes without compromising speed or security. This is particularly crucial for blockchain's adoption in mainstream financial services and other sectors where high transaction throughput is essential.

The future of blockchain technology is marked by significant advancements that aim to address current challenges and unlock new possibilities. From developing more efficient consensus algorithms and integrating with AI and IoT to enhancing scalability and speed, these trends indicate a rapidly maturing technology poised to impact various domains substantially. As these advancements unfold, they will pave the way for broader adoption and more innovative applications of blockchain technology.

Emerging Security Technologies

As blockchain technology evolves, emerging security technologies are increasingly important to address new challenges and threats. These advancements include developing quantum-resistant algorithms, implementing layered security models, and continuous innovations in cryptographic techniques. Each of these areas plays a crucial role in ensuring blockchain networks' ongoing security and reliability.

One of the most pressing concerns in blockchain security is the potential threat posed by quantum computing. Quantum computers, with their ability to solve complex mathematical problems much faster than traditional computers, could potentially break the cryptographic algorithms currently used in blockchain technology. The development of quantum-resistant algorithms is underway to counter this threat. These algorithms are designed to be secure against the capabilities of quantum computers, ensuring that blockchain networks remain secure even as quantum computing technology advances. Adopting quantum-resistant algorithms is essential for blockchain systems' long-term security and viability.

The concept of layered security models in blockchain refers to using multiple security measures at different levels of the network. Instead of relying on a single line of defense, layered security models employ various techniques and protocols to provide comprehensive protection against various threats. This approach can include network-level security measures, transaction-level security protocols, and user-level security practices. Blockchain networks can achieve greater resilience against attacks and system failures by implementing security at multiple layers.

Continuous innovation in cryptographic techniques is essential to stay ahead of evolving cyber threats. Blockchain technology relies heavily on cryptographic methods for securing transactions and maintaining the ledger's integrity. Innovations in this area include the development of more efficient and secure cryptographic algorithms, enhanced privacy-preserving techniques such as zero-knowledge proofs, and advanced critical management systems. These innovations improve the security of blockchain networks and enhance user privacy and trust.

The future of blockchain security is marked by rapid advancements in response to emerging threats and challenges. The development of quantum-resistant algorithms, the adoption of layered security models, and continuous innovations in cryptographic techniques are all critical in ensuring that blockchain technology remains secure and trustworthy. As these security technologies evolve, they will play a key role in enabling blockchain's safe and widespread adoption across various industries and applications.

Societal Impact

The societal impact of blockchain technology extends far beyond its technical and economic aspects, influencing governance, public services, ethical considerations, societal challenges, and contributing to social good and sustainability. These dimensions highlight the transformative potential of blockchain in reshaping various facets of society.

Blockchain's application in governance and public services is poised to introduce unprecedented transparency, efficiency, and trust. Governments worldwide are exploring blockchain for various uses, such as secure and transparent voting systems, immutable public registries, and efficient management of public resources. For example, blockchain can streamline processes in public administration, reducing bureaucracy and corruption by securely recording transactions and data, which are then accessible for public verification. This technology also offers innovative solutions for civic engagement and policymaking, potentially leading to more participatory and responsive governance models.

As blockchain technology becomes more integrated into societal infrastructures, it raises significant ethical and societal questions. Issues such as data privacy, the digital divide, and the centralization of power in blockchain ecosystems are of paramount concern. Ensuring that blockchain technologies are developed and implemented in an inclusive and equitable way is crucial. There is also a need for clear regulatory frameworks to address these ethical concerns and to ensure that blockchain applications do not exacerbate existing societal inequalities but rather contribute to fair and just outcomes.

Blockchain has the potential to contribute significantly to social good and sustainability. Its application in supply chain transparency can help enforce labor rights and environmental standards. Blockchain platforms can facilitate the tracking of ethically sourced materials or verify the authenticity of fair trade products. In sustainability, blockchain can be pivotal in managing renewable energy sources, carbon credits, and environmental monitoring. By providing transparent and immutable records, blockchain technology can foster greater accountability and encourage practices that benefit the environment and society.

The societal impact of blockchain technology is multifaceted, touching upon aspects of governance, ethical considerations, and contributions to social good and sustainability. As blockchain continues to evolve, its role in shaping societal structures and addressing global challenges becomes increasingly significant. The technology promises to foster a more transparent, equitable, and sustainable world, but this requires thoughtful implementation, inclusive policies, and a commitment to addressing the ethical and societal challenges it presents.

Predictions and Speculations

The future landscape of blockchain technology is rife with predictions and speculations about its potential impact on various industries, the broader economy, and its evolving role in the digital world. These projections range from transformative disruptions across numerous sectors to long-term economic implications and a reshaped digital ecosystem.

Blockchain technology is anticipated to cause significant disruptions across various industries. In the financial sector, blockchain could revolutionize traditional banking, lending, and payment systems, making them more decentralized, efficient, and secure. The healthcare industry might see groundbreaking changes in how patient data and medical records are stored and shared, enhancing privacy and interoperability. Supply chain management could be transformed with increased transparency and traceability, reducing fraud and improving efficiency. Additionally, sectors like real estate, education, and entertainment could undergo substantial changes with the introduction of blockchain, from streamlining transactions to altering how content is created and consumed.

The long-term economic impacts of blockchain technology could be profound. By enabling more direct and efficient transactions, blockchain has the potential to reduce costs and remove intermediaries, leading to a more streamlined economy. Its ability to create new business models and revenue streams, particularly in the digital economy, is another area where blockchain could have a significant economic impact. Moreover, technology could play a crucial role in creating more inclusive financial systems, offering access to financial services for unbanked or underbanked populations worldwide, thus contributing to global economic development.

Blockchain's role in the digital world is expected to evolve substantially. As the technology matures, it could become a foundational element for the next generation of digital services and platforms.

Blockchain's potential to enhance data security, ensure privacy, and create trust in digital transactions positions it as a cornerstone technology in the emerging digital landscape. Its integration with advancing technologies like AI, IoT, and 5G could further expand its capabilities and applications, leading to new digital interactions and services.

The predictions and speculations surrounding blockchain technology point toward a future where it plays a pivotal role in reshaping industries, impacting the economy, and evolving the digital world. While the full extent of these changes remains to be seen, it is clear that blockchain has the potential to drive significant transformation and innovation in the coming years.

Case Study: The ZCash 51% Attack Risk and Coinbase's Response

ZCash, a cryptocurrency operating on a Proof of Work (PoW) consensus mechanism, encountered a significant security threat. ViaBTC, a crypto mining pool, gained control of over half of ZCash's hash power, raising concerns about a potential 51% attack on the network.

A 51% attack in a blockchain network occurs when a single entity gains control of more than 50% of the network's hash power. This dominance enables the entity to manipulate the network, potentially reversing transactions and double-spending coins. This risk became evident for ZCash, which shares Bitcoin's PoW mechanism, when ViaBTC's mining pool crossed the 51% threshold.

Coinbase, a major cryptocurrency exchange, took proactive measures to safeguard its users in response to this looming threat. The exchange increased the confirmation threshold for ZCash transactions to 110 blocks, extending deposit times from 40 minutes to approximately 2.5 hours. Additionally, Coinbase imposed restrictions on ZCash trades, moving the market into limit-only mode to mitigate any potential volatility .

ViaBTC addressed the concerns by clarifying its position. The firm stated that although the hash rates in its pool exceeded 51% of the ZCash network's total, ViaBTC did not control this hash power. The power was attributed to individual pool participants. ViaBTC temporarily hosted the hash rates and remained committed to defending miners' rights to switch pools as desired. The company acknowledged the risks of a 51% attack but asserted it had neither the motivation nor the capability to launch such an attack.

This incident highlights the inherent vulnerabilities in PoW-based blockchain networks, especially those with concentrated mining power. It also underscores the importance of vigilance by exchanges and network participants to proactively monitor and respond to such risks.

The ZCash incident with ViaBTC is a cautionary tale about the potential dangers of hash power concentration in blockchain networks. It also demonstrates the critical role of exchanges like Coinbase in mitigating these risks through swift and decisive actions, thereby protecting the integrity of the blockchain and the interests of its users.

The ZCash situation with ViaBTC was a pivotal moment in the cryptocurrency world, shedding light on the vulnerabilities of blockchain networks to 51% attacks and the crucial role of exchanges in safeguarding the ecosystem. It underscores the need for continuous monitoring and readiness to implement protective measures against such threats.

Career Corner

A career in blockchain technology is an innovative and rapidly growing field within the tech industry, focused on developing and managing distributed ledger systems that offer security, transparency, and decentralization. This specialization is particularly significant in the digital transformation era, offering numerous opportunities for those interested in cryptography, distributed computing, and financial technology.

One of the primary roles in blockchain technology is that of a Blockchain Developer. These professionals are responsible for developing and implementing blockchain-based applications and solutions. Their tasks include designing blockchain protocols, developing smart contracts, and creating the architecture for decentralized applications (DApps). They play a critical role in transforming blockchain concepts into practical applications that can be used in various industries.

Another critical position is that of a Blockchain Architect. Individuals in this role focus on designing the overall structure of blockchain systems, considering aspects like network design, blockchain consensus mechanisms, and security protocols. Their work is crucial in ensuring that the blockchain solutions are scalable, secure, and aligned with the organization's business objectives.

For those interested in the financial applications of blockchain, a career as a Cryptocurrency Analyst or a Blockchain Financial Analyst is highly relevant. These professionals analyze cryptocurrency markets and blockchain financial systems, providing insights and strategies for investment and financial applications. Their expertise is essential in navigating digital currencies' complex and rapidly evolving world.

The role of a Blockchain Project Manager is also increasingly significant. These individuals oversee blockchain projects, coordinating between developers, stakeholders, and users. They ensure that projects meet specified requirements and are completed on time and within budget. Their ability to understand both technical and business aspects of blockchain projects is critical for successful implementation.

Given blockchain's technical and specialized nature, pursuing relevant certifications and continuous learning is vital. Certifications such as the Certified Blockchain Developer offered by various organizations can provide foundational and advanced knowledge in blockchain technology. Additionally, courses and certifications in programming languages, cryptography, and distributed systems are beneficial for those seeking a career in this field.

Blockchain technology professionals must have strong programming skills, a solid understanding of cryptographic principles, and familiarity with distributed computing concepts. They should also possess excellent problem-solving abilities and the capacity to think innovatively to leverage blockchain technology in various applications.

A career in blockchain technology offers a wide range of exciting opportunities. From developing blockchain applications and designing blockchain systems to analyzing financial trends in cryptocurrencies and managing blockchain projects, professionals in this field are at the forefront of advancing a technology that has the potential to revolutionize multiple industries. Keeping up to date with the latest developments and trends in blockchain technology is crucial in this dynamic and burgeoning field.

Chapter Questions

1. What is the fundamental purpose of blockchain technology?

   A. To provide online banking services

   B. To record transactions across a network of computers

   C. To facilitate international travel

   D. To improve social media platforms

2. What unique feature does a block in a blockchain contain?

   A. User's personal information

   B. A cryptographic hash of the previous block

   C. The IP addresses of the network nodes

   D. A digital signature of the blockchain creator

3. What key characteristic distinguishes blockchain from traditional recordkeeping?

   A. Centralization

   B. Decentralization

   C. Limited transparency

   D. Single point of failure

4. Why is transparency important in blockchain networks?

   A. To increase computational power

   B. To ensure the privacy of transactions

   C. To facilitate accountability and trust

   D. To reduce the size of the blockchain

5. What is the consequence of modifying transaction data in a blockchain?

   A. Increased efficiency

   B. Change in the hash, signaling data breach

   C. Faster transaction times

   D. Reduction in data storage requirements

6. Which type of blockchain is typically used within organizations for private transactions?

   A. Public

   B. Private

   C. Consortium

   D. Hybrid

7. Who introduced blockchain technology to the world in 2008?

   A. Elon Musk

   B. A group known as Satoshi Nakamoto

   C. The United Nations

   D. IBM Corporation

8. What sector first utilized blockchain technology?

   A. Healthcare

   B. Cryptocurrency

   C. Agriculture

   D. Online retail

9. What is a significant challenge facing public blockchains like Bitcoin and Ethereum?

   A. Scalability

   B. Lack of transparency

   C. Overcentralization

   D. Excessive security measures

10. What does the term "tokenomics" refer to in the context of cryptocurrencies?

    A. The artistic design of digital tokens

    B. The economic principles governing a cryptocurrency

    C. The legal framework for digital tokens

    D. The technological infrastructure of cryptocurrencies

11. What type of blockchain consensus mechanism is less energy intensive?

    A. Proof of Work

    B. Proof of Stake

    C. Proof of Authority

    D. Proof of Identity

12. What technology do intelligent contracts on blockchain utilize?

    A. Artificial intelligence

    B. Quantum computing

    C. Virtual reality

    D. Self-executing code

13. What is a significant benefit of using blockchain in supply chain management?

    A. Reducing the need for physical storage

    B. Enhanced tracking and transparency

    C. Automating employee payroll

    D. Eliminating the need for transportation

14. How does blockchain technology potentially transform voting systems?

    A. By making them more entertaining

    B. By making them less accessible

    C. By increasing security and transparency

    D. By reducing voter participation

15. What is a critical issue to address when implementing blockchain technology?

   A. Choosing the suitable color scheme

   B. Ensuring scalability and energy efficiency

   C. Focusing solely on financial applications

   D. Avoiding the use of cryptography

CHAPTER 17

Risk and Compliance in Cybersecurity

In the dynamic and ever-evolving landscape of digital technology, the importance of risk management in cybersecurity cannot be overstated. It acts as the bedrock for safeguarding information systems and assets from the threats looming in the cyber world. Risk management, in the context of cybersecurity, involves identifying, assessing, and prioritizing risks to ensure that an organization's information assets are protected with adequate security. The key to effective risk management lies in understanding the technical aspects of cybersecurity and recognizing how cyber risks can impact an organization's broader objectives and strategies.

Defining cybersecurity risk is a nuanced process that involves considering the probability of cyber incidents occurring and their impact on the organization. This definition extends beyond technical vulnerabilities; it encompasses the potential for financial loss, reputational damage, legal liabilities, and operational disruptions. Cybersecurity risks are unique in their ability to evolve rapidly as threat actors continually adapt their tactics, techniques, and procedures. This fluid nature of cyber risks demands a dynamic approach to risk management that is flexible and responsive to the changing threat landscape.

The role of cybersecurity risk management in organizational strategy is pivotal. It goes beyond protecting IT assets; it is about ensuring business continuity, protecting intellectual property, maintaining customer trust,

© Dr. Jason Edwards 2024, corrected publication 2024
Dr. J. Edwards, *Mastering Cybersecurity*, https://doi.org/10.1007/979-8-8688-0297-3_17

and compliance with regulatory requirements. Effective risk management strategies are aligned with the organization's overall goals and objectives, providing a secure foundation that enables the organization to pursue innovation and growth without undue exposure to cyber threats.

Integrating risk management into the broader spectrum of cybersecurity efforts is crucial for building a resilient cybersecurity posture. This integration involves embedding risk management principles into every aspect of cybersecurity practices, from policy formulation and implementation to incident response and recovery. By doing so, organizations create a comprehensive approach that addresses the technical aspects of security and aligns with organizational risk tolerance and strategy. This holistic approach ensures that cybersecurity initiatives are not siloed but integral to the organization's overall risk management framework.

The introduction to cybersecurity risk and compliance sets the stage for a deeper exploration into how organizations can effectively manage these challenges in a world where cyber threats are ever-present. The subsequent sections delve into the principles of risk management, compliance with cybersecurity standards, developing a compliance framework, risk mitigation strategies, and the critical role of auditing and reporting in cybersecurity. Each section provides insights and practical guidance on navigating cybersecurity risk and compliance's complex and critical domain.

Basics of Compliance in Cybersecurity

The basics of compliance in cybersecurity form an essential component of an organization's overall security strategy. Compliance refers to the adherence to established guidelines, standards, and laws that govern cybersecurity practices. These guidelines are often set by industry groups, regulatory bodies, or governments and are designed to protect sensitive data, ensure privacy, and maintain the integrity and availability of information systems. Understanding and implementing these compliance requirements is critical for organizations to protect themselves from cyber threats and avoid legal and financial penalties associated with non-compliance.

Several factors drive the need for compliance in the cybersecurity realm. Firstly, the increasing frequency and sophistication of cyber-attacks necessitate robust security measures, and compliance frameworks offer a structured approach to achieving this. Secondly, in an era where data breaches can have far-reaching consequences, compliance helps safeguard sensitive information, thus maintaining customer trust and business reputation. Additionally, for many organizations, compliance is not optional; it is a legal requirement, particularly in industries like healthcare, finance, and ecommerce, where the handling of sensitive data is subject to stringent regulations.

Several key compliance frameworks and standards are pivotal in shaping cybersecurity practices. These include the General Data Protection Regulation (GDPR) in the European Union, which sets guidelines for data protection and privacy; the Payment Card Industry Data Security Standard (PCI DSS), which outlines security standards for organizations that handle credit card transactions; and the Health Insurance Portability and Accountability Act (HIPAA) in the United States, which provides data privacy and security provisions for safeguarding medical information. Other vital standards include ISO 27001, which provides specifications for an information security management system (ISMS), and the National Institute of Standards and Technology (NIST) frameworks, which offer comprehensive guidelines for improving cybersecurity.

The relationship between compliance and security is intricate. While compliance involves adhering to specific regulations and standards, security is a broader concept focused on protecting information assets from threats and vulnerabilities. Compliance can be seen as a subset of security; it provides a baseline of required practices and controls. However, simply being compliant does not guarantee security. While compliance sets the minimum standards, organizations must recognize that adequate security often requires going beyond these standards to address their unique risks and challenges. Compliance should be integrated into a broader security strategy that includes risk assessment, threat intelligence, incident response, and continuous monitoring to ensure a robust defense against cyber threats.

Understanding Risk Management in Cybersecurity

Risk management in cybersecurity is a fundamental process that involves identifying, analyzing, and prioritizing risks to ensure the security and integrity of information systems. This process is guided by principles that provide a structured approach to managing cybersecurity risks. The first principle is the continuous nature of risk management; it is not a one-time activity but an ongoing process that evolves as new threats emerge and organizational priorities change. Another critical principle is aligning risk management with business objectives, ensuring cybersecurity measures support the organization's goals.

Risk identification is the first step in the risk management process. It involves systematically identifying potential threats that could exploit vulnerabilities in the organization's information systems. This step requires understanding the organization's assets, including hardware, software, data, and people, as well as the various external and internal threats to these assets. Familiar sources of cyber risk include malware, phishing attacks, insider threats, and natural disasters. Risk identification should be comprehensive and regularly updated to reflect the changing cybersecurity landscape.

Risk assessment is conducted following identification to evaluate the potential impact and likelihood of identified risks. This assessment is crucial in understanding how each risk could affect the organization regarding operational disruption and financial loss. Risk assessment methodologies vary, ranging from qualitative approaches, such as expert judgment and scenario analysis, to quantitative methods, like statistical analysis and modeling. The goal is to understand the magnitude of each risk and how it could affect the organization's operations, reputation, and bottom line.

Risk prioritization is the process of ranking identified risks based on their assessed impact and likelihood. This step is critical in allocating resources effectively, allowing organizations to focus on managing the most significant risks. Prioritization considers factors such as the severity of potential outcomes, the effectiveness of existing controls, and the organization's risk appetite. High-priority risks pose the greatest threat to the organization's critical assets and objectives. By prioritizing risks, organizations can develop targeted strategies to mitigate, transfer, accept, or avoid risks in line with their overall risk management strategy.

Understanding these core aspects of risk management in cybersecurity is essential for organizations to build a robust defense against the evolving threats in the cyber landscape. It enables them to make informed decisions about where to invest resources, how to strengthen their security posture, and how to align their cybersecurity efforts with their strategic objectives.

The Risk Management Process

The risk management process in cybersecurity is a structured approach that guides organizations through the complexities of identifying, assessing, and mitigating cyber risks. This process is not static; it adapts to the changing cyber environment and the evolving objectives of the organization. At its core, the risk management process is about understanding the landscape of potential cyber threats and taking proactive steps to minimize their impact on the organization.

Planning and scoping form the foundational stage of the risk management process. This step involves defining the scope of the risk management efforts, setting clear objectives, and determining the resources and tools required. Effective planning ensures that the risk management process is aligned with the organization's overall business strategy and cybersecurity goals. This stage also includes identifying the stakeholders and determining their roles and responsibilities. Organizations can ensure a focused and efficient approach to managing cybersecurity risks by establishing a clear plan and scope.

Implementation strategies are the actionable steps taken to address the identified risks. These strategies vary based on the nature and severity of the risks and the organization's overall risk tolerance. Common implementation strategies include deploying technical security controls, such as firewalls and encryption, implementing policies and procedures, conducting training and awareness programs, and establishing incident response and recovery plans. The choice of implementation strategies should be guided by the outcomes of the risk assessment process, ensuring that the most critical risks are addressed effectively and efficiently.

Monitoring and review are critical components of the risk management process. This stage involves continuously tracking the effectiveness of implemented strategies, detecting changes in the risk environment, and assessing the organization's overall security posture. Regular monitoring helps identify new or evolving risks and determine whether the existing risk management strategies are effective or need adjustment. The review process also involves analyzing the lessons learned from security incidents and updating the risk management plan. This cycle of monitoring and reviewing ensures that the risk management process remains dynamic and responsive to the changing cybersecurity landscape.

The risk management process in cybersecurity is an ongoing cycle of planning, implementation, monitoring, and review. This structured approach enables organizations to proactively manage their cyber risks, adapt to new threats, and align their cybersecurity efforts with their strategic objectives. By continuously refining their risk management practices, organizations can build a resilient cybersecurity posture that protects their assets and supports their long-term success.

Risk Management Tools and Techniques

Various tools and techniques are employed in cybersecurity risk management to ensure a thorough and practical approach to identifying, assessing, and mitigating risks. These methods range from advanced software tools to strategic analytical approaches, each vital in comprehensively managing cyber risks.

The choice between quantitative and qualitative approaches in risk assessment is a critical decision in the risk management process. Quantitative methods involve using numerical data and statistical models to assess risk. These methods are practical in providing measurable and comparable risk data, which can be especially helpful in prioritizing risks and making informed decisions about resource allocation. However, quantitative methods often require substantial, reliable data and can be complex to implement. On the other hand, qualitative approaches rely on subjective analysis based on expertise and experience. These methods are typically more straightforward and are particularly useful when numerical data is limited. They involve categorizing risks based on severity and likelihood, using scales like "high," "medium," and "low." While less precise than quantitative methods, qualitative approaches offer valuable insights, especially in rapidly changing risk environments where data may not be readily available.

Risk management software tools are integral in facilitating the risk management process. These tools offer a range of functionalities, including risk identification, assessment, prioritization, and tracking. They can automate many aspects of risk management, such as aggregating data, tracking risk metrics, and generating reports. This automation enhances efficiency, accuracy, and consistency in risk management practices. Standard features of these tools include dashboards for real-time risk monitoring, compliance management modules, and incident response tracking. The selection of appropriate software tools depends on the organization's specific needs, the complexity of its IT environment, and the nature of the risks it faces.

Adhering to best practices in risk analysis is critical for the success of the risk management process. This includes maintaining an up-to-date inventory of assets and vulnerabilities, ensuring stakeholder involvement in risk management, and continuously updating risk assessments to reflect the changing cyber threat landscape. Effective communication and documentation are also essential, as they ensure that all stakeholders know the risks and the measures being taken to mitigate them. Additionally, organizations should strive to integrate risk management into their broader business processes and decision-making, ensuring that cybersecurity considerations are integral to the organization's operational strategy.

The tools and techniques for risk management in cybersecurity are diverse and must be carefully selected and applied to match each organization's unique needs and challenges. By combining quantitative and qualitative approaches, leveraging advanced software tools, and adhering to best practices, organizations can develop a robust risk management framework that effectively protects against cyber threats while supporting their overall business objectives.

Compliance with Cybersecurity Standards and Regulations

Compliance with cybersecurity standards and regulations is crucial to an organization's cybersecurity strategy. Implementing compliance measures involves more than just adhering to laws and regulations; it's about integrating these requirements into the organization's processes and culture. This integration ensures compliance is not an afterthought but a fundamental component of the organization's operations. Effective compliance measures include establishing policies and procedures that align with regulatory standards, training employees on compliance-related matters, and deploying technical controls to meet specific regulatory requirements.

Understanding compliance requirements is a complex task, given the variety of global standards and regulations. Organizations must first identify which regulations apply to their operations, which can vary based on factors such as the industry sector, type of data handled, and geographical location. For instance, companies handling the personal data of EU citizens must comply with the GDPR, while those in the healthcare sector in the United States must adhere to HIPAA regulations. Understanding these requirements is crucial for developing a compliance strategy that addresses all relevant legal and regulatory obligations.

Developing a compliance road map is an essential step in managing cybersecurity compliance efforts. This road map acts as a strategic plan that outlines the steps needed to achieve and maintain compliance. It includes setting clear goals, identifying the resources required, and establishing timelines for implementation. The road map should cover all compliance aspects, from technical measures and employee training to policy development and incident response planning. A well-structured compliance road map guides the organization toward compliance and helps monitor progress and make necessary adjustments.

However, implementing compliance is not without its challenges. One of the primary challenges is the ever-changing nature of cybersecurity threats and regulations. Keeping up with these changes requires constant vigilance and adaptability. Another challenge is the resource constraints, particularly for smaller organizations, which may lack the necessary expertise or financial resources to implement compliance measures fully. Additionally, there can be resistance to change within organizations, as compliance efforts may require significant modifications to existing processes and systems. Overcoming these challenges requires a committed approach from the organization's leadership, adequate resource allocation, and a culture that values and understands the importance of cybersecurity compliance.

Achieving compliance with cybersecurity standards and regulations is a multifaceted process that requires a deep understanding of the applicable requirements, a strategic road map for implementation, and the ability to navigate various challenges. By effectively managing these aspects, organizations can ensure that they comply with necessary regulations and strengthen their overall cybersecurity posture.

Key Cybersecurity Standards and Regulations

Essential cybersecurity standards and regulations are critical in shaping how organizations approach and manage their cybersecurity defenses. These standards provide structured frameworks and guidelines that help organizations protect their information assets and respond to cyber threats. They vary in scope and focus, addressing different aspects of cybersecurity, from data protection and privacy to information security management.

An overview of significant frameworks reveals the diversity and specificity of these standards. The General Data Protection Regulation (GDPR) is a prominent example, primarily focused on data protection and privacy for individuals within the European Union. It imposes strict rules on data handling and grants individuals significant rights over their data, impacting organizations worldwide that process EU citizens' data. Another critical framework is ISO 27001, a globally recognized standard that provides specifications for an information security management system (ISMS). ISO 27001 emphasizes a risk-based approach to securing information assets, requiring organizations to implement comprehensive information security controls tailored to their specific risk landscape.

Industry-specific regulations also play a pivotal role in defining cybersecurity compliance. For instance, the Payment Card Industry Data Security Standard (PCI DSS) applies to all entities that store, process, or transmit credit card information, dictating strict security measures to protect cardholder data. In the healthcare sector, the Health Insurance Portability and Accountability Act (HIPAA) in the United States sets standards for protecting sensitive patient data. These industry-specific regulations reflect different sectors' unique risks and requirements, necessitating tailored compliance strategies.

Navigating international compliance adds a layer of complexity. With the globalization of business operations, many organizations are subject to multiple, sometimes conflicting, cybersecurity regulations from different countries or regions. Compliance in this international context requires a thorough understanding of the various legal requirements across jurisdictions and reconciling them into a cohesive cybersecurity strategy. This challenge often necessitates a flexible approach to compliance that can accommodate different regulatory environments while maintaining a consistent level of cybersecurity protection.

Compliance with crucial cybersecurity standards and regulations is a multifaceted task that requires organizations to be well-versed in various frameworks and requirements. Whether adhering to broad frameworks like GDPR and ISO 27001, industry-specific regulations like PCI DSS and HIPAA, or managing the complexities of international compliance, organizations must navigate this landscape thoughtfully. Doing so ensures legal and regulatory compliance and significantly strengthens their cybersecurity posture.

The Role of Policy and Governance

The role of policy and governance in cybersecurity is pivotal in establishing a structured and practical approach to managing cyber risks and ensuring compliance with relevant standards and regulations.

Policies and governance structures are the backbone of an organization's cybersecurity efforts, providing a clear framework for managing and enforcing cybersecurity within the organization.

Policy development is a crucial step in this process. Cybersecurity policies are formal documents that outline an organization's approach to managing and protecting its information assets. These policies cover many areas, including access control, data protection, incident response, and employee conduct regarding cybersecurity. Developing these policies involves understanding the organization's risk landscape, legal and regulatory requirements, and business objectives. Effective cybersecurity policies are clear, concise, and tailored to the specific needs and context of the organization. They should be regularly reviewed and updated to reflect changes in the cybersecurity environment and the organization's operations.

Governance structures are equally important in ensuring cybersecurity policies are effectively implemented and adhered to. These structures define the roles, responsibilities, and decision-making processes related to cybersecurity within an organization. Effective governance involves establishing a dedicated cybersecurity governance body, such as a cybersecurity committee or a Chief Information Security Officer (CISO), who oversees the organization's cybersecurity strategy and ensures alignment with overall business objectives. This governance body ensures that cybersecurity policies are effectively communicated, understood, and enforced across the organization.

Aligning policies with compliance is a critical aspect of cybersecurity governance. This alignment ensures that the organization's cybersecurity policies meet internal security objectives and comply with external regulatory and legal requirements. It involves regularly assessing the alignment of policies with relevant standards and regulations, such as GDPR, ISO 27001, or industry-specific requirements like HIPAA. This alignment is not a one-time effort but a continuous process, as internal and external environments are subject to change. Regular review and policy updates, in light of new compliance requirements or changes in the threat landscape, are essential for maintaining effective alignment.

The role of policy and governance in cybersecurity is central to establishing and maintaining an effective cybersecurity posture. Through thoughtful policy development, the establishment of robust governance structures, and the alignment of policies with compliance requirements, organizations can ensure that they protect their information assets and meet their legal and regulatory obligations. This integrated approach to policy, governance, and compliance is fundamental to the overall success of an organization's cybersecurity strategy.

Developing a Compliance Framework

Developing a compliance framework is a strategic undertaking that requires careful planning and execution. It involves creating a structured program that meets regulatory requirements and aligns with the organization's business objectives and risk profile. This framework serves as the blueprint for how an organization approaches compliance, ensuring consistent and effective management of regulatory obligations across all levels of the organization.

The first step in building and maintaining a compliance program is to define its scope and objectives. This involves understanding the specific regulatory requirements the organization must comply with and identifying the internal and external risks that could impact compliance. The program should set clear, achievable objectives that address these requirements and risks, focusing on protecting critical assets and data. It's essential to assess the current state of the organization's compliance posture, identifying gaps and areas for improvement. This assessment forms the basis for developing a tailored compliance program that addresses the organization's unique needs.

Program design and setup are crucial in laying a solid foundation for the compliance program. This phase involves developing the policies, procedures, and controls that will be used to achieve compliance. The program design should consider the organization's structure, processes, technology, and culture to ensure that the compliance measures are practical and effective. Establishing clear governance structures and roles is also essential, ensuring accountability and oversight of the compliance efforts. Additionally, integrating the compliance program into existing business processes can help in embedding compliance into the organization's daily operations.

Stakeholder engagement is a crucial aspect of developing a compliance framework. It involves involving various stakeholders in the compliance process, including leadership, employees, and potentially external parties like customers or suppliers. Effective communication and training ensure that all stakeholders understand their roles and responsibilities in achieving compliance. Engaging stakeholders early and regularly can also help gain their support and commitment, which is crucial for the successful implementation and sustainability of the compliance program.

Program implementation is the stage where the compliance framework is put into action. This involves deploying the defined policies, procedures, and controls across the organization. Effective implementation requires careful planning, resource allocation, and coordination. It's essential to monitor the implementation process, addressing any challenges or resistance. Training and awareness programs should be conducted to ensure that employees understand the compliance requirements and how they apply to their roles. Continuous monitoring and regular program reviews are essential to ensure it remains adequate and relevant in changing regulatory landscapes and business environments.

Developing a compliance framework is a comprehensive process that involves defining objectives, designing and setting up the program, engaging stakeholders, and implementing the program effectively.

A well-developed compliance framework ensures regulatory adherence and strengthens the organization's overall cybersecurity posture by integrating compliance into every aspect of its operations.

Integrating Compliance with Business Processes

Integrating compliance with business processes is essential in ensuring compliance becomes a seamless part of an organization's daily operations. This integration requires a strategic approach where compliance measures are not seen as separate or external to business activities but are interwoven with the organization's processes and workflows. The aim is to create a compliance-conscious culture where adherence to regulations and standards is a natural part of business practices rather than a burdensome add-on.

Aligning compliance with business goals is critical for this integration to be successful. Compliance efforts should support and enhance the organization's overall objectives, not hinder them. This alignment involves understanding the business's strategic direction and ensuring compliance initiatives contribute positively to achieving these goals. For instance, if a business prioritizes customer trust, its compliance program should focus on data protection and privacy regulations, enhancing customer confidence. By aligning compliance with business objectives, organizations can ensure that their compliance efforts add value and drive the business forward.

Incorporating compliance into day-to-day operations involves practical steps to ensure that employees know and adhere to compliance requirements in their routine activities. This can be achieved through regular training, clear communication of policies and procedures, and integrating compliance checks into standard operational processes, for example, incorporating data protection measures into the customer service process or ensuring that IT staff routinely check for compliance with cybersecurity standards. Making compliance a part of everyday activities helps embed it into the organizational culture and ensures sustained adherence over time.

Change management in compliance integration is another crucial aspect. Introducing new compliance measures or updating existing ones often requires changes to current processes, systems, and potentially organizational structures. Effective change management strategies are necessary to facilitate these changes smoothly. This includes communicating the need for change, involving key stakeholders in the change process, providing training and support, and addressing any resistance to change. Change management ensures that transitions to new or updated compliance measures are accepted and adopted by the organization, enabling a more effective and efficient compliance framework.

Integrating compliance with business processes is a multifaceted endeavor that requires aligning compliance with business goals, embedding compliance into day-to-day operations, and effectively managing change. By successfully integrating compliance, organizations ensure adherence to necessary regulations and standards and create a more agile, responsive, and responsible business environment. This integration is vital for organizations to thrive in an increasingly regulated and risk-prone business landscape.

Measuring Compliance Program Effectiveness

Measuring the effectiveness of a compliance program is crucial for ensuring that it meets regulatory requirements and supports the organization's overall objectives. Effective measurement involves setting up mechanisms to regularly assess and evaluate the performance of the compliance program, ensuring that it remains relevant, effective, and aligned with both the internal and external environments.

Key Performance Indicators (KPIs) are vital tools in this measurement process. KPIs for a compliance program should be carefully selected to provide meaningful insights into the program's performance. Examples of KPIs might include the number of compliance incidents reported, the time taken to resolve these incidents, employee compliance training completion rates, and the results of compliance audits. These indicators help quantify the effectiveness of the compliance program and can highlight areas that require attention or improvement. These KPIs must be aligned with the compliance program's specific objectives and the organization's broader goals.

Regular assessments and reviews are also essential components of measuring program effectiveness. This involves conducting periodic audits and reviews of the compliance program to ensure that policies and procedures are being followed and that they remain effective in the face of changing regulations and business processes. These assessments can be internal, conducted by the organization's audit team, or external, carried out by independent auditors. The findings from these assessments provide valuable feedback on the performance of the compliance program and help identify areas for improvement.

Continuous improvement strategies are integral to the long-term success of a compliance program. Organizations should implement strategies to address any identified gaps or weaknesses based on the insights gained from KPIs and regular assessments. This might involve updating policies and procedures, enhancing training programs, or implementing new technologies to strengthen compliance. Continuous improvement is a proactive approach that helps organizations stay ahead of regulatory changes and evolving cybersecurity threats. It ensures that the compliance program meets current standards and is prepared to adapt to future requirements.

Measuring the effectiveness of a compliance program is a dynamic process that involves setting appropriate KPIs, conducting regular assessments and reviews, and implementing continuous improvement strategies. By effectively measuring and continually enhancing their compliance programs, organizations can ensure that they meet regulatory requirements and contribute to the organization's overall security and success.

Risk Mitigation Strategies

Risk mitigation strategies in cybersecurity involve a comprehensive approach to reduce the likelihood and impact of cyber threats. Effective risk mitigation requires a blend of technical, administrative, and physical controls, each addressing different aspects of cybersecurity.

Techniques for reducing cyber risk are diverse and should be tailored to an organization's specific threats and vulnerabilities. These techniques include implementing robust security protocols, regularly updating and patching systems, encrypting sensitive data, and conducting continuous threat monitoring. An essential aspect of risk reduction is developing a comprehensive incident response plan, which prepares the organization to respond to and recover from cyber incidents quickly and effectively. Additionally, organizations should adopt a layered security approach, where multiple defensive mechanisms are employed in a coordinated manner to protect against various threats.

Technical controls are essential components of risk mitigation. These controls involve the use of technology to protect information systems and data. Examples include firewalls, intrusion detection and prevention systems, antivirus and anti-malware software, and secure configurations of IT systems and networks. Technical controls also encompass encryption to protect data in transit and at rest, and strong authentication mechanisms, like multifactor authentication, control access to sensitive systems and data. The effectiveness of technical controls depends on their correct configuration, regular updates, and continuous monitoring to ensure they are functioning as intended.

Administrative controls are policies, procedures, and practices designed to manage the overall conduct of employees and the organization with regard to cybersecurity. These controls include cybersecurity policies, user training and awareness programs, access control policies, and regular security audits and assessments. Administrative controls are crucial for creating a culture of security awareness within the organization and ensuring that employees understand their role in maintaining cybersecurity. Regular training and awareness programs help to keep employees informed about the latest cyber threats and the best practices for avoiding them.

Though sometimes overlooked in cybersecurity, physical security measures are vital in protecting the physical assets that store or access digital information. These measures include securing data centers, server rooms, and other areas where sensitive information is stored against unauthorized access and environmental hazards. Physical security also involves using surveillance cameras, security guards, and access control systems, like badge readers or biometric scanners, to monitor and control access to physical facilities. Ensuring the physical security of IT assets is a critical aspect of a holistic cybersecurity strategy.

Risk mitigation strategies in cybersecurity involve a combination of techniques for reducing cyber risk, including implementing technical, administrative, and physical controls. These strategies should be integrated and coordinated to protect against cyber threats comprehensively. Organizations can significantly reduce their cybersecurity risks and enhance their overall security posture by employing these diverse measures.

Balancing Risk with Business Objectives

Balancing risk with business objectives is critical to effective cybersecurity risk management. It involves aligning the organization's risk mitigation efforts with its goals and strategic direction. This balance ensures cybersecurity measures support business growth and innovation rather than impede them. The key is to achieve a state where the level of security is commensurate with the value of the assets being protected and the potential impact on the business.

Risk appetite and tolerance are fundamental concepts in this balancing act. Risk appetite refers to the risk an organization accepts to pursue its objectives. In contrast, risk tolerance is the level of risk the organization can withstand without significant impact. Understanding and defining the organization's risk appetite and tolerance helps make informed decisions about which risks to accept, mitigate, or transfer. This clarity enables the organization to allocate resources more effectively and avoid over- or under-investing in cybersecurity measures.

Cost-benefit analysis is a valuable tool in balancing risk with business objectives. This analysis involves weighing the costs of implementing specific cybersecurity measures against their benefits regarding reduced risk. The aim is to identify solutions that offer the best return on investment, considering the financial costs and the potential impact on business operations. This approach helps prioritize cybersecurity initiatives based on their effectiveness in reducing risk and aligning with business goals.

Decision-making frameworks are essential for guiding these balancing efforts. These frameworks provide a structured approach for evaluating and making decisions about cybersecurity risks. They typically involve assessing the likelihood and impact of different risks, considering the organization's risk appetite and tolerance, and evaluating the costs and benefits of various mitigation strategies. Decision-making frameworks help ensure that decisions about cybersecurity risks are consistent, rational, and aligned with the organization's strategic objectives.

Balancing risk with business objectives in cybersecurity is a complex but essential task. Organizations can ensure that their cybersecurity efforts are aligned with their business goals by understanding and defining their risk appetite and tolerance, conducting thorough cost-benefit analyses, and employing structured decision-making frameworks. This alignment enhances the organization's security posture and supports its overall growth and success.

Advanced Risk Mitigation Approaches

Advanced risk mitigation approaches in cybersecurity involve leveraging cutting-edge technologies and methodologies to protect against sophisticated cyber threats. These advanced approaches are becoming increasingly important as the cyber threat landscape evolves and becomes more complex.

Artificial intelligence (AI) and machine learning (ML) are at the forefront of these advanced approaches. AI and ML can significantly enhance an organization's real-time ability to detect and respond to cyber threats. By analyzing vast amounts of data, these technologies can identify patterns and anomalies that may indicate a security breach, often much faster and more accurately than traditional methods. AI-driven security systems can adapt and learn from new threats, continuously improving their effectiveness. Furthermore, AI can assist in automating routine cybersecurity tasks, freeing up human resources to focus on more complex security challenges.

Cloud security is another critical area in advanced risk mitigation strategies. As more organizations move their data and operations to the cloud, the security of cloud-based systems and data becomes paramount. Cloud security involves implementing controls specific to the cloud environment, such as identity and access management, data encryption, and secure application interfaces. It also includes ensuring the security of the cloud infrastructure itself and managing the shared responsibility model between the cloud service provider and the organization. Adequate cloud security requires a thorough understanding of the cloud environment and its unique challenges, along with deploying specialized tools and practices designed for cloud security.

Incident response and recovery planning is an essential component of advanced risk mitigation. Despite the best preventive measures, the possibility of a security incident can never be eliminated. An effective incident response plan ensures that an organization can quickly and effectively respond to a security incident, minimizing its impact. This plan should include clear procedures for detecting, containing, and eradicating threats and recovering affected systems and data. Recovery planning is equally important, ensuring the organization can resume operations immediately after an incident. Both incident response and recovery planning should be regularly tested and updated to ensure they remain effective in the face of new and evolving cyber threats.

Advanced risk mitigation approaches in cybersecurity, including AI and ML, cloud security, and robust incident response and recovery planning, are crucial for protecting against today's sophisticated cyber threats. These approaches represent the cutting edge of cybersecurity and are essential for organizations looking to enhance their security posture in an increasingly complex and dynamic threat landscape.

Auditing and Reporting in Cybersecurity

Auditing and reporting are critical components of an effective cybersecurity strategy, ensuring that security controls are functioning as intended and that the organization complies with relevant laws and regulations.

Conducting cybersecurity audits is critical in evaluating the robustness and effectiveness of an organization's cybersecurity measures. These audits involve systematically examining the security controls, policies, and procedures to ensure they adequately and effectively mitigate cyber risks. Cybersecurity audits can be internal, conducted by the organization's audit team, or external, carried out by independent auditors. The purpose of these audits is to identify vulnerabilities and gaps in the security posture and to provide recommendations for improvement.

Audit planning and execution are crucial steps in the auditing process. Planning involves defining the scope, objectives, and methodology of the audit. This includes selecting the areas to be audited, such as network security, data protection, or incident response capabilities, and determining the criteria against which these areas will be evaluated. During the execution phase, auditors collect and analyze data, interview relevant personnel, and review documentation and systems. Effective execution requires a thorough understanding of cybersecurity principles and practices and the ability to assess the security controls in place objectively.

Assessing control effectiveness is a core part of the audit process. This assessment evaluates whether the cybersecurity controls are appropriate, properly implemented, and effectively reduce risk to an acceptable level. It involves testing the controls to see how they perform under different scenarios and identifying any areas where they may fall short. The effectiveness assessment provides valuable insights into the strengths and weaknesses of the organization's cybersecurity measures and helps identify improvement areas.

Dealing with non-compliance is another critical aspect of cybersecurity auditing and reporting. The organization must respond appropriately when audits reveal non-compliance with internal policies or external regulations. This response may involve implementing corrective actions to address the identified issues, reevaluating risk assessments, updating policies and procedures, and, if necessary, conducting retraining for staff. An effective response to non-compliance not only addresses the immediate issues but also helps strengthen the organization's overall cybersecurity posture.

Auditing and reporting in cybersecurity are essential practices that comprehensively assess an organization's cybersecurity health. Conducting regular audits, properly planning and executing these audits, assessing the effectiveness of controls, and effectively dealing with non-compliance are all integral to maintaining a strong and responsive cybersecurity posture. These activities help ensure that organizations are compliant with regulations and adequately protected against cyber threats.

Reporting Compliance and Risk Status

Reporting compliance and risk status is a crucial aspect of cybersecurity management, as it provides transparency and accountability in how an organization manages its cyber risks and adheres to regulatory requirements. Effective reporting involves regularly communicating the current compliance status and risk to relevant stakeholders within and outside the organization.

Internal reporting mechanisms are essential for keeping an organization's management and relevant personnel informed about cybersecurity. These mechanisms typically involve regular reports to senior management or a dedicated cybersecurity governance body, such as a security committee or board of directors. Internal reports should provide a clear and concise overview of the current risk status, including any identified vulnerabilities, incidents, and the effectiveness of controls. They should also include updates on compliance with internal policies and external regulations. Effective internal reporting ensures that decision-makers are well-informed about cybersecurity and can make decisions based on current information.

External reporting requirements vary depending on industry regulations and legal obligations. Many organizations must report certain types of cybersecurity incidents to regulatory authorities. For example, under GDPR, organizations must report data breaches involving personal data to the relevant supervisory authority. External reporting may also involve disclosing cybersecurity information to stakeholders such as customers, partners, or shareholders, particularly after a significant security incident. Adhering to these external reporting requirements is crucial not only for compliance purposes but also for maintaining trust and transparency with external stakeholders.

Communicating with stakeholders is an integral part of the reporting process. Effective communication involves providing the necessary information and ensuring that it is understandable and relevant to the audience. This might involve translating technical cybersecurity issues into business terms for internal stakeholders, highlighting the organization's impact. For external stakeholders, communication should focus on demonstrating that the organization is managing cybersecurity risks effectively and is committed to protecting their interests. Clear and effective communication helps build and maintain confidence among stakeholders in the organization's ability to manage cybersecurity risks and compliance.

Reporting compliance and risk status, both internally and externally, is vital for effective cybersecurity management. It involves developing robust internal reporting mechanisms, adhering to external reporting requirements, and communicating effectively with all relevant stakeholders. These activities ensure compliance with regulatory requirements, build trust, and support informed decision-making within the organization.

Best Practices in Cybersecurity Reporting

Best practices in cybersecurity reporting are fundamental to ensuring that the insights gained from cybersecurity activities effectively inform decision-making and strategy development. These practices revolve around transparency, accuracy, continual improvement, and leveraging reporting for strategic decisions.

Transparency and accuracy are the cornerstones of effective cybersecurity reporting. Reports should provide a clear and honest view of the organization's cybersecurity posture, including strengths and weaknesses. Accuracy is crucial to ensure that decisions are made based on reliable and valid information. This means that data presented in reports should be carefully verified and derived from credible sources. Transparent and accurate reporting builds trust among stakeholders and ensures that the organization has a realistic understanding of its cybersecurity status.

Continual improvement is another crucial aspect of best practices in reporting. Cybersecurity is a dynamic field with evolving threats and changing regulatory landscapes. Effective reporting should, therefore, not only highlight the current state of affairs but also suggest areas for improvement and growth. This could involve recommendations for enhancing security controls, updating policies, or increasing cybersecurity awareness and training. Reports should be used as a tool for continuous learning and development, helping the organization to adapt and strengthen its cybersecurity posture over time.

Leveraging reporting for strategic decisions is essential to transforming cybersecurity reporting from a compliance activity into a strategic asset. Reports should provide insights that guide decision-making at the highest levels, helping to shape the organization's overall strategy. This involves using the data and analyses from reports to identify trends, forecast potential security challenges, and make informed decisions about resource allocation, investment in new technologies, and strategic initiatives. By integrating cybersecurity reporting into the broader business strategy, organizations can ensure that their cybersecurity efforts align with and support their overall objectives.

Best practices in cybersecurity reporting are about much more than meeting compliance requirements. They involve ensuring transparency and accuracy, fostering continual improvement, and leveraging the insights from reporting to inform strategic decisions. By adhering to these practices, organizations can enhance their cybersecurity reporting processes, making them valuable tools for managing cyber risks and supporting the organization's strategic goals.

Auditing and Reporting in Cybersecurity

Conducting cybersecurity audits is a vital aspect of maintaining a robust cybersecurity posture. These audits systematically evaluate an organization's cybersecurity policies, procedures, and practices. They aim to ensure that security controls protect the organization's information systems and data. Cybersecurity audits can be internal, conducted by the organization's staff, or external, carried out by independent entities. These audits help identify vulnerabilities, ensure compliance with regulations and standards, and verify that cybersecurity practices align with the organization's strategic objectives.

Audit planning and execution form the backbone of the cybersecurity auditing process. Effective planning entails defining the scope of the audit, determining the methodologies to be used, and identifying the key areas and systems to be evaluated. This phase also involves gathering relevant documentation, such as policies, procedures, and previous audit reports. During the execution phase, auditors systematically review and assess the organization's cybersecurity measures. This involves examining technical controls, evaluating procedural and administrative measures, interviewing staff, and analyzing compliance with established standards and policies.

Assessing control effectiveness is a core objective of cybersecurity audits. This assessment focuses on determining whether the cybersecurity controls are appropriate, properly implemented, and effective in mitigating identified risks. It involves testing and evaluating security measures to identify weaknesses or gaps in the organization's cybersecurity framework. The effectiveness of controls is assessed against the backdrop of the organization's risk environment and the evolving threat landscape, ensuring that controls are adequate for today's needs and resilient to future challenges.

Dealing with non-compliance is an essential aspect of the audit process. When audits reveal gaps or instances where the organization does not comply with internal policies or external regulations, addressing

661

these findings promptly and effectively is critical. This involves developing and implementing corrective action plans to remediate identified issues, revising policies and procedures as necessary, and, where required, retraining staff to ensure compliance. Addressing non-compliance is about rectifying immediate issues and strengthening the overall cybersecurity framework to prevent future occurrences.

Auditing and reporting in cybersecurity are crucial in ensuring that an organization's cybersecurity measures are effective and compliant with necessary standards and regulations. Conducting thorough audits, effectively planning and executing these audits, assessing the effectiveness of controls, and adequately addressing non-compliance are key elements in maintaining a strong cybersecurity posture. These activities safeguard against cyber threats and align cybersecurity practices with the organization's broader goals and objectives.

Reporting Compliance and Risk Status

Reporting compliance and risk status is critical to an organization's cybersecurity strategy. This process involves regularly updating key stakeholders on the organization's compliance with cybersecurity standards and the current status of cybersecurity risks. Effective reporting ensures that both management and relevant external parties know how cybersecurity risks are managed and how they align with compliance requirements. This transparency is essential for informed decision-making and maintaining trust among stakeholders.

Internal reporting mechanisms play a key role in the cybersecurity governance framework. These mechanisms typically involve regular reports to senior management, the board of directors, or a dedicated cybersecurity committee. Internal reports should provide a comprehensive overview of the organization's cybersecurity posture, including compliance with policies and regulations, the effectiveness of security controls, and any incidents or breaches. These reports are vital for ensuring that the organization's leadership is informed about cybersecurity issues and can provide the necessary support and resources for cybersecurity initiatives.

Various regulatory bodies and industry standards dictate external reporting requirements. Depending on the organization's location, industry, and the type of data it handles, it may be required to report certain cybersecurity information to external regulatory agencies. For example, companies subject to GDPR may need to report data breaches involving personal data to regulatory authorities. External reporting can also extend to customers, partners, and other stakeholders, especially in a security incident that may impact them. Complying with these external reporting requirements is crucial for legal compliance, maintaining business relationships, and upholding the organization's reputation.

Communicating with stakeholders about cybersecurity issues is a critical aspect of reporting. Effective communication involves not only providing relevant information but also ensuring that it is presented in a clear, concise, and understandable manner. For internal stakeholders, this may include translating technical cybersecurity issues into business impacts. Communication should reassure external stakeholders that the organization is managing cybersecurity risks effectively and is committed to protecting their interests. Good communication practices help in building trust and can play a significant role in how stakeholders perceive the organization's cybersecurity efforts.

Reporting on compliance and risk status, both internally and externally, is essential for effective cybersecurity management. It involves developing robust reporting mechanisms, adhering to external reporting requirements, and communicating effectively with all relevant stakeholders. These activities ensure regulatory compliance, support informed decision-making, and build trust in the organization's ability to manage cybersecurity risks.

The Future of Cybersecurity Risk and Compliance

The future of cybersecurity risk and compliance is an area of dynamic and continual evolution, shaped by emerging trends and technologies. Understanding these developments is crucial for organizations to stay ahead of threats and maintain compliance in an increasingly complex digital landscape.

Emerging trends and technologies in cybersecurity are driving significant changes in how organizations protect their digital assets and comply with regulations. These trends include the growing adoption of cloud computing, the proliferation of Internet of Things (IoT) devices, and the increasing sophistication of cyber threats. Cybersecurity strategies are evolving to become more proactive and intelligence driven, leveraging advanced technologies to anticipate and mitigate risks before they materialize.

Predictive analytics is becoming a cornerstone of modern cybersecurity strategies. Predictive analytics tools can forecast potential security incidents and vulnerabilities by analyzing historical data and identifying patterns. This proactive approach allows organizations to prioritize risks and implement preventive measures more effectively. Predictive analytics can also play a vital role in compliance, helping organizations anticipate and adapt to regulatory changes and ensure ongoing adherence to standards.

Blockchain technology is increasingly being explored for its potential to enhance cybersecurity and compliance. With its inherent decentralization, transparency, and immutability properties, blockchain can provide a secure and tamper-proof way of storing and managing data. This makes it particularly useful for identity and access management applications, secure transaction processing, and maintaining auditable records. Blockchain's ability to provide a verifiable and permanent record of transactions can also aid in compliance management, ensuring the integrity and traceability of data.

Next-generation threat intelligence is another area of focus in the future of cybersecurity. This involves using advanced algorithms, machine learning, and AI to analyze vast amounts of data from various sources to identify emerging threats. Next-generation threat intelligence goes beyond traditional signature-based detection, offering more sophisticated and contextual insights into threats. This intelligence is crucial for organizations to understand the rapidly changing threat landscape and to implement more effective, targeted security measures.

The future of cybersecurity risk and compliance is being shaped by integrating emerging technologies like predictive analytics, blockchain, and next-generation threat intelligence. These technologies offer new opportunities for organizations to enhance their security posture, improve compliance, and stay one step ahead of cyber threats. As the digital landscape continues to evolve, staying abreast of these developments and incorporating them into cybersecurity strategies will be essential for organizations looking to protect their digital assets and maintain compliance.

Preparing for Future Challenges

Preparing for future challenges in cybersecurity requires organizations to be forward-thinking and adaptive. As the digital landscape evolves, so must the approaches to managing cyber risks and maintaining compliance.

Training and skill development are essential in equipping the workforce to handle emerging cybersecurity challenges. As cyber threats become more sophisticated, the skills needed to combat them must evolve. Organizations must invest in ongoing training and professional development programs to ensure their cybersecurity teams are well-versed in the latest technologies and threat mitigation strategies. Beyond technical training, educating the broader workforce on cybersecurity best practices is crucial, as human error remains a significant vulnerability. Regular awareness programs and training sessions can help in building a more security-conscious culture among all employees.

Policy evolution is a critical aspect of preparing for the future. Cybersecurity policies should be dynamic and flexible enough to adapt to new threats, technologies, and regulatory changes. Regular reviews and updates of policies and procedures ensure that they remain relevant and practical. This includes revising incident response plans, data protection policies, and compliance frameworks to reflect new risks and requirements. An agile policy framework allows organizations to respond quickly to changes in the cybersecurity landscape and maintain a strong defensive posture.

Building resilient cybersecurity cultures fosters an organizational environment where cybersecurity is a shared responsibility. This culture emphasizes the importance of security at every level of the organization, from the executive suite to the front lines. A resilient cybersecurity culture values vigilance, collaboration, and continuous learning. It involves encouraging open communication about cybersecurity issues, sharing knowledge and insights, and promoting a proactive approach to identifying and addressing security vulnerabilities. Organizations can enhance their security posture by cultivating a resilient cybersecurity culture and better preparing for future challenges.

Preparing for future challenges in cybersecurity involves a multifaceted approach that includes investing in training and skill development, evolving policies and procedures, and building resilient cybersecurity cultures. These efforts will equip organizations to navigate the complex and ever-changing cybersecurity landscape, ensuring they remain well-prepared to manage risks and maintain compliance in the face of future challenges.

Final Thoughts: The Road Ahead

As we look toward the future of cybersecurity risk and compliance, it's evident that the road ahead will be marked by continuous change and the need for adaptability. Organizations must remain vigilant and proactive in their approach to cybersecurity, integrating lessons learned, anticipating the unanticipated, and building a proactive cybersecurity posture.

Integrating lessons learned is crucial for continuous improvement in cybersecurity practices. Organizations should regularly analyze cybersecurity incidents and near misses within their own environments and from external sources to identify patterns and areas for improvement. This analysis can reveal valuable insights into the effectiveness of current security measures and highlight potential vulnerabilities. By learning from past experiences, organizations can adapt their strategies to better protect against future threats and ensure compliance with evolving regulations.

Anticipating the unanticipated is a challenging but essential aspect of cybersecurity. The threat landscape constantly evolves, with new types of attacks emerging regularly. Organizations must, therefore, cultivate a mindset of preparedness for the unexpected. This involves staying informed about the latest threats and trends and conducting regular risk assessments and scenario planning exercises. Organizations can develop more robust and flexible strategies to respond to unforeseen challenges by considering a wide range of potential scenarios.

Building a proactive cybersecurity posture is moving from a reactive, incident-driven approach to a more strategic, anticipatory one. This proactive posture involves implementing advanced technologies like AI and machine learning for predictive threat detection, investing in regular training and awareness programs, and developing agile policies and procedures. A proactive approach also emphasizes the importance of collaboration and information sharing with other organizations and industry groups, as collective knowledge is a powerful tool in combating cyber threats.

The future of cybersecurity risk and compliance will require organizations to be dynamic, insightful, and forward-thinking. By integrating lessons learned, preparing for the unexpected, and adopting a proactive approach, organizations can navigate the complexities of the digital world more effectively. The road ahead in cybersecurity is continuous learning, adaptation, and vigilance, focusing on building resilient and robust defenses against an ever-evolving array of cyber threats.

Case Study: T-Mobile's $500 Million Fine

T-Mobile, one of the leading telecommunications companies, encountered a significant operational and reputational challenge when subjected to a $500 million fine. This substantial fine culminated in various incidents and failures in their cybersecurity and data protection practices, leading to a severe data breach.

The pivotal incident leading to this consequential fine was a major data breach that compromised sensitive customer data, including personal and financial details. This breach wasn't a stand-alone event but a peak in a series of security lapses that T-Mobile had experienced over time.

The breach was attributed to several key factors. T-Mobile's security infrastructure had critical vulnerabilities that were not identified and addressed in time, allowing cyber attackers to exploit these weaknesses. Additionally, the company exhibited considerable gaps in conducting regular and comprehensive risk assessments, which are crucial in identifying potential security threats. A lack of adequate employee training in cybersecurity best practices contributed significantly to the breach. This training deficit heightened the risk of human error and susceptibility to sophisticated cyber-attacks. Moreover, the response to the breach was not as prompt and effective as required, exacerbating the situation and its impact.

This significant data breach drew the attention of regulatory authorities, leading to an extensive investigation into the company's practices. The investigation uncovered that T-Mobile had not complied with several critical industry standards and data protection and cybersecurity regulations. As a result of these non-compliance issues and the harm inflicted on consumers, T-Mobile has levied a fine of $500 million.

In the aftermath of the incident and the subsequent fine, T-Mobile embarked on remedial actions. The company significantly enhanced its cybersecurity infrastructure by integrating more robust security measures to safeguard against future breaches. Recognizing the gaps in their risk management strategies, T-Mobile revised and improved these practices, introducing more frequent and comprehensive risk assessments and proactive risk mitigation measures. They also initiated comprehensive training programs for their employees to raise awareness about cybersecurity and instill best practices. Additionally, T-Mobile developed more effective incident response protocols to ensure quicker and more coordinated responses in future security incidents.

The case of T-Mobile's $500 million fine is a crucial lesson for the industry, emphasizing the importance of maintaining robust cybersecurity measures, conducting regular risk assessments, properly training employees, and having swift incident response mechanisms. The experience of T-Mobile highlights the severe financial and reputational repercussions that can result from neglecting these aspects of cybersecurity.

The substantial fine imposed on T-Mobile is a stark reminder of the critical importance of cybersecurity vigilance and regulatory compliance. It underscores the necessity for continuous improvement and adaptation in cybersecurity practices to protect against the dynamically evolving digital threats adequately.

Career Corner

A cyber risk and compliance career is a crucial and increasingly relevant field within the cybersecurity sector, focusing on identifying, assessing, and managing risks associated with digital information and technology. This area is vital for ensuring organizations comply with regulatory requirements while safeguarding against cyber threats. It offers diverse opportunities for those interested in bridging the gap between cybersecurity, legal compliance, and risk management.

One of the primary roles in this domain is that of a Cyber Risk Analyst or Risk Management Specialist. These professionals are tasked with identifying and assessing cyber risks that an organization may face. They analyze potential threats, vulnerabilities, and impacts and recommend strategies to mitigate these risks. Their work is central to developing and maintaining an effective risk management framework that aligns with organizational objectives and compliance requirements.

Another significant role is that of a Compliance Analyst or Officer. Individuals in this position ensure that the organization adheres to external regulatory requirements and internal policies. This includes understanding and interpreting relevant laws and standards, such as GDPR, HIPAA, or ISO 27001, and implementing policies and procedures to ensure compliance. They also conduct regular audits and assessments to identify compliance gaps and areas for improvement.

For those interested in a strategic approach to risk and compliance, the role of a Cyber Risk and Compliance Manager or Director is vital. These professionals oversee the development and implementation of risk management and compliance programs. They ensure that risk and compliance efforts are integrated with the organization's overall cybersecurity strategy and are aligned with business goals. Their leadership fosters a culture of risk awareness and compliance throughout the organization.

The role of a Data Protection Officer (DPO), especially in organizations that handle large amounts of sensitive data, is also increasingly important. DPOs are responsible for overseeing data protection strategies, ensuring compliance with data protection laws, and serving as the point of contact between the organization and regulatory authorities on matters related to data privacy.

Cyber risk and compliance professionals often pursue certifications to enhance their expertise and credibility. Certifications such as the Certified Information Systems Auditor (CISA), Certified Information Security Manager (CISM), and Certified Information Systems Security Professional (CISSP) are highly valued. Additionally, certifications specific to compliance and risk, like the Certified in Risk and Information Systems Control (CRISC) and the Certified Compliance & Ethics Professional (CCEP), can provide specialized knowledge in this field.

Individuals in this career path must understand cybersecurity principles, risk management practices, and legal and regulatory frameworks. They should have excellent analytical skills, attention to detail, and the ability to effectively communicate complex compliance and risk-related issues.

In summary, a cyber risk and compliance career offers a range of challenging and impactful opportunities. From analyzing and managing cyber risks to ensuring regulatory compliance and overseeing data protection strategies, professionals in this field play a crucial role in protecting organizations from cyber threats and legal repercussions. Staying current with the ever-evolving landscape of cybersecurity threats, technologies, and regulatory changes is essential in this vital and dynamic field.

Chapter Questions

1. What is the primary goal of risk management in cybersecurity?

    A. Increasing financial profits

    B. Enhancing business reputation

    C. Protecting information systems and assets from threats

    D. Streamlining operational processes

2. Which of the following aspects of cybersecurity risk are involved?

    A. Only technical vulnerabilities

    B. Financial loss and reputational damage

    C. Solely focusing on malware attacks

    D. Reducing operational costs

3. What is crucial for building a resilient cybersecurity posture?

    A. Focusing only on external threats

    B. Integrating risk management into all cybersecurity efforts

    C. Limiting cybersecurity to IT departments

    D. Prioritizing financial objectives over security

4. What is the need for compliance in cybersecurity primarily driven by?

    A. The desire to increase market share

    B. The increasing sophistication of cyber attacks

    C. The goal of reducing employee workload

D. Simplifying business processes

5. What does GDPR focus on in cybersecurity?

   A. Data encryption standards

   B. Data protection and privacy

   C. Network security optimization

   D. Hardware vulnerabilities

6. In risk management, what does risk prioritization involve?

   A. Disregarding low-impact risks

   B. Focusing on internal risks only

   C. Ranking risks based on impact and likelihood

   D. Ignoring long-term risks

7. Why are regular assessments and reviews critical in risk management?

   A. To focus solely on past incidents

   B. To ensure the continued effectiveness of strategies

   C. To reduce training requirements

   D. For public relations purposes

8. In cybersecurity, what is the primary function of technical controls?

   A. Increasing operational efficiency

   B. Protecting information systems and data

   C. Reducing the need for policies

   D. Enhancing organizational culture

9. Which approach is vital in managing cybersecurity risks?

    A. Reactive response to incidents

    B. Proactive and anticipatory stance

    C. Sole reliance on technology

    D. Outsourcing risk management tasks

10. The use of AI and ML in cybersecurity primarily aims to

    A. Replace human cybersecurity teams

    B. Predict and respond to threats in real time

    C. Focus on hardware security

    D. Cut down operational costs

11. What is the key to balancing risk with business objectives in cybersecurity?

    A. Ignoring low-probability risks

    B. Focusing only on short-term goals

    C. Aligning risk mitigation efforts with business goals

    D. Prioritizing risk management over business objectives

12. How does blockchain technology contribute to cybersecurity?

    A. By simplifying compliance processes

    B. Through its decentralization and immutability

    C. By focusing solely on financial transactions

    D. Reducing the need for threat intelligence

13. What role does predictive analytics play in cybersecurity?

    A. Decreasing dependence on technology

    B. Forecasting potential security incidents

    C. Focusing on historical data analysis only

    D. Eliminating the need for incident response plans

14. In cybersecurity reporting, why is accuracy important?

    A. To ensure decisions are based on reliable data

    B. To simplify reporting processes

    C. For enhancing organizational culture

    D. To reduce the need for further analysis

15. The future of cybersecurity risk and compliance emphasizes

    A. Relying on past strategies

    B. Static policy frameworks

    C. Adapting to emerging trends and technologies

    D. Reducing collaboration with industry groups

CHAPTER 18

Incident Response

Incident Response (IR) is a vital component of cybersecurity, focused on immediately and effectively handling security breaches and cyber-attacks. Its main goal is to manage the repercussions of a security incident while establishing protocols to prevent future threats. IR involves a series of defined steps and procedures aimed at minimizing the impact of the incident, maintaining business continuity, and integrating technical, managerial, and strategic elements to address modern cyber threats effectively.

The definition and scope of Incident Response are extensive. It is defined as an organization's methodology to respond to and manage a cyberattack or data breach. The scope covers the detection, analysis, containment, eradication, and incident recovery. IR extends beyond the technical aspects, encompassing legal, public relations, and human resources components. IR is a comprehensive process beyond technical fixes, including managing communication, reputation, legal issues, and organizational resilience.

In cybersecurity, the importance of Incident Response is paramount. In an era of increasingly sophisticated cyber threats, the ability of an organization to respond effectively to incidents is crucial. A robust IR strategy mitigates the damages of an attack and builds the trust of customers and stakeholders in the organization's ability to protect data. It is a critical component in maintaining information integrity, availability, and confidentiality, highlighting its essential role in the cybersecurity landscape.

© Dr. Jason Edwards 2024, corrected publication 2024
Dr. J. Edwards, *Mastering Cybersecurity*, https://doi.org/10.1007/979-8-8688-0297-3_18

The evolution of Incident Response has been significant over the years. Initially focused on reactive measures post incident, it has evolved to include proactive strategies like threat hunting and predictive analytics. This evolution reflects the changing nature of cyber threats and the need for more sophisticated and anticipatory approaches to cybersecurity. Today, IR involves a balance of reactive and proactive measures, ensuring that organizations are prepared to handle incidents as they occur and prevent potential threats before they materialize.

Key principles and best practices in Incident Response include preparedness, rapid detection, effective communication, and continuous improvement. Preparedness involves regular training and simulation exercises, while rapid detection requires robust monitoring and alert systems. Effective communication is crucial for coordinating response efforts and managing stakeholder expectations. Continuous improvement, gained from lessons learned from past incidents, ensures that IR strategies evolve and adapt to the ever-changing cyber threat landscape. These principles are fundamental to building an organization's resilient and effective IR capability.

Steps in the Incident Response Process

The Incident Response Process is structured into several critical steps, each playing a unique role in handling cyber threats. It starts with identifying threats, where the focus is on the early detection of potential security incidents. This involves monitoring network traffic, analyzing security alerts, and recognizing signs of unauthorized access or malicious activities. Early identification is crucial in limiting the impact of an incident and is heavily reliant on advanced monitoring systems and skilled personnel.

Once a threat is identified, containment strategies are implemented. The goal here is to limit the spread and impact of the incident. This involves isolating affected systems, blocking malicious traffic, and temporarily shutting down certain services. Containment is a delicate balance between halting the progression of the threat and maintaining as much operational functionality as possible. It's a critical step in preventing larger-scale damage and stabilizing the situation for further analysis and action.

The next step is eradicating risks, which involves removing the threat from the organization's systems. This could include deleting malicious files, closing security loopholes, or updating vulnerable software. It's a phase where thoroughness is key, as any oversight can lead to the resurgence of the threat. Teams often collaborate with external experts and utilize specialized tools to ensure that the threat is wholly eradicated.

Following the eradication, the focus shifts to recovery measures. This step is about restoring affected services and systems to their full functionality. It involves careful planning to ensure that reintroducing systems do not reopen security vulnerabilities. The recovery process is often phased and closely monitored, with a keen eye on ensuring that no aspects of the threat remain in the system.

Post-incident activities are the final step in the Incident Response Process. This phase involves thoroughly analyzing the incident to learn from it and improve future responses. Key activities include documenting the incident, analyzing the effectiveness of the response, and implementing changes to prevent similar incidents. This step is critical for evolving an organization's cybersecurity defenses and involves technical review and adjustments in policies, procedures, and potentially even training and awareness programs. The goal is to strengthen the organization's security posture and resilience against future cyber threats.

Building an Incident Response Team

Building an effective Incident Response Team is critical in preparing an organization to handle cyber threats efficiently. This team comprises individuals with diverse skills and expertise who respond to and manage security incidents. The foundation of a strong team lies in clearly defined roles and responsibilities. This delineation ensures that each member knows their specific duties during an incident, ranging from technical response to communication with stakeholders.

The composition of the team and the skills required are varied. It typically includes IT professionals skilled in cybersecurity, network and system administration, and forensic analysis. Additionally, legal, public relations, and human resources department members are often included to address the broader implications of incidents. This diversity in skills and backgrounds enables the team to tackle all aspects of an incident, from the technical response to legal compliance and communication with affected parties.

Training and development are crucial for maintaining the effectiveness of the Incident Response Team. Regular training sessions, workshops, and simulation exercises are necessary to update the team on the latest threats and response strategies. This ongoing development ensures the team is always prepared to respond to new and evolving cyber threats with the most current knowledge and techniques.

Effective communication and coordination are vital during an incident. The team must have established protocols for internal communication to ensure that information is shared efficiently and decisions are made promptly. Coordination with other departments is also essential, ensuring a cohesive and comprehensive response to incidents.

Lastly, external support and collaboration significantly affect the team's effectiveness. This can include partnerships with external cybersecurity experts, law enforcement agencies, and other organizations. These collaborations can provide additional expertise, resources, and perspectives, particularly valuable in handling complex or large-scale incidents. External partnerships also offer opportunities for sharing best practices and learning from the experiences of others in the field, further strengthening the team's capabilities.

Tools and Technologies for Incident Response

The use of specialized tools and technologies significantly enhances the effectiveness of an Incident Response Process. These tools streamline the process and provide critical insights and capabilities that allow for a more effective and efficient response to cybersecurity incidents.

Incident Tracking Systems are fundamental in managing and documenting incidents from detection to resolution. These systems enable teams to log incidents, track their status, assign tasks, and document actions taken. This ensures a coordinated response and provides valuable data for post-incident analysis. Effective tracking is crucial for understanding an incident's lifecycle and identifying areas for improvement in the response process.

Forensic tools play a critical role in understanding and mitigating cyber threats. These tools allow teams to conduct in-depth analyses of incidents, uncovering how a breach occurred, what data was affected, and the source of the attack. They enable digital evidence extraction, preservation, and analysis, which is vital for identifying vulnerabilities and preventing future incidents. Forensic tools are essential for uncovering the root cause of incidents and providing evidence in cases where legal action is necessary.

Threat Intelligence Platforms are instrumental in providing actionable information about emerging threats. These platforms collect and analyze data from various sources to identify potential threats and vulnerabilities. This information allows Incident Response Teams to anticipate and prepare for specific attacks, making their response more targeted and effective.

Automation and orchestration solutions are increasingly important in managing the complexity and volume of tasks involved in Incident Response. Automation allows for rapid response to common incidents, while orchestration ensures that different tools and processes work together seamlessly. These solutions help reduce the response time, minimize the impact of incidents, and allow human responders to focus on more complex aspects of incident management.

Security Information and Event Management (SIEM) systems provide a holistic view of an organization's security posture. SIEM systems aggregate and analyze data from various sources within the organization, providing real-time analysis of security alerts. They are essential for the early detection of incidents and for providing insights that guide the response process. SIEM systems are the backbone of many Incident Response strategies, offering a centralized platform for monitoring and managing security events.

Preparing for Cybersecurity Incidents

Preparing for cybersecurity incidents is a proactive measure crucial for any organization's security strategy. This preparation phase is centered around comprehensive Incident Response planning and readiness, ensuring the organization can handle potential cyber threats effectively.

Creating a robust Incident Response Plan is the first step in this preparation. This plan outlines the procedures and protocols to be followed during a cyber incident. It details the roles and responsibilities of the Incident Response Team, the steps for assessing and responding to incidents, and the communication strategies to be employed. A well-crafted plan is specific, actionable, and tailored to the unique needs and structure of the organization.

Regular updates and maintenance of the response plan are vital to ensure its effectiveness. Cyber threats evolve rapidly, and a plan that is not regularly reviewed and updated can quickly become obsolete. This process involves revising the plan to incorporate new threats, technologies, and lessons learned from recent incidents. Regular audits and reviews help in keeping the plan relevant and effective in the dynamic landscape of cybersecurity threats.

The integration of the Incident Response Plan with Business Continuity Plans is essential. This ensures that the organization can maintain critical operations even in the face of a cyber incident. It involves identifying critical business processes, understanding how a cyber incident could impact these processes, and developing strategies to maintain operations during and after an incident. This integration helps in minimizing the operational and financial impact of cyber incidents.

Resource allocation is a critical component of Incident Response planning. This involves ensuring that the Incident Response Team can access the tools, technologies, and personnel required to respond to incidents effectively. Adequate resources include budgetary considerations, ensuring the team can procure and maintain necessary security tools and services.

Finally, legal and regulatory considerations are integral to preparing for cybersecurity incidents. Organizations must understand and comply with relevant laws and regulations related to cybersecurity and data protection. This includes requirements for reporting incidents, handling customer data, and cooperating with authorities. Compliance with these legal and regulatory requirements is critical to avoid legal repercussions and maintain customer and stakeholder trust.

Establishing Communication Protocols

Training and simulation exercises are crucial components in preparing for cybersecurity incidents, equipping the Incident Response Team and relevant staff with the skills and experience needed to handle real-world threats effectively.

Designing comprehensive training programs is the first step in this preparatory phase. These programs are tailored to team members' specific roles and responsibilities, ensuring that each participant is equipped with the necessary knowledge and skills. The training covers various aspects of Incident Response, from technical skills required for threat detection and mitigation to decision-making processes during a crisis. The objective is to build a competent team that is well-versed in the protocols and procedures outlined in the Incident Response Plan.

Scenario-based simulations are an effective method for applying theoretical knowledge to practical situations. These simulations involve creating realistic cyber threat scenarios that the team may encounter. Participants are tasked with responding to these simulated incidents, allowing them to apply their training in a controlled environment. These simulations provide valuable hands-on experience and help identify potential skills or response strategy gaps.

Tabletop exercises are another key component of training. Unlike scenario-based simulations, tabletop exercises are more discussion-focused and less technically intensive. They typically involve team members walking through a hypothetical incident step by step to discuss their response strategies. This type of exercise is invaluable for testing the Incident Response Plan's theoretical aspects and fostering team communication and decision-making skills.

Full-scale drills take training further by simulating an entire incident in real time. These drills are the most comprehensive training involving the Incident Response Team and other parts of the organization. They provide a realistic experience of what an actual cyber incident would feel like, testing the technical response and the organization's ability to maintain operations during a crisis.

Finally, the feedback and improvement processes are vital to the success of these training and simulation exercises. After each exercise, detailed debriefings and feedback sessions are conducted to analyze the response and identify areas for improvement. Lessons learned are then incorporated into the training programs and Incident Response Plan, ensuring continuous improvement and adaptation to new threats. This training, testing, feedback, and improvement cycle is essential in building and maintaining an effective response capability against cyber threats.

Building a Culture of Security Awareness

Building a culture of security awareness within an organization is fundamental to preparing for cybersecurity incidents. This culture is not just about having policies in place; it's about ingraining security as a core value in every employee's daily activities and decision-making processes.

Employee training and education form the bedrock of this culture. Regular training sessions are essential to keep all employees, not just the IT staff, informed about the latest security threats and best practices. These sessions should cover various topics, from basic cybersecurity hygiene to more advanced concepts, depending on the employee's role and level of access to sensitive information. The aim is to ensure that every organization member understands cybersecurity's importance and role in maintaining it.

Promoting a security-first mindset is about embedding security considerations into every aspect of the business. This means encouraging employees to think proactively about security, whether developing new products, engaging with customers, or managing day-to-day operations. A security-first mindset also involves leadership setting an example, demonstrating a commitment to security in their actions and decisions, and fostering an environment where security is everyone's responsibility.

Regular security briefings are vital for keeping the organization updated on current cybersecurity trends, potential threats, and recent incidents within and in the broader industry. These briefings help maintain employee awareness and vigilance and can be a platform for sharing best practices and reinforcing key security messages.

Phishing and social engineering awareness are critical as these attacks target individuals within the organization. Employees should be trained to recognize and respond appropriately to phishing attempts and other forms of social engineering. This training often includes simulations of phishing emails or social engineering attacks to test employees' awareness and provide practical experience in identifying these threats.

Reporting and escalation procedures are critical components of a security-aware culture. Employees should be clear about what constitutes a security incident and whom to report it to. Clear and straightforward reporting channels should be established and communicated to all employees. Additionally, there should be well-defined escalation procedures to ensure that the appropriate personnel address potential security incidents swiftly and appropriately. Ensuring employees are comfortable and encouraged to report suspicious activities without fear of reprisal is vital to early detection and response to security threats.

Managing Cybersecurity Incidents

The process begins with effective management of actual incidents. This involves activating the Incident Response Plan when a potential threat is detected. The Incident Response Team takes the lead, assessing the situation and implementing the predefined procedures. The key here is to manage the incident efficiently while minimizing organizational disruption. This management includes assessing the severity of the incident, determining the resources needed, and executing the response plan effectively.

Incident detection and validation are the initial steps in managing an incident. This phase involves accurately identifying a potential security threat and confirming its legitimacy. Advanced monitoring systems, alert mechanisms, and skilled cybersecurity personnel are crucial in detecting anomalies that could indicate a cybersecurity incident. Once detected, it's vital to validate these alerts to avoid misallocating resources to false alarms.

Immediate response actions are taken once an incident is validated. These actions are designed to reduce damage as quickly as possible. It could involve isolating affected systems, blocking malicious traffic, or implementing other emergency measures to prevent the spread of the threat. The speed and efficiency of these initial actions can significantly impact the overall severity of the incident.

Coordination of efforts across teams is essential during an incident. While the Incident Response Team leads the charge, coordination with other departments – such as IT, legal, public relations, and human resources – is crucial. This coordination ensures a unified approach to the incident, addressing the technical aspects and legal, communicational, and personnel-related implications.

Documentation and recordkeeping throughout the incident management process are crucial for several reasons. They provide a detailed account of the incident's timeline, actions taken, and resources used. This documentation is invaluable for post-incident analysis, legal compliance, and potential use in criminal investigations. Keeping detailed records also aids in identifying areas for improvement in the organization's response capabilities.

Finally, decision-making under pressure is a critical skill for the Incident Response Team. Cybersecurity incidents often unfold rapidly and can be unpredictable, requiring quick and decisive actions under stressful conditions. Making informed decisions based on the available data and the team's expertise is essential in managing the incident effectively while minimizing its impact on the organization.

Communication Strategies During a Crisis

Internal communication management is the first critical step. It involves disseminating accurate information about the incident to all relevant internal parties, including management, staff, and the IT team. This communication ensures everyone knows the situation and understands their role in the response effort. Effective internal communication helps prevent misinformation and panic, maintains morale, and ensures a unified response to the incident.

External stakeholder notifications are equally important. This involves informing customers, partners, suppliers, and possibly regulators about the incident, particularly if their data or operations could be affected. Timely and transparent communication with these stakeholders is crucial for maintaining trust and meeting regulatory reporting obligations. It's essential to tailor the message to each group, ensuring that it's relevant and clear and addresses their specific concerns or the impact on them.

Media and public relations come into play when the incident gains public attention or is of a nature that requires public disclosure. Handling media relations effectively is crucial for maintaining the organization's reputation. This involves preparing press releases, conducting press conferences if needed, and providing regular updates as more information becomes available. The aim is to be transparent and factual, avoiding speculation and overpromising resolutions.

Crisis communication teams are often formed to manage complex communication tasks during a cybersecurity incident. This team, typically comprising members from communications, legal, and IT departments, is responsible for crafting the message, deciding the communication channels, and timing the release of information. They work closely with the Incident Response Team to ensure the information communicated is accurate and current.

Ensuring message consistency and accuracy throughout the crisis is crucial. Inconsistent or inaccurate messages can lead to confusion, erode trust, and potentially cause legal issues for the organization. All communication should be carefully vetted to ensure it aligns with the facts of the incident and the organization's response strategy. Consistent messaging across all channels and updates is critical to managing the narrative of the incident and upholding the organization's credibility during a crisis.

Technical Aspects of Incident Management

The technical aspects of incident management play a pivotal role in effectively responding to and resolving cybersecurity incidents. These aspects encompass a range of specialized activities and processes focused on understanding, containing, and mitigating the impact of cyber threats.

Network and system forensics are essential components of technical incident management. This process involves examining affected systems and networks to uncover the incident's root cause. Forensic analysis helps in identifying the source of the attack, the method used, and the extent of the damage. This analysis is crucial for understanding how the breach occurred and preventing similar future incidents. Forensic experts utilize specialized tools to collect and analyze digital evidence, ensuring that it is handled in a manner that preserves its integrity for potential legal proceedings.

Data analysis and interpretation are critical in making informed decisions during and after an incident. This involves analyzing the data collected from various sources, such as logs, network traffic, and security alerts, to gain insights into the incident. Effective data analysis helps in identifying patterns and anomalies that could indicate the presence of a cyber threat. Interpreting this data accurately is vital for understanding the incident's scope and guiding the response efforts.

Utilizing cybersecurity tools is integral to managing cybersecurity incidents. These tools range from antivirus software and firewalls to advanced intrusion detection and prevention systems. They are essential for detecting threats, protecting vulnerable assets, and responding to active security incidents. Incident Response Teams rely heavily on these tools to automate certain aspects of the response process, enabling them to focus on more complex tasks that require human intervention.

Containment and mitigation techniques are implemented once a threat is identified. Containment involves isolating affected systems to prevent the spread of the threat, while mitigation refers to the steps taken to reduce the impact of the incident. These techniques are crucial for minimizing damage and restoring normal operations quickly. They require a deep understanding of the organization's network and systems and the ability to implement effective countermeasures rapidly.

Long-term security enhancements are the final step in the technical aspect of incident management. Following an incident, it's essential to analyze the effectiveness of the existing security measures and make improvements where necessary. This could involve updating security policies, enhancing network defenses, or implementing new security technologies. The goal is to strengthen the organization's security posture to withstand future cyber threats better. This proactive approach ensures that lessons learned from incidents are applied to enhance long-term security and resilience.

Legal and Ethical Considerations

Managing cybersecurity incidents involves technical and strategic aspects and crucial legal and ethical considerations. Navigating these considerations effectively is essential to ensure compliance, maintain trust, and minimize legal risks.

Compliance with laws and regulations is a foundational legal consideration. Organizations must adhere to various laws and regulations related to cybersecurity and data protection. These may include industry-specific regulations, national data protection laws, and international frameworks. Non-compliance can lead to significant legal penalties and reputational damage. Therefore, Incident Response Teams must be well-versed in relevant legal requirements and ensure their response strategies align with these regulations.

Ethical handling of sensitive data is a key aspect of managing cybersecurity incidents. Organizations often handle large amounts of sensitive data, including the personal information of customers and employees. During and after a cybersecurity incident, it's crucial to handle this data ethically and responsibly. This includes ensuring the confidentiality of personal information, preventing unauthorized access, and being transparent about any data breaches that may impact individuals' privacy.

Cooperation with law enforcement is often necessary, especially in severe or criminal cyber incidents. This involves working with local, national, or even international law enforcement agencies to support investigations and legal proceedings. Organizations need to establish procedures for how and when to engage with law enforcement, ensuring that they do so in a way that is helpful to the investigation while also protecting their legal interests.

Reporting obligations are a critical legal consideration in incident management. Many jurisdictions require organizations to report certain types of cybersecurity incidents, especially those that involve data breaches or significant threats to user privacy. Understanding these reporting obligations is essential for compliance. Timely and accurate reporting can help mitigate legal repercussions and maintain trust with customers and regulatory bodies.

Finally, managing legal risks and liabilities is an ongoing process. Cybersecurity incidents can expose organizations to various legal risks, including lawsuits from affected parties or penalties from regulatory bodies. Properly managing these risks involves adhering to legal and regulatory requirements and implementing comprehensive cybersecurity measures to prevent incidents. In the event of an incident, it's crucial to have legal experts involved in the response process to navigate any potential legal issues and minimize liabilities.

Psychological and Human Factors

The psychological and human factors in managing cybersecurity incidents are often overlooked but are crucial for the well-being of the Incident Response Team and the effectiveness of their response. These factors significantly shape the team's ability to handle stress, uncertainty, and the demanding nature of crisis situations.

Stress management for responders is paramount. Individuals involved in Incident Response often face high-pressure situations, long hours, and the burden of high-stakes decision-making. Providing resources for stress management, such as counseling services or stress-reduction training, can help responders cope with these pressures. Ensuring team members take breaks and have support mechanisms is vital for maintaining their effectiveness and preventing burnout.

Dealing with uncertainty and chaos is a common challenge in cybersecurity incidents. These situations are often unpredictable, with information changing rapidly and many unknowns. Training responders to manage and operate effectively in such environments is essential. This includes developing flexible response plans, practicing adaptive thinking, and preparing for various scenarios so teams are better equipped to handle unexpected developments.

Leadership in crisis situations is crucial for guiding teams through challenging incidents. Leaders must demonstrate calmness, decisiveness, and clear communication during a crisis. They play a crucial role in setting the tone for the response, managing the flow of information, and ensuring that team members remain focused and coordinated. Effective leadership can significantly impact the team's ability to respond efficiently and maintain morale.

Team dynamics and morale are critical components of a successful response effort. Encouraging collaboration, open communication, and mutual support among team members can enhance the overall response capability. Recognizing and celebrating small victories and learning from setbacks can also help maintain morale. A cohesive team that works well together is more resilient and effective in managing complex incidents.

Supporting mental health is a vital aspect that should not be neglected. Cybersecurity incidents can be stressful and may psychologically impact those involved in the response. Access to mental health resources, such as counseling or peer support programs, is essential. Creating an environment where team members feel comfortable discussing mental health issues and seeking help can contribute significantly to their overall well-being and the effectiveness of the response team.

Addressing the psychological and human factors in incident management is key to maintaining the Incident Response Team's health, morale, and effectiveness. These factors are integral to ensuring that the team is technically capable and psychologically prepared to handle the challenges of cybersecurity incidents.

Post-Incident Analysis and Recovery

The post-incident analysis and recovery phase is critical in the cybersecurity incident management lifecycle. This phase not only aids in understanding what transpired but also in fortifying defenses against future incidents.

Conducting post-incident reviews is the initial step in this phase. These reviews are comprehensive meetings where the Incident Response Team and relevant stakeholders dissect the details of the incident. The objective is to understand the incident's timeline, the effectiveness of the response, and the overall impact on the organization. These reviews are essential for learning from the incident and preparing more robust future response strategies.

Gathering and analyzing incident data is a crucial part of the review process. This involves collecting data from various sources, such as logs, system reports, and team member accounts. Analyzing this data helps in piecing together the sequence of events and understanding how the incident occurred and was subsequently managed. This in-depth analysis is vital for uncovering the incident's root causes and identifying potential areas of vulnerability within the organization's systems and processes.

Identifying successes and shortcomings in the Incident Response is a key outcome of the post-incident review. Successes, such as effective containment measures or efficient team coordination, should be recognized and used as benchmarks for future incidents. Equally important is identifying shortcomings in the response, be it delayed detection, inadequate communication, or any other gaps that might have hindered an adequate response. Acknowledging successes and shortcomings is crucial for a balanced and constructive review process.

Developing improvement plans based on the insights gained from the post-incident analysis is a proactive step toward enhancing cybersecurity resilience. These plans may involve training initiatives, updates to response strategies, investments in new technologies, or changes to internal protocols. The focus is addressing the identified shortcomings and strengthening the organization's cybersecurity posture.

Sharing lessons learned with the broader organization, sometimes even with external partners or industry groups, is beneficial. Disseminating the knowledge and insights gained from the incident helps build a more informed and prepared community. This sharing can be formal reports, training sessions, or informal discussions and contributes to a culture of continuous learning and improvement.

Finally, updating policies and procedures is an essential step in the post-incident recovery process. This involves revising existing security policies, response protocols, and operational procedures based on the lessons learned. Regular updates ensure that these policies and procedures remain effective and relevant, considering the evolving nature of cyber threats. This continual refinement process is key to maintaining an agile and robust cybersecurity framework within the organization.

Recovery Strategies and Resilience Building

The recovery strategies and resilience building phase is an integral component of the post-incident process, focusing on restoring operations and strengthening the organization's defenses against future cyber threats.

System restoration and data recovery are the immediate priorities following an incident. This involves restoring affected systems and data to their original or new, secure state. The process is often challenging, requiring careful planning to ensure no remnants of the threat remain. Data recovery efforts are critical if sensitive information is compromised or lost. The goal is to minimize downtime and data loss, ensuring business operations can resume quickly and smoothly.

Strengthening defenses is a proactive step taken after an incident. This may include upgrading security software, patching vulnerabilities, and enhancing network security measures. It's also about reviewing and improving the organization's cybersecurity policies and practices. The idea is to close the gaps that were exploited in the incident and to fortify defenses against new types of threats that have been identified.

Monitoring for potential reoccurrences is crucial in the aftermath of an incident. Enhanced monitoring helps detect any similar threats or residual impacts from the original incident early. This continuous vigilance is essential, as attackers often attempt to exploit the same vulnerabilities multiple times or may have embedded mechanisms to enable future access.

Building organizational resilience is about developing the capability to respond to and recover from future incidents effectively. This involves not just technological solutions but also cultivating a culture of security awareness, training employees, and implementing robust Incident Response processes. Organizational resilience is enhanced by fostering an environment that can adapt to the changing landscape of cyber threats and withstand and recover from disruptions.

Continual learning and adaptation are key to maintaining and improving cybersecurity posture over time. This involves staying informed about the latest cybersecurity trends, threats, and best practices. Organizations should regularly review and update their cybersecurity strategies, learn from past incidents, and adapt their defenses accordingly. This continuous improvement process ensures that the organization remains prepared and resilient against the evolving nature of cyber threats.

In summary, recovery strategies and resilience building focus on restoring operations post incident, fortifying defenses, maintaining vigilant monitoring, enhancing organizational resilience, and fostering a culture of continual learning and adaptation. This comprehensive approach is essential for organizations to rebound from cyber incidents and to safeguard themselves against future threats.

Impact Assessment and Reporting

The impact assessment and reporting stage is a critical part of the post-incident process, focusing on understanding the full extent of the incident's consequences and communicating these findings to relevant parties.

Assessing financial and operational impacts is the initial step. This assessment quantifies the direct and indirect costs incurred due to the incident. Direct costs may include system repairs, data recovery efforts, and legal fees. In contrast, indirect costs can encompass lost productivity, business disruption, and potential loss of future revenue due to damaged trust. Operational impacts involve evaluating the extent to which the incident disrupted normal business operations and identifying any long-term operational challenges that may have arisen.

Reporting to stakeholders is a crucial aspect of post-incident management. Stakeholders must be informed about the incident and its impacts, including customers, partners, investors, and employees. This communication should be clear, transparent, and timely. It's important to outline the steps taken to address the incident and measures implemented to prevent future occurrences. Effective stakeholder communication helps maintain trust and confidence in the organization's ability to manage cyber threats.

Legal and regulatory reporting is also an essential part of the process. Many jurisdictions require organizations to report specific cyber incidents, especially data breaches or privacy violations. Compliance with these legal and regulatory requirements is critical. Organizations must ensure their reporting is accurate, timely, and in line with the legal obligations specific to their industry and operational location.

Reputation management post-incident is critical to restoring and maintaining public confidence. Cyber incidents can significantly impact an organization's reputation if handled poorly. Proactive reputation management involves addressing the incident and communicating effectively with the public and media. This might include press releases, media briefings, and active engagement on social media platforms.

Future risk assessments are integral to improving cybersecurity posture. After an incident, organizations should reassess their risk landscape. This involves identifying new vulnerabilities or threats, evaluating the effectiveness of current security measures, and determining the likelihood of similar incidents occurring in the future. Regular risk assessments are crucial for avoiding potential threats and ensuring that cybersecurity strategies and defenses are aligned with the evolving risk environment.

In summary, impact assessment and reporting involve a thorough analysis of a cyber incident's financial, operational, and reputational impacts, comprehensive reporting to stakeholders and regulatory bodies, active management of the organization's reputation, and conducting future risk assessments to inform and enhance cybersecurity measures. This comprehensive evaluation and communication process is vital for recovery and strengthening defenses against future cyber threats.

Long-Term Security Strategy Development

Developing a long-term security strategy is an essential component of an organization's overarching approach to cybersecurity, ensuring sustained protection against evolving cyber threats.

Strategic planning for cybersecurity involves setting long-term goals and objectives for an organization's cybersecurity posture. This planning process encompasses assessing current security capabilities, identifying potential threats, and determining the resources required to address these challenges. It's about aligning cybersecurity initiatives with the organization's overall mission and objectives, ensuring that security considerations are integrated into all business operations.

Integrating security into business strategy is crucial for creating a resilient organization. This integration means that cybersecurity is not treated as an isolated IT issue but as a critical business function that impacts all areas of the organization. By embedding security considerations into business decisions, processes, and culture, organizations can ensure a more holistic and effective approach to managing cyber risks.

Investing in advanced security measures is a key part of long-term strategy development. This involves investing in the latest technology solutions, such as AI-driven security tools or advanced threat detection systems, and the human capital and training necessary to use these tools effectively. The aim is to stay ahead of cybercriminals by employing sophisticated defenses that can adapt to the changing tactics and techniques used in cyber attacks.

Fostering a culture of continuous improvement in cybersecurity is vital. This culture encourages regular review and refinement of security policies, procedures, and technologies. It involves learning from past incidents, staying abreast of the latest cybersecurity trends and innovations, and continuously evaluating the organization's security posture. This mindset of ongoing improvement helps organizations stay resilient in the face of an ever-evolving cyber threat landscape.

Collaborating with industry and government entities is also an important element of long-term strategy. Such collaborations can provide insights into emerging threats, best practices, and regulatory expectations. They can also offer opportunities for sharing resources and intelligence, benefiting smaller organizations. Engaging in public-private partnerships, industry groups, and cybersecurity alliances helps build a stronger, more united front against cyber threats.

In summary, developing a long-term security strategy involves strategic planning that aligns cybersecurity with overall business objectives, integrating security into every facet of the business, investing in advanced technologies and skilled personnel, fostering a culture of continuous improvement, and collaborating with external entities. This comprehensive approach is key to building and maintaining a robust, agile cybersecurity posture that can adapt to and withstand future challenges.

The Future and Emerging Trends in Incident Response

In the ever-evolving cybersecurity domain, Incident Response (IR) has become a pivotal aspect of organizational defense strategies. The current landscape of Incident Response is characterized by a complex blend of advanced technologies, skilled professionals, and sophisticated methodologies designed to tackle an array of cyber threats. Today's IR teams are equipped with various tools ranging from intrusion detection systems to comprehensive threat intelligence platforms, enabling them to detect, analyze, and respond to incidents more effectively than ever. However, as cyber threats become increasingly sophisticated, the pressure on these teams to adapt and respond quickly is continually mounting. The current landscape sees a constant cat-and-mouse game between attackers and defenders, with each side continuously evolving its tactics and technologies.

The nature of cybersecurity threats has undergone significant transformation over the years. Initially, cyber-attacks were primarily the work of individual hackers driven by curiosity or a desire for recognition. Today, the threat landscape includes highly organized cybercriminal groups, state-sponsored actors, and advanced persistent threats (APTs). These adversaries employ a range of tactics, from ransomware and phishing to sophisticated supply chain attacks and IoT vulnerabilities. The evolution of these threats has increased the complexity of Incident Response and raised the stakes, with potential impacts ranging from financial losses to national security risks. This evolution demands a proactive and dynamic approach to IR that continuously adapts to the changing tactics and techniques used by cyber adversaries.

The Rise of Artificial Intelligence and Machine Learning

Integrating artificial intelligence (AI) and machine learning (ML) in cybersecurity represents a paradigm shift in approaching threat detection and Incident Response. These technologies are rapidly becoming central to the strategies employed by organizations to defend against increasingly sophisticated cyber threats.

AI and ML have revolutionized threat detection by enabling the analysis of vast amounts of data at speeds and scales unattainable by human analysts. These technologies learn from patterns and anomalies in data, continually improving their ability to detect potential threats. ML algorithms, for instance, can sift through network traffic to identify unusual behaviors that may indicate a breach, such as unusual login attempts or unexpected data exfiltration. AI enhances this capability by identifying threats and suggesting the best course of action to mitigate these threats, thereby augmenting the decision-making process of Incident Response teams.

Predictive analytics, powered by AI and ML, takes a proactive stance in cybersecurity. Instead of merely reacting to incidents as they occur, predictive analytics enables organizations to anticipate and prepare for potential threats. These systems can predict where vulnerabilities will likely be exploited by analyzing historical data and current trends and suggest measures to prevent breaches. This foresight is invaluable in a landscape where preemptive action can save organizations from significant losses and reputational damage.

AI's role in automating Incident Response is perhaps one of its most transformative impacts. Traditional Incident Response can be a resource-intensive and time-consuming process. AI dramatically changes this by automating various aspects of Incident Response, from initial threat detection to implementing mitigation strategies. Automated systems can immediately isolate affected systems, deploy patches, or change access controls in response to a detected threat. This rapid response capability significantly reduces the window of opportunity for attackers to cause damage. Moreover, AI-driven automation frees human responders to focus on more complex tasks that require nuanced judgment and expertise, thereby enhancing the overall efficiency and effectiveness of the Incident Response process.

Cybersecurity in the Era of the Internet of Things (IoT)

The Internet of Things (IoT) proliferation has significantly expanded the cybersecurity landscape. With billions of interconnected devices, each potentially a point of vulnerability, the IoT era presents unique challenges and opportunities for cybersecurity professionals.

IoT devices often lack robust built-in security, making them susceptible to attacks. These vulnerabilities can lead to unauthorized access, data breaches, and even the commandeering of devices for malicious purposes. The heterogeneous nature of IoT devices and their widespread use across various sectors complicates the Incident Response process. Responders must deal with a vast array of device types, each with its configuration, operating system, and security protocols, making standardization of response procedures difficult.

Securing these devices becomes a priority as the IoT landscape continues to grow. This involves implementing stronger security protocols at the device level and ensuring secure communication channels between devices. Manufacturers and developers play a critical role in integrating security into the design phase of IoT products. Additionally, regular firmware updates and patches are essential to address emerging vulnerabilities.

Developing effective Incident Response strategies for IoT environments requires a specialized approach. This includes creating an inventory of all IoT devices within the network to monitor and manage them effectively. Incident Response in IoT also involves segmenting networks to prevent the spread of attacks across devices and deploying IoT-specific security solutions, like specialized intrusion detection systems, to monitor and protect these devices.

The IoT will continue to be a focal point in cybersecurity discussions. Integrating AI and ML for enhanced detection and response in IoT environments and developing more standardized security frameworks specific to IoT are likely to be key focus areas. As IoT technology evolves, so will the strategies and technologies to secure these devices.

Blockchain Technology in Incident Response

Blockchain technology, known for its use in cryptocurrencies, is emerging as a potential solution for enhancing cybersecurity and Incident Response.

Blockchain's decentralized nature and inherent features, like immutability and transparency, offer new ways to secure data and networks. For instance, blockchain can create tamper-proof network activity logs, making detecting and analyzing cyber-attacks easier. Its decentralized structure makes it less susceptible to single points of failure, common targets in cyber attacks.

Incorporating blockchain into incident detection and reporting can enhance the integrity and reliability of these processes. By storing incident data on a blockchain, organizations can ensure that the data is not altered post incident, providing a clear and unchangeable record of events. This can be invaluable in forensic analysis and in cases where legal evidence is required.

While blockchain presents significant opportunities for cybersecurity, it's not without its limitations. The technology is still in its nascent stages, and there are concerns about scalability, speed, and the resource-intensive nature of some blockchain implementations. Additionally, the integration of blockchain into existing cybersecurity infrastructures can be challenging. Despite these challenges, the potential of blockchain in transforming Incident Response and cybersecurity remains a promising area for future development.

Preparing for the Future of Incident Response

As we look to the future, the Incident Response field is poised for significant transformations driven by technological advancements and shifts in the cyber threat landscape. Emerging technologies like artificial intelligence (AI) and machine learning (ML) are set to redefine how IR teams detect and respond to threats, offering unprecedented speed and efficiency. The increasing interconnectedness of devices and systems through the Internet of Things (IoT) presents new challenges and opportunities for Incident Response. Additionally, the growing emphasis on regulatory compliance and data privacy shapes how organizations approach IR, making it more structured and accountable. The future of Incident Response is not just about technological advancements; it also encompasses a broader understanding of cybersecurity's social, political, and ethical implications. Preparing for this future requires a holistic approach that integrates cutting-edge technology with a deep understanding of the evolving cyber threat landscape and its broader impacts on society.

Case Study: The Cash App Breach and Its Incident Response Shortcomings

Cash App, a widely used mobile payment service, experienced a significant data breach that compromised the sensitive information of millions of its users. The breach was initiated through a sophisticated phishing attack targeting the company's employees, leading to unauthorized access to Cash App's internal systems. This case study delves into the Incident Response efforts of Cash App, highlighting the shortcomings and the lessons that can be learned.

The breach unfolded with a phishing attack, where cybercriminals successfully tricked Cash App employees into revealing their credentials. This breach of security protocols allowed the attackers to access the company's internal customer support systems. Consequently, they accessed a wealth of personal information, including users' names, account numbers, and transaction histories.

Incident Response Shortcomings

1. **Delayed Detection and Response**: The breach initially went undetected for a considerable period, giving attackers enough time to harvest sensitive data. This delay in detection indicated a deficiency in effective monitoring and alert systems, which should have been capable of promptly identifying unusual activities within the internal systems.

2. **Inadequate Employee Training**: The susceptibility of employees to the phishing attack pointed to a lack of robust training in recognizing and responding to cybersecurity threats. Regular and comprehensive cybersecurity awareness programs for employees, particularly those with access to sensitive information, were lacking.

3. **Communication Failures**: The communication with users following the breach was neither prompt nor clear, leading to widespread confusion and erosion of trust among customers. Internally, the communication was also fragmented, resulting in an uncoordinated and ineffective response to the incident.

4. **Poor Coordination of Response Efforts**: The response to the breach was marked by a lack of cohesive strategy, with various departments operating independently rather than as part of a unified response team. This disorganization led to delays in containing the breach and mitigating its impacts.

5. **Ineffective Public Relations Strategy**: The company's approach to public relations after the breach was more reactive than proactive, failing to manage the public narrative effectively. This inadequacy in handling public relations further harmed the company's reputation and eroded customer trust.

The Cash App breach underscores the importance of robust detection and monitoring tools to identify and respond to breaches swiftly. It highlights the necessity of regular and comprehensive employee cybersecurity training, especially for those with access to critical systems and data. Effective communication, both internally and with customers, is crucial in managing the aftermath of a breach. A coordinated Incident Response effort is essential for efficient containment and recovery. Lastly, a proactive public relations strategy is vital in maintaining trust and managing the narrative during a crisis.

Career Corner

A career in Incident Response is a critical and dynamic area within cybersecurity, focusing on addressing and managing the aftermath of security breaches and cyber-attacks. This field is essential for rapidly identifying, containing, and mitigating the impact of security incidents, thereby protecting organizational assets and reputation. It offers opportunities for those interested in fast-paced, problem-solving roles within cybersecurity.

One of the critical roles in Incident Response is that of an Incident Responder or Incident Response Analyst. These professionals are the frontline defenders when a cybersecurity incident occurs. They are responsible for quickly identifying and analyzing security breaches, conducting initial investigations, and executing steps to contain and mitigate the impact. Their swift actions are crucial in preventing further damage and beginning the recovery process.

Another significant position is that of an Incident Response Manager or Coordinator. Individuals in this role oversee the Incident Response process and team. They ensure that response strategies are implemented effectively and that the incident is managed according to established procedures. Their role includes coordinating with different departments, managing communications during a crisis, and ensuring a systematic and organized approach to handling incidents.

The role of a Forensic Analyst is also vital in the Incident Response lifecycle. Post-incident Forensic Analysts delve deep into the cause and method of the breach. They analyze compromised systems, uncover how an attack was carried out, and gather evidence for potential legal action. Their detailed analysis is crucial for understanding the attack vector and preventing future incidents.

For those interested in a broader strategic view, the Cyber Incident Response Director or Chief Information Security Officer (CISO) position focusing on Incident Response might be appealing. These senior professionals develop and oversee the organization's Incident Response strategy. They ensure that the organization is prepared to respond to incidents and that robust response plans align Incident Response with the overall cybersecurity strategy.

Professionals in Incident Response often pursue relevant certifications to enhance their skills and career prospects. Certifications such as the Certified Incident Handler (GCIH), Certified Computer Security Incident Handler (CSIH), and Certified Information Systems Security Professional (CISSP) are widely recognized in the field. These certifications provide knowledge on handling and responding to security incidents and understanding broader cybersecurity principles.

Individuals in this career path must possess strong problem-solving skills, the ability to work under pressure, and excellent communication abilities. They need to deeply understand cybersecurity threats, attack methodologies, and a broad array of defensive technologies. They should also be adept at collaborating with various organizational teams and departments.

A career in Incident Response offers a range of challenging and rewarding opportunities. From being on the front lines addressing security breaches to managing the overall Incident Response strategy, professionals in this field play a crucial role in protecting organizations from the evolving landscape of cyber threats. Continuous learning and staying abreast of cybersecurity trends and technologies are essential in this vital, fast-paced field.

Chapter Questions

1. What is the primary goal of Incident Response (IR) in cybersecurity?

    A. To improve network speed

    B. To manage and handle security breaches effectively

    C. To enhance software development

    D. To increase sales and marketing efforts

2. What does the scope of Incident Response cover?

    A. Only technical aspects

    B. Only legal aspects

    C. Detection, analysis, containment, eradication, and recovery

    D. Only public relations

3. What is crucial for an effective Incident Response strategy in modern cybersecurity?

    A. Focusing only on reactive measures

    B. Mitigating attack damages and building customer trust

    C. Ignoring proactive strategies

    D. Reducing training exercises

4. What has been a significant change in the evolution of Incident Response?

    A. Moving from proactive to only reactive measures

    B. Inclusion of proactive strategies like threat hunting

    C. Decreasing the use of technology in response

    D. Limiting the response to technical teams only

5. What is a critical principle in Incident Response?

    A. Avoiding communication with stakeholders

    B. Prioritizing cost over security

    C. Rapid detection of threats

    D. Decreasing the frequency of training

6. What is the first step in the Incident Response Process?

    A. Eradication of risks

    B. Recovery measures

    C. Identification of threats

    D. Post-incident activities

7. What is critical during the containment stage of Incident Response?

    A. Increasing the spread of the incident

    B. Limiting the impact of the incident

    C. Ignoring affected systems

    D. Permanent shutdown of services

8. What is essential for the eradication of risks in Incident Response?

    A. Keeping vulnerable software un-updated

    B. Collaboration with external experts

    C. Avoiding the use of specialized tools

    D. Overlooking security loopholes

9. What is vital for an effective Incident
    Response Team?

    A. Having a team with identical skills

    B. Diverse skills and clear roles

    C. Limited training and development

    D. Working without external support

10. What role do AI and ML play in Incident Response?

    A. Slowing down the threat detection process

    B. Enhancing threat detection and response

    C. Reducing the accuracy of data analysis

    D. Ignoring predictive analytics

11. Why is securing IoT devices a challenge in Incident
    Response?

    A. Due to their robust built-in security

    B. IoT devices lack robust built-in security

    C. IoT devices are not used widely

    D. IoT devices do not connect to networks

12. What is the benefit of incorporating blockchain in
    Incident Response?

    A. Decreasing data transparency

    B. Creating tamper-proof logs

    C. Centralizing data storage

    D. Reducing data integrity

13. What is a critical consideration in the post-incident analysis and recovery phase?

    A. Avoiding the analysis of incident data

    B. Identifying successes and shortcomings

    C. Not updating policies and procedures

    D. Limiting lessons learned to internal teams

14. What is a critical aspect of long-term security strategy development?

    A. Separating security from business strategy

    B. Investing in outdated security measures

    C. Integrating security into business strategy

    D. Avoiding collaboration with external entities

15. What marks a significant transformation in the future of Incident Response?

    A. Reducing the use of emerging technologies

    B. Embracing emerging technologies like AI and ML

    C. Ignoring the evolution of cyber threats

    D. Solely focusing on traditional methods

Correction to: Mastering Cybersecurity

Correction to:

Dr. Jason Edwards, Mastering Cybersecurity,
https://doi.org/10.1007/979-8-8688-0297-3

This book was published with an incorrect copyright holder name **The Editor(s) (if applicable) and The Author(s), under exclusive license to APress Media, LLC, part of Springer Nature** in the Front matter copyright page and all the chapter-opening pages. This has now been updated with the correct copyright holder name **Dr. Jason Edwards** in the Front matter copyright page and all the chapter-opening pages.

The updated version of this book can be found at
https://doi.org/10.1007/979-8-8688-0297-3

Answers with Explanations

Chapter 2

1. **Correct Answer: A. To encrypt a victim's data and demand a ransom for decryption.** Ransomware is a type of malware that encrypts the victim's files, making them inaccessible, and then demands a ransom from the victim to decrypt the files. This type of attack primarily aims at financial gain through the ransom paid by the victim.

2. **Correct Answer: B. Intercepting and possibly altering communication.** Man-in-the-middle (MitM) attacks involve an attacker secretly intercepting and possibly altering the communication between two parties who believe they are directly communicating with each other. These attacks exploit security weaknesses to eavesdrop or manipulate the data being exchanged.

Dr. J. Edwards, *Mastering Cybersecurity*, https://doi.org/10.1007/979-8-8688-0297-3

3. **Correct Answer: B. An attack that targets vulnerabilities unknown to the vendor.** A zero-day exploit is a cyberattack that targets vulnerabilities in software or hardware that are unknown to the vendor or the public. These vulnerabilities have not been patched or addressed because they are not yet known to the vendor.

4. **Correct Answer: B. Phishing.** Phishing is a deceptive tactic used by cybercriminals to obtain sensitive information from victims. It typically involves sending fraudulent emails or messages that mimic legitimate sources to trick recipients into revealing personal information like login credentials and credit card numbers.

5. **Correct Answer: C. Prolonged and stealthy presence in a network.** Advanced persistent threats (APTs) represent a category of cyberattacks where an unauthorized user gains access to a network and remains undetected for an extended period. The key characteristic of APTs is their stealthy and prolonged nature, aiming to steal data or monitor network activity over time.

6. **Correct Answer: C. Phishing, malware, and hacking of personal accounts.** Individuals often face cyber threats such as phishing, malware, and hacking due to a lack of cybersecurity awareness and the personal nature of their online activities.

7. **Correct Answer: C. Threats to operational integrity and data security.** Businesses face cyber threats aiming at financial gain, data theft, and disruption of operations, posing risks to their operational integrity and data security.

8. **Correct Answer: C. State-sponsored cyber espionage.** Governmental bodies are susceptible to sophisticated state-sponsored cyber espionage targeting critical national infrastructure and sensitive government data.

9. **Correct Answer: B. The sensitive nature of patient data.** Healthcare institutions hold sensitive patient data, making them attractive targets for cybercriminals looking to exploit this information.

10. **Correct Answer: B. Intellectual property and personal data.** Educational institutions are targeted for cyberattacks due to the valuable intellectual property and personal information they possess.

11. **Correct Answer: B. Financial gain from assets and data.** Financial institutions are prime targets for cyberattacks due to the significant monetary assets and financial data they manage, offering lucrative payoffs for cybercriminals.

12. **Correct Answer: B. System slowdowns and file corruption.** Early viruses and worms primarily caused inconvenience by slowing down systems and corrupting files, rather than being designed for financial gain or espionage.

13. **Correct Answer: B. Proliferation of online banking and ecommerce.** The rise of financially motivated malware coincided with the growth of online banking and ecommerce, targeting financial assets and personal identities.

14. **Correct Answer: C. National infrastructure and sensitive data.** State-sponsored cyber espionage typically focuses on disrupting national security and stealing sensitive information related to government operations.

15. **Correct Answer: B. Increased use of AI-powered attacks.** Over time, cyberattacks have become more sophisticated, with increased utilization of advanced technologies like AI to make attacks more effective and adaptive.

Chapter 3

1. **Correct Answer: B. To manipulate people into divulging confidential information.** Social engineering in cybersecurity is primarily about manipulating individuals to break security protocols and reveal sensitive information, exploiting the human tendency to trust.

2. **Correct Answer: C. Impersonation.** Impersonation is a common tactic in social engineering, where attackers pretend to be someone else to gain trust and manipulate their target into taking undesirable actions.

3. **Correct Answer: B. Focus on exploiting human psychology.** Social engineering sets itself apart from other cyber threats by exploiting human psychology, leveraging emotions and cognitive biases rather than relying on technical hacking techniques.

4. **Correct Answer: C. Appearing to be from reputable sources.** Phishing attacks, a form of social engineering, typically involve emails that appear to be from reputable sources to trick recipients into divulging sensitive information.

5. **Correct Answer: B. Fabricating a situation to gain information.** Pretexting in social engineering involves creating a false scenario to deceive someone into providing confidential information, exploiting their trust or authority.

6. **Correct Answer: B. Confirmation bias.** Confirmation bias, a tendency to favor information that confirms existing beliefs, is commonly exploited in social engineering to manipulate targets' decisions and actions.

7. **Correct Answer: B. Gaining physical access to restricted areas.** Tailgating in social engineering refers to unauthorized persons gaining physical access to restricted areas by following closely behind authorized individuals, exploiting social norms of politeness.

8. **Correct Answer: B. By leveraging feelings like fear and trust.** Emotional manipulation in social engineering leverages emotions such as fear and trust to influence targets' behavior, often bypassing rational decision-making processes.

717

9. **Correct Answer: B. Reciprocity.** The principle of reciprocity is exploited in social engineering when attackers do small favors for their targets, expecting that this will make the targets more inclined to assist them in return.

10. **Correct Answer: B. Identity theft.** Identity theft is a significant risk in the digital age due to social engineering, where attackers use deceptive means to impersonate individuals and access their financial or personal information.

11. **Correct Answer: C. Develop critical thinking skills.** Developing critical thinking skills is essential in safeguarding against social engineering, as it involves questioning information and motives, thereby reducing susceptibility to manipulation.

12. **Correct Answer: C. Employee awareness programs.** Employee awareness programs are crucial in combating social engineering in the workplace as they educate staff about recognizing and responding to various forms of attacks.

13. **Correct Answer: B. Artificial intelligence (AI).** Artificial intelligence (AI) poses new risks for social engineering, offering tools that can automate and personalize attacks, making them more convincing and harder to detect.

14. **Correct Answer: B. More sophisticated deception methods.** Technological advancements are expected to lead to more sophisticated deception methods in social engineering, enhancing the complexity and effectiveness of attacks.

15. **Correct Answer: D. Detecting and responding to attacks.** AI plays a significant role in preventing social engineering by helping to detect and respond to attacks more efficiently, analyzing patterns and predicting potential threats.

Chapter 4

1. **Correct Answer: A. Encrypting and decrypting information.** Cyber cryptography focuses on encrypting (coding) and decrypting (decoding) information to secure data from unauthorized access, manipulation, or theft.

2. **Correct Answer: B. Information is hidden from unauthorized users.** Confidentiality in cryptography ensures that sensitive information is kept secret and inaccessible to unauthorized users, protecting private data.

3. **Correct Answer: B. SSL/TLS.** SSL (Secure Sockets Layer) and TLS (Transport Layer Security) are protocols used in web browsing to secure online transactions by encrypting the data transmitted between web servers and clients.

4. **Correct Answer: C. Simple substitution cipher.** Early methods of cryptography, such as those used by Egyptians and Spartans, included simple substitution ciphers, where letters in a message were systematically replaced with other letters.

5. **Correct Answer: C. Allied decryption of the Enigma machine.** During World War II, a significant advancement in cryptographic history was the Allied forces' decryption of the German Enigma machine, which had a profound impact on the war's outcome.

6. **Correct Answer: B. The same key for both processes.** Symmetric cryptography uses the same key for both encryption and decryption processes, making it efficient for scenarios where large volumes of data need to be encrypted.

7. **Correct Answer: B. Key length.** In symmetric algorithms, the length of the key is a critical factor in determining the security level. Longer keys are harder to crack using brute-force methods, providing greater security.

8. **Correct Answer: B. Asymmetric.** Asymmetric cryptography uses two different keys for encryption and decryption processes: a public key for encryption and a private key for decryption.

9. **Correct Answer: B. To create a unique, fixed-size hash value from input data.** Hash functions in cryptography are used to convert input data into a unique, fixed-size string (hash), ensuring data integrity and making it nearly impossible to derive the original input from the hash.

10. **Correct Answer: B. Public Key Infrastructure (PKI).** In PKI systems, root Certificate Authorities are at the top of the trust hierarchy, issuing certificates to subordinate CAs and establishing a chain of trust.

11. **Correct Answer: B. To develop algorithms secure against quantum attacks.** The goal of post-quantum cryptography is to create cryptographic algorithms that can withstand the potential capabilities of quantum computers, which may be able to break current encryption methods.

12. **Correct Answer: A. Computations on encrypted data.** Homomorphic encryption allows for performing computations on encrypted data without needing to decrypt it first, maintaining data privacy and security even during processing.

13. **Correct Answer: A. To prove a statement is true without revealing any information about the statement.** Zero-knowledge proofs are used in cryptography to verify the truth of a statement without disclosing any information other than the fact that the statement is true, enhancing privacy and security in authentication and transactions.

14. **Correct Answer: B. The complexity of cryptographic systems for user adoption.** The challenge of balancing security with usability in cryptography involves designing systems that are both robustly secure and user-friendly to encourage wider adoption and correct usage.

15. **Correct Answer: A. The balance between security and individual rights.** Ethical considerations in cryptography include addressing how cryptographic technologies impact privacy and security, ensuring they benefit society while respecting individual rights and freedoms.

Chapter 5

1. **Correct Answer: B. To ensure business continuity and success.** Network security is crucial for the continuity and success of modern enterprises, as it protects against threats that can disrupt business operations and cause financial and reputational damage.

2. **Correct Answer: B. Protecting sensitive data.** At the core of network security is the protection of sensitive data, including personal information, financial records, and intellectual property, from unauthorized access and breaches.

3. **Correct Answer: C. Network threats.** Network threats have evolved significantly over time, transitioning from simple viruses and worms to more sophisticated forms such as advanced persistent threats (APTs).

4. **Correct Answer: D. To continuously verify every access request.** The Zero Trust model operates on the principle of continuous verification of every access request, ensuring only authenticated and authorized users and devices can access network resources.

5. **Correct Answer: B. Confidentiality, integrity, and availability.** The CIA triad in network security stands for confidentiality, integrity, and availability, representing the foundational principles for securing information systems.

6. **Correct Answer: B. Artificial intelligence and machine learning.** AI and ML are increasingly used in network security for threat detection and analysis, leveraging their capabilities to identify patterns and anomalies indicative of cyber threats.

7. **Correct Answer: B. Filters devices based on their unique MAC address.** MAC address filtering in Wi-Fi networks is a security measure that allows or blocks devices from accessing the network based on their unique Media Access Control (MAC) address.

8. **Correct Answer: B. Stateful firewall.** A stateful firewall keeps track of the state of active connections and makes decisions based on the context of the traffic, unlike stateless firewalls which filter traffic solely based on source and destination.

9. **Correct Answer: B. To create secure, encrypted connections over public networks.** VPNs are used in network security to create secure, encrypted connections over public networks, ensuring safe and private data transmission, especially important for remote access.

10. **Correct Answer: B. To identify potential weaknesses in a network.** Vulnerability scanning is a proactive security measure that uses specialized tools to identify known vulnerabilities in a network, helping organizations to address security risks.

11. **Correct Answer: C. Role-based access control (RBAC).** Role-based access control (RBAC) assigns access rights based on roles within an organization, streamlining permission management based on job functions.

723

12. **Correct Answer: B. To address vulnerabilities that attackers could exploit.** Patch management strategies involve identifying, testing, and installing patches to address vulnerabilities in systems and software, crucial for protecting against potential cyber attacks.

13. **Correct Answer: B. Blocking suspicious traffic.** Intrusion prevention systems (IPS) are designed to block suspicious traffic, actively preventing potential threats from causing harm to the network.

14. **Correct Answer: B. Dealing with scalability and integration with existing systems.** One of the main challenges in adopting blockchain technology in network security is managing scalability and effectively integrating it with existing network systems.

15. **Correct Answer: C. Increased use of AI and quantum computing.** The future of network security is likely to involve increased use of advanced technologies like AI and quantum computing to counter sophisticated cyber threats.

Chapter 6

1. **Correct Answer: B. To protect digital assets from threats.** Application security aims to safeguard applications from various cyber threats and vulnerabilities, ensuring the protection of both data and the functionality of applications.

2. **Correct Answer: B. Loss of sensitive data.** Security breaches can lead to the loss of sensitive data, which can have severe consequences for organizations, including financial loss and damage to their reputation.

3. **Correct Answer: C. To sustain customer trust and relationships.** Robust application security is essential for maintaining customer trust and relationships, as security breaches can lead to a loss of confidence and negatively impact the business's bottom line.

4. **Correct Answer: B. Legal actions and financial penalties.** Besides losing data, organizations may face legal actions and financial penalties due to a security breach, highlighting the importance of proactive application security measures.

5. **Correct Answer: B. To keep up with evolving cyber threats.** Organizations need to continuously adapt their security strategies to address the constantly changing nature of cyber threats and to protect their digital assets effectively.

6. **Correct Answer: B. Understanding fundamental security principles.** The foundation of effective defense strategies in application security is understanding and implementing fundamental security principles and best practices.

7. **Correct Answer: C. Only authorized individuals access sensitive information.** The "confidentiality" aspect of the CIA triad ensures that sensitive information is accessible only to those who are authorized, protecting it from unauthorized access.

8. **Correct Answer: C. Incorporating security from the start.** Integrating the security development lifecycle (SDLC) into application development is beneficial because it incorporates security considerations right from the planning stage, making the process more effective.

9. **Correct Answer: B. To identify and assess potential security threats.** Threat modeling is a process used in application security to systematically identify and assess potential security threats, which helps in prioritizing security efforts.

10. **Correct Answer: C. Incorporating security measures from the design phase.** A principle of Security by Design is to incorporate security measures from the outset of application design, ensuring that security is an integral part of the application.

11. **Correct Answer: B. To protect against malicious inputs.** Input validation in secure coding practices is crucial for protecting applications from malicious inputs, which helps in maintaining data integrity and reliability.

12. **Correct Answer: B. To test the application without internal knowledge.** Black-box testing involves testing an application without any prior knowledge of its internal workings, effectively simulating an external hacking attempt.

13. **Correct Answer: B. To provide an in-depth security analysis.** Manual code reviews in white-box testing are important because they provide an in-depth and nuanced view of potential security issues that automated tools might miss.

14. **Correct Answer: B. They identify runtime vulnerabilities.** Dynamic Application Security Testing (DAST) tools are valuable because they identify vulnerabilities in web applications in their running state, which might not be apparent in the static code.

15. **Correct Answer: B. To ensure security considerations throughout the development.** Integrating threat modeling into the software development lifecycle (SDLC) is important as it ensures that security is considered at every phase of development, from planning to maintenance.

Chapter 7

1. **Correct Answer: C. Flexible resources and rapid innovation.** Cloud computing offers flexible resources and rapid innovation, allowing users to scale and innovate faster than traditional computing methods.

2. **Correct Answer: B. On-demand availability.** Cloud computing is characterized by on-demand availability, allowing users to access resources whenever needed without upfront costs or complexity.

3. **Correct Answer: C. Hosted by third-party providers and shared among organizations.** Public clouds are hosted and managed by third-party providers and are shared across multiple organizations, offering scalability and cost-effectiveness.

4. **Correct Answer: B. Platform as a Service (PaaS).** PaaS includes operating systems, middleware, and development tools, providing a platform for software development without managing underlying infrastructure.

5. **Correct Answer: B. Delivering software over the internet on a subscription basis.** SaaS delivers software applications over the internet, eliminating the need for installations and maintenance on user devices.

6. **Correct Answer: B. An intergalactic computer network.** J.C.R. Licklider's vision of an "intergalactic computer network" laid the foundational concept for what would become cloud computing.

7. **Correct Answer: B. A form of distributed and parallel computing.** Grid computing is a type of distributed and parallel computing involving a network of loosely connected computers working together.

8. **Correct Answer: B. Microsoft Azure.** Microsoft Azure is known for its strong emphasis on hybrid cloud capabilities, allowing businesses to integrate on-premises data centers with the Azure cloud.

9. **Correct Answer: B. Data security and privacy.**
With the increasing adoption of cloud technologies, data security and privacy have become primary concerns, requiring robust protection measures.

10. **Correct Answer: C. Securing their data within the cloud.** In the shared responsibility model, customers are responsible for securing their data within the cloud, including managing access and protecting client-side data.

11. **Correct Answer: A. Assigns users to specific roles and grants access based on those roles.**
RBAC in cloud security assigns users to roles and grants access accordingly, minimizing the risk of unauthorized access.

12. **Correct Answer: B. Effective key management.**
Key management is critical in data encryption, ensuring secure storage, distribution, and access control of encryption keys.

13. **Correct Answer: B. To secure data during transmission.** TLS is used to secure data as it moves across networks, ensuring confidentiality and integrity during transmission.

14. **Correct Answer: B. Zero Trust Architecture.** Zero Trust Architecture represents a fundamental shift in cybersecurity, operating under the assumption that trust must always be verified, regardless of location or network.

15. **Correct Answer: A. To simulate real-world attacks and identify vulnerabilities.** Ethical hacking and red teaming simulate real-world attacks to identify and address vulnerabilities in cloud environments proactively.

Chapter 8

1. **Correct Answer: C. Flexible resources and rapid innovation.** Cloud computing offers flexible resources and rapid innovation, allowing users to scale and innovate faster than traditional computing methods.

2. **Correct Answer: B. On-demand availability.** Cloud computing is characterized by on-demand availability, allowing users to access resources whenever needed without up-front costs or complexity.

3. **Correct Answer: C. Hosted by third-party providers and shared among organizations.** Public clouds are hosted and managed by third-party providers and are shared across multiple organizations, offering scalability and cost-effectiveness.

4. **Correct Answer: B. Platform as a Service (PaaS).** PaaS includes operating systems, middleware, and development tools, providing a platform for software development without managing underlying infrastructure.

5. **Correct Answer: B. Delivering software over the Internet on a subscription basis.** SaaS delivers software applications over the Internet, eliminating the need for installations and maintenance on user devices.

6. **Correct Answer: B. An intergalactic computer network.** J.C.R. Licklider's vision of an "intergalactic computer network" laid the foundational concept for what would become cloud computing.

7. **Correct Answer: B. A form of distributed and parallel computing.** Grid computing is a type of distributed and parallel computing involving a network of loosely connected computers working together.

8. **Correct Answer: B. Microsoft Azure.** Microsoft Azure is known for its strong emphasis on hybrid cloud capabilities, allowing businesses to integrate on-premises data centers with the Azure cloud.

9. **Correct Answer: B. Data security and privacy.** With the increasing adoption of cloud technologies, data security and privacy have become primary concerns, requiring robust protection measures.

10. **Correct Answer: C. Securing their data within the cloud.** In the shared responsibility model, customers are responsible for securing their data within the cloud, including managing access and protecting client-side data.

11. **Correct Answer: A. Assigns users to specific roles and grants access based on those roles.** RBAC in cloud security assigns users to roles and grants access accordingly, minimizing the risk of unauthorized access.

12. **Correct Answer: B. Effective key management.** Key management is critical in data encryption, ensuring secure storage, distribution, and access control of encryption keys.

13. **Correct Answer: B. To secure data during transmission.** TLS is used to secure data as it moves across networks, ensuring confidentiality and integrity during transmission.

14. **Correct Answer: B. Zero Trust Architecture.** Zero Trust Architecture represents a fundamental shift in cybersecurity, operating under the assumption that trust must always be verified, regardless of location or network.

15. **Correct Answer: A. To simulate real-world attacks and identify vulnerabilities.** Ethical hacking and red teaming simulate real-world attacks to proactively identify and address vulnerabilities in cloud environments.

Chapter 9

1. **Correct Answer: B. To connect physical devices to the Internet.** IoT aims to extend Internet connectivity to a diverse range of physical devices, enabling them to collect and exchange data, thus integrating the digital and physical worlds.

2. **Correct Answer: C. Ability to connect and exchange data.** IoT devices are characterized by their ability to connect to the Internet and other devices, facilitating data exchange and communication within the IoT ecosystem.

3. **Correct Answer: B. Industrial automation.** IoT technology is extensively used in industrial automation to improve efficiency and safety, with devices such as sensors and actuators playing a key role in monitoring and controlling industrial processes.

4. **Correct Answer: B. Confidentiality, integrity, and availability of data.** IoT security focuses on protecting the data collected and transmitted by IoT devices, ensuring its confidentiality, integrity, and availability against cyber threats.

5. **Correct Answer: B. Diverse range of devices with limited security.** One of the main challenges in IoT security is securing a wide array of devices, many of which have limited processing power and memory, making them vulnerable to cyberattacks.

6. **Correct Answer: B. Cloud computing.** Cloud computing provides the computational power and resources necessary for processing and analyzing the large volumes of data generated by IoT devices.

7. **Correct Answer: B. To reduce data processing time by processing data near the source.** Edge computing in IoT involves processing data close to where it is generated, reducing latency and bandwidth usage, and enhancing the responsiveness of IoT applications.

8. **Correct Answer: B. Lightweight messaging.** MQTT is a protocol designed for low-bandwidth, high-latency environments in IoT, offering an efficient and lightweight messaging system for device communication.

9. **Correct Answer: C. To detect and prevent threats.** AI and ML are used in IoT security to analyze data and identify patterns that indicate potential security threats, enabling proactive threat detection and prevention.

10. **Correct Answer: B. Breaking traditional cryptographic algorithms.** Quantum computing presents a threat to IoT security by potentially breaking many of the cryptographic algorithms currently used to secure data and communications.

11. **Correct Answer: C. To control resource access based on user roles.** Role-based access control in IoT is important for managing access to resources, ensuring that users and devices only have access to the information and functionalities necessary for their specific roles.

12. **Correct Answer: B. Starting devices with verified and trusted software.** The secure boot process in IoT devices ensures that they start up with software that has been verified as authentic and secure, protecting against the execution of malicious code.

13. **Correct Answer: B. To protect data confidentiality during transmission.** Data encryption in IoT is used to secure data as it is transmitted between devices and systems, ensuring that it remains confidential and protected from unauthorized access.

14. **Correct Answer: B. To protect against unauthorized data access.** Secure API design in IoT backend systems is crucial for protecting APIs from security threats such as unauthorized access, data breaches, and denial-of-service attacks.

15. **Correct Answer: B. To effectively address security incidents.** Incident response planning in IoT is essential for quickly and effectively identifying, containing, and recovering from security incidents, minimizing their impact on IoT systems and operations.

Chapter 10

1. **Correct Answer: B. Collecting and analyzing data for legal evidence.** Digital forensics combines elements of law and computer science to analyze data from various digital sources for use as evidence in legal contexts.

2. **Correct Answer: C. A broad range of devices and data types.** Digital forensics has expanded beyond computer crime to encompass a wide range of digital devices and data sources, reflecting the diverse nature of modern technology.

3. **Correct Answer: C. The increasing sophistication of technology and cybercriminals.** The field of digital forensics evolved to keep pace with the advanced techniques employed by cybercriminals and the rapid growth in digital technology.

4. **Correct Answer: C. Owing to the proliferation of digital devices and data.** The growing volume of digital data and the widespread use of digital devices have made forensic expertise more crucial in various legal and investigative scenarios.

5. **Correct Answer: C. The increasing use of computers in society.** The growing need to analyze data from computers and digital storage for legal purposes was a key factor in the development of digital forensics.

6. **Correct Answer: B. Metadata and logs.** Metadata and logs are foundational elements in digital forensics, providing critical information about file activities and system operations.

7. **Correct Answer: C. Maintaining the integrity of data.** Ensuring that digital evidence remains unaltered from the point of collection to presentation in court is essential for its admissibility and credibility.

8. **Correct Answer: C. The diversity of devices and operating systems.** The wide range of mobile devices and operating systems presents a significant challenge in mobile forensics, requiring a broad knowledge base and diverse tools.

9. **Correct Answer: B. Examining network traffic and logs.** Analyzing network data is crucial in identifying signs of unauthorized access or malicious activities within a network.

10. **Correct Answer: C. Dynamic nature of cloud environments.** The constantly changing and distributed nature of cloud services poses significant challenges in forensic investigations.

11. **Correct Answer: C. Introduction of AI and machine learning.** The use of AI and machine learning has brought advanced analytical capabilities to digital forensics, aiding in the efficient processing and analysis of large datasets.

12. **Correct Answer: C. IoT forensics.** IoT forensics involves investigating interconnected devices that are constantly exchanging data, presenting unique forensic challenges.

13. **Correct Answer: C. Adapting to sophisticated cybercrimes.** Anticipated future trends in digital forensics include adapting investigative techniques to handle increasingly complex and sophisticated cybercrimes.

14. **Correct Answer: B. Developing tools for novel types of data.** As emerging technologies create new types of digital evidence, developing appropriate forensic tools and methods is crucial.

15. **Correct Answer: B. Navigating evolving laws and ethical dilemmas.** Digital forensics professionals must continually adapt to changing legal and ethical landscapes, particularly in areas of privacy and data protection.

Chapter 11

1. **Correct Answer: B. To streamline cybersecurity efforts.** The identification and categorization of system vulnerabilities are essential for understanding the security landscape and prioritizing which vulnerabilities require immediate attention and remediation, thereby streamlining cybersecurity efforts.

2. **Correct Answer: C. Software bugs.** Software bugs, often resulting from coding errors, can lead to unexpected and exploitable system behaviors, making them a common form of system vulnerability.

3. **Correct Answer: C. They detect known vulnerabilities efficiently.** Automated vulnerability scanners play a crucial role in cybersecurity by efficiently detecting known vulnerabilities in software and network configurations.

4. **Correct Answer: B. It uncovers more nuanced and complex vulnerabilities.** Manual testing is indispensable in vulnerability assessment as it helps in uncovering more nuanced and complex vulnerabilities that automated tools might miss.

5. **Correct Answer: B. They may not detect zero-day exploits.** One limitation of relying solely on automated vulnerability scanners is that they may not always identify zero-day exploits or highly complex security weaknesses that require a nuanced understanding.

6. **Correct Answer: C. To keep up with evolving threats and vulnerabilities.** Continuous monitoring and routine security assessments are essential in cybersecurity to adapt to new threats and vulnerabilities as systems evolve.

7. **Correct Answer: B. To identify vulnerabilities in a system.** Penetration testing, or ethical hacking, is used to identify vulnerabilities in a system by simulating cyberattacks to exploit these vulnerabilities.

8. **Correct Answer: B. It gathers detailed information about the target system.** The reconnaissance phase in ethical hacking is crucial as it involves amassing a wealth of information about the target system, which forms the foundation for all subsequent testing activities.

9. **Correct Answer: B. To simulate real-world attacks.** Exploitation tools in penetration testing are designed to take advantage of known weaknesses in systems, allowing testers to simulate attacks and assess the potential impact of real-world breaches.

10. **Correct Answer: B. Documenting findings from assessments.** A key component of reporting in cybersecurity is creating a detailed and comprehensive report of the findings from vulnerability assessments and penetration tests, including identified vulnerabilities and their potential impacts.

11. **Correct Answer: B. By evaluating the potential impact of vulnerabilities.** Risk assessment is crucial in cybersecurity as it evaluates the likelihood and potential consequences of vulnerabilities being exploited, guiding strategic resource allocation.

12. **Correct Answer: C. It creates a more resilient defense system.** A multilayered security approach combines different types of security controls to create a more resilient and comprehensive defense system against cyber threats.

13. **Correct Answer: B. To ensure alignment with business goals.** Mitigation strategy development should be a collaborative effort involving various departments and stakeholders to ensure that the strategies are not only technically sound but also align with the organization's operational needs and business goals.

14. **Correct Answer: B. To keep up with changing cyber threats.** Continuous adaptation of mitigation strategies is important to maintain robust defenses against the constantly evolving landscape of cyber threats.

15. **Correct Answer: B. To create a security-conscious culture.** Comprehensive communication and training in cybersecurity are essential to create a security-conscious culture within the organization, making every employee a part of the cybersecurity defense.

Chapter 12

1. **Correct Answer: C. To guide the safeguarding of digital assets.** Security policies are essential in an organization's cybersecurity strategy as they provide fundamental guiding principles for protecting digital assets against cyber threats.

2. **Correct Answer: C. A constitution.** Within an organization, security policies are akin to a constitution, establishing fundamental laws and principles for governing digital operations and ensuring cybersecurity.

3. **Correct Answer: C. Adaptation to dynamic threats.** Security policies demonstrate an organization's proactive approach to managing cyber risks by being adaptable and responsive to the dynamic nature of cyber threats.

4. **Correct Answer: C. By assuring the protection of sensitive information.** Effective security policies provide assurance to stakeholders outside the organization, such as customers and partners, by demonstrating the organization's commitment to protecting sensitive information.

5. **Correct Answer: B. To adapt to the evolving digital environment.** The adaptability of security policies is crucial to maintain their relevance and effectiveness in the face of the ever-changing digital environment and emerging cyber threats.

6. **Correct Answer: C. Comprehensive coverage of the digital ecosystem.** The scope of a robust security policy is characterized by its comprehensive coverage, ensuring that every relevant aspect of the organization's digital operations is protected.

7. **Correct Answer: B. Adherence to the SMART criteria.** Objectives in a security policy should adhere to the SMART criteria – specific, measurable, achievable, relevant, and time-bound – to ensure they provide clear, actionable targets.

8. **Correct Answer: B. Stakeholder engagement.** Engaging stakeholders in the development of security policies ensures that the policies are effective, practical, and aligned with the organization's specific needs and challenges.

9. **Correct Answer: B. Regular reviews and updates.** Regular reviews and updates are vital for maintaining the relevance and effectiveness of security policies, ensuring they continue to address emerging threats and organizational changes.

10. **Correct Answer: C. Clear communication of policy violations' consequences.** An effective enforcement mechanism in a security policy includes clearly communicating the consequences of policy violations, acting as a deterrent and maintaining policy integrity.

11. **Correct Answer: B. To keep up with changing cyber threats.** Continuous monitoring is essential in the context of security policies to ensure they remain effective against the constantly evolving landscape of cyber threats.

12. **Correct Answer: B. To ensure understanding and adherence across the organization.** Training and awareness programs are key to ensuring that all members of the organization understand and adhere to the security policies, thereby enhancing overall cybersecurity.

13. **Correct Answer: B. It ensures that policies fit the organization's unique attributes.** Tailoring security policies to an organization's unique structure, culture, and risk profile ensures that they are practical, relevant, and effective.

14. **Correct Answer: B. To ensure policies are practical and widely accepted.** Stakeholder engagement in security policy development is a multilayered strategy that ensures the resulting policies are practical and relevant and enjoy broad acceptance within the organization.

15. **Correct Answer: C. Integrating proactive strategies for threat anticipation and mitigation.** Incorporating proactive strategies in security policies helps manage the dynamic nature of cyber threats by anticipating and mitigating potential risks.

Chapter 13

1. **Correct Answer: B. To safeguard personal information in the digital realm.** Data privacy laws are designed to protect personal information in the digital environment, ensuring that entities handle this data responsibly and ethically.

2. **Correct Answer: B. Cultural, political, and social factors.** The design of data privacy regulations is shaped by various factors unique to each region, influencing how these laws are formulated and implemented globally.

3. **Correct Answer: C. The European Union's GDPR.** GDPR is recognized as a pioneering model in data protection and privacy, setting stringent standards that have significantly influenced data privacy legislation worldwide.

4. **Correct Answer: A. Data minimization.** GDPR emphasizes principles like explicit consent and data portability, guiding other laws to focus on minimizing the amount of personal data collected and processed.

5. **Correct Answer: B. Strict penalties for non-compliance.** GDPR mandates organizations to follow stringent data handling practices and imposes severe penalties for non-compliance, ensuring adherence to data protection standards.

6. **Correct Answer: C. It compels them to reassess global data handling practices.** GDPR has a global impact, requiring multinational corporations to reevaluate and align their data handling practices with GDPR standards, even outside Europe.

7. **Correct Answer: C. Complexity in navigating diverse compliance requirements.** Different jurisdictions have unique data privacy laws, creating a complex landscape for global organizations to navigate and comply with various regulations.

8. **Correct Answer: B. Consumer rights regarding personal information.** The CCPA focuses on empowering consumers with rights related to their personal information, such as the right to know, delete, and opt out of the sale of their data.

9. **Correct Answer: B. They add complexity due to specific data requirements.** Sector-specific regulations like HIPAA introduce additional layers of complexity in data privacy management due to their specific requirements for handling sensitive data.

10. **Correct Answer: C. The evolving nature of data privacy regulations.** As technology advances, data privacy laws must evolve to address new challenges and ensure effective protection of personal data.

11. **Correct Answer: B. They regulate cross-border data flow.** International data privacy agreements play a crucial role in harmonizing data protection standards and regulating the flow of data across national borders for multinational companies.

12. **Correct Answer: B. To ensure compliance with data privacy laws.** Regular data audits help organizations verify their adherence to data privacy regulations and identify areas needing improvement.

13. **Correct Answer: B. Retaining only necessary data for intended purposes.** Data minimization involves collecting and retaining only the data that is absolutely necessary for the specific purposes for which it was gathered.

14. **Correct Answer: B. Privacy considerations are integrated from the outset.** "Privacy by design" is an approach where privacy and data protection considerations are embedded into the development of products and services from the beginning.

15. **Correct Answer: C. To mitigate the risk of data breaches.** Employee training in data protection is essential to reduce the likelihood of data breaches, often caused by human error or lack of awareness.

Chapter 14

1. **Correct Answer: B. They originate from individuals within the organization.** Insider threats are unique because they come from individuals who have legitimate access to an organization's systems and data.

2. **Correct Answer: B. They intentionally cause harm to the organization.** Malicious insiders deliberately inflict harm through actions like data theft or system sabotage, motivated by various factors such as revenge or financial gain.

3. **Correct Answer: C. It analyzes patterns in user behavior to detect threats.** UBA is crucial for detecting insider threats as it identifies deviations from normal behavior patterns within an organization's network.

4. **Correct Answer: C. Anomaly detection.** This method is crucial for identifying unusual patterns in network activities that may indicate insider threats, including malicious actions or inadvertent mistakes.

5. **Correct Answer: B. It detects and prevents unauthorized data access and transmission.** DLP is key in combating insider threats by ensuring sensitive information is not accessed or transmitted without authorization.

6. **Correct Answer: C. To limit access to information based on job requirements.** Access controls ensure employees only access necessary information for their job, reducing the risk of insider threats.

7. **Correct Answer: B. They define procedures to handle detected threats.** Incident Response Plans are essential for outlining the steps to take when an insider threat is detected, including containment and investigation procedures.

8. **Correct Answer: B. Phishing awareness training.** This training is critical in educating employees about recognizing and responding to phishing attempts, a common tactic used in cyber-attacks.

9. **Correct Answer: B. They identify and address security vulnerabilities.** Regular security audits and assessments are crucial for continuously evaluating and improving an organization's cybersecurity measures.

10. **Correct Answer: B. They cause breaches through negligence or lack of awareness.** Careless insiders inadvertently cause security breaches, often due to lack of proper cybersecurity awareness or negligence.

11. **Correct Answer: B. It encourages proactive identification and reporting of threats.** A trusting but vigilant atmosphere ensures employees feel valued and supported in identifying and reporting security threats.

12. **Correct Answer: C. They prevent sensitive information from being compromised.** Secure communication practices are critical for ensuring that all organizational communication is conducted through secure channels, thus protecting sensitive information.

13. **Correct Answer: B. Collaboration with external entities to compromise security.** Collaborative insiders pose a threat by working with external parties, such as competitors or cybercriminals, to undermine an organization's security.

14. **Correct Answer: B. It can lead to intentional or unintentional security breaches.** Employee dissatisfaction is a critical factor in insider threat management as it can lead to harmful actions against the organization.

15. **Correct Answer: B. It aids in the early detection and mitigation of potential threats.** Encouraging employees to report security concerns is vital for early detection and effective mitigation of insider threats.

Chapter 15

1. **Correct Answer: B. Faster data processing and threat identification.** AI enhances cybersecurity by processing and analyzing large amounts of data rapidly, identifying potential threats quicker than human analysts.

2. **Correct Answer: C. Learning from new data to identify emerging threats.** ML algorithms continuously learn from new data, enhancing their capability to adapt and respond to new cybersecurity challenges.

3. **Correct Answer: C. Continuously evolving.** The cyber threat landscape is constantly changing, with hackers developing new techniques to breach security systems.

4. **Correct Answer: B. Dependence on high-quality data.** AI and ML's effectiveness in cybersecurity heavily relies on the quality of the data used for training, making accurate and unbiased data crucial.

5. **Correct Answer: B. Analyzing email patterns and content.** AI aids in phishing detection by analyzing the patterns and content in emails to identify potential phishing attempts.

6. **Correct Answer: B. Alan Turing, to test if a machine can mimic human intelligence.** Alan Turing proposed the Turing Test to determine if a machine's behavior is indistinguishable from that of a human.

7. **Correct Answer: B. Reduced interest and investment in AI research.** The first AI winter occurred due to disillusionment with AI's progress, leading to decreased funding and interest.

8. **Correct Answer: C. Advanced pattern recognition and prediction.** Deep learning, a subset of machine learning, has significantly advanced AI's capabilities in image and speech recognition, contributing to the current AI boom.

9. **Correct Answer: B. Inherent biases in AI algorithms.** A key ethical concern in AI is the potential for biases in algorithms, which can lead to unfair and discriminatory outcomes.

10. **Correct Answer: C. AI, whose decision-making process is understandable.** Explainable AI refers to AI systems where the decision-making process is transparent and understandable to users.

11. **Correct Answer: B. Leading to workforce disruptions due to automation.** AI and robotics automation can significantly disrupt the workforce, potentially leading to job losses and economic inequality.

12. **Correct Answer: B. Response to identified threats.** AI-driven systems in cybersecurity can automate the response to identified threats, enabling quicker mitigation and reducing the window of opportunity for attackers.

13. **Correct Answer: B. Threat detection and response.** Machine learning enhances threat detection and response mechanisms in cybersecurity by recognizing patterns and anomalies indicative of cyber-attacks.

14. **Correct Answer: B. Generative Adversarial Networks (GANs) and Variational Autoencoders (VAEs).** These models are central to generative AI, enabling the creation of new, original content across various forms.

15. **Correct Answer: B. To govern AI's influence on privacy, autonomy, and fairness.** Ethical guidelines in AI are necessary to address its impact on key societal values like privacy, autonomy, and fairness.

Chapter 16

1. **Correct Answer: B. To record transactions across a network of computers.** Blockchain's primary function is to securely record and store transactions across a distributed network, offering security and transparency.

2. **Correct Answer: B. A cryptographic hash of the previous block.** Each block in a blockchain contains a unique cryptographic hash of the previous block, linking them in a secure and tamper-evident manner.

3. **Correct Answer: B. Decentralization.** Blockchain technology is decentralized, meaning no single entity controls the data, in contrast to traditional centralized systems.

4. **Correct Answer: C. To facilitate accountability and trust.** Transparency in blockchain networks allows all participants to view transactions, fostering trust and accountability among users.

5. **Correct Answer: B. Change in the hash, signaling data breach.** Altering transaction data in a block changes its hash value, indicating a breach in the blockchain's integrity.

6. **Correct Answer: B. Private.** Private blockchains are used within organizations for confidential and controlled transaction recording.

7. **Correct Answer: B. A group known as Satoshi Nakamoto.** Blockchain was introduced in a 2008 whitepaper by an entity or group using the pseudonym Satoshi Nakamoto.

8. **Correct Answer: B. Cryptocurrency.** Blockchain was first implemented as the underlying technology for Bitcoin, a cryptocurrency.

9. **Correct Answer: A. Scalability.** Public blockchains like Bitcoin and Ethereum face challenges with transaction processing speed and capacity, affecting scalability.

10. **Correct Answer: B. The economic principles governing a cryptocurrency.** Tokenomics refers to the economic models and incentives that dictate the creation and distribution of cryptocurrencies.

11. **Correct Answer: B. Proof of Stake.** Proof of Stake is a consensus mechanism that is more energy efficient compared to Proof of Work, as it does not involve intensive computational tasks.

12. **Correct Answer: D. Self-executing code.** Smart contracts on blockchain are based on self-executing code, which automatically enforces the terms of a contract.

13. **Correct Answer: B. Enhanced tracking and transparency.** Blockchain technology provides enhanced transparency and traceability in supply chain management, improving accountability and efficiency.

14. **Correct Answer: C. By increasing security and transparency.** Blockchain can make voting systems more secure and transparent, mitigating issues like fraud and tampering.

15. **Correct Answer: B. Ensuring scalability and energy efficiency.** Addressing scalability and energy efficiency is crucial for the widespread adoption and sustainability of blockchain technology.

Chapter 17

1. **Correct Answer: C. Protecting information systems and assets from threats.** Risk management in cybersecurity aims to safeguard information systems and assets from a wide range of cyber threats, ensuring the security of organizational data and infrastructure.

2. **Correct Answer: B. Financial loss and reputational damage.** Cybersecurity risk encompasses more than just technical vulnerabilities; it includes the potential for financial loss, reputational damage, legal liabilities, and operational disruptions.

3. **Correct Answer: B. Integrating risk management into all cybersecurity efforts.** Building a resilient cybersecurity posture requires integrating risk management principles into every aspect of cybersecurity practices, ensuring a comprehensive and holistic approach to security.

4. **Correct Answer: B. The increasing sophistication of cyber attacks.** The need for compliance in cybersecurity is driven by the growing sophistication and frequency of cyber attacks, necessitating robust security measures to protect sensitive information.

5. **Correct Answer: B. Data protection and privacy.** The General Data Protection Regulation (GDPR) focuses on setting guidelines for data protection and privacy, particularly for individuals within the European Union.

6. **Correct Answer: C. Ranking risks based on impact and likelihood.** Risk prioritization in risk management involves evaluating and ranking identified risks based on their potential impact and likelihood, enabling effective allocation of resources.

7. **Correct Answer: B. To ensure the continued effectiveness of strategies.** Regular assessments and reviews in risk management are important to ensure that the implemented strategies continue to be effective in the face of changing threats and business environments.

8. **Correct Answer: B. Protecting information systems and data.** Technical controls in cybersecurity are used to protect information systems and data from threats and vulnerabilities through measures like firewalls and encryption.

9. **Correct Answer: B. Proactive and anticipatory stance.** A proactive and anticipatory approach in managing cybersecurity risks involves predicting and preparing for potential threats, rather than just reacting to incidents.

10. **Correct Answer: B. Predict and respond to threats in real time.** The use of AI and machine learning in cybersecurity aims to enhance the ability to detect and respond to cyber threats in real time, improving overall security response.

11. **Correct Answer: C. Aligning risk mitigation efforts with business goals.** Balancing risk with business objectives involves aligning risk mitigation efforts with the organization's overall goals and strategic direction, ensuring that security supports business growth.

12. **Correct Answer: B. Through its decentralization and immutability.** Blockchain contributes to cybersecurity through its properties of decentralization and immutability, providing a secure and tamper-proof way of managing data.

13. **Correct Answer: B. Forecasting potential security incidents.** Predictive analytics in cybersecurity is used to analyze data and identify patterns that can help forecast potential security incidents, allowing for proactive risk management.

14. **Correct Answer: A. To ensure decisions are based on reliable data.** Accuracy in cybersecurity reporting is important to ensure that decisions are made based on reliable and valid information, enhancing the effectiveness of decision-making processes.

15. **Correct Answer: C. Adapting to emerging trends and technologies.** The future of cybersecurity risk and compliance emphasizes the need for

organizations to be dynamic and adaptive, staying abreast of emerging trends and technologies to effectively manage risks and maintain compliance.

Chapter 18

1. **Correct Answer: B. To manage and handle security breaches effectively.** The primary goal of Incident Response is to effectively manage and mitigate the effects of security breaches and cyber attacks, ensuring organizational resilience.

2. **Correct Answer: C. Detection, analysis, containment, eradication, and recovery.** Incident Response covers a comprehensive scope including the detection of incidents, their analysis, containment, eradication, and recovery, making it a multifaceted process.

3. **Correct Answer: B. Mitigating attack damages and building customer trust.** An effective Incident Response strategy aims to mitigate the damages of cyber attacks and build customer trust in the organization's capability to protect data.

4. **Correct Answer: B. Inclusion of proactive strategies like threat hunting.** The evolution of Incident Response has included the adoption of proactive strategies such as threat hunting and predictive analytics, reflecting the changing nature of cyber threats.

5. **Correct Answer: C. Rapid detection of threats.**
Rapid detection is a key principle in Incident
Response, crucial for timely and effective handling
of security incidents.

6. **Correct Answer: C. Identification of threats.** The
first step in the Incident Response Process is the
identification of threats, which is essential for early
intervention and effective management of incidents.

7. **Correct Answer: B. Limiting the impact of the
incident.** During containment, it's crucial to limit
the spread and impact of the incident to prevent
larger-scale damage.

8. **Correct Answer: B. Collaboration with external
experts.** Collaborating with external experts and
using specialized tools are essential for thoroughly
eradicating risks and ensuring comprehensive
resolution of security incidents.

9. **Correct Answer: B. Diverse skills and clear roles.**
An effective Incident Response Team requires a
diversity of skills and clearly defined roles to address
all aspects of an incident comprehensively.

10. **Correct Answer: B. Enhancing threat detection
and response.** AI and ML play a crucial role in
enhancing the capabilities of Incident Response
Teams in threat detection and response, providing
speed and efficiency.

11. **Correct Answer: B. IoT devices lack robust built-in security.** The lack of robust built-in security in IoT devices poses significant challenges in securing them and complicates the Incident Response Process.

12. **Correct Answer: B. Creating tamper-proof logs.** Blockchain technology can be used to create tamper-proof logs of network activity, enhancing the integrity and reliability of incident data.

13. **Correct Answer: B. Identifying successes and shortcomings.** In the post-incident analysis and recovery phase, it is crucial to identify both the successes and shortcomings of the incident response to improve future strategies.

14. **Correct Answer: C. Integrating security into business strategy.** Integrating security considerations into the overall business strategy is key in developing a resilient and comprehensive long-term security strategy.

15. **Correct Answer: B. Embracing emerging technologies like AI and ML.** The future of Incident Response is marked by the adoption of emerging technologies like AI and ML, which are set to transform how threats are detected and managed.

Index

A

Access control lists (ACLs), 115, 248, 306

Advanced Encryption Standard (AES), 77, 187

Advanced persistent threats (APTs), 16, 104, 174, 271, 558, 700, 714, 722

Advanced Research Projects Agency Network (ARPANET), 225

Advanced Social Engineering and Manipulation (ASEM), 97

AI-driven attacks, 129

AI-driven security systems, 537

AI-driven systems, 751

AI-powered attacks, 30, 31

Amazon Web Services (AWS), 224, 226, 273

Anonymization, 438, 454

Apple File System (APFS), 350

Application Programming Interface (API), 307

Application security, 724
- APIs/web services, 154, 156, 157
- CIA triad, 140
- definition, 139
- development lifecycle, 151, 153, 154
- dynamic analysis/vulnerability scanning, 148–150
- mobile application, 158, 159
- OWASP/web application, 159–161
- secure coding practices, 141–144
- security breaches, 139
- software developers, 167
- SQL injection attack, case study, 165, 166
- testing and assessment, 144, 145, 147
- threat intelligence, 162, 164
- threat modeling and risk assessment, 140

App store security, 179

Artificial intelligence (AI), 31, 125, 267, 319, 402, 458, 537, 718
- automation, 566
- career, 590, 591
- case study, 589
- cyber resilience, 567
- future of work, 558
- future, 583–588

© Dr. Jason Edwards 2024, corrected publication 2024
Dr. J. Edwards, *Mastering Cybersecurity*, https://doi.org/10.1007/979-8-8688-0297-3

N

Printed in the United States
by Baker & Taylor Publisher Services